Perspectives on the Measurement of Human Performance

The Century Psychology Series

Kenneth MacCorquodale
Gardner Lindzey
Kenneth E. Clark

Editors

PERSPECTIVES ON THE MEASUREMENT OF HUMAN PERFORMANCE

W. W. RONAN
Georgia Institute of Technology

ERICH P. PRIEN
Memphis State University

APPLETON-CENTURY-CROFTS
EDUCATIONAL DIVISION
MEREDITH CORPORATION

Copyright © 1971 by

MEREDITH CORPORATION

All rights reserved

This book, or parts thereof, must not be used or reproduced in any manner without written permission. For information address the publisher, Appleton-Century-Crofts, Educational Division, Meredith Corporation, 440 Park Avenue South, New York, N. Y. 10016.

7120-1

Library of Congress Card Number: 72-133192

PRINTED IN THE UNITED STATES OF AMERICA

390-75690-3

Preface

For many years, all behavioral research has recognized the importance of the criterion in any investigative field. Research reports usually offer a quite detailed description of the criterion that was used in any particular study. Industrial psychology, in particular, has accorded major importance to the "criterion problem" through a great deal of discussion and, spasmodically, some research effort. If anything, with the passage of years and effort the problem has become more and more apparent and more and more a block to progress in our knowledge.

The compilers of this anthology have attempted to show in a review of the relevant literature[1] that the problem is actually that of shifting research emphasis from individual differences (as in psychological tests) to understanding human performance in the "real" world. In a sense it is to devote our time to what most psychologists say they do, "study behavior." It is our contention that the criterion, as an evaluative index of performance behavior, is really a subproblem in the field of understanding human performance. We also submit that the study of human performance, *per se*, has been a sadly neglected area of research and, in consequence, future progress must involve the shift in research mentioned above if any significant progress in performance prediction is to be accomplished.

The introductory section offers evidence that similar conceptions and perceptions have been presented by others. Unfortunately their efforts seem to have had little noticeable effect either in formulating relevant research hypotheses, or in altering the practice of using the most available criterion. However, they do delineate the general area of concern, the world of work, and discuss many of the specific problems that are of importance. In general, they indicate both the importance and the neglect of the study of human performance. In addition to the selections which are included in their entirety, reference is made to other articles in this and each of the following part introductions. The reader who wishes to pursue the specific topic in greater depth will find these and other additional references listed by part at the end of the text.

[1] Ronan, W. W. and Prien, E. P. *Toward a Criterion Theory: A Review and Analysis of Research and Opinion.* (Greensboro, N. C.: The Richardson Foundation, 1966.)

Related to the shift in research efforts are four basic problems that require solution before human performance can be more fully studied and comprehended. The first of these is the reliability of performance. Such an obvious requisite to prediction of performance as its *reliability* would seem to have received considerable attention. The fact is that a real dearth of information on the topic exists, and, furthermore, such data as are in existence indicate that human performance tends to be unreliable.

Related to the reliability of performance is the reliability of its observance. It is a fact that all performance or the results, in order to be measured, must be observed in some way. The question is, can such observation achieve an acceptable level of reliability? The question is moot at present, but, the weight of the evidence seems to be that performance observation has questionable reliability.

Another important question is that of the dimensions of performance, that is, in performing any tasks, no matter how simple, do various aspects of "success" exist in the task and are these aspects related or unrelated? In this area, past research efforts have often used a single or "global" index to measure performance in any task in spite of studies that demonstrate the existence of more than *one* performance dimension in even relatively simple tasks.

Finally there is the question of how performance on the same task may be affected by being required in different situations. Broadly, "situation" can mean any change in the stimulus context. This may be a relatively simple change, as the addition of a new work-group member, or a quite drastic change as in moving a plant to a new location. In any case, there is remarkably little information concerning this particular problem area although it would appear that performance can be altered by changing its environment context.

These four problems constitute the material of separate parts of the text and in no way can any final answers be implied. In essence they are presented in an heuristic sense because there is such a comparative lack of verified information on these topics. Before performance can be more fully understood it is essential that the formulated questions are answered.

Building on the problems and assumptions of the preceding paragraphs, Part VI is devoted to studies of organization indices of performance. To say that organizations perform in the same way individuals do is erroneous, the output is simply the summated result of the composite of individual behaviors of those who constitute the organization.

The articles in Part VII are concerned with the development of the most efficacious designs leading to a better understanding of performance. Our present knowledge is based largely upon quite limited "one-shot" studies; in particular, the interrelationships of the variables determining performance are only dimly understood. The studies presented are those incorporating multivariate designs which, it is hoped, will serve as models for future study.

The selections included in Part VIII are concerned with work toward a theory of criteria. As our knowledge stands today this is a most difficult area—in a sense, "the blind leading the blind." However, the development of theories, with testable hypotheses, is intended both as an appreciation of past efforts and as a guide to future theoretical formulations.

One final point is that of the previous reference to the "real" world. The performance of interest here is that which occurs in connection with work at actual jobs and tasks, and we believe that the study of such performance in laboratory or simulated situations really cannot be meaningful. When performance is seen as occurring in the individual-workgroup-organization matrix the relevent stimuli must be present if "real" performance is to be fully studied. In general, it is questionable whether findings from isolated studies, no matter how well done, can be generalized to the actual performance situations. Furthermore, it is believed, that personal and organization indices such as accidents, absenteeism, a measure of relative profit, and many others will, of necessity, be used to analyze performance in the present embryonic situation. Future research may reveal better measurement methodology, but at present there appears no alternative.

We are indebted to the many authors who agreed to reprinting their work. We are indebted to the publishers who provided special permission to reprint the articles from the various journals. The authors and publishers are acknowledged on the title page of each article.

W. W. Ronan
Erich P. Prien

Contents

Preface v

I THE BACKGROUND OF THE PROBLEM 1

1. Human Effectiveness   *Arthur H. Brayfield*   5
2. A Research Utopia in Industrial Psychology   *Herbert A. Toops*   17
3. Criteria for What?   *S. Rains Wallace*   46
4. The Placement of Workers: Concepts and Problems   *Edwin E. Ghiselli*   57
5. A Modified Model for Test Validation and Selection Research   *Marvin D. Dunnette*   69
6. Whose Criterion?   *Jay L. Otis*   79

II RELIABILITY OF PERFORMANCE 87

7. Moderating Effects and Differential Reliability and Validity   *Edwin E. Ghiselli*   93
8. Output Rates Among Coil Winders   *Harold F. Rothe and Charles T. Nye*   102
9. Productivity and Errors in Two Keying Tasks: A Field Study   *T. Klemmer and R. Lockhead*   110
10. Work Methods: An Often Neglected Factor Underlying Individual Differences   *Robert H. Seashore*   121
11. Reliability of Absence Measures   *Edgar F. Huse and Erwin K. Taylor*   135
12. Some Hypotheses for the Analysis of Qualitative Variables   *Clyde H. Coombs*   138

III RELIABILITY OF PERFORMANCE OBSERVATION 149

13. The Ability to Judge People   *Ronald Taft*   153
14. Some Determinants of Supervisory Esteem   *David Kipnis*   182
15. Performance Tests of Educational Achievement   *David G. Ryans and Norman Frederiksen*   195
16. The Check List as a Criterion of Proficiency   *Arthur I. Siegel*   231
17. The Predictability of Various Kinds of Criteria   *Daryl Severin*   236
18. Errors in Time-Study Judgements of Industrial Work Pace   *Kalman A. Lifson*   247

IV DIMENSIONS OF PERFORMANCE 269

19 A Factorial Study of Sales Criteria   *Carl H. Rush, Jr.*   273
20 A Factor Analysis of Eleven Job Performance Measures
    William W. Ronan   286
21 Dimensions of Foreman Performance: A Factor Analysis of
    Criterion Measures   *Weld W. Turner*   298
22 A Psychological Study of Occupational Adjustment   *Alastair Heron*   311
23 An Investigation of the Criterion Problem for One Group of Medical
    Specialists   *James M. Richards, Jr., Calvin W. Taylor, Philip B. Price,
    and Tony L. Jacobsen*   317
24 Salary Growth as a Criterion of Career Progress   *Thomas L. Hilton
    and William R. Dill*   337
25 An Analysis of Pilot Flying Performance in Terms of Component
    Abilities   *Edwin A. Fleishman and George N. Ornstein*   346
26 Development of a Clerical Position Description Questionnaire
    Erich P. Prien   363

V PERFORMANCE AND EXTRA-INDIVIDUAL CONDITIONS 371

27 Contingency Factors   374
28 Methods of Evaluating the Efficiency of Door-to-Door Salesmen of
    Bakery Products   *Roy M. Dorcus*   377
29 Management Quality and Its Effect on Selection Test Validity
    Leonard W. Ferguson (assisted by John J. Hopkins)   383
30 A Factorial Study of Administrative Behavior   *Ralph M. Stogdill,
    Carroll L. Shartle, Robert J. Wherry and William E. Jaynes*   391
31 A Further Analysis of the Relations Among Job Performance and
    Situational Variables   *Edward E. Cureton and Raymond A. Katzell*   404
32 Organizational Conditions and Behavior in 234 Industrial Manufacturing
    Organizations   *George H. Dunteman*   406
33 The Predictability of Occupational Level from Intelligence
    Richard S. Ball   415
34 Test Validity over a Seventeen-Year Period   *B. Knauft*   419

VI ORGANIZATION PERFORMANCE 421

35 Ultimate Criteria of Organizational Worth   *Bernard M. Bass*   424
36 Criteria of Organizational Effectiveness   *Stanley E. Seashore*   438
37 Incentive Conditions and Behavior in 188 Industrial Manufacturing
    Organizations   *George J. Palmer, Jr., and Ronald H. Schroeder*   445
38 Factorial Analysis of Organizational Performance   *Stanley E. Seashore
    and Ephraim Yuchtman*   469
39 The Study of Organizational and Relevant Small Group and
    Individual Dimensions   *Bernard P. Indik*   485

40 An Analysis of Organization Characteristics   *Erich P. Prien and W. W. Ronan*   506

VII MODEL STUDIES FOR PERFORMANCE ANALYSIS   521

41 Design of the Experiment   *S. E. Seashore and D. G. Bowers*   523
42 Relationships among Measures of Supervisory Behavior, Group Behavior, and Situational Characteristics   *Treadway C. Parker*   532
43 Seven Societal Criteria of Organizational Success   *Hal Pickle and Frank Friedlander*   546

VIII SOME GENERAL CONSIDERATIONS   559

44 The Use of Criterional Measures   *Joseph Weitz*   562
45 Criterion Development   *Bryant Nagle*   579
46 The Past and Future of Criterion Evaluation   *Robert J. Wherry*   594
47 Criterion Measurement and Personnel Judgments   *Robert M. Guion*   598
48 Studies in Synthetic Validity: An Exploratory Investigation of Clerical Jobs   *C. H. Lawshe and Martin D. Steinberg*   606
49 A Research Strategy for Partial Knowledge Useful in the Selection of Executives   *Harold Guetzkow and Garlie A. Forehand*   615
50 Synthetic Validity in a Small Company: A Demonstration   *Robert M. Guion*   627

Name Index   641

Subject Index   649

Perspectives on the
Measurement of Human Performance

I THE BACKGROUND OF THE PROBLEM

The actual study of performance as such has been rather limited in spite of the unanimity of opinion as to the importance of criteria to research in the social and behavorial sciences. However, there has been some excellent work presented that encompasses the problems presented by study of the phenomena in the area, such as variables related to effective and ineffective performance, the dimensions of behavior, and techniques of evaluation. In general, the requirements in terms of hypotheses, techniques, and research designs involved in an attack are a relatively unexplored area.

The first article, Brayfield (1965), is one of the most recent discussions of the area and is generalized to a much broader domain of interest than that of industrial psychology. For example, Brayfield uses as an illustration the possibility, in clinical work, of having a patient with professional assistance set goals as a basis for a planned program of individual development. Unfortunately, our present knowledge of how to establish goals with operationally defined parameters is virtually nil. The point is that behavioral analyses are required so that *behavioral* goals can be established on some research based information. This point of view can be considered as the major thesis of this book—that behavior, in all its facets, must be explored and understood before it is possible to make accurate predictions.

The remaining articles in this part are concerned primarily with the field of industrial psychology. The article by Toops (1959) is a wide ranging treatise that discusses the entire area of performance and its prediction in the world of work. One of the major points is the most important for the context here, that "success" is not a unitary concept but is better described in terms of a "profile." Additionally, the dimensions required by such profiles are not known but must be if prediction is ever to be done with any degree of accuracy and comprehensiveness. Further points of emphasis are the need for research on "environments," that economic efficiency is not the only possible criterion in terms of human adjustment to work, the possibility of nonlinear relationships, various technical measuring problems, and the possibility of many known and unknown moderator variables that affect performance. In total, the article provides a most comprehensive overview of the general points of interest in the study of human performance in whatever context of interest.

The statement by Wallace (1965) of the *criterion* is almost evangelical—but probably not enough so—in decrying past research emphasis on utility as opposed to understanding that has characterized most of the work in industrial psychology. Past failures to predict performance adequately are most forcefully described, the use of available rather than relevant criteria, the questionable use of ratings, and the general need to reevaluate our entire orientation are all quite convincingly scrutinized. Wallace's points serve to direct attention to the past shortcomings of industrial psychology as is intended here, and, it is hoped, their seriousness and urgency will be shown by the readings included in this text.

Ghiselli (1956) in a somewhat earlier statement has discussed many of the "concepts and problems" in the "placement of workers," a seemingly more restricted area. Actually, many of the same problems are recognized in the more comprehensive statements, for example, the lack of research concerning knowledge about performance criteria. The implications of a criterion score are explored, the need for occupational profiles again expressed (see Toops), and the possible effects of the work situation on individual job performance are discussed. Other concepts are mentioned, but again many of the more important are described in a slightly different context. One specific determiner that appears to have a marked effect on predictor/performance relations is the passage of time and the sequential measures of such relations over a period of time. That the predictor-criteria relation does change over time, sometimes quite drastically, has been demonstrated by a few studies. Actually, the literature is remarkable for the paucity of studies involving any extended time periods. This is specifically emphasized in some articles included here and, in the authors' opinion, has been grossly neglected in planning and executing research projects.

The next article in this part, by Dunnette (1963), is a concise formulation of the entire general domain of human performance and prediction. In particular the Guetzkow and Forehand model cited in the text of the article is seen as crucial. The model delineates clearly the variables involved along with stress on their interrelationships to show the complexity of the needed models, hypotheses, and vital research. In addition, Dunnette emphasizes the need for multiple criteria, the need for typologies, and he questions most seriously the continued acceptance of *global* models as appropriate.

The final presentation in this section by Otis (1953) provides suggestions to broaden our perspective or to shift our emphasis in personnel research. His message essentially is to immerse ourselves in the criterion side of the predictor-criterion equation to the extent that research has focused on the development of predictors.

The entire part is intended to indicate our present virtual cul-de-sac position along with the fact that seemingly fruitful conceptualizations have been made and—with consistent complacency—ignored by most workers in the field.

A distinct exception is Weitz (1961), (1964, reprinted in Part VIII) who provides results which show that the selection of the most appropriate criterion is at least partly determined by task difficulty and induced motivational level. This is obviously consistent with the position espoused by Wherry (1957, reprinted in Part VIII) in rejecting the criteria proposed by Bellows (1941). What seems to be essential is less slavish adherence to the whims and predilections of the research sponsor and a clearer focus on the principles of scientific theory for industrial psychology. This point is very clearly drawn by Baxter (1965) in his Division 14, Presidential Address.

Perhaps the repetition of the obvious needs by Otis, Ghiselli, Wallace and Baxter will eventually lead to a turn out of the cul-de-sac.

REFERENCES

BAXTER, B. "Quo Vadis," Presidential Address, Div. 14, American Psychological Association, 1961.

BELLOWS, R. M. "Procedures For Evaluating Vocational Criteria." *Journal of Applied Psychology*, 1941, 25, 499-513.

1 Human Effectiveness

ARTHUR H. BRAYFIELD

I propose in this Memorial Lecture to examine, briefly and at a somewhat abstract level, the social and cultural setting in which the psychology enterprise goes forward, to propose a social orientation for psychology's efforts, to illustrate the potential impact of such an orientation on psychological practice and research, and to suggest possible sources of psychology's leverage on human affairs.

As the sociologists and anthropologists have conceptualized it, human affairs become organized and structured as social institutions. An institution is defined as a "set of folkways and mores integrated around a principal function of society [Young & Mack, 1959, p. 75]." Thus, all of the folkways and mores which control the production of goods and services are called the economic institution. The folkways and mores, frequently supported by law, establish the norms for a group whose members are to have certain regulated role behavior toward one another in carrying out their responsibilities for an essential social function.

It has been instructive to me, in considering the development of psychology as a *profession*, to examine the major social institutions with a view to identifying the institutional basis for the profession of psychology. Selectively, for example, we may consider the following major social functions: religion, education, government, economics, law, health.

Sociologists have developed numerous ideas from institutional analysis such as: the persistence of certain basic institutions as universal features of social organization; the transference and shifting of functions over time from one institution to another; the interdependence of institutions so that changes in one create changes in another; and the tendency of institutions to persist through organization for self-perpetuation (Alpert, 1963). These ideas, however, serve mainly as a backdrop for our immediate concern.

Even a casual survey of most of the major social institutions suggests that they become the base for the development of relatively unique and specialized professions. Thus there have emerged the clergy, teachers,

From *American Psychologist* 1965, 20, 645–657. Presented as the Donald G. Paterson Memorial Lecture at Minnesota State Psychological Association, Minneapolis, April 29, 1965.

public administrators, economists and business administrators, lawyers, and physicians.

Next we note that the social institution, through its characteristic or predominant profession, establishes the "rules of the game" and the controls for the profession or professions serving it. The folkways and mores become codified and regulate professional entry, training, and performance and conduct.

Finally, it seems clear that institutions, and the professions serving them, are established, developed, and maintained because they meet some essential human need.

The question which I now pose is an obvious one: What is the institutional base for the profession of psychology?

It is apparent that psychology is not *uniquely* linked to any single existing social institution.

In language appropriate to the season, psychology plays always in someone else's ball park. The rules of the game and the umpires are, in the main, controlled by the host team.

We see this most clearly, of course, in the health field, especially mental health. Let me here report to you as relevant to the *magnitude*, at least, of this circumstance some data recently brought together in a preliminary fashion by Forrest Vance.

In the 1964 *National Register of Scientific and Technical Personnel* questionnaire which went out in the spring and summer of 1964, one question asked: "Please give the principal service you perform or product on which you work." Following this item, we were able to add the following: "Is this service or product related to the field of mental health?" Of somewhat more than 18,000 psychologist respondents, some 71% answered "Yes." Vance's rough estimate, from extrapolations based on *National Register* and National Institute of Mental Health data, is that approximately 8,000 psychologists provide some 13,000,000 man-hours per year of clinical services and another 7,500 psychologists spend another 13,000,000 man-hours per year of psychological effort, primarily teaching and research, related to mental health. Thus some 15,000–16,000 psychologists perceive their work as related to the field of mental health and contribute the staggering total of 26,000,000 man-hours per year of work so defined.

It is understandable, then, that psychology's role in the health domain is of interest to many psychologists and of great concern to some.

It is interesting to see how the relationship of psychology to the institution of health and the profession of medicine is viewed by sociologists. Such a view is afforded in the 1963 *Handbook of Medical Sociology* edited by three behavioral scientists (Freeman, Levine, & Reeder, 1963). In this *Handbook,* Walter I. Wardwell (1963), a well-known sociologist with a special competence in the sociology of the professions, classifies clinical psychologists as among the *limited independent health-related practitioners* who

> function independently of the medical profession but limit their area of practice to specified conditions and/or parts of the human body. . . . In so doing [he says] they implicitly accept the authority of the physician over general conditions or systemic disorders [p. 219].

In his view, the best established limited practitioners in the United States are dentists, psychologists, optometrists, and podiatrists.

Wardwell's specific observations regarding clinical psychologists are relevant:

> Despite formal protestations, medicine appears to have given psychology *de facto* acceptance as a limited health profession rather than merely as an ancillary one. One reason for this may be that the psychologist does not touch the patient's body. Although mind and body are intertwined in any conceptualization of the malfunctioning of psyche or soma, the very concrete distinction between mere conversing and "the laying on of hands" permits drawing a clear line of professional responsibility which the psychologist has no desire to cross. An additional reason for medical acceptance of psychology has probably been the high standards of professional competence in psychology that have resulted from its historic locus in the graduate schools of established universities. Although psychologists have sometimes been criticized for having an inadequate clinical background, they have often been more intellectually alert and research-oriented than most practicing physicians or psychiatrists—probably as a consequence of broad training in academic psychology and related subjects and because of the requirement that they submit a comprehensive research dissertation for the doctorate [pp. 223–224].

Wardwell concludes that psychology appears to have gained high standing as a profession and cites the relevant evidence from several studies of occupational prestige.

For the present purpose, it may be useful also to briefly assess the profession of social work and its relation to social institutions. Some writers classify social welfare as a social institution and consider social work to be its representative profession. However, Sidney Levenstein (1964), in a recent book titled *Private Practice in Social Work*, takes a contrary view. He makes the point, for example, that "economic security in old age is being met more or less adequately through three institutions: family, government and industry [p. 8]." In his view, "This does not put these three institutions into the category of 'social welfare' [p. 8]."

Rather, according to Levenstein's analysis, social work itself is an institution which is designed

> to help people with problems that prevent people from achieving an optimum standard of social and economic well-being; to provide goods and services to all those who require or request help in achieving optimum social life, through an institution so structurally patterned as to afford an ongoing evaluation of social problems and work toward means to alleviate and prevent them [p. 9].

My reaction is that social work is not necessarily an institution itself but that it has institutionalized the *social pathology* which itself is a product of the malfunctioning of the major social institutions, perhaps especially the family, the law, and the economic institutions, and has developed a profession of social work. At any rate, its historic linkage is to social pathology.

This appraisal of social institutions and professional function leads me to suggest a possible orienting approach which would clarify psychology's unique role in human affairs and enable psychologists to make more explicit and understandable their contribution to society.

My "provisional try" is that psychology's unique concern, both as profession and as science, is with the establishment and maintenance of the effective performance of the members of society in all their required tasks, their social roles, and their human relationships. *Human effectiveness* is the target for our effort.

It is my estimate that society is caught up in a gigantic tide of *rising expectations* and that this cultural phenomenon is not limited to the underdeveloped countries or to the civil rights movement. Indeed it is a pervasive imperative that has found expression in many of the elements of the "Great Society." I think it no accident—nor sheer political design—that these rising expectations were articulated by two of our foremost political leaders of recent times and that they focus upon programs devoted, in their essence, to effective human functioning in both a broad and narrow sense.

Psychology shares this zeitgeist and individual psychologists seek to be useful and to serve this vast social concern. And we have our own great expectations for psychology itself.

It would, I believe, clarify psychology's contribution and focus the efforts of psychologists if our predominant orientation was to the establishment and maintenance of effective behavior in all realms of human endeavor.

Our scientific interest would be to identify and describe the conditions for effective performance; our professional interest would be to test and use this knowledge with individuals and groups.

The introduction of the concept of human effectiveness into our discourse is no mere play on words, no simple semantic maneuver, no limited political ploy, and I propose now to illustrate its potential impact on research and practice.

A human-effectiveness orientation would, I believe, energize the search for an adequate taxonomy of human behavior and of behavior settings. This I consider to be a long-neglected necessity. Let me illustrate by drawing upon some experiences in the field of mental retardation.

In a series of discussions with representatives of the President's advisory group on mental retardation it became clear that professional manpower shortages impose serious limitations upon programs, and that programs themselves require for their design and carrying out a type of information not presently available. The crux of the matter is the need to specify the common task requirements for effective functioning as an individual in a complex society. We presently are without a useful systematic analysis of environmental demands and concomitant behaviors (Bloom, 1964, pp. 183–201; Sells, 1963). If some such classificatory scheme were available it would be possible to make more intelligent provisions for training experiences for the mentally retarded and to restructure the jobs of professional and related personnel working in mental retardation programs. A tentative beginning has been made along this line at the Parsons (Kansas) State Hospital and Training Center (Leland, 1964, p. 43).

Several years ago, Robert Gagné (1963) discussed this proposition under the title "Task Analysis and the Establishment of Human Performances." Task description was suggested as a starting point with the purpose of providing a "clear, complete, consistent, and unequivocal communication of human performances, using words that have definite operational meanings [p. 1]." Given a satisfactory set of task descriptions applying to a job or to some other collection of human functions, it would then be possible to make an analysis of these descriptions for a variety of purposes. Gagné singles out a purpose served by such *classifying of human functions* which he believes has not been systematically investigated but which is of considerable importance. He suggests that a classification could be made of the *conditions for establishment of human performances*. Gagné summarizes his discussion as follows:

> 1. Human tasks can be described accurately, reliably, and unambiguously.
> 2. Suppose we take as a problem the question, "How do we get this task done in the best possible way by a human being?" This question leads us to identify the factors which can be worked with to bring about what I have called the "establishment of performance."
> 3. These factors are as follows. First, there must be learning of performances. Second, there must be motivation to perform the task. Third, there must be proper attention to the task. Fourth, different

people, equally well trained, will differ in their capacities for performance. And fifth, something in the situation must tell the performer what he is supposed to do.

4. None of these factors is novel—they are all well known. If there is something new in what I am saying, it lies in the possibility that the great variety of human tasks can be classified in *all* of these ways independently. They can be classified as to what is necessary for learning to occur; what is necessary for attention to be insured; what are the necessary capacities; and what must be done to have the individual "set" to do the task.

5. If we were able to make all these kinds of classifications, we should have the beginnings of a model of human performance, perhaps one which would ultimately permit quantitative prediction. But even before that, some one could come to us and say: Here is a task. What has to be done to get it performed? And we could answer: This task requires learning conditions as follows, attentional conditions of this particular sort, capacities of such and such a nature, and instructions of this kind.

6. Finally, I have tried to suggest that these pieces will not fall together of their own accord. Someone must try to do research of the sort which deliberately puts them together; which attempts to answer the total question, what are the conditions for establishment of human performances [pp. 11–12]?

It is obvious that the same considerations may apply to the maintenance of performance over time.

The utilities of this general approach are self-evident. However, I should like to suggest as illustrative two uses which are quite different in many respects.

Is it conceivable that this is a potentially useful approach for a counseling or clinical psychologist working with an individual client? Would it be clarifying and helpful if the individual undertook to do a task description and analysis of those areas of human functioning which were most salient for him? In short, the client, with the assistance of the professional, would do his own task description and analysis as a basis for (*a*) the clarification of personal goals and (*b*) a planned program of personal development.

Consider a more general problem in the design of environments. I am thinking here of the current interest in "planned communities" as in some of the communities established for older persons or some of the "new cities" which are on the drawing boards or are in being, such as Columbia City near Washington, D. C. The planning of Columbia has involved psychologists, sociologists, and psychiatrists. Would this be a useful conceptual scheme and working tool for such an effort? Particularly if it were combined with some of the notions embodied in Roger Barker's (1960) work in psychological ecology with its emphasis upon behavior settings and environmental "claims"?

The human-effectiveness orientation puts many of the substantive problems of psychology in a somewhat different light. Two examples from the study of motivation illustrate this.

Psychoanalytic ego psychology has, I believe, been given a new thrust by the publication of Robert W. White's (1963) monograph titled "Ego and Reality in Psychoanalytic Theory." In this extension of his paper in the *Psychological Review* (1959), White proposes an energy source which he designates as *effectance*. Drawing upon work in animal and developmental psychology, he notes a general relationship of effectiveness which the animal or child seeks to maintain or establish between itself or its environment. He assumes, as crucial to adaptation and survival, an energy (effectance) intrinsic to the organism's apparatus which guarantees its constant use in finding out about the environment and in learning what effects can be had upon it. The accompanying experience is termed a *feeling of efficacy* which White says may be described as a feeling of doing something, of being active or effective, of having an influence on something. His thesis is that "the feeling of efficacy is a primitive biological endowment as basic as the satisfactions that accompany feeding or sexual gratification, though not nearly as intense [1963, p.35]." (And parenthetically I am tempted to suggest that the literature and lore of sexual behavior indicate that effectance and feelings of efficacy may be importantly involved in that behavior domain.) I am reminded by White's work that Donald Super some years ago suggested that the exercise of ability might in and of itself be an important satisfier.

White introduces the term *competence* to describe a person's existing capacity to interact effectively with his environment. He finds this concept useful to describe the cumulative result of the whole history of the individual's transactions with the environment, no matter *how* they were motivated. Finally, he uses *sense of competence* to describe the subjective side of one's actual competence and notes that it does not always accurately reflect what others judge to be our actual competence. Competence, for White, becomes a highly important *nucleus of motivation*. He expresses the hope that

> the concepts of effectance, feeling of efficacy, competence, and sense of competence will be experienced by clinical workers as helpful, as tools which will enable them to form a clearer and more consistent picture of just what it is that goes wrong in early ego deviation [1963, p. 92].

More generally, his conceptualization

> is held to improve our comprehension of reality testing, early ego deviations, identification as a growth process, self-esteem, and ego strength [1963, p. 182].

His proposals give an interesting cast to psychoanalytic theory and perhaps practice.

An interesting example of human-effectiveness-oriented research on motivation is afforded by the recent work of David C. McClelland and associates on the establishment and maintenance of the achievement motive in adults. The acquisition or change of a complex human characteristic like a motive in adulthood is indeed a challenging and significant venture. Drawing upon animal-learning experiments, human-learning experiments, experiences with psychotherapy, and from the attitude-change research literature, McClelland has designed a "motive acquisition" program and has been in the process of trying it out with business executives and management trainees. There has evolved gradually from these pilot efforts a set of 12 theoretical propositions which he is attempting to test. The novelty of this approach is suggested by McClelland's report that the investigators were encouraged in their belief that motives could be acquired in adulthood by the successful efforts of two quite different groups of "change agents"—operant conditioners and missionaries! The initial and preliminary data suggest that significant behavioral changes do occur among their subjects. This is a fascinating undertaking, an account of which appeared in the May 1965 *American Psychologist* (McClelland, 1965).

The utility of the concept of human effectiveness in clarifying a theory of psychopathology is suggested in the work of Phillips and Zigler and colleagues over the past few years. They have developed gross indices of social competence composed of six variables each of which is divided into three categories with each category conceptualized as representing a step along a *social-effectiveness* continuum (Phillips & Zigler, 1961). The variables are age, intelligence, education, occupation, employment history, and marital status. From a series of investigations they have suggested that "level of maturity" as defined by the social-competence or social-effectiveness indices is related to the incidence of mental disorders, symptoms manifested, diagnosis received, and prognosis; and they have advanced a developmental approach which appears to have considerable value for the understanding of psychopathology (Zigler & Phillips, 1961). In their words (Zigler & Phillips, 1962), "In such a schema the various disorders are viewed as inappropriate solutions to the problems of living at various levels of development [p. 220]."

Actually, much work in psychology is readily interpreted as fitting within a framework which emphasizes the establishment and maintenance of effective human performance. I was struck by this fact recently in reading Neal E. Miller's (1963) Royal Society paper in which he described and assessed recent developments in experimental psychology with particular emphasis upon investigations of how organisms process and act upon information. His report ranges from sensory functioning to the effects of infantile experience. Interestingly, in discussing experiments which agree in demonstrating that interference and filtering are phenomena of the central nervous system rather than involving peripheral masking or adjustments in the muscles of the ear, he observes that "the next time you arrive at a crowded airport, the application of such research to the control tower may well influence the safety of your landing [p. 485]." Elsewhere in his paper he cites research on the problem of "trouble-shooting" complex electronic equipment such as the radars used in the armed services to illustrate the value of heuristic principles in human problem solving and the test of their value by methods other than computer simulation. He also notes that a significant development in experimental psychology has been the increase in interaction between the clinic and laboratory with the clinic furnishing interesting problems. It is apparent that this distinguished scientist finds it congenial and easy to think within a human-effectiveness orientation.

These examples suggest to me that a human-effectiveness orientation could give new and fruitful directions to research and could give a new and useful dimension to the interpretation of research.

It is tempting to speculate upon the ways in which psychologists, oriented to human effectiveness as their predominant concern, could maximize their contribution to human affairs. I shall succumb to the temptation to speculate.

One attractive strategy would be to "capture" an ongoing social institution in which the leadership of psychologists would be predominant and which would give full expression to their interest and competence. There is one such social institution in which psychologists earlier defaulted their opportunity for leadership but where they are now making a comeback. I refer, of course, to *education.* This seems to be a natural source of cultural support for the contributions of psychology particularly, although not necessarily only, through its formal organized social structure—the school.

In passing, it might be noted that we may see the emergence of new social structures concerned with education as in some elements of the poverty program. It is too early to assess their potential impact or to identify the role of psychologists in them. With a few notable exceptions, particularly among researchers, the scanty evidence to date suggests that psychologists are somewhat more likely to talk about their role than to actively participate in specific work settings and projects. In fact, it sometimes seems that there are psychologists who believe that recognition should be bestowed rather than earned.

In any event, no other social institution seems quite so compatible with the basic interests of psychologists or so generally hospitable to present and potential contributions as does education.

It is, of course, possible to fantasy the emergence of a social institution which would have human effectiveness at its core and in which psychologists would play the leading role. There is, indeed, much in the vision and program of the "Great Society" which might seemingly betoken such a development over time. Perhaps the operational test of its emergence would be the act of a President—when he (or she) sends a message to the Congress calling for the enactment of a program of *Psychicare*.

It is admittedly difficult, however, to discern trends or events which would presage the development of a single social institution revolving around human effectiveness. In matter of fact, a possible trend is the envelopment of human effectiveness as a part of the health institution and the particular province of medicine. The restorative and habilitative emphasis of medicine, along with the rise of the public health movement, lends itself to this development. Thus a respected sociologist, Talcott Parsons (1958), examines the concept of health with reference to the individual's participation in the social system and defines health as "the state of optimum *capacity* of an individual for the effective performance of the roles and tasks for which he has been socialized [p. 176]." The rapid development of community and preventive psychiatry indexes the extension of the domain of health to include concerns with such matters as poverty, juvenile delinquency, education, urban renewal, and the like (Caplan, 1964, p. 304).

A middle-ground strategy to enhance the contribution of psychology to human affairs would be to evolve a new social structure or organizational entity as part of or even outside any existing social institution. Such an entity would offer to the public services which draw from a wide range of subfields of psychology including, for example, engineering, industrial, counseling, clinical, educational. It could engage in grant- and contract-supported research in all substantive areas of psychology. Although there is no existing prototype (in all its possible ramifications) for such an organization or structure, there are elements presently in existence. Perhaps the closest approximation is the Psychological Corporation, which during its existence had included research and services in test development, market research, industrial and engineering psychology, counseling, and audio-visual instructional programs. Psychological Services in Pittsburgh is, in part, such an entity. There are, of course, a number of nonprofit psychological research organizations as, for example, the American Institutes for Research.

If such an entity were developed under university auspices, it would readily lend itself to instructional purposes. Albee (1964) has proposed and discussed such a psychological center as part of a university program with particular emphasis upon its desirability as a practicum agency controlled by psychologists. He does not, however, link it exclusively to a university but also urges the consideration of this pattern by private practitioners. More than 15 years ago, Milton E. Hahn and Raymond A. Katzell operated a Psychological Services Center at Syracuse University which contained many of the elements of Albee's proposal; and several groups of clinical psychologists, mainly in private practice, are developing possible forerunners of such a Center in Los Angeles and in New York State, although the emphasis presently is on clinical services to individuals.

There has been sufficient experience with most of the elements of such a comprehensive psychological entity or social structure to suggest that the concept is a viable one.

There remains, of course, the alternative of continuing to work within the framework of existing social institutions and present organizations while remaining alert to new and emerging opportunities.

Whatever the future development of the role of psychology in our culture, it will be in response to *social demand* as expressed in opportunities for service through research, teaching, practice, and advice and consultation. And this in turn should be conditioned largely by the following importance which I attach to them:

1. The tested knowledge which psychologists have at their command and can communicate to others or themselves apply.
2. The demonstrated competence of individual psychologists.
3. The efforts which psychologists make as individuals and, as appropriate, through their various organizations to clarify their unique contributions and to insure the existence of optimal conditions for making their contributions.

My primary and limited purpose in this paper has been to suggest an orientation which is congenial and relevant to the interests of diverse psychologists and responsive to the perceived needs of our culture and the members of our society. We are, in my view, a science and profession uniquely concerned with human effectiveness—with the establishment and maintenance of the effective performance of the members of society in all their required tasks, their social roles, and their human relationships. This is our challenge—and our opportunity.

REFERENCES

ALBEE, G. President's message: A declaration of independence for psychology. *Ohio Psychologist,* 1964, 10, No. 4.

ALPERT, H. Sociology: Its present interests. In B. Berelson (Ed.), *The behavorial sciences today.* New York: Harper & Row, 1963. Pp. 52–62.

BARKER, R. G. Ecology and motivation. In M. R. Jones (Ed.), *Nebraska symposium on motivation: 1960.* Lincoln: Univer. Nebraska Press, 1960. Pp. 1–49.

Bloom, B. S. *Stability and change in human characteristics.* New York: Wiley, 1964.
Caplan, G. *Principles of preventive psychiatry.* New York: Basic Books, 1964.
Freeman, H. E., Levine, S., & Reeder, L. G. (Eds.) *Handbook of medical sociology.* Englewood Cliffs, N. J.: Prentice-Hall, 1963.
Gagne, R. Task analysis and the establishment of human performances. In A. Melton (Chm.), Criteria for a broad scale map of human functions. Symposium presented at American Psychological Association, Philadelphia, September 1963.
Leland, H. (Ed.) Conference on measurement of adaptive behavior. Parsons, Kans.: Parsons State Hospital and Training Center, Rehabilitation Center, 1964. (Mimeo)
Levenstein, S. *Private practice in social work.* New York: Columbia Univer. Press, 1964.
McClelland, D. C. Toward a theory of motive acquisition. *American Psychologist,* 1965, 20, 321–333.
Miller, N. E. Certain recent developments in experimental psychology *Proceedings of the Royal Society, London,* (Series B) 1963, 158, 481–497.
Parsons, T. Definitions of health and illness in the light of American values and social structure. In E. G. Jaco (Ed.), *Patients, physicians and illness.* Glencoe, Ill.: Free Press, 1958. Pp. 165–187.
Phillips, L., & Zigler, E. Social competence: The action-thought parameter and vicariousness in normal and pathological behaviors. *Journal of Abnormal and Social Psychology,* 1961, 63, 137–146.
Sells, S. B. (Ed.) *Stimulus determinants of behavior.* New York: Ronald Press, 1963.
Wardwell, W. I. Limited, marginal, and quasi-practitioners. In H. E. Freeman, S. Levine, & L. G. Reeder (Eds.), *Handbook of medical sociology.* Englewood Cliffs, N. J.: Prentice-Hall, 1963. Pp. 213-239.
White, R. W. Motivation reconsidered: The concept of competence. *Psychological Review,* 1959, 66, 297–333.
White, R. W. Ego and reality in psychoanalytical theory. *Psychological Issues,* 1963, 3(3, Monogr. No. 11).
Young, K., & Mack, R. W. *Sociology and social life.* New York: American Book Company, 1959.
Zigler, E., & Phillips, L. Social competence and outcome in psychiatric disorders. *Journal of Abnormal and Social Psychology,* 1961, 63, 264–271.
Zigler, E., & Phillips, L. Social competence and the process-reactive distinction in psychopathology. *Journal of Abnormal and Social Psychology,* 1962, 65, 215–222.

2 A Research Utopia in Industrial Psychology

HERBERT A. TOOPS

The reminiscing sometimes deemed appropriate to be indulged in by a grandfather can be disposed of quickly. In 1919, **Mr. Mitten, progressive president of the Philadelphia street railway system,** hired Mr. Max Watson and myself to "look his street cars over for a week as psychologists."

It developed later what he really wanted to know was how to paint the interior of his cars so two ends would be served: (a) Passengers wouldn't congregate up front but would move to the back relieving the congestion; (b) They would be more cheerful and willingly ride the cars more often.

We knew nothing then about the psychology of street-car painting—I wonder if that still wouldn't be quite an order—but we accomplished to his satisfaction part of the second objective by telling him that in our opinion the passengers would like it if the company would press the uniforms of their employees. So, in 1919, nearly forty years ago, I helped put the creases in the pants of Philadelphia's streetcarmen! I have been on the ragged edge of industrial psychology ever since!

On this occasion—the first of its kind, and I hope there will be many more—I don't want to bore you to tears, as grandfathers are wont to do, telling you how bad life was back in December, 1917. That was my first APA meeting. There were then only some 350 psychologists in America with about half of them in attendance. Being a psychologist then was a hard life, but in all a very good one. Everybody knew everyone, by sight if not by first name.

We have grown some in the intervening forty years! In fact, just a few minutes ago out in the lobby I overheard someone say that if psychology continues to grow as it has been, there will shortly be more psychologists than people!

Nor do I want to tell you how good, absolutely or relatively, life is

From *Personnel Psychology*, 1959, 12, 189–225. Revision of a paper presented before the Grandfathers' Meeting, Industrial Psychology Section, APA, Washington, D. C., September 1, 1958.

today—in some respects it is terrible; but rather do I crave to share with you some of my thoughts about how good life could be in the Utopian future, in my opinion, if we put our heads and backs together, carefully planned what we wanted to do, and joined efforts to clear away the obstacles.

Talking to industrial psychologists, if, like a preacher, I were to take a text for my discourse, I would say that the profile, the scoring key, and the selective regression equation are three of our profoundest tools—comparable to fire, the wheel, the steel plow, and the jet engine in the life of man generally—and therefore worthy of considerable detailed examination. I see a tremendous need for their increased employment.

I base that judgment on the fact that not only are these instruments eminently sound theoretically as I shall attempt to show herein, but also because the end products are so easy for the man of the street to understand. He, of course, is a very important part of the picture of acceptance or rejection of a profession. It is he in general who pays the bills.

I. THE PROFILE

First, the profile. The profile does not necessarily consist of a number, n, of picturized comparable test scores on an individual, but rather, generalized: A profile consists of a number, n, of scores on an individual; period. This greater generality will be important to my central thesis. Nothing is said there about the scores being comparable; nothing is said about picturization; nothing is said even about their being *test* scores, for any old scores, if valid, will do, quantitative or qualitative, the latter of course being the more general.[1] Qualitative terms are of course far more generally understood by people who have only words in which to express their meanings and that includes most of us. I shall endeavor then to prove to you with qualitative scores my central point, namely, that the profile is basic, because only it, of all proposals to date, comes close to representing as a scientific schema the whole functioning individual.

Let me assert then that the most profound remark a psychologist can make is to say, "A kind of people acts alike, thinks alike, even tends to emote alike." Obviously I am defining "kind" as a subsociety (statistical, not geographical) of people who have a common profile of categories. An ulstrith, to which I shall refer repeatedly hereinafter, is any one such subsociety, when all the traits involved in a study are broken down statistically into compound trait-category patterns to the utmost degree.

Go beyond *two* compound breakdowns of the categories of people,

---

[1] Quantitative scores are qualitative scores having intrinsic order of the several categories with the intervening intervals equal or assumed equal, which may be quite another matter.

looking for a criterion as well, and only Kinsey and the Detroit police suicide reports seem to have seen the need for as many as four trait breakdowns. Both of these have four trait breakdowns on the test side; both have at least one criterion.

Table 2.1 below will serve as well as most to present a point of view. You can't prove in 45 minutes what here I shall simply have to assert.

You cannot predict at all well with regression equations the behavior of those three ulstrith groups, inclusive of course of quite a number of other ulstriths of coordinate mode of origin. Yet there is, I feel, indeed a curious rationality behind it all. Let us look into the matter meticulously.

I need not tell psychologists—or should I?—that we should look for the causation involved. The Detroit police, actuated somewhat by the same considerations as the US Census, specifically, here to print a basic report on both sides of a 2-foot by 3-foot sheet of paper—instead of one very much larger and incidentally much more useful for our purposes—employed the reverse side of the sheet for additional compound breakdowns of (a) method (firearms, sleeping pills, etc.) and (b) motive, so far as known. Of course the two sides of the sheet of necessity are independent, unrelated.

All six (sex, color, age, marital condition, method, and motive) if put on one side of the paper in a six-breakdown analysis would have enabled us, perhaps, to see that even suicide is a lawful human behavior—even if legally a crime.

Let us take a bold step, go beyond our data and infer the causation involved in *motives* and *methods* of the three groups (A, B, C) above.

The first two groups (A and B), I submit, really are not seriously attempting suicide; they only seem to do so. Perhaps they are employing suicide as a tool, the first to influence an intractable young man; the second, to influence a man who as a youth married a maiden who one day would reach the menopause and would suspect her man of running out on her. (The "rationality" of the motivational tool is not beyond suspicion but is not the issue here.)

Group C for the most part, I take it, made man-sized efforts to succeed at the business at hand. (No pun intended.) But I suspect the

TABLE 2.1. *The relative success of Ulstrith groups attempting suicide, Detroit*

Group	Ulstrith Description (Sex, color, age, marital condition)	Number Attempting Suicide	Per Cent Successful
A	F, W, 18, S	x	0
B	F, B, 45, M	y	1
C	M, W, 65–70, M	z	75

different success-figure also involved more than motive. We ask why 25 per cent of the aged men failed; why it was not 100 per cent. As theoreticians we need to know something about that.

If you will speculate a little further with me, then, I think you can also picture a possible, nay plausible, difference in means or method: "To commit suicide" groups A and B probably used sleeping pills—far too few to accomplish results—while the third, C, probably in the main employed firearms—a rather effective method, the aim being good, anatomical knowledge adequate, the attempt bona fide. Just possibly most of the unsuccessful 25 per cent of group C employed the methods preferred by groups A and B. The published data, on different sides of the sheet, unfortunately cannot tell us. Obviously we need at least a breakdown of five "traits," inclusive of method. Such reports are never written by statistical psychologists trying to probe the causes of suicide. They should be.

The above example proves (if with me for the moment you will forget a lot of sectarian orthodoxies):

1. That like-traited, like-minded people think alike, act alike, and perhaps even emote alike in their gross behaviors, not excepting the most bizarre, suicide.
2. That to know the ulstrith, the pattern, is virtually to know the behavior. To predict it, you simply compute the percentages of Table 2.1. The result is a highly useful empirical probability. You largely or entirely duck problems of weighting, combining scores, regression equations, norms, normal correlation surfaces, curvilinearity, type-equations, and the like. The price you pay for this, of course, is a very large N.
3. That every one of us belongs to some one of the ulstriths in the complete analysis from which the above three groups were extracted. Everyone of us, then, *if* we attempt suicide, has a probability of successful suicide, given numerical value in the "per cent successful" column[2] of the larger, inclusive, Table 2.1. Note that Table 2.1 does not say much of anything about what some want to know; namely, what are John A. Citizen's chances of successfully committing suicide. There are one or more similar "ifs" in every prediction ever made. It would be both interesting and useful to dwell on this but we must hasten on.
4. That it follows that every living person is fair game for inclusion in many of the possible proposable researches of psychologists, perhaps in almost all. I am merely giving the law of the single variable a new twist— but the languishing critter, research, has needed a sartorial operation on its caudal appendage for some time in my opinion. (That's what manufacturing intelligence tests and owning cows does to you.)
5. That irrespective of whether we can presently do it or not, psycholo-

---

[2] This column of course did not occur in the original report; it had to be computed; and the word "successful" also was missing from the report. You can't employ a word implying merit in an official report on suicide.

gists must begin shortly to talk the language of causation; not only must we look for "causes" of human behavior but equally important we must not be content until we have found them.

We must begin to do something about our findings. The day is over, in my opinion, when a psychologist, or an "ologist" of any other name, can usefully say, "Behold me: I have solved another batch of ten thousand correlations; have performed another factor analysis and found five factors. I have named them Ammonia, Begonia, Chalcedonia—I am now content to rest on my laurels." Why, I am old enough to remember the thrill I got when Simpson solved all 28 of the possible intercorrelations (think of it!) of his 37 cases. That feat was the beginning of the end. All later records pale into insignificance, relatively.

6. That we need to project experiments of heroic size, macrostudies. Obviously ulstriths consume persons like jets consume fuel, and, in my opinion, the analogy does not stop there. Both get phenomenal results, the one in understanding human behavior, the other in speed of transportation.

Our research problems require for their solution bold thinking. The requirements, so it seems to me, are:

(1) The collection, on a very large group of persons (100,000 to 250,000 perhaps, or even more) of very extensive data, test-variables, on all aspects of their lives, almost surely by successive periodic inventories to involve the very important relativity factor, time, growth, maturity. The past ten years I have devised some 17,000 Yes–No questions (288 pages) of the types I think might be useful. These touch virtually every facet of life. I guess that there may be 30,000 more worth collecting but it is much harder to concoct new items now than ten years ago. Yes–No questions readily are amenable to electronic manipulation.

(2) A follow-up, equally bold in its conception, in which from fifty to a hundred or more criteria are accumulated on every person periodically for at least 40 years. We need to know:

What kinds of people succeed at specific occupations.
What kinds of people go insane. (Specific insanities, of course.)
What kinds of people commit *specific* kinds of crime, and under what *situations*.
(Those words "specific" and "situations," I am sure, are keys to research on the causes of crime.)
What kinds of people go to specific types of colleges. What kinds do not go at all.
What kinds of people get specific college degrees.
What kinds of people go on to graduate school.
What kinds of people become Pasteurs, Edisons, and Einsteins.
What kinds of people die before 30; before 40.
And a hundred others.

As for details regarding the analysis of data:

(a) There is on file in this capitol city a manuscript of plans for a research invention which will speed up the sorting of ulstriths and facilitate the criterion-analysis by 25,000 to 50,000 times over the very great efficiency (25,000 cases sorted per hour on one trait) of IBM sorting procedures. Though mechanical mainly or only, it dwarfs electronics-only devices for the purpose at hand. It is based on the principle of conjunctions of *categories* of traits.[3]

(b) The machine to which I have just referred will locate patterns [1] of any degree of complexity and [2] ascertain the conjunctions of such patterns with one or many simple or compound follow-up patterns of categories. The principle is simple: For the compounds merely superimpose two or more stencils. There are, for example, 144,491,500 possible two-category patterns among 17,000 such questions. Of these, presumably, we need compute only a very few: First, those pairs of categories which contain the most valid single variable as a component, by aid of which we determine the second "most important" variable; second, those trios which have the above selected pair as a component of the pattern and so on. Once we have learned what are the "prime causes" and the referrent variables of human capacity and ability. (See 8. below), the process presumably can be substantially shortened. The aim of course is maximum prediction with a minimum of variables.

(c) The collection of such data will be of utmost interest and value to researchers in sister sciences, who quickly and easily can be supplied with complete duplications of our data. (The genealogist and even the geneticist, for example, years later, can have something about ancestors more substantial than their names, occupations, dates of birth, ages at death, and causes of demise.)

Obviously the more scientists we can induce to employ our data, the more insight about "people" we shall achieve. The value of a study is greater the larger the number of intercorrelations produced in that study. With n variables we have $n(n-1)/2$ intercorrelations; but with $n+1$ variables we have $(n+1)n/2$ intercorrelations, an appreciably larger number. Or, finally, the value of a research is directly proportional to the square of the number of variables analyzed.

7. That (please be charitable!) a man reacts as a whole personality, as

---

[3] The aim in good design is to make it possible to sort "cases" and make needed analyses visually without necessarily involving a counting of noses. By and large we want to know what is the profile of (A) the successes and the co-profile of (B) the failures on a minimum number selected out of 45,000 Yes-No questions. Before employment of our selections on individuals we shall need the usual cross-validation.

Personally, I feel that in time we shall learn that cross-validation is unnecessary because with a little manipulation every ulstrith group is in effect a cross-validation of others. Large populations, when treated as ulstriths, have a way of "telling the truth" the first time.

a member, as a first approximation, of an ulstrith population. It follows that any one member thereof, is, presumably, almost as good a representative of an ulstrith as any other. Accordingly, smaller ulstrith frequencies, smaller x's, y's, and z's (Table 2.1) than we are accustomed to guess will be necessary, presumably will yield dependable results. This means in the aggregate very much larger N's than now appear in studies —in many cases N's so large that they can be accumulated only by cooperative sharing of the burden of data-collecting. Facts cost money. If that is the cost, well then that is the cost! Many indispensable facts have cost the human race blood as well as money.

Obviously, employing ulstriths, we need representativeness as to the ulstrith population only. Thus, we largely duck problems of population-representativeness, normal curves, normal correlation surfaces, and of course problems such as curvilinearity, interaction and the like. Yet, withal, we take full account of interaction and curvilinearity, and still we get results that a man of the street can understand.

8. That the meaning of all or most of an individual's responses is *relative* to the ulstrith group to which the individual in question belongs.

They also are relative in a very special way to certain status and environmental variables which may be called *referent variables*:

Age (maturity)
Socio-economic status (income)
Marital condition
Education
And others[4]

These are variables which modify the *meaning*—the causal potency—of other variables.

Interaction "in the Library"

For the discovery of these variables *in the literature* we look for the key words "if" and "provided"; these, of course, implying an interaction: This conclusion "is true *if* only bright young people are considered," or "*provided* they are not athletes and are not employed." Such statements always refer to categories of referent variables.

Trait Interaction

All such imply interactions, of course; that is to say, where the weight of an aptitude-variable is not a constant, as implied in ordinary regression equations, but rather is a mathematical function of a referent

---

[4] Those here enumerated alter the action-potential of a man of a given basic profile with the onset of *time, attainment,* and *fortune.*

variable. The simplest form of such an equation, involving two variables, is the simple warped plane, with linear elements in both predictors,

$$Y_0 = A + BX_1 + CX_2 + (DX_1X_2) \tag{1}$$

The constants A, B, C, D are easily found by least-squares normal equations. The added term, (DX_1X_2) is, here, the single interaction term.

The complete equation can be factored into:

$$Y_0 + \frac{BC}{D} - A = X_1 + \frac{C}{D}(DX_2 + B), \tag{2}$$

or

$$Y_0' = X_1'X_2'', \tag{3}$$

where a prime sign indicates a correction for zero-point; a double prime indicates a correction both for length of unit and for zero-point in our measuremental system [2].

In both (2) and (3) it may be seen that the weight of either variable is a multiplicative function of the other. I have located a few examples where such equations prevail.

Equation (1) is easily fitted by least squares, and the lower limit of the validity of the Y_0's in equations (1), (2), and (3) is the multiple-r appropriate to:

$$Y_{00} = A + BX_1 + CX_2, \tag{4}$$

the ordinary multiple regression equation. If the multiple correlation for (1) is not appreciably larger than the multiple for (4), then we may conclude that interaction does not prevail.

All this leads to the presumption that the multiplication of trait scores (3) is a more basic mode of combination of traits, for predictive purposes generally [3], than is their addition in ordinary regression equations, (4). Equation (1) degenerates into (4) when D is zero.

So far I have not been successful in generalizing the factoring for three or more predictive variables. The simplest interaction involving three predictor-variables is:

$$Y_{000} = A + BX_1 + CX_2 + DX_3$$
$$+ (EX_1X_2 + FX_1X_3 + GX_2X_3 + HX_1X_2X_3) \tag{5}$$

where the parenthetical expression contains four interaction terms. Equation (5) also is easily solved by least squares; requires a rather large number of cases, N, to secure low probable errors for the several constant coefficients; but apparently is not easily factorable. Perhaps I have only been unfortunate in my mathematical manipulations.

The chief importance of (3) lies in the fact that a zero-score in one variable can reduce to a zero-prophecy even a very favorable score in another variable; and also that *two* or more favorable values in two or more variables may "cooperate," in the individual, in the production of "genius." (In words, "The potency of a good and virtuous trait is multiplied enormously when associated with a high value in a second compatible trait.") Accordingly, we may conclude that (5) is at least minimally capable, as a type, of handling most cases observed to date of the dependence of a criterion score upon three test-variables. As a type equation both equation (5) and equation (1) are capable minimally of "explaining" special disability, special ability, and genius—all of which, like suicide, are assumed by many to be lawless.

Empirically Determined Interaction

In discovering interactions *experimentally*, one needs to think as logically as possible about what variables—particularly in very large or very small amounts—*ought* to modify the meaning of a score; such variables, perhaps, as:

> Difficulty or complexity (of environment)
> Experience (perhaps a curvilinear interaction [3] in industry generally)
> Intellect
> Energy
> Health (I have worked with such an instrument with an approximate validity of .40, a validity as high as was that of Army Alpha in 1919 in the prediction of university scholastic success.)
> Growth (time changes, both positive and negative).

I discover no one working in such realms. Students these days seem to prefer dissertations "bound to arrive."

If we were to get really serious, I contend, the price of one flat-top would go far in ascertaining not only what are the basic aptitude variables but also what are these referrent variables. We would need to hire a few scores of competent persons, a lot of clerks, a dozen or so IBM outfits, and an electronic computer or two, and start industriously to work, first reading the literature.[5]

---

[5] The device to which I referred above is capable, with a great deal of preliminary work in classification of books, articles, monographs, etc., of finding in a trice all articles out of a million which are pertinent to one's inquiries if his need can be couched in terms of the complete, or any part-pattern, of the compound knowledge-classification system of rubrics.

An industrial research institute tells me that they budget some 30 per cent of their client fees to finding out what is already known about problems they undertake. If this could be reduced to 2 per cent or less, the productivity in research of clients' money would approach 140 per cent. The situation of course will get very much worse before it gets any better.

The interested reader will get much stimulus to thinking from: Walker, Fred F., Jr. Blueprint for knowledge. *Scientific Monthly*, 1951, 72, 90–101.

Applications to Industrial Personnel Problems

I conjecture that no expenditure of such an amount of money could be industrially more important. Consider with me the importance for productivity, progress, and human happiness generally, of having most boys and girls:

(1) Enter the right occupation;
(2) Progress therein as they individually are capable;
(3) Get pay proportional to their present but ever-changing deserts;
(4) Unfailingly get a chance to be called, without personal application, to any part of the world to do what only a person of their pattern of aptitudes and achievements can do best (a perpetual national roster);
(5) And finally, after a lifetime of highly productive industrial effort, retire to that part of the country (or the world) where they, individually, would find life most salubrious. (Nature does not dictate that a man's usefulness to his fellowmen stops abruptly at 65! Society may reward old men with what such men regard as "good living.")

These are big ends. Their achievement is a first, and potent, step toward Utopia.

How could we accomplish such? The solution of all these implies specialized applications of profiles and two tools for ascertaining and utilizing them, the selective regression equation and scoring keys. Let us discuss some of these applications in detail.

(1) *Entering the right occupation.* Let us first ascertain a half dozen or more nearly-unique traits. Consider the human aptitude profile of Table 2.2, which here involves addends.

TABLE 2.2. *Coding unique profiles on basic unique tests*
(The boldfaced, small, numbers are addends)

Tertile	"Abstract Intelligence" Trait 1	"Mechanical Ability" Trait 2	"Social Intelligence" Trait 3	"Energy" Trait 4	... Trait 5	... Trait 6
3	68–100 **2**	288–500 **6**	91–150 **18**	— **54**	— **162**	— **486**
2	34–67 **1**	123–278 **3**	46–90 **9**	— **27**	— **81**	— **243**
1	1–33 **0**	0–122 **0**	0–45 **0**	— **0**	— **0**	— **0**
Raw Scores of Tom Jones............	28	327	72	—	—	—

Tom Jones' profile = $0 + 6 + 9 + 0 + 162 + 0 = 177$

A RESEARCH UTOPIA IN INDUSTRIAL PSYCHOLOGY 27

TABLE 2.3. *Positive guidance probabilities*
Thirty or Fifty Families of Occupations:

Ulstrith	1	2........15........20........50	Total
0			
1			
2			
—			
—			
—			
177............................No.		No. in the compartment succeeding to 75-percentile (success standard) Per cent so succeeding (success-probability)	
—			
—			
—			
727			
728			
Total			

The six tests could be scorings of selected items from the 17,000 or 47,000 question test. (A stencil may be applied six times, with or without item-weights (see below) to the 17,000 items.) Some of them may be referrent variables that modify the meaning of an individual's basic aptitude scores. In any case they are basic—highly valid as profiles—"causal."

Tom Jones, whose profile is indicated by ovals in Table 2.2, may have his pattern easily ascertained as a code number, 177. All persons whose test scores plot as do his also are 177's; collectively they comprise an ulstrith, one of the patterns of an ultimate statistical breakdown of the six traits. [1]

The code numbers enable us to specify each person by a single individual code number between 0 and 728. Every possible pattern has a number, and every number between 0 and 728 has a corresponding pattern. The code numbers are unique. There are no duplicates.

Perhaps 729 kinds of humans are enough? By such a conception we may hope ultimately to have a taxonomy, causally, of humans.

What can we do, specifically, with Tom's 177? Well, for one thing, we can have positive guidance, guidance of an individual *into* the one or two or at most a very few occupations in which his chances for success truly are greatest, not the present negative guidance, *away from* the individual's proposed "obviously bad" choice of occupation. One tally-mark, in a compartment of a two-way table (Table 2.3), may stand for both a person's basic profile and his occupational status. Aggregated they produce the representative compartment illustrated in Table 2.3.

(A) Table 2.3 obviously will cost some tens (or scores) of millions; occupational success being one of the most important and also most difficult (diversified) of the one hundred failure-success criteria. Its cost can be minimized by ascertaining families of occupations, perhaps a few dozen in number rather than tens of thousands.

I think there are additional possibilities of reducing the cost by the expedient of *introducing the criterion into the tests*. Whatever questions can be asked of an employer may also be asked (in perhaps a different form) of the employee, and more besides (e.g., trade-test questions). Most tradesmen, for example, in 1958 are literate. That statement was not equally true forty years ago. Trade tests can be given by paper-and-pencil methods.

We have found that university students almost without exception know their cumulative point-hour ratio (scholastic average) correct to within a few hundredths of the value one obtains from an evaluation of their records on file in the Registrar's Office. For item-evaluation purposes, where the object is to throw away some 40 per cent, more or less, of the less useful items, a relatively correct validity coefficient serves our purposes quite as well as a perfectly correct one since the errors, if any, are small and presumably affect all items correspondingly—raising or lowering all coefficients by a very small amount, if indeed the errors in the aggregate are not compensative.

As an illustration of what I mean, in a criterion for construction of intelligence tests one may include in the experimental test battery such questions as:

In grade school I failed, or was held back, one or more times.	Yes	No
In grade school, pupils often asked me to help them with their lessons	Yes	No
I graduated from high school.	Yes	No
I was salutatorian of my high school class.	Yes	No
I was valedictorian of my high school class.	Yes	No
In college I always tried to study with a brighter student if I could.	Yes	No
In high school I took as little mathematics as I could get away with.	Yes	No
In undergraduate college I took all the mathematics courses in the college catalog.	Yes	No
I think I could get a college degree.	Yes	No
I would like to get an M.A. degree.	Yes	No
I belong to Phi Beta Kappa.	Yes	No
I like foreign languages.	Yes	No
I once took a course in Greek.	Yes	No
To be a second Einstein would be the height of attainment for me.	Yes	No

And a hundred other such! This technique takes lots of questions, but presumably saves oceans of work.[6]

[6] A universal statistical machine, which somebody ought shortly to invent, presumably would aggregate selected patterns of items for criterion and other analysis as

Now to return to Tom, patiently waiting:

(a) By looking under column 15, say, Tom notes (in row 177) whether he has much chance of succeeding in Family 15 of occupations, *which he thinks he would like to enter*. If the percentage is low, we have negative guidance: Obviously he ought not to enter occupational family 15. The guidee himself initiates this inquiry.

(b) Then in the same row of Table 2.3 he also notes the two or three occupational families with highest success probabilities.[7] He ought to think seriously about entering one of these. Probably expert vocational counsellors will initiate the ensuing *positive* guidance. With the table available they no longer are soothsayers, and in time will come to be believed, trusted, and followed. Table 2.3 is on a far firmer basis than is presently, the underwriting of life insurance.

Emotions, interests, beliefs, and such are not the prerogative of those professions now monopolizing them. They belong to Man, not to professions. By 2000 A.D. we ought as individuals to take vocational medicine as objectively, as uncomplainingly, as usefully, and as successfully as we now take medicine for disease. A vocational recommendation ought to be as objective and valid as any diagnosis in the world. It means so much to the individual in a world where, as now, we live to work. Soon enough on this planet we probably shall have to work to live.

(2) *Pay according to deserts*. In the scheme of human values in our world, pay looms large. "What does it cost?" is almost the most interesting question there is. Possessions—speaking in the large—are the tools of personality. Our aspirations to own, to become, to be thought of, to be are of course highly relative to our income. Everyone of us, without exception, employs pay or profit—in any case money—as a tool to construct the stage on which we individually choose to dance through life.

It strikes me that industrial psychologists are in the best possible position to work on this problem. Salary or wages paid is the criterion; the tests are the tests of Table 2.2 plus additional ones of age, experience, education, marital condition, dependents, etc. The selective regression equation strikes me as a very simple, very easy, and probably adequate statistical technique. It has the additional merit of being, when solved, the most easily understood of the regression techniques. The aim, of

---

well as score tests, ascertain patterns, gross moments, product-moments and the like. One feels small sympathy for an over-worked electronic machine. Such a machine in turn expects none!

[7] This table also exemplifies selection. By going down a column an employer can locate what ulstrith of people will do his job best, the highest entry; and second best the second highest probability. Appropriately, he will learn what kind of people are of the highest aptitude for his job and are most worth training and which are second best. Of course he will have to compete in the market place for them. A thousand years from now he may be expected to procure central clearance before hiring them and provide assurance to society that the proffered employment is in the public interest.

course, is to ascertain if possible a highly valid minimal (as to numbers of variables) regression equation for, ideally, every occupation; but, practically, and in the long run, for every occupational family.

Then if (a) these selections usually or even generally should happen to involve the same "test" variables, any guidee (employed or unemployed) can be told where people of his talents may receive the most money; and if, in addition, (b) these should happen to include one or more easily amenable-to-change variables, such as specific trade-education, a guidee (employee) can be advised what is most efficacious in general for him personally (as a member of an ulstrith, of course) to do to improve his wage worth for promotion and get more money. With experience and effectiveness one is worth more.

It strikes me that the solution would tend to solve wage disputes. Now it's "If carpenters are worth that, we plumbers should strike for more money." There is little logic in that. It is emotional only. Clearly, if the profile of talents is identical in the two occupations, if plumbers are cut off the same bolt of goods as carpenters, some considerable undesirable pressures would tend to be relieved. That would be a healthy antidote to the insidious creeping inflation of America.

The end result would be healthy also in other realms. We hear too little of ambition, hard work, and perseverance these sad days; rather is the situation verbalizeable in: "I'm going to get myself a racket, just like his (a telescreen hero's)!" I am assuming of course that the industrial virtues of thrift, honesty, perseverance, ambition, punctuality, and industriousness will demonstrate themselves to be positive virtues. (The statistician of course does not take these for granted. Some advisers of the government at Washington don't either, but for a different reason!)

I have found it possible to teach "practical bricklaying" to a wide variety of people. I have not myself mastered plastering, but several of my "students" have. This observation is included to suggest that the aptitude pattern for success in a lot of high-paid occupations may be common enough in America and, incidentally, that *perhaps* some occupations have preponderantly the wrong kinds of people in them.

(3) *Retirement in Utopia.* A man's friends and associates, his community, his neighborhood, his home, his car, and his possessions are a vital part of his "pay for working." Each of these add to or subtract from his happiness and well-being as he sees it as a representative of the ulstrith to which he belongs, and their value to him is highly relative thereto.[8] (It is surprising how often that word "relative" crops up. I think that some of the sociologists realize the importance of this more than most psychologists do, but they don't quite seem to be able to say it clearly.)

[8] I can personally attest to the correctness of the principle, "*Other things equal* the fewer farms, houses, furniture, books, and cars you own the better!" That is philosophical. I think there is no contradiction here.

As a matter of logic, then, clearly if a person presently employed considers himself to be living in Utopia, even though his salary is low he may be hard to budge by salary inducements. After all, all that one can buy with a salary is an approximation to one's personal ideas of Utopia: cars, clothes, houses, food, lipstick, dancing pumps, gasoline, etc.

Obviously then, it is useful for psychologists to find out what people *do* with their money, what possessions they have, what they *would like to own*. A 1000-item possessions test, unanalyzed as yet, seems to contain indubitable evidence that possessions are highly relative to income, age, sex, education, occupational competence, and marital condition.

For the reason mentioned above, namely, that we all dance on a stage of our own construction, test scores (patterns?) on this "test' probably are a highly valid index to personality, minimally subject to malingering.

But to return to our theme: For a person about to retire, obviously a Utopian environment—Utopian for *him*—is a "must." Inwardly he mulls the thought, "Where can I and my wife be best contented, happiest?" I conceive that if industrial psychologists took serious steps to solve this problem, they would also solve an equally important one, namely, "Where should a recent school graduate strive to settle down where he too will be most content, be best paid an unearned dividend by his environment?"

I conceive it would work out this way:

(a) Mr. and Mrs. Smith, about to retire, would each answer 3000 Yes-No questions (already in existence) about what features they would like in an ideal retirement-community, viz:

The lowest temperature and the highest temperature of the year are seldom more than ten to twenty degrees apart.	Yes	No
There are rattlesnakes in the community.	Yes	No
The trout fishing is superb.	Yes	No
The drinking water as drawn from the tap is always ice cold.	Yes	No

Their answers as a geometrical pattern are a *test stencil*. It contains their hopes and aspirations, both for and against features of "Utopia." They now want to know how the 6000 communities of America score-up on this stencil.

(b) The same 3000 questions will have been asked previously (and officially) of the some 6000 communities of America and the answers recorded on some 6000 cards. These are the *tests*. These cards may now be scored a million times for a million about-to-retire individuals by the aid of a million personal stencils of which the Smith's is one such. (Why should stencils always come out of dictionaries and encyclopaedias? Why *not* have more stencils than tests?)

(c) At this point we would strive to enlist Dr. Lindquist to our venture since obviously we have here a big test-scoring and recording project. As our mandate from client Smith, we need to score every community card by the Smith Stencil and acquire on a tape some 6000 units long the recorded highly-legible total scores of every American community.

(d) Then inspecting the tape, Mr. and Mrs. Smith pick out the four or five highest scoring and go to live at each a few months before selling the family homestead and taking the irretrievable step. Like our vocational guidee of a previous example, if they have already set covetous eyes on Florida, being human they first ascertain its score—the result being negative guidance if a Floridian community logically is not for them.

Research on "Environments"

I contend that research on environments, communities, homes, and work-places should multiply an hundredfold.

And while we are talking in this vein, by the same token we should consider the functions which go on in houses; for example, eating. An 800-item taste test revealed that the average college sophomore feels that steak, bread, tomatoes, corn, and potatoes are "good to eat"; he wants nothing of game, products of the forest, river or sea, nor even such esoteric products of the garden as asparagus, artichokes, endive, and brussels sprouts. Either for the most part he has never tasted the latter class, or he doesn't like them if he has; and mostly if they are strangers to him he is unwilling to try them for the first time, or, if he didn't like them on the first trial to try them again. His taste A.Q. is pretty low. That is bad!

Ought not psychology do something about ascertaining our tastes and prejudices to the end that the proper education may attempt to render us all more cosmopolitan? Society, if not employers, has a concern for how we spend our wages. We want an ever-expanding market. It doesn't take an economist to tell us that. A capitalistic economy is premised on that.

Psychologically it occurs to us that venturesomeness in foods may be highly related to research aptitude, engineering success, and to certain personality (creative) traits that are highly important. If so, then one may determine an important index to individual personality by noting what pattern of foods one eats and what "new" items he is willing or unwilling to try out.

No one presently knows whether, or to what extent, the paper-and-pencil situation is a substitute for the real life situation. I have tried many times to get laboring men at noon to try chop suey with me. Only the most venturesome will try it once. I have never had a repeat; I have no convert! I don't think the working clothes had anything to do with it.

The economic end of such, of course, is that, if we were much more cosmopolitan, Central America which has some 150 native fruits we have never tasted, Brazil which has at least 25 *varieties* of bananas, and India which has 20 *varieties* of mangoes would then exchange these for our cars, television outfits, and road-building machinery to the material good of us all. If only we would learn to like their products and they ours, what might not be the end of it! Emigration, intercontinental touring, international education, among other things, would take on new statuses. Isn't there a research problem here for import (industrial) psychologists? I assume that we, rather than they, need to take the first step.

II. THE STENCIL

Let us pass on to a brief consideration of the stencil, which I conceive has untold ramifications awaiting our discovery [4]. We have just had one example of its use in a novel fashion. Stencils—I am sure—can accomplish other things too.

To make a long story short, I may say that if you will write out as many truths as you can about scoring stencils, most of them can be successfully and usefully refuted. I shall here content myself with two.

1. *Relativity applications of stencils.*

The oft-quoted "truth": Every examinee is scored in uniform manner by the same objective (if possible) scoring stencil.

The refutation: Not necessarily so; perhaps ideally every person should be scored by "his own" personal scoring stencil: And a first approximation to that, of course, is "the stencil appropriate to persons of his ulstrith." We are asserting here only what the clinician for decades has considered his domain and prerogative; namely, the necessity of a *personal* re-interpretation of the meaning of a score.

To our own satisfaction at least we have proved above that the importance of many scores is *relative* to something else. We can put that "something else" into stencils. All we need is a pretest to determine which stencil, or which stencils of a compound system, to apply to John Jones' test performance. All that rigorous science requires of us then is that if we had a thousand scoring clerks, every one of the thousand would apply the same objective stencil system to John Jones' performance.

A hundred objective test performances of other persons identical in geometrical pattern with that of John Jones in the recorded answers, but differing from him in basic ulstrith, conceivably could result then in a hundred different predictions, a different one for each specific individual concerned. The predictions, of course, would be more valid than the one prediction we now make *in common* for every one of the hundred, very much more valid if the basic profile is highly causal—encompasses most of the things we ought to measure.

As tactics, obviously test responses should be so set up that they may be resurrected from the files with a flip of a switch whenever any new scoring hypothesis is generated. This is a job for inventing (industrial) psychologists?

That statement, of course, is useful only if we also systematically collect criteria. Why don't schools and businesses so set up their "cash registers" as to automatically collect cumulative records for criteria?

2. *Weighting applications of stencils.*

Now consider a second use of stencils, for *weighting individual test items.*

The oft-quoted truism: Every right answer counts 1, and every wrong answer counts zero, in ascertaining the total score of an individual.

The refutation: Every right answer of *each individual* item may be scored from 0, 1, 2 ... 9 (integral weights pre-calculated to give optimal prediction.)

The above end may rather easily become a function of stencils, thus:

> Let us devise four stencils severally labeled 1, 2, 4, 7. Then all test items having a weight of 9, as an example, will have their right answer stencil-positions punched in *both* the 7 and 2 stencils; and all having a weight of 8 will have the right answer stencil positions punched in *both* the 7 and 1 stencils, and so on. No item will be punched in more than *two stencils.*[9]
>
> Now, the scoring machine, employing all 4 stencils in turn, produces four scores for each individual (it takes two double-runs of present stencil-scoring machines): the extended sum of which weights every individual's item response on every question, with a weight 0, 1, 2, 3, ... 9. The zero omits an item entirely and enables us "to weight-score" the 168 items, say, of our 17,000 most pertinent to Trait A but ignore 16,832 of them. (Of course, we must have all 17,000 answers in one card.)

The weight in relative scoring is in the legends of the scoring stencils. Accordingly, relative scoring, interaction scoring, curvilinearity scoring, I conceive, require only previous computation and incorporation into the scoring stencils. (I have not eliminated all work for psychologists; I have not reduced them to the status of laborers, whose future industrial plight is precarious, to my way of thinking.)

The stencil has many other potentialities commending it to our attention. The true potentialities of stencils are almost wholly discoveries for the future in my opinion. No one seems to be working in this area.

[9] There may be greater merit in employing 1-2-4-8 stencils, where as many as four holes are punched in four stencils, this series yielding integral item weights 0–15 inclusive. The work in making extensions is no greater. The proofing of stencils, at worst, is done once for all and is easily accomplished by a routine process.

III. THE SELECTIVE EQUATION

The selective regression equation is important because its solution is the best approximation to causation, when we have quantitative[10] traits, that we have at the moment. It locates a minimum of traits or tests or variables which yields the highest multiple correlation. It deserves, in my opinion, to be the father-idea of a hundred years of intense application by industrial psychologists. Witness:

(A) Salary Formula for Every Occupation

One by-product of our above proposed gigantic follow-up should be salary formulae for all occupations. The "traits" most "causative" of success and failure are singled out by the selective regression equation. To know these would be of utmost value for guidance. They would be equally useful to the employer to know when to promote a man, to tell him how to advise his employees how to prepare for and when to seek a promotion, perhaps even when to change employer or to shift occupation. (In Utopia, good employers do that!)

The more "causal" are the basic traits, including referrent variables, and the more general they are in the sense of including environmental, situational, and other variables, the more valuable.

(B) Business Failure

As an example of the problems they would help to solve, Mr. Babson tells us that less than a third of all new businesses started this year will be in business three years hence. This phenomenon has little or nothing to do with the "recession." It is the universal occupational hazard of new businesses. Who pays the debt for business failure? The account does not stop with the bankrupt and his family. The community chest is not the solution. It is our concern, the consumers'.

Who are the business failures by ulstriths? Whose business as a profession is it to discover this? Business-planning (industrial) psychologists?

(C) The Features of a Product Which Make It "Good"

As another example, house-builders who build hundreds of houses on ten different basic blue-print plans with scores of individual variations

---

[10] If we have qualitative scores at the start, we first may quantify them; thus the application is general. We have been quantifying qualitative variables in our laboratory for at least two decades [6].

find that they sell them after various intervals from minus 60 days to plus 360 days after being "ready to move into." It is an ideal set-up for the selective regression equation to discover what minimal pattern of features makes a house a "ready sale" or a "dud."

(D) Theoretical Considerations

It is the function of industrial psychology, as I see it, to aid the individual to get the most out of life by so manipulating his personal talents, his associates, and his environment that he and all others involved will have the most happiness in the natural course of events. If you agree, then values come in for scrutiny. What is the value of an education? "Why educate girls?—they only get married anyhow." If automation dooms the occupation of labor, what then? The world has problems cut out for it.

Ask a thousand men at random what are the ends and values of life. The answer, and the resultant publication, make no sense. Read a thousand such treatises and you will be but little the wiser. About the only conclusion you will reach is that "Men differ!" But, alternatively, perform a selective regression analysis for one occupation in one locality and the results, I contend, will be illuminating for local carpenters, or local plumbers, say. Or again, perform the analysis on men *in general* by the method of ulstriths based on basic traits and referent variables, and the results will be intelligible, meaningful, yes insightful, for Man.

(E) As an Antidote for Bad Thinking

The greatest contribution of selective regression equations, of course, derives from their value as a stimulus to thinking. As an example, in the three multiple correlation studies known to me in which wage-worth (salary, etc.) are predicted as a criterion, amount of education (number of school grades completed) has a negative weight: the more of education the less the wage-worth. And this obtains despite the fact that in a hundred studies education always correlates positively with wages. Now I would be the last to contend that three swallows make a summer, but I would be curious, if this finding were found generally true, to know why. I have often wondered whether anything I try to teach students ever sticks!

As another application—in a report on some hundreds of questionnaires, promulgated by as many individual researchers, the NEA deduced that length of questionnaire is the chief factor in getting returns. Make them short, say they.

The correlation was negative—no doubt about that. The computed selective regression, however, tells us that the influence of length is negligible in getting returns if the questionnaire techniques employed are good. Of course one should not cite individual cases, but I cannot resist the temptation. I personally received 101 per cent of returns on one questionnaire. Another researcher got over 80 per cent of replies to a questionnaire containing over 1800 questions. Clearly so long as questionnaires anywhere stop short of 100 per cent of returns our techniques still are improvable. The selective regression equation tells us what (of the proffered hypotheses) matters, but it does not at all tell us how to optimalize the effect.

As still another application of this technique, a national magazine printed in parallel columns some fourteen "traits" about the "laws" of the 48 states (and D. C.) regarding automobiles together with two criterion variables, the number of accidents per state and the number per 100,000,000 gallons of gas consumed. N, of course, was 49. The analysis showed that "speed" was the thirteenth or next to least important of fourteen variables in a selective regression equation having a validity of about .35. In Wherry's sense, speed added only "error."

Haven and I [5], from sheer logic, anticipated that result twenty years ago. Our reasoning about strata of drivers could easily be verified if we had a common, adequate report form on every fatal accident. To what extent are industrial psychologists responsible for the public having newspapers print only "correct" ideas about the cause of auto accidents? Are not most of the commonly held ideas erroneous? And what do we do to reduce the average of 40,000 deaths annually on our highways? The figure doesn't get smaller.

The above are a fair sample of the insight one may obtain from selective regression equations. It singles out "causes" better, in my opinion, than any other technique.

All my arguments to date hinge on the general desirability of truly ascertaining the practical behavior expectations of individuality by a new macro-approach in which the above tools are all important in the exploratory and pre-exploratory periods. Coded ulstriths are of most use and value *after* we have ascertained the "causal" variables.

IV. MICRO-RESEARCHES ALSO NEEDED

Let me now present just a few micro-jobs of research needing doing.

Selling Things

Goods made often are not readily sold by the print of the catalogue or by the ad on the billboard or the speech emanating from the telescreen. Goods made should always be wanted, and, according to present philosophy, save as samples should not be made until they are wanted. If we had consulted the consumer first, classifying all subjects by ulstriths, I contend that to state the problem properly is all but to solve it. Somebody ought to start planning that better. Why not industrial psychologists?

In my attic, I have at least 30 cubic feet of "letters" received in the last fifteen years—epistles I shall never open. To judge from the envelopes, some of the appeals were duplicated seven or eight times! All offer Utopia, their Utopia—not mine, for a price. If advertisers had generally available ulstriths on all people *most* of that pile could have been sent to people more interested than I. Those envelopes could just as well have gone to the people who *ought* to be logical purchasers of the products offered.

I also wish to refer again to the fact that by employing eight follow-ups I once got 101 per cent of replies to one questionnaire I promulgated. Can books, slide-rules, cars be sold cheaper by the ulstrith approach (but then, if people don't respond "as they should," resort not to a seventh or an eighth duplication of a bad appeal but rather employ the eight-follow-up technique on them—each follow-up appealing to a different motive for buying)? In the questionnaire situation the cost *per reply received* became cheaper the longer we followed up.

Sellers of things in America are paid far too much for their services; inventors, designers and even manufacturers far too little. In my opinion, we ought to do studies of things offered for sale, the mode of selling, the probable utility of a given good to ulstrith groups of consumers, as well as of the traits of salesmen. The consumers' research services make a bad assumption; namely, that all consumers are alike. Industrial psychologists, in my opinion, ought to enter that field.

I seem to remember that people of my ulstrith—when an epistle arrives—are distracted by work, are out of money sometimes, take vacations sometimes, and sometimes feel for the moment just simply cussed and "agin" everything. Four or five later ads, each with a new but valid angle, would probably get from me a sympathetic reception if I really needed the thing offered. Most of my ulstrith, my thesis is, have roughly what I have; want roughly what I want; buy mainly what I buy; are appealed to by the novel, the useful, the efficient just as am I.

Persons as "Tests"

I personally think highly of my next observation. I have observed that the traits of persons who bear a fixed relationship to a particular subject often influence greatly his acts, his behavior, his successes and failures, his happiness. It has been my good fortune in the past forty years to have been in contact with a lot of people of divers kinds (who hasn't)—college students, professors, research workers, government officials, military personnel, farm tenants, apartment-renters, businessmen. Summing up my experiences with them I would now hazard the guess that the failure of a married man, financially, industrially, professionally, morally, is about as often a failure of his wife as of the man. In the case of acquiring a new farm tenant, for example, if through great emergency I were given a choice of interviewing only the wife or the husband but not both, my conclusion is that I would choose to interview the former. It is not alone in detective thrillers that "cherchez la femme" is the best of tactics. All of us personally know a case or two where we are sure the man would have been a dismal failure, occupationally or professionally, save for his wife. To ask a working man, "What is your wife like?" is analogous to asking a mental hospital inmate "What day of the week is it?" and, I suspect, is a far more valid query. The inmate often doesn't care what day of the week it is!

To us as a profession, I feel sure it means that we should introduce into our multiple regression equations of aptitude, wages, promotions, etc., variables *regarding persons who bear* to our subjects *a fixed relationship*—traits and scores of the man's wife, his children, his supervisor, and the like. And while talking in this vein, we ought also to involve variables measuring *situations* (badly in debt to finance companies, unemployed and has used up his twenty-six weeks pay, unable to finance a much-needed operation, overfat, etc.) and also *environmental variables*. A lot of things in this world need optimalizing besides belt measures! Psychologists ought to know what *classes* of variables should be introduced to multiple regression analysis.

Honors and Titles as Pay

Industrial psychologists, in my opinion, need to look into the role of honors, titles, mentions, and such as motivational coin of the realm, with pretty big denominations printed on each. I would suggest that these values are *relative* to the basic personality profile or to some pattern of the *referrent* variables. (For most of us life is made up of petty successes—little incidents which in themselves are nothing spectacular in Saint Peter's ledger but for us spell happiness.) In fifty years, in my opinion, we ought to have an applied industrial psychology of honors and emoluments.

Vacations

Let us veer off into a different realm. While I, an Ohio workman, try to meet the rising costs of a vacation in Florida, some equally worried long-time inhabitant of that state would like very much to take a vacation in Ohio. Obviously then, if only somehow we could swap houses for a month, we would both profit; if in addition I were challenged by the opportunity I could help make his short-time tenancy more worthwhile. Perhaps I could leave in odd places about the house little discoveries for him to make at unpredictable times in that month—"Dear Prof. Smith: This fruit cake, when you discover it, is made by Aunt Jemima's recipe that has been in our family for three generations. That's why we want you to try it—but please leave us a note and tell us if you like it as much as we do." Ask yourself if your personal happiness isn't compounded mainly out of such little incidents as this!

My vacation in Oregon could be so much more pleasant if almost any vacationing or unemployed geologist could be induced to swap geological knowledge with me for psychological for a few weeks. Just try to imagine the lure of the mountains and of the nightly campfires under such circumstances! Nowadays such golden opportunities generally happen only by chance rather than by prearrangement, and then only rarely.

There is indeed a science of vacationing. Whose business is it to develop it? Travel could be a prescribed dose for personality improvement.[11] Perhaps that should be a joint effort of clinical, industrial, and other psychologists? (Travel-culture psychologists)

Changing Opportunity

The take of the movie box office reveals that either our wants change or the ulstriths attending movies change, or both. Let me remind you that as to frequencies ulstriths are of unequal size. Wouldn't it be useful to psychological theoreticians, as well as to Mr. Babson, to know the answer?

For generations farming was an occupation of opportunity for tens of millions and, as recently as the thirties, was a means of subsistence for myriads of unemployed who went home to father on the farm when depression struck. Farming as an occupation nowadays requires so much capital and so much specialized knowledge, while small farms are becoming nonexistent or financially unobtainable, that it has lost much of its former safety-valve function. Talking in a larger vein, who systematically notes shifts in vocational opportunity? Why not industrial psychologists? (Vocational-Opportunity Psychologists)

Some thirty years ago a thousand architects' families sent Ohio State University 45 times as many students as a thousand laborers' families. (Here we found the US Census indispensable.) There is no adequate explanation in terms of intellectual differences in the two occupations. I suggest that a study of the changing college opportunity ratios of parental occupations, controlled by ulstriths, might reveal even more startling indices. Certainly industry is interested in the answer.

There is one study which indicates that we have a great plenty of

---

[11] We might collect some of other nations' uncollectible national debts by charging off what they feed our selected vacationers!

engineers if only we used them for engineering rather than for drafting, clerical work, and the like. Such studies should be generalized to cover all occupations. We now tend to try to solve only immediate problems by calamity-expedients typified by passing another law. And as everyone—excluding only legislators—knows, law is a comparatively weak social instrumentality for effective and satisfactory human motivation.

Prophecies that universities, of 25,000 presently, will be meg-universities by 1970 are a big shot-in-the-arm for local business. What about the economic letdown if they are not realized?

Who knows, for example, from what ulstriths the college-going population comes? (Hollingshead tells us that both the "very rich" and the "very poor" know in common that college is a waste-of-time, of course for *them*.) If we knew that, we could make a more realistic prophecy. Personally, I have my doubts that meg-universities will be realized, but without facts I can't conscientiously or safely be very vociferous.

Criticism

Hotels often request the departing guest to leave behind criticisms of the service. Obviously the viewpoint of the departing "guest" is very precious to those whose aim sincerely is improvement. May I suggest that our national *suggestion* box be increased greatly in size to include also "criticisms" and "commendations"? Most of us want in the main to conform to what others want of us. Most of us are pleased, rather than annoyed, by the plaudits of even the most humble. Why don't we find out in wholesale fashion what others want, have to suggest, or feel "is good"? I venture to say that if we did, we should have less need for phony wars, import duties, foreign aid or AAA regulations to bolster up the industrial system. Must "normal" progress always require even larger and larger economic and political shots-in-the-arm? Temporary expedients have a sad way of becoming permanent policy. They get larger and larger—not smaller and smaller. The shots in that case shortly become worse than the disease! (Human-want psychologists?)

Public "Service"

Of 36,000 Ohio high school seniors' parents, in 1936, ten per cent were employed in government. Not one of the 36,000 seniors proposed to enter government for an occupation. (Occupations, as well as babies, ought to be wanted when they arrive.) Whose business and concern is that? I say that it concerns all of us. What will it profit us if we all labor mightily and gain the whole world only to have it squandered by untrained, ignorant politicians and irresponsible governments?

The Special Problem of Counties and Aggregates

Ohio has a great script Y of white territory up through the state where the good things, 36 "success" indices, of life prevail—for example, good roads, good schools, good books, good doctors. It has an equal block of black territory in the southern and southeastern area. There presently is much migration from black to white territory, and from states neighboring on the south. Whose business is it to see that that migration is orderly and for the good of all concerned?

The statistics of counties, county-indices, I have found, seem to yield the same analytical results as observation equations (profiles of scores) derived from individuals. In two states we have found procurable from 250 to 350 county indices. Probably we didn't discover half of those available. If I am right, the solution of many human problems then does not require us to collect data on individuals; instead, just put the available indices of counties into our regression equations, factor analyses, and the like. (Probably counties should be induced to collect some indices they now do not collect.)

Since the war, the northern one-third of Minnesota counties has lost some 30 per cent of its former population. Factor-analysis (one possible system of search for "causes") on the statistics of counties could throw much light on the "causes" of that labor mobility.

Other areas than the county are the obvious logical bases for collection of statistics for the planning of the welfare of the state. Shall we leave the planning of that to our sister border-disciplines, ask them to help us, or by lack of initiative toss the problem squarely in their laps? Gerrymandering, redistricting, solves nothing.

Ohio has 88 counties. The historical reasons for that go back 150 years. They were horseback travel and knee-deep mud; the county-seat should not be more than one horseback-day's travel away for anyone. There are today no *rural* schools in Ohio. That's consolidation.

Tennessee some time ago eliminated some two-thirds of its counties by consolidation. Under the larger-county system it suddenly found it could build good roads, good schools, and employ competent personnel with the money formerly paid to incapable but multitudinous public servants, relatives of voters. How big should a county be? I doubt whether Ohio, in 1958, "needs" more than 8 or 9 "counties." Again I ask the unavoidable question, whose is the first step? (Consolidation psychologists)

Other Problems

It strikes me that indices of factories (sub-branches) which have some variation in organization and control, when analyzed, could usefully find things of worth from the subfactory indices. In such analyses, in a certain sense you analyze for "causes" the behavior of all the people in the communities in question.

We are all agreed, of course, that the payroll office should be so set up as to afford us numerous criteria on workers without having to make a special, often unrewarded and very expensive, search for them. These could be the source of indices not now collected, even though the dividend rate depends upon them.

Communication in Industry and Occupation

The signs on superhighways are deplorable. You can't read them at 90 miles an hour. They wouldn't tell you what you wanted to know if you could!

The directions given employees are often misunderstood; even the bright employee when told to "clean out the shrubbery" succumbs with the dumb to the obvious by getting a grubbing hoe and really cleaning well the yard, the shrubbery with the sprouts and weeds!

Factories spew out goods, medicines, foods. The container tries to tell you how to use it. Often the best method uppermost in the mind of the maker is not communicated to the purchaser by the directions on the carton or bottle. A Philadelphia lawyer couldn't make sense out of a lot of them!

The directions for assembling and for using machines can be as confusing as they now are, or they could be so clear that only the dullest could fail to understand.

Isn't this realm a research career and a field of application for hundreds of psychologists? The adequate research answer will also have solved the central problem of the educational psychologist, I think.

Need for Principles of Human Motivation

The older I get, the more people I meet, the more I travel, the more I see of the lives of my 30 apartment-house tenants, the more do I feel that the techniques of normal human motivation should be ascertained as quickly as possible, and the more important ones become a part of the elementary school curriculum, even if we had to abbreviate some of the traditional content. I could go on in similar vein at great length, but the capacity of an audience to enjoy, vicariously, Utopia is limited.

If I were to summarize in a few words all that I have tried to say, I would say:

1. People behave as members of ulstriths. (Of course they also behave as individuals, but I have tried to show that this is relatively unimportant for our science at its present stage.)

2. The meaning—the behavior potential of traits—is often relative—to

other traits (nearly all of which relativity is still to be discovered). Like the bad apple in the barrel, one bad trait in a man can spoil the whole individual. And two, or more, good and virtuous traits can produce genius.

3. By techniques already largely known to us the tremendous amounts of data on individuals, needing to be gathered and analyzed, can both be had and effectively analyzed in our generation. Such studies will be costly, but we cannot afford not to do them. Ideas for national salvation bear high price-tags.

4. Anyone wanting to work at research can easily find a hundred jobs badly needing doing, any one of which could usefully change life on this planet in a fundamental manner.

5. The research jobs undertaken should fit into a general plan of those which most need doing; they should not be a mere by-product of university teaching nor something a personnel worker does only when he wants to present a paper at a professional society.

6. Big scale cooperative data-gathering is imminent. Data-analysis should be similarly organized. The philosophy of US census-taking is due, in my opinion, for a fundamental overhauling.

7. Research on people in the long run will pay off just as surely and probably even more bountifully than does industrial research, which has become the warp and woof, the heart and brain of industrial life in America in the last few decades.

8. We must put our knowledge and our principles to work. Industrial psychology cannot succeed as an armchair science.

9. We must go further; we must try to infer causes. As a nation, teachers, publicists, politicians, and lawmakers must learn that most results are multiply-causated; stop looking for panaceas—all-potent individual variable—and look instead for causal profiles.

10. In the next half century we must develop psychology as a logical science with logical, as versus empirical, equations. Above all, we must start to begin.

REFERENCES

1. Toops, H. A. The use of addends in experimental control, social census and managerial research. *Psychol. Bull.*, 1948, 45, 41–74.
2. Toops, H. A. On the validity of two multiplied traits as compared with two added traits, fundamental equality of the units of measurement within the given scale of the several variables being assumed. *Ohio College Asssociation Bulletin* No. 85, 1932, 1057–1062.
3. Toops, H. A. Empirical psychology and the "generalized" regression equation. *Ohio College Association Bulletin*, No. 81, 1932, 1003–1011.

4. Toops, H. A. The generalization of objective scoring keys. Mimeographed paper. Ohio State University, 1956.
5. Toops, H. A. & Haven, S. *Psychology and the Motorist.* Columbus: R. G. Adams and Co., 1938.
6. Wherry, R. J. Maximal weighting of qualitative data. *Psychometrika,* 1946, 9, 263–266.

3 Criteria for What?

S. RAINS WALLACE

All of the older of us remember with a feeling of debt the short article which John G. Jenkins published in 1946 with the title, "Validity for What?" It was the first powerful plea to those who would apply tests and talk about their validities to recognize the key position of criteria in determining how they interpret and use them. No one disagreed with Jenkins' position then and no one would now, even though his statements that

> psychologists in general tended to accept the tacit assumption that criteria were either given of God or just to be found lying about ... [p. 93].

> The novice of 1940, searching through many textbooks and much journal literature would have been led to conclude that expediency dictated the choice of criteria and that the convenient availability of a criterion was more important than its adequacy [p. 94].

are not conducive to complacency.

In the 18 years which have followed, we have become wiser and sadder about the criterion problem. If we have not accomplished a great deal, if we tend to use the expedient criterion with the comforting thought that some day we will get down to constructing better ones, if we concentrate on criteria that are predictable rather than appropriate, we do operate with varying levels of guilt feelings. We have not done much about it, but we know we should.

It is interesting to note that what Jenkins perceived as a relatively straightforward and well-understood problem, i.e., the validation process itself, has become the subject of considerable, diverse, and rewarding discussion. We have progressed from the folly of saying that the validity of a test is its correlation with a single other measure to the point where we now recognize many different kinds of validity which can be and are classified in varying ways. Some of these classificatory systems are based upon processes of validation—i.e., expert (or inexpert) examination or opinion, concurrent, predictive, synthetic, construct, convergent, or dis-

Presidential Address, Division 14, American Psychological Association, 1964.

criminant—while others (e.g., Cattell's recently proposed system) are based upon the nature of the criteria employed—i.e., direct *versus* circumstantial, particular *versus* conceptual, and natural *versus* artifactual. Thus while Jenkins' concern with "Validity for What?" led him to address himself mainly to the criterion problem, my title "Criteria for What?" leads me largely to a concern for the meaning of validation and the implications of various methods of arriving at it.

Validity for industrial psychology has largely consisted of what Cattell (1964) has called "utility" and has banned from the validation universe entirely. We have been, and continue to be, primarily concerned with demonstrating some relation between our selective, evaluative, or training procedures and measures of desired performances in the real world. This concern is certainly defensible and, I believe, necessary. However, its acceptance as the sole interest of the industrial psychologist has dangers which we shall examine in due course.

The concern for demonstrating utility is necessary because the industrial psychologist must show that, at a minimum, his services are not doing harm. The possibility of this macabre event has been softpedaled. Somehow, we seem to have convinced our clients, and even ourselves, that the application of our selection techniques is, at worst, neutral in its effect. This is probably the reason that we are allowed and allow ourselves to install selection tests and other procedures by which prospective employees are rejected for initial employment, even though we have no evidence that those rejected are any different from those who are employed in potential success for the job.

Except in the rare situation where recruiting of suitable employees is no problem for management, this is patently absurd. If we apply a rejection instrument that, for example, eliminates 50 percent of available applicants, we double the recruiting problem. This is a high cost to pay for a selection procedure. If it is not accompanied by some measurable increase in the proportion of men hired who reach an acceptable level of performance, it is a cost without a return—and not even our longest-haired brethren in the psychological world would attempt to defend such a state of affairs. Despite this, we and our sponsors continue to "give a test a whirl" in blissful oblivion of its true cost, i.e., the rejection of potentially adequate employees.

Indeed, since the efficient use of our selection procedures is so dependent upon the interrelationship of recruiting, selection, and training costs, and since these may change as changes in local or general economic and demographic factors occur, the establishment and specification of utility demands that we have up-to-date knowledge of the relation between the number of potential recruits and the number of open jobs, the distribution of selection measures within the applicant population, and the proportion of successful performers which can be expected from any possible selection ratio incurred by the application of such measures. To accomplish this, we must have estimates of the predictive validity of our procedures. We cannot substitute any other type of validity for this purpose. Concurrent validity, the device whose attractiveness in terms of time saving and production of statistically significant relationships has led us to employ it to an inordinate degree, is irrelevant to questions of utility, i.e., to the prediction problem. As a validation process, it has some qualities which deserve our attention and which will be mentioned later. But let us make no mistake. The determination of the utility of our procedures includes predictive validation as a necessary factor.

Necessary? Certainly. Sufficient? Perhaps—for utility. But for progress, probably not. Let us pause for a moment and take quick stock of our current posture with regard to test prediction of performance in the real world. I think we must look at some discouraging facts. The first and most disturbing one is that what success has been achieved in test prediction is largely old hat. Before Jenkins' article appeared, a group of psychologists developed a test battery which had high validity for predicting performance in pilot training. Even before that, tests were doing a good job of predicting performance in schools and colleges. The hope that these techniques would lead to equally accurate predictions in the less well-structured, controlled, and specific situations of post-training performance in the real world of business and industry has not been fulfilled. The predictive test validities reported for vocations today are little, if any, higher than those reported 15 years ago. What improvements have been made have resulted from refinements of existing techniques or methods or from the abandonment of unreliable, invalid techniques and instruments, with a corresponding elimination of chance or extraneous variance, rather than from any new approaches or philosophies.

As was true in the past, it is true today that the major successes for tests in posttraining prediction have occurred for jobs requiring readily recognized physical-skill components, such as typing, various pursuit or tracking jobs, or machine manipulation. As soon as we begin to think about so-called "higher-level" jobs (selling, supervising, copywriting, teaching, etc.), our validities become more and more discouraging.

Let me remind you that I am speaking of prediction of reliable and objective measures of performance. These are, in themselves, hard to come by, and this has led us to turn with ill-concealed delight to other criteria which are readily available and rather generally predictable. We have found that what we or our tests say about people often agrees to a statistically significant degree with what other people say about them. In short, while we cannot accurately predict what a man does, we can predict what other people say about what he does. The implications of this lotus which we are gulping down in great quantities are disturbing to say the least. Would a systematic study of the intercorrelations of the many tests which are valid for rating criteria reveal that we have only found a "good-guy" or "impressive-fellow" factor, and then busily created a large stable of predictors for it? Do we, in applying such tests, tend to maintain any mythology, irrelevance, and inaccuracy which now underlie management's evaluation of performance? I think the answer to these questions is affirmative, and thus refuse to be comforted by some of the impressive coefficients of correlation presented in our validity information exchanges by government agencies and others. The fact that we can predict ratings is a significant one and deserves much more investigation—and a different type—than it has received. It does not demonstrate that we have made any considerable progress in achieving utility for our predictive instruments.

Of course, it would be unfairly pessimistic to say that we do not have some success in predicting performance. Many of us employ devices for which we can demonstrate utility of both statistical and practical significance. It should be noted that with very few exceptions, such as the good old Strong (Strong Vocational Interest Blank), these do not fit into our own mythology that applied psychology takes principles or instruments developed by our purer brethren and puts them to work in the everyday world. To the contrary, the attempt to demonstrate utility of so-called standard aptitude or personality tests for selection in specific jobs has an impressive record of failure. Instead, the tests which have demonstrated utility have tended to be those developed for a specific application.

This is exemplified by the comparative success of devices based on the biographical-data or personal-history approach. I think it can be shown that this type of test is about the only one which has demonstrated usable predictive validity in a wide variety of vocational tasks and situations ranging from clerical employees, airman assignments, salesmen, and even managerial personnel. I believe that almost any knowledgeable industrial psychologist confronted with the assignment of developing a predictive instrument in a new business, industrial, or government situation would put his first investment into the development of a biographical data blank. Let us not quibble at this juncture about the specific content of such devices. Whether the items they include verge into those we may think of as interest or personality items is not germane, since it is the approach in terms of device construction that concerns us here. In brief, I suggest that the device is completely tailor-made for the job situation and the specific performance criterion for which it is to be used. In addition, it is totally empirical and, therefore, free from the constraints of any hypothesis or of the demands imposed by the desire for generality. And, finally, the contribution of each item to the final prediction of the specific performance involved, measured in a specific and pre-determined way.

Such instruments are likely to have demonstrable predictive validity as long as our boot straps hold out. They thus meet the necessary requirement for utility. What about progress? As one who has for years been associated with the hard-nosed, empirical approach to the selection problem, I must confess to the belief that it is rapidly approaching the end of its tether. We are sterile because we are farming better than we know how. Sterile because our empiricism has prevented us from developing even the rudiments of new insights or generalizable concepts. Our progress has been cheerfully based on luck and, not surprisingly, our luck appears to be running out.

Now before you decide that I have changed sides, let me point out that the other side is no better off. By the other side, I mean those test constructors or appliers who do attempt to develop concepts concerning the nature of traits, jobs, and criteria, but who have embraced the procedure of predictive validity for job-oriented criteria.

A psychologist develops a theoretical framework which convinces him that certain attributes of people can be defined, identified, and measured. His definition leads him to hypothesize that certain responses to certain kinds of items will serve as a sort of measure of an attribute which he has in mind. In some cases, he reinforces his hypothesis by finding that people who he believes exhibit an unusually high or low degree of the attribute do, in fact, make very high or low scores on his, or some other psychologist's, test. Thus, schizoids make high scores on a test for introversion, or psychopaths do very poorly on a test for emotional stability. In other cases, where, for instance, his test is of the interest variety, he finds that artists as a group show a different pattern of responses on a test than do engineers.

Or, he may operate at a higher level of sophistication, put his test into a battery of many other different tests, and attempt to determine through factor analysis what kind of trait or attribute his testing is getting at. This gives him a basis for hypothesizing the existence of and (unfortunately) naming a factor which these tests measure in common. Whichever of these methods is employed, the psychologist now has a test or battery with a name which represents a hypothesis.

Unfortunately, the classical validation procedures do not test the hypothesis. If the psychologist decides on the basis of a job analysis that the attribute his test is hypothesized to measure is required for a particular performance, and determines its predictive validity for such performance, he may get significant or nonsignificant validation. Suppose it is the former. Does this mean that his test actually measures the attribute he has defined, and this attribute is, in fact, important for the performance? Certainly not. It may mean that his test measures something quite different from what he had in mind, and that he has stumbled upon a predictor of which he has no clear concept. If he gets zero validity, does it falsify the hypothesis? Again, the answer is no. The test may fail to validate because it does not measure the attribute identified in the job analysis and named by hypothesis or because the attribute is not, in fact, related to the performance. Furthermore, we must reiterate the awful truth that nonsignificant validities against performance criteria are the general rule, and that significant validities are notoriously unlikely to lead to generalizability—in other words, validities anticipated on the basis of job taxonomies very rarely come through.

So I cry a plague on both our houses—empirical and hypothetical alike—in the way that they are currently constructed. Both may achieve utility—both will fail to achieve progress. When we have no hypothesis or basis for generalization, we are likely to obtain predictive validity. When we have a hypothesis or concept, we are unlikely to obtain validity and we also fail, in the process, to obtain information about our concept. Something must be wrong.

One thing that is wrong is that we have yet to pay enough attention to the processes by which we use our criteria to establish predictive relationships. In the rare cases, where we have examined different types of criteria for the same job and against the same predictors, we have failed to arrive at interpretations of the different validity functions which emerge. We have long recognized that relationships between predictors and criteria can be greatly affected (moderated, if you will) by an unrecognized number and variety of situational factors, but only a very few of us have made any effort to manipulate or examine these factors in a systematic way so as to throw more light on the basic nature of our prediction problem. Only recently have we interested ourselves in the manner in which validity relationships may be moderated by population variables, and even when we have, there has been a tendency to exhibit with pride the higher validities which can be shown for subgroups of a population rather than to perceive the existence of such moderator variables as a challenge to and a potential for an enhanced understanding of predictive validity per se. We have published thousands of concurrent validities and somewhat less predictive validities, and yet little has been done to develop an understanding of the relationship between these two concepts by longitudinal follow-ups or systematic testings and criterion determinations through a temporal continuum.

But all these do not, I believe, constitute the true villain of the piece. Paradoxically enough, I think that our villain is a kind of Mr. Hyde to Jenkins' Dr. Jekyll. He is the performance criterion with relevance. He is so desirable in providing us with the satisfaction and security that come from the demonstration of utility that we are likely to do two things. First, we tend to overlook some of the weaknesses in criteria which Jenkins talked about, and to compromise our goal of reliability and freedom from bias in order to maintain criteria which are clearly relevant to management's ultimate goals. Second, we are likely to ignore the possibility that criteria which are largely irrelevant to a particular job may be highly relevant for a concept upon which our original predictive hypothesis was based.

Let me pause, here, to reiterate that I embrace without question the proposition that utility must be demonstrated in a particular job situation before a predictive instrument can be put into use, and that only predictive validity against a criterion of accepted job relevance can serve this purpose. The question I am raising has to do with allowing relevance to become such a preponent factor in our thinking that it begins to serve as a substitute for reliability, freedom from bias, etc., or that it prevents us from examining the usefulness of criteria which lack apparent relevance to a specific job. I suggest, in short, that we ought to get our eyes off the ball.

Recently, I heard one of our most knowledgeable people in the field of management criteria (Hemphill, 1964) shock a mixed group of research workers and executives in the life insurance field by stating that he has just about decided that the only hope for evaluating management lies in the establishment of a family of simulated criteria for the various aspects of the managerial job. The reasons he gave for this position were highly realistic. In brief, he asserted that any measure of managerial performance is either so subjectively biased, or so contaminated by chance or by factors over which the manager has no control, as to be largely worthless as a criterion for evaluating a selection, training, or supervisory process. He implied that our experience indicates that where high reliability of a criterion is found by any of the classical procedures, it is more likely to indicate the existence of systematic contamination than of reliability of the performance measure itself. He also pointed out that even where we have criteria of sufficient reliability to allow predictive validity, it takes so long to find this out that the nature of the job under consideration is very likely to have undergone considerable change so that we end up with a predictor for something that no longer exists. Thus, the only hope he can see for the future is to cut the Gordian knot and develop simulated situations in which the subject's performance can be compared to some known standards under highly controlled and standardized conditions. After the smoke had cleared and the blood had been mopped from the floor, one thing emerged clearly. For that audience, at least, the idea of removing criteria from the real world was so threatening as to lead to some irrationality of discussion.

Admittedly, our history has made us shy of the repercussions of dependence on irrelevant criteria. Even in Jenkins' day, there was recognition that using a paper-and-pencil test as a criterion in determining a validity for a predictor of success in aerial gunnery may produce high correlations and poor gunners. In the life insurance business, we can predict training school grades with considerable accuracy, and we also demonstrate that they have no relation to how many sales the students will eventually make. However, before we let these traumatic episodes associated with irrelevant criteria paralyze our thinking, let us remember that, in most of these situations, we have paid the price of accepting criteria because they were at hand rather than because we had some good reason for employing them.

But, you may say, what good reason can we have for employing a criterion whose relevance to the ultimate desired performance is not apparent? This question is implied by Jenkins' (1946) statement that

> the researcher must devote much time and thought to determining that the performance he selects as a source of criterion data is an adequate representation of the total field performance desired by the sponsor [p. 97].

It has led us not only to insist upon the real-life situation for our criteria but also to concentrate on the more global, single type of criterion and to avoid partial criteria even though analyses of sets of partial and global criteria have demonstrated that their interrelationships are extremely complex and produce multifactors.

I propose that it is time to reexamine our position in this regard if we are to break out from the sterility which results from our current procedures of determining utility. Perhaps such a breakout might occur if we look at the concept of relevance itself. Thus far, we have thought of a criterion as having relevance for the ultimate job. But a criterion can have a different, if equally and perhaps more important, relevance. It can be relevant to the hypotheses or concepts underlying the predictor. It can be relevant to the question of why a predictive validity against a job-oriented criterion does or does not exist. It can be relevant to the formation of a concept which is generalizable to prediction in a number of job situations rather than in one specific task. Indeed, a criterion with relevance for the ultimate job may be quite inappropriate for the investigator who seeks an understanding of that job and of its various relationships to predictors.

For example, the obvious and most frequently used performance criterion for salesmen is how much they sell. It is apparent that salesmen who fail to ask anyone to buy their product will, in general, not sell as much as those who do. It also seems probable that some salesmen may ask a great many people and yet fail to sell as much as others who ask relatively few. Suppose we have a test or item which is based upon the hypothesis that it will differentiate men who have varying degrees of willingness to ask people to buy. This intervening variable we designate "call reluctance." Validating the test against the criterion of total sales gives us something we can use now, but it does not give us a basis for work in the future. It gives us something that works but no basis for knowing why it works. What we need to do is to examine a criterion which is more relevant to the hypothesis and less relevant to the job, i.e., how many people each man asked to buy his product. Note that an examination of the correlation between this hypothesis criterion and the job criterion, and of the different validities of our predictors for the two different criteria, can go far in telling us whether our concept of call reluctance has theoretical value or not. Of course, we should set up other criteria relating to call reluctance. In any case, the result could be measured in terms of the development of new and broader concepts rather than of a new test gimmick.

This is the use of a partial but job-oriented criterion with hypothesis relevance rather than ultimate performance relevance. But why should we stop with partial criteria? Why not get out of the job situation entirely if, in so doing, we can enrich our understanding? Suppose we have the hypothesis that a test predicts aggressive behavior. Before we develop the further hypothesis that aggressive behavior is a favorable trait for salesmen and see whether the test predicts selling ability, could we not define aggressive behavior in an operational manner and in a variety of settings and measures so that a behavioral set of criteria can be developed and validity defined as the support or falsification our hypothesis receives from the relationship of such criteria to the test prediction?

The difficulties of defining criteria for the many hypothetical attributes or factors found in our test files today and of setting up situations in which they can be observed are admittedly great. However, the attempt might, in and of itself, have a healthy effect upon the thinking of many of our test constructors. It might also attract the interest of our experimentalists and research-minded clinicians.

Many of us have, to speak frankly, deplored what we regarded as the naive and soft-headed methods by which our clinical brethren (as well as some test and measurement savants) have attempted to validate their tests by correlation with other tests, with diagnoses, or with ratings almost always on a concurrent basis. We have, quite properly, expressed scorn of the position taken by some writers that validation for instruments employed in diagnosis and therapy is unnecessary so long as they provide the clinician with a sense of security about what he is doing. But while we have been basking in our purity and hardheadedness, a number of thoughtful, conceptually oriented people have passed us by. While we have high-heartedly applied whatever test came to hand against whatever job-situation criterion was available, they have recognized that tests can be invalidated conceptually, so far as potential utility or generalizability is concerned, by demonstration of too high or too low correlation with other tests. While we have all but reconciled ourselves to the fact that, at the present state of the art, knowledge of the utility of a test for one criterion in one job aids us little, if at all, in building a predictor for another job or even for a different criterion in the same job, they have proceeded to systematic manipulation of multiple and varied predictors in conjunction with multiple and varied criteria to the end of establishing a basis for some concepts about what is being measured and how it may be operationally defined and identified.

You will recognize, of course, that I am speaking of what is called construct validity. It is not new in the testing field. It is even older in the experimental and physiological fields where it has been a truism that a useful theoretical construct can only result from the employment of different and independent measurement procedures in its investigation.

Miller (1961), in his Presidential Address at the American Psychological Association, showed the pitfalls that may be encountered in psychophysiological investigations if assumed intervening variables are not manipulated by a variety of techniques and measured by a variety of criteria. In a study of thirst, for example, he found that while three methods of manipulating thirst had consistent effects when measured by the amount of water drunk normally by the animal or the amount of quinine in the water required to suppress drinking, their interrelationships were considerably altered when the measurement was made in terms of the rate of work at pressing a bar to obtain a water reward. He concludes that the use of the last measure in some of his previous work probably trapped him

> into greatly overestimating the reduction in drive, if any, produced by the inflation of a balloon in the stomach. . . . the overall results cannot be explained by the assumption of a single intervening variable . . . [p. 747].

Weitz (1961) has recently shown that the conclusions derived from an experiment on the role of verbal association in mediating transfer of learning may be radically different, depending on the criteria employed in determining the effect of experimental variations. He makes a plea for the use of varying criterion measures as a method of gaining more insight into the operations of the independent and intervening variables.

As you know, Patricia C. Smith and her colleagues at Cornell have made real strides in the measurement and understanding of job attributes through the application of this type of model. However, in studies of training of the more applied type, the recognition has only rarely occurred and everything that has been said about our selection of criteria and our validation concepts for selection predictors applies equally to our evaluations of various training procedures.

It seems probable that industrial psychology, particularly as it relates to selection, appraisal, and training procedures, is approaching Armageddon. The popular books which accuse us of perpetuating conformity, comfort, and the status quo, penalizing the thorough and creative, and doing it through indefensible invasions of privacy have too much wheat in their large load of chaff to be smugly ignored. Even more important to all psychologists of good will is the maintenance of a balance between our present contributions to the national productivity and the increasing demands for immediate unselective employment and specialized training of culturally deprived groups. If there was ever a time in which we require conceptual foundations for what we are currently doing and what we hope to do in the future, it is now.,

In the effort to provide such foundations, I believe we must expand our thinking about criteria and validity beyond the point of utility alone. We must reexamine our relations to and communications with psychologists in the test-and-measurement, experimental, and clinical fields. We must question our current fertility in the generation of psychological thought. We must somehow convince our sponsors and ourselves that it is as important to gain insight into why our procedures do or do not work as it is to produce a tried-and-true predictive gimmick. Doing this involves many steps, but the first and most important is to recognize that the answer to the question "Criteria for What?" must always include—for understanding!

REFERENCES

CATTEL, R. B. Validity and reliability: A proposed more basic set of concepts. *Journal of Educational Psychology*, 1964, 55, 1–22.

HEMPHILL, J. K. Criteria for evaluating managerial performance. Speech presented at Life Insurance Agency Management Association Research Planning Conference, Hartford, June 1964.

JENKINS, J. G. Validity for what? *Journal of Consulting Psychology*, 1946, 10, 93–98.

MILLER, N. E. Analytical studies of drive and reward. *American Psychologist*, 1961, 16, 739-754.

WEITZ, J. Criteria for criteria. *American Psychologist*, 1961, 16, 228–231.

4 The Placement of Workers: Concepts and Problems

EDWIN E. GHISELLI

One of the oldest areas of industrial psychology, if not the oldest, is the selection and placement of workers. Its history extends back over half a century and its literature would fill at least a small library. Our knowledge and experience in this area is extensive. As a result, many of us think of worker placement as a field where basic concepts have been crystalized and the fundamental problems solved. From this point of view it follows that all that remains is the minor matter of tightening up on a few technical details. As a consequence, the field of worker placement no longer provides the stimulus it once did. The cake of yesteryear appears as but a few dry crumbs today. How much more alluring are the meadows of human relations where unfettered one can joyously gallop off in 19 different directions simultaneously.

Yet my thesis is that worker placement is not a fallow field. The exploring plow of science has barely broken the surface ground. There are many exciting discoveries yet to be made. Basic concepts in fact have not been adequately formulated nor fundamental problems solved. I am reminded of the story, doubtless apocryphal, told of a famous scientist whose name escapes me. "How nice," someone said, "to have thoroughly investigated one field and to have discovered all there is to know about it." "Your view of the situation is completely inaccurate and your understanding is small," he replied. "Only now as a result of our many years of work can I really begin to ask the questions and state the problems." This is the way I view the field of worker placement. Our half century of thought and research puts us in an advantageous position whereby we can obtain a better perspective of both the trees and the woods. Past work has not solved our problems, but merely permits us to state the problems a little bit more effectively.

Therefore, I should like to reexplore the area of worker selection, breaking it up into smaller portions and examining the wonders of each. Time limits me to three: namely, criteria, occupational analysis, and per-

From *Personnel Psychology*, 1956, 9, 1–16. Presidential address, Division 14, meeting of the American Psychological Association, 1955.

sonnel classification. I believe that many gems of intellectual challenge will be revealed. And I hope to show that what is indicated is not only the muscle work of research but also the cortical activity of conceptualizing.

CRITERIA

When the industrial psychologist sets about developing a selection program he invariably seeks criteria of job proficiency to use as bases for evaluating and refining his assessment procedures. So great is his compulsion in this connection that he is fraught with guilt feelings when he fails to obtain criterial measures. In those situations where criteria are available for continuous validation he becomes deliriously manic.

One would therefore expect to find that the criterion problem has attracted a great deal of attention. Yet this does not seem to be true. Otis (17), Bellows (2), Toops (27), and Thorndike (23) have set the stage for us but we have failed to supply the lines. Such concern as we have evidenced has been with technical details rather than with conceptual formulations. As Jenkins (16) once said, we act as though criteria are either God given or just to be found lying about.

I think that part of the difficulty lies in the fact that we have been far more interested in predictors than in that which is to be predicted. It perhaps is unfortunate that we ever used the term criteria to denote measurements of job success. The implication is that evaluation of the performance of workers on the job is of lesser importance than their performance on tests and other similar devices. Behavior, wherever it is manifest, falls within the province of the psychologist, and as persons interested in quantitative descriptions of behavior, we should regard job performance as a fertile field of study in and of itself.

Since criteria are ways of measuring certain aspects of behavior, it has seemed to me both necessary and desirable to consider its dimensional aspects. Elsewhere I (9) have said that we must concern ourselves with three kinds of criterion dimensionality—static dimensionality, dynamic dimensionality, and individual dimensionality.

Let me first consider what I have termed static dimensionality. I fear that we have tended to consider the criterion as a simple affair. This tendency has masked the importance of the work that has been done in the area, and at the same time has prevented the emergence of fruitful ideas. For one thing, we act as though for each job there is *a* criterion. We get it and use it in validating our selection devices. Sometimes we find ourselves in the embarrassing circumstance of having not one but several different criterion measures. What shall we do? I expect that most of you do as I have done, solve the problem nicely by discarding all but the one that appears most "pertinent" and "reasonable."

When we do face the problem squarely, we seek ways and means for combining the various measures into a single differentially weighted composite. But what shall be the logic that leads us to some particular differential set of weights? Shall we, as Horst (12) and Edgerton and Kolbe (7) propose, weight the component variates in terms of their principal component? We will thereby maximize differences between individuals in terms of composite criterion scores and minimize difference in scores on the different variates within an individual. But is this good? Are we willing to assume that there is kind of g running through all of the various criterion measures and that its weight is high? Certainly the results of factorial studies of criteria point in quite a different direction. Such studies rather clearly show that the different measures of performance on a job are unlikely to be explainable on the basis of a single factor, but rather represent manifestations of a number of different factors, (e.g., 4, 19, 29).

If we accept the proposition that criteria are indeed multidimensional, we are faced with a variety of new problems. It is apparent that the scores of an individual on a number of variables cannot be combined into a single index number that will describe him uniquely. Consequently it is necessary to locate his position in a multidimensional criterion space. We could handle this situation either by attempting to predict each criterion and dimension separately and then estimate the individual's position in the space, or we could divide the space into parts and by the discriminate function estimate into which part the individual is most likely to fall.

We have tended to think of criteria as static phenomena. Thus production is production—whether it be early or late production. But it is apparent that criterion performance may be determined by quite different sets of factors in different individuals and in the same individual at different times. It is therefore apparent that we must concern ourselves with the dynamic aspects of job performance.

My colleague Mason Haire and I collected certain data which are pertinent in this connection. We obtained records of production on a group of new taxicab drivers for their first 18 weeks of employment. The correlations between production on the various weeks was a little lower for distant than for closer weeks. However, all correlations were quite substantial. A factor analysis of these data would necessarily yield a fairly heavy general factor and would indicate that production was determined by very nearly the same factors through the time period studied. We also had on these people scores on a variety of tests taken at the time of hiring. The correlations between scores on these tests and weekly production at different stages revealed some remarkable things. The validity coefficients of some tests remained at exactly the same level throughout the entire period. For others, validity coefficients that initially were high dropped to zero, and for still others validity coefficients that were initially low rose to a substantial level. One test even showed cyclical changes, with its validity alternately rising to levels of over .40 and subsiding quietly to zero.

If these results are substantiated by other investigations, it will mean that conceptionalizations of the selection problem will be extremely difficult, and extremely complex. General predictions of jobs success will be not only poor but also meaningless.

Finally, I bring up the perplexing problem that I have termed individual dimensionality. We have been presuming up to now that all workers on the same job should be measured on exactly the same dimensions. Yet some 15 years ago Otis (17) called to our attention the fact that different workers performing exactly the same job may make equally important contributions to their organization but in quite different ways. Thus one salesperson may sell yards and yards of cotton goods and therefore be considered a good worker, while another whose sales are much less may be considered equally good because she motivates customers to purchase merchandise in other departments. The organization may profit equally from the efforts of both workers.

I confess that I do not have much to suggest here. I would think however, that we might begin by investigating the critical dimensionality of individual workers, asking such questions as the extent to which workers on the same job vary in the same dimensions. Perhaps Stephenson's (21) Q-technique or Cattell's (5) P-technique would be useful in this connection. Analysis of the dimensionality of the individual brings to mind Horst's (13) proposal to measure traits within the person, and this in turn recalls Hull's (14) old concept of trait variability.

Individual dimensionality is important in the selection of workers because it means that different factors underlie the performance of different individuals performing exactly the same job. It therefore follows that we should use different devices in appraising different persons who are candidates for one and the same job. For one type of candidate we would use one type of selective device, and for another type of candidate we would use a different selective device. This suggests that the point may come where we shall have to administer tests to applicants to determine which other tests we shall use as a basis for determining their qualifications.

OCCUPATIONAL ANALYSIS

We speak blithely of tests for clerks, salesmen, or punchpress operators, without fully realizing the implications of our statements. When we make such statements we are saying there are a number of positions so similar in nature that they are almost identical and therefore can readily be grouped together into the same class, a job. We recognize that there may be some differences in duties and requirements for different positions falling into the same job, and that these differences are likely to be greater when the positions occur in different organizations. While these differences may worry us some, they do not worry us enough. If they did, and we thought about the matter as carefully as Shartle (20) has, some fascinating conceptual and research problems would emerge.

Why is the grouping of positions into classes a problem of any pertinence for worker selection and placement? The answer to this question is that we are interested in establishing certain kinds of generalizations, generalizations with respect to the relationships between predictor scores and criteria. It makes little difference whether our concern is with different classes of positions in the same organizations, or with the same class of positions in different organizations. We are seeking principles that will serve as bases for the more effective placement of workers.

It appears to me that there are three sets of problems that need to be dealt with in connection with occupational analysis. One involves the kinds of characteristics that are to be used in determining similarity among positions. The second is concerned with the types of arrangements or organizations of positions into classes. And the third has to do with ways for determining similarity among jobs. Let us see what we can make of each of these.

As I review discussion of occupational families it appears to me that groupings have been made on three bases (11). First, there are administrative characteristics such as duties, responsibilities, hours of work, and tools and equipment. Second, there are characteristics which are acquired by workers in the performance of their work, such as specific skills and knowledges. Finally, there are a variety of personal characteristics, such as aptitudes and personality traits, that are related to effectiveness of job performance.

Each of these poses problems which I cannot now detail. A few illustrations will suffice. When is a duty a duty and when is it two duties? What are the elemental characteristics of a duty? Is it true that the amount of time a duty is performed is its important dimension? Shall we take the position Brown and I (11) have propounded to the effect that the relative importance of abilities and traits for various jobs is to be gauged only on the basis of the extent to which they are related to appropriate criteria? Or with Jaspen (15) shall we say that such correlations are so mutilated by restrictions of range and inadequate criteria that they reveal little or nothing, and that therefore we should study job profiles drawn through the average scores on various tests earned by workers on different jobs?

But I am not sure that the three aforementioned types of formal characteristics, the administrative, the learned skills and knowledges, and the essential abilities and traits are sufficient. There are, I believe, other factors of a truly psychological nature that are pertinent and important.

As one reaches advanced years, one is permitted, yes, even expected, to indulge in certain esoterica. Therefore recently I have permitted myself to play around with the concept of role perception, particularly in relation to job specification. Our reaction to the statement that two observers may perceive the same stimulus differently would be that this is elemental. But our reaction to the statement that two workers performing the same job perceive it differently probably would be either that the statement is false or the workers should be put on the couch. Yet as I have just said in discussing individual dimensionality of criteria, it is apparent that people performing exactly the same tasks may in fact view their jobs quite differently. One of my former students, W. N. McBain, tried to study the job role perceptions of a group of maintenance workers. The findings rather clearly showed wide discrepancies in the perceptions of duties and responsibilities of persons with the same work assignments.

This phenomenological approach is most suggestive. A group of positions might be exactly the same in terms of the three sets of formal characteristics I mentioned earlier, and yet performance on them might bear little relationship to some predictor variable because of the different job perceptions of the workers filling them who consequently adopt different roles. If we considered only those positions filled by persons with similar perceptions of their jobs, and validated our predictors just with these people, our relationships might be much higher.

The arrangements or organizations of positions into classes is a problem of taxonomy. In seeking to gain some insight into this matter, I consulted with biologists of various stripes. But they seem more concerned with end products, ultimate classes, rather than with the means by which such classes are, and can be, formed. So I turned to a patient philosopher. As a result of my discussion with him it appears that in forming occupational families we have rigidly and compulsively held to the type or organization termed logical product. We group positions into jobs, jobs into occupations, and lower order occupations into higher order ones, on the basis of a decreasing number of assumed common elements. Thus comptometer operators and bookkeepers are grouped together into the same class called computational clerks because both have two characteristics in common: arithemetic calculation and paper work. These two jobs, together with those of file clerk and coding clerk, are grouped together into the more general class of office workers because all four have in common the single element of paper work.

Perhaps we should be looking for other types or organizations. In certain instances a logical summation might be more appropriate. With this system our organization involves an increasing number of elements. It is not unlikely that such an arrangement will be helpful in viewing certain industrial jobs. For example, the jobs of buffing machine and drill press operator might be subsumed under the job of machinist, since the latter involves all of the elements of the former. A logical summation has important implications for selection and placement of workers. It suggests that a job can be broken up into chunks of activities, and that proficiency in each chunk is to be predicted separately.

It may well be that there is no nice ordering of jobs. The relationships among jobs might be something like the relationships among the stars in the heavens. No clear and distinct groupings occur, but rather there is a continuous distribution with modal regions or constellations. Three studies support this notion. Coombs and Satter (6), Thorndike and Norris (25) and I (10), using quite different methods attempted to determine the similarity among jobs. None of these studies showed any clear cut groupings of jobs. Rather, if the jobs were plotted in multidimensional space, and we had the appropriate vision, we would see jobs positioned relative to one another in the same manner that we find celestial bodies positioned, a continuous distribution with various areas in which there tends to be a certain clustering.

This clustering notion leads to some interesting and complex inferences with respect to selection. First of all it does, of course, suggest a great deal of specificity with respect to the validity of selection devices. If we could ascertain some dimensionality of this complex space, we might be able to set up sliding multiple regression equations for our predictors. We would change the constants in the equation in some systematic fashion as we moved its aim from one point to another in the solar system of jobs.

CLASSIFICATION AND DIFFERENTIAL PLACEMENT

The recent war brought forcibly to our attention the matter of effective manpower utilization. We saw that selection is only one aspect of the larger problem of worker placement. The determination of which individuals to accept and which to reject for a given job was not as important as the determination of which job an individual could be placed in most effectively. This latter we term the classification problem.

Classification is not just a problem during national emergencies. There are a number of situations where the selection or rejection of persons is not a consideration at all. Instead we are confronted with a number of persons on the one hand and a number of vacant positions on the other. The task is to make the most effective matching of men and positions. Transfer of workers is such a case. For example when a job is eliminated and because of a particular union contract or a particular management philosophy the workers are not to be terminated, they must be placed elsewhere in the organization. In many instances upgrading and promotion is a true classification problem. Executive trainees in an organization ultimately are to be placed in an operations, sales, or staff position; and this is a straightforward classification problem.

While from time to time there are easy labor markets, it is unquestionably true that we can look forward to a future of a tight manpower situation. Increased production demands, shorter hours of work, cold wars, and the like, will require fuller realization of the potentialities of workers. We will not be able to afford the luxury of rejecting persons who thereby on their own must seek other employment. Instead we shall have to discover where in the world of work each can make a significant contribution.

When we consider personnel classification we are in a curious position. I am reminded of the story told of Einstein. Seeing him pace up and down obviously in deep thought a bystander remarked, "What's the trouble, Professor, can't you solve your problem?" To which Einstein replied, "No, that's not it. My difficulty is that I cannot state the problem. If I can state it I can solve it." We probably would be much further ahead in our thinking about personnel classification if we had not devoted so much of our attention to solutions, of which a number have been offered, but rather had given more thought to stating the problem. As it is we have procedures available but inadequate statements of concepts and objectives.

Discussions of personnel classification have overlooked what to me is a very important consideration, namely, the type of work situation. The focus of attention has largely been the individual and the job performance that he will attain. Yet it is quite obvious that in many instances classification must deal with work situations where the individual does not perform in isolation. The need may be to place workers in jobs where his activities have a limiting effect upon the performance of others, or in teams where there is a more dynamic interaction. Therefore I have sought to differentiate three types of jobs, independent jobs, successive jobs, and coordinate jobs (8). For each of these three types of jobs we have a different classification problem.

There are a large number of jobs where the workers' contributions are largely independent. In a department store, for example, the work of a sales clerk in one department generally has little bearing upon that of a sales clerk in another department. Here the classification problem is seen in its simplest form, and it is the problem for which solutions have been developed.

Yet we immediately have difficulties. What are objectives? These, I think, have not been stated clearly enough. As Brown and I see it there are three possible objectives: to place each person in that job on which his performance will be highest, to place persons in jobs so that all jobs are filled by persons who meet some minimum standards of performance, or to place persons so that the highest total criterion scores will result (11).

Now let us see how adequately the solutions that have been developed achieve these objectives. We can classify the solutions into four major types, those that involve non-exact cut-and-fit methods, those that involve differential prediction, those that involve the placement of individuals into classes via the discriminant function, and the simplex solution.

Thirty-five years ago the late Edward Lee Thorndike (22) considered the problem of differential placement. He developed a routine by means of which the more able individuals are dealt with first by placing them in jobs in accordance with their highest talents, but not placing any individual in a job for which he fails to meet minimum qualifications. Less able individuals are distributed among jobs pretty much at random. There is no assurance that this routine gives the best solution in terms of any of the three objectives. But the placement clearly is better than that which would be accomplished on a chance basis. I suspect that many of us either formally or informally have used a cut-and-fit method similar to Thorndike's.

Differential prediction essentially involves the separate prediction of success for each individual on each job, and then, other things being equal, placing each person on that job for which he has highest talent. However, in personnel classification things are never equal. For different jobs there are different quotas, different jobs have different degrees of predictability, and different jobs have different degrees of importance or different minimum standards of performance. Robert Thorndike (23, 24) and Brogden (3), in separate treatments, have sought exact solutions bearing in mind the complicating factors just mentioned. While mathematically more elegant, their solutions achieve little more than the beautifully simple system of Edward Thorndike. Robert Thorndike and Brogden try to achieve the impossible, a simultaneous attainment of the three objectives of placing persons in accordance with their highest talents, not filling jobs with unqualified individuals, and highest total criterion scores. None of these objectives is completely achieved, so that the result is a sort of compromise and approximation of the maximal result.

Personnel classification involves the placement of individuals into one or another of several classes, the classes in this case being jobs. It is therefore not unexpected to find that many have sought to apply the discriminant function. This type of solution has been discussed by Rulon (18), Tiedeman (26), and Anderson (1). While unquestionably the discriminant function is a lovely statistical device, its sheer nicety should not be grounds for accepting it as the final solution, or even a partial solution. To apply the discriminant function, clearly defined classes of individuals are necessary. What are classes in personnel classification? Some have said that they are given by the persons now placed in jobs in question. But obviously many such persons are misplaced and hence the classes are incorrectly defined. Others have said that the classes are "successful" workers in the specified jobs. But an individual who in fact is a failure on all of the jobs in question, would by this procedure necessarily be classified as a success on at least one of them. The discriminant function, then, is not the answer—at least until we can specify our classes of individuals.

So far as I have been able to discover, Votaw and Dailey (28) are the only ones who have sought to achieve a single objective. This, they specify as the maximal total criterion scores—or the highest total productivity. I must take it entirely on faith that their mathematical procedure accomplishes this. Their simplex solution is far beyond me. It has something to do with tensors. But these little items occur neither in my perceptual field, my life space, or my subconscious. Granting the method, then, we have at least one exact solution for personnel classification when it is concerned with independent jobs.

Let us consider now the case of successive jobs. Here the work passes from one individual to another. The performance of those whose activities occur late in the sequence is directly conditioned by the performance of those who play a part earlier in the sequence. A simple example is the case of the orange sorter and the orange packer. If the sorter is too slow the packers production is limited. On the other hand, if the sorter is too fast the packer's bin overflows. I know of no systematic consideration of this type of work situation. However, I would presume that the objective would be to assign workers to the two jobs so that the speed of production of each is exactly the same. We would seek to allocate talent to each job in such degrees as to maintain a flow of production that is orderly and at a maximal rate. I suppose that we would be placing persons in accordance with predicted raw criterion scores rather than standard criterion scores. I do see questions that I am unable to answer when proficiency on the various jobs differ in predictability. If you think of regression lines with different slopes you will see what I mean.

I have said that classification also must deal with jobs that are coordinate in nature. An example are the coordinate jobs of riveter and bucker-upper. In work situations of this kind the end result is a function of the group effort and is not just an additive function of individual capabilities. No matter how well either the riveter or the bucker-upper performs his job, the work will be poorly done if the performance of the other is not satisfactory. There are many such teams in industry—repair crews, airplane crews, administrative staffs, to name a few.

The important characteristic of coordinate jobs is that in addition to individual talents, they involve interpersonal relationships of various kinds. Again I must confess that the solution, and indeed the problem, escapes me. I presume that the task is to discover the levels of group productivity that are achieved by teams comprised of individuals with different combinations of characteristics. However, somehow, we must state an objective such as maximal total productivity of all groups, or whatever, and this objective should dictate our solution.

CONCLUSION

I stated at the beginning that my thesis is that worker placement is an exciting field jam-packed with challenges. Perhaps I have not convinced you. If that is the case, the fault is mine, for in the domain of worker placement most mountains are yet unclimbed and most channels yet unswum. New ideas and concepts are necessary if we are to achieve further improvements. Factual research alone will not be sufficient.

REFERENCES

1. ANDERSON, T. W. Classification of multivariate analysis. *Psychometrica*, 1951, 16, 31–49.
2. BELLOWS, R. M. Procedures for evaluating vocational criteria. *Journ. Appl. Psychol.*, 1941, 25, 499–513.
3. BROGDEN, H. E. An approach to the problem of differential prediction. *Psychometrica*, 1946, 11, 139–154.
4. CARTER, L. F. Psychological Research on Navigator Training. A.A.F. Aviation Psychology Research Report, No. 10, 1947.
5. CATTELL, R. B. *Factor Analysis.* Harper, 1952.
6. COOMBS, C. H. & SATTER, G. A. A factorial approach to job families. *Psychometrica*, 1949, 14, 33–42.
7. EDGERTON, H. A., & KOLBE, L. E. The method of minimum variation in the coordination of criteria. *Psychometrica*, 1936, 1, 185–187.
8. GHISELLI, E. E. New ideas in industrial psychology. *Journ. Appl. Psychol.*, 1951, 35, 229–235.
9. GHISELLI, E. E. Dimensional problems of criteria. *Journ. Appl. Psychol.*, 1956, 40, 1–4.
10. GHISELLI, E. E. The measurement of occupational aptitude. University of California Publications in Psychology, 1955, 8, 101–216.
11. GHISELLI, E. E., & BROWN, C. W. *Personnel and Industrial Psychology.* 2nd ed. McGraw-Hill, 1955.
12. HORST, A. P. Obtaining a composite measure from different measures of the same attributes. *Psychometrica*, 1936, 1, 53–60.

13. Horst, A. P. *The Prediction of Personal Adjustment.* Social Science Research Council, 1941.
14. Hull, C. L. Variability in amount of different traits possessed by an individual. *Journ. Educ. Psychol.*, 1927, 18, 97–104.
15. Jaspen, N. Symposium: Development of useful criteria in industrial research. A.P.A. meetings, 1954.
16. Jenkins, J. G. Validity for what? *Journ. Consult. Psychol.*, 1946, 10, 93–98.
17. Otis, J. L. The criterion. In W. H. Stead, *et al., Occupational Counseling Techniques,* American Book Co., 1940.
18. Rulon, P. J. Distinctions between discriminant analysis and a geometric interpretation of the discriminant function. *Harvard Educ. Rev.*, 1951, 21, 80–90.
19. Rush, C. H. A factorial study of sales criteria. *Personnel Psychol.*, 1953, 6, 9–24.
20. Shartle, C. L. *Occupational Information.* 2nd ed. Prentice-Hall, 1952.
21. Stephenson, W. *The Study of Behavior Q-Technique and its Methodology.* Univ. Chicago Press, 1953.
22. Thorndike, E. L. In *The Personnel System of the United States Army,* Vol. II, *The Personnel Manual.* 1919, pp. 276–333.
23. Thorndike, R. L. *Personnel Selection.* Wiley, 1949.
24. Thorndike, R. L. The problem of classification of personnel. *Psychometrica,* 1950, 15, 215–235.
25. Thorndike, R. L., & Norris, R. C. Empirical evidence on Air Force Career Fields. Air Training Command, Human Resources Research Center Research Bull. 52–13, 1952.
26. Tiedeman, D. V. The utility of the discriminant function in psychological and guidance investigations. *Harvard Educ. Rev.*, 1951, 21, 71–80.
27. Toops, H. A. The criterion. *Educ. Psychol. Measmt.*, 1944, 4, 271–297.
28. Votaw, D. F., & Dailey, J. T. Assignment of personel to jobs. Air Training Command, Human Resources Research Center, *Research Bull.*, 1952, 52–54.
29. Wrigley, C. The prediction of a complex aptitude. *Brit. Journ. Psychol.*, Statistical Section, 1952, 5, 93–104.

5 A Modified Model for Test Validation and Selection Research

MARVIN D. DUNNETTE

It is argued that the classic prediction model is grossly oversimplified and has resulted in corresponding oversimplifications in the design of most validation studies. A modified and more complex prediction model is presented. Implications for future validation research are discussed in the context of the kinds of behaviors to be predicted, the necessity for investigating heteroscedastic and nonlinear relationships, and the important advantages in prediction which may be realized by discovering homogeneous subsets of jobs, tests, people, and behaviors within which prediction equations may be developed and crossvalidated.

Nearly 35 years ago, Clark Hull (1928) discussed the level of forecasting efficiency shown by the so-called modern tests of the time. He noted that the upper limit for tests was represented by validity coefficients of about .50 corresponding to a forecasting efficiency of only 13%. He regarded the region of forecasting efficiency lying above this point as being inaccessible to the test batteries of the day, and he viewed with pessimism the use of test batteries for predicting occupational criteria. Hull, of course, failed to emphasize that the accuracy of practical decisions might better be assessed against zones of behavior (e.g., passing versus failing in a training program) rather than against the metrical continuum assumed in the calculation of his index of forecasting efficiency. Further, he gave no attention to the varying effects of different selection ratios on the accuracies obtainable with even rather low correlation coefficients. Even so, we should be somewhat dismayed by the fact that today our tests have still not penetrated the region of inaccessibility defined so long ago by Hull. Ghiselli's (1955) comprehensive review of both published and unpublished studies showed average validities ranging in the .30s and low .40s; an average validity of .50 or above was a distinct rarity. These low validities have apparently led many psychologists to become disenchanted with test and selection research. Some have

From *Journal of Applied Psychology*, 1963, 47, 317-332. This paper was read at the seventieth annual convention of the American Psychological Association held in St. Louis in the fall of 1962.

disappeared into other endeavors such as the study of group influences, interaction patterns, and the like. Others have sought refuge in the hypothesis testing models of statistical inference and have implied validity for tests showing *statistically* (but often not *practically*) significant differences between contrasting groups (see Dunnette & Kirchner, 1962). Nunnally (1960) comments:

> We should not feel proud when we see the psychologist smile and say "the correlation is significant beyond the .01 level." Perhaps that is the most he can say, but he has no reason to smile [p. 649].

Even less defensible, perhaps, has been the tendency for many to persist in doing selection *without* conducting selection research or test validation. The ordinary defenses for such practice run the gamut—from claiming near miracles of clinical insight in personnel assessment to the recounting of anecdotes about instances of selective accuracy (counting the "hits" and forgetting the "misses") and finally to the old cliché that "management is well-satisfied with the methods being employed." We cannot and should not try to avoid the fact that the statistics of selection (i.e., validity coefficients) are far from gratifying and offer little support to anyone claiming to do *much* better than chance in the selection process.

It seems wise, therefore, to discuss the possibility of improving our batting average in test validation and selection research. Selection programs will go on—with or without psychologists—but I believe we now have the capability for penetrating the region of inaccessibility outlined by Hull.

First, let us examine the classic validation or prediction model. This model has sought simply to link predictors, on the one hand, with criteria, on the other, through a simple index of relationship, the correlation coefficient. Such a simple linkage of predictors and criteria is grossly oversimplified in comparison with the complexities actually involved in predicting human behavior. Most competent investigators readily recognize this fact and design their validation studies to take account of the possible complexities—job differences, criterion differences, etc.—present in the prediction situation. Even so, the appealing simplicity, false though it is, of the classic model has led many researchers to be satisfied with a correspondingly simplified design for conducting selection research. Thus, the usual validation effort has ignored the events—on the job behavior, situational differences, dynamic factors influencing definitions of success, etc.—intervening between predictor and criterion behavior. I believe that the lure of this seemingly simple model is, to a great extent, responsible for the low order of validities reported in the Ghiselli (1955) review. It is noteworthy that the studies reviewed by Ghiselli show no typical level of prediction for any given test or type of job. In fact, there seems to be little consistency among various studies using similar tests and purporting to predict similar criteria. The review also suggests that the magnitude of validity coefficients is inversely proportional to the sample size employed in the studies. This can perhaps be explained, in part, by sampling error, but it may also be due to the relatively greater homogeneity possible within smaller groups of subjects. It appears, in other words, that the varying levels of prediction shown by the various studies are related somehow to the appropriateness (or lack thereof) of the classic prediction model for the particular set of conditions in the study being reported. It seems wise, therefore, to consider a prediction model which more fully presents the complexities which are only implied by the classic model.

Guetzkow and Forehand (1961) have suggested a modification of the classic validation model which provides a richer schematization for prediction research and which offers important implications for the direction of future research. Their model along with certain additional modifications is shown in Figure 5.1. Note that the modified prediction model takes account of the complex interactions which may occur between predictors and various predictor combinations, different groups (or types) of individuals, different behaviors on the job, and the consequences of these behaviors relative to the goals of the organization. The model permits the possibility of predictors being differentially useful for

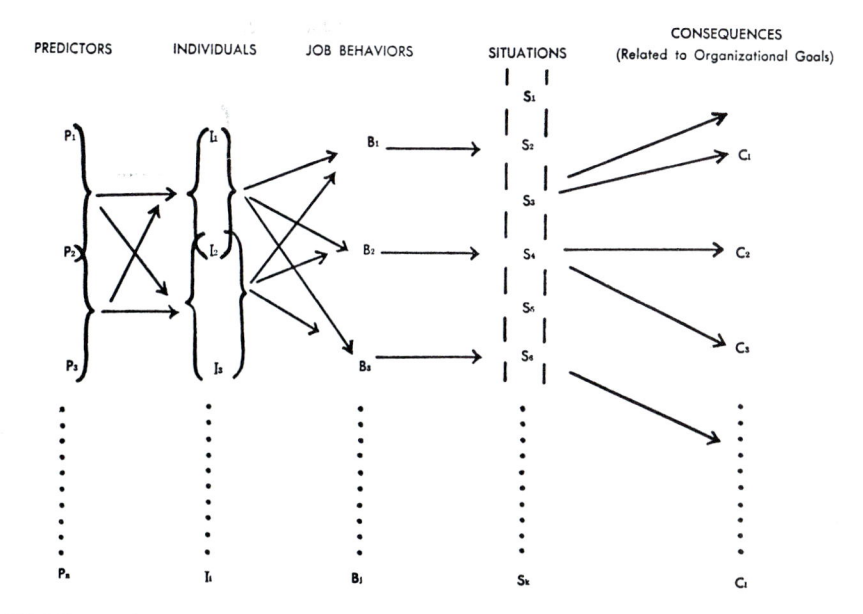

FIGURE 5.1. *A modified model for test validation and selection research.*

predicting the behaviors of different subsets of individuals. Further, it shows that similar job behaviors may be predictable by quite different patterns of interaction between groupings of predictors and individuals or even that the same level of performance on predictors can lead to substantially different patterns of job behavior for different individuals. Finally, the model recognizes the annoying reality that the same or similar job behaviors can, after passing through the situational filter, lead to quite different organizational consequences.

This modified and more complex prediction model leads to a number of important considerations involving the emphases to be followed by future validation research:

First, we must be willing to back off a step or two from global measures of occupational effectiveness—ratings, volume of output, and other so-called criteria of organizational worth, and do a more careful job of studying actual job behavior—with particular focus on behavioral or stylistic variations among different individuals with the same jobs. Most previous validation research has been overly concerned with predicting organizational consequences without first determining the nature of possible linkages between such consequences and differences in actual job behavior. It is true that industrial psychologists should continue to be concerned about predicting organizational consequences. Certainly, the modified model implies no lessening of such an interest. What is hoped, however, is that the more careful analysis of the behavioral correlates of differences in organizational consequences will lead to broader understanding of them and, eventually, to their more accurate prediction.

Secondly, as implied by the point just made, the modified model demands that we give up our worship of *the* criterion (Dunnette, 1963). I believe that our concept of *the* criterion has suggested the existence of some single, all encompassing measure of occupational success against which predictors must be compared. Our modified model demands that we work with multiple measures of individual behavior and organizational consequences. I suggest therefore that we cease talking about *the* criterion problem and that we discard the notion of a so-called ultimate criterion. Such action should result in a research emphasis which will be less restrictive and less simple-minded and more aware of the necessity of analyzing and predicting the many facets of occupational success.

Thirdly, the modified model implies nothing concerning the form of the relationships to be expected. One of the unfortunate consequences of utilizing the classic validation model was its overemphasis on the correlation coefficient as almost the sole statistic of validation research. The notion of a simple linkage between predictor and criterion led easily to the equally simple assumption of the applicability of the linear, homoscedastic model for expressing the magnitude of relationships. Kahneman and Ghiselli (1962), in investigating relationships between 60 aptitude variables and various criteria, showed that 40 per cent of the scatter diagrams departed significantly from the linear, homoscedastic model, and 90 per cent of these departures held up on cross-validation. This is an important finding for it points up the necessity in future validation research of adopting a methodology taking account of the very great likelihood of nonlinear, heteroscedastic models. Our more complex prediction model, focusing as it does on the complex linkages between predictors and consequences, implies also the necessity of adopting more complex and sophisticated tools of analysis in studying these linkages.

Fourth, and most obviously, our modified model demands that we develop a sort of typology for classifying people, tests, job situations, and behaviors according to their relative predictability. Future validation research must define the unique conditions under which certain predictors may be used for certain jobs and for certain purposes. Research studies should, therefore, be devoted to the definition of homogeneous subsets within which appropriate prediction equations may be developed and cross-validated. This idea is not particularly startling nor even new. But it has *not* been applied widely in the conduct of selection research. The modified model rather explicitly directs us to carry out such subgrouping studies in order to learn more about the complex linkages between predictors and consequences. Fortunately several studies already are available which confirm the advantages of studying differential patterns of validity for various subgroups. A brief review of some of these research approaches should illustrate the utility of applying our more complicated model to validation research.

With respect to job groupings, Dunnette and Kirchner (Dunnette, 1958; Dunnette & Kirchner, 1958, 1960) have studied the different patterns of validities obtained when careful techniques of job analysis are used to discover groupings of jobs which are relatively homogeneous in terms of actual responsibilities. Substantial different validities were obtained for engineers grouped according to functional similarities (research, development, production, and sales), salesmen (industrial and retail), and clerical employees (stenographers and clerk typists). These studies highlight the necessity of studying job differences and the differential predictability of effectiveness in various job groupings. More generally, an emphasis on the varying predictability of different job activities is inherent in the methods of synthetic validity (Balma, Ghiselli, McCormick, Primoff, & Griffin, 1959) and in the use of the *J* coefficient developed by Primoff (1955).

Everyone recognizes the possibility of situational effects on the validity of psychological predictions, but there is a paucity of research designed to estimate systematically the magnitude of such effects. Perhaps the best example of such research is provided by Vroom (1960). He showed that various aptitude tests (verbal and nonverbal reasoning, arithmetic reasoning) predicted ratings of job success most effectively for persons who were highly motivated. Job effectiveness in nonmotivating situations showed either no relationship or negative relationships with tested abilities. In a second study with Mann (Vroom & Mann, 1960), it was shown that the size of work groups strongly influence employee attitudes toward their supervisors. Employees in small groups preferred democratic or equalitarian supervisors; employees in large work groups preferred authoritarian supervisors. In a significant series of studies, Porter (1962) is also investigating situational factors such as hierarchical level, firm size, and job function as they affect managerial perceptions of their jobs. More emphasis needs to be given to these and other situational factors in validation studies, particularly as they serve to operate as moderating variables (Saunders, 1956) in behavioral predictions.

Many studies have shown different validities for different subgroups of individuals. For example, Seashore (1961) summarized a vast number of scholastic success studies which show almost uniformly that the grades of women (in both high school and college) are significantly more predictable than those of men. It is also well established that differing patterns of validity are typically obtained for subgroups differing in amounts of education and/or years of job experience. It may seem obvious that such factors as sex, education, and experience provide useful moderating variables in validation research. However, researchers also have identified variables which are much less *obvious* but which *do* make substantial differences in the patterns and magnitudes of validities obtained. For example, Grooms and Endler (1960) showed that the grades of anxious college students were much more predictable ($r = .63$) with aptitude and achievement measures than were the grades of nonanxious students ($r = .19$); and Frederiksen, Melville, and Gilbert (Frederiksen & Gilbert, 1960; Frederiksen & Melville, 1954) have shown that interest in engineering (as measured by the Strong test) has a higher validity for predicting grades for noncompulsive engineers than for compulsive ones. Berdie (1961) showed that the grades of engineering students with relatively consistent scores on an algebra test were more predictable from the total test score than were the grades of students with less consistent scores.[1] Ghiselli (1956, 1962) has developed a method for dividing persons, on the basis of a screening test, into more and less predictable subgroups. The advantage of his method is that no a priori basis is necessary for the identification of subgroups; the method depends simply on the development of one or more predictor tests to facilitate the subgrouping process.

The identification of more and less predictable subgroups of persons, whether based on logical factors (such as sex, education, or experience)

---

[1] The algebra test of 100 items was divided into 10 subtests of equal difficulty. The measure of consistency for each student was simply the sum of squares of the deviations of his 10 scores from his mean score on all 10 subtests.

or on methods such as those employed by Berdie and Ghiselli, places a special burden on the investigator to demonstrate the stability of his results. Although the studies cited above were cross-validated (i.e., checked on holdout groups), the validity generalization and/or extension of such results has not often been measured. This needs to be done. The results so far reported with these methods are promising indeed, but they will take on greatly added significance when it is demonstrated that they hold up over time.

Less research has been directed at identifying subsets of predictors showing differential patterns of validity. However, Ghiselli (1960, 1962) has also contributed methodology in this area and has succeeded in significantly enhancing prediction by identifying, again through the development and use of screening tests, the particular predictor which will do the most valid job for each individual.

General approaches to the development of "types" have been made by a number of investigators. Gaier and Lee (1953) and Cronbach and Gleser (1953) summarize a variety of methods of assessing profile similarity and conclude that available indexes are simply variants of the general Pythagorean formula for the linear distance between two points in n-dimensional space. Lykken (1956) has questioned the psychological meaning of such "geometric similarity" and he proposes a method of actuarial pattern analysis which requires no assumptions concerning the form of the distribution and which defines similarity in psychological rather than geometric terms. His method consists simply of investigating criterial outcomes for subjects classified together into cells on the basis of similar test scores. In a recent study, he and Rose (Lykken & Rose, in press) demonstrate that the method is more accurate in discriminating between neurotics and psychotics on the basis of MMPI scores than either clinicians' judgments or a statistical technique based on equations derived from a discriminant function analysis. Lykken's method of actuarial pattern analysis is the same as Toops' (1959) method of developing subgroups or "ulstriths" based on biographical and test similarities and then writing different prediction equations for each of the subgroups so identified. It is interesting to note that computers have now given us the capability for carrying out many of Toops' suggestions—which at one time were regarded as wild-eyed, idealistic, and unrealistic. McQuitty (1957, 1960, 1961) also has developed methods for discovering the diagnostic and predictive significance of various response patterns. His techniques, in addition to the methods proposed by Lykken and Toops, constitute the most extensive attack made to date on the problem of developing differentially predictable subsets or types.

These studies and methods mark the bare beginnings of efforts to take account of complexities which have been ignored by the oversimplified prediction model of the past. It appears that subgrouping of tests, people, jobs, situations, and consequences is necessary to a thorough understanding of what is going on in a prediction situation. The widespread acceptance of the modified model which we have been discussing should lead to a new and refreshing series of questions about problems of selection and placement. Instead of asking whether or not a particular selection technique (test, interview, or what have you) is any good, we will ask under *what circumstances* different techniques may be useful. What sorts of persons should be screened with each of the methods available, and how may the various subgroups of persons be identified and assigned to optimal screening devices? Finally, what job behaviors may be expected of various people and how may these behaviors be expected to aid or to detract from accomplishing different organizational objectives which may, in turn, vary according to different value systems and preferred outcomes?

What are the implications of these trends for the selection function in industry? Primarily, I believe they suggest the possibility of a new kind of selection process in the firm of the future. The selection expert of tomorrow will no longer be attempting to utilize the same procedure for all his selection problems. Instead, he will be armed with an array of prediction equations. He will have developed, through research, a wealth of evidence showing the patterns of validities for different linkages in the modified prediction model—for different predictors, candidates, jobs, and criteria. He will be a flexible operator, attentive always to the accumulating information on any given candidate, and ready to apply, at each stage, the tests and procedures shown to be optimal.

REFERENCES

BALMA, M. J., GHISELLI, E. E., MCCORMICK, E. J., PRIMOFF, E. S., & GRIFFIN, C. H. The development of processes for indirect or synthetic validity: A symposium. *Personnel Psychol.*, 1959, 12, 395–400.

BERDIE, R. F. Intra-individual variability and predictability. *Educ. psychol. Measmt.*, 1961, 21, 663–676.

CRONBACH, L. J., & GLESER, G. Assessing similarity between profiles. *Psychol. Bull.*, 1953, 50, 456–473.

DUNNETTE, M. D. Validity of interviewer's ratings and psychological tests for predicting the job effectiveness of engineers. St. Paul: Minnesota Mining and Manufacturing Company, 1958. (Mimeo)

DUNNETTE, M. D. A note on *the* criterion. *J. appl. Psychol.*, 1963, 47, 251–254.

DUNNETTE, M. D., & KIRCHNER, W. K. Validation of psychological tests in industry. *Personnel Admin.*, 1958, 21, 20–27.

DUNNETTE, M. D., & KIRCHNER, W. K. Psychological test differences between industrial salesmen and retail salesmen. *J. appl. Psychol.*, 1960, 44, 121–125.

Dunnette, M. D., & Kirchner, W. K. Validities, vectors, and verities. *J. appl. Psychol.*, 1962, 46, 296–299.

Frederiksen, N., & Gilbert, A. C. Replication of a study of differential predictability *Educ. psychol. Measmt.*, 1960, 20, 759–767.

Frederiksen, N., & Melville, S. D. Differential predictability in the use of test scores. *Educ. psychol. Measmt.*, 1954, 14, 647–656.

Gaier, E. L., & Lee, M. Pattern analysis: The configural approach to predictive measurement. *Psychol. Bull.*, 1953, 50, 140–148.

Ghiselli, E. E. The measurement of occupational aptitude. Berkeley: Univer. California Press, 1955.

Ghiselli, E. E. Differentiation of individuals in terms of their predictability. *J. appl. Psychol.*, 1956, 40, 374–377.

Ghiselli, E. E. Differentiation of tests in terms of the accuracy with which they predict for a given individual. *Educ. psychol. Measmt.*, 1960, 20, 675–684.

Ghiselli, E. E. The prediction of predictability and the predictability of prediction. Paper read at American Psychological Association, St. Louis, September 1962.

Grooms, R. R., & Endler, N. S. The effect of anxiety on academic achievement. *J. educ. Psychol.*, 1960, 51, 299–304.

Guetzkow, H., & Forehand, G. A. A research strategy for partial knowledge useful in the selection of executives. In R. Taguiri (Ed.), *Research needs in executive selection.* Boston: Harvard Graduate School of Business Administration, 1961.

Hull, C. L. Aptitude testing. Yonkers, N. Y.: World Book, 1928.

Kahneman, D., & Ghiselli, E. E. Validity and non-linear heteroscedastic models. *Personnel Psychol.*, 1962, 15, 1–11.

Lykken, D. T. A method of actuarial pattern analysis. *Psychol. Bull.*, 1956, 53, 102–107.

Lykken, D. T., & Rose, R. J. Psychological prediction from actuarial tables. *J. clin. Psychol.*, in press.

McQuitty, L. L. Isolating predictor patterns associated with major criterion patterns. *Educ. psychol. Measmt.*, 1957, 17, 3–42.

McQuitty, L. L. Hierarchical linkage analysis for the isolation of types. *Educ. psychol. Measmt.*, 1960, 20, 55–67.

McQuitty, L. L. A method for selecting patterns to differentiate categories of people. *Educ. psychol. Measmt.*, 1961, 21, 85–94.

Nunnally, J. The place of statistics in psychology. *Educ. psychol. Measmt.*, 1960, 20, 641–650.

Porter, L. W. Some recent explorations in the study of management attitudes. Paper read at American Psychological Association, St. Louis, September 1962.

Primoff, E. S. *Test selection by job analysis.* Washington, D. C.: United States Civil Service Commission, Test Developmental Section, 1955.

Saunders, D. R. Moderator variables in prediction. *Educ. psychol. Measmt.*, 1956, 16, 209–222.

Seashore, H. G. Women are more predictable than men. Presidential address, Division 7, American Psychological Association, New York, September 1961.

Toops, H. A. A research utopia in industrial psychology. *Personnel Psychol.*, 1959, 12, 189–227.

Vroom, V. H. *Some personality determinants of the effects of participation.* Englewood Cliffs, N. J.: Prentice-Hall, 1960.

Vroom, V. H., & Mann, F. C. Leader authoritarianism and employee attitudes. *Personnel Psychol.*, 1960, 13, 125–139.

6 Whose Criterion?

JAY L. OTIS

The task of addressing a group such as the one assembled here is difficult, because it would be presumptuous to attempt to inform and inappropriate to attempt to entertain. Perhaps my assignment is to present a point of view which may stimulate some, irritate others, and create the condition of boredom in only a few.

Each person in this field of ours has a conception of his job and the role he believes he should play, which determines the way he practices his profession, and also serves as a criterion by which he evaluates the status of his colleagues. In fact, much of this presentation has to do with job concepts and their role in the establishment of suitable criterion variables for use in the work we undertake in both research and service. The job concept presented here is not new, but it may be somewhat controversial. We may be asking the industrial psychologist to play a role which he does not wish to assume.

It is not surprising that business executives are unaware of the duties and functions of an industrial psychologist; in fact, some of our colleagues in other divisions are no better informed than our present and potential employers. By definition, a psychologist is a specialist in industrial and business behavior. Perhaps what I am suggesting is that we interest ourselves in industrial behavior and not in predicting and studying the nonpsychological conception of industrial behavior.

Today a majority of the membership in our division is employed by industry and business, and the academic domination no longer exists. The work assignments of our members vary from research positions in both large and small industry to staff positions in personnel and industrial relations departments. Some of our colleagues are in line assignments and devote their talents to actual business operations. We are now close to industry, we are informed about industry, and we are in a position to use many of our own observations of industrial behavior and depend less and less on management opinions and observations for both data and explanations.

Presidential address, Division 14, American Psychological Association, 1953.

It has been said that an industrial psychologist must have not only a criterion acceptable to himself, he also must have one that is acceptable to management as well. We hear such terms as management criteria, acceptable to management, use of those standards which management judges to be important, management ratings, production records, supervisory judgment, sales quotas, and judgements of ability. But we rarely hear of a criterion of industrial behavior constructed by those who are expert in the field of industrial behavior—industrial psychologists.

We spend the majority of our time on predictors, measurements of attitudes, and training programs, and only a small fraction of our research time on the criterion variables themselves. We leave that to management and spend countless hours in "teaching management how to give ratings we can use," correcting production records for machine capacity, experience influence, and all of those conditions which contaminate the criterion. Whether we like it or not, many of the criteria we now use have been so modified by our attempts to correct, that for a wide variety of purposes we are using criteria in which we ourselves have had considerable say and which bear little resemblance to the data given to us by management. Some of the methods of treating criterion variables obtained from management sources result in individual-criterion scores which management itself might question without the psychologist being able to make an adequate, meaningful defense.

I am suggesting that many of us might find profit in crossing over the fence from the predictor side of the equation and study, derive, and construct the things to be predicted. I once suggested to a group of my colleagues that it might be profitable to divide a research team in half and put one half to work constructing predictors for the criterion variables obtained in a work situation by the other half of the team. I am suggesting the desirability of coming close enough to the daily work situation to be able to make judgments about workers and working conditions which not only approximate, but perhaps surpass, management judgements in validity. This is not a common role for industrial psychologists to play. I can say from personal experience that a psychologist working in a single firm for an extended period of time can accumulate job-behavior information which will permit him to make judgments concerning job proficiency for a large number of employees working at different job levels in many of the major departments.

If the psychologists have direct access to the workers through counseling or a function such as job evaluation, we may obtain information not possessed by management itself. As we become more active in industry we find that the usual criterion variables become less desirable, and we can educate management so that significant job behavior can be substituted for those judged to be less desirable.

JOB ANALYSIS AND CRITERION RESEARCH

For the most part, criterion research has been closely associated with validity research and little has been done to work on criterion problems alone. Most of us, when called to work on practically any industrial problem, begin by using the job-analysis approach. Just what is the task that seems to be the center of the problem? It is an inventory of job facts. Job analysis may be defined as the process of obtaining job information or job facts to be used in the various operations in the field of personnel management. It is the process of determining the tasks which comprise the job and of the skills, knowledges, abilities, and responsibilities required of the worker for successful performance. One operation in personnel management and supervision is the determination of the performance or performances which may be used to differentiate the good and poor workers. Job analysis should be of value here. It may be true that we have depended too little on job analysis to aid us in selecting criterion variables and too much on the opinions of administrators and supervisors as to what constitutes significant job performance. Certainly a thorough job analysis should precede the selection of variables as criteria or the acceptance of criteria submitted by management.

Those who work in the field of job analysis soon discover the elusive nature of a job. It is true in industry that the job a man is performing today can change radically tomorrow and still retain the same title, the same wage, the same labor grade, merely through the issuance of a standard practice instruction altering a major task while forgetting to make the changes in title, pay, and labor grade which we need for identification purposes. What a job is and what responsible authorities think it is are not always the same. Each job must be carefully identified. In describing the tasks and determining job content, interest is directed toward what the workers do, not what they are *expected* to do, not what the supervisors *say* they do, but what the workers actually do during the normal course of a day's work. A knowledge of job content is highly important in building a criterion, because some duties are essential for success and others may be disregarded. There are some duties which do not affect job proficiency, but which can become management annoyances and may influence management's judgement of the worker's ability to perform his skilled assignments.

The job is the unit of research. It is essential that the job be held relatively constant if criteria are to apply equally well to all employees assigned to the job. For example, foreman jobs in one large manufacturing plant have been classified into six labor grades; laborers in the same organization fall into the first three labor grades, and the job known as machine set-up operator is found from labor grade 2 to labor grade 6. It is possible that many studies not preceded by job analysis classify as "identical" many jobs of widely different content and difficulty.

The job analysis should reveal the nature of the job and the workers who can be classified as being in that job. It should also reveal the criterion variables which are available or which should be developed. The job analysis should show the kind of job performances which are essential for workers to demonstrate high proficiency on criterion variables. A careful and thorough analysis should reveal the job performances which are characteristic of success and those performances characteristic of failure. Rarely are job analyses carried out so that this kind of criterion information is available. This is one way the industrial psychologist can begin to develop his criteria and acquire an intensive knowledge of individual worker performance, which management itself does not possess.

AN ILLUSTRATION OF JOB ANALYSIS

It might be desirable to see the result of an intensive analysis and the modifications in criterion development based on this intensive study. An industrial psychologist working on the selection of salesmen followed management desire and established a criterion of earnings as the measure which best differentiated poor and good salesmen. Later this criterion was dropped and net sales was chosen as a more representative measure. Predictors correlated as well with the second criterion as with the first, but since prediction was not as accurate as desired, an analysis of the criterion variables was begun, based in part upon a job analysis and in part upon an analysis of the way each man performed his job.

For example, two of the salesmen, each selling $60,000 worth of merchandise a year, were discovered to be different kinds of salesmen with quite different job performances. These facts were known to management, but were considered less important than the fact that both men were considered superior in sales effectiveness. One salesman, working in the midwest, worked very hard during the summer months selling a single product out of an extensive line. He liked a long winter vacation. The second salesman, living in the east, spent considerable time "at the shore" during the summer months but worked very hard during the winter selling a different company product. A third salesman, working in central New York, was very effective because he sold the complete line during the twelve months of the year, but neither his total sales nor his earnings were appreciably higher than the sales and earnings of the first two men. As the study of the behavior of each salesman continued, additional facts revealed that the roads to success differed, that behavior leading to success as defined by management resulted in numerous types of sales jobs and the prediction was low because of the different behaviors which resulted in the same, or nearly the same, criterion scores. The thorough job analysis provided information about the duties the salesmen were supposed to perform. The detailed analysis of each job the salesman was performing resulted in a true picture of actual job performance.

In addition, the job behaviors of successes and failures were studied, and the causes of success and failure were isolated wherever possible. There is even now a continuing search for job behavior that leads to success and by success is meant net sales. The activities of the industrial psychologist have revealed to the company that there are certain basic criteria or basic job performances which underlie success. This was not a statistical study; it involved the reading of every report on every man. It involved traveling in the field. It involved participating in the seasonal reviews of job performance. It involved attending training sessions, sales meetings, and general sales conferences. It involved actual participation in sales management committee meetings where policies were reviewed and new policies established.

Call it what you will, the purpose was first to understand the job and the performances necessary for success, and second, to watch the performance of every salesman so that his job behavior could be not only described, but also evaluated. There is a continuing search for job behavior that leads to success.

PREDICTING WHOSE CRITERIA?

Who establishes the criterion variables used in selection as well as other types of research? Production records rarely contain comparable data; they are maintained for production control and sometimes for payroll use, but rarely are kept for criterion purposes. Rating scales are constructed by psychologists, but the ratings are made by supervisors. No research person is ever quite satisfied with his criterion. It comes to him from the dusty storage room in the form of incomplete records, poorly identified numbers, or it comes from the desk of the hurried, often disinterested supervisor who complains of the time required to complete this unimportant task. It is refined by statistical methods, corrected for rater bias, modified in terms of machine capacity, size of product produced, materials used, and even then may be a poor estimate of actual job behavior.

As psychologists, we have always attempted to predict management criteria based upon management raw data. As industrial psychologists we have too often neglected to establish our own criteria. Our job concept has caused us to apply our research skills to the development of predictors which we have carefully constructed and standardized. Thousands of research articles—even journals—are devoted to tests and measurements, but few are the reports on criterion development. Research energy has been expended on half of the job. We have left the creation of a suitable criterion score for each person or each group being studied to persons who cannot be classified as students of industrial behavior. Can we find methods which will permit us to derive our own criterion variables without devoting a large portion of our time to a single job?

THE JOB CONCEPT INTERVIEW

The Department of the Army, through the Personnel Research Branch of the Adjutant General's Office, has provided research funds and technical collaboration which have made it possible for psychologically trained individuals to make a criterion study of a relatively large group of company grade officers. Quoting from the objectives of this study, we find material of interest to us.

> Those who have engaged in intensive job analyses have observed that it is difficult to avoid making judgments about the incumbents on the jobs being analyzed. When a person describes his job, he gives information which reveals his conception of the job and the role he plays in performing it. As an analyst becomes skilled in analyzing a certain kind of job, he finds it possible to compare these conceptions and roles and to make both comparative and absolute judgments about the several incumbents. It is possible to assume that a more carefully constructed analysis directed not only toward the job duties and surroundings, but also toward the incumbent and his attitudes and feelings about his job and the people with whom he works, would result in judgments about the incumbents that would be somewhat better derived than those based on a straightforward job analysis.
> An analysis of the job and the incumbent's conception of his job in comparison with analyses of similar jobs and different concepts provides a framework for judgment that is worthy of exploration. Since the analysis technique used in this study differs in many respects from traditional job analysis and since the differences are primarily psychological, this method should be considered as one type of Psychological Requirements Analysis. It is identified in the report as the Personnel Research Institute Job Concept Interview. This Job Concept Interview form covers the following job analysis areas:
>
>   1. Incumbent Information
>   2. Description of Duties and Tasks
>   3. Check List of Weapons and Equipment
>   4. Job Functions

5. Relationships with Others
6. Knowledges and Skills Required
7. Personal Characteristics Required
8. Opinion Survey Form, covering attitude toward supervision and general officer behavior

With this background in mind, the primary objective of this study is methodological. As a methodological study it is designed to explore the possibilities of this particular psychological requirements analysis method in an attempt to determine what a detailed study of a sample of incumbents on the same job would reveal about criterion and predictor data. In other words, is this method of value in the identification of variables of differentiation which may be used to determine differences in level of performance of the incumbents studied? Is it possible, through this method, to give each incumbent a criterion score or an estimated criterion score for each variable isolated?

On the basis of a comprehensive search of the available literature including the historical records of the Department of the Army and perusal of citations for numerous awards, areas of concern were tentatively identified. On the basis of these, preliminary forms of interviews were constructed. These were administered to a pilot population of active reservists. Extensive revision of the interview was then undertaken. In the main study, 102 company grade officers on duty with troops were interviewed. Each interview lasted approximately six hours. In addition, the immediate superior and a selected subordinate of the concerned officer were interviewed. Interviews with superiors and subordinates generally took from two to four hours. Interview results were quantified. A total of 76 criterion variables was derived. These were subjected to statistical analysis in which they were related to both the Army OEI and to an overall psychological evaluation derived by the interviewer.

A finding of this study is the identification of behavioral areas which may be used to serve as indexes of officer excellence. These should be considered in the development of future officer effectiveness reporting systems. The Job Concept Interview method shows definite promise in the criterion area.

The method of having psychologically trained job analysts attempt to evaluate and describe job performance has been refined and an additional military sample studied. The criterion scores will be correlated with predictor data for the same sample secured by another research team in another university. A preliminary study of a nonmilitary group is underway. This study uses a clerical and administrative sample. Job analysts making a job evaluation of the clerical and administrative jobs have written an evaluative summary of each job incumbent interviewed. A follow-up validity study will be conducted this year.

A method such as this makes it possible for industrial psychologists to derive criterion variables on a sample of workers without spending a tremendous amount of time on the job, much of which may be unproductive. Although this is not a completely new method, it is still in the stage of development where neither its full possibilities nor its limitations are fully known. In the future, criterion-construction teams may be used in somewhat the same manner as test-construction teams are now used. As pointed out previously, with the more conventional techniques of criterion construction, the primary source of criterion data has been supervisors and official records, and both bias and contamination have tended to make the criteria less useful than we would like. Perhaps much of the bias and contamination can be eliminated by using data derived specifically for criterion purposes by skilled technicians using methods that have been standardized and developed in a variety of situations. This approach extends the frontiers of research in this area.

CONCLUSION

"Whose Criteria?" is a question which cannot be answered now. If I may indulge in a personal opinion, I believe that improvement in the collection of basic data in this area will follow an active attempt to participate in the criterion-construction process by those of us with research responsibilities in this area.

In conclusion, the character of our membership is changing. Most of us have gained industrial acceptance, and are now face to face with daily operating problems and decisions. We need methods and techniques suitable to our training and skills so that our estimates of worker proficiency will contain fewer biases and less contamination than the management criteria of today.

II RELIABILITY OF PERFORMANCE

The preceding part has given an overview of the concepts and problems of measurement in the prediction of human performance. Explicitly mentioned at times but always implicit is the basic requirement that such performance must be reliable if prediction is to succeed. From the amount of research done in the area one might contend that this requirement had been established beyond even the most trifling cavil. The fact is that it has not been established and furthermore, such evidence as does exist most definitely indicates that human performance is not reliable. Actually it is remarkable how little research attention has been given to performance reliability. Less than twenty-five studies were found by the authors stressing the direct problem, although it is given more or less direct attention in many other studies particularly in the field of testing. However, the authors postulate this as a major research area because of the lack of systematic study and its significance for the study of performance.

These points are made in an extensive review of the experimental literature by Fiske and Rice (1955) wherein three types of behavioral variability are discussed along with possible sources of such variability. These authors also emphasize the lack of knowledge in the area, in the field of interest here in particular—well-learned acts. Considering the fact that in any research study the interpretation of results is directly dependent upon the reliability of the criteria used, it is quite disconcerting to find so little research attention given to criterion reliability in both specific studies and as a general area of research interest.

Fiske and Rice posit three types of behaviorial variability. Type I is spontaneous or random and corresponds to what is here referred to as an individual characteristic or capability. Type II consists of systematic variability, which in this context corresponds to the style of performance variability. Type III consists of changes in response associated with changes in the stimulus or the stimulus situation and here corresponds roughly to the concept of the moderator variable relation. However, in personnel research Type III seems to represent task differences which in turn require new learning, a principle specifically rejected by Fiske and Rice. In this respect, the concept would seem to represent a separate and distinct type of behaviorial variability. Perhaps this is uniquely of interest in industrial psychology.

The research results showing variability of performance under some circumstances and no variability under other circumstances constitutes a distinct and important measurement problem. In particular, the practice of using group indices to estimate individual performace reliability can be questioned quite seriously. It is in fact conceivable that a major part of "errors of measurement" is due to individual variability that is concealed by measurements of group behavior. The general conceptual area is explicitly or implicitly recognized in the studies presented.

The major research effort designed to study performance reliability as one of its central hypotheses is the series of studies by H. F. Rothe and C. T. Nye. The study presented, Rothe and Nye (1958), calls into quite serious question the assumption present in all prediction studies that human performance is reliable. In particular, the concluding paragraph brings out the perils involved in the unquestioning or untested assumption of such reliability. The presented study makes the point quite well but study of the full series makes one cease to question why validity coefficients are generally so low but rather why they are so high. Another major point brought out by the studies is that any validity coefficient obtained is virtually a chance product of the specific time any performance measure might be made. This "chance" element is introduced by the fact of fluctuating performance levels by individuals and the resultant coefficient is determined by the point measured on the performance cycle and may be high, low, or zero.

A point concerning individual performance reliability that has received limited study outside laboratory tasks is the possibility that performance variability is an individual difference as a trait of individuals. However, that such might be the situation can be inferred from some research. The presented article by Klemmer and Lockhead (1962) is a case in point. The study of over 1000 operators of key punch and bank proof machines involved literally millions of responses. One of the key findings was that performance variability was 6 to 10 per cent of the group mean, but the variability was independent of production level. Actually there were two criteria in the study, production of cards and checks and errors made, and the ratios were for production 2/1 and errors 10/1 for best and poorest performances; however, on the production criterion, level of production and performance variability were independent while mean error level and error variability were correlated. Related to this latter is also the point that fast operators made fewer errors ($r =$ about -0.50). We have then the situation that understanding, or even determining, individual performance variability is not obviously manifested as separate from task criterion.

The early article by Seashore (1939) conceptualizes the bases for individual performance in a frame that indicates that performance reliability may be a quite gratuitous assumption. In summarizing the knowledge of sensory capacities, "adjustment," and motor abilities, Seashore asserted that different individuals must use different work methods because of different levels and interrelations of the various capacities, abilities, aptitudes, and so forth. He mentioned that much of the work done in industrial engineering shows there are vast differences in individual work methods. In effect we are always dealing with a quite distinctive individual approach to every specific task and, as a result, can question the entire concept of individual performance reliability because different performances arrive at the same goal but by different methods. Obviously, if this is so, the performance measurement becomes crucial; it must be reliable if we are to work back to the human characteristics functioning as bases for the performance.

Further evidence that approaches to tasks are highly individual is contained in the article reprinted here by Cohen and Strauss (1946). The study investigated a relatively simple task, folding sheets. Cohen and Strauss used both observation and movies to analyze performance on the job in question on a rather small number of subjects—twenty-one. They found a large ratio of actual performance levels, about 3/1, and a great variety of methods of doing the job. In fact they conclude, "From the point of view of the methods analyst, there are as many different methods of performance as there are operators." In general, the study indicates that a quite simple task involves variable performance by different individuals. One can only imagine the variability inherent in extremely complex tasks, for example, navigating an aircraft as described by Carter and Dudek (1947).

The above studies can be used to call into question a generalized concept reliability. People are performing, to arrive at a rather limited outcome, but they get there using different performances or responses to what is apparently the same objective stimulus situation. In effect, one aspect of the total performance may result in the same outcome but the responses leading to this outcome are different for different individuals and thus performance reliability is an individual, not group, phenomenon. In fact, it is not impossible that the same individual could use different behaviors at different times to achieve a specified objective.

A brief article by Huse and Taylor (1962) follows. The results show that at different levels of difficulty of a criterion (here absences), reliability of the criterion varies. The hypothesis suggested is that the incidents have different underlying behavioral antecedents. This particular hypothesis has been discussed by Prien and Ronan (1967) as pertinent to the general area of incident measure of performance, but, as far as the authors are aware, there is no research evidence to identify differing behavioral antecedents.

The study by Coombs (1948) which is reprinted here discusses the use of six possible scores from measures designed to assess some individual psychological variables, as presented—test scores, but the principles apply to performances other than tests. Coombs speaks of the usual measures of group performance in terms of averages and variability but also presents other possible scores relating to *individual* performance. The two of interest are "dispersion" of an individual's score within a single measure and individual score dispersion over several different measures. Essentially Coombs is referring to the point of this section, the measurement of individual performance reliability, and he makes the points that little research has been attempted with the presumed phenomenon and also that the significance of any possible findings is unknown. To judge from the amount of research inspired, this article has not received the attention it deserves since the implication is that individual performance reliability is easily determined, but little has been done, particularly in relation to performances on actual tasks as contrasted with psychological tests where a great deal of such work has been reported.

Ghiselli (1956, 1960a, 1960b), in a series of articles, has discussed individual performance reliability and presented research results to depict the many ramifications of reformulating some "basic principles" in the light of performance variability data. Two of the studies (Ghiselli 1960a, 1960b) concern the "predictability" of individual's performance in terms of "D-scores," that is, differences between standard predictor and criterion scores. The results have shown that such scores vary markedly for different individuals and result in a regular pattern of higher and lower validities as groups are split into subgroups on the basis of D-scores.

Incidentally, one of the major implications of these findings is that the traits related to success in a given activity are not those related to failure in the same activity. In the third article presented here (Ghiselli, 1963) the general implications of the findings of the first two are discussed. Of special importance is that Ghiselli questions quite seriously the classic psychometric theory that errors of measurement and prediction are the same for all individuals. Conclusive evidence is presented to show that this assumption is not so, and, related to later sections of this book, that moderators have quite varying effects on different individuals and are of more serious concern in understanding performance than for classic errors of measurement of whatever kind. Basically, Ghiselli has shown that reliability of performance is better understood as an individual difference, that it does seriously distort the more commonly used prediction methods and, as a general implication, is worthy of much more serious research investigation than it has received to date.

Considering the basic importance of performance reliability to prediction there is rather meager evidence on this basic topic. What does exist tends toward the conclusion that performance is *not* reliable and has the implication that performance variability may be a basic individual difference, possibly the result of some personality trait or traits acting as moderators. Whatever the case, the glaring fact is that performance reliability is not understood and requires concentrated research effort to determine whether or not performance prediction is even possible at any acceptable level or, alternatively that we deal with the "unique individual."

REFERENCES

CARTER, L. F. & DUDEK, F. J. The use of psychological techniques in measuring and critically analysing navigator's flight performance. *Psychometrika*, 1947, 12, 31–42.

FISKE, D. W. & RICE, L. N. Intra-individual response-variability, *Psychological Bulletin*, 1955, 52, 217–250.

GHISELLI, E. E. Differentiation of tests in terms of accuracy with which they predict a given individual. *Educational and Psychological Measurement*, 1960b, 20, 675–684.

GHISELLI, E. E. The prediction of predictability. *Educational and Psychological Measurement*, 1960a, 20, 3–8.

GHISELLI, E. E. Differentiation of individuals in terms of their predictability. *Journal of Applied Psychology*, 1956, 40, 374–377.

PRIEN, E. P. & RONAN, W. W. *The limitations of incident measurement of performance*. Pittsburgh, Pa. American Institutes for Research, 1967.

7 Moderating Effects and Differential Reliability and Validity

EDWIN E. GHISELLI

Classic psychometric theory holds that errors of measurement and of prediction are of the same magnitude for all individuals. Interactive effects are not recognized, and the psychological structure of all individuals is taken to be the same. To increase reliability and validity of measurement, then, attention is entirely focused on improvement of measuring devices. However, a substantial body of evidence indicates there are systematic individual differences in error, and in the importance a given trait has in determining a particular performance. Reliability and validity of measurement can be increased by the use of moderator variables which predict individual differences in error and in the importance of traits.

For more than half a century the notions of Yule and Spearman have dominated theoretical formulations in psychometrics. Pursuant to these classical notions errors are taken to be random and scores are combined additively. The possibility of interactive effects among variables is not recognized. Because in the linear combination of variables their weights are the same for all individuals, it is presumed that the psychological structure of all individuals is precisely the same.

On any one administration of a test, error scores are taken to vary from individual to individual. Hence for some individuals the error of measurement is smaller and for others it is larger. However, over many parallel tests the standard deviation of the errors is taken to be the same for all individuals. More correctly it should be said that as the number of parallel tests increases without limit the standard error of measurement approaches the same value for all individuals. Hence it is concluded that for all individuals. More correctly it should be said that as the number of reliability.

Similarly, for any one administration of a given criterion and a test the error with which the test predicts the criterion is taken to vary from

From *Journal of Applied Psychology*, 1963, 47, 81–86.

individual to individual. Hence for some individuals the error of prediction is smaller and for others it is larger. However, over many parallel criteria and tests the standard deviation of the errors is taken to be the same for all individuals. Again, more correctly it should be said that as the number of parallel criteria and tests increases without limit the standard error of prediction approaches the same value for all individuals. Hence it is concluded that for a given criterion and test all individuals are measured with the same degree of validity.

Because it is held that errors are random and equal for all individuals, and scores are additive with no interactive effects, it follows that neither reliability nor validity can be improved by selecting out from the total group those individuals for whom error is smaller. Reliability can be improved only by increasing the number of measurements, elimination of elements of lesser reliability, or better "housekeeping" procedures designed to reduce random error. Validity can be improved only by increasing the reliability of the criterion and predictor, or adding other predictors which cover aspects of the criterion not measured by the original predictor or aspects of the original predictor which are independent of the criterion.

Classic psychometric theory deals with a large number of sets of measurements, but let us concern ourselves only with two as we ordinarily do in the practical situation. Consider the bivariate distribution of scores on two variables where the relationship is less than unity. The two variables can be either two parallel tests or a criterion and a predictor. Running from the upper right hand to the lower left hand of the bivariate distribution chart is a group of individuals for whom scores are highly related. For this group the differences, regardless of sign, between standard scores on the two variables and the error of measurement or of prediction are small. For the remainder of the individuals the difference between the two standard scores are greater and hence the error is greater. If it could be demonstrated that these differences, or some other measure of error such as the standard error or the correlation coefficient, were related to another variable then some modification of classic psychometric theory would appear to be in order. Ghiselli (1960b) has called this other variable a predictability variable, but Saunders (1956) has better termed it a moderator thus drawing attention to the interactive effects.

Fiske and Rice (1955) have summarized early evidence indicating that individual error of measurement may be predicted by a moderator. More recent demonstrations are provided by Fiske (1957a) and Berdie (1961). Stagner (1933), Abelson (1952), Hoyt and Norman (1954), Holzman, Brown, and Farquhar (1954), Fredericksen and Melville (1954), Saunders (1956), Ghiselli (1956), Fredericksen and Gilbert (1960), and Ghiselli (1960b), among others, have shown that the error of prediction itself may be predicted by a moderator.

Using the procedure he employed to study moderating effects on validity (Ghiselli, 1960b), the present author further examined moderating effects in reliability of measurement. Two parallel forms of a complex reactions test were administered to 775 semiskilled workers, 517 of whom were used as an experimental group and 258 as a crossvalidation group. Each person took both forms of the test on the same occasion. For each member of the experimental group the difference, regardless of sign, between standard scores on the two forms was determined. It was found that age, education, and scores on a tapping and dotting test were related to these differences. A combination of scores on these variables was taken to form a moderator. The reliability coefficient, the correlation between the two parallel forms, was .92 for the entire group, whereas for the 9% of subjects earning the lowest moderator scores it was only .82 and for the 15% earning the highest moderator scores it was .97.

Three other instances of moderating effects in validity also may be described. A 64-item forced-choice inventory was administered to 96 factory workers on whom criterion scores in the form of supervisors' ratings were available. Seventeen of the items were used in a scale designed to measure "Sociometric Popularity." Half of the workers were used as an experimental group and half as a cross-validation group. For the experimental group the differences, regardless of sign, were determined for each individual between standard criterion and standard test scores. For the 47 items not used in the predictor scale an item analysis was performed against these differences. Responses to 15 of these items were found to be significantly related to the differences and were formed into a moderator to be applied to the cross-validation group. For the entire cross-validation group the validity of the scale as given by the Pearsonian coefficient was—.01, whereas for the 19% earning the lowest moderator scores the validity was −.47 and for the 32% earning the highest scores it was .39.

A group of 144 foremen and a group of 154 executives were rated by their superiors who divided them into two groups, the more and the less successful. Forty per cent of the foremen and 42% of the executives were placed in the upper category. All men took the 64-item forced-choice inventory, 24 items of which were scored in a supervisory ability scale. Critical test scores had been set for the two groups such that the scores of 43% of the foremen fell above their critical score and 39% of the executives fell above theirs. In both groups half of the men were placed in an experimental group and the other half in a cross-validation group. Each of the two experimental groups were further subdivided into two groups, one consisting of those individuals who were either high or low on both variables, the "on quadrant" cases, and those who were high on one variable and low on the other, the "off quadrant" cases. An item analysis was performed using the 40 nonscored items. For the foremen, 9 items, and for the executives, 13 items, were found to differentiate significantly between the on quadrant and off quadrant cases, and they were formed into two moderators to be applied to the cross-validation groups. Only three items were common to both moderators. For the entire cross-validation group of foremen the phi coefficient between the criterion and predictor was .26, whereas for the 17% earning the lowest moderator scores the coefficient was .10 and for the highest it was .41. For the entire group of executives the phi coefficient between the criterion and predictor was .41, whereas for the 21% earning the lowest moderator scores the coefficient was .10 and for the 26% earning the highest scores it was .68.

There is, then, a substantial body of evidence indicating that it is possible to predict individual error of measurement and error of prediction. Clearly those individuals for whom a test has a greater degree of reliability or validity can be systematically differentiated from those for whom it has a lesser degree. The higher the cutting score on the moderator is set the higher is the reliability or validity of the test for those individuals who fall above it. The choice of a cutting score is a matter of how many individuals one is willing to eliminate in order to achieve a higher degree of reliability or validity.

Even recognizing that it is possible to differentiate within a group those individuals whose scores are more reliable from those whose scores are less reliable, the practical value of such a differentiation might well be questioned. However, purely for descriptive purposes it might be desirable to know how reliably an individual is measured. Thus if administrative decisions are to be made on the basis of some test or other measuring device, it would be very helpful in borderline cases to have some indication of whether a given individual is measured with a small or large error. Furthermore, with a lower error of measurement validity should be enhanced. Classic psychometric theory itself teaches this, and Berdie (1961) has given an empirical demonstration. Finally, in some situations it might be highly desirable to be able to predict the extent of intraindividual variability in performance. In personnel selection ordinarily the aim is to pick out those individuals whose performance is high. But for planning purposes or to insure the smooth flow of work it might be equally important to select individuals whose rate of work does not vary greatly from one period to another, that is, has a high degree of self-consistency or reliability.

The case for validity is much clearer since a reduction in error means more accurate prediction and hence the selection of higher performing individuals. But even here the use of moderators might be criticized on the grounds that it necessitates the elimination of a substantial proportion of cases from the appraisal procedures which in turn eliminates even more. However, this is not necessarily the case. Ghiselli (1956) has shown that if a given percentage of individuals is to be selected and the rest eliminated, selecting that given percentage on the combined basis of their moderator and test scores yields a substantially superior group of individuals than that selected on the basis of test scores alone.

Furthermore, in some instances, especially those where the validity for the total group is low or zero, for those individuals who earn low scores on the moderator and who might therefore be eliminated from the appraisal, the validity coefficient may be of respectable magnitude and negative. For example, with the factory workers mentioned earlier the validity of the predictor for the 32% earning the highest moderator scores was .39. But in addition, for the 19% who earned the lowest moderator scores the validity coefficient was −.47. So for these latter individuals high predictor scores were associated with low criterion scores. Consequently for half of the total group, the 32% earning high moderator scores and 19% earning low moderator scores, the validity of the predictor is of the order of 40. It may seem peculiar, but a given score on a test may indicate the promise of success for some individuals, whereas for others it may indicate the liklihood of failure.

Another way to use a moderator, and a way which permits an assessment of all individuals, is to determine which of two predictors to use in selection. Ghiselli (1960a) accomplished this by determining for each individual the difference between his standard criterion score on Predictor 1, and also the difference between his standard criterion score and his standard score on Predictor 2. These differences were taken regardless of sign. Thus for each individual the difference between the two differences was determined. For a given individual a positive difference indicates that the one test gives the better prediction and a negative difference that the other is better. Moderators were then developed which were related to these differences and could be applied to cross-validation groups. For some individuals the moderator selects Predictor 1 and for the others it selects Predictor 2, but the standard scores for all individuals are thrown together regardless of predictor.

Ghiselli presents three instances where this proved to be an effective procedure. In one the validity coefficients for two predictors for a particular criterion were .02 and .20, and using predictors selected by the moderator the coefficient was .33. In another instance the validity coefficients of the two predictors were .55 and .61, with predictors selected by the moderator having a validity of .73. Finally, in an instance where the two validity coefficients were .17 and .51, using a moderator to select the better predictor for each individual gave a coefficient of .73.

Obviously the nature of the traits which function as moderators is a matter of considerable importance. Clearly it would be most helpful if all moderators had characteristics in common. Some of the research does suggest that "undesirable" traits such as a lack of personality integration and low motivation are associated with larger error. But certainly many of the traits which have been found to be effective as moderators are of quite a different sort such as age, education, type of interest, and manual dexterity. In a number of Ghiselli's studies moderators were developed through item analyses of the same inventory so that similarity of items which form different moderators can be examined. His results indicate that there is a high degree of specificity. With two different tests predicting the same criterion for a given group, and with the same test predicting different though similar criteria for two different groups, the items which form the moderators are quite different. While moderator variables are by no means as elusive as suppressor variables, since so many investigators have been able to find or develop them, they do seem to be just as specific. It would therefore appear to be impossible to state any general principles about the nature of the traits which act as moderators. Of course when the bivariate distribution of criterion and test scores is heteroscedastic then test scores themselves serve as a moderator because they are related to error of prediction (Kahneman & Ghiselli, 1962).

Some of the findings indicate that the relationships between moderator scores and scores both on criteria and predictors are quite low. Therefore, they do not add to prediction in a multiple correlation sense. The contribution of moderators is of an entirely different order, differentiating those individuals for whom error is smaller from those for whom it is larger. Their contribution, then, is unique.

As has been seen, there is a substantial body of empirical evidence indicating that moderator effects do occur. Convincing though these findings may be, one would be much more persuaded of moderating effects if some theoretical foundation of them were provided. It could be, as Saunders (1956) and Berdie (1961) have suggested, that moderators operate by sorting a heterogeneous aggregation of individuals into homogeneous groups. The magnitude and pattern of intercorrelations among variables, and hence reliability and validity, vary from group to group. Heterogeneity would be indicated by systematic variation of error from individual to individual whereas homogeneity would be indicated by all individuals having the same error. This notion permits retention of the classic psychometric concepts of randomness of errors and the linear combination of variables. What it adds is the admission that the magnitude of error and the differential weights carried by the components in a composite, the psychological structure, may vary from group to group. However, within a group the error of measurement and of prediction, and the relative weights carried by a set of tests in predicting a criterion are the same for all individuals.

Thus, women might be less distracted than men by environmental changes during a testing session and hence be more reliably measured. In this case, sex would moderate error of measurement. Intelligence might be more related to grades in engineering school for those students who have substantial interest in engineering than for those whose interest is low. Engineering interest, then, moderates error of prediction. For younger factory workers finger dexterity might be more important than spatial ability in predicting rate of production on the job, and the reverse might be true for older workers. So age would function to moderate the relative weights finger dexterity and spatial ability have in predicting rate of production.

This notion that moderators sort heterogeneous aggregations of individuals into homogeneous groups is a very useful way of conceptualizing moderator effects. It focuses attention on the kinds of differences which exist among individuals who in some given respect are homogeneous thereby suggesting types of moderators. Furthermore, it does little violence to classic psychometric theory. However, it presumes individuals can be divided into clear and distinct classes. Yet in actual practice moderators distribute individuals along a continuum. Individuals are not sorted into separate classes and a "group" is merely those individuals who fall at the same point on the continuum.

Another possible explanation of moderator effects is that the common elements which account for the correlation between two variables differ from individual to individual rather than just from group to group. What in the first point of view were considered as classes are now thought of as class intervals. Interactions among variables of the sort proposed by Lee (1961) are involved.

Error of measurement would be taken as varying from being quite small for some individuals to being quite large for others. Consequently error scores would carry less weight in determining fallible scores for some individuals than for others. Obviously a necessary condition is that individual differences in error scores possess some consistency or reliability over parallel tests. Evidence supporting this is provided by Fiske and Rice (1955), Fiske (1957b), and Berdie (1961). Such a position would not require that all variation commonly termed error of measurement is predictable by the moderator, but only a portion of it. The remainder would still be thought of as being random error. The reliability coefficient, then, would be an average description of precision of measurement.

The importance of a given trait in determining performance on some criterion is taken to differ among individuals. The trait varies from being of prime importance in determining criterion performance for some individuals to being of little or no importance for others. At the one extreme, then, error of prediction is smaller and test validity higher and at the other error is larger and test validity lower. Consequently the weight a test carries in prediction varies from individual to individual. Ghiselli's (1961) demonstration that two tests can be differentiated in terms of the accuracy with which they predict a criterion for a given individual is evidence of this effect. In effect Ghiselli weighted one test 1 and the other 0 for some individuals and the reverse for the remaining. Applying the optimally predicted pattern of weights for each individual accounted for a greater proportion of criterion variance. Pursuant to this position validity coefficients are average descriptions of predictive accuracy and multiple regression weights indicators of the average relative importance of the different predictors.

With respect to validity, the function of the moderator is to predict for a given individual the weight a test carries in determining criterion performance. It is not necessary that the moderator account for all criterion variance unpredicted by the tests, since some of this variance can be due to unreliability and the rest to unmeasured but important traits. The individuals' weights might be unrelated both to their criterion and test scores, or related to one or both. But nothing in this concept indicates what such correlations should be. Perhaps the correlations between the weights and the criterion and test differ from situation to situation.

Moderators are most attractive since they promise significant improvements in reliability and especially in predictive validity. However, that other subtle variable, the suppressor, also promises much in adding to prediction but in practice seldom makes much of a contribution nor holds up well from sample to sample. Hence some counsel of caution might be in order. It is quite possible that the time and effort required to develop moderators might be more fruitfully spent in seeking improvements in reliability and validity of the sort that follow from classic psychometric theory (Ghiselli, 1960). Furthermore, since the indications are that moderators are rather specific it might be that they, like suppressors, do not hold up well from sample to sample.

REFERENCES

ABELSON, R. P. Sex differences in predictability of college grades. *Educ. psychol. Measmt.*, 1952, 12, 638–644.

BERDIE, R. F. Intra-individual variability and predictability. *Educ. psychol. Measmt.*, 1961, 21, 663–676.

FISKE, D. W. The constraints of intra-individual variability in test response. *Educ. psychol. Measmt.*, 1957, 17, 327–337. (a)

FISKE, D. W. An intensive study of variability scores. *Educ. psychol. Measmt.*, 1957, 17, 453–465. (b)

FISKE, D. W., & RICE, L. Intra-individual response variability. *Psychol. Bull.*, 1955, 52, 217–250.

FREDERICKSEN, N., & GILBERT, A. C. F. Replication of differential predictability. *Educ. psychol. Measmt.*, 1960, 10, 759–767.

FREDERICKSEN, N., & MELVILLE, S. D. Differential predictability in the use of test scores. *Educ. psychol. Measmt.*, 1954, 14, 647–656.

GHISELLI, E. E. Differentiation of individuals in terms of their predictability. *J. appl. Psychol.*, 1956, 40, 374–377.

GHISELLI, E. E. Differentiation of tests in terms of the accuracy with which they predict for a given individual. *Educ. psychol. Measmt.*, 1960, 20, 615–684. (a)

GHISELLI, E. E. The prediction of preditability. *Educ. psychol. Measmt.*, 1960, 20, 3–8. (b)

HOLZMAN, W. H., BROWN, W. F., & FARQUHAR, W. G. The survey of study habits and attitudes: A new instrument for the prediction of academic success. *Educ. psychol. Measmt.*, 1954, 14, 726–732.

HOYT, D. P., & NORMAN, W. T. Adjustment and academic predictability. *J. counsel. Psychol.*, 1954, 1, 96–99.

KAHNEMAN, D., & GHISELLI, E. E. Validity and nonlinear heteroscedastic models. *Personnel Psychol.*, 1962, 15, 1–11.

LEE, M. C. Interactions, configurations, and nonadditive models. *Educ. psychol. Measmt.*, 1961, 2, 797–805.

SAUNDERS, D. R. Moderator variables in prediction. *Educ. psychol. Measmt.*, 1956, 16, 209–222.

STAGNER, R. The relation of personality to academic aptitude and achievement. *J. educ. Res.*, 1933, 26, 648–660.

8 Output Rates Among Coil Winders

HAROLD F. ROTHE
and CHARLES T. NYE

A series of previous papers has shown that the output rates, or production, of various groups of industrial employees tends to be relatively inconsistent from one period of time to another. It has been hypothesized that this inconsistency might be a function of the incentivation, or lack of incentivation, in the various situations. It has also been suggested that this inconsistency is not the same thing as low "reliability"; rather, that output is itself a phenomenon deserving study. "The proper subject for the study of industrial output is industrial output itself."

One study revealed different daily work curves from one day to another rather than a "typical daily work curve" (1). A second study showed a low correlation between the average production for one two-week period compared with the average production for the following two-week period. There was no financial incentive system in operation in that plant (3). The third study showed a higher correlation between the average production of one week compared with the average production of the next week, covering a period of 16 weeks, in a plant that did have a financial incentive system (4). Even in this latter situation, however, the week to week consistency was lower than the consistency commonly described in textbooks (5).

In the present study, data were again taken from the official books of a manufacturing concern and the week to week consistency for a group of employees was determined. The ratio of interindividual differences and the ratio of intra-individual differences were also obtained. These two measures, the consistency and the ratios, were analyzed in the light of the hypotheses previously put forth.

BACKGROUND OF THE STUDY

The data used here were taken from the books of a Midwest manufacturing plant. They cover a group of 27 employees and a period of 38 successive weeks from June 1956 to March 1957. (Actually 39 weeks

From *Journal of Applied Psychology*, 1958, 42, 182–186.

TABLE 8.1. *Weekly average output (Percentage performance of standard) for group of coil winders*

Week Ending		Percentage Performance	Number of Employees Weekly
June	17	76.1	27
	24	76.2	27
July	1	78.9	27
	8	80.6	21
	15	78.6	27
	22	82.2	27
	29	84.7	27
August	5	83.3	25
	12	83.7	26
	19	88.0	26
	26	78.5	24
September	2	85.3	24
	9	82.0	25
	16	82.9	26
	23	90.6	26
	30	84.0	27
October	7	92.2	25
	14	92.0	25
	21	91.9	27
	28	90.4	27
November	4	93.3	26
	11	94.2	25
	18	92.1	26
	25	93.2	26
December	2	87.5	27
	9	92.7	27
	16	90.1	27
	23	87.7	26
	—	—	—
January	6	89.2	27
	13	91.2	27
	20	88.2	27
	27	90.6	25
February	3	88.0	25
	10	91.3	27
	17	88.0	27
	24	89.8	25
March	3	90.7	27
	10	91.2	27

were covered but one week in December was omitted because the plant closed for inventory.) The employees were mainly women and all were experienced on their jobs. There were no "learners" in the group. Although there were some slight variations in the jobs they fall into three basic jobs described in the U.S.E.S. Dictionary of Occupational Titles as Coil Winder, 6–99.014, Rotor-Coil Winder, 6–99.112, and Stator-Coil Winder, 6–99.131. All employees in the plant, including those involved in this study, were members of a national union under a union-shop contract.

There was no financial incentive system in effect. There had been one, but it had been removed about five years earlier. The employees were performing their regular jobs in their regular workplaces, and each employee governed her own work pace. (No moving belts, no long machine runs, etc.) The data were used for each week in which the employee worked 32 or more hours. Thus, from time to time, the size of the sample dropped below 27 employees. However, in no week were there fewer than 21 employees.

MAIN FINDINGS

The weekly average output for the group, and also the number of employees whose data were used in this analysis for each week, is shown in Table 8.1. Inspection of this table shows there was an increase in performance early in the period studied and that the group performance later stabilized at a plateau. It is noteworthy that there was a change in departmental foremen at the beginning of this study. A forelady who had

TABLE 8.2. *Frequency distribution of r's between successive week's output. Individual performance for group of coil winders*

r	Frequency
.91–1.00	1
.81– .90	7
.71– .80	8
.61– .70	5
.51– .60	5
.41– .50	3
.31– .40	5
.21– .30	1
.11– .20	0
.01– .10	1
−.09– .00	1

Note.—Median r = .64.

previously supervised this department but who had been transferred to another department was transferred back to the Coil Winding Department at the time that happened to be selected for this study. Output climbed immediately upon her return and stabilized again at the high level it had reached previously when this forelady was supervising operations. Although this improved production is undoubtedly a tribute to this forelady, it is also an uncontrolled variable in this study. It is doubtful if the rise in productivity affected the results of this study, but this does indicate the difficulties involved in attempting to do scientific research in an industrial situation.

The correlation of each employee's performance for one week with his or her performance for the following week was determined by the

TABLE 8.3. *Highest and lowest average weekly performances and their ratios, for individual coil winders during 38-week period*

Employee	Highest Weekly Average	Lowest Weekly Average	Ratio of Highest to Lowest
A	108	43	2.51
B	144	20	7.20
C	97	26	3.73
D	91	56	1.63
E	140	67	2.09
F	97	37	2.62
G	154	58	2.66
H	100	33	3.33
I	103	46	2.24
J	127	75	1.69
K	118	51	2.31
L	114	75	1.52
M	136	43	3.16
N	119	59	2.02
O	113	61	1.85
P	117	60	1.95
Q	180	76	2.37
R	198	60	3.30
S	151	62	2.44
T	110	58	1.90
U	115	61	1.89
V	94	60	1.57
W	91	56	1.63
X	142	81	1.75
Y	114	61	1.87
Z	106	46	2.30
AA	107	41	2.61

Note.—Median intra-individual ratio = 2.24.

method of Pearsonian r. The distribution of the obtained r's is shown in Table 8.2. The median r is .64; the highest r is .91 and the lowest r is — .03. Thus it is concluded that the week to week output was not particularly consistent, and also that there was an extremely large variation in consistency. This latter point is important for psychologists attempting to validate tests (or other activities) against production data. It shows the need for taking production data over a fairly long period of time. If a psychologist happened to select the two weeks correlating .91 he would undoubtedly be most happy, and if he happened to select the two weeks correlating — .03, he would be most unhappy.

The greatest and least amount of productivity for each employee for any one of the 38 weeks is shown in Table 8.3, together with the ratio of best to worst performance of each employee. The average (median) ratio of best to worst performance or intra-individual ratio is 2.24.

The ratio of best operator to worst operator for each week—the inter-individual ratio—is shown in Table 8.4 where the average (median) ratio is 2.06. Thus the average ratio of the range of intraindividual performances exceeds the average ratio of the range of inter-individual performance. This was also true in the study of butter-wrappers who were also working under nonincentive conditions (2). But the opposite was true (i.e., the average ratio of the range of *inter*-individual performance exceeded the average ratio of the range of *intra*-individual performance), in the study of chocolate-dippers who, perhaps by no coincidence, were on a financial incentive system (4).

It is also perhaps important to note that the ratios found in this situation were much larger than the ratios found in the study of chocolate-dippers (although smaller than the ratios found in laboratory studies). In that study, the median inter-individual ratio was 1.475 and the median intra-individual ratio was 1.18, as contrasted with the 2.06 and 2.24 found here, respectively.

OTHER FINDINGS

Since the correlation of output from one week to the next week was so low, ($r = .64$) the data were combined in various ways to determine the effect of using longer periods of time. The most obvious combination was to split the data—to correlate the average production of each of the 27 operators for the first 19 weeks with their average production for the second 19 weeks. The Pearsonian r is .71 which is low for a work sample of this size.

Another r was obtained using the average production of each operator for the four week periods of greatest plant employment (i.e., when the number of employees in the plant was greatest). The employees

TABLE 8.4 *Highest and lowest average individual weekly performances, and their ratios, for group of coil winders during 38-week period*

Week Ending		Highest Employee's Average	Lowest Employee's Average	Ratio of Highest to Lowest
June	17	97	51	1.90
	24	98	49	2.00
July	1	102	33	3.09
	8	110	56	1.96
	15	111	46	2.41
	22	105	59	1.78
	29	105	26	4.04
August	5	119	47	2.53
	12	114	67	1.70
	19	180	50	3.60
	26	116	54	2.15
September	2	118	49	2.41
	9	115	58	1.98
	16	114	56	2.04
	23	142	63	2.25
	30	154	43	3.58
October	7	198	57	3.47
	14	115	37	3.11
	21	113	20	5.65
	28	117	28	4.18
November	4	151	55	2.75
	11	127	71	1.79
	18	117	74	1.58
	25	105	69	1.52
December	2	108	59	1.83
	9	116	44	2.64
	16	126	61	2.07
	23	134	71	1.89
	—	—	—	—
January	6	144	58	2.48
	13	119	63	1.89
	20	118	51	2.31
	27	121	61	1.99
February	3	111	59	1.88
	10	114	73	1.56
	17	116	43	2.70
	24	115	57	2.02
March	3	117	68	1.72
	10	116	71	1.63

Note.—Median interindividual ratio = 2.06.

whose output data were used in this study formed only a part of one department in a very large plant. Here, as probably almost everywhere, the grapevine carries stories of increasing or decreasing sales and corresponding rises and falls in employment. Thus it was believed that there may be some relationship between output and size of the plant labor force. There were two peaks of employment in the period covered by this study. Production data for the four weeks leading up to and including each of the two peaks were used. The peaks were about six months apart from each other. The obtained $r = .25$ which suggests a lack of common variables influencing output during those two periods.

Along the same line of reasoning, the average output for each operator during a five-week period of decreasing employment was correlated with the five-week average during a period of increasing employment. The obtained $r = .60$. The writers suspect that the r of .60 found here, and the r of .25 in the preceding paragraph are merely chance variations.

The average production for the entire group of 27 operators for each week was correlated with the size of the total plant labor force for that week, and the resulting $r = -.39$. This means that as the employee force decreases the average production of these coil winders increases, and vice versa. Although this correlation $-.39$ is statistically significant at between the 1% and 5% levels, it should be realized that it is an indication from one department in one plant. Other data from other situations are needed before much meaning can be attached to these data.

The correlation between total weekly plant employment and weekly output variance of these coil winders is $-.02$; between number of total plant's employees on layoff and average production of these coil winders, $r = -.03$; between total number on layoff and variance of coil winders production, $r = .02$; between number employed in coil winding department and average production of these 27 operators, $r = .07$; and between number employed in this department and variance of output of these 27 operators $r = -.16$. All of these correlations are, of course, insignificant.

DISCUSSION

It has been hypothesized that "... *the incentives to work may be considered ineffective when the ratio of the range of intra-individual differences is greater than the ratio of the range of inter-individual differences*" (2, p. 326). In the present situation, where there was no financial incentive system, the intra-individual ratio did exceed the inter-individual ratio. And in a previous study, with no incentive system in effect, this same relationship between the ratios of inter- and intra-individual differences was found, while in a situation where an incentive system was in effect, the opposite relationship was found. The hypothesis is clearly not proven by this study, but these various studies do seem to point clearly toward a relationship between incentivation and inter- and intra-individual differences.

A second hypothesis was "if the intercorrelation of output rates for two periods closely related in time is less than .50, the incentivation is not highly effective, while intercorrelation higher than .80 indicates very effective incentivation" (4, p. 96). The present facts are generally consistent with this hypothesis, but they vary in amount (or size of coefficient). In the light of the present study this hypothesis is now changed to say that an intercorrelation of .80 or above indicates effective incentivation and an intercorrelation of .70 or less indicates ineffective incentivation. This leaves a twilight zone of between .80 and .70 that needs clarification from further research. (It also tempts one to speculate on the chaos that might exist if a negative or insignificant intercorrelation were to exist!)

The output data were correlated with various other variables such as size of employee force and number of employees on layoff, but the obtained r's were insignificant.

Grouping the weekly output data into 4, 5, and 19 week periods and correlating the data for these longer periods did not increase the r significantly over the r for single weeks' outputs correlated.

This study, along with the other output studies (1, 2, 3, 4) again shows that production data cannot be picked up casually and used to validate tests or other procedures. In this entire series of studies of industrial output the most striking single result is the lack of consistency from time to time, especially when there is no financial incentive system in operation. A second important result is the wide range of "consistency coefficients" of output data, such that a researcher could be entirely misled by tests of statistical significance if he just happened to select a period of unusually high or low consistency.

REFERENCES

1. ROTHE, H. F. Output rates among butter wrappers: I. *J. appl. Psychol.*, 1946, 30, 199–211.
2. ROTHE, H. F. Output rates among butter wrappers: II. *J. appl. Psychol.*, 1946, 30, 320–327.
3. ROTHE, H. F. Output rates among machine operators: I. *J. appl. Psychol.*, 1947, 31, 484–489.
4. ROTHE, H. F. Output rates among chocolate dippers. *J. appl. Psychol.*, 1951, 35, 94–97.
5. TIFFIN, J. *Industrial psychology*. New York: Prentice-Hall, 1942.

9 Productivity and Errors in Two Keying Tasks: A Field Study

E. T. KLEMMER and G. R. LOCKHEAD

Productivity and error rates were measured for a billion responses by more than a thousand operators of IBM card punches and bank proof machines in 20 different installations. Productivity increases and errors decrease during the 1st year on the job, sometimes longer. Experienced card punch operators average 56,000 to 83,000 keystrokes per day with 1600 to 4300 strokes per undetected error. Experienced bank proof machine operators average 4350 to 6600 checks per day with about 3500 checks per undetected error. The fastest operators at any installation produce twice as much as the slowest. The least accurate operators make 10 times as many errors as the most accurate. Fast operators tend to make fewer errors ($r = -.5$).

A conservative estimate is that two million people spend a large part of each day before a keyboard driven machine: typewriter, keypunch, adding machine, teletype, bank proof machine, linotype, etc. The productivity and error rates of these operators are of interest to the companies that employ them, the companies that design and build the machines, and the psychologists who are interested in this form of human behavior.

There is a long history of studies concerning keyboards and keying, mostly centered around the typewriter. Many studies looked at training (e.g., West, 1957) and several comprehensive publications provide rules for setting work standards for keyboard driven machines based on time and motion analyses (e.g., Colver, 1960). Studies have been aimed at designing new and better keyboards (e.g., Hillix & Coburn, 1961), and several papers review the work done thus far with typewriters (e.g., Rahe, 1954).

The present study does not add laboratory or theoretical data to this field but rather presents data on production and error rates from a large number of operators in the course of their actual daily work. These data will be useful in providing a baseline for experimental work as well as

From *Journal of Applied Psychology*, 1942, 46, 401–408.

describing the distribution of production and error rates for keyboard operators.

The data in this report were drawn from more than a billion responses made by more than a thousand operators in 20 installations. The experience of the operators ranged from 1 week to several years. All of the data presented are from two types of machines: the IBM card punch Models 024 and 026, and the IBM bank proof machines, Models 802 and 803.

Most of the current report is based on records routinely kept by large installations of card punches and bank proof machines. The operators were not told that their performance records would be subjected to special analysis. In addition, the results of two special speed tests are given for comparative purposes.

Few installations keep uniform records of the errors made by operators in addition to their production records. Since error rates are less easy for the research worker to determine than are production rates, considerable attention has been given to errors. Fortunately, two large installations did keep regular and uniform records of both production and error rates for all operators.[1] The error analyses presented are based largely on the data from these: one keypunch and one bank proof machine installation.

Production and error figures are treated separately with each broken

FIGURE 9.1. *Distribution of 271 card-punch operators according to average daily production rate.*

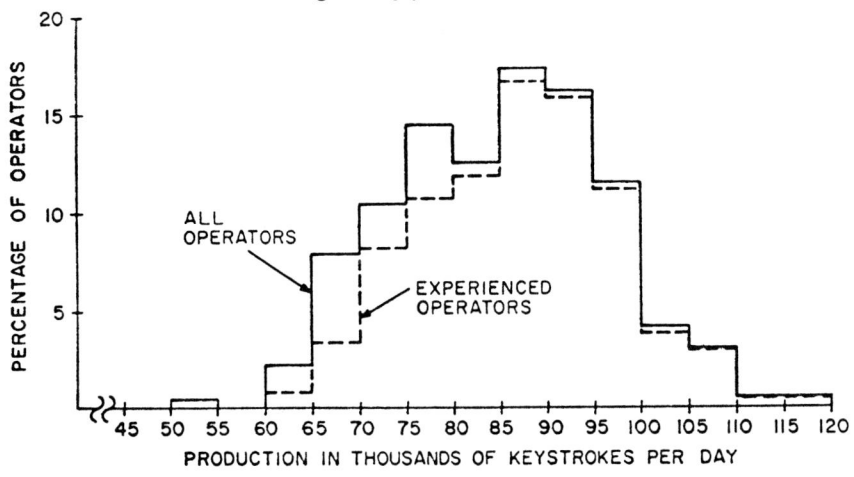

---

[1] We are particularly indebted to C. R. Pricher of the New York Federal Reserve Bank, and S. Kreps and J. Roarty of the Social Security Administration for their cooperation in making comprehensive records available for this study.

down according to differences occuring between installations, differences between operators in the same installation, and variability within operators. Many reasons could be cited to explain these differences but most would be speculative. We shall refrain from such speculation as much as possible.

Some interesting consistencies in error rates are shown which immediately raise the hope of a simple model to describe at least some of human error making.

DESCRIPTION OF MACHINES

The card punch, or keypunch, machine is the size of a small desk and produces punched cards under keyboard control. It has an alphanumeric keyboard similar to a typewriter keyboard except that the numerals are located in a 3×3 matrix with the top row of the matrix at Keys u, i, and o on the right hand side of the alphabetic keyboard. The shift key serves to shift between alphabetic and numeric information rather than between upper and lower case. The card punch is capable of automatically punching information on one card which it reads from the preceding card. This duplicated information is not liable to keying errors and is not counted in measures of production on a keystroke basis.

The bank proof machine is a device for sorting and totaling bank checks. It has two keyboards: one numeric 3×3 keyboard with a zero bar (similar to an adding machine), and one 4×6 or 4×8 sorting keyboard coded by bank numbers. The operator keys the amount of the check into the numeric key board, presses the appropriate sorting key, and drops the check in a slot in the machine. Because of the use of two keyboards and the check handling required, productivity on the bank proof machine can not be compared directly with card punching.

PRODUCTION RATES

Seven different card punch installations provided sufficient data to make reasonable estimates of the average daily production of the average operator. These estimates range from 56,000 to 83,000 keystrokes per day, with 5 of the 7 in the 66,000 to 74,000 range. The average operator spends about 7 hours per day at the machine. The differences between installations are due largely to differences in the work to be punched.

Two card punch installations ran special speed tests of 20–30 minutes on 5 or more operators. Average performance on the 2 tests was 18,000 strokes per hour, or about twice that of the maintained rate over the working day.

Six different banking installations provided sufficient production data to allow estimates of keying rates on bank proof machines. The range in daily production was about 4,350 to 6,600 checks, or about 20,000 to 30,000 keystrokes per day when an average of 4.5 keystrokes is assumed for each check (this does not include the sorting keystroke). The operators spend an average of about 5 hours per day actually entering checks. The differences in production among installations is largely a matter of sorting requirements and face amounts of the checks handled.

Distributions over Operators

The individual differences among keypunch operators and proof machine operators are similar and may be considered together. Figures 9.1 and 9.2 show the distribution of production rates over operators on card punch and bank proof machines, respectively. Both show the number of operators who fall into class intervals of production rates. The effect of excluding operators with less than a year on the job is shown by the dashed line.

Figures 9.1 and 9.2 tell the story which seems to hold for large installations. The frequency distribution curves are nearly bell-shaped and symmetrical. Since the distribution curves for production are close to normal it is reasonable to state a standard deviation for their variability. For the experienced keypunch operators of Figure 9.1 the mean is 87,000 keystrokes per day with a standard deviation of 10,000 keystrokes. For the experienced proof machine operators of Figure 9.2 the mean production rate is 6,400 checks per day with a standard deviation of 860 checks. Thus, for both keypunch and bank proof operators the standard deviation is approximately 12 per cent of the group mean.

Variability within Operators

In brief, the data of the present study provide the following estimates for within-operator variability in production: week-to-week production averages, for individual operators, fluctuate such that the standard deviation of these averages for each operator is about 6–10% of the group mean production, while monthly averages fluctuate with a standard deviation of about 3–5% of the group mean production (based on variance averaged over operators). This implies that the variability of an operator's production is relatively independent of her mean production level.

This variability within the individual operators contributes to the spread of the distribution in Figures 9.1 and 9.2, but it accounts for only a small fraction of the total variance observed between operators. This does not mean that within-operator variability is negligible. Performance measures from keyboard operators do vary sufficiently from day-to-day, week-to-week, and even month-to-month to make consideration of this source of variance important, particularly in evaluating individual performance.

FIGURE 9.2. *Distribution of 459 bank-proof machine operators according to average daily production rate.*

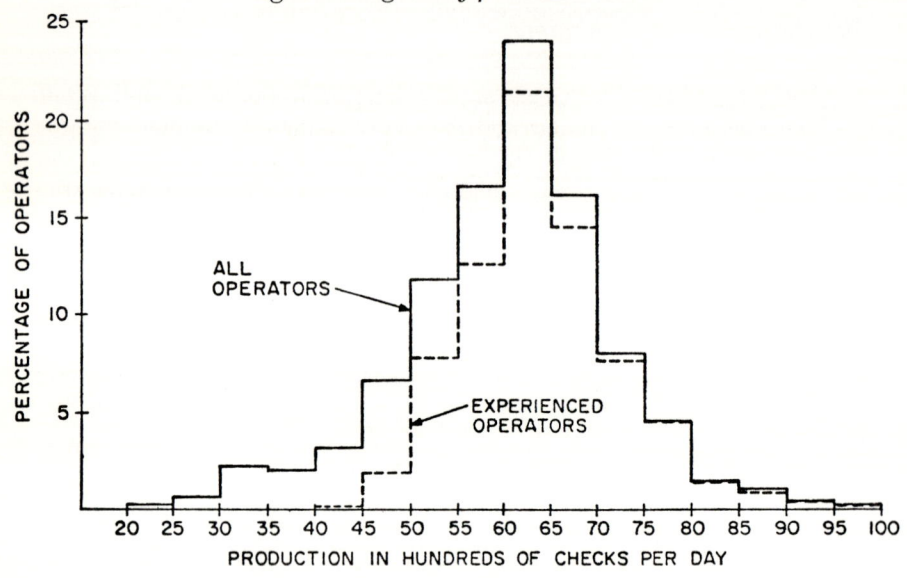

ERROR RATES

The average error estimates, in terms of number of keystrokes per error, range from 1,600 to 4,300 for four different card punching installations. In terms of percentage error, this is a range of .02% to .06%. These figures are for errors caught in an independent verifying procedure. No data were available on errors which the operator herself detected and corrected.

Only two of the bank proof machine installations visited keep a record of errors and these records require a few words of explanation. Errors which are not detected by the operator immediately are caught by the operator herself in checking the total of her machine with supplied totals. These are the errors considered here. No errors in the cents position are recorded and some errors in the dimes position are also not counted (usually errors of 10 cents and 20 cents). No sorting errors are counted. Errors which could conceivably be due to poorly written numerals are also not counted. Within these rules, the counted errors average about 3,500 checks per error or .03% error per check. This error is considerably lower than that of any keypunch installation on which we have data. The difference in accuracy may be due to increased emphasis on accuracy, more immediate knowledge of errors, and different criteria for excusing errors in the proof machine installations.

Distribution over Operators

The ranges of individual differences in errors among keypunch operators and proof machine operators are similar and may be considered together. Unlike production data, the units for measuring errors are not straightforward. Two error measures are commonly used by the installations: (a) the percentage of items (cards or checks) in errors, and (b) the number of items per error (or mean free path between errors).

If the frequency distribution of operators were plotted against intervals of percentage-error, a skewed distribution results with most operators clustered at the low error end. If the number of items per error is used, an even more skewed distribution results with most of the operators clustered at the high error end. Thus, we could apparently show that most operators clustered together in error rate with a few poor operators out in the tail of the distribution, or that most operators clustered together except for a few good operators out in the tail of the distribution. Actually, each of these conclusions is valid for its own measure of error but the resulting skewed distributions do not allow the application of normal curve statistics. In addition, the within-operator variability, as measured by standard deviation of percentage-error, is a linear function of the operator's mean error rate (as described below). Both of these findings suggest a logarithmic transformation. The log transform also has the nice property that the log distribution of errors is the same whether the raw scores are percentage-error or items per error. Since it is difficult to interpret error measures in logarithmic units, it may be better to plot percentage-error on a logarithmic scale. The distributions of undetected errors by operators on card punches and proof machines are plotted in this fashion in Figures 9.3 and 9.4. Again, operators with 1 year or more of experience are plotted separately from the entire group.

The difference in performance between the best and worst operators is much more striking in errors than in production. Namely, the ninetieth percentile operator makes 6-10 times as many errors as the tenth percentile operator. The dotted lines indicate the tenth and ninetieth percentile points for each distribution.

There is a similarity in the *shape* of error distributions over operators at different installations which is quite impressive even when the average error rates of the installations are widely different. This similarity can be shown by transforming the error rates for several installations, so that the median error rates are all the same, and superimposing the resulting error distributions. Four sets of data are used to show this similarity: the experienced operators of Figures 9.3 and 9.4, the trainees of Figure 9.3 and a large group of students from a keypunch school after just 1 week of training. The four distributions are shown together after transformation in Figure 9.5.

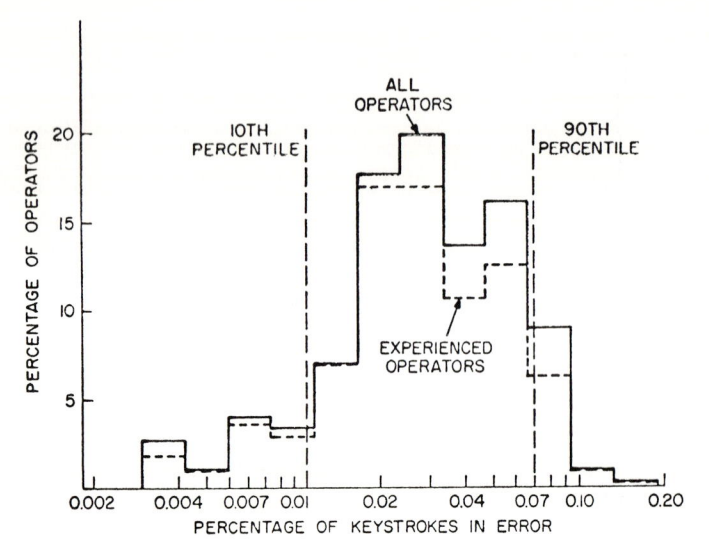

FIGURE 9.3. *Distribution of 271 card punch operators according to error rate determined by 10 percent sample verification over a 1-week period. (Only those errors found in verification are included.)*

The four tasks are all similar—that is, they involve keyboard entry. However, they involve two different keyboards, different types of source documents, and the populations are quite different. So it seems curious that the shape of the distributions is so nearly the same. Indeed, the only striking difference between the distributions is in average error rates before the data were transformed.

Variability within Operators

As in production distributions, the within-operator variability contributes to the spread of the distributions in Figures 9.3 and 9.4, but only accounts for about 10% of the total variance. Unlike the production data, however, the variability of an operator's error rate is not independent of her mean error rate.

The observed within-operator variability as a function of mean error

PRODUCTIVITY AND ERRORS IN TWO KEYING TASKS 117

rate is shown in Figure 9.6 for bank proof operators grouped according to mean error rate. The standard deviation for these operators is obtained by averaging the variance based on scores for 6 consecutive months and taking the square root of the average variance. Figure 9.6 shows that the

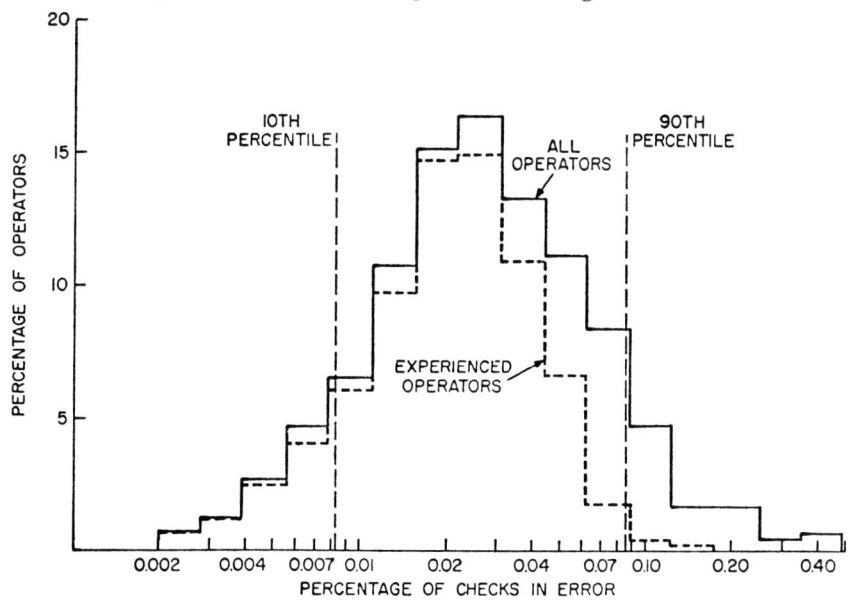

FIGURE 9.4. *Distribution of 459 bank proof machine operators according to error rate measured over a 1-month period. (Only those errors found in verification are included.)*

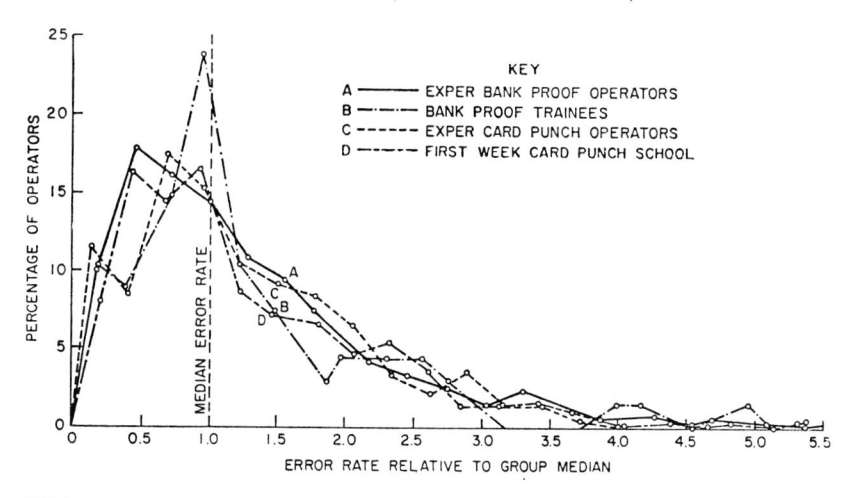

FIGURE 9.5. *Distribution of operators according to error rate for four different groups of operators. (Sampling periods range from 1 hour to 1 month with over 100 operators in each classification.)*

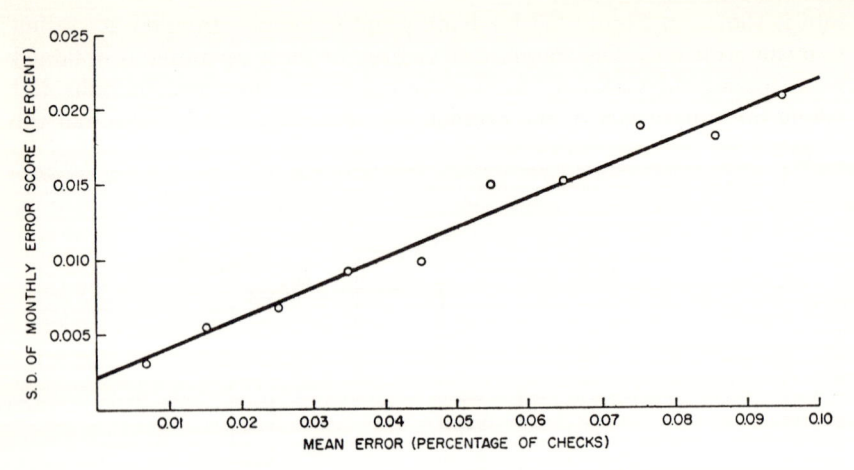

FIGURE 9.6. *Within-operator variability of error score as a function of mean error for 459 bank proof machine operators. (Mean error is based on 6 months of data for each operator.)*

within-operator standard deviation of percentage-error approximates a linear function of *her* mean error rate.

Poisson Model

Since keying errors are low probability events, it is interesting to ask if observed differences in error rates were due to random fluctuations in observed frequency of a fixed probability event. The answer is that for between-operator differences, the fixed-probability model would predict less than 5 per cent of the observed variance. For within-operator variability the assumption of fixed within-operator error-probability predicts less than half of the observed variance. Thus, the differences in error-probability between operators, and variation of error-probability within operators, are real and cannot be attributed to sampling fluctuations.

RELATION OF SPEED AND ERRORS

Since there is a 2-1 range in speed and a 10-1 range in errors between operators, it is immediately interesting to ask if the fast operators make more errors. Analysis show just the opposite to be true. The operators who are better in speed also make fewer errors, although the correlations are far from perfect. For the keypunch data (one installation) the correlation between speed and errors over all operators is $-.42$ and for bank proof machines this correlation is $-.53$.

IMPROVEMENT WITH TRAINING

First we must make a distinction between two methods of obtaining the learning curves. The best way to follow change in performance with practice is to follow the same operators over many months or years of work. Unfortunately, this is not always possible since records are not usually available in this manner. Particularly for data over periods of years, we must depend upon another method. That is, to look at how long each operator has been on the job and to group operators by time intervals according to their starting dates. The intervals must be chosen so as to have a reasonable number of operators in each interval in order to reduce the variability due to individual differences. This consideration dictates a set of intervals increasing in size with increasing months-on-the-job, since normal turnover produces a lesser density of operators at the longer experience end of the curve. The main disadvantage of this second method is that the natural selectivity factors which cause operators to leave must operate differentially to some extent as a function of skill. Learning curves plotted by this second method include the influence of such selectivity factors as well as time on the job.

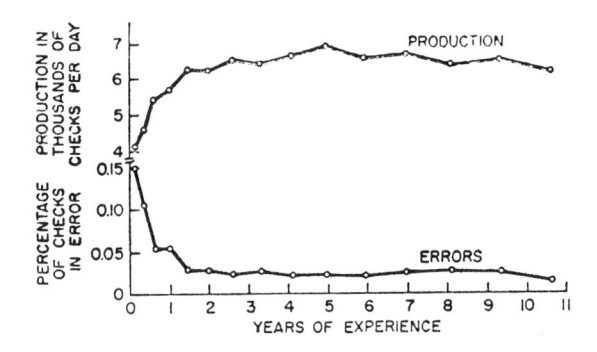

FIGURE 9.7. *Improvement in performance as a function of time on the job for 459 bank proof machine operators in one bank. (Plotted points are means for all operators falling within that interval of time on the job. Different operators are represented at each point.)*

Production and error rates, as a function of time on the job, are plotted in Figure 9.7 for one bank proof machine installation using the second method. The mean production and error rates for operators falling within each time interval are plotted against time-on-the-job. This, and similar plots for other installations, clearly shows continued significant improvement in both speed and accuracy during the first year on the job. Improvement after the first year is not clear in all installations and may well be related to job difficulty.

Comparison with Typing

For short-run tests, speed on the card punch averages more than five strokes per second on tasks with no complications. Over the regular working day, averaging over jobs and operators leads to an average production of 2.8 strokes per second during time actually spent on the machine. For 7 hours per day actually at the machine (out of an 8-hour day) this means about 70,000 strokes per day. Translated into typewriter language, these figures are equivalent to 60 words per minute for short runs with a daily average of 34 words per minute for 7 hours of typing. It should be noted, however, that these figures are averages over time and that operators often key easy on highly practiced combinations (e.g., "the") at rates pressing the limiting speed of the machine (18–20 strokes per second).

REFERENCES

COLVER, G. (Ed.) *A guide to office clerical time standards.* Detroit, Mich.: Systems and Procedures Association, 1960.

HILLIX, W. A., & COBURN, R. Human factors in key set design. *USN Electron. Lab. res. Rep.*, 1961, No. 1023.

RAHE, H. *Typewriting research index: 1900–1954.* Carbondale, Ill.: 807 Twisdale Avenue, 1954.

WEST, L. J. Review of research in typewriting learning with recommendations for training. *USAF Train. Res. Cent. tech. Note,* 1957, No. 57–69.

10 Work Methods: An Often Neglected Factor Underlying Individual Differences

ROBERT H. SEASHORE

Current explanations of the origin of individual differences in human abilities tend in two main directions, (1) a dependence upon certain *biological bases,* such as the most favorable anatomical structures for effective physiological functioning of sense organs, nerves and effectors, and (2) a dependence upon *amount of previous training* (sometimes indirectly through extent of environmental opportunity for learning). To these two factors we may well add an intermediate factor, namely, (3) the particular *work methods* or patterns of behavior which are adopted by each individual in the course of utilizing his biological equipment during learning. Learning consists of (1) the preliminary adoption of various work methods, sometimes discarded in favor of others, and (2) the refinement of the final work method by such processes as overlapping of component parts, or redintegrations (conditioning of responses to some part of the situation instead of the entire situation as was necessary in early stages). It is quite possible that (2) is really a variation of (1). In measuring individual differences it is not sufficient to control the instructions or working situation, for the observer's previous incidental background may lead him to adopt very different work methods from those expected. It follows that "control" limited to ordinary instructions and demonstrations is incomplete, and that other unnoticed factors operate to modify the work method actually adopted. The actual kind of work method itself must be observed, recorded, and analyzed if we are to have any adequate understanding of the influence of training. Our studies of individual differences have all too frequently been carried out with inadequate qualitative analysis.

The terms, work methods or behavior patterns are here used to include any variation in set, attitude, approach, trick of the trade, adjustment mechanism, etc., in other words qualitative variations in *ways* of reacting to a situation. The observer may frequently be unaware of the nature or plan of his work method. Probably the best known example of

From *Psychological Review*, 1939, 46, 123–141.

the importance of work methods comes from the photographic motion studies of Gilbreth (7) who reduced the average number of movements in laying a brick from 16 to 4, and thereby helped to lay the foundation for a new applied science of time and motion studies. These have become a recognized service of specialized firms in industrial engineering but have received little attention from psychologists. Slow motion pictures now afford an excellent method for such investigations, and are also widely used in athletic coaching, to diagnose correct and incorrect playing form and strategy.

The purpose of this paper is to show how these work methods are important in determining individual differences in *all* psychological activities, *sensory, affective,* and *intellectual fields* as well as the *motor fields* from which our first illustrations were taken. The concept of work methods is by no means limited to serial or complex performances but applies equally to even the simplest performances such as sensory threshold discriminations and simple reaction times. The range of possible behavior patterns is determined in part by the structural limitations of the particular species or individual but it is also a matter of learning, often of the informal trial-and-error variety, and only vaguely understood even by highly skilled performers.

According to our analysis learning includes (1) the discovery or development of work methods, and (2) the perfection of the particular methods by such processes as overlapping of component processes and the development of 'higher units,' such as responding to words or phrases instead of separate letters as in typing, telegraphy, and piano playing. In some cases the essential work method is hit upon during the early stages of learning and subsequent practice results largely in the improvement of details for greater speed and precision of efficiency. In other cases nearly the whole course of learning is concerned with a shifting from one method or set of methods to another and only in the last stages do the effects of repetition become important for polishing details.

It is not the purpose of this paper to deny the inheritance of individual differences in anatomical or physiological development. Both inheritance and environment are well demonstrated as determinants of such basic biological factors. It is likewise agreed that these variations in biological makeup are important as one set of factors determining individual differences in psychological activities, but we need to know more of their relative importance in comparison with the factors of the particular work methods adopted and the subsequent improvement of the method by repeated practice.

If our hypothesis as to the importance of work methods is correct then we cannot simply control amount of training and attribute all else to biological capacities as has been attempted so often in the past. The third variable, the *work methods employed,* is the unknown factor which we shall seek to evaluate in relation to the other two.

The importance of work methods may now be stated as follows: In responding to a given task an individual may utilize his anatomical and physiological characteristics in *a number of more or less equivalent patterns* of behavior. These various patterns (attitudes, approaches, tricks of the trade, adjustment mechanisms such as sublimation, etc.) may involve the use of the same body structures but frequently emphasize the importance of some other structures. Where a new pattern of action avoids the use of some body structure or functional mechanism in which the individual is deficient it may easily compensate for this deficiency. The patterns also differ widely as to their effectiveness in terms of the end results, such as fineness of sensory discrimination, adequacy of emotional adjustment, or effectiveness in terms of speed or precision of work performed. In simpler terms this theory would emphasize not so much "what you are born with," as "what you do with it." In any given case, however, the variations in biological equipment might be of either greater, equal, or less importance than the behavior pattern in determining end results.

To use a mechanical analogy, the *capacity* of a simple mechanism such as a pump can be predicted from a knowledge of its measurements because except for minor variations the pump can usually operate in only one fixed way. The corresponding capacity of the human mechanism *cannot* be predicted unless the particular mode of operation is also clearly specified and controlled. The human mechanism is sufficiently complicated to permit *many different modes of operation.* Furthermore, the results of introspective analyses and motion studies indicate that even the most carefully standardized instructions and controls of psychological experiments only partially guarantee the selection of a given mode of operation, and in fact, frequently result in indirect complications which may not even be suspected unless the usual quantitative methods are supplemented by qualitative analyses such as introspection.

Let us now examine the evidence from the major fields of psychology to evaluate the relative importance of these three types of determinants, the biological capacities, the patterns of behavior, and quantitative variations (*e.g.* overlapping of movements, coordination of simultaneous operations, etc.) in the same general pattern of behavior.

In the sensory field, we find one of the largest bodies of experimental facts on individual differences in audition. The Seashore measures of musical talent provide six standardized experiments on the measurement of auditory discriminations. In this field we find very representative results on individual differences, *viz., wide variations* in individual thresholds, which are *relatively independent of the amount of previous training*, and *relatively stable* after even extensive amounts of professional musical training. Stanton's (24) careful experiments at the Eastman school of music have shown that such tests are valuable in predicting probable success or failure of students during the standard course, and that four years of training in the school did not result in significant improvement in scores on the tests themselves. Thus far, the evidence would seem to be very favorable to a theory of biological capacities as determinants of acquired skill in a complex vocational activity.

It happens, however, that a number of incidental findings have arisen to suggest important limitations to the theory of biological factors, though they do not deny the results of this particular vocational guidance. First, we should expect that if there were all-important anatomical or physiological bases for individual differences in auditory discrimination thresholds, these should affect more than one type of discriminations. However, it is found that for a given age range, such as college students, the various measures of pitch, intensity, time, rhythm, consonance, and tonal memory are only slightly correlated and highly specific, with the single exception of pitch and tonal memory. Rhythm, for instance, is not predictable from the scores on time and intensity, a very difficult thing to explain on the basis of any known characteristic of either the sense organs or nerve structure. It is still possible, of course, that there may be a large number of biological correlates, one or more for each such functional difference. If this is the case, it would explain the low intercorrelations between similar tests, but it should be noted that none of the hypothetical biological correlates have yet been discovered for these various types of sensory discriminations. If true, it also vastly complicates both theory and practice of vocational guidance and personnel selection because of the enormous number of factors involved.

If we seek a learned basis for these individual differences, the observed intercorrelations between various types of auditory discriminations would be quite in keeping with the results on transfer of training in other fields, where fairly effective transfer is found in a few relatively narrow fields and little or no transfer between most activities, even those which in a qualitative way seem *a priori* to be almost as closely related as the tests which do fall within the narrow group clusters. This point is to be treated in a parallel paper by the writer (20) on the factorial analysis of fine motor skills.

The previously cited findings of Stanton as to the absence of improvement in auditory acuities with extensive standard musical training may simply indicate that the particular types of training did not produce an effective transfer to the test situation. In a study at Oregon on the improvability of pitch discrimination under individual training specifically designed for that purpose, the writer (19) has in fact produced a rather significant amount of improvement within a limited period of time. Twelve students whose initial thresholds on the Seashore phonograph record of pitch were 30 d.v. or poorer, at a basal frequency of 435 d.v. (placing them roughly in the lowest decile on adult norms), were given from three to five hours of intensive training at or close to the thresholds of the individual on this same frequency. This small amount of specific training produced an improvement up to the average of 5 d.v.

with a range of from 17 to 1 d.v. These figures, however, are not as significant as they appear to be because the normal average threshold is about 3 d.v. and the distribution is markedly skewed toward the superior levels. Its significance, however, is enhanced by the fact that it included all of the poorest scorers, and that class, theoretically at least, should be expected to include all those persons with the more serious anatomical handicaps, if such handicaps existed at all.

C. E. Seashore (16) had previously distinguished between *cognitive* thresholds, governed by ability in understanding the procedures, and *physiological* thresholds, which theoretically are determined by the biological limitations of the sense organ and nervous system. If this distinction be accepted, it should then follow that a good many of the poorer thresholds are due to cognitive factors and subject to improvement by the appropriate techniques. It is not yet known whether such intensive training on one note, 435 d.v., will transfer to other parts of the pitch range or whether each part of the range must be trained separately. Tone qualities and particular types of discriminative responses might also involve specific abilities.

In a further study we obtained preliminary introspections which strengthened the assumption that individuals differ as to work methods in activities even as simple as pitch discrimination. Some observers attempted to retain a clear auditory image of the first tone for comparison with the second, others employed a visual image of a vertical scale, still others attempted to reproduce the tone by implicit throat action, and so on. Further study on this problem is to be continued along with the studies on transfer of training in pitch discrimination. The crucial experiment will be to determine whether individuals who are instructed in superior work methods can significantly improve their own thresholds.

From these experiments we need not conclude that there are no physiological limits, but merely that these limits, if any, are valid *only for a given work method*, and that by the use of other work methods a significant improvement may be obtained. The results on the improvement of pitch control through use of visual cues in the Seashore tonoscope illustrate a work method in which improvement may be achieved by utilizing another structure, the eyes, in conjunction with the training of the principal structures of ears and proprioceptors.

In the field of affective processes, the term *adjustment mechanisms* has been applied to the various ways of solving emotional situations. Such mechanisms are synonymous with work methods in the other fields. Up to the present time objective measurements of individual differences in emotional adjustments have been stated in terms of hypothetical *traits* such as introversion-extroversion which are inferred from the occurrence of certain symptoms, or end results.

Recent analyses of I-E tests have shown however that nearly the same quantitative scores (end result in terms of number of symptoms) may be produced by very different mechanisms having very different significance for adjustment to practical situations. Thus an individual may attain a given I-E score by being primarily interested in abstract types of work, or by fear of social contacts, or still other causes. The partial or complete failure of I-E tests to predict success in various practical situations seems quite logical in view of the diversity of underlying behavior patterns which may be involved, even though these mechanisms are sometimes causally related.

Personality inventories have usually emphasized classifications based on addition of numerous end results or *symptoms* which are considered *a priori* to be indicative of certain types of emotional adjustment. The qualitative study of the adjustment mechanisms underlying conflicts or frustrations, *e.g.* compensation, rationalization, substitution, sublimation, etc., which has recently been extended by Lewin, Shaffer, Wallin, Hull, and others has been almost entirely overlooked as a source of objective test construction, but the writer and Katz (21) have presented a classification of such adjustment mechanisms which goes deeper than the current symptomological approach.

The basic theory here presented suggests that in proceding toward a goal, an individual may be blocked or frustrated in his drive by some other conflicting drive, social custom, or environmental obstacle. In this conflicting situation, he is faced with a number of alternative procedures or solutions of the problem. These solution mechanisms are equivalent to the *work methods* in other fields, *e.g.,* motor skills. If the drive is weak, the individual may simply turn aside and give up the particular goal in favor of another goal (*substitution*). Even if the drive is strong he may see no possible solution and give up. If the drive is a continuing one, giving up is only temporary, and he will later have to either strongly *repress* it, *regress* to an earlier, perhaps even an infantile or sick person's type of solution (sympathism), respond negatively by refusing to recognize the situation or conventional solutions of it (negativism), or revert to imaginary solutions (phantasy, or Lewin's irreal solutions).

If the drive is strong, he may simply redouble his energy in the original type of behavior (compensation) which may go so far as to be called over-compensation, often becoming ridiculous socially. A second type of compensation is that which transfers to another activity, as when a dull student attempts to compensate in athletics or some other outside activity. Various other mechanisms include *rationalization, egocentrism* (attention getting), *identification* with some more successful persons or groups, and dissociation or the use of 'logic tight compartments' in refusing to recognize the inconsistency of separate adjustments to each of the conflicting forces.

Each of the twelve qualitatively different adjustment mechanisms (behavior patterns) for the solution of emotional problems can also be rated quantitatively on its effectiveness as a work method with respect to

(1) the extent of achievement of the individual's original goal or a satisfactory substitute, (2) the attainment of social approval or disapproval as a secondary goal, (3) the usefulness or undesirability of the behavior to his social group, and (4) the building up of habits of effective or ineffective adjustment mechanisms for the solution of future conflicts.

Two or more mechanisms which are qualitatively very unlike in some instances achieve practically equivalent *end results* in terms of these four criteria, but their probabilities of attaining the desired results vary widely from one mechanism to another. This hypothesis of different mechanisms is quite different from the simpler idea often implied in personality adjustments that we differ mainly in quantitative aspects of the same hypothetical larger pattern of behavior, *e.g.*, 'neuroticism.'

Another value arising from the analysis of such affective behavior patterns is the fact that the mechanisms can be simply described in terms of the individual aims, behavior, and results. Alternative solutions may then be presented in terms of other mechanisms which are equally understandable in terms of *what to do* and their probable results.

The continuity between these normal adjustment mechanisms and the psychopathic behavior which results from their exaggerated development suggests also the basis for the psychiatric classification of mental disease based upon underlying mechanisms in place of the current symptomological classifications which are widely recognized to be unsatisfactory.

Various typological theories have suggested a correlation between, *e.g.*, body build and personality characteristics. The principal theory in this field, that of Kretschmer, seems to be largely invalidated by the quantitative studies of Klineberg, Asch, and Block (10) who found that what little evidence there was could be explained upon the basis of changes in body proportions with increasing age. It is not at all necessary that all such biological bases for affective characteristics be disproved. On the contrary, it is quite possible that some such bases as glandular balance may be quite important even within the normal range of variation. It may be significant, however, that to date few of the possible relationships which have been studied have been verified.

Even when biological bases are discovered, however, it is still important to find whether the end result is mediated by *different degrees of the same type of behavior or by qualitatively different mechanisms* with overlapping ranges of effectiveness.

In the intellectual processes we have a considerable body of experimental evidence as to the relationships between possible biological bases and functional effectiveness, *e.g.*, in tests of 'general intelligence.' The work summarized in Paterson's *Physique and Intellect* (13) indicates that except for a few pathological cases at the lower extreme of the distribution, there is no significant correlation between intelligence and the body size, height-weight ratio, head size, brain weight, or other structural measurements. Certain neurologists believe that they can distinguish structural differences in the cortical cell development of feebleminded and highly intelligent individuals, but this point is still controversial, and even if valid for distinguishing pathological cases on the lower extreme of the distribution it is by no means certain to be the basis for the large differences within the main portion of the normal distribution of intelligence scores.

The lack of correlation between intelligence and any known characteristic of size, proportions or weight of the brain is perhaps not so disturbing as the corresponding lack of any known correlation with a functional aspect of the nervous system such as speed of conduction. This extensive literature has been reviewed by Farnsworth, Seashore, and Tinker (8), but one of the more recent studies may be cited to illustrate the total lack of correspondence. Travis and Dorsey (26) have shown that the time for neural conduction in the knee jerk (electrical action current technique, eliminating the slower muscular component) is no faster for male inmates of a feebleminded hospital than for superior children of comparable age 7–10 yrs. When no difference is found between such extremes of a distribution it becomes very unlikely that any will be found anywhere within the normal range of intelligence. However, the idea is a favorite among many psychologists and continues to crop up at rather frequent intervals, in disregard of the large body of evidence against it.

Perhaps the strongest evidence for some neurological basis for intelligence is found in superior families where the best of individual care given to a feebleminded child has been insufficient to produce any significant improvement over a period of years. At least some of these cases are definitely accounted for as cases of birth injury or other definite physical handicaps such as glandular imbalance in cretinism. Harlow (8) has recently reviewed the field of neuro-intellectual correlations.

It may be that outside of these cases where normal anatomical growth has failed or degeneration has set in there are also cases of individuals whose nervous systems contain the normal number and arrangement of nerve cells in healthy condition, but who have not yet learned efficient work methods for the solution of verbal problems such as are found in most intelligence tests. The results of the Wellman experiments (27) on pre-school children at the University of Iowa indicate that moderately superior children do increase very significantly in measured intelligence as a result of continued attendance in superior school environment, and that control groups placed in ordinary schools do not show this improvement. Skeels and Fillmore (21) also showed that children placed in a state institution, which evidently constitutes an inferior environment, likewise show significant decreases in measured intelligence as a result of continued stay in this environment. They also showed that illegitimate children of mothers of low I.Q.'s develop superior I.Q.'s when raised in superior foster homes. Furthermore Skodak (22) has shown that illegitimate children of a group of definitely feebleminded mothers did not show feeblemindedness themselves but were approximately normal when raised in superior foster homes.

Again, one need not conclude that hereditary or any other biological bases are of no importance, but merely that the range of possible improvement in intelligence in any given individual is considerably greater than we have previously believed.

The improvability of intelligence test scores might be considered to represent either increasing speed or effectiveness in the same work methods, or the adoption of superior work methods or both. One of the interpretations of the historical imageless thought controversy is that the two sides simply found observers having individual differences in methods of thinking, some with strong imagery and others without it, or at least unable to verbalize about it without training such as Titchener gave in introspective procedures. Ruger's (15) classical study on the solution of mechanical puzzles has indicated some of the specific attitudes, cues and work methods which were found to be most effective in solving such problems. A somewhat similar study by Husband (9) indicated that in human learning of a lengthy finger maze there was so much difference in the effectiveness of different methods that practically no one succeeded in learning it by either rote kinesthetic or visual imagery methods, but instead everyone eventually hit upon a verbal method of counting, and the sooner an individual adopted this method the sooner he learned the maze. Various sub-types of the verbal method also appeared, with varying degrees of effectiveness.

The author (18) has recently shown that in the solution of the simple disc transfer or pyramid puzzle, students exhibited all degrees of insight from an almost random trial-and-error, through vague unanalyzed hunches, to visually imagined series of steps and on up to verbal rules of various degrees of adequacy and completeness. In the most difficult levels of the problem neither overt trial and error nor casual insights were anywhere nearly as effective as a formal inductive method of analyzing the major variables, systematically recording and classifying the data, and examining the summaries for recurrent patterns or principles underlying solutions. The technical methods of solving intellectual problems in the various sciences, professions, and trades are of course excellent examples of specialized work methods.

The principal theories as to the origin of individual differences in motor skills have been summarized by the writer (17, 20). Within the group of high speed manual skills low correlations of about .20 are the rule, and the only significant correlations occur in very restricted groups, *e.g.*, one group of visual and auditory reaction times, and two sub-groups of tapping tests which however are relatively independent of each other and of simple reaction time. The fact that different musculatures, *e.g.*, hand, jaw, foot, are closely intercorrelated in a single skill, *e.g.*, reaction time, is of no help in the practical problem of predicting success in other more practical skills. It is therefore difficult to postulate any general neuro-muscular factor or even any group factors of significant breadth which might account for the observed large and relatively stable individual differences in various skilled manual speed performances.

As a crucial test, Buxton and Humphreys (3) tested and then further trained a larger number of subjects on four motor tests including the two different kinds of tapping tests until plateaus were reached on the learning curves. If there were some fundamental biological factors such as speed of nerve conduction or muscular contraction operating as determinants of skill in movements of the right arm these physiological limits should appear in both types of tapping tests after the extensive training. Instead of the expected rise in correlations from the pre-training to the post-training series there was actually a slight though insignificant decrease in five of the six correlations and no significant change in the other. So far as the writer can see, the only remaining type of hypothesis for a biological basis of individual differences in motor skills is to suppose that there is a different set of biological factors underlying almost every separate test, or at least for each narrow group, as in the tapping tests.

The work of McNemar (11) on the intercorrelation of motor scores on identical and fraternal twin boys does in fact support such a theory although it can also be interpreted as at least partially due to similarities in training of the twins. This important experiment should be extended and varied to determine more exactly its real significance. The principal reasons for questioning or minimizing the biological interpretation are that no known biological basis has been suggested, and that practically all of the other evidence in this field of manual speed skills tends to minimize its possible importance in favor of the explanation of differences in work methods.

The classic experiments of Book (1) on typewriting suggested a compromise interpretation which seems most reasonable, *viz.*, a given set of physiological limits, *e.g.*, maximum speed of muscular contraction, determine the end result *only for a given work method. If other work methods are introduced* so as to minimize the importance of the limiting factors then further progress may follow. The classic learning plateaus found by Bryan and Harter (2) in the acquisition of motor skills in telegraphy were, in fact, attributed to successive changes from single letter to syllable, word, and even phrase grouping patterns. The classic tachistoscopic experiments of Cattell on 'higher units' of perception, and overlapping of processes likewise fit closely into this explanation. (*Cf.* Dearborn (5), for an interesting summary of these experiments presenting views similar to those of the present writer.) For example in a range of attention experiment, ten unrelated letters cannot be accurately reported, but ten letters in the word UNIVERSITY represent a higher (learned) unit which can be reported with little difficulty. Hollingworth's theory of integration suggests that a single cue comes to evoke a pattern of response which originally was evoked only by a whole situation. Such a change in method may also be analogous to shifting to a higher gear in driving an automobile. The inductive methods of scientific research might then be thought of as a super 'low gear' having tremendous power, but with low speed.

The historical collapse of mental chronometry in the 1890's further illustrates a major difficulty of explaining complex performances on the basis of physiological limits. Thus, if there are five steps in unlocking and opening a door (*e.g.*, extract key ring, select key, insert in lock, turn knob, push door), the sum of the minimum times for each step will not predict the minimum time for the total movement because the steps can be so greatly *overlapped* as to obscure the importance of each element. Lange, Ach, Messer, and others mentioned by Murphy (12), have shown by introspection that various attitudes or 'sets' produce significant variations in reaction time. The order from slowest to fastest was the sensory attitude (attention to stimulus), central (or divided attention), and motor attitude (attention primarily to making responses). It was further indicated that inexperienced observers often change from the sensory to the motor attitude after extensive practice, which is usually accompanied by some improvement in reaction time.

Probably the simplest example of the significance of work methods is given by Perrin (14) in an experiment on speed of card sorting. Simple observation revealed that a number of techniques or 'tricks of the trade' were employed by certain of the observers, *e.g.*, (1) holding the deck in the left hand *close* to the sorting trays rather than several inches away, (2) edging the top card off with the left thumb so as to be easily grasped by the right hand, (3) moving the card toward the trays while turning it over for inspection, and (4) tossing the card rather than placing it on the trays. The superior half of the group, as judged by average speed, utilized a larger number of these techniques than did the slower half. Such casual observation could not of course be expected to show complete differentiation of the groups and in fact one member of the slower half of the group used all of these techniques and still did not get above average. This might be attributed to the absence of still other unnoticed methods, and perhaps to an incomplete degree of overlapping of the movements. It is only fair to add that it might also indicate that the combination of the best methods might not have been sufficient to completely overcome the hypothetical physiological limits which might have been involved in the test.

The clearest and most extensive evidence for the importance of work methods comes from the well-known but largely neglected findings of Gilbreth on the elimination of useless movements. Such studies have been repeated and extended in large numbers of other motor skills, principally by industrial engineers, but unfortunately the results have attracted very little attention in psychology, perhaps because the results are frequently unpublished trade secrets. Gilbreth later checked his analyses by constructing wire models of the hand movements of skilled and unskilled operators to show the difference in techniques to beginners and to aid in their training along the most effective lines. Various minor points have arisen, as to whether there is *one best way* for all persons to use, and, even if there is, whether it can be used continuously without undue fatigue. These, however, are trivial questions, and the evidence is clear that such analysis of work methods can and does produce very significant improvements in motor skills. Slow motion pictures have now largely supplanted Gilbreth's earlier methods of still photography, but the principles are much the same. Gilbreth developed a standard terminology of 'therbligs' or unit types of best movements as a shorthand method for describing various types of skilled movements, but this need not imply any neglect of the factor of overlapping of the movements.

Cox (3) has shown that whereas training in one type of factory assembling operation did not transfer to a second similar operation under ordinary conditions it was possible within the same length of time to introduce efficient work methods on the first skill which did produce very marked transfer to the second operation. Furthermore the workers trained in superior methods continued to become even more superior as time went on. This study is of the greatest importance for applied psychology in all fields.

The significance of these sample results on the analysis of sensory, affective, intellectual, and motor skills may be summarized in a few sentences. (1) *Individual differences in attainment of various practical skills may be in part determined by anatomical or physiological limitations of the individual's receptors, connectors and effectors.* (2) *Such limitations, however, apply to specific behavior patterns or work methods including attitudes and 'sets' as well as the main activities*, and (3) *changing to a different behavior pattern may partially or completely overcome any one or several of these limiting factors, thus permitting further progress in learning of the new skill.* These changes occur even from trial to trial.

Such a view helps to explain the very commonly observed specificity of individual differences in human abilities which placed so great a strain on theories of biological determinants of aptitudes. The concept of qualitative differences in behavior patterns or work methods is in keeping with both the quantitative findings on individual differences and the related fields of learning and adjustment.

An adequate recognition of work methods further minimizes the present 'fatalistic' attitude of vocational guidance, that a person is biologically endowed with certain basic aptitudes for success or failure in various fields. In place of this fatalistic theory it suggests that while these limitations may exist for any given work method, they may be overcome by employing a different work method which is less subject to these same limitations. This fact has been recognized in a recent study by Thurstone (25). Qualitative analysis has already indicated the nature of the preferred methods in certain fields, and the same type of experimental methods, principally verbal report and photographic motion study, can be used wherever needed for other fields.

Selection of workers on the basis of initial tests may still be useful in certain fields where learning is very difficult, but in many other fields vocational guidance should come to emphasize more and more the possibilities of attaining a given skill by experimentally evaluated work methods. Furthermore, the real significance of biological factors underlying a given skill can only be determined by controlling the other major variables of behavior patterns *as well* as the amount of previous training, both formal and informal. Such behavior patterns may even in many cases be adopted as a result of unrecognized chance discovery, as in golf, where the behavior pattern is frequently not well understood even by the skilled professional performer himself. The discovery and teaching of such effective work methods should henceforth become one of the major functions of the applied psychologist in all fields. Gestalt psychology has so far emphasized the idea that these important patterns simply appear as forced reactions to the total situation. Consulting engineers and teachers interested in diagnostic learning have long shown however that such patterns can be analyzed and redirected as an effective aid to learning.

REFERENCES

1. Book, W. F. *Learning to typewrite: with a discussion of the psychology and pedagogy of skill.* New York: Gregg Publ. Co., 1925.
2. Bryan, W. L. & Harter, N. Studies in the physiology and psychology of the telegraphic language. Psychol. Rev., 1897, 4, 27–53.
3. Buxton, C. E. & Humphreys, L. G. The effect of practice upon intercorrelations in motor skills. *Science*, 1935, 81, 441–443.
4. Cox, J. W. *Manual skill, its organization and development.* New York: Macmillan, 1934, 268 pp.
5. Dearborn, W. F. Professor Cattell's studies of perception. *Arch. Psychol.*, No. 30, 4, 1914, 34–35.
6. Farnsworth, P. R., Seashore, R. H., Tinker, M. A. Speed in simple and serial action as related to performance in certain 'intelligence' tests. *Ped. Sem.*, 1927, 34, 537–551.
7. Gilbreth, F. B. & Gilbreth, L. M. *Fatigue study.* (2nd Ed. Rev.) New York: Macmillan, 1919. Pp. 175.
8. Harlow, H. The neuro-physiological correlates of learning and intelligence. *Psychol. Bull.*, 1936, 33, 479–525.
9. Husband, R. W. Human learning in four section elevated finger maze. *J. gen. Psychol.*, 1928, 1, 15-28.

10. KLINEBERG, O., ASCH, S. E., & BLOCK, H. An experimental study of constitutional types. *Genet. Psychol. Monogr.,* 1934, 16, 141–221.
11. MCNEMAR, Q. Twin resemblances in motor skills and the effect of practice thereon. *J. genet. Psychol.,* 1933, 42, 70–99.
12. MURPHY, G. *An historical introduction to modern psychology.* New York: Harcourt Brace Co. (3rd Ed. Rev.), 1932.
13. PATERSON, D. G. *Physique and intellect.* New York: Century Co., 1932. Pp. 304.
14. PERRIN, F. A. C. An experimental study of motor ability. *J. exp. Psychol.* 1921, 4, 24–57.
15. RUGER, H. The psychology of efficiency: an experimental study of the processes involved in the solution of mechanical puzzles and in the acquisition of skill in their manipulation. *Arch. Psychol.,* No. 15, 1910, pp. 88.
16. SEASHORE, C. E. *Psychology of musical talent.* New York: Silver Burdett Company, 1919. Pp. 288.
17. SEASHORE, R. H. Individual differences in motor skills. *J. gen. Psychol.,* 1930, 3, 38–65.
18. SEASHORE, R. H. The pyramid puzzle: a useful device in studying thought. *Amer. J. Psychol.,* 1938, 51, 549–557.
19. SEASHORE, R. H. Improvability of pitch discrimination (abstract), W.P.A. meetings. *Psychol. Bull.,* 1935, 32, 546.
20. SEASHORE, R. H. Factorial analysis of fine motor skills. I. Theoretical, historical, and minor experiments (not yet published).
21. SEASHORE, R. H. & KATZ, B. An operational definition and classifiction of mental mechanisms. *Psychol. Rec.,* 1937, I, No. 1, 3–24.
22. SKEELS, H. M. & FILLMORE, E. A. The mental development of children from underprivileged homes. Report presented before Mid-Western Psychol. Assoc., Madison, Wisconsin, 1938.
23. SKODAK, M. The mental development of children whose true mothers are feebleminded. Report presented before Mid-Western Psychol. Assoc., Madison, Wisconsin, 1938.
24. STANTON, H. M. Musical capacity measures of adults repeated after music education. Iowa City. *Univ. of Iowa Studies.* Series on aims and progress of research. 1930, No. 30. Pp. 18.
25. THURSTONE, L. L. Shifty and mathematical components. A critique of Anastasi's monograph on the influence of specific experience upon mental organization. *Psychol. Bull.,* 1938, 35, No. 4, 223–236.
26. TRAVIS, L. E. & DORSEY, J. M. Conduction rate as found in hypophrenic children. *J. exp. Psychol.,* 1930, 13, 370–372.
27. WELLMAN, B. Mental development from pre-school to college (abstract). 45th Annual Meeting of American Psychological Association, 1937, p. 78.

11 Reliability of Absence Measures

EDGAR F. HUSE
and ERWIN K. TAYLOR

Four different absence measures were defined and examined: attitudinal absences, absence frequency, absence severity, and medical absences. Attitudinal absences and absence frequency were sufficiently reliable to be used as criterion measures; absence severity and medical absences were considered to be too unreliable for use as criterion measures.

Absenteeism has been frequently studied as either a criterion or a predictor measure. However, relatively little attempt has been made to systematically examine the reliability of absenteeism as such.

The present study was undertaken to investigate the reliability of absenteeism as a criterion measure. Specifically, the study was designed to determine which of several different types of absence measures had sufficient reliability to be used as criterion variables.

METHOD

Subjects. The subjects (Ss) were 393 truck drivers of a large oil company. At the time of the study, the Ss were engaged in delivering fluid petroleum products, primarily gasoline, to retail and industrial outlets, usually service stations. All drove tractors and semitrailers. They reported to terminal superintendents in each of 12 marketing divisions located in a single midwestern state. The mean age of the Ss was 38, with the age range from 23 to 64 years. The range of job experience as truck driver with the firm was from 1 to 26 years, with a mean experience as driver of 8 years.

Procedure. A recording form was used to record all nonoccupational illness or injury absences for the full years 1957 and 1958. The recording form was designed to provide information regarding the number of 1-day absences, the number of 2-day absences, and so on, up to absences of 6 months and over.

Definition of absenteeism. Prior to analysis of the data, several different types of absence measures were defined: (a) absence frequency —total number of times absent; (b) absence severity—total number of days absent; (c) attitudinal absences—frequency of 1-day absences; and (d) medical absences—frequency of absences of 3 days or longer.

These definitions were built from the assumption that absence, as such, can be composed of both attitudinal absences and medical absences. In other words, in the former the worker avoids coming to work; in the latter, the worker is sufficiently ill that he is unable to come to work. Any individual absence, of course, can be a combination of different factors. No attempt was made in this study to prove or disprove these assumptions. Rather, the four differently defined absence measures were examined to determine their relative reliability.

Analysis of data. The intercorrelation matrix for the four different absence measures was computed for the years 1957 and 1958, using product-moment correlation coefficients. The matrix is given in Table 11.1.

RESULTS AND DISCUSSION

As shown in Table 11.1, total absence frequency has the highest reliability for the 2 years, .61. Attitudinal absences have a reliability of .52, while severity and medical absences have reliabilities of .23 and .19, respectively.

TABLE 11.1. *Intercorrelation of absence variables*

	Frequency 1958	Frequency 1957	Severity 1958	Severity 1957	Attitudinal 1958	Attitudinal 1957	Medical 1958	Medical 1957
Frequency 1958	—	.61	.63	.28	.77	.47	.63	.18
Frequency 1957		—	.55	.61	.60	.88	.33	.46
Severity 1958			—	.23	.37	.40	.80	.14
Severity 1957				—	.24	.31	.18	.79
Attitudinal 1958					—	.52	.15	.00
Attitudinal 1957						—	.18	.06
Medical 1958							—	.19
Medical 1957								—

The relationship between the variables is even more illuminating. Absence frequency is not only the most reliable measure; it appears to hold more variance in common with the other variables. On the other hand, medical absences are relatively unique with little common variance with any other measures, with the exception of severity. As expected, attitudinal absences show a high degree of relationship with total absence frequency, a much lower relationship with severity, and an even lower relationship with medical absences.

The reliability of medical absences and absence severity makes them suspect for use as criterion variables. The reliability of both additional absences and absence frequency is sufficiently high that either can be used as a criterion. The question of which one should be used in any particular study would, of course, be dependent upon the aims of the investigator.

12 Some Hypotheses for the Analysis of Qualitative Variables

CLYDE H. COOMBS

I. INTRODUCTION

The advancement of psychology as a science rests primarily upon the advancement of measurement theory. New advances, like all inventions, are fundamentally a repatterning of existing concepts; old ideas are put together in a new perspective and new concepts emerge. These new concepts are then buffeted about on paper and in the laboratory. Some, perhaps most, get knocked out of the ring and the rest take their place among the accepted concepts in scientific psychology. Examples of the latter are the foundation stones (too numerous to list) laid by Thurstone in the fields of psychophysics and factor analysis. Guttman (3, 4) has extended these basic contributions in some papers on the theory and technique of scaling qualitative data, and Festinger (2) has recently published a review of the literature in this field.

The concept of a scale has been made clear by Thurstone's (6) development of the law of comparative judgments. In his review Festinger (2) illustrates the concept in detail and the manner in which it is applied by Guttman and his co-workers. The contributions of Guttman have all been pointed in the direction of how to purify a set of items in a questionnaire in order to select that subset of items the responses to which are generated by the same function. This, unfortunately, is a rare event in the domain of psychological traits. There is a tendency in Guttman's papers to the effect that an instrument is not worthwhile if the above criterion is not met. In the opinion of the writer this is a serious error. We will point out in this paper that the responses of a group of

From *Psychological Review*, 1948, 55, 167–174.
This study was made possible by the Bureau of Psychological Services, Institute for Human Adjustment, Horace H. Rackham School of Graduate Studies, University of Michigan

individuals to an instrument, be it a personality questionnaire, attitude scale, or paper and pencil test, potentially contain the essential elements for six separate scores. Each of these scores has its particular significance. Psychological measurement theory already contains the basic concepts necessary to the proper design of instruments to permit the determination of these six scores and their significance. One of these scores, here called the trait status score, is indicative of the degree to which the trait or variable measured by the instrument is generated by a unified function. Hence, the trait status score is an index of the degree to which the performance of a sample of individuals on an instrument has met Guttman's concept of a perfect scale.

The general procedure in searching for scales is to administer a questionnaire containing items believed, on more or less a priori grounds, to belong to or to measure the same domain. The responses of the subjects to these items are then analyzed to see if, among this sample of items, there is a subsample which forms a scale. If a scale is found, all the remaining items are then thrown out and the scale items only are used. It is the writer's conviction that much of the potential value of the instrument is lost.

One of the dangers of this procedure lies in the likelihood that the domain defined by the subsample of scalable items is a restricted partition of the domain originally intended to be measured. For example, a questionnaire composed of items designed to measure attitude toward the British may, with one population sample, yield a scale only among those items that measure attitude toward British foreign policy. In another instance, a collection of behavior items belonging to the domain of honesty may, in that population sample, yield a scale only among those items pertaining to lying or stealing.

Another consequence of selecting only scalable items is the restriction, if not the almost complete destruction, of the potential clinical value of the questionnaire for the analysis of an individual. Guttman appears to recognize the clinical significance of deviants from a scale when he says, "As a matter of fact a study of the deviants is an interesting by-product of the scale analysis. Scale analysis actually picks out individuals for case studies" (4, p. 149). And yet by restricting his final measuring instruments to the truly scalable items he has eliminated the possibility of deviants among individuals who are from the same universe as the original sample. To the degree to which the instrument is confined to scalable items its potential clinical significance is also confined.

II. THE GENESIS OF PSYCHOLOGICAL TRAITS

To make these matters clearer let us digress and consider what gives rise to a scale in the first place. In the infant the psychological domains of mental abilities, personality traits, character, and attitudes are either nonexistent or a relatively undifferentiated mass of potentialities. As the child approaches maturity some of these potentialities come to be realized. Separate mental abilities, various personality traits, and a variety of attitudes differentially develop. One might say that these domains become structured. The degree to which this organization or structuring arises through the mutual influence of maturation and environment is not relevant to our problem. Probably both types of influences enter to different degrees into the organization of different domains and even within a given domain. In the domain of personality, for example, some traits may be more the result of biological differences and others more the result of cultural or educational differences. The important thing for the understanding of scales is that organization and structure appear as unified psychological traits in these various domains. Some traits may be found to be common to various cultures and some peculiar to a particular cultural framework.

Because of the variety of influences which generate them, psychological traits are unique to some extent in every individual. But in a highly organized social order with standardized education there will tend to be certain traits generated which will be common to the population subjected to the same pattern of forces. There is, however, at the same time, opposition, contradiction, and interaction of these forces on organisms that are not equally endowed in the first place—with the result that the structuring of a psychological trait is less complete in some individuals than in others. The degree to which this structuring has occurred in a particular individual with respect to a particular psychological trait should be of considerable clinical significance.

A psychological trait, in other words, may or may not be a functional unity and it may or may not be general, *i.e.*, common to a large number of individuals. A psychological trait is a collection of related behavior elements in which a psychologist is interested. These elements may be integrated or organized to a varying extent in different individuals. The more completely integrated the elements are in an individual the greater is the dynamic functional force of the trait. For example, a collection of items in an arithmetic test defines a psychological trait. Unpublished studies of such tests by scale analysis have indicated the existence of remarkably good scales. This is to be understood in terms of the high standardization of educational procedures and progression of training which give rise to the functional unity we call arithmetic ability.

On the other hand, a psychologist may be interested in the state of morale of a group of workers in a company. He assembles a collection of items sampling specific attitudes toward many phases of the company's policies and operation. The questionnaire might contain items sampling the employees' attitudes toward hours of work, environmental conditions, wages, personnel policies, etc. These items may or may not be related to each other, that is, comprise a scale. The morale of an individual worker may be regarded as a distillation or resolution of a heterogeneous assembly of a number of these lesser attitudes toward the company. An individual worker is regarded as having high morale if he indicates a favorable attitude toward the company on a high proportion of specific attitudes, and as having low morale if he has a high proportion of unfavorable attitudes.

It may be noted here in passing that the writer is in complete agreement with Conrad (1) with respect to his position on uni-dimensional scales. It is highly desirable to search for such instruments, but sometimes we appear to act as if uni-dimensionality were a property of the instrument instead of a property of a group of individuals. For one group of individuals the collection of items in a questionnaire may represent a cohesive series of steps in a psychological continuum. For the members of this group, that collection of items represents a psychological trait which is common to the group and integrated into a functional unity. This situation is rarely found in practice; what is needed, in part, is an index of the extent to which the scale exists for an individual, for a group of individuals, and for the trait itself. We shall propose certain indices which may be so interpreted.

III. THE STATUS SCORES

We are applying the term 'status' to the score obtained in the conventional manner on a test of mental ability, a neurotic inventory, or other instrument. This is done, for the purposes of this paper, to prevent confusion with several other kinds of scores which may be obtained from the same instrument at the same time, because each of these scores is subject to different interpretations. The status scores are conventionally interpreted as the relative position of individuals with respect to what is being measured by the instrument. A status score may be interpreted roughly as the position of an individual relative to other individuals.

There is a status score for each individual and a status score for a group of individuals as a whole—the latter being merely the average of the status scores of the individuals comprising the group.

IV. THE DISPERSION SCORES

The status score theoretically represents the amount of some trait or ability which an individual possesses. Hence, if a trait were perfectly integrated and organized, the individual would pass correctly every item sampling a level of ability below his and fail every item at a level of ability above his. But because psychological traits are not usually so well structured, individuals' performances are inconsistent. An individual may fail some items which are below his ability as determined by the performance of a group of individuals and may pass some items which are above his ability. The score which represents the degree of this inconsistency we call the 'dispersion' score. This score may be obtained by computing the mean deviation or standard deviation or some other measure of variability of the inconsistent responses.

The dispersion score, consequently, is a measure of the degree of structuring or integration of the trait within the individual. This score is significant of something rather different from the status score but perhaps nonlinearly related. This is a matter for experimental study.

Thurstone (7) in one of his early articles on the measurement of attitudes suggests that the dispersion of the items endorsed by an individual is an index of his tolerance on the issue measured by the attitude scale. This hypothesis has been undeservedly neglected in later experimental studies.

Let us return to the example of the morale questionnaire. The items of the questionnaire could be ordered on the basis of the proportions of the population indicating favorableness or unfavorableness on each. Then for each individual there would be two scores; one would be the proportion of items in which he indicates a favorable attitude, representing his status score, and the other would be his dispersion score. The latter score would be determined by the individual's unfavorable responses on items to which he could be expected to respond favorably (in view of his status score), and also by his favorable responses on items to which he could be expected to respond unfavorably. The significance of a dispersion score would be different for different psychological traits and has to be investigated separately for each. In the case of the psychological trait of morale, the writer would be inclined to test the hypothesis that the dispersion score of an individual would be indicative of the rigidity or susceptibility of the morale of this worker to change—the degree to which his morale is a functional unity—a dynamic psychological trait.

The potential clinical significance of this concept of scales might be made clear by a further example. A personality trait is created in an individual as a result of a variety of forces over a period of time. The extent to which a particular personality trait is formed, such as honesty for example, will vary among individuals. A collection of behavioral items pertaining to honesty could be ordered in terms of the prevailing standards of society. An individual's over-all degree of honesty would be reflected by the proportion of situations in which he would behave honestly. Two individuals may have the same honesty (status) scores, and yet differ widely in their dispersion on the ordering of these situations as determined by society. The individual with very small dispersion has accepted the precepts of society and has an integrated trait of honesty to the degree indicated by his dispersion score. The individual with wide dispersion is in conflict with society's values in this domain or has not formulated a generalized principle of honesty.

The dispersion score of a group as distinguished from that of an individual is determined by the *dispersion of the status scores* of the individuals comprising the group. A high dispersion score signifies that the members of the group do not have similar positions on a scale but are diversified. A low dispersion score signifies that the members of a group all have similar positions on the scale, that the group is unified. It would be indicative, for example, of the extent to which the group could be expected to exhibit a united front in the domain tapped by the instrument. It is the group dispersion score that Conrad (1, p. 587) is speaking of when he says, "Our purpose was to discover whether the sample's current attitudes were homogeneous and unified, or heterogeneous and divergent. For this purpose we are inclined to agree with McNemar's (5, p. 328) statement, . . . that 'variation within groups indicates the relative homogeneity of groups in their opinion about an issue.'"

V. THE TRAIT STATUS SCORE

The 'trait status' score is in some ways one of the most important scores of all. It is determined by the *average of the dispersion scores of the individuals comprising the group*. A low trait status score indicates that the trait in question exists as a functional unity, that it is a *common* psychological trait within that group. A high trait status score indicates that the function being measured is not an organized integrated trait, but rather that the elements in the instrument are a heterogeneous unrelated collection. The trait status score is directly related to the degree to which a scale exists. If a scale exists the trait status score is low, *i.e.*, the respective members of a group have low dispersion scores.

Let us return to the morale questionnaire and assume it was administered to the workers in two separate plants. The interrelation of the specific attitudes contained in the questionnaire may be high in one plant and low in another. In that plant in which the trait status score reveals the existence of a scale running through the elements the morale of the workers is a highly structured functional unity. The experimenter would be motivated to see what in the situation was bringing about this 'halo' effect, what had created this generalized attitude which was being reflected in all the elements. The low trait status score might also indicate that the attitudes or morale of the group would be less subject to change under the influences of propaganda. There might even be the basis here for experimentally determining a rational origin for "indifference' in the morale scale. If a scale exists in the items measuring morale, those individuals on the favorable side of morale would be more affected by favorable propaganda than unfavorable. Similarly those individuals on the unfavorable side of the morale scale would be more influenced by unfavorable propaganda. This effect may make itself apparent in a shift of the status score of the individual or a contraction of his dispersion. In a plant in which no scale is found in the morale elements comprising the questionnaire, two workers may have the same score or proportion of favorable attitudes but have very different specific attitudes. If a scale were not found to exist in the morale questionnaire for this group of workers, it would indicate the lack of any organizing or structuring force, and hence that the workers might be more susceptible to either favorable or unfavorable influences.

In a recent paper Thurstone (8) emphasizes the potentialities of the discriminal dispersion in the prediction of conduct. He says, "In the measurement of social attitudes of a group it is not only the average affective value of a proposal or idea that is of significance but also the dispersion of affective values within the group. It may even be possible to *define the morale of a group in terms of the sum of affective dispersions of all its debatable issues.* . . . Measurement of the seriousness of crimes can be made by psychophysical methods in which the dispersions are signs of heterogeneity or lack of unity in the group and its code" (8, p. 248).

This is almost identically the thesis of this paper except that where Thurstone is talking about the discriminal dispersion of items on the scale, we are talking of the dispersion of the items for an individual and the dispersion among individuals. We would define the morale of a group as the status score of the group. But in predicting the behavior of the group in terms of the likelihood of a strike, for example, the group dispersion score would be very significant. Other things being equal, the greater the group dispersion score the less the likelihood of any concerted action by the group. In other words, the group status score would be indicative of the direction the group would take if it took action and the group dispersion score would be indicative of the likelihood of any action being taken. We would hypothesize further that the trait status score for this same group would be indicative of the amount of effort that would need to be expended to change the direction of the group's action. A low trait status score would indicate that the individual members hold firm convictions, that their morale, whether it be good or bad, is a highly structured functional unity. Their morale is not as susceptible to change as that of a group of individuals whose average dispersion score (trait status score) is greater.

The trait status score, representing the degree of integration or scalability, will differ among the infinity of psychological traits, just as, for a given trait, individuals will vary in their degree of integration as represented by their dispersion scores. From the point of view of factor analysis, the fact that a scale does not exist in a collection of items means that the total score is a function of more than one factor, it is not a unitary trait. But the fact that a scale does exist in the collection of items and reveals a unitary factor in a factor analysis of the items, does not necessarily mean that the psychological variable being measured is primary. What it could mean is that the pattern of primary factor loadings of all items is the same.

It is this fact that adds to the confusion on the subject of uni-dimensionality. It is possible for a psychological trait to act as an integrated functional unity (low trait status score—uni-dimensional) and yet be a function of a number of independent or related factors. This would only be revealed if the battery being factored included relatively pure measures of the factors. For example, the score of an individual i on item q is defined as follows:

$$s_{iq} = a_{q1}x_{1i} + a_{q2}x_{2i} + \ldots + a_{qr}x_{ri},$$

where the a's are the loadings of the item q on each of the r factors, and the x's are the loadings of the individual in each of the respective r factors.

The individual's score on a trait t may be defined factorially as

$$S_{it} = \beta_{t1}x_{1i} + \beta_{t2}x_{2i} + \ldots + \beta_{tr}x_{ri},$$

where the β's are the loadings of the test on each of the r factors.

The condition that a psychological trait be perfectly integrated into a functional unity is the condition that

$$a_{11} = a_{21} = \ldots = a_{q1} = \ldots = \beta_{t1}$$
$$a_{12} = a_{22} = \ldots = a_{q2} = \ldots = \beta_{t2}$$
$$\vdots$$
$$a_{1r} = a_{2r} = \ldots = a_{qr} = \ldots = \beta_{tr}$$

This condition, of course, would rarely, if ever, be met. The degree to which this condition is met, however, would signify the degree to which a functional field is integrated.

VI. THE TRAIT DISPERSION SCORE

The 'trait dispersion' score is defined as the dispersion of the individuals' dispersion scores. The significance and interpretation to be given this score is more speculative than any of the others and, like the others, should be subjected to intensive experimental validation. In line with the hypotheses already presented, however, it may be suggested that this score may be indicative of heterogeneity of the strength of forces bringing about integration of a psychological trait. The dispersion score of an individual, it will be recalled, is interpreted as the degree to which the psychological trait in question is integrated into a functional unity in the individual. If the trait dispersion score is high, this would indicate wide variability among individuals in the degree to which this has occurred. One of the possible reasons for this would be the lack of standardized forces influencing the integration of the trait from individual to individual.

VII. CONCLUSIONS

There are inherent, then, in any instrument designed to measure a psychological trait, six separate scores. Hypotheses are presented as to the significance of each of these scores for different aspects of the trait.

1. There is the individual's 'status' score which is the conventional score in an objective test of mental ability or the number of favorable responses in an attitude questionnaire or similar instrument.

2. There is the 'status' score of the group which is simply an *average of the individuals' status scores*. This represents the average ability, average attitude, or average value of the group taken as a whole with respect to the trait in question.

3. There is the individual's 'dispersion' score which is a measure of his dispersion over the items and is indicative of the extent to which the trait being measured is a functional unity for *him*. Because the absolute magnitude of this score would be a function of essentially irrelevant matters—such as the number of items in the scale and their distribution of scale values—it perhaps should be expressed as a ratio of the 'trait status' score below. This would indicate the extent to which the trait was a functional unity for the individual as compared with the average individual of the group.

4. There is the 'dispersion' score of the group which is the *dispersion of the individuals' status scores*. This represents the cohesion or uniformity or rigidity of the group—the similarity of the individuals in the group with respect to the trait in question.

5. There is the 'trait status' score of the group which is the *average of the individuals' dispersion scores*. This represents the extent to which the trait in question exists as a functional unity in the group. It is only if this value is sufficiently low that the instrument may be said to measure a unitary trait. This is, in effect, the score that Guttman tries to make as low as possible by scale analysis. It is desirable that psychologists isolate these traits in the domain of personality and develop measuring instruments for them, for these are general personality traits. As has been

pointed out, however, an instrument is not worthless because the trait status score does not indicate the trait to be a general functional unity. So long as the items meet some suitable criterion for inclusion in the domain, the other four scores are still significant in their own right and for their special purposes.

6. There is the 'trait dispersion' score which is the dispersion of the individuals' dispersion scores. This score may be interpreted as indicative of the heterogeneity of the strength of forces from one individual to another bringing about integration of a psychological trait.

VIII. SUMMARY

Potentially, then, any mental ability test, personality questionnaire, neurotic or adjustment inventory, or attitude questionnaire could be made to yield six scores. Two of these are the conventional scores usually obtained—the individual's status score and the group's status score. The other four scores are derivatives of the dispersion within the individual and between individuals. They are indices of the extent to which a trait exists as a functional unity in general (the trait status score); the extent to which there is integration (rigidity, conformity or maturity) of the trait in the individual (the individual's dispersion score); the extent to which there is organization, cohesion, or uniformity within the group (the group dispersion score); and the degree to which there is uniformity or heterogeneity in the strength of the forces bringing about integration of a trait from individual to individual (the trait dispersion score). The particular significance or interpretation of these scores is dependent upon the nature of the psychological trait in question. The explanation of integration or lack of it may be in terms of maturity, conflict or uniformity of social forces, standardization of education, or other dynamics.

REFERENCES

1. CONRAD, H. S. Some principles of attitude-measurement: a reply to 'Opinion-attitude methodology.' *Psychol. Bull*, 1946, 43, 570–589.
2. FESTINGER, L. The treatment of qualitative data by 'Scale analysis.' *Psychol. Bull.*, 1947, 44, 149–161.
3. GUTTMAN, L. An outline of the statistical theory of prediction. In *The prediction of personal adjustment* (P. Horst, *et al.*). New York: Social Science Research Council, 1941. Pp. 250–364.
4. GUTTMAN, L. A basis for scaling qualitative data. *Amer. sociol. Rev.*, 1944, 9, 139–150.

5. McNemar, Q. Opinion-attitude methodology. *Psychol. Bull.*, 1946, 43, 289–374.
6. Thurstone, L. L. A law of comparative judgment. Psychol. Rev., 1927, 34, 273–286.
7. Thurstone, L. L. Attitudes can be measured. *Amer. J. Soc.*, 1928, 33, 529–554.
8. Thurstone, L. L. The prediction of choice. *Psychometrika*, 1945, 10, 237–253.

III RELIABILITY OF PERFORMANCE OBSERVATION

Ultimately the assessment of performance depends upon an observation by some person. This may be as simple as counting the number of pieces made in one hour or as complex as the elaborate "performance review" files for individuals that are current in some organizaitons. Whatever the observation may be, the question of reliability recurs. Can performance be reliably observed and reported? This question is discussed and illustrated in the materials presented in this section.

Two general reviews of performance observation are presented in the studies by Taft (1955) and Kipnis (1960). The first is a review of the literature and reports attempts to have persons using all sorts of direct and indirect information concerning the persons to be judged make relevant assessments of performance. There are several important conclusions reached by the article but most relevant here is that the performance judgment situation is highly complex in terms of descriptive variables. In addition, the review emphasizes distorting traits within an observer, as intelligence or "social skill." In general, such judgments are so dependent upon many modifying individual traits and situational characteristics that they are of questionable utility. From the orientation of this book, it appears again that despite a disturbing lack of knowledge, observation of performance is continually in use, as in performance rating.

The Kipnis article is specifically concerned with ratings and discusses the uncertainties and distortions possible when ratings are used in situations where some extraneous value (promotion or merit increase) is dependent upon the rating. The general tenor of the article is that any such ratings are suspect and that the commonly found global rating, in particular, *cannot* be used in predictive validity studies with any degree of confidence.

The third presentation by Ryans and Frederiksen (1951) discusses performance tests as measures of achievement but incorporates an exposition of considerations that are applicable much more widely in the general realm of performance observation. One, more pertinent to the present purpose, is the distinction made between reliability of performance and reliability of performance observation. The authors make the statement, "It is possible to study the *reliability of performance* (as distinguished from judging performance) only when the reliability of judging performance has been shown to be adequate." Aside from this, some considerations are presented in constructing a performance test that are generally pertinent to the adoption of any performance measure. Of especial interest is the fact that there are many ways of "observing" the same act as is illustrated by the unidentified study where ratings of performance on the construction of "metal objects" varied in reliability from 0.11 to 0.55; whereas, by using taper gauges to measure, the same judges showed reliabilities in the 0.90's.

Related to this point are studies showing that objective and subjective appraisals of the same performance tend to show low correlations. The pattern is that subjective measures show fairly substantial correlations, and objective and subjective measures low correlations and objective measures very low or even negative relationships.

A search of the literature actually shows relatively few studies illustrating the patterns of relationships of subjective and objective measures of performance. The studies by Siegel (1954) and by Siegel, Schultz, and Benson (1960) are among the more recent that do so. In the first study which is reprinted here (1954) the correlations between ratings of four performances and "check list" scores of the same performances range from 0.26 to 0.66 and in the second, the same general finding is made in a much more complex research effort. Of particular note in the second study is that the correlation between proficiency ratings and training needed was 0.35; one would expect a much higher value if proficiency was being evaluated effectively.

A survey article by Severin (1952) summarizing the literature to 1952, but still most relevant, incorporates the major theme of this section by showing the low relationships between various observations of performance. Well over one hundred studies are evaluated and one of the major conclusions is, "The median of all correlations in the table was 0.28, which seems to be further evidence that one cannot properly substitute one measure of job performance for another without first knowing the degree of equivalence." Examination of the data presented will show the previously mentioned relations of high correlations among ratings, low with ratings and objective measures, and very low or negative between objective indices.

A quite ingenious study by Lifson (1953) is next presented which seems to be quite definitive as a basis for questioning the reliability of human observation in the evaluation of performance. The observers here were trained time-study men who evaluated "workers" (students who worked while paced by a metronome) and who were to rate work pace as compared to a "normal" pace. The studies revealed rater leniency, some ratees were more reliably evaluated, as were some jobs, some raters showed the "central tendency error," interactions were of importance, and, most significantly, one third of the variance resulted from rater-to-rater differences. Judging by the fact that most studies in the field continue to use ratings as performance criteria, this study has not received the attention it deserves. The finding that one third of the performance-measurement variance was due to rater differences in a controlled experimental situation makes it conceivable that even more such unwanted variance occurs in field studies having less stringent attempts at control.

The studies presented here along with those in the part concerned with the dimensions of performance would appear to raise some quite serious questions that must be answered before any further progress can be made in industrial psychology.

The first question concerns the utility of ratings of performance. In spite of many years of effort, ratings continue to show low or even negative relationships with objective performance measures. The question is, what do ratings really rate?

Another question concerns the possibility that humans *cannot* rate performance in any meaningful manner. When it is considered that all performances involve several dimensions, that usually a group of persons is rated, and that rating studies continue to show halo, central tendency, and other errors; plus the fact that all humans are subject to biases, prejudices, and other limitations, the authors submit that any global ratings of performance are uninterpretable. Furthermore, such efforts give the misconception that something has been measured but actually what has been measured is unknown.

That ratings can be made with some reliability is shown in a recent study by Prien and Woodley (unpublished). Peer ratings were obtained on class members during a six-week summer course after 1, 3, 5, 7, 9, 15, 20, 25, and 30 days of contact. Intraclass correlations of interjudge consistency show a linear relation to time with the r_{kk} of early ratings about 0.15 and of later ratings about 0.70. Thus early ratings are unreliable but become more reliable with time, however, the question of just what is being rated is unknown.

Some positive actions that might be taken to make performance measurement more relevant are, first, to recognize in planning research efforts that even the simplest performances have more than one dimension and interrelate with other aspects of performance. Second, people are performing and records are being or can be kept of absenteeism, disciplinary actions, grievances, production, and a great variety of other indices of their behavior. Measurements here, of course, present difficulties, but they do measure "real" things in contrast to global ratings of performance. The third point is that as far as can be determined at present some behaviors can only be assessed by ratings. However, these are somewhat limited and should probably be confined to simple yes-no dichotomies. In general, the frame of reference is to keep individual measures of each performance as simple as possible and minimize human involvement in the assessment and measurement facets that are relevant to behaviors. It is to be hoped that working within such a frame of reference will bring progress toward a better understanding of the behaviors underlying performance and thus allow better predictions of the performance.

REFERENCES

SIEGEL, A. I., SCHULTZ, D. G., & BENSON, S. *Post-training Performance criterion development and application.* Wayne, Pa. Applied Psychological Services, 1960.

PRIEN, E. P. & WOODLEY, K. The reliability of peer ratings of classroom performance. Unpublished study, 1967.

13 The Ability to Judge People

RONALD TAFT

What are the factors related to the ability to judge accurately such behavioral characteristics as the abilities, traits, action tendencies, motives, and emotions of other people?[1] Are there some persons who consistently demonstrate good ability to judge others accurately and, if so, what are the correlates of such ability? These are the general questions to which this review is addressed. The practical importance of the above questions in psychology is obvious, especially when we consider the role of the psychologist's personality in determining the validity of the observations and inferences with which he works.

METHODS OF MEASURING ABILITY TO JUDGE OTHERS

The number of differing methods of measuring ability to judge others that have been used in the experiments in this area may partly account for the varied and sometimes conflicting results found. The distinction between analytic and nonanalytic judgments (Wallin, 75) appears to be a particularly important one. In analytic judgments, the judge (J) is required to conceptualize, and often to quantify, specific characteristics of the subject (S) in terms of a given frame of reference.[2] This mainly involves the process of inference, typical performances of J being rating traits, writing personality descriptions, and predicting the percentage of a group making a given response. In nonanalytic judgments, J responds in a global fashion, as in matching persons with personality descriptions and in making predictions of behavior. An empathetic process is usually involved in nonanalytic judgments.

From *Psychological Bulletin*, 1955, 52, 1–23. The major part of this review was prepared by the writer while he was a research assistant at the Institute of Personality Assessment at the University of California. He wishes to thank Professors D. W. MacKinnon and T. R. Sarbin for their advice and assistance which have been given unstintingly.

[1] The review is confined to judgments about the emotional, personality, and behavioral characteristics of others, not their physical or sociological characteristics.

[2] J stands for judge and S for subject. Throughout this review, the term "subject" refers to the person being judged.

A Classification of Tests of Ability to Judge Others

The classification that follows is based on that suggested by Notcutt and Silva's review of the experimental approaches (54).

1. *Perception of emotional expressions in photographs, drawings, models, and movies.* This method has been used to study ability to judge in a number of studies (2 [ch. 8-10], 3, 13, 18, 25, 26, 30, 33, 37, 38, 39, 73, 76, 78). The required response may be a multiple choice, a one-word free response, or a completely free response. The criteria are usually S's intention, or the judgment of psychologists. Less controversial criteria were used by Coleman (18), where J had to select from a check list the situation to which S was responding. This type of test usually evokes a nonanalytic judgment, although, as F. H. Allport (2) has demonstrated, these judgments can be made analytically. The method has the advantage of being neat, but the expressions tend to be culturally stereotyped. In real-life situations the expression of emotions may be idiosyncratic (38, 42) and thus their recognition may require a different type of ability from the recognition of stereotyped responses.

2. *Rating and ranking of traits.* This is an analytic method, and has the advantage of clear-cut quantification. It also has the virtue of requiring a performance which is frequently used in psychological work. It suffers from all the drawbacks of ratings in general, particularly the lack of consensus about the meaning of terms and the quantitative standards to be used.

A further difficulty with this method of measuring ability to judge others is the establishment of criteria. Two different approaches to these criteria may be distinguished: (*a*) Peer judgments, i.e., pooled judgments made by the Ss themselves, which may or may not include the self-ratings (1, 6, 17, 24, 27, 32, 60, 67, 73, 81). The use of this type of criterion suffers from the doubt whether we are measuring ability to judge or simply the degree to which J conforms to the criterion group; the nonconformist would score poorly, but might in fact be a good judge. (*b*) External criteria—these may be judgments made by other observers who may or may not be well acquainted with the Ss; or they may be derived from test results (3, 17, 23, 40, 52, 53, 67, 71, 73, 78). (Only Cogan *et al.* [17], Estes [23], and Vernon [73] used tests as well as ratings to provide the criteria.) Taft (67) obtained an intercorrelation of .72 between ratings using each of the two types of judgmental criteria, peer judgments and external judgments.

3. *Personality descriptions.* The J is provided with some data about S and required to write a description of his personality. The data provided

might be a brief interview with S, observation of S in some standard situation, or some descriptive material concerning him. This method, in general, involves analytic judgments but suffers from the vagueness of J's task; also the criterion lacks precision, and is usually based on the opinions of persons who are arbitrarily regarded as "expert judges" (9, 12, 55).

4. *Personality matchings.* In this method, J is required to match some data concerning S with some other data concerning him. Where the S's are known personally to J, the task may be to match S with the relevant data. The method lends itself readily to nonanalytic judgments, but some Js may use analytic modes of inference to assist them to make the matchings. The matching method (23, 67, 73, 81) has the great advantage over the previously described methods of studying the ability to judge others in that its criterion is completely objective, but it has the weakness that it constitutes an artificial situation not paralleled in everyday life or in psychological practice.

5. *Prediction of behavior or life-history data.* The J has some acquaintance with S or is given data about him, and his task is to predict S's performance on various test items or his responses to personality and attitude inventories, or to predict specified aspects of his life history. These are the co-called "empathy" tests (20) and are probably primarily nonanalytic. A related test is the "mass-empathy" test (72) in which J predicts the combined responses of a group of people. It is suggested that the "mass-empathy" test of prediction is more likely to be tackled analytically than is the empathy test, as it does not lend itself so readily to empathizing with any particular person. Thus the empathy test will be regarded as nonanalytic, and the mass-empathy test as analytic, wherever such a distinction is cogent to our argument. It is perhaps significant in this reference that a mass-empathy test (Kerr) and an empathy test (Dymond) were found to be uncorrelated for 87 subjects (8). The empathy method was used in fifteen other studies analyzed (9, 10, 20, 21, 28, 34, 40 [ch. IIIC], 44, 54, 56, 57, 59, 73, 78, 79) and the mass-empathy method in ten (16, 40, 41, 66, 67, 68, 69, 70, 72, 74).

The method of behavioral prediction, like the matching method, has the advantage of possessing an objective criterion. The reliability of the predictions on any one item tends to be low, and, therefore, the test should preferably consist of a number of items or behavioral events to be predicted. One weakness of the empathy method, demonstrated by Hastorf and Bender (11, 35) is the spurious effect of projection; the predictions made by J are often partly the result of projection of his own personality, and, consequently, an accidental resemblance between J and S will render the predictions more accurate than they otherwise would be. Hastorf and Bender suggest the use of an index separating the effect of projection, similarity, and empathy. A further weakness of the "empathy" method is the possibility that judgments may often be made correctly by using cultural stereotype responses without attempting to predict the responses of the particular S. Gage (28) has demonstrated how accuracy of stereotype predictions can be kept separate from accuracy of individual predictions.

6. A few miscellaneous techniques should also be mentioned, although studies based on them, in general, fall outside the scope of this review. Most of these techniques employ indices that attempt to measure the ability to judge others in an indirect manner, e.g., Dymond's empathy index on the TAT (17), Walton's generalized empathy test (76), and McClelland's "role-playing ability" scale (46). Even more remote are the tests devised by Chapin (15), Moreno and Moreno (49), Sherriffs (61), Moss Social Intelligence Test (50 used in 73). Most of these measures are either assumed to possess face validity or have been validated against one of the first five methods of testing ability to judge others.

IS THERE A GENERAL ABILITY TO JUDGE OTHERS?

Is there sufficient consistency in the ability to judge others for persons to be characterized as good or poor judges? We are here concerned with the generality and specificity of the ability to judge others and with test-retest reliability of the measures used. G. W. Allport suggests that the ability to judge others is analogous to artistic ability in that it is neither entirely general nor entirely specific. "It would be unreasonable, therefore, to expect a judge of people to be uniformly successful in estimating every quality of every person ... It seems more of an error, however, to consider the ability entirely specific than to consider it entirely general" (5, p. 512 and footnote). Let us now look at the experimental evidence which, on the whole, supports Allport's contention.

Consistency Between Different Types of Tests

Some persons may be better at judging others on analytical tests while others may be better on nonanalytic tests. F. H. Allport (2) found that, in judging emotional expression (Rudolph poses), some Js were superior at judging the intended emotion when using a naive type of intuitive method, while other Js were superior after receiving a training in the use of analytic methods of making the same judgments. Using 44 measures of ability to judge, Vernon (73) obtained significant correlations of over .30 for S's ability to rate strangers (analytic) and his performance on subtests of the Moss Social Situations Test involving nonanalytic judgments about people (Social Situations and Observation of Human Behavior). Wedeck (78) obtained significant positive correlations ranging from .18 to .56 (mean .31) between a test of ability to rate the personality traits of verbally described persons and seven other tests of ability to judge emotions and personal qualities of persons depicted in various ways, both pictorial and verbal. The Ss consisted of 203 adolescent school girls. A factor analysis revealed a "psychological factor" with a high saturation in the judgment of emotion tests (nonanalytic) but a negligible one in the trait-rating tests (analytic). Wolf and Murray (81) using four Js found a "fairly consistent" rank order between the accuracy of Js predictions of the 15 Ss' rank order on three objective tests and J's ability to match the Ss with their Dramatic Production Test records. Taft (67) obtained a significant correlation of .36 between the ability to rate others on traits and the ability to predict group responses on an inventory. On the other hand, a test of ability to match the Ss with their mosaic productions did not correlate significantly with these two analytic tests. Neither did an empathy test with a mass-empathy test (see p. 3 *supra*). In general then, significant but low consistency has usually been found between one test of ability to judge others and another, but some studies suggest that analytic and nonanalytic tests tend to differ in their results. We shall therefore need to note in our review the type of test used in the particular experiments reported.

Reliability of Tests

Adams (1) reports an average test-retest reliability of .55 for the accuracy of sorority girls in ranking nine of their "sisters" on 63 personality traits, the interval between the two tests being approximately three weeks. The criteria were the pooled rankings. This index of realiability indicates that there is some consistency for a particular judge in making specific judgments, but the consistency is not high. If this is typical, the influence of attenuation on correlation coefficients using such data would be considerable. In fact, only a few of the studies report even moderately high reliabilities. Dymond (21) reports a split-half reliability for her empathy test (predictions of S's ratings of himself and of J on six characteristics) of .82 and a test-retest reliability after six weeks of .60 (20). Travers (69) asked his Ss to predict the percentage of a specified population who would answer "true" or "false" to each of 25 items, and the split-half reliability of the accuracy scores for this test was .64.

Taft (67) obtained a test-retest reliability coefficient of .82 for a 30-item prediction test similar to that of Travers but this contrasted with a split-half reliability of only .20. Correlations between single items tend to be even lower than .20 (67, 69, 74), a further indication of the low reliability of any one item. We thus see the necessity for tests of this nature to include a large number of items in order to ensure reliability.

Consistency in Accuracy Between Traits and Between Subjects

Travers, in a further experiment (70), found correlations of .44 and .47 respectively for two groups of students (N, 26 and 31) between ability to judge the word knowledge of S's own group and ability to judge that of the general population. "The evidence then indicates that some subjects are generally good at judging what various groups of men know, while others are poor" (70, p. 98). Taft's study yielded a corresponding correlation of .31 for 40 Ss on tests analogous to those of Travers.

Vernon (73) did not compute the reliabilities of the tests which he used, but, on the basis of "logically related aggregates," i.e., clusters, he suggests that his data show four independent dimensions—ability to judge self, to judge acquaintances, to rate strangers, and to judge character sketches of strangers. Kelly and Fiske (40, ch. IIIC) attempted to devise a test of the ability of psychologists to predict inventory responses of two patients whom the latter had diagnosed. The respective accuracies achieved in judging each patient intercorrelated .23 for 100 Js. In contrast to this low consistency, Estes (23) reports that his ten best judges in a test of ability to rate the traits of persons depicted in short movies were consistently more accurate than the ten poorest judges on all 23 variables and for all eight Ss. The criteria of accuracy were the ratings assigned by clinical psychologists.

Gage (28) also reports high generality in the ability of his Js to judge the responses of six strangers on the Kuder Preference Inventory after they had directly observed Ss expressive behavior for a short time. He found high consistency in J's ability to judge irrespective of the specific items or Ss on which he was being tested. Consistency (correlation of .71) was also shown between ability to predict the responses of the six strangers and those of three randomly selected classmates. Similar findings, with regard to consistency in Js accuracy between different Ss are reported by Bender and Hastorf (11).

Luft (45) suggests that there might be individual differences in consistency amongst Js. In one of his experiments using 74 Js, all persons with various degrees of training in psychology, he found that 27 per cent of the Js were able to predict the personal inventory responses of both of two Ss with above chance accuracy. The predictions were made on the basis of case-record material. However, the accuracy scores of the total sample of 74 Js did not correlate significantly from one S to the other. These findings may be taken in conjunction with those of Dymond (20) in her experiment referred to above. She found that the capable judges tended to show less variation in the accuracy with which they could judge the S's self-rating on each of six traits than did poorer judges. Thus, good judges, at least, seem to show some consistency in ability to judge irrespective of the type of S or the type of qualities being judged. We could not expect, however, that even a capable judge would be able to judge members of another culture as well as he can judge members of his own; there is evidence that judgments are more accurate when J and S are similar in cultural backgrounds, also in age and sex (34, 36, 67, 71 81). Nor could even a good judge be expected to judge all areas of the personality or use different kinds of "clinical evidence" equally well. (Space does not permit the inclusion of a systematic review of the experiments that have been performed on these specific factors in judging [67, pp. 12-23]).

Conclusion. Allport's dictum at the beginning of this section seems to be justified by the data. A reasonable conclusion might be stated as follows: the degree to which a person can make accurate judgments about others is a function of his general ability to judge and of specific situational and interactional factors, but the greater his general ability to judge, the less will be the relative influence of the specific factors. The specific factors concerned are the type of S, the relationship between J and S, the type of judgment demanded, the traits being judged, and the material available to J. In addition, the consistency in the performance of any individual J is limited by the low reliability that characterizes many of the tests used to measure ability to judge. In view of the effect of specific factors we must be cautious in drawing general conclusions from studies that do not require J to make a variety of judgments about a variety of Ss.

THE CHARACTERISTICS OF GOOD JUDGES OF OTHERS

In consequence of the above conclusions, some of the findings quoted in the review that follows should be limited to the actual Ss, judging situations, traits, or modes used in the particular experiments. Wherever similar findings are obtained over several situations, we may expect that the individual characteristics of the good judges concerned can be generalized, but where contradictory findings are obtained between one study and another the variation may merely be due to the specific factors involved in the experiments. Our plan has been to report findings as conclusions where the weight of the evidence clearly supports them, even though some contradictory findings may raise doubts.

Age

Gates (30) found a progressive increase from the ages of 3 to 14 years in the ability to judge the intended emotional expressions in six of the Ruckmick poses. Walton (76), using various tests of empathy with emotional expression, obtained similar results for *J*s ranging from kindergarten to university age. His published tables seem to suggest that the greatest improvements occur between 9 and 11, and between 14 and adulthood. Further support for the development of empathy in children is provided by Dymond *et al.* (22) where a marked increase in signs of empathy is reported between 7 and 11 years. The test consisted of predictions by the *J*s of whether their classmates liked or disliked them.

On the other hand a number of studies using adults as *J*s failed to find any increase with age in ability to judge others (16, 23, 41, 56, 64, 67). These studies employed *J*s ranging from 18 to at least the late thirties, but the tests mostly tested their ability to predict the responses of college age *S*s. Consequently, the older *J*s would be less similar to their *S*s than would the younger *J*s and the former may therefore have been under a handicap.

Conclusions. While ability to judge emotional expressions increases with age in children—probably through experience—no increase with age has been found in adults on various tests of ability to judge others. This latter finding, however, is subject to the limitation that the subjects being judged have mostly been closer in age to the younger judges.

Sex

It has been contended that "Experimental studies, so far as they go, establish only a slight margin in favor of women" (5, p. 517). This seems to be a reasonable summary of the many studies that have been conducted on sex differences in ability to judge people. One study (37) reports a significant superiority for women students in judging the emotional expressions in the Rudolph poses, but in the other studies of judging emotional expressions in photographs, models, and movies, no significant or consistent sex differences are reported. In five studies (2, 18, 25, 30, 33) the authors report no differences; in three (13, 26, 39) a slight, but apparently insignificant, superiority for women; and in one (38) a slight superiority for men. The results are not related to the sex of the person whose emotions were being judged.

Similar results have been found in other tests of judging ability. Dymond (20) reports no sex differences at first in the ability of students to predict how other members of their group rated themselves and *J*; however, in a second administration, six weeks later, the female *J*s were significantly better than the males. In a further experiment (21), she found female students significantly superior to males in making judgments similar to those in her first experiment. These two studies differed from most of the other ones on sex differences in that the Js were well acquainted with the Ss. However, where husbands and wives predicted each other's responses to an inventory (54), sex differences in accuracy were not significant; if anything, the males were the more accurate.

None of the other five reported experiments (46, 56, 64, 69, 71) which compare the ability of males and females either to rate their S's traits or to predict their responses found significant differences. It is also interesting to note that no relationship was found between the ability of males on these types of tests of judging and their scores on inventory and projective tests of femininity (67).

Conclusions. The weight of evidence is in favor of no sex difference in ability to judge, or perhaps a slightly superior ability in women. The reported studies do not suggest any convincing explanations for this possible superiority of women, and until further evidence suggests a changed view, it would be wise to conclude that there are no differences.

Family Background and Sibling Rank

In a study of ability to predict how other boys would answer personal inventory questions (mass-empathy), Sweet (66) found a positive relationship between judging ability and the socioeconomic status of the Js. These results, however, could have been due to the influence of intelligence. The only other study reported on this topic, Taft (67), found no correlation among graduate students between ability to judge and socioeconomic status, where the test required J to rate S on six traits, and to predict their personal inventory responses. The criteria for the ratings were both peer and psychological assessments.

Regarding size of family and order of birth, an earlier suggestion by F. H. Allport (2) that Js from larger families are better at judging emotional expression has not been supported. (Allport used only 26 Js and does not report significance. Estes (23) found no relation between "sibling status" and ability to judge on a trait-rating test and in Taft's study (67) there was actually a negative correlation between ability to judge and number of siblings. In this latter study it was also found that the best Js were only children; then came eldest, middle, and youngest children in that order. The explanation given is that the fewer the older siblings, the more likely is a child to be brought into contact early with adult modes of judging others.

Taft also found that those Js who had a rural background were poorer at judging than the urban ones but this might be explicable again in terms of sibling status. Minority group status showed an interesting pattern in this study: Negroes and foreign students were poorer and Jewish students better than the average in judging (see above for the details of the test used). The explanation given is that the former groups are too isolated and dissimilar from the others to judge them accurately, but the Jewish group possesses a marginal position in the American culture as a whole which provides both the opportunity and the stimulus for making accurate judgments.

Conclusions. The findings reported on the influences of background factors on ability to judge are derived from very few studies, and almost entirely from one. Thus no consistencies can be educed until we have more evidence.

Intelligence and Perception

G. W. Allport sums up the studies up to 1937 on the relationship between ability to judge others and intelligence as follows: "Experimental studies have found repeatedly that some relationship exists between superior intelligence and the ability to judge others ... even within a high and narrow range of intelligence. ... Understanding people is largely a matter of perceiving relations between past and present activities, between expressive behavior and inner traits, between cause and effect, and intelligence *is* the ability to perceive just such relations as these" (5, p. 514).

In an early study, Cogan *et al.* (17) found a significant correlation between J's intelligence and his ability to rate the intelligence of others, and also to rate sense of humor. The criteria were pooled ratings. The correlations between intelligence and ability to rate seven other personality traits were not significant. Adams' study (1) was similar but more complex. He studied 80 female students living together in groups of 10. They ranked themselves and each other on 63 traits, including seven related to intellectual functioning; the pooled rankings acted as the criterion both for measuring the accuracy of the judgments and for measuring the characteristics of the Js. The seven intellectual characteristics had an average correlation of only .12 with ability to judge others, the highest correlations being .21 for "observation" and for "mentally bright" (significant at 5 per cent level). We should note, however, the possibility that the use of peer ratings as the criterion may have provided a measure of J's conformity to his group, rather than of his ability to judge his peers.

Where some independent measure of the criterion was used (21, 55, 67, 73), the accuracy of analytic judgments of personality traits showed significant positive correlations with intelligence fairly generally. Vernon obtained significant correlations of approximately .30 between intelligence and various analytic measures of ability to judge strangers. For other judgments, however, involving nonanalytic modes, the correlations obtained with intelligence were approximately zero.

Taft (67) scored the intelligence of his 40 Js according to their best performance in any of a number of various cognitive tests. This index of intelligence correlated .37 with their ability to judge the traits of their peers and to predict their peers' responses to an inventory (analytic). Academic ability also showed low positive correlations with these tests of ability to judge others but the sample was highly selected in this regard (senior graduate students). Wedeck (78), using 203 girls, reported saturations of g factor ranging from .18 to .34 for his seven varied tests of ability to judge others. There were no consistent differences in this respect between the analytic and the nonanalytic tests.

The results of other studies correlating intelligence and ability on nonanalytic modes of judging are contradictory. In Sweet's study (66), 12- to 14-year-old boys at a YMCA camp predicted how their peers would respond to a questionnaire on 22 different activities. There was a "high relationship" between their accuracy and their CAVI scores. The assessees in the OSS procedures (55) wrote personality sketches of their peers and these were rated by the assessment staff for accuracy. Despite the admitted unreliability of the criteria, the assessees' ability to judge correlated significantly with various verbal intelligence tests (.32 to .48) and .54 with the final staff rating on Effective Intelligence. The latter rating, however, was contaminated both with the scoring of the judging test and with the intelligence test results.

The only other study found that reported a significant positive correlation between judging ability and verbal intelligence (.21) was that of Kanner (38) which correlated the ability of students to judge the intended emotions in the Feleky poses and their Thorndike intelligence scores. Dymond (21) reports a positive correlation between her J's ability to predict the S's self and other ratings on six traits and J's scores on the Wechsler Performance Scale. However, a further study repeating the same technique (43) found no correlation with the ACE Group Test. Similarly Kelly and Fiske (40) found a significant correlation between ability to predict inventory responses and score on the fluency subtest of the PMA but not with any of the other subtests or with the Miller Analogies test.

All the other studies correlating nonanalytic modes of judging with intelligence found no correlation, for example, between (a) the accuracy of predictions of the questionnaire responses of eight psychology students and the J's ACE scores (9), (b) ability to "throw" scores on masculinity-femininity test and Thorndike "intelligence score" or grade point ratio (41), (c) Army Alpha scores and the ability of Js to match correctly a short behavior record with personality sketches (23), (d) ability to predict group responses and the Otis, Cooperative General Culture Test, or Thorndike Reading Test scores of the Js (69, 70), (e) various intelligence tests and the ability of graduate students to match mosaic productions with acquaintances (67), and (f) various group intelligence tests and ability to predict inventory responses on the basis of a brief observation of S's expressive behavior (28).

Conclusions There seems to be a positive relationship between intelligence and ability to judge others analytically. The highest correlation reported is .55 but the use of intellectually homogeneous groups in most of the studies would have reduced the correlations obtained. The superiority of more intelligent Js is probably the most pronounced in ability to rate the intelligence of others. The results for analytic modes do not appear surprising as such modes require a precise understanding of the meaning and application of abstract terms (traits).

Nonanalytic modes of judging tend to manifest lower correlations between intelligence and accuracy of judgment. It is possible that accurate nonanalytic judgments of others are more a function of good perceptual and judgmental attitudes than of the use of abstract intelligence, provided the mode of making the judgments is clearly within the level of comprehension of J.

Training in Psychology

It is often assumed that qualified psychologists are more capable than laymen of making unbiased judgments, since they receive training in the dynamics of personality and also in the correct manner of making judgments, e.g., using fixed standards, considering only relevant evidence, avoiding projection, combining probabilities in their correct weight, etc. On the other hand, some writers argue the opposite. For example, Murray (51) claims that the use of analytic perception and induction together with the repression of emotion and feeling leads to poor ability to judge others.

Let us now turn to the experimental evidence on the question. Are those who have taken courses in psychology more accurate judges than those who have not? In a test of judging emotional expressions in the Boring-Titchener models on an adjective check-list, students who had completed at least one course in psychology were, if anything, less accurate than students just taking their first course (13). Hanks (34) found no relationship between training in psychology and the ability to predict S's answers to inventory questions from biographical and other inventory data. Polansky (56), on the other hand, found graduate students in psychology to be better judges than those without psychological training when judging Ss who were friends of the author. Whether the

Ss, as well as the Js, were also trained in psychology is not stated. The tests required Js to make specific behavioral predictions about three Ss whose actual behavior was known.

Studies comparing the ability of professional psychologists with nonpsychologists do not, in general, suggest that those trained in psychology are better judges. If anything, the contrary seems to be the case. In Estes' experiment (23) psychologists were significantly poorer than the average of a wide variety of Js (professional and nonprofessional persons) in judging others on ratings, check lists, and matching tests. The material presented consisted of brief samples of S's expressive behavior recorded in a movie. These findings are supported by Wedell and Smith (79) who compared qualified, experienced clinicians with untrained, inexperienced interviewers on their ability to predict the responses of 200 interviewees to an attitude questionnaire. The untrained Js made the more accurate predictions.

Luft (44, 45) compared the ability of clinicians (psychiatrists, psychologists and social workers), graduate psychology students, and physical science students on a series of tests in which they were required to predict the responses of individuals to objective and projective test items. The physical scientists were superior to all the other groups of Js on the tasks taken as a whole. On the other hand, Taft (67) found psychologists to be superior to graduate students in various other disciplines. In a study of ability to rate traits and to predict the inventory responses of graduate students participating in an assessment program, judgments made by the assessment staff (psychologists) were more accurate than similar judgments made by the assessees themselves (both staff and peer ratings being used as criteria for the ratings). The assessees did not include psychology graduate students, but the assessment psychologists were "definitely" superior to social science students and "probably" superior to physical science students in judging. In this latter respect, the results appear to contradict those of Luft, but there was some evidence (not reported by Taft [67]) that the superiority of the psychologists in Taft's study was due primarily to the accuracy of the experimental psychologists rather than the clinical. In Luft's study the psychologists were clinicians.

Let us now consider some studies in which Js with different degrees of training in psychology are compared. Kelly and Fiske (40) did not find advanced graduate students of clinical psychology any more accurate at predicting the personality inventory responses of patients whom they had diagnosed through normal psychological techniques than similar students with one year less training. Kelly and Fiske were also able to compare the validity of the assessments of the professional promise of clinical psychology trainees made by other graduate students in clinical psychology with similar assessments made by professional psychologists and psychiatrists. The judgments were made on the basis of test protocols and interview reports and the Ss were actually unknown to the Js. The validity of the assessments was determined by S's later performance as a clinical psychologist. The authors conclude that the students "utilized the materials as effectively as the more mature 1947 staff [psychologists]" (40, p. 175). However, the students had certain advantages over the psychologists—they had greater similarity to the Ss and had themselves undergone the experience of assessment; also, being in training themselves, they had a more appropriate frame of reference for interpreting the criterion (as the authors point out). These factors are less likely to explain Soskin's finding (62) that experienced clinical psychologists were not more accurate than graduate students in predicting the inventory responses of a 26-year-old mother, from her projective test protocols.

Professional psychologists were more successful than psychology students in correctly diagnosing the psychiatric patients depicted in the Szondi Test (57). The superiority, however, could well be due to the psychologists greater familiarity with the diagnostic categories used in the test. Technical knowledge could also account for the clinicians' superiority in Luft's experiment referred to above. Luft found that the clinicians were significantly superior to psychology students in predicting two Ss' responses to a projective test (but not to an objective test) after they had been provided with written interview data about the Ss.

Conclusions. The results on the comparative ability of nonpsychologists, psychology students, and professional psychologists to judge other people are partly obscured by the effect of similarity in age and academic status between J and S. Attempting to allow for this effect in the reported results, physical scientists, and possibly other nonpsychologists, e.g., personnel workers, appear to be more capable of judging others accurately than are either psychology students or clinical psychologists. There is a suggestion that experimental psychologists may be superior as judges to clinical psychologists, but this conclusion must await further evidence.

There is also evidence that suggests that courses in psychology do not improve ability to judge others and there is considerable doubt whether professional psychologists show better ability to judge than do graduate students in psychology.[3] Do these findings necessarily lead to the conclusion that training in psychology blunts a judge's ability? Actually, the results could be wholly attributed to selective factors operating (a) in the accreditation of graduate students as psychologists

---

[3] In spite of this finding there is reason to believe that ability to judge others can be improved by specific training in judging and repeated specific practice, except where the person already has good ability to judge others (3, 4, 14, 20, 33, 37, 47).

and (b) in the selection of psychology as a career. On this latter point, there are some interesting but unanswered questions. Perhaps those taking up psychology, especially clinical psychology, are too concerned about social relations (see below, *Attitude Toward Social Relations*) to be good judges, or perhaps they have had insufficient experience with a wide range of people. Watson (77) has pointed out that many professors and clinicians tend to live in isolation from the general life experiences of the people whom they are endeavoring to understand.

Esthetic Ability and Sensitivity

G. W. Allport claims that of all the characteristics of a good judge of others "esthetic" ability stands above the others, and can even compensate for such things as lack of intelligence and experience (5, p. 538).

Allport and Allport (3) reported that the only correlation found for "susceptibility to social stimuli" (ability to judge emotional expression—Rudolph poses?) was with artistic ability. Of the nine best judges on the test, seven had literary productions to their credit. Unfortunately, no comparable figures are given for those low on the test. Vernon (73) found that the more accurate raters of strangers and of acquaintances (analytic) tended to be more artistic according to their scores on various musical and art judgment tests and were rated high on esthetic values by their peers. Ability to match character sketches with case history material did not correlate with esthetic judgments. Bender (9) reports on a test of ability to write accurate descriptions of the Ss on the basis of test profiles. The author acted as a referee for accuracy. He states that all the good judges were interested in literary or dramatic activity but again no statement is furnished regarding the poor judges in this respect. On another test by Bender in which J was required to rate S's standing on various opinion scales, ability to judge did not correlate significantly with the Meier-Seashore Art judgment test. Estes (23), however, found clear evidence that good ability to match character sketches was related to painting and dramatic avocations but not musical.

Taft (67) concluded that the ability to rate traits accurately and to predict the Ss' inventory responses (analytic) correlates positively with "simple, traditional, artistic sensitivity." This was measured by are judgment tests similar to those used by Vernon and Bender in which high scores are allotted for ability to follow traditional artistic rules. On the other hand, the same Js' scores, on a test in which their preferences for various patterns were compared with the preferences of actual artists,[4] correlated negatively with analytic judging ability. None of the artistic tests correlated with performance on a nonanalytic test (matching).

[4] The distinction between these two types of esthetic judgment corresponds roughly with the symmetrical and asymmetrical types described by Barron (7).

There was also zero correlation between all the tests of ability to judge others and an index of dramatic ability, i.e., ratings of the *J*'s ability to empathize with roles in a role-playing test.

Conclusions. The ability to judge others seems to be higher in those persons who have dramatic and artistic *interests*, but the relationship is not as clear-cut in the case of dramatic and artistic *ability*.

The evidence on dramatic ability is too limited as yet, but in view of role-playing theory, this would seem to be an important area for study, particularly in its relationship to the ability to make accurate nonanalytic judgments of others.

The conclusion on artistic ability must turn on the definition of such ability; while there may be a positive correlation between ability to judge others on analytic modes and ability to endorse traditionally accepted esthetic rules this may possibly be a function of intelligence and interest. The above relationship is not found where the sophisticated standards of professional artists are used and it might well be that professional artists, if tested, would perform poorly on tests of ability to judge others. The accuracy of nonanalytic judgments seems to be even less dependent on artistic ability—with the possible exception of literary ability—than are analytic judgments. (This is explicit in Taft and implicit in Vernon.)

Emotional Stability and Character Integration

It may be argued that the well-adjusted person is less subject to projecting himself into others than a poorly adjusted person and therefore he is able to judge them better. However, it is also possible to argue that a poorly adjusted person, who at the same time is aware of his emotional difficulties, is more sensitive to similar difficulties in others. Most of the findings in this area indicate that the first argument is the more correct, but the evidence is not unequivocal.

Where the tests of ability to judge are analytic in nature, the studies have reported a significant positive relationship between accuracy and emotional adjustment. The only possible exception is that of Adams (1) who reports that his good raters of personality traits tend to be rated high by their peers on the following: touchy, lack courage, work for present, independent, talkative, egotistic. These are signs of poor superficial adjustment, but do not necessarily point to a fundamental maladjustment. The other experiments reveal a positive relationship between analytic tests of judging and (*a*) the Bell Adjustment Inventory (69, 70), (*b*) the Character Education Test (66), (*c*) teacher's ratings that children need psychological help (32), (*d*) steel-workers' accident-proneness (63), (*e*) the California Authoritarian Scale (59), and (*f*) ratings of graduate students by their faculty on "personal soundness" (67). The latter study also reported a positive correlation between ability to make accurate analytic judgments and the "psychotic" scales on the MMPI (*Pa, Pt, Sc*).

The relationship between various measures of adjustment and nonanalytic tests of judging are more equivocal. Studies using the MMPI support the results quoted above: the ability of clinical psychologists to predict the inventory responses of their patients correlated negatively with their scores on the *Pt* scale (41); good judges (undergraduates) on Dymond's empathy test (43) tended to be low on *Pd, Pa, Pt*, and *Sc*, and psychology graduate students who were rated high by their peers on "role-playing ability" (nonanalytic?) also were low on these latter scales and on the *D* scale (46).

Emotional adjustment as measured by the Bell Scale correlated positively with ability to match the Ruckmick and Frois-Wittman emotional expression pictures (26) but not with ability to predict inventory responses after observing S's expressive behavior (28). A test of matching a short film of expressive behavior with character sketches showed zero correlation with the Bernreuter (23) whereas matching mosaic productions with the acquaintances who produced them showed a significant *negative* correlation with ratings on "personal soundness" (67).

Conclusion. Ability to judge others on analytic modes correlates positively with emotional adjustment; presumably the more psychologically significant aspect of this correlation is that poor judges tend to be poorly adjusted, and therefore, probably more likely to allow personal biases to affect their judgments. Studies are still needed in this area using Ss who are more heterogeneous on emotional adjustment than the highly selected groups used in most of the experiments reported. Such studies would perhaps throw light on the connection between poor adjustment and poor ability to judge. The need for further studies is even more evident in the case of nonanalytic modes of judging in which the evidence is more contradictory. There is, however, a clear trend for the MMPI on both analytic and nonanalytic judgments—the poorer judges tend to be elevated on the psychotic scales, in particular, "psychasthenia."

Self-Insight

Is there any relationship between having a good knowledge of oneself and being an accurate judge of others? The inference that there is such a relationship seems reasonable if we accept the theory that we learn to know ourselves by our acceptance of the attitudes of others toward ourselves, and that we learn to know others by observations and inferences deriving from our introjection of the behavior of others.

According to this formulation the acquiring of self-knowledge and knowledge of others are indispensable to each other. Writers who have stressed this viewpoint include Mead (48), Sullivan (65), and Cottrell (19).

Before looking at the experimental evidence on this question, we should refer briefly to a difficulty involved in handling the concept of insight experimentally. For experimental purposes self-insight is usually defined operationally as the ability of J to judge himself accurately, using as the criteria of accuracy judgments made by some other persons. However, it is possible, especially in the case of persons with complex, recondite personalities, that the self-judgments may be more veridical than those made by others. The use of tests, objective and projective, as the criteria can somewhat ameliorate this difficulty (e.g., 73). Other steps that might be taken are: (a) to use, as criteria, judgments made by "experts" (e.g., 53) defined either as persons who know the person well or as professional psychologists—although as we have seen there is considerable doubt whether these latter Js are, in fact, more expert than lay Js; (b) to require S to judge himself as he predicts he will be judged by the other Ss, and then to use these latter judgments as the criteria (e.g., 20)—this method has the disadvantage of contaminating judgments of self with judgments of others; and (c) to use over-all clinical judgments of the person's "self-insight" (e.g., 73, 80).

In many studies it has been found that the Js tend to rate themselves high on admirable traits and low on reprehensible ones (3, 17, 32, 60, 67). Consequently, those who are *actually* high on admirable or low on reprehensible traits will tend to be scored higher than others on self-insight. This artifact operates in all studies of self-insight, no matter how measured, and could affect the relationship found between self-insight and ability to judge others.

Let us now look at the results of experiments in this area:

1. Do good judges of self possess the same personality characteristics as good judges of others? Adams tests the ability of girls to rank themselves and acquaintances on 63 traits, using the pooled rankings as the criterion (1). He concluded that good judges of self and good judges of others possess quite different personality syndromes—strangely enough, the former were oriented towards society, whereas the latter were more egotistic. Compared with the good judge of others, the good self-judge is more intelligent, possesses the more desirable emotional attributes, and is much more socially minded. Vernon (73) obtained substantially the same findings as Adams, using ratings by the Js of themselves, friends, and strangers. He used both pooled judgments and tests as criteria, but note the weakness that these tests were mainly of the inventory, i.e., self-rating, type. When he grouped the intercorrelations between his data into "logically related aggregates," self-ratings formed a different cluster from ratings of others. The good self-raters tended to have a good sense

of humor and good abstract intelligence and were sociable, whereas the good judges of others were less sociable and intelligent, but more artistic than good self-raters.

The Ss (graduate students taking part in a "living-in" assessment procedure) in Taft's experiment (67) predicted their sociometric standing, their relative status in the group on inventory time responses, and also how their peers would rate them on six traits. Good judges of self were taken as those assessees who were accurate in making these predictions. The assessees were rated by the staff on the Gough check list of 279 descriptive adjectives, and the characteristics of good judges of self were thus compared with the characteristics of those assessees who were good judges of the traits and the inventory responses of their fellow assessees. Sixteen of the adjectives distinguished good judges of self from good judges of others, at the 1 per cent level of confidence. Similarly, ten adjectives distinguished the poor judges of self from the poor judges of others. The qualitative differences confirmed Adams' and Vernon's finding that good judges of self tend to be more sociable than good judges of others.

2. What relationship has been found between self-insight and ability to judge others? In the most simplified instance, where the correlations are based on Js ability to judge himself and his peers on single traits, a high positive relationship has been found consistently. Traits on which this relationship has been established include both socially approved and socially disapproved characteristics as follows: beauty (58), leadership (32), empathy (19), obstinacy and disorderliness (60). Evidence has also been presented demonstrating that Js possessing disapproved traits but lacking insight into them tend to project these traits into persons whom they are judging more than do other Js who possess the same traits but do not lack insight (60, 80). Where self-insight has been measured over a number of traits, or in a "global" fashion, the results quoted are conflicting. For example, in a further experiment, Vernon used peer ratings of his J's self-insight as the measure; this measure correlated significantly with the objective measure of ability to rate self accurately described above, and correspondingly these peer-ratings showed no correlation with various measures of ability to judge (ability to rate traits, to make predictions about the behavior of friends and strangers, and to match character sketches with case study material). Similarly, Frenkel-Brunswik (27) found "no consistent relationship" between three psychologists' self-insight and their accuracy in rating adolescents on the Murray needs. The criteria for measuring accuracy of both self and other ratings were the judgments made by the other two psychologists. Taft (67) also failed to find a significant correlation between J's scores on the overall index of ability to judge others (rating the Ss on six traits and predicting their responses to inventory items) and the index of ability to

judge self, described above. On the other hand, Norman (53) did obtain significant correlations in a very similar study, using as Ss 72 graduate students in psychology who were taking part in an assessment program. Their over-all ability to judge themselves on 31 personality traits correlated positively with their ability to judge their peers on the same traits, both when peer ratings and when staff ratings were used as the criteria.

The reason for the clear-cut differences in the results of the above experiments is not obvious. One difference between Norman's study and the others is that, in his experiment, ability to judge self and others is measured by *J*'s accuracy in rating himself and his peers on the same list of traits. In Vernon's and Taft's studies the measure of ability to judge included more than tests of ability to rate self and others on a list of traits. Frenkel-Brunswik's study differs in that the *J*s were not rating their peers.

Taft's results also suggest one subtlety not mentioned by Norman; a chi-square analysis revealed a significant relationship that would not show up in either a linear or a curvilinear correlation: dividing the *J*s into three groups on the basis of their accuracy, it was found that whereas good judges of others tended to be average on ability to judge self and average judges of others tended to be good judges of self, poor judges of others tended to be either good or poor judges of self (rather than average).

Conclusion. Persons who show insight into their own status with respect to their peers on individual traits tend also to rate their peers accurately on those traits. However, when over-all indices are obtained of the subject's self-insight and of ability to judge others, using a variety of tests of these abilities, the relationship is not so clean-cut.

Good judges of self have been shown to possess a number of traits that differentiate them from good judges of others: in particular, greater social orientation. A more mature consideration is required in future work on this topic of the extent to which motivational forces that cause *J* to be accurate in his judgments of himself also cause him to distort his judgments of others.

Social Relations

SOCIAL SKILL AND POPULARITY

Common sense would suggest that a person who possesses good ability to judge people is able to use this ability to advantage in situations requiring social skill, e.g., in leadership or salesmanship. It may be argued that ability to empathize with others and to play their roles, particularly in their relationships to oneself, is positively related to social skill. While there is some evidence to support this viewpoint, there is sufficient evidence to the contrary to force us to seek a more sophisticated attitude. In a study related to the area of role playing and social judgment, Moreno and Moreno (49) found that those children who were able to perceive social roles more accurately than others (according to the psychologist's judgment) were not necessarily those who could enact them best.

Vernon (73) found that the ability to judge strangers is related positively and significantly to scores on the Social Situations and the Memory for Names and Faces subtests of the George Washington Test of Social Intelligence, and negatively to scores on the Observation of Human Behavior subtest. In the OSS study (55), however, scores on the Judgment of Others Test (ability to write accurate personality descriptions of one's peers) had such a low correlation with the staff ratings of the candidates on Social Relations that it was discarded as a measure of this trait. Taft (67) used several tests and ratings to measure the social skills of his subjects; in a role-playing test the good judges of others were rated significantly lower on "ingenuity" than were the poor judges; there were no differences between good and poor judges in the ratings made by the assessment staff on "persuasiveness" in discussion nor on "likeability" as defined by peer sociometric choices. Both analytic and nonanalytic judgments showed the same pattern.

Norman, in the Clinical Psychologist Assessment Study described above, also failed to obtain a linear correlation between ability to judge and a sociometric measure of the acceptability of his Js as professional co-workers. There was, however, a curvilinear relationship; those who received a medium score on acceptability were significantly better at judging than those who received a low score on acceptability. There is a hint here that a study which included more socially maladjusted persons than is usually found among Js in these types of investigation would reveal the expected positive correlation between social skill and ability to judge others.

Studies of the ability to predict group responses have found almost without exception a positive relationship between ability to judge and popularity; also good leaders and salesmen tend to be good judges. The study by Chowdhry and Newcomb (16) finds that those chosen as leaders in a sociometric test are good judges of group opinion only on topics relevant to the group. Ability on the "mass empathy" test (Psychometric Affiliates) correlates positively with various measures of the popularity and efficiency of union officials (72), with the ability of new car salesmen to sell (68), with the sociometric scores of steel workers as working companions (63), and with sociometric ratings of students on leadership after a half-hour discussion (8). In this latter study the Dymond test also correlated significantly with these ratings on leadership. Gage (29) reviews several studies (by Gage and Suci, Wood, and Sprunger) that confirm the positive relationship between the degree to which a group accepts J and his ability to predict the responses of this group to various opinion items. The one exception quoted is a Naval Leadership Project study which failed to find a correlation between the popularity of leaders on a ship and their ability to predict their crew's opinions on an attitude scale. Gage also found a positive correlation with popularity among high school students when the item responses were predicted by the Js for each individual S separately instead of for the group as a whole (28).

Conclusions. The ability to predict how Ss will respond to opinion items shows a consistent positive relationship with measures of social skill, such as leadership, salesmanship, and popularity. This relationship would follow logically from the probability that these types of social skill are aided by the ability to predict how people will behave. Unfortunately, this relationship could also be due simply to a combination of J's tendency to project his own responses onto his S and his being in fact similar to S in his responses. Until these factors have been more carefully isolated, it is impossible to know which explanation is the correct one. Recently a method has been proposed (11) for separating the effects of projection, similarity, and empathy in such tests of judging ability. Other tests of ability to judge others, e.g., rating traits or matching expressive behavior, do not show this same consistent relationship with social skills.

ATTITUDE TOWARDS SOCIAL RELATIONS

In addition to considering the ability to judge others as a social "capacity" it should also be considered as an "attitude." An interest in social relations does not, however, mean good ability to judge the personality of others.

Adams working with the judgment of traits (see above) found that the good judges were independent but "talkative." "The good judge tends towards the egotistic . . . is cold-blooded towards others and not interested in them . . . he develops a shrewd ability to measure others, not as human beings, but as tools" (1, p. 181). This is consistent with the findings already mentioned that good judges of others tend to be less sociable than good judges of self (1, 67, 73).

Dymond (21) reports characteristics for her "high empathy" group that were more comparable to Adams' good self-raters than his good raters of others. On the basis of a TAT analysis, they are described as "outgoing, optimistic, warm, emotional people, who have a strong interest in others," while those low in empathy are "either self-centered and demanding in their emotional contacts or else lone wolves who prefer to get along without strong ties to other people" (21, p. 349). Possibly this finding results from Dymond's method of measuring "empathy" which includes in the score the ability to predict how the Ss will rate J as well as how they will rate themselves. This former measure is close to what we have called ability to judge self.

Taft asked his Js to check their own traits on the Gough Adjective Check List; the poor judges selected socially relevant traits almost exclusively, e.g., *egotistical, noisy*, whereas the good judges put far more stress on traits concerned with executing tasks, e.g., *industrious, patient*. In the tests of judging, the poor judges were significantly more likely to make their errors in the direction of generosity to their Ss than were the good judges. These and other data lead to the conclusion that the poor judges were more socially oriented than the good judges, while the latter were more task oriented. The social dependence of the poor judges makes them unwilling—or, perhaps, unable—to judge their Ss in a "hard-headed," extraceptive manner.

Conclusion. The evidence supports the contention that social detachment is a necessary prerequisite for making accurate judgments of others. This social detachment of the good judge of others could well account for the superior ability in this respect of physical scientists, referred to previously (45, 67), since this group might be thought to be less concerned with social matters than psychologists or social scientists.

JUDGABILITY

Are good judges those who are themselves more difficult to judge? On two grounds it might be expected that this would be the case: first, "As a rule people cannot comprehend others who are more complex and subtle than they" (5, p. 515), and, second, good judges are less socially expressive than poor judges, as we have just seen. Actually, Bender states that the better judges in his study were, in his opinion, persons whom others would have found more difficult to judge (9). His test required the Js to predict, on the basis of character sketches of eight Ss, their scores on seven opinion scales. Taft also found that his good judges were less accurately judged by their peers than were the poor judges.

Dymond found the contrary in her study, but since her good judges were *more* sociable than the poor ones, this suggests that the judgability of good and poor judges is possibly a function of their respective sociability. The validity of this explanation is borne out by the fact that, in an unreported part of Taft's experiment, the sociability of the Ss was positively correlated with the accuracy with which they were judged by both the assessment staff and their peers.

OVER-ALL SUMMARY AND CONCLUSIONS

The ability to judge others has been considered as a personality trait, and its correlates have been discussed. Five different methods of measuring this ability have been described, and it was suggested that the results of the studies quoted may vary according to the operational definition used. This would seem to apply particularly to the distinction between analytic and nonanalytic techniques, although, when we review the findings on the correlates of the ability to judge, we find few that reveal a definite difference between these two types of techniques.

The contradictions found between studies may be due partly to the low reliability of the measures used, and partly to the effect of specific factors such as the type of judgment required, the traits being judged, and the Ss used. This problem of specificity arises with all traits, but it seems to be particularly marked in the case of the ability to judge others; nevertheless, there does seem to be sufficient generality on this ability to justify describing at least some judges as "good" or "poor."

A great deal of carefully designed investigation is obviously required in the area of judging ability, both with respect to this ability as a general trait, and with respect to differences in the ability under specific conditions. Future experiments should employ longer, more reliable tests of the ability to judge the characteristics of others, and should systematically vary the types of tests used, the types of Ss being judged, and the range of Js. Studies are also required in which the effect of motivational factors can be observed.

Our review of the literature suggests that the following characteristics are fairly consistently found to be positively correlated with the ability to judge the personality characteristics of others: (*a*) age (children), (*b*) high intelligence and academic ability (with analytic judgments especially), (*c*) specialization in the physical sciences, (*d*) esthetic and dramatic interests, (*e*) insight into one's status with respect to one's peers on specific traits, (*f*) good emotional adjustment and integration (analytic tests only), and (*g*) social skill (only with tests of ability to predict S's behavior). The ability to judge correlates negatively with J's social dependence and his "psychasthenic" score on the MMPI. Characteristics showing fairly consistent lack of correlation are age (in adults), sex, and training in psychology. Some possible relationships on which more evidence is still required before we can substantiate the possible correlation with ability to judge mentioned in parentheses are number of older siblings (negative), literary ability (positive with analytic judgments), and being a clinical psychologist (negative). Two characteristics that may hold for especially poor judges only are poor social adjustment, and either good or poor (not average) ability to judge self.

The main attributes of the ability to judge others seem to lie in three areas: possessing appropriate judgmental norms, judging ability, and motivation. Where J is similar in background to S he has the advantage of being readily able to use appropriate *norms* for making his judgment. The relevant *judging ability* seems to be a combination of general intelligence and social intelligence, with the possibility of an additional specific factor for nonanalytic judgments ("intuition")—so far only Wedeck has distinguished such a factor. But probably the most important area of all is that of *motivation:* if the judge is motivated to make accurate judgments about his subject and if he feels himself free to be objective, then he has a good chance of achieving his aim, provided of course that he has the requisite ability and can use the appropriate judgmental norms. The act of judging one's fellows is a purposive piece of behavior that involves not only conscious motivation but also ingrained attitudes towards social relationships, including the relationships inherent in the act of judging itself.

REFERENCES

1. ADAMS, H. F. The good judge of personality. *J abnorm. soc. Psychol.*, 1927, 22, 172-181.
2. ALLPORT, F. H. *Social psychology.* Cambridge: Riverside Press, 1924.
3. ALLPORT, F. H., & ALLPORT, G. W. Personality traits: their classification and measurement *J. abnorm. soc. Psychol.*, 1921, 16, 6–40.
4. ALLPORT, F. H., & MUSGRAVE, R. S. Teleonomic description in the study of behavior. *Charact. & Pers.*, 1941, 9, 326–343.
5. ALLPORT, G. W. *Personality: a psychological interpretation.* New York: Henry Holt, 1937.
6. ARGELANDER, ANNALIES. The personal factor in judging human character. *Charact. & Pers.*, 1937, 5, 285–296.
7. BARRON, F. Personality style and perceptual choice. *J. Pers.*, 1952, 20, 385–401.
8. BELL, G. B., & HALL, H. E., JR. The relationship between leadership and empathy. *J. abnorm. soc. Psychol.*, 1954, 49, 156–157.
9. BENDER, I. E. A study in integrations of personalities by prediction and matching. Unpublished doctor's dissertation, Univer. of Syracuse, 1935.
10. BENDER, I. E., & HASTORF, A. H. The perception of persons: forecasting another person's responses on three personality scales. *J. abnorm. soc. Psychol.*, 1950, 45, 556–561.
11. BENDER, I. E., & HASTORF, A. H. On measuring generalized empathic ability (social sensitivity). *J. abnorm. soc. Psychol.*, 1953, 48, 503–506.
12. BRACKEN VON, H. Persönlichkeitsfassung auf Grund von Persönlichkeitsbeschreibungen. *Jenaer. Beit Z. Jugend und Erzihungspsychologie*, 1925, 1–50. Reported in reference 5, 459–460.

13. Buzby, D. E. The interpretation of facial expression. *Amer. J. Psychol.*, 1924, 35, 602–604.
14. Cantor, R. R. An experimental study of a human relations training program. Unpublished doctor's dissertation. The Ohio State Univer., 1949.
15. Chapin, F. S. Preliminary standardization of a social insight scale. *Amer. soc. Rev.*, 1942, 7, 214–225.
16. Chowdhry, K., & Newcomb, T. M. The relative abilities of leaders and non-leaders to estimate opinions of their own group. *J. abnorm. soc. Psychol.*, 1952, 47, 51–57.
17. Cogan, L. G., Conklin, R. M., & Hollingworth, H. L. An experimental study of self-analysis, estimates of associates and the results of tests. *Sch. & Soc.*, 1915, 2, 171–179.
18. Coleman, J. C. Facial expressions of emotion. *Psychol Monogr.*, 1949, 63, No. 1 (Whole No. 296).
19. Dymond, Rosalind F. A preliminary investigation of the relationship of insight and empathy. *J. consult. Psychol.*, 1948, 12, 228–233.
20. Dymond, Rosalind F. A scale for the measurement of empathic ability. *J. consult. Psychol.*, 1949, 13, 127–133.
21. Dymond, Rosalind, F. Personality and empathy. *J. consult Psychol.*, 1950, 14, 343–350.
22. Dymond, Rosalind F., Hughes, Anne S., & Raabe, Virginia L. Measurable changes in empathy with age. *J. consult. Psychol.*, 1952, 16, 202–206.
23. Estes, S. G. Judging personality from expressive behavior. *J. abnorm. soc. Psychol.*, 1938, 33, 217–236.
24. Ferguson, L. W. The value of acquaintance ratings in criteria research. *Personnel Psychol.*, 1949, 2, 93–102.
25. Fernberger, S. W. False suggestion and the Piderit model. *Amer. J. Psychol.*, 1928, 40, 562–568.
26. Fields, S. J. Discrimination of facial expression and its relation to personal adjustment. *J. soc. Psychol.*, 1953, 38, 63–71.
27. Frenkel-Brunswik, Else. Motivation and behavior. *Genet. Psychol. Monogr.* 1942, 26, 121–265.
28. Gage, N. L. Judging interests from expressive behavior. *Psychol. Monogr.*, 1952, 66, No. 18 (Whole No. 350).
29. Gage, N. L. Explorations in the understanding of others. *Educ. psychol. Measmt.*, 1953, 13, 14–26.
30. Gates, G. S. An experimental study of the growth of social perception. *J. educ. Psychol.*, 1923, 14, 449–462.
31. Goodenough, Florence L. Sex differences in judging the sex of handwriting. *J. soc. Psychol.*, 1945, 22, 61–68.
32. Green, G. H. Insight and group adjustment. *J. abnorm. soc. Psychol.*, 1948, 43, 49–61.

33. GUILFORD, J. P. An experiment in learning to read facial expression. *J. abnorm. soc. Psychol.*, 1929, 24, 191–202.
34. HANKS, L. M., JR. Prediction from case material to personality data. *Arch. Psychol., N.Y.*, 1936, 29, No. 207.
35. HASTORF, A. H., & BENDER, I. E. A caution respecting the measurement of empathic ability. *J. abnorm. soc. Psychol.*, 1952, 47, 574–576.
36. HEYMANS, G., & WIERSMA, E. Beitrage zur speziellen Psychologie auf Grund einer Massenuntersuchung. *Z. Psychol.*, 1906, 42. Reported in reference 6.
37. JENNESS, A. The recognition of facial expressions of emotions. *Psychol. Bull.*, 1932, 29, 324–350.
38. KANNER, L. Judging emotions from facial expressions. *Psychol. Monogr.*, 1931, 41, No. 3 (Whole No. 186).
39. KELLOGG, W. N., & EAGLESON, B. M. The growth of social perception in different racial groups. *J. educ. Psychol.*, 1931, 22, 367–375.
40. KELLY, E. L. & FISKE, D. W. *The prediction of performance in clinical psychology.* Ann Arbor: Univer. of Michigan Press, 1951.
41. KELLY, E. L., MILES, C. C., & TERMAN, L. Ability to influence one's score on a typical pencil and paper test of personality. *Charact. & Pers.*, 1936, 4, 206–215.
42. LANDIS, C. The interpretation of facial expression in emotion. *J. gen. Psychol.*, 1929, 2, 59–72.
43. LINDGREN, H. C., & ROBINSON, JACQUELINE. The evaluation of Dymond's test of insight and empathy. *J. consult. Psychol.*, 1953, 17, 172–176.
44. LUFT, J. Some relationships between clinical specialization and the understanding and prediction of an individual's behavior. Unpublished doctor's dissertation, Univ. of California, Los Angeles, 1949.
45. LUFT, J. Implicit hypotheses and clinical predictions. *J. abnorm. soc. Psychol.*, 1950, 45, 756–760.
46. MCCLELLAND, W. A preliminary test of role-playing ability. *J. consult. Psychol.*, 1951, 15, 102–108.
47. MARTIN, H. W. Effects of practice on judging various traits of individuals. *Psychol. Bull.*, 1938, 35, 690. (Abstract)
48. MEAD, G. H. *Mind, self and society.* Chicago: Univer. of Chicago Press, 1934.
49. MORENO, J. L., & MORENO, FLORENCE B. Role tests and role diagrams of children. In J. L. MORENO (Ed.), *Group psychotherapy.* New York: Beacon House, 1945. Pp. 188–203.
50. MOSS, F. A., HUNT, T., OMWAKE, K. T., & BONNING, M. M. *Social intelligence test.* Washington: Center for Psychological Service, 1927.

51. Murray, H. A. *Explorations in personality.* New York: Oxford Univer. Press, 1938.
52. Newcomb, T. M. An experiment designed to test the validity of a rating technique. *J. educ. Psychol.*, 1931, 22, 279–289.
53. Norman, R. D. The interrelationships among acceptance-rejection, self-other identity, insight into self, and realistic perception of others. *J. soc. Psychol.*, 1953, 37, 205–235.
54. Notcutt, B., & Silva, A. L. M. Knowledge of other people. *J. abnorm. soc. Psychol.*, 1951, 46, 30–37.
55. OSS Assessment Staff. *Assessment of men.* New York: Rinehart, 1948.
56. Polansky, N. A. How shall a life history be written? *Charact. & Pers.*, 1941, 9, 188–207.
57. Rabin, A. I. Szondi's pictures: identification of diagnoses. *J. abnorm. soc., Psychol.*, 1950, 45, 392–395.
58. Rokeach, M. Studies in beauty. II. Some determiners of the perception of beauty in women. *J. soc. Psychol.*, 1945, 22, 155–169.
59. Scodell, A., & Mussen, P. Social perceptions of authoritarians and non-authoritarians. *J. abnorm. soc. Psychol.*, 1953, 43, 181–184.
60. Sears, R. R. Experimental studies of projection. I. Attribution of traits. *J. soc. Psychol.*, 1936, 7, 151–163.
61. Sherriffs, A. C. The "intuition questionnaire." A new projective test. *J. abnorm. soc. Psychol.*, 1948, 43, 326–337.
62. Soskin, W F. Bias in postdiction from projective tests. *J. abnorm. soc Psychol.*, 1954, 49, 60–74.
63. Speroff, B. J. Empathic ability and accident rate among steel workers. *Personnel Psychol.*, 1953, 6, 297–300.
64. Steinmetz, H. C. A study of the ability to predict test responses. Unpublished doctor's dissertation, Purdue Univer., 1947.
65. Sullivan, H. S. Conceptions of modern psychiatry. *Psychiatry*, 1940, 3, 1–117.
66. Sweet, Lennig. *The measurement of personal attitudes in younger boys.* New York: Association Press, 1929.
67. Taft, R. Some correlates of the ability to make accurate social judgments. Unpublished doctor's dissertation, Univer. of California, 1950.
68. Tobolski, F. P., & Kerr, W. A. Predictive value of the empathy test in automobile salesmanship. *J. Appl. Psychol.*, 1952, 310–311.
69. Travers, R. M. W. A study in judging the opinions of groups. *Arch. Psychol., N.Y.*, 1941, No. 266, 1–73.
70. Travers, R. M. W. A study of the ability to judge group-knowledge. *Amer. J. Psychol.*, 1943, 56, 54–65.
71. Valentine, C. W. The relative reliability of men and women in intuitive judgments of character. *Brit. J. Psychol.*, 1929, 19, 213–238.
72. Van Zelst, R. H. Empathy test scores of union leaders. *J. appl. Psychol.*, 1952, 36, 293–295.

73. VERNON, P. E. Some characteristics of the good judge of personality. *J. soc. Psychol.*, 1933, 4, 42–57.
74. WALLEN, R. Individual's estimates of group opinion. *J. soc. Psychol.*, 1943, 17, 269–274.
75. WALLIN, R. The prediction of individual behavior from case studies. *Soc. Sci. Res. Coun. Bull.*, 1941, No. 48, 181–250.
76. WALTON, W. E. Empathic responses in children. *Psychol. Monogr.*, 1936, 48, No. 1 (Whole No. 213), 40–67.
77. WATSON, D. L. On the role of insight in the study of mankind. *Psychoanal. Rev.*, 1938, 25, 358–371.
78. WEDECK, J. The relationship between personality and "psychological ability." *Brit. J. Psychol.*, 1947, 37, 133–151.
79. WEDELL, C., & SMITH, K. U. Consistency of interview methods in appraisal of attitudes. *J. appl. Psychol.*, 1951, 35, 392–396.
80. WEINGARTEN, ERICA M. A study of selective perception in clinical judgment. *J. Pers.*, 1949, 17, 396–406.
81. WOLF, R., & MURRAY, H. A. An experiment in judging personality. *J. Psychol.*, 1937, 3, 345–365.

14 Some Determinants of Supervisory Esteem

DAVID KIPNIS

Research on processes by which impressions and opinions of other persons are formed appears to have implications for problems of rating research. In this review, conditions external to the behavior of subordinates, which have been found to promote interpersonal liking in general, have been suggested which may affect the extent of leniency in ratings. Among variables related to leniency may be the degree of propinquity between rater and ratee, amount of pressure under which the supervisor is working, and the extent to which the supervisor expresses criticism of subordinates.

It is contended that many logical and practical problems of measuring job performance originate in the expectation that supervisor's ratings will provide information on most of the important aspects of subordinate job performance. More general studies strongly suggest that impressions of other persons are based upon considerably less than the total information available. An alternate view considered herein is that evaluations of performance are primarily determined by a single class of subordinate behaviors. The success of the subordinate in carrying out this class of behaviors determines how he will be judged in all aspects of performance.

This view has the advantage of describing rather well the presence of halo in ratings as well as the frequent finding that objective measures of performance do not correlate highly with ratings. In addition, it provides a basis for the inclusion of other measures of performance, without the logical necessity that these measures correlate with ratings. A significant problem for ratings becomes the identification of the class of subordinate behaviors which primarily determine over-all evaluations. An initial guess is that these behaviors are related to the "support" shown supervisors by subordinates when carrying out directions and orders.

From *Personnel Psychology*, 1960, 13, 377–391. Many constructive discussions were held with Albert S. Glickman on problems of ratings prior to and during the writing of this paper. Thanks are also extended to Dorothy M. Kipnis whose careful criticisms resulted in many improvements in the paper.

INTRODUCTION

Few topics in industrial psychology have received more attention than the use of supervisory evaluations of performance as a source of criterion data. The simple and still appealing notion that supervisors are in the best position to evaluate various aspects of the subordinate's performance has been made suspect by the prevalence of errors of halo and leniency as well as the lack of equivalence often found between supervisory ratings and other estimates of production efficiency (e.g., Gaylord, Russell, Johnson & Severin, 1951; Mackie, Wilson & Buckner, 1954; Severin, 1952). In general, research on supervisory evaluations of performance, rather than resolving problems of criteria, have pointed out their complexities. This lack of clarification remains a major stumbling block to progress in selection and classification (Haire, 1959).

It is often profitable when one is stalled on some problem to attempt to approach it from a different point of view. For the most part, research on supervisory ratings has concentrated on the practical problem of developing procedures and instruments to objectify raters' judgments and to eliminate sources of errors from their ratings. Not as much attention has been paid to the processes by which supervisors arrive at their judgments of performance. Here an attempt will be made to specify such processes by relating supervisory ratings to the broader area of research on interpersonal perception. Since supervisory ratings are basically the impressions that one person has of another, it is reasonable that these areas should overlap. And since research on interpersonal perceptions has been specifically concerned with the processes by which we build up information about and form relationships with others, many of the findings may be directly applicable to ratings.

Specifically, two problems of concern in both industrial ratings and the larger area of interpersonal perception are reviewed.[1] The first deals with factors external to the behavior of the person evaluated which may be expected to promote rater leniency. The second presents some suggestions as to what kinds of subordinate behaviors may promote favorable supervisory evaluations.

---

[1] While not covered in the paper, it may be noted that the works of Asch (1946) and Kogan and Tagiuri (1958) on processes by which impressions of individuals are formed, as well as the works of Bieri (1955), Gollins and Rosenberg (1956), Haire and Grunes (1950), Kelly (1955), Leventhal (1957), Pepitone and Hayden (1955), and Steiner (1954) on the conditions under which complex or discrepant behaviors of an individual are perceived and reported, have direct implications for problems usually associated with halo in ratings. These studies, in addition to their general implications, suggest that the extent of halo in ratings may be conditioned in part, at least, by identifiable and measurable individual differences among raters.

EXTERNAL FACTORS

Glickman (1955) notes reasons for a supervisor to rate leniently. By and large, these concern the raters' appraisal of the consequence to himself and the ratee of giving harsh ratings. In addition to such considerations as these, the following three sources of influence upon the promotion of leniency have been noted—although not specifically in terms of merit rating. However, to the extent that the variables have promoted liking between persons in other situations, they may be suspected of operating in the rating situation.

Propinquity. Sheer physical proximity between two persons will affect the probability of friendship developing between them. The pervasiveness of propinquity in promoting friendships has caused Caplow and Forman (1950) to speak of the "mechanical effects of accessibility upon intimacy." For example, Byrne and Buehler (1955) found that friendships made in a classroom were strongly conditioned by whether or not students sat next to each other. Festinger, Schachter, and Back (1950) in a study of friendship formations in a veterans' housing project found that such details as the floor on which one lived, and the way one's door faced on a court affected the likelihood of friendship formation.

The studies cited have been done mostly among relatively homogeneous groups where no formal barriers to the establishment of friendship existed. Within industrial settings, however, interaction between supervisors and subordinates is monitored by formal status differentials which might well militate against propinquity affecting liking. On the other hand, such factors as the arrangement of working space and duty assignments, which require the supervisor to spend more time with some employees than with others, suggest that different opportunities for contact may lead to differences in leniency. This point was tangentially investigated by Dorothy Kipnis (1957) in a study of the prediction of sociometric choices of B-29 Bomber crews, which found that officers' evaluations of enlisted men were clearly affected by the physical distance that separated them in the aircraft. More lenient ratings were given to men who worked nearest the officers.

While length of acquaintance is usually thought of as causing leniency in ratings (Guilford, 1954, p. 295), it is suspected that the time period per se is not an important factor—to the extent it does not facilitate increased interaction between rater and ratee. For instance, given two subordinates, the first employed 10 years but seeing his supervisor only once a week, and the second employed for 5 years but in constant interaction with the supervisor, it would be guessed that the supervisor might evaluate higher the latter employee, all other factors between the two employees being equal.

Social Setting. A second set of conditions which may affect leniency is the "social setting" under which the ratings are made. In general, a setting which encourages cooperation (Deutsch, 1949), participation (Bovard, 1951; Morse & Reimer, 1956), or is free from arbitrary sanctions (Lewin, Lippitt & White, 1939) may be expected to result in more congenial interpersonal relationships and the promotion of greater liking among participants. These findings are based upon ratings of co-equals or of subordinates rating superiors, and they cannot be expected to apply directly to the supervisor rating subordinates. However, the significant point of these studies with reference to ratings is that changes in social structural variables can affect interpersonal liking.

Along these lines, a variable which probably has great consequences for rater leniency is the degree of pressure from the social structure that is placed upon the rater. It is assumed that such pressure increases stress. Among others, Murray (1933) and Feshbach and Singer (1957) have studied the effects of stress upon the perception of other people. The main results indicate that the arousal of stress produces significant changes in the liking of others. Concomitant with stress is greater projection of maliciousness and aggression by the perceiver onto those he was rating. In industry, departments and work units vary widely in the degree of pressure under which employees are working. This pressure may be short-term or an inherent aspect of the work. A shortage of work personnel with no corresponding decrease in the necessity for work output will increase the degree of pressure placed upon subordinates and supervisors. A sudden increase in the work load, or work where the consequences of error are costly, are other examples of situations involving heightened pressure. As pressure increases, less leniency in ratings is to be expected—due not only to projective factors, but also because as work load demands increase there will be greater likelihood of errors and mistakes being made by subordinates.

Expression of Criticism. A third variable which may affect rater leniency has to do with the finding that expressions of criticism are found to have a cathartic effect which reduces interpersonal hostility. Thibaut and Coules (1952) and Pepitone and Kleiner (1957) report that, when individuals are restrained from directly criticizing others, they retain less friendly feelings toward these individuals. Since supervisory duties usually involve the criticism of subordinates' work, it may prove that inhibition of this criticism on the part of the rater is reflected in harder ratings at some later date. The findings of Spector (1954) in this area most closely approximate the industrial rating situation. He directly investigated the effects of blocking rater criticism of an individual's performance on later evaluations of this performance. The most lenient ratings were given by raters who were allowed to criticize the ratee and this criticism was accepted by the ratee as being helpful. The most severe ratings of performance were assigned by raters who were given no chance to express criticism of the performance. For the most part, personal qualities of the rater may determine the extent to which he will openly criticize subordinates. However, blockages to direct criticism may inadvertently occur through "human relations" training wherein supervisors are cautioned to temper criticism of subordinates with understanding of the motivations underlying their behavior, or through assigning this function to the personnel department.

BEHAVIORS OF SUBORDINATES AFFECTING RATINGS

To this point, sources external to the behavior of subordinates which may influence ratings have been discussed. Of course it has long been recognized that ratings are sensitive to such external influences, if not specifically to the foregoing. The conversion of ratings to rankings, for instance, to eliminate between-rater variations is one method used to control these factors.

Less recognition has been given, however, to the possibility that some subordinate behaviors may be more influential than others in determining supervisors' evaluations. This lack of recognition is primarily due to the current conceptualization of the rating process. As ordinarily stated, the rating problem centers around means of objectifying ratings. It is expected that, given guidance, the rater can evaluate impartially, if imperfectly, the more important aspects of a subordinate's job proficiency. As such, no special subordinate behaviors are expected to be more influential than others. The facts of halo, leniency, lack of equivalence between ratings and other measures are considered errors to be minimized by the development of scales and procedures which will objectify and guide the supervisor's observations toward those aspects of performance which he logically should see. The lack of success achieved to date through this approach suggests that a reexamination of the nature of these ratings may prove profitable.

One possibility is that the content of ratings is mainly determined by a restricted class of subordinate behaviors. To the extent that the subordinate successfully carries out this class of behavior, perceptions and judgments of other aspects of his work are distorted in the direction of greater leniency. It follows that the remaining aspects of work are not measured as validly as the class of subordinate behavior which primarily influenced the supervisor's judgment.

There is evidence from various sources to support the proposition that a restricted class of behaviors can determine evaluations of other aspects of an individual's performance. Asch (1946), and Haire and

Grunes (1955), studying processes by which impressions and opinions of other persons are formed, have found that the total impression of another person is frequently based upon limited aspects of the other person's behavior. Less central behaviors are distorted to make them consistent with the core behaviors around which impressions have been formed. Barrett (1958), investigating the processes by which psychologists were able to integrate information about an industrial applicant into one over-all appraisal, found that total impressions were based upon only a limited portion of the information available. Interviews and a clinical rating of the applicant were the main determinants of over-all ratings. Objective test data, which presumably gave new and independent information about the candidate, were not influential in determining opinions.

Mackie, Wilson, and Buckner (1954) and Sherif, White, and Harvey (1955) have also presented data which illustrate how perceptions of directly-observed behavior are distorted to conform to previous notions. Judges in Mackie's study were supervisors of Navy-enlisted submariners; in Sherif's study groups of boys judged each other's performance. In both instances, negligible correlations were found between judges' ratings of subjects' performance on tasks (job sample tests for submarines, target throw for boys) and actual performance on these tasks (correlations from .01 to .18). On the other hand, correlations ranging from .42 to .74 were found between ratings of task performance and the over-all ratings or status accorded the subjects by the judges. The higher the status, the more performance was overestimated. The lower the status, the more performance was underestimated. In addition, Sherif and his co-workers found that the longer a group had been organized, the more judges' estimates of performance were distorted towards over-all status.

What subordinate behaviors, then, may be most influential in determining status in the eyes of supervisors?[2] Some guide to this problem may be found by considering the role of the supervisor. Haire (1957, Chapter 12), Steiner (1954, 1955) and others (Jones & deCharms, 1958; Kelley, cited in Bruner & Tagiuri, 1954, Chapter 17, p. 642) have shown that a judge will pay attention to different aspects of an individual's behavior depending upon the judge's own role, and the goals of his position, at the time he makes his observations. Within the military, Moore (1953) found that superiors of noncommissioned officers based their

---

[2] While, logically, technical proficiency should be high on the list of behaviors that promote lenient ratings, this is not often found to be the case. One possible reason for this may be that most employees can do their work, at least at the minimum level of technical competence demanded by the job. In addition, attrition of the most incompetent from the job, as well as raising of the general proficiency level of those who remain on the job through training and previous experience, may serve to reduce noticeable differences among men. Finally, the observations of Cronbach (1957), that applied technology is constantly striving to reduce individual differences among men through introduction of improved machinery, would also lead to reduced variance associated with technical proficiency.

evaluations of them upon their ability to get out the work. Conversely, the subordinates of these noncommissioned officers based their evaluations of them primarily in terms of their human relations ability. Clearly, markedly different bases for the evaluation of the same person may be found depending upon the position of the evaluator. In general, given knowledge of the perceiver's role, predictions can be made concerning the salient behaviors of the object person that will most influence the perceiver.

It is fairly well agreed that the supervisor's role is a difficult one. Balma, Maloney, and Lawshe (1958) have indicated some of the problems faced by the supervisor as a result of scientific management and the growth of unions. In his role the supervisor is subjected to a variety of pressures from his superiors to maintain production and efficiency; at the same time he has responsibilities to his subordinates which are often in conflict with these pressures from above. While these pressures may vary in intensity, they are present in most hierarchical structures. Mann (1954) in referring to these conflicting obligations has aptly termed the supervisor a "member of two families."

If the supervisor had no personal stake in the outcome of these conflicting elements, it could still be argued that he could maintain the necessary objectivity to evaluate performance. However, a final element which contributes to "subjectivity" in ratings is the fact that the supervisor's own reputation and chances for success are primarily dependent upon the work of his subordinates. Subordinate delinquencies mean that the supervisor's work schedules and goals have been delayed, and they reflect upon his effectiveness to his superiors. Under these conditions the supervisor may be described as highly involved with those he is reporting upon, and evaluations of their work may be strongly conditioned by the nature of the interaction between himself and subordinates.

Returning to the question of what subordinate behaviors may be most likely to promote supervisory esteem, as a first approximation the author suggests that supervisors may be most influenced by behaviors in subordinates that show support for himself and his goals. By supportive behaviors are meant behaviors that reflect a willingness to accept the supervisor's influence or which promote confidence in the subordinate's ability to carry out the work.

In themselves, of course, such behaviors are an important component of job performance. Subordinates, who are lazy, insolent, forgetful or argumentative, or misinterpret the range of the responsibilities (Lawshe, 1959) for instance, tend to be disruptive and impede the flow of work. However, to the extent that these behaviors become the basis for the interpretation of other behaviors of the subordinate, limits are placed on the range of behaviors which we may expect the supervisor to reliably evaluate. This is because evaluations may be more affected by the diligence with which the subordinate supports the supervisor than by the subordinate's technical knowledge. For instance, the oft-noted, but little investigated, success of "yesman" behavior in winning supervisory esteem is an example of supportive behavior which serves to alleviate supervisory anxiety rather than promote production.

Whether the specific behaviors designated here as the content of ratings are correct is a matter of empirical research. Beyond this question, further discussion is in order concerning the general question of implications for rating research brought about by postulating that supervisory evaluations are mainly determined by a limited number of subordinate behaviors.

1. *Assumptions and Data of Ratings*

One useful standard for the evaluation of theory is the necessity for it to be consistent with existing data (Allport, 1955, Chapter 1). Applying this standard, it may be seen that the proposition, that over-all evaluations are determined by a specific class of subordinate behaviors, can accommodate rather well two important findings of rating research. It describes the conditions giving rise to halo and, secondly, it does not require that the supervisor's description of subordinate behaviors be congruent with more objective measures. In fact, it predicts little relationship insofar as the supervisor is not describing the central class of subordinate behaviors which primarily determined the rating. From this point of view, significant problems of rating research are the identification of the specific class of subordinate behaviors determining ratings, as well as the conditions under which these behaviors will be most influential. Two such conditions may be a) the extent the supervisor is dependent upon the work of subordinates to maintain his own reputation as against only nominal supervision without involvement and b) the length of time the supervisor has led the group he is rating. The longer the time, the higher the probability that perceptions of specific behaviors will be distorted (Sherif, White & Harvey, 1955).

Finally, this assumption can be readily coordinated with current research in interpersonal perception. As findings accumulate in that area, it seems more and more likely that ratings cannot be excepted from general uniformities of interpersonal perception. Similar factors may determine ratings in the case of the supervisor evaluating subordinates and in the case of the college sophomore rating his friends on maturity. As this point becomes recognized, the interaction between the two areas should provide two beneficial effects. First, an important industrial field setting for research in interpersonal perceptions will be provided. Second, the results of such studies in turn may clarify many problems currently associated with supervisors' ratings.

2. Measurement of Performance

Ghiselli (1956) has recently pointed out that performance on any given job may be best described in terms of at least several independent dimensions. As a corollary, it can be added that no one measure of performance may be adequate to describe these independent dimensions. While we recognize this, our efforts to measure performance are usually limited to the use of one measuring instrument. In part, dissatisfaction with ratings as a criterion measure stems from this practice of expecting them to measure total job performance. For instance, Taylor, Parker, and Ford (1959) concluded, after an unsuccessful attempt to cross-validate a rating scale format found less subject to "bias" in a prior methodological research project:

> We rather question the ability of the average supervisor in industrial management to provide an appraisal of his subordinates adequate to the needs of predictor validation. From this, it necessarily follows that ordinary appraisals by superiors are probably even less adequate to provide a basis for personnel action, particularly those of promotion or transfer (p. 266).

If the proposition is valid that supervisor's ratings are measuring only an aspect of job performance, then some progress toward salvaging ratings as a measure of performance can be made. This more modest definition allows room for the development of other measures of job performance without expectation that the measures should correlate with each other, or more importantly, correlate with supervisors' ratings. If technical knowledge is an important component of the criterion, then job knowledge tests might be used. If willingness and diligence are important, supervisors' ratings could be included (assuming for the moment that the guess as to the class of behaviors is correct). If human relations skills are to be measured, the opinions of peers or subordinates might be solicited. Certainly the gathering of these data is no easy task. The identification and measurement of the various dimensions of performance in itself presents many challenging and difficult problems. Beyond that problem, the monumental task of combining the various sources of information into an over-all description of subordinate performance must be solved. These problems are, of course, beyond the scope of this paper. Ghiselli (1956) has addressed himself to the logical and methodological considerations involved here.

3. Prediction of Performance

A third consequence of distinguishing between performance as perceived by the supervisor, and performance as estimated by other measures, may be noted in terms of the development and validation of selection tests. Such tests are, of course, constructed from an analysis of the abilities and temperamental qualities needed on the job. While the specific nature of the tests may vary according to the orientation or insightfulness of the test constructor, the focus is usually on the job elements.

In validating these tests, however, the most frequent criterion is supervisory ratings of performance. The disappointing validities so often obtained with this criterion may stem from the dubious assumption that supervisors' ratings are equivalent with the performance the investigator is attempting to predict. To the extent that ratings are used as criterion measures, it may be more appropriate to develop tests to measure how the subordinate accommodates his actions to the supervisor. Kipnis and Glickman (1958, 1959) have attempted to do this in developing a battery of tests to predict Navy sailors performance evaluations. Tests to measure such hypothesized "support" behaviors as insolence (lack of), decisiveness, and willingness to work beyond minimum standards on tiring jobs were developed. In two small pilot studies multiple correlations with supervisors' ratings of over .40 were obtained. Larger scale studies with these tests are now in progress.

In general, greater flexibility of choice of criteria for test validation follows from the assumption that supervisors' evaluations cover only an aspect of job performance. Balancing this gain, however, is the fact that many of the problems, discussed in the previous section on the measurement of performance, apply as well to its prediction. As Ghiselli (1956) has indicated, the prediction of any one dimension of job performance cannot be taken as synonymous with the prediction of job performance in its entirety. At best more limited statements about validity are required. The multi-dimensionality of job performance is not likely to be completely described by either single tests and/or single criterion measures.

REFERENCES

Asch, S. E. "Forming Impressions of Personality." *Journal of Abnormal and Social Psychology*, XLI (1946), 258–290.

Allport, F. H. *Theories of Perception and the Concept of Structure.* New York: John Wiley & Sons, 1955.

Balma, M. J., Maloney, J. C., & Lawshe, C. H. "The Role of the Foreman in Modern Industry." *Personnel Psychology*, XI (1958), 195–206.

Barrett, R. S. "The Process of Predicting Job Performance." *Personnel Psychology*, XI (1958), 39–58.

Bieri, J. "Cognitive Complexity-Simplicity and Predictive Behavior." *Journal of Abnormal and Social Psychology*, LI (1955), 263–268.

Bovard, E. W., Jr. "The Experimental Production of Interpersonal Affect." *Journal of Abnormal and Social Psychology*, XLVI (1951), 521–528.

Bruner, J. S. & Tagiuri, R. "The Perception of People." In G. Lindzey (Ed.), *Handbook of Social Psychology*. Cambridge, Mass.: Addison Wesley, 1954.

Byrne, D. & Buehler, J. A. "A Note on the Influence of Propinquity upon Acquaintanceship." *Journal of Abnormal and Social Psychology*, LI (1955), 147–148.

Caplow, T. & Forman, R. "Neighborhood Interaction in a Homogeneous Community." *American Sociological Review*, XV (1950), 357–366.

Cronbach, L. J. "The Two Disciplines of Scientific Psychology." *American Psychologist*, XII (1957), 671–685.

Deutsch, M. "An Experimental Study of the Effects of Cooperation and Competition upon Group Process." *Human Relations*, II (1949), 199–231.

Feshbach, S. & Singer, R. D. "The Effects of Fear Arousal and Suppression of Fear upon Social Perception." *Journal of Abnormal and Social Psychology*, LV (1957), 283–288.

Festinger, L., Schachter, S., & Back, K. *Social Pressures in Informal Groups*. New York: Harper and Brothers, 1950.

Gaylord, R. H., Russell, E., Johnson, C., & Severin, D. "The Relationship of Ratings to Production Records: An Empirical Study." *Personnel Psychology*, IV (1951), 363–371.

Ghiselli, E. E. "Dimensional Problems of Criteria." *Journal of Applied Psychology*, XL (1956), 1–4.

Glickman, A. S. "Effects of Negatively Skewed Ratings on Motivation of the Rated." *Personnel Psychology*, VIII (1955), 39–47.

Gollins, E. S. & Rosenberg, S. "Concept Formation and Impressions of Personality." *Journal of Abnormal and Social Psychology*, LVI (1956), 39–42.

Guilford, J. P. *Psychometric Methods*. New York: McGraw-Hill Book Company, 1954.

Haire, M. "Interpersonal Relations in Collective Bargaining." In Arensberg, C. M., Barkin, S., *et al.* (Eds.), *Research in Industrial Human Relations. A Critical Appraisal*. New York: Harper and Brothers, 1957.

Haire, M. "Psychological Problems Relevant to Business and Industry." *Psychological Bulletin*, LVI (1959), 169–194.

Haire, M. & Grunes, W. "Perceptual Defenses: Processes Protecting an Organized Perception of Another Personality." *Human Relations*, III (1950), 403–412.

Jones, E. E. & deCharms, R. "The Organizing Function of Interaction

Roles in Person Perception." *Journal of Abnormal and Social Psychology*, LVI (1958), 155–164.

KELLY, G. A. *The Psychology of Personal Constructs*. Vol. I. *A Theory of Personality*. New York: W. W. Norton, 1955.

KIPNIS, DOROTHY M. "Interaction Between Members of Bomber Crews as a Determinant of Sociometric Choice." *Human Relations*, X (1957), 263–270.

KIPNIS, D. & GLICKMAN, A. S. "The Development of a Non-Cognitive Battery to Predict Enlisted Performance." *Technical Bulletin 58-9*, Washington, D.C.: U.S. Naval Personnel Research Field Activity, 1958.

KIPNIS, D. & GLICKMAN, A. S. "The Development of a Non-Cognitive Battery: Prediction of Radioman Performance." *Technical Bulletin 59-11*, Washington, D.C.: U.S. Naval Personnel Research Field Activity, 1959.

KOGAN, N. & TAGIURI, R. "Interpersonal Preference and Cognitive Organization." *Journal of Abnormal and Social Psychology*, LVI (1958), 113–116.

LAWSHE, C. H. "Of Management and Measurement." *American Psychologist*, XIV (1959), 290–294.

LEVENTHAL, H. "Cognitive Processes and Interpersonal Predictions." *Journal of Abnormal and Social Psychology*, LV (1957), 176–180.

LEWIN, K., LIPPITT, R., & WHITE, R. T. "Patterns of Aggressive Behavior in Experimentally Created 'Social Climates'." *Journal of Social Psychology*, X (1939), 271–299.

MACKIE, R. R., WILSON, C. L. & BUCKNER, D. N. *Research on the Development of Shipboard Performance Measures*. I–V. ONR Contracts Nonr-7001 and Nonr 1241(00). Los Angeles, California: Management and Marketing Research Corp., 1954.

MANN, R. & DENT, J. "The Supervisor: Member of Two Organizational Families." *Harvard Business Review*, XXXII (1954), 103–112.

MOORE, J. V. Factor Analytic Comparison of Superior and Subordinate Ratings of the Same NCO Supervisors. Washington, D.C.: Human Resources Research Center. Technical Report 53-29, 1953.

MORSE, N. C. & REIMER, E. "The Experimental Change of a Major Organization Variable." *Journal of Abnormal and Social Psychology*, LVI (1956), 120–129.

MURRAY, H. A. "The Effects of Fear upon Estimates of Maliciousness of Other Personalities." *Journal of Social Psychology*, IV (1933), 310–329.

PEPITONE, A. & HAYDEN, R. G. "Some Evidence for Conflict Resolution in Impression Formation." *Journal of Abnormal and Social Psychology*, LI (1955), 302–307.

PEPITONE, A. & KLEINER, R. "The Effects of Threat and Frustration on

Group Cohesiveness." *Journal of Abnormal and Social Psychology,* LIV (1957), 192–199.

Severin, D. "The Predictability of Various Kinds of Criteria." *Personnel Psychology,* V (1952), 93–103.

Sherif, M., White, J. B., & Harvey, O. J. "Status in Experimentally Produced Groups." *American Journal of Sociology,* LX (1955), 370–379.

Spector, A. J. "Influences on Merit Ratings." *Journal of Applied Psychology,* XXXVIII (1954), 393–396.

Steiner, I. D. "Ethnocentrism and Tolerance of Trait Inconsistency." *Journal of Abnormal and Social Psychology,* XLIX (1954), 349–354.

Steiner, I. D. "Interpersonal Behavior as Influenced by Accuracy of Social Perception." *Psychological Review,* LXII (1955), 268–274.

Taylor, E. K., Parker, J. W., & Ford, G. L. "Rating Scale Content. IV. Predictability of Structured and Unstructured Scales." *Personnel Psychology,* XII (1959), 247–266.

Thibaut, J. & Coules, J. "The Role of Communication in the Reduction of Interpersonal Hostility." *Journal of Abnormal and Social Psychology,* XLVII (1952), 770–777.

15 Performance Tests of Educational Achievement

DAVID G. RYANS and
NORMAN FREDERIKSEN

Collaborators: George K. Bennett, Harold O. Gulliksen, G. F. Kuder, Leo Smith, Joseph Tiffin.

From the standpoint of validity one of the most serious errors committed in the field of human measurement has been that which assumes the high correlation of knowledge of facts and principles on the one hand and performance on the other. Nevertheless, examinations for admission to the bar, for medical practice, for teaching, and even tests of ability to cook and sew, are predominantly verbal tests of fact and principle in the respective fields. Relatively little attention has been paid to the testing of performance as such.

Tests of information or knowledge are not, of course, to be discredited. They have an important place in education and industry for purposes of identifying certain kinds of individual differences. These tests are economical to use since they can be administered to large groups of persons and since they may be quickly and accurately scored. However, while they may provide important information about an individual's school progress, his general information background, and his knowledge of facts and principles, they often tell only part of the story. Many situations to which an individual is required to respond are very complex, and effective behavior in those situations demands something in addition to the knowledge of facts and principles.

Knowing the recipe for preparing food (the prescribed ingredients, the proper amounts of each, when each is to be introduced into the mixture, and the conditions under which the preparation should take place) does not, as any novice knows, assure the success of the finished product. Similarly, knowing the names and locations of the clutch, brake, accelerator, steering gear, starter, and gear shift, and knowing the chronology of the operation of these parts does not insure, without practice, that an

From E. F. Lindquist (Ed), *Educational Measurement.* Washington, D. C., American Council on Education, 1951.

individual can drive an automobile. Still again, extensive knowledge of vocabulary and rules of grammar do not, in themselves, assure a student of the ability to express himself and his ideas in literary endeavors. It is for these reasons that performance tests are sometimes important devices for assessing educational achievement.

WHAT IS A PERFORMANCE TEST?

Use of the Term "Performance Test" in the Measurement of Aptitude and the Measurement of Achievement

The term "performance test" has been used in connection with both the measurement of aptitude and the measurement of achievement. An *aptitude test* is commonly thought of as a device for measuring the capacity or potentiality of an individual for a particular kind of behavior. In the measurement of aptitude, previous experience or training on the part of the individual is assumed either to be lacking or to be constant for all individuals comprising the population considered.

It is in the testing of aptitude rather than achievement that performance tests probably have been most frequently mentioned in the literature of psychology. Thus, performance tests have been used extensively for the determination of the general intellectual background or general level of ability of individuals who suffer from language deficiencies. In this sense *performance test* is more or less synonymous with "nonverbal test" and is used primarily to distinguish this type of measurement from that requiring ability to comprehend and respond verbally. Familiar examples of such performance tests of general intellectual ability are those requiring reproduction of patterns of tapping (the Knox Cube Test), those involving the fitting of blocks or forms of differing geometrical shapes into the proper depressions in a form board (the Seguin Form Board), and those involving the tracing of a maze (Porteus Maze Test). Such tests have been widely used in seeking to estimate the capacity for learning of deaf children, foreign-born persons who are unfamiliar with the language in use, and persons who have not had the benefit of instruction in reading and writing.

Other performance tests of aptitude of a somewhat different nature and purpose have been used in the testing of capacity for training with respect to specific skills. Tests of this type are not used primarily as a substitute for intelligence tests, but rather to supplement paper-and-pencil tests of verbal and quantitative abilities in determining the individual's neuromuscular coordination, manual dexterity, spatial perception, etc. Data derived from such tests have been found to be useful in the prediction of ability to learn various mechanical skills and operations.

An achievement test, as contrasted with an aptitude test, presupposes training and is intended to provide a continuum upon which the relative proficiency of different individuals at a particular sort of acquired behavior may be judged.

Performance tests of achievement purport to provide objective means for estimating the proficiency with which a task is performed. The situations involved are functional to a high degree and are likely to be complex. Because of the complexity of the situation, administrative control is often difficult. In spite of such problems associated with the measurement of performance, however, performance tests of achievement have been successfully developed in certain areas of behavior. Perhaps the most familiar tests of this type are those used in determining the progress of students of typewriting. The objective determination of errors, and of units of work produced per unit of time, serves to reveal the accuracy and speed of typewriting performance. Other commonly known performance tests of achievement are those used by state motor vehicle departments in the licensing of automobile drivers. In such tests the operator is required to start, stop, and maneuver the automobile as prescribed by an examiner. Additional examples might be drawn from the fields of industrial arts education, music, and other areas.

It should be noted here that the measurement of aptitude and the measurement of achievement can never be considered entirely separately. Achievement presupposes aptitude, and it is usually impossible to measure aptitude except in terms of previous experience of the individual, even though such experience may not be highly specific. Although this inherent relationship is recognized, the present chapter will, nevertheless, make a practical distinction between the two (aptitude and achievement) for purposes of discussion, and henceforth will consider the topic of performance tests exclusively as they are used in the measurement of achievement.

The Kinds of Performance Tests of Achievement

Performance tests are not at all new in the measurement of achievement. Athletic competition has a long history dating back at least to the Greek games and races 800 years before Christ. Athletic games, meets, and tournaments employ the principles of performance testing to reveal differences in skill of trained individuals or teams. Similarly, musical performance and literary and artistic endeavors have been judged and rated for many years. Although the techniques often may have lacked refinement, and although the control of conditions of administration has not always been adequate, the procedures employed actually were those of performance testing.

More recently, performance tests have been used in industry in determining the proficiency of an employee, or prospective employee, at a particular skill. In these industrial situations, performance tests have been devised for the measurement of ability to "do the job" or to produce some industrial product.

One of the first applications of performance testing in education came with the adaptation of certain psychophysical methods for the judgment of quality of handwriting. The usefulness of performance tests of achievement is obvious in vocational curriculums involving the teaching of such skills as typewriting, machine operations, and food preparation.

In general, performance tests may be divided into three major types: (1) *recognition tests*; (2) *tests involving simulated conditions*; and (3) *work sample tests*.

RECOGNITION TESTS

The recognition type of performance test, as the label implies, attempts to measure the individual's ability to recognize essential characteristics of a performance or product of performance, or to identify objects such as geological or botanical specimens.

A musical selection is played on an instrument and the examinee is required to indicate errors or deficiencies in execution or interpretation. A series of splices of electrical wires is presented and the examinee is required to determine those that are correctly done and those that may be inadequate. The examinee is presented with a piece of mechanical equipment into which certain defects (breakage of parts, poor adjustments, etc.) have been introduced, and he is required to locate and identify the defect. All of these are examples of performance tests involving the recognition of the wrongness or rightness of equipment, a process, or a product.

In other performance tests of the recognition type, the examinee is asked to identify mechanical parts and their functions in a particular assembly, to choose the proper tool or equipment for a defined operation, or to judge the quality of specimens of material or work. In the natural sciences students may be required to identify certain geological specimens, or to describe trees from leaves, twigs, and bark. Similarly, students of art or literature may be required to judge and select superior and inferior artistic and literary productions.

Performance tests of the recognition type are relatively easy to prepare and are adaptable to a fairly wide range of situations. Although they measure important aspects of performance, they do not measure directly the individual's mastery of a skill, technique, or procedure.

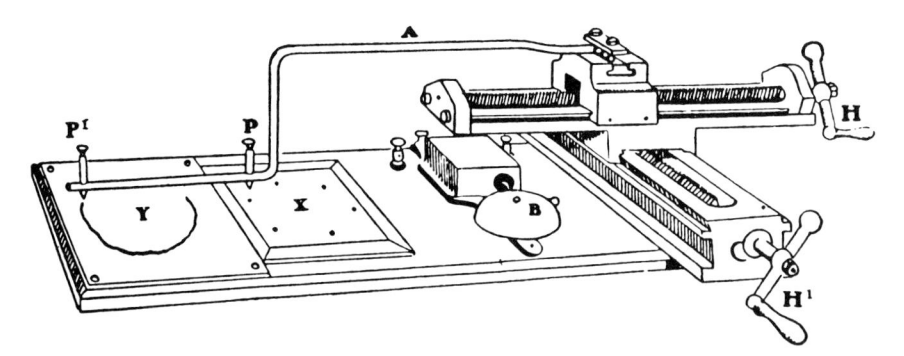

FIGURE 15.1. *Wisconsin Miniature Test for Engine-Lathe Operation. (Reported by Patten [20, p. 451]; illustration reproduced from Viteles [30, p. 229].)*

TESTS INVOLVING SIMULATED CONDITIONS

Performance tests sometimes are designed to copy or simulate the real-life situations or operations that the test is devised to measure. Such tests seek to isolate and duplicate the essential activities of an operation or task. From the examinee's performance in this representative situation, judgment is made regarding his ability or skill in the real situation.

"Simulated condition tests" sometimes have been referred to as miniature tests.[1] Such a test as used in industry, for example, involves apparatus that has been especially constructed for the purpose. Although the test situation is artificial in a sense, it has certain advantages of administration (mock equipment may be provided in multiple sets for testing purposes with greater economy and convenience than can the more expensive and often scarce machinery), and of safety (use of the specially constructed device minimizes dangers that might be involved in the operation of a production machine by a novice or unskilled worker who is being tested).

A number of tests involving simulated conditions have been devised. Figure 15.1 shows the Wisconsin Miniature Test for Engine-Lathe Operation reported by Patten (20). The test apparatus is so constructed that various aspects of the examinee's behavior may be recorded in a convenient manner.

A miniature punch press for measuring ability to operate an industrial punch press, has been described by Tiffin and Greenly (27).

A Vigilance Test described by DeSilva and Channell (8) is used for measuring steering, braking reaction, and combined braking and steering in automobile drivers.

---

[1] Viteles (30) makes a distinction between "miniature" tests and "simulated job" testing, defining the former as a test which reproduces the job in miniature and the latter as a test that simulates the job without reproducing it.

It should be noted that although the use of simulated conditions tests and miniature tests in the measurement of performance has certain advantages, the method must be used with caution and with as complete knowledge as possible of the relationship between the results of the miniature test and the more complete performance with actual equipment and under actual conditions. In the training of gunners' mates for the Navy, for example, the situations involved in repairing a 20-mm. gun on a work table in a land-based training school may be quite different from those that apply when repairing the same gun on a pitching and rolling ship under battle conditions. During World War II the Army Air Forces found that a performance test for bombardiers consisting of bombing desert targets made up of concentric circles, or even a simulated factory or building, was not satisfactory as a measure of an individual's accuracy in bombing a defended target in an actual air raid. And in schoolteaching, performance tests requiring a prospective teacher to conduct a strange class through a day's study may result in quite different estimates of the teacher's ability as compared with judgments and evidences based upon the continuous conduct of a class throughout a term or year.

Obviously then, what may seem to be a valid sample of an isolated task or procedure—the miniature test—may not be a valid sample of the situation *in toto*. This may be due to a number of causes. The physical conditions of the simulated test may not actually reproduce those of the performance in question. Furthermore, it may not be possible to duplicate important psychological conditions of the examinee, such as those related to emotional components of the situation (which often affect performance to a considerable degree) in the simulated test.

Simulated conditions tests of performance, then, may have a useful place in achievement testing, but their limitations must be recognized and overcome if they are to serve the purposes intended.

WORK SAMPLE TESTS

The work sample test of performance consists essentially of a "controlled" tryout under the actual conditions of the work situation. The examinee is required, under normal conditions, to carry through the operations that the job demands.

The work sample test illustrates the "identical elements" test previously described. This type of test is realistic; it has greater face validity than any other type of test or examination. When administered under standard conditions with standardized scoring procedures that have been carefully worked out, the work sample test may provide valid and reliable estimates of achievement for many kinds of behavior or performance.

TESTS OF EDUCATIONAL ACHIEVEMENT   201

In use, the work sample test may include the complete sequence of behavior or operation required by a given job or piece of work, or it may consist only of selected samples of job behavior. Obviously, for many types of activity the former is not economical of time and expense. In general, the more limited the sample of behavior that will predict the whole of that behavior, the greater the advantage so far as economy in test administration is concerned. Therefore, it is common practice to seek

FIGURE 15.2. *Blum Sewing Machine Test. (Reproduced from Blum [4, p. 36].)*

selected samples of performance that are sufficiently predictive of the behavior as a whole to insure adequate measurement of individual proficiency. The problem of sampling in the development of work sample tests will be discussed in greater detail later in this chapter (pages 206–208).

Work sample tests are of two principal kinds: (1) those in which a clear-cut distinction between the "rightness" or "wrongness" of the execution of a skill is possible, and which, therefore, are more or less automatic in scoring; and (2) those which must depend upon the judgment of observers for evaluation and assignment of a score or rank. Target shooting, foot races, mechanical assembly tests, and typewriting tests generally fall into the first category. They are capable of very objective scoring. In contrast, the proficiency demonstrated by an individual at automobile driving or violin playing, or the quality of performance reflected by some product of that performance such as a painting, a novel, a wire splice, or a chest of drawers, are measurable principally in terms of judgments made by presumably competent observers and with the aid of adapted psychophysical methods.

Illustrations of work samples are readily available. The classroom English theme is a work sample of the student's ability to think and express his ideas in verbal form. A pattern employed by the Blum Sewing Machine Test (4) is shown in Figure 15.2. It is designed so that the basic elements of sewing may be directly measured with a work sample. (In this test the examinee is required to sew on the line in situation A and between the lines in situation B. The line is zigzagged to resemble changes in direction required in actual sewing jobs.)

Again, when a student of music is required to play or sing a musical selection for purposes of judgment and criticism, his performance is a work sample.

Among the best-known work sample performance tests are those which require stenographers to take dictation and transcribe their shorthand notes, and those which require the typist to prepare a sample of copy for grading with respect to quality and speed of performance.

USES OF PERFORMANCE TESTS OF ACHIEVEMENT

The immediate purpose of performance tests is the measurement of individual differences in proficiency of performance. But the ultimate purposes or *applications of performance tests* are the principal interest of education and industry. In general, the uses of performance tests of achievement may be classified in four categories: (1) their use for the prediction of successful execution of skills; (2) their use in the diagnosis of deficiencies in performance; (3) their use as a teaching aid; and (4) their use for providing a criterion measure.

For the Prediction of the Successful Execution of Skills

The most obvious use of a performance test is in the determination of the relative proficiency of individuals with respect to a particular procedure or operation—the estimation of job effectiveness. Such estimates of proficiency have important applications in education, industry, and everyday life.

One such use is in the *selection* of personnel in industry. It is generally true that the selection of employees can be significantly improved if the results of an appropriate performance test, or tryout at the operation or job for which the candidate is applying, are employed. A carefully prepared performance test may approximate quite closely the task required in a job situation.

A second use of proficiency data yielded by performance tests is in educational and industrial classification and placement. Since students and employees vary greatly with respect to proficiency at a given skill or type of job behavior, it is important for purposes of economy of time and cost that individuals be "placed" as nearly as possible at the level of their achievement. In the school, and for industrial training, *further instruction should always begin at the level already attained by the individual.* In job placement, *both efficiency of operation and individual satisfaction are enhanced* by placement according to level of ability.

Still another use of determinations of proficiency yielded by performance tests is in the licensing of operators of mechanical equipment. Perhaps the best known of such procedures is the driving test for automobile operators.

For Diagnosis of Deficiencies in Performance

The use of performance tests for the diagnosis of deficiencies in performance also is important. Basically, diagnosis involves an analysis of aspects of behavior (of an individual's strength, of his arithmetic skill, of his industrial productivity, etc.) into observable units and the assessment of the quality of the behavior thus scrutinized. In the diagnosis of achievement the performance test provides standardized conditions for such analysis and for the determination of difficulties or deficiencies in behavior.

A number of years ago Freeman (9) called attention to the possibility of diagnosing faults in handwriting through the measurement of performance. The handwriting performance of the individual (writing arm too near body, thumb too stiff, index finger pressing too heavily, movement too slow, too much lateral movement, etc.) was observed and certain of the difficulties identified.

As a Teaching Aid

Although this use is one that perhaps is less commonly recognized, performance tests may contribute significantly to educational programs as *teaching aids*. They are of particular importance in that they provide motivation to the student through the direct revelation of success or failure in execution of the function toward which training is directed. And, of equal importance, they provide the instructor with a clean-cut means of evaluating his teaching—that is, revealing areas in which the students are, or are not, attaining desired objectives. Both experiment and experience have called attention to the effect of "knowledge of progress" upon learning. The performance test provides a direct and unequivocal indication of satisfactory or unsatisfactory performance and also stimulates the student to try to improve his skill.

During World War II, performance tests were found to be particularly effective in bringing about the improvement of instruction and learning. Despite the fact that skills required of service personnel were usually of a distinctly practical nature, instruction in the service schools was sometimes dominated by lectures and verbal descriptions of apparatus and its operations, or at best by demonstrations which were *assumed* to be useful in acquainting the trainee with the necessary techniques or understanding. Even when "learning by doing" was undertaken, its purpose was often defeated by the lack of individual supervision and attention required to avoid wrong learning. The introduction of performance tests in many of these schools focused attention upon familiarity with equipment and on the skills and understanding of procedures necessary for its proper maintenance, operation, and repair.

Regardless of what the teacher or course syllabus may describe as the course objectives, the efforts of the students will be directed mainly toward passing the examinations. The *course objectives, therefore, are likely to be achieved to the extent that they are reflected in the testing program*. Recognition of this fact, provided it results in examinations which truly reflect the objectives of the course, will go a long way toward improving learning. If a course or curriculum has as its aim the development of skills other than those of a verbal nature, the use of performance tests is essential to effective learning.

Providing a Criterion Measure

When the behavior involved in a situation is broad enough and representative enough of the situation as a whole, the performance is itself the criterion behavior for that situation. Consequently, performance test data, particularly when they refer to work samples, provide a more satisfactory measure of criterion behavior than is usually available. Because performance tests serve as a measure of the criterion, they may be of use in several important ways.

Performance test data may provide, first of all, *a criterion for research*. Information yielded by performance tests makes possible the validation of other measures which, although of a more indirect nature, may be more convenient for use and more economical in administration. In many situations it is difficult and expensive to administer performance tests to large numbers of examinees. Such situations demand the construction of psychometric instruments that will yield measurements related to the criterion and which also will be practicable. In the construction of aptitude tests for various skills and operations, performance tests may provide the criterion against which the available second-order measures can be judged (19).

Again, performance test results may be used as a *criterion for advancement* or promotion of individuals in training and in service. The most usable index of present level of attainment, and, by inference, of the qualifications of the individual for successive levels of training or job activity, is provided by the performance test.

Finally, performance tests provide a *criterion for the general evaluation of a training program* in school or industry. Since the primary purpose of many educational activities is the progressive development of skill, the accomplishments of such a program can best be evaluated in terms of the proficiency in such skills attained by the students.

DEVELOPMENT OF THE PERFORMANCE TEST

Many performance tests have a high degree of "face validity"; they appear to duplicate the job situation so closely that there seems to be no question that they are measuring the intended abilities and measuring them well. Face validity alone, however, is no guarantee of real validity or of high accuracy of measurement. An individual might, for example, drive an automobile over a standard driving course with satisfactory proficiency, but still experience considerable difficulty in the more confused emotional and operational situation involved in driving his automobile along certain outlet routes at five o'clock in the afternoon in New York City. While the performance test, requiring operation of the vehicle over a standard course, may have sampled satisfactorily certain aspects of driving ability, the sampling may have been too narrow to be sufficiently valid. Again, a typist who has drilled intensively on a particular paragraph of copy, or a pianist who has practiced diligently on a particular selection for a recital, may satisfactorily "pass" a performance test involving skill at the particular copy or musical selection studied. Such a test probably would not be a valid or reliable test, however, of the one individual's typing skill or the other's musical accomplishment. Performance tests must be submitted to the same empirical checks of reliability and validity as are paper-and-pencil tests of aptitude and achievement, and with the same degree of rigor.

The Problem of Sampling

The validity of a performance test will depend to a large extent on the particular tasks which are chosen to be included in it to represent the more general abilities which the test is designed to measure. The choice of these tasks should be made in the light of thorough knowledge of the job as a whole, as exemplified by a job analysis, as well as upon various practical considerations.

In selecting sample tasks for inclusion in a performance test, limitations often are imposed by such factors as time and amount of equipment and personnel available. If it is desired to develop a performance test to measure ability of trainees in disassembling and assembling diesel engines, where only four engines are available for fifty trainees, and where the total job might require several hours for a team of men working together, building a test which can be individually administered to all trainees within a reasonable amount of time and with the supervision of only two or three instructors would seem to be impossible. But it is in situations of this sort that performance tests are badly needed for such purposes as the evaluation of training, the motivation of trainees, and individual guidance and placement.

The problem may be solved by choosing parts of the total job to represent the task as a whole. In choosing jobs to be included in a test, the test constructor probably would not select them on a random basis or on the basis of the proportion of the total time devoted to certain jobs. Much of the task might be of routine nature, such as assembling nuts and bolts to hold a housing in place. It probably would be more desirable to choose the salient parts of the task, those which are especially important because they are difficult or because they are crucial to the proper operation of the equipment. One should be guided in this selection by a careful job analysis, by the opinions of experts, and by his own experience in learning to perform the task.

In the interests of economy of time, it would be desirable to include in each task a minimum of easy, routine operations. There is little to be gained by requiring an examinee in a test situation to remove and replace a whole series of nuts and bolts when one or two such operations might be sufficient to demonstrate knowledge of the correct procedure.

As many of the really salient tasks should be included in the performance test as is possible with the time and equipment available. If amount of equipment is a limiting factor, this condition may sometimes be overcome by breaking each piece of equipment up into subassemblies, so that different people can work on the same equipment simultaneously.

Various specific recommendations have been made for the selection of samples for performance test situations. Chapman (6), for example, makes several suggestions for choosing a work sample for a performance test in industry. He states that: the operation should be sufficiently exact to admit of accurate standardization and to enable objective judgments to be made; the task chosen should have face validity, and should be of a nature to command respect and establish the confidence of tradesmen; the materials, tools, and equipment should be reduced to the smallest practical quantity and should be capable of standardization so that all tests may be given under uniform conditions; the performance should not require an undue length of time; the performance should involve as little repetition of identical procedures as possible; and a preliminary tryout of a performance test should always be made using experts as the examinees to detect possible problems or difficulties. Adkins and Primoff (1) suggest further that the sampling of activities should be as wide as is practical; that each workpiece (test situation) should be used to test as many of the activities involved in the behavior as possible; and that the work sample should be designed for ease of measurement with available devices as well as with a view to its representativeness.

If the number of separate jobs which can be included in a test situation is small and represents only a small proportion of the possible jobs, then coaching in these specific tasks to the exclusion of the job as a whole becomes a possibility. Instructors who are interested in having a good test record might be guilty of such coaching, or information about the tests might be passed on from one generation of students to the next. The difficulties in this problem can be minimized by developing sets of alternative forms of a test which in the aggregate cover all the important features of the total job. Then if information as to which form of the test will be given is withheld, students and instructors must be prepared for all possibilities.

On the other hand, it may be that there are only a few really important features in the total job, and that all of these can be included in the test. If this is true, then there is no objection to specific coaching, and it would in fact be desirable for trainees to know in advance exactly what comprises their test. One of the characteristics of a good performance test is that practice or "cramming" for the test results in improvement in ability to do a job. In contrast, cramming for an oral trade test probably would result in little or no improvement in job performance.

The ideal method of investigating the validity of a performance test is, as is true of any achievement test, to study its relationship to a suitable criterion measure. The difficulty, of course, is that a criterion that is more satisfactory than the performance test results themselves is usually lacking. The development of a criterion based on "on-the-job performance" is highly desirable as a check on the success with which good judgment has been employed in selecting appropriate tasks for inclusion in the test. It will also be of direct assistance for the development of satisfactory scoring standards.

Evaluating the Results of Performance Testing

The scoring of a performance test obviously will depend upon the kind of skill being measured. The relative importance of speed, accuracy, use of approved methods, or quality of the product must be weighed, and a scoring procedure must be developed which will adequately reflect the decisions reached. In filing a block of metal to meet certain specifications, for example, one may ask if it is more important that the job be done quickly, that the specifications be exactly met, that the file be held in a prescribed manner, or that the finish of the product be free of scratches. The relative importance of these and other characteristics of the performance must be decided, and each must be adequately represented and properly weighted on a score sheet. The decision as to the nature of the judgments to be made will ordinarily be based on the evidence from job analysis, expert judgment, and one's own experience in learning to perform the job. Final evaluation of the procedures developed should ideally be based on the relationship of the various test "items" to a satisfactory external criterion.

In many situations the choices are offered of measuring *performance in process* or of measuring the results of the performance, the *product*. Thus, in the hand-tool shop an individual's performance in filing a piece of metal may be judged either from the way he holds the file, the kind of strokes he uses, etc., or it may be judged from the quality of the finished product. Similarly, in typewriting, the typist's position, touch, etc., may be observed and rated; or the typed copy may be graded for conformance to prescribed standards. Even in schoolteaching performance there is often a choice between observing and rating a teacher as she guides her pupils in learning, and judging the proficiency of her teaching from the product, the improvement in learning evidenced by the pupils (in relation to their ability).

Measurable characteristics of the performance in process. What are the measurable characteristics of performance in process? A number of specialized scoring methods might be mentioned, but these resolve themselves generally into two major categories: (1) those relating to the estimation of quality of performance; and (2) those having to do with the speed, or rate, of performance.

In some situations one of these characteristics is definitely more important than the other. In many kinds of behavior they are both important and serve to complement each other. Thus, in the familiar example of typewriting it is highly desirable that the typist prepare copy *both* accurately and rapidly. A rapidly typed letter that is inaccurate will be of little use; on the other hand, since a principal purpose in using a typewriter is to increase efficiency, there is also a premium on speed.

If success on the job is dependent largely on the speed with which it is carried out, as in taking dictation or loading magazines on a 20-mm. gun, then obviously speed should figure strongly in the scoring of the test. If errors are important, then appropriate penalties should be substracted or separate speed and error scores reported. If quality is the primary consideration, as in machining metal parts to close tolerances or in playing a musical instrument, then speed should be given little or no weight in the score.

It might be mentioned here that in certain types of training situations the use of speed scores has proved to be an excellent motivating device, even though improving speed was not considered a major objective of the teaching. Competition for low time-scores among gunner's mate trainees in Navy schools, for example, proved to be an excellent incentive for practice in the disassembling and assembling of guns.

In the measurement of speed or rate of production, the primary scoring concern is that accuracy and uniformity in counting and timing be attained. The use of automatic counting devices, such as the Veeder counter, is often possible. In other situations the counting process is facilitated by assembling the finished products in cases or racks that are constructed to hold a given number of units. For timing purposes, chronoscopes or kymographs may be used, but the stop watch will be satisfactory for most situations where production rate is a major concern.

Time required to produce a single *unit of work* may be used as a measure of production rate, particularly when the time required to produce a sample is relatively long, but it is usually less satisfactory because of the greater unreliability of this method than counting the *number of units produced during a given time*. In either case an average time required to produce a unit of work may readily be computed. Timing separate units does, of course, have the advantage of making possible the computation of a measure of variability in production rate.

Although quality and speed of performance are the two major measurable characteristics of performance in process, it may be noted that performance is sometimes judged from such additional correlates of performance as learning time, accident rate, attitude toward job, etc. These will not be discussed here in greater detail.

Measurable characteristics of the product of performance. In measuring the product of performance, the principal characteristics to be considered relate to the *quality* of the product. In measuring quality, certain standards (standards of appearance, usability, etc.) are adopted and the product is judged in relation to such standards.

In the case of a piece of metal turned on a lathe, for example, the product must conform to prescribed measurements or dimensions in order to serve the purpose intended. Somewhat similarly, a typing specimen will be judged in light of certain standards of spacing, position on the page, and freedom from error. Thus, conformance to prescribed dimensions, standards of general appearance, freedom from error, strength, and suitability for use may be used to judge the quality of a product and, by inference, the quality of the performance of an individual.

Often it is possible to objectify the measurement of quality of the product through the use of patterns, gauges, and scoring keys; the product may be classified, and scored, as it does or does not conform to the pattern or key. For some work samples such automatic scoring is less feasible, and it is necessary to resort to the judgments of qualified observers of the relative goodness or poorness of the product as it is compared with some agreed-upon standard or as it is compared with other similar products.

Should measurement of performance be directed at the process or the product? While performance may often be measured either in process or in terms of the product, some situations are more limited and offer less choice. Occasionally the product of performance *is not* measurable apart from the performance in process. Playing a musical instrument is an example of such a case. Driving a car (unless driving record over a period of time, and in terms of such recordable data as number of fender dents, number of accidents, or number of traffic violations, is considered) is another. In still other situations, analysis of the process is difficult and it is generally not possible to measure the performance in process except by judging the product of the performance. Examples of this sort are the writing of musical selections, the composition of literary products, etc.

In other instances, *both* the performance in process and the product of the performance may be measured by judging an individual's proficiency at a given sort of behavior. Certain advantages, and also certain disadvantages, are attached to each.

For example, it will be recalled that while the objective measurement of performance in process is possible in some situations, many times it is necessary to resort to subjective judgments which tend to be unreliable. Even when such ratings are refined and when they are made by trained and competent judges, there may be uncertainty as to whether the reported differences in performance are due to differences between the performances being judged or to the variability of the judges. For such reasons, it may be of doubtful value in some situations to attempt to measure the performance in process.

On the other hand, it *is* highly *desirable* to measure *actual operation*, or performance in process, in many cases. The final product of performance may appear to be of satisfactory quality, but the operational methods or procedures employed may have been unsatisfactory, even to the extent of creating a hazard to personnel or equipment. A taxi driver, for example, may successfully and speedily negotiate a route through traffic, but may at the same time constitute a problem for other drivers and pedestrians along the way. In such an instance, some attempt must be made to measure performance in process.

Again, as has already been noted, it is impossible in some situations to measure the product of performance apart from the process. Musical performance provides a case in point. Such performance may be recorded, it is true, but measurements of that performance must always relate to judgments made *during* the execution. Examples of a similar nature indicate the obvious need for measures of performance in process.

In general, measurement of the product of performance is likely to be somewhat more reliable than the measurement of the performance in process. Through the use of patterns, gauges, graded sample quality scales, etc., a relatively high degree of accuracy of measurement can be attained. Another advantage of the measurement of the product of performance over the measurement of performance in process lies in the relatively more convenient administrative procedures of the former. Fewer proctors or administrative assists are required for judging the product, and lesser demands are made upon them. Usually the product can be judged or graded at any time following completion of the performance.

However, an important consideration in measuring the product of performance has to do with the irreparability or irrevocability of errors or flaws that may have been introduced at some early stage of workmanship on the product. Such errors may be impossible to correct and may influence all later operations. While a major portion of the workmanship may have been of superior quality, the early mistake may detract seriously from the product as a whole.

Techniques for the measurement of performance in process. In the measurement of the *quality* of performance in process, the methods available are largely subjective in nature and usually consist of ratings of behavior made by presumably competent judges.

Objective recording devices have been constructed in a few instances. For example, Barens and Amrine (3) describe a method and apparatus for automatic scoring, in terms of time and errors, of the performance of driving a screw down into a tapped hole. Behavior of the subject of the workpiece is transmitted over an electric circuit and a record of performance produced on a kymograph. Similarly, Lindahl (15) developed a procedure for analyzing the foot movements of cutoff machine operators, obtaining an objective recording of individual patterns of performance on a moving paper tape. With a certain amount of ingenuity similar automatic devices employing the kymograph, Veeder counters, or other available recording instruments may be developed.

For the most part, however, variations of the psychophysical method of single stimuli, or absolute judgment, have been employed in the past, and remain a principal source of data, in scoring quality of performance in process. The performance is simply "rated," with reference to some specified continuum, by a qualified observer. In practice, the use of such methods ranges all the way from relatively superficial judgments of the "satisfactory-unsatisfactory" type to fairly detailed ratings which provide for the breaking-down of operations and the judgment of separate processes or operations entering into the performance. Perhaps the most common of these procedures is that which is based upon analysis of the performance into "steps" or operations and which makes use of a point-scale with certain values arbitrarily assigned for the successful completion

---

To Saw to a Line with a Rip and Cross-Cut Saw

Tools and Materials: Sharp rip saw and cross-cut saw, bench, wood vise, and piece of wood.

Directions: Observe pupil as he works, and rate him on the following points

1. *Clamping stock:* 1 2 3 4 5 6 7 8 9 10
Stock should be so held that it will not be loosened or cracked, and that its position will facilitate sawing.
2. *Starting cut:* 1 2 3 4 5 6 7 8 9 10
With thumb at line, saw should be placed against the thumb. Saw should be pulled back slowly a few times to make a groove, then pushed forward.
3. *Holding saw:* 1 2 3 4 5 6 7 8 9 10
Saw should be held firmly. For cross-cut saw, angle should be 45 degrees; for rip saw, 60 degrees.
4. *Stroke:* 1 2 3 4 5 6 7 8 9 10
Stroke should be long and even, not too fast. Proper angle should be kept during sawing. Line should be followed.
5. *Ending cut:* 1 2 3 4 5 6 7 8 9 10
The piece being cut off should be held with the free hand. Saw strokes should be slow and with little pressure so as to prevent breaking off the end.

FIGURE 15.3. *A rough point-scale for judging ability to saw a line with a rip and crosscut saw. (From Proffitt, Ericson, and Newkirk [21].)*

of given operations. A rough scale[2] of this sort, devised for judging ability to use a saw, is shown in Figure 15.3 (21).

In measuring efficiency of performance in terms of the *time required to complete* a phase or cycle of the operation, various timing devices may be used. In some instances very exact measurements requiring precision timing may be necessary. However, under most conditions of performance testing the use of a stop watch for timing will provide entirely satisfactory and useful score units. When the speed of performance of a group of examinees is to be tested, it may be desirable to utilize the services of a central timekeeper who, in addition to giving the starting signal for the test, will, at intervals, indicate the amount of elapsed time. This method was used to advantage in the administration of performance tests in Navy gunnery schools during World War II.

Techniques for measuring the product of performance. A number of devices have been used for measuring relatively accurately the *quality* of the product of performance insofar as such activities as typing, handwriting, woodworking, electrical wiring, mechanical assembly, etc., are concerned. Error scores have been used in typewriting, patterns and gauges in wood and metal work, and graded sample quality scales in handwriting, electrical work, metal work, etc.

In judging the quality of many products that must conform to prescribed dimensions, devices such as rulers, combination squares, Vernier scales, and micrometer calipers may be employed. However, the use of such instruments, which require relatively precise reading, may be very unreliable (due to observer errors) particularly when a fairly large number of samples are being measured. Lawshe and Tiffin (14), for example, found the use of precision measuring instruments in industrial plants very inaccurate.

In order to facilitate and objectify the evaluation of a product, patterns and gauges often may be developed, permitting relatively automatic scoring. Such instruments may be devised to indicate clearly on a "pass-fail" basis whether or not certain standards are met by the product. (24).

In Figure 15.4 is shown a relatively simple device revealing "wind" or unevenness of a flat surface (19). This device was constructed in developing criterion measures for tests of mechanical ability.

Mechanical and electrical devices also may be employed in determining the relative quality of the product. Thus, a soldered joint may be

[2] The question may be raised whether or not such an arbitrary rating device properly may be called a "scale." Certainly the requirements of a scale as it is viewed technically (an established zero point and equality of intervals) are lacking. However, sufficiently high reliability is often obtained with such relatively crude instruments, and if such is the case, there is justification for their use in practical situations.

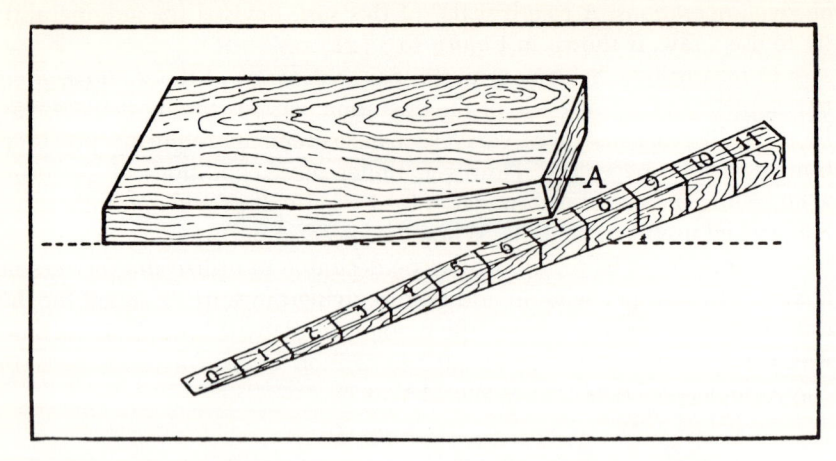

FIGURE 15.4. *Simple device for revealing "wind" or unevenness of a flat surface. (From Paterson and Elliott [19, p. 190].)*

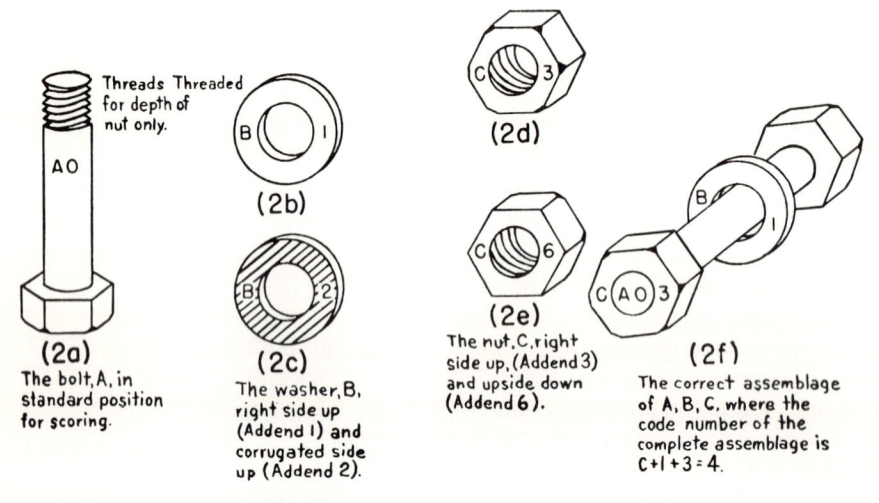

FIGURE 15.5. *Assembly of bolt, nut, and washer, illustrating use of code numbers in scoring performance tests. (From Toops [28, p. 147].)*

measured for its conductivity with special types of galvanometers. Similarly, appropriate apparatus may be applied to determine the fastness of a joint in woodwork, the tensile strength of a metal product, and the like.

Toops (28) has proposed a method which employs code numbers to objectify and facilitate the scoring of the product of performance tests. Through the use of this rather simple but ingenious procedure, parts of the product are identified by numbers and letters, and the scoring becomes a simple clerical operation requiring little or no mechanical skill or understanding on the part of the proctor or recorder. Figure 15.5 illustrates Toops's proposal, showing an assembly of a hexagonal bolt, machine nut, and washer with corrugated side. The score is the sum of the weights assigned to individual elements, and only the correct combination of operations gives the correct sum.

Although it is possible to measure many products of performance objectively, more subjective methods must be resorted to in some cases. In the judgment of handwriting or freehand drawing, for example, there is no pattern or gauge or scale that can be used to yield a direct measurement of goodness or satisfactoriness of the product. In such situations, rating devices of various sorts may be employed. While the estimates derived from such methods are likely to be less reliable than those of more objective techniques, they frequently can be refined to a point where their use can be defended.

The Minnesota Food Score Cards (5) were devised to measure the quality of foods that had been prepared in home economics classes. The procedure is not highly refined from a psychophysical standpoint. In use, a score or rating is simply assigned to each of various characteristics or qualities of the food prepared. Figure 15.6 shows the score card used in rating the cooking of bacon.

BACON			2
	1	2	3	Score
Appearance	1. Curled or has decided humps	Fairly straight and flat	1.
Color	2. Too light or dark brown	Even, light golden brown	2.
Tenderness	3. Brittle or tough	Crisp, easily cut with fork	3.
Flavor	4. Burned, acrid, raw	Mild, meaty, well done	4.
			SCORE

FIGURE 15.6. *Score card used in rating the cooking of bacon. (From Brown[5].)*

A somewhat similar point-scale rating form for "fastening" in woodworking, as described by Adkins (1), is shown in Figure 15.7.

Some products of performance are not as readily analyzed and broken down into units or segments as those just described. In order to achieve maximum objectivity and reliability in the judgment of such

(a) Nails:
- (1) Straightness.......... 1 2 3 4 5 6 7 8 9 10
Are nails driven straight, heads square with wood, no evidence of bending?
- (2) Hammer marks....... 1 2 3 4 5 6 7 8 9 10
Is wood free of hammer marks around nails?
- (3) Splitting............. 1 2 3 4 5 6 7 8 9 10
Is wood free of splits radiating from nail holes?
- (4) Depth................ 1 2 3 4 5 6 7 8 9 10
Are depths of nails uniform and of pleasing appearance?
- (5) Spacing.............. 1 2 3 4 5 6 7 8 9 10
Are nails spaced too close or too far apart?
- (6) Utility............... 1 2 3 4 5 6 7 8 9 10
Will the nails hold?

(b) Screws:
- (1) Slots................. 1 2 3 4 5 6 7 8 9 10
Are slots free of splitting and other evidence of driving strains?
- (2) Straightness.......... 1 2 3 4 5 6 7 8 9 10
Are screws straight, heads parallel with surface?
- (3) Splitting............. 1 2 3 4 5 6 7 8 9 10
Is wood free of splits in the area of screws?
- (4) Screw driver marks.... 1 2 3 4 5 6 7 8 9 10
Is wood free of screw driver marks near screws?
- (5) Countersinking....... 1 2 3 4 5 6 7 8 9 10
Is countersinking neat and of satisfactory depth?
- (6) Spacing.............. 1 2 3 4 5 6 7 8 9 10
Are screws spaced too close or too far apart?
- (7) Utility............... 1 2 3 4 5 6 7 8 9 10
Will the screws hold?

FIGURE 15.7. *Point-scale rating form for "fastening" in woodworking. (From Adkins [1, p. 231].)*

products, a series of samples of the product, ranked in order of quality, may be used as a standard against which any given product can be compared and scored. Rating scales of this type have been referred to as "graded sample quality scales."

Such psychophysical methods as the *method of equal appearing intervals* and the *paired comparisons method* may be employed to establish scale values for samples of products of varying grades of qual-

TESTS OF EDUCATIONAL ACHIEVEMENT 217

ity. The judgment of the quality of a particular product may then be made by comparing the product in question with the graded samples and assigning the value, or score, of the sample that the product most closely resembles.

One of the most familiar examples of such a scale of samples of graded quality is that which has been used for assessing the quality of handwriting. An example of the Ayres Handwriting Scale is shown in Figure 15.8 (2).

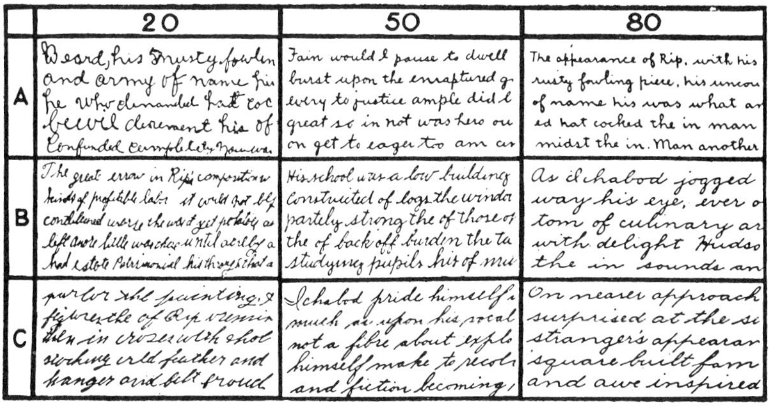

FIGURE 15.8. *Ayres Handwriting Scale (From Ayres [2].)*

The graded sample quality is relatively easy to devise, although some acquaintance with psychophysical methods is necessary. A large number of samples of the product are assembled, and these are ranked in order of quality by experts. Samples may then be selected in accordance with the judgments of the experts and with regard to clear-cut and consistent differences in judged quality.

The problem of scoring standards. Ordinarily, it is desirable to employ a scoring procedure which will satisfactorily distribute (or spread out) the scores of examinees with respect to the performance being measured. In using the results of a test which thus distributes the scores, an important problem is always that of determining the point in the distribution that will define satisfactory performance—in other words, the "passing point." It is one thing to say that an individual's performance netted him a given number of points or that these points were equivalent to a certain percentile rank, and sometimes quite another to attempt to translate the score points into terms of "satisfactory" or "unsatisfactory" performance.

Setting a "passing point" for performance tests may be accomplished by relating the score distribution to the criterion in some cases, but this often is an uncertain undertaking. Just what total score on the Rating Form for Fastening shown in Figure 15.7 represents satisfactory performance? Would the performance an individual who received a rating of 10 on all of the "screws" items except items 3 and 7, and who hopelessly split the wood into which the screw was being driven, be considered satisfactory? Would his raw score of 50 represent approximately the same level of attainment as the score of another individual who received ratings of 7 on each of the seven items? Usually one must resort to the judgment of competent persons and arbitrarily decide upon the pass-fail point or other defined points of a score distribution.

In many situations in which performance tests are used, the "minimum essentials" of the performance may be considered in establishing the satisfactory-unsatisfactory point. Such a test might consist of selected essential operations, or qualities, all of which must be properly demonstrated in order for the performance to be satisfactory. During the war, for example, tests of this sort were developed for use at one of the amphibious training bases, where it was necessary that every trainee be able to recognize beachmarker signals indicating where certain types of cargo were to be unloaded, signals identifying various types of landing craft, and the like. A minimum essentials test would be appropriately used in situations involving relatively simple operations without mastery of all of which it would be dangerous or impossible for a person to carry out the activity in question.

Reliability

In scoring any test, the judgment of an observer is to some degree involved, even though the scoring may consist only of counting the dots that appear through a scoring stencil or reading the dial of a test-scoring machine. In performance testing, the role of the observer may become considerably enhanced in importance. Not everyone is qualified, for example, to grade the performance of a piano concerto or to judge the skill of a trainee in using a lathe. If the over-all reliability of a performance test is found to be high, one need not be concerned about the reliability of observer judgment; but if the reliability is low, it is necessary to study the relative contributions to a reliability coefficient of (1) consistency of performance of the testee and (2) consistency of judgments of the observer who is making the evaluations.

Data for studying observer reliability may easily be obtained, if some *product* of the performance such as a theme or a hand-tool project is to be rated, merely by having the same set of products independently judged by several observers. If the performance itself is to be judged, it is ordinarily possible to arrange for several observers to view the performance simultaneously and make independent judgments. If the intercorrelations of the several sets of ratings are on the average high (say, .90), reliability of the observers may be said to be satisfactory. This method also permits the identification of the poorest judge on the basis of lower correlations of his ratings with those of other judges. In the event that the intercorrelations are on the average low, steps must be taken to improve the reliability of judging the performance.

The nature of the steps to be taken will, of course, depend on the characteristics of the testing situation. (1) In some instances, selection of better-trained observers might be sufficient. (2) Even with well-qualified observers, it might also be necessary to give special training with respect to definitions of the characteristics to be rated and of the items on the scale used in rating in order to insure agreement among judges on these points. (3) Designing a rating sheet such that various aspects of the performance are objectively defined and independently judged and on which instructions for use are clearly stated may improve consistency of rating. (4) Development of instruments for objectively measuring the products may bring about the desired improvement in reliability.

For example, in one shop training situation it was found that the correlations among raters in judging metal objects constructed to certain specifications by trainees varied from .11 to .55. When a set of simple taper gauges was constructed for use in measuring the products and when the raters were instructed in their use, the correlations for the same judges increased to .93 and .94. When the same raters repeated the measurements after an interval of ten days, the correlation of first ratings with second ratings was found to be .97.

It is possible to study the *reliability of performance* (as distinguished from judging performance) only when the reliability of judging performance has been shown to be adequate. When this condition has been satisfactorily met, the special problems having to do with measuring the consistency of performance of the examinee should be considered.

When a performance test is made up of a series of tasks involving, let us say, the disassembly and assembly of a machine, its adjustment and operation, and the analysis of defects in the machine, a high degree of specificity is often found in ability to perform the various tasks, particularly in a training situation. An individual who can do one task well may do poorly on other tasks. Such specificity may indicate a real lack of generalized ability in the area of mechanical manipulation, or it may merely reflect irregularities in the training program. Whatever the cause, such a situation would appear to show low test reliability when reliability is measured by correlating scores on one set of tasks with scores on a second set of tasks (split-half or alternate-form reliability). It may sometimes be necessary to make a special investigation to determine whether the low reliability is the fault of the test or the fault of a training situation which does not consistently give the same amount and quality of instruction to each student on each part of the curriculum. In such cases the use of test-retest reliability may be appropriate.

However, test-retest reliability also has distinct limitations in certain situations. In a training situation it may be found that a test-retest type of reliability may not be feasible because participation in the first test situation may constitute a significant amount of additional practice for some of the trainees, but not for others. The test-retest correlation may be seriously affected by such circumstances.

Variation in condition of the equipment used in a performance test is still another source of unreliability which must be taken into account and guarded against, particularly when complex operations, such as difficult assembly jobs or precise adjustments, are involved.

Perhaps the essential difficulty in the development of performance tests of high reliability is that relatively few tasks or items are likely to be involved in the testing. In cases where many simple short operations are required, as in operating a typewriter, it is not difficult to build tests of satisfactory reliability; but in any operation involving relatively long, complex tasks, such as in the assembly of an engine or the construction of a woodwork sample, the performance test is likely to be of a lower reliability unless it is an exceptionally lengthy one.

Steps in Developing a Performance Test

1. *Making a job analysis.* The first step in the development of a performance test is to make a very careful study of the specific skills and abilities involved in activities the test is intended to measure. Such a study might best culminate in a formal job analysis report. Methods of job analysis have been adequately described elsewhere, and it will not be necessary to discuss the procedures here. If at all feasible, the test constructor might well be advised to learn the job himself. He may thus come to understand better some of the more subtle aspects of the performance which are difficult to convey in words. The usual observational methods involved in making the job analysis might also be supplemented by such devices as time-and-motion studies and analyses of causes of failure on the job.

If the performance test is to be employed in a training situation, it usually is desirable to go beyond the stated objectives of the curriculum, and study the job for which training is being given. It is quite possible that the curriculum is in some respects unrealistic, and that tests which would adequately assess school achievement might not be as closely related to job success as would be possible or desirable. In developing tests of school achievement, it is entirely possible that contributions can thus be made which will lead to the improvement of the training situation.

2. *Selecting tasks to represent the job.* The next step in performance test construction is to determine which of the operations or skills are to be tested among those described in the job analysis, and what specific tasks are to be chosen to represent those skills. In general, as wide a variety of specific tasks should be included in the test as is feasible from the standpoint of such practical considerations as amount of time and equipment available. Special care should probably be taken to insure that any skills which are commonly responsible for failures are included. Short tasks usually are preferable to long ones, since a larger number of items can be included in the test and higher reliability probably secured.

After it is decided what abilities are to be tested, it is necessary to determine whether the performance of the task itself (performance in process) or some product of that performance should be evaluated. Sometimes the solution is obvious; if a test for truck drivers is to be developed, there is no product to be judged and the only possibility is to observe the performance itself. On the other hand, the product may be of primary importance and the process by which that object is produced of no particular consequence. In a test of English composition where the product is an essay, one would not ordinarily be concerned with the time required, the revising and rewriting indulged in, or the frustrations and blocks experienced during the preparation of the essay. In still other situations both the performance in process and the characteristics of the product may be of importance; for a given type of performance it might be desirable to note whether or not safety precautions were observed, if procedures likely to damage equipment were employed, or if wasteful errors had been made (even though later corrected), as well as to rate the product on its important characteristics.

In the event that a product is to be evaluated, it is necessary to decide what workpieces or job samples will be produced. The specifications of the product must be described in sufficient detail so that variability among products of different examinees is a function of differences in ability of testees rather than differences in interpretations of the job specifications. In the measurement of proficiency in use of hand tools, a test situation might be developed which would require the use of layout tools, hack saw, and files. On completion of the workpiece, the product could be measured and inspected and ratings made to describe success in using these tools. A still better method might be to rate the product at the end of each of various stages in its production—after layout, sawing, rough filing, etc. Such a procedure probably would yield more reliable scores and would furnish information which might have greater diagnostic value. Other test situations might similarly be arranged to yield measures of proficiency in the use of other hand tools.

In setting up the job specifications for a test, it should be kept in mind that *time* is an important consideration in performance testing. If a testee is required to spend a large proportion of his testing time in routine or repetitive operations, fewer items can be included in the test and its reliability will necessarily suffer. Ordinarily, for example, a half-inch hack saw cut would be as good as one inch for testing purposes and would take roughly half the time, perhaps allowing an opportunity for adding another test item.

Similar considerations are involved in selecting tasks where the performance in process is to be observed. As wide as possible a coverage of the basic skills revealed by the job analysis should be sought, including particularly any tasks which give opportunity for errors which have been found to be common causes of failure. Testing time should be used to the fullest possible extent for performing the crucial or difficult aspects of the job, rather than routine operations.

3. *Developing the rating form.* Having selected a series of tasks or qualities to be included in the performance test, the next procedure is to determine the features of the performance, or of the product, which are to be rated, and to devise suitable rating forms.

The rating form or record sheet may consist merely of a listing in correct order of the operations which must be carried out to perform the job assigned, with space to check whether or not each operation was correctly performed. It is possible also to permit the judge to rate the quality of the performance of each operation, but in many situations it is preferable to reduce the scoring to a yes-no check on each characteristic of the performance considered important, making sure that the performance description is sufficiently unambiguous as to permit high observer agreement.

The performance descriptions employed may be given differential weighting if it is desired to increase the variance in total score contributed by certain operations or qualities.

If time required to perform the task is important, this may also be recorded and used in the scoring of the test.

When the product of the performance is to be rated, a list of the characteristics which serve to differentiate a good from a poor product should be compiled. Some of these characteristics may be amenable to direct measurement with a gauge or other measuring device; others may require a more subjective judgment. The accuracy of such judgments may be increased by the use of graphic or descriptive rating scales, or by comparison with a series of products which have been scaled with respect to the attribute under consideration. These topics have been discussed in some detail in an earlier section of this chapter.

4. *Surveying the practical limitations.* Before developing an "operating plan" for administering a performance test, due account should be taken of various factors in the situation which impose limitations upon the

"ideal" procedure which might otherwise be outlined. These restrictions are likely to be related to such factors as amount of time, equipment, and personnel available.

One of the first considerations at this point is the amount of time which can reasonably be devoted to performance testing. This decision will hinge on such questions as the importance of the task, the probable validity of the test, the number of applicants, and the cost of equipment and personnel needed for the test administration. In a school situation it would perhaps be necessary also to estimate what proportion of the total time scheduled for instruction may be devoted to performance testing. Again, the conclusion would depend upon the particular situation. In certain kinds of instruction such as typewriting, it might be advisable to spend as much as three-fourths of the time in performance testing, that is, in timed trials. In other areas of study the proportion obviously would be much smaller.

Some investigation also will be necessary to determine how much equipment may be available in relation to the number of candidates to be tested; and how many persons may be available who will be qualified to administer the test or to make the required evaluations of performance. The operating plan will be prepared in the light of such considerations as these.

5. *Developing the tentative "operating plan."* After having analyzed the job, selected tasks to represent the job in the test situation, developed trial forms for rating or recording performance, and surveyed the practical limitations imposed by considerations such as time, personnel, and equipment, the next procedure in developing a performance test is to organize the data and materials—to formulate an operating plan. This plan will be tentative in nature at the beginning and will become more crystallized as the construction of the test progresses. Numerous trial runs of portions or all of the test may be required to establish suitable time allowances, adequate instructions, feasible means of judging certain aspects of performance, and the like.

In developing the operating plan, the exercise of ingenuity may sometimes enable one to overcome obstacles related to limitations in time, personnel, and equipment, which might otherwise reduce the proposed testing program to dimensions which would be fatal to its success. Where the amount of equipment is too small to permit testing of more than a few examinees at one time, it may be possible to break down each piece of equipment into subassemblies, permitting one man to work at each subassembly. Since it is not always essential that the jobs be done in any particular order, examinees can rotate from one subassembly to another, and thus a larger number may be tested simultaneously than would otherwise be possible.

The administration of several types of tests also can sometimes be carried out simultaneously in order to make maximum use of the testing time and equipment available. For example, a performance test might be given to successive small groups (of a size that can be accommodated by the amount of available equipment), drawing them out of a larger group which is occupied with, say, a paper-pencil test. In some school situations as many as three tests have been simultaneously administered, following a scheme which is diagrammatically shown in Figure 15.9 (24.).

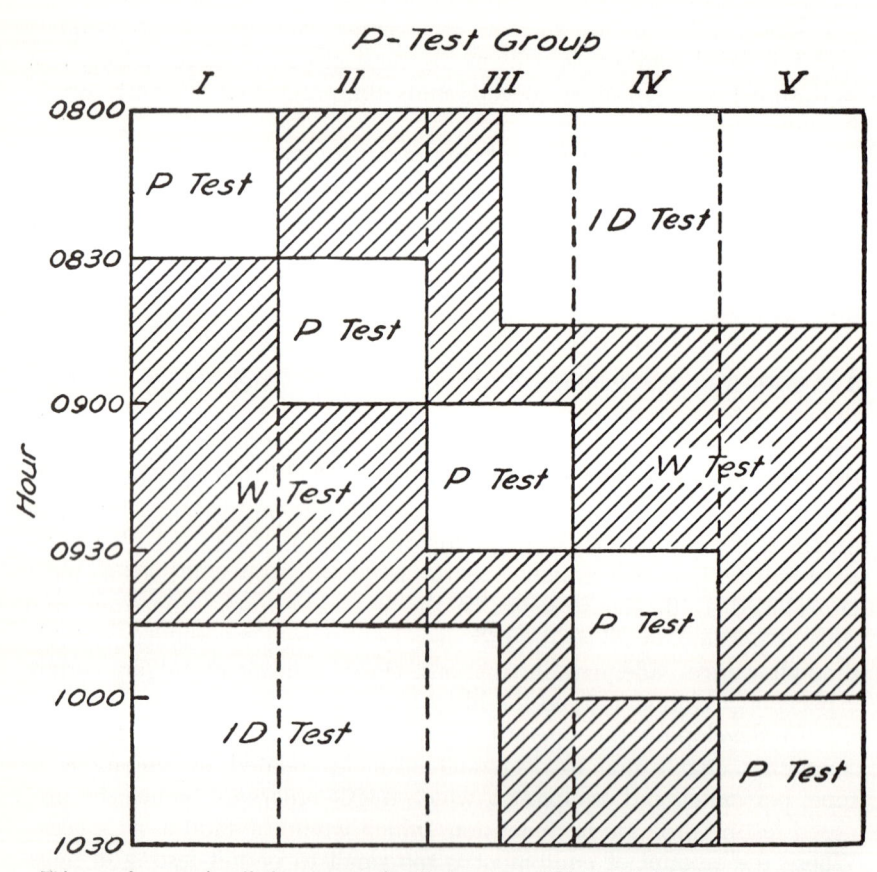

This procedure permits all the men to take all three tests within a period of three hours without conflict. Maximum use is made of the available testing time. It is necessary that all groups except the first and last group taking the performance test be interrupted once in their written test; this is not a serious objection if the written examination is of the short-answer or objective type.

FIGURE 15.9. *Diagram illustrating the method of coordinating the administration of identification, performance, and written tests.* (From Stuit [24, p. 475].)

If it is necessary to make on-the-spot evaluations of the performance exhibited during the test (performance in process), the lack of well-trained judges may restrict the number of examinees who can be tested at one time. This difficulty can sometimes be overcome by preparing rating forms that are adaptable for personnel who lack the full amount of training. Advanced students, for example, can sometimes be used to judge the performance of elementary students, provided they are adequately supervised and given a sufficient amount of special instructions for the task. Such a procedure should, of course, be justified by making suitable studies of the agreement of such judges with the best judges available.

There are, of course, likely to be limitations in the scope of the program even after all possible economies in the use of time, personnel, and equipment have been considered. In the initial stages of the development of a testing program, the test constructor probably should not permit himself to be handicapped unduly by these practical considerations; but it is essential that the operating plan as finally developed be a reasonable and practical one.

The tentative operating plan should provide as complete a description of the procedures as it is possible to make before a full-scale trial run has been made. The plan should include directions (1) for preparing the equipment or other materials for administration of the test, (2) for training the test administrator and other assistants or judges who may be involved, (3) for checking the condition of the equipment, and (4) for the actual conduct of the test. After this operating plan has been subjected to scrutiny by qualified critics, and suitable revisions have been made, the test is ready for its full-scale tryout.

6. *Tryout and revision of the test.* Before its use for purposes of measurement the performance test should be thoroughly studied under realistic conditions of administration. A trial run should be arranged, permitting the test to be tried out on samples of examinees drawn from the population for which the test is ultimately intended. The samples used in the tryout should be as representative as possible, and large enough to yield stable statistical results.

During the tryout, the tentative operating plan should be carefully followed in all details. Arrangements should be made to have the examinees' behavior and all procedures observed in detail to detect possible shortcomings and to suggest improvements. Special precautions should be taken to see that the equipment is adequately prepared and the test administrators thoroughly trained; otherwise the usefulness of the test cannot be properly determined.

The value of the trial administration for confirming the usefulness of the test, or for suggesting improvements, depends upon the careful observation of the procedures and the keeping of complete records. The test scores themselves constitute an important part of these records, but they should be supplemented by notes of undesirable aspects of the testing and unexpected behavior of the examinees as they are observed.

If judgments of the performance in process are involved in the test, provision should be made for two or more judges to make independent ratings of each candidate's performance, so that the reliability of the test may be studied.

The difficulty of the test situations or items, as revealed by the tryout, will be of particular interest. If the test is of the minimum essentials type and the group tested has been well trained, most of the items or tasks probably will be successfully passed by a large proportion of the candidates. If it is not a minimum essentials test, the proportion passing each item ordinarily will be smaller. Certain items may be found which are passed by very few of the candidates. Before discarding these items on the grounds that they are "too hard," the test constructor should be sure that their elimination will not harm the test from the standpoint of validity. In the performance testing in Navy service schools, it occasionally was found that instructors had failed to teach certain skills, although that aspect of the training had been assumed to be satisfactory. Items which are failed by a large proportion of the candidates may reveal deficiencies in training rather than in the test itself. On the other hand, it may be that the test item requires an unreasonably high level of proficiency for the candidates being tested, and the item then should be revised or eliminated. Still another possibility, if the item involves evaluation of the quality of performance by a judge, is that the standards of judgment involved in the rating are unrealistic, and that the descriptive rating scale needs revision or the judges should be given more adequate instructions. In general, the principles of item selection presented earlier apply equally to performance tests.

In situations where subjective ratings of performance are involved, the agreement of the various judges who have independently made observations should be studied. This probably can best be accomplished by computing correlations for each pair of judges for the ratings of performance on each item or task. Ideally more than two judges should be used, making it possible to compare the judges' estimates with respect to their agreement with each other. If the correlation is high for certain judges, it would seem to establish the possiblity of achieving reliable evaluation of performance, even though correlations were low for other judges. If the reliability of judgment as measured by correlations between judges is consistently low, then steps must be taken to improve reliability. Additional experimentation may be necessary to discover what steps should be taken—improve the training of the judges, revise the rating form, or change the nature of the task performed by the examinees.

Study of the internal consistency of a performance test may or may not be relevant to the problem of the test's reliability. It would probably be useful in any case to study the tryout data to determine the extent to which success on one task is associated with success on other tasks. But high internal consistency is not to be expected for certain types of tests, particularly if they are of a composite nature or if they are used in a training situation. If a split-half correlation is high, it does not necessarily mean that the test is highly reliable; it may be desirable to attempt to obtain other evidence of reliability. A test-retest correlation, for example, might furnish a better estimate of the reliability of the tests, although if the test is used in a training program, the test itself might furnish a significant amount of additional practice in the case of some trainees and thus spuriously affect the obtained reliability coefficient. In general, the principles and procedures described previously, apply equally to performance and other types of tests.

A study of the evidence bearing on the question of reliability may suggest improvements in the test or in a training program in which it is used. Uneven learning, as shown by trainees who do well in some tasks but poorly in others, may direct attention to the training program and reveal that some students are given better training in certain areas than others. If the unreliability is clearly a function of the test itself, and not due to uneven preparation of trainees or to unreliability of ratings made by the judges, then some modification of the test is necessary. The most obvious solution of the problem would be to lengthen the test. If this is impossible, then an alternative might be to increase the number of scorable units of performance in the time available.

Evidence as to the validity of the performance may be particularly difficult to obtain. If the test is used in a training program, it may be possible to correlate test scores with other measures of achievement such as course grades. But such correlations must be interpreted with caution. For course grades often reflect verbal ability or mathematical ability more than skill in performance; so low correlations will not necessarily indicate low validity. Another possibility would be to select the highest and lowest examinees in the group on the basis of performance test scores, and ascertain from instructors or supervisors whether or not in their opinion these individuals were clearly in different categories of achievement. Such a rough type of validation should reveal gross failure of the test to measure what it is supposed to measure.

7. *Preparation of directions for administration and use of the test.* After the test has gone through at least one trial administration and revision, and when the test is judged to be ready for use, a complete manual of directions should be prepared. The importance of such a detailed manual is often underestimated; it is easy to believe that instructions will be remembered by proctors and that the details regarding

preparation of equipment and the like will be carried out uniformly from time to time. People do forget, however, and personnel may change. A complete, detailed description of the procedures in manual form will help to insure uniformity of conditions and procedures from one test administration to the next.

The preparation of a manual of directions has been considered in general earlier. The following points should be especially considered in the performance testing situation.

1. *Preparations for administering the test.* Under this heading should be included specific directions for: (1) training proctors or other assistants who may assist in giving the test or in judging the performance of the candidates; (2) the arrangement of equipment and the materials which are to be used in testing; (3) preparing the equipment for testing, by making whatever adjustments or maladjustments that may be necessary, introducing defects or misassembling parts, if required, and checking on deterioration of equipment; (4) providing for a thoroughgoing practice session with proctors or other examining assistants; and (5) arranging for the coordination of performance testing with other testing sessions.

2. *Conduct of the test.* Under this heading should be discussed the detailed directions for administering the test, including instructions for giving directions to the examiners, for maintaining standard conditions, for timing the test and recording time and other records of performance, and for resetting the apparatus for the next group of examinees.

3. *Scoring the test.* Here should be outlined the directions for grading performance or a product, for recording the scores on appropriate forms, for checking the scoring, and for converting the raw scores to standard scores, percentiles, or other types of measures.

Many paper-and-pencil tests are essentially self administering. Performance tests very seldom can be so considered. The control of testing conditions is basic to the success of a procedure, and care must be exercised constantly to assure uniform administration. In some situations, such as radio code receiving and stenography (23), the possibility of uniform testing conditions may be increased through the use of recordings which permit a high degree of control over the presentation of test materials.

Performance tests in many respects may be considered laboratory experiments. As such, they require the same insight in designing and the same vigilance in administering.

SELECTED REFERENCES

1. ADKINS, D. C., et al. *Construction and Analysis of Achievement Tests.* Washington: Government Printing Office, 1948. 292 pp.

2. AYRES, L. P. *A Scale for Measuring the Quality of Handwriting of School Children.* New York: Russell Sage Foundation, 1915. 16 pp.
3. BARNES, R. M., & AMRINE, H. T. "The Effect of Practice on Various Elements Used in Screw-Driver Work," *Journal of Applied Psychology,* 26: 197–209, 1942.
4. BLUM, M. L. "Selection of Sewing Machine Operators," *Journal of Applied Psychology,* 27: 35-40, 1943.
5. BROWN, C. M., et al. *Minnesota Food Score Cards.* Minneapolis: University of Minnesota Press, 1946.
6. CHAPMAN, J. C. *Trade Tests.* New York: Henry Holt, 1921. 431 pp.
7. CURETON, T. K.; BOOKWALTER, K. W.; GLASSOW, R.; & MCCORMICK, H. G. "The Measurement of Understanding in Physical Education," *The Measurement of Understanding: Forty-fifth Yearbook of the National Society for the Study of Education,* Part I. Chicago: National Society for the Study of Education, 1946. Chap. 12, pp. 232–52.
8. DESILVA, H. R., & CHANNELL, R. "Driver Clinics in the Field," *Journal of Applied Psychology,* 22: 59–69, 1938.
9. FREEMAN, F. N. *Freeman Chart for Diagnosing Faults in Handwriting.* Boston: Houghton Mifflin, 1914.
10. FRUTCHEY, F. P.; DEYOE, G. P.; & LATHROP, F. W. "The Measurement of Understanding in Agriculture," *The Measurement of Understanding, Forty-fifth Yearbook of the National Society for the Study of Education,* Part I. Chicago: National Society for the Study of Education, 1946. Chap. 14, pp. 270-80.
11. HAY, E. N. "Predicting Success in Machine Bookkeeping," *Journal of Applied Psychology,* 27: 483–93, 1943.
12. HULL, C. L. *Aptitude Testing.* Yonkers, N.Y.: World Book Co., 1928. 535 pp.
13. LAWSHE, C. H. *Principles of Personnel Testing,* New York: McGraw-Hill, 1948. 227 pp.
14. LAWSHE, C. H., & TIFFIN, J. "The Accuracy of Precision Instrument Measurement in Industrial Inspection," *Journal of Applied Psychology,* 29:413–19, 1945.
15. LINDAHL, L. G. "Movement Analysis as an Industrial Training Method," *Journal of Applied Psychology,* 29:420-36, 1945.
16. MCCLOY, C. H. *Tests and Measurements in Health and Physical Education.* New York: Crofts & Co., 1942. 412 pp.
17. MCPHERSON, M. W. "A Method of Objectively Measuring Shop Performance," *Journal of Applied Psychology,* 29: 22-26, 1945.
18. NEWKIRK, L. V., & GREENE, H. A. *Tests and Measurements in Industrial Education.* New York: John Wiley & Sons, 1935. 253 pp.
19. PATERSON, D. G.; ELLIOTT, R. M.; et al. *Minnesota Mechanical Ability Tests.* Minneapolis: University of Minnesota Press, 1930. 560 pp.

20. Patten, E. F. "An Experiment in Testing Engine Lathe Aptitude," *Journal of Applied Psychology*, 1923, 7: 16–29.
21. Proffitt, M. M.; Ericson, E. E.; & Newkirk, L. V. "The Measurement of Understanding in Industrial Arts," *The Measurement of Understanding, Forty-fifth Yearbook of the National Society for the Study of Education*, Part I. Chicago: National Society for the Study of Education, 1946. Chap. 16, pp. 302–20.
22. Scott, M. G., & French, E. *Better Teaching Through Testing*. New York: A. S. Barnes Co., 1945. 247 pp.
23. Seashore, H., & Bennett, G. K. *Stenographic Proficiency Tests*. New York: Psychological Corporation, 1946.
24. Stuit, D. B. (ed.). *Personnel Research and Test Development in the Bureau of Naval Personnel*. Princeton, N.J.: Princeton University Press, 1947.
25. Thorndike, R. L. *Personnel Selection*. New York: John Wiley & Sons, 1949. 358 pp.
26. Tiffin, J. *Industrial Psychology*, New York: Prentice-Hall, 1947. 554 pp.
27. Tiffin, J., & Greenly, R. J. "Experiments in the Operation of a Punch Press," *Journal of Applied Psychology*, 23:450–60, 1939.
28. Toops, H. A. "Code Numbers as a Means of Scoring Group-Administered Performance Test Products," *Journal of Applied Psychology*, 26: 136–50, 1942.
29. Toops, H. A. *Trade Tests in Education*. New York: Teachers College, Columbia University, 1921. 118 pp.
30. Viteles, M. S. *Industrial Psychology*. New York: W. W. Norton & Co., 1932, 652 pp.

16 The Check List as a Criterion of Proficiency

ARTHUR I. SIEGEL

The check list represents a particularly attractive tool for measuring a man's ability to perform a task. A performance check list is prepared by analyzing a task into the component actions which a man performs in order to complete the task. In some cases the task involves making something. In this case an end product evolves and the end product is also analyzed in terms of its adherence to certain prescribed standards and its freedom from defect. An examinee receives credit for each of the analytic performance components with which he conforms and each of the elementalistic aspects of his end product that meets prescribed standards. A total task score is derived by adding a man's credits on each of the analytic components of performance and end product adherence to prescribed standards.

For instance, a performance check list for welding consists of items relating to the way the welder performs his job (e.g., "cleans base metal and rods," "adjusts oxyacetylene regulators to 4–5 pounds," "preheats base metal," etc.); the safety precautions the welder follows (e.g., "does not open acetylene cylinder valve more than 1½ turns," "uses goggles when welding," "makes sure fire extinguisher in area before igniting torch"); and items relating to adherence of the final weld to prescribed standards (e.g., "bead width 3–5 times metal thickness," "bead height 25–50% of metal thickness," etc.). The welder is given credit for each of the items with which his performance or final weld conforms, and his total score is the sum of these credits. The problem, as mentioned by Thorndike,[1] is that there *may* be aspects of a job that are lost in the analytic approach, so that scoring the elementary items does not give an entirely adequate evaluation. Specifically, the scores obtained by subjects scored in an analytic manner may not correlate highly with the over-all,

From *Journal of Applied Psychology*, 1954, 38, 93–95. The data herein reported are a small portion of the data gathered under Contract Nonr-872(00) between the Institute for Research in Human Relations and the Office of Naval Research. The opinions expressed are those of the author and do not necessarily represent the opinions of the Office of Naval Research or of the Naval Service.

[1] Thorndike, R. *Personnel selection*, New York: John Wiley, 1949.

"clinical" judgments of experts as to the quality of a final product produced.

If performance check list scores do correlate highly with expert, "clinical" judgments or rankings of end products, the performance "check list" is to be preferred. This follows since more objectivity may be introduced into the check list, examiner reliability may be increased by the check list, test reliability may be increased by the check list and less background and less experience in the particular test task is required by the examiner who uses the check list than by the examiner who makes a "clinical" appraisal. Moreover, if performance in process is checked as well as the quality of the final product, certain insights may be gained, which could be missed by only an over-all, final appraisal of end products.

METHOD

Performance check lists[2] were constructed for four tasks: aluminum butt welding; patching a hole in plastic; splicing a cracked aircraft channel; and aircraft fabric repair. The inter-examiner reliabilities for both the aluminum butt welding and fabrics lists were coincidently at .92. The inter-examiner reliabilities for the plastics and channel splicing lists were not ascertained. However, the inter-examiner reliabilities on four other check lists similar to the ones herein discussed ranged from .91 to .97. Likewise, the intra-examiner reliability by retest methods for measurements made on the adherence of end products to prescribed standards was ascertained only by the welding and fabrics lists. These intra-examiner reliabilities were .93 and .87 respectively. Intra-examiner reliability for observations made of performance in process is difficult to obtain by the retest method. This difficulty follows because of the relative impossibility of having an examinee perform the same task in exactly the same manner on two separate occasions. However, by a motion picture technique, the intra-examiner reliability for performance in process was found to be .93 for the welding test. The intra-examiner reliabilities for performance in process of the remaining lists were not determined.

The aluminum butt welding, plastic patching, channel splicing, and fabric repair tasks were first administered to 15 aviation structural mechanics at the Naval Air Technical Training Unit, Memphis. Four of the subjects held the Naval rate of "striker," four held the rate of third class, four the rate of second class and three the rate of first class Aviation Structural Mechanic. All of the jobs represented in these tests are

[2] To save printing costs, the performance check lists as well as the correlational matrices upon which our discussion is based have been deposited with the ADI Auxiliary Publications Project. Order Document No. 4038 from Chief, Photoduplication Service, ADI Auxiliary Publications Project, Library of Congress, Washington, D. C., remitting $1.75 for 35 mm. microfilm or $2.50 for 6 by 8 inch photocopies.

tasks which Naval Aviation Structural Mechanics typically perform. The mean service length of the examinees was 54.6 months with a standard deviation of 38.3 months. The mean scores and standard deviations for the group on each of the tests follow: aluminum butt welding, mean 15.0, sigma 6.9; splicing a cracked channel, mean 44.3, sigma 6.8; plastic repair, mean 20.8, sigma 6.5; and fabric repair, mean 33.4, sigma 9.0. The examiners were Chief Aviation Structural Mechanics who held instructors' billets at the Naval Aviation Structural Mechanics School, Memphis. The examinees were unknown to the examiners prior to the testing situation.

The end products produced by each examinee on each of these tests were taken to the Naval Air Station, Atlantic City. At Atlantic City, five Chief Aviation Structural Mechanics were asked to rank, from best to worst, the end products produced by the examinees on each of the tests.

RESULTS

The correlations of the rankings of the Chief Petty Officers who ranked the end products from each test with the rankings produced by our analytic and synthetic approach and also the correlations *between* the rankings of the various chiefs who ranked the end products at Atlantic City were calculated. All of these correlations were rank difference correlations. If the experts (Naval Chief Aviation Structural Mechanics) agreed among themselves more than they agreed with the rankings produced by the analytic and synthetic approach, then the analytic and synthetic approach has lost something that these experts considered to be important in making their rankings. On the other hand if the experts agreed with the rankings produced by the check list as much as they agreed among themselves, then little has been lost by the analytic and synthetic approach.

The median rank difference correlation between the rankings of the chiefs at Atlantic City of the end products from each test was then obtained. The median rank difference correlation of the chiefs' rankings with the rankings produced by our analytic and synthetic check list approach was also calculated. These *rhos* are presented in Table 16.1.

For the welding test, the median rank difference correlation of the chiefs' rankings with the rankings produced by the analytic and synthetic approach was .41. For the plastics test, the structural maintenance test and the fabrics test, the median rank difference correlations of the chiefs' rankings with the rankings produced by the analytic and synthetic approach were .66, .26 and .33, respectively. For the welding test, the plastics test and the structural maintenance test, the median rank difference correlations between the chief's rankings were .95, .89, and .29, re-

TABLE 16.1. *Median correlations between chiefs and between rankings of chiefs with analytic approach*

Test	Median Rho Between Chiefs	Median Rho of Chiefs with Analytic Approach
Welding	.95	.41
Plastics	.89	.66
Structural Maintenance	.37	.26
Fabrics	.29	.33

spectively, and these three *rhos* were greater than the correlation of the chiefs' rankings with the rankings produced by the analytic and synthetic approach. However, the reverse was true for the fabrics test; median *rho* between chiefs .29, median *rho* of chiefs with analytic approach .33. All median rank difference correlations were then converted to product moment correlations and the product moment correlations transformed to z's (r to z' transformation). The significance of the difference was then calculated between the z's which represented the median correlations between the chiefs' rankings of the end products of each test and the z's which represented median correlations of the chiefs' rankings with the rankings produced by the analytic and synthetic approach for the same tests.

Of the four tests of significance calculated, only the difference between the median correlation between the rankings of the chiefs and the median correlation of the chiefs' rankings with the rankings produced by the analytic and synthetic approach for the welding test was statistically significant. However, at this juncture, it is well to point out that three of the four median rank difference correlations between the chiefs' rankings were greater than the median correlations of the chiefs' rankings with the rankings produced by the analytic and synthetic approach.

Thus it seems that we were not able to demonstrate conclusively that the Chief Petty Officers in our sample agreed with the rankings produced by the analytic and synthetic approach more than they agreed with each other. On the other hand, in view of the bias (here controlled) that usually enters into judgments of end products, when judgments are made in actual work situations, it seems probable that any loss indicated by the three lower correlations of the chiefs' rankings with the rankings produced by the analytic and synthetic approach as compared with the correlations between the chiefs' rankings would be compensated for if this bias had been allowed to operate here as a confounding variable. Moreover, some procedural elements were not apparent to the chiefs when they made their judgments of the final products. For instance, a man may break safety rules and lose a certain amount of credit. Infractions such as these are not seen when making appraisals of end products, but may be too important to omit from consideration when estimating a man's real work ability. Since the chiefs who did the ranking had only end products to evaluate, it seems probable that part of the loss indicated by the lower correlations between the chiefs' rankings and the rankings produced by the analytic and synthetic approach as compared with the between-chiefs' correlations may also be assignable to distortions in the rankings of the analytic and synthetic approach due to poor care and use of equipment, violation of safety precautions, etc. on the part of the examinees.

SUMMARY

As mentioned by Thorndike, there *may* be aspects of a job that are lost in breaking down a job in terms of the elemental, analytic components comprising the job. If this is so, then scoring the elemental, analytic components of a task does not give an entirely adequate evaluation. Therefore, an investigation was performed into the relationship between total scores assigned via a scoring of the elemental components of a job (performance check list approach) and over-all, "clinical" judgments of experts (Naval Chief Petty Officers) as to the quality of a final product produced. Rank difference correlations were calculated between the scores assigned via a performance check list and judgments of experts as to the quality of final products. Inter-correlations between the rankings of the experts on the quality of end products produced were also calculated. The following conclusions seem warranted.

1. Three out of four median correlations *between* the rankings of Naval Chief Aviation Structural Mechanics were not significantly different from correlations of the chiefs' rankings with scores obtained by an analytic and synthetic approach.

2. Although no statistical differences were shown in three of the four pairs of rank difference correlations under consideration, the tendency was toward greater agreement between experts' rankings than between the rankings of the experts and the rankings of the analytic and synthetic approach.

17 The Predictability of Various Kinds of Criteria

DARYL SEVERIN

SUMMARY

This investigation was undertaken in an attempt to generalize regarding (1) the relationships of several measures of job performance for the same people, and (2) the usefulness of several kinds of tests for predicting job performance. This was accomplished by utilizing correlation coefficients from the following five sources: a) Dorcus and Jones' *Handbook of Employee Selection,* b) the Army Air Force, c) the Navy, d) the Personnel Research Section, Department of the Army, and e) articles which have appeared in the literature since the publication of Dorcus and Jones (1950).

Some of the generalizations that seem warranted are as follows:

(1) Various job performance scores correlated very low (median correlation of .28) with other measures of performance of the same job by the same people. This finding emphasizes the danger in substituting an "easy to obtain" measure of performance for a "hard to get" measure without knowing their degree of equivalence.

(2) Non-personality tests such as intelligence, performance, and achievement gave higher correlations (median of .33) than personality tests (median of .15) for predicting job performance.

(3) "Ready-made" *non-personality* tests appeared to be neither better nor poorer on the average for predicting job performance than "tailor-made" *non-personality* tests. However, "tailor-made" *personality* tests seemed more satisfactory for predicting job performance than "ready-made" *personality* tests. This does not obviate the necessity to validate each test for a specific job, neither is it evidence that one kind of test would be just as effective as another in any specific situation.

(4) The median correlation obtained when predicting job performance with various kinds of tests was .25.

From *Personnel Psychology,* 1952, 5, 93–104. The author is indebted to Dr. H. E. Brogden and Dr. R. H. Gaylord for their aid in the planning of this study. The opinions expressed are those of the author and do not necessarily express the official views of the Department of the Army.

NATURE OF THE PROBLEMS

Substituting one criterion for the other. In the validation of tests for predicting job performance, it is frequently found that the desired criterion cannot be easily obtained. This often results in another criterion being used in its place without any knowledge of the degree of equivalence of the two. The assumption is made, however, that the workers will have about the same relative standing on the two measures. The problem then is to learn to what degree one measure of job performance correlates with other measures of the same job. The present research was undertaken in order to determine what relationships existed among several criterion measures of the same jobs.

Usefulness of certain kinds of tests for predicting job performance. The other problem to which the present study was addressed involved the classification of tests and job performance measures to ascertain whether certain types of tests were generally better than others for the prediction of job performance. In the present study personality tests were compared with non-personality tests (intelligence, aptitude, achievement, etc.); ratings were compared with production records; and "ready-made" tests were compared with "tailor-made" tests.

METHOD

Correlations used. Most of the information was obtained from Dorcus and Jones' *Handbook of Employee Selection* (2). This is a reference book for both the layman and the professional psychologist. It consists of 426 abstracts of research studies using psychological tests conducted from 1906 to 1948 with a primary emphasis on employee selection. Since many of the authors did not report their findings in terms of correlations these abstracts were not used in the tabulations. Similar research conducted by psychologists in the three military organizations the publication of Dorcus and Jones' *Handbook of Employee Selection* previously mentioned as well as research appearing in the literature since was also included in the computations.

It should be emphasized that the information obtained can be considered representative only of the studies reported inasmuch as any tendency to withhold certain correlations from the literature would change the results to that extent. However, no evidence was found that this happened.

Tables of correlations. The first table presents correlation coefficients of criteria with other criteria. Nine criteria were included in

TABLE 17.1. *Correlation of various criterion measures.*

r	ON THE JOB RATINGS BY SUPERIORS WITH						r	ON THE JOB RATINGS BY ASSOCIATES WITH		ON THE JOB RATINGS BY SUBORDINATES WITH PROD. RECORDS	TRAINING GRADES WITH PROD. RECORDS
	Prod. Rec.	Job. Rat. by Assoc.	Prof. Tests	Train. by Assoc.	Rat. by Super.	Train. Records		Subor. Rat.	Prof. Tests		
.90–.94							.90–.94				
.85–.89							.85–.89				
.80–.84							.80–.84	2			
.75–.79							.75–.79	2			
.70–.74							.70–.74	2*			
.65–.69							.65–.69	2			
.60–.64				2			.60–.64	3			4
.55–.59				1			.55–.59	1			4
.50–.54	1	1		2			.50–.54		1		5
.45–.49	1*	4		1*	1		.45–.49				4
.40–.44	1	2			1		.40–.44				2
.35–.39		8*			1		.35–.39		1		3
.30–.34		3	1	1			.30–.34		1*	4*	3
.25–.29			1	1	2		.25–.29		2	1	3
.20–.24			3*	3	6*	1	.20–.24			1	9*
.15–.19					1		.15–.19			1	4
.10–.14			1		1	6*	.10–.14			1	3
.05–.09						3	.05–.09				1
.00–.04							.00–.04				7
(−.05)–(−.01)							(−.05)–(−.01)				3
(−.10)–(−.06)							(−.10)–(−.06)				3
Number	3	18	6	11	13	10	Number	12	5	8	58
Median	.47	.38	.23	.47	.23	.11	Median	.70	.32	.30	.24

* Median correlation

the present study. Some of these correlations were on-the-job ratings by superiors with production records, on-the-job ratings by superiors with proficiency tests, etc.

All the other tables deal with the correlations of the predictors (tests) with the various criteria measures. Since negative correlations are as valuable for prediction purposes as positive ones, the correlations are reported regardless of sign in Tables 17.2 through 17.5. Personality tests are tabulated separately from non-personality tests and this division then tabulated separately for production records and ratings. Further breakdowns of the above are by numbers of cases in the study, whether

RESULTS

Table 17.1 shows the correlations between various criterion measures. For example, column 1 shows three different correlations between on-the-job ratings by superiors and production records, with a median correlation of .48. The table gives the range and median correlation of various criteria, as well as the number of correlations which serves as indication of the frequency with which psychologists have made studies of this type. If this table is a fair representation of such correlations then

TABLE 17.2. *Personality and non-personality tests predicting job performance as judged by ratings and production records*

r	PERSONALITY TESTS WITH			r	NON-PERSONALITY TESTS WITH		
	Ratings	Prod. Rec.	Ratings & Rec.		Ratings	Prod. Rec.	Ratings & Rec.
.85–.89[1]	1		1	.85–.89		1	1
.80–.84				.80–.84			
.75–.79				.75–.79		2	2
.70–.74	3		3	.70–.74	2	1	3
.65–.69	2		2	.65–.69	1	2	3
.60–.64	4		4	.60–.64	7	2	9
.55–.59	3		3	.55–.59	6	1	7
.50–.54	4		4	.50–.54	2	2	4
.45–.49	1	2	3	.45–.49	11	2	13
.40–.44	3	1	4	.40–.44	5	4	9
.35–.39	4		4	.35–.39	10*	5	15
.30–.34	7	5	12	.30–.34	10	7	17*
.25–.29	5	1	6	.25–.29	6	4*	10
.20–.24	6*		6	.20–.24	7	10	17
.15–.19	5	6	11*	.15–.19	5	5	10
.10–.14	8	8*	16	.10–.14	5	5	10
.05–.09	15	5	20	.05–.09	4	4	8
.00–.04	13	13	26	.00–.04	1	6	7
Number	84	41	125	Number	82	63	145
Median	.20	.11	.15	Median	.36	.26	.33

Average of medians .20 and .26 = .23
Average of medians .36 and .11 = .24

[1] Since negative correlations are as valuable for predictive purposes as positive correlations the correlations have been tabulated in this and the following tables regardless of sign.

training records and on-the-job ratings by superiors seem to have a low degree of relationship, with a median correlation of only .11. In contrast with this, ratings by associates correlated quite highly with ratings by subordinates, the median correlation being .70. One fairly clear finding appears to be that training grades correlate low with various measures of on-the-job performance (median correlation of .22). The median of all correlations in the table was .28, which seems to be further evidence that one cannot properly substitute one measure of job performance for another without first knowing their degree of equivalence. For example,

TABLE 17.3. *Comparison of personality tests and non-personality tests (intelligence, performance, achievement, etc.) for predicting job performance as judged by ratings and production records*

	PERSONALITY TESTS WITH			NON-PERSONALITY TESTS WITH		
r	Ratings Cross Val.	Prod. Rec. Cross Val.	r	Ratings		Prod. Rec. Cross Val.
^	^	^	^	Cross Val.	Not Cross Val.	^
.85–.89			.85–.89		3	1
.80–.84			.80–.84			
.75–.79			.75–.79			2
.70–.74	5		.70–.74	2	2	1
.65–.69	3		.65–.69		2	1
.60–.64	2		.60–.64	5	2	1
.55–.59	1		.55–.59	6	2	1
.50–.54	1		.50–.54	2		2
.45–.49		2	.45–.49	11	1	
.40–.44	2	1	.40–.44	3*	2	1
.35–.39	2		.35–.39	7	2*	4
.30–.34	6	5	.30–.34	7	3	5*
.25–.29	3	1	.25–.29	4	1	1
.20–.24	4*		.20–.24	3	2	2
.15–.19	1	4	.15–.19	2	3	3
.10–.14	9	7*	.10–.14	2	2	2
.05–.09	10	5	.05–.09	3	2	1
.00–.04	8	12	.00–.04	1		
Number	57	37	Number	58	29	29
Median	.20	.11	Median	.40	.38	.34

if a company does not keep production records as a measure of performance, and grades received in training are used as an estimate of the performance, it is very doubtful that the employees would have anywhere near the same relative standing on the two measures.

Table 17.2 shows correlations of tests with on-the-job ratings and production records. The chief reason for making the tabulations in this

TABLE 17.4. *Personality and non-personality tests predicting job performance as judged by ratings and production records broken down by number of cases in the experiment*

	PERSONALITY TESTS WITH						NON-PERSONALITY TESTS WITH						TOTAL OF ALL TESTS AND JOB PERFORMANCE COMBINED		
	Ratings			Production Records			Ratings			Production Records					
r	0–40	41–80	81+	0–40	41–80	81+	0–40	41–80	81+	0–40	41–80	81+	0–40	41–80	81+
.90–.94	1														
.85–.89		3											2		
.80–.84		2	1						1				2	4	1
.75–.79		2	2				1	1					2	2	3
.70–.74		1	1						2	2			2	6	4
.65–.69	1			1			2	3	2	1	1		4	3	2
.60–.64							2	2	2	2			3	1	3
.55–.59	2						1		1	1			5		
.50–.54	1						4	5*	2	1			7	6	4
.45–.49	2	1		1				2	3	1	3		3	6	4
.40–.44	1	1	2			1	5	3	2*	4*	1	1	10	5	4
.35–.39	4	2*	1				6*	3	3	4	2		15	5	8
.30–.34	4	1		1		3*	5	1	1	1	2	1	11*	3	2
.25–.29	1	1	3	1			3		3	2	8*	*	6	11*	6*
.20–.24		2	2	2	3		1	1	3	2	1	2	8	5	8
.15–.19	3*		2*	1	6*	1	1	1	3	1	4		8	13	5
.10–.14	5	1	6	1*	3	1	1	2	2		3		8	12	8
.05–.09	3	6	6		3	1	3		1	1	3		8	12	8
.00–.04	7	2	4	7	6		1				6		15	14	4
Number	35	25	24	14	18	8	35	21	26	27	32	4	111	96	62
Median	.19	.31	.15	.05	.10	.31	.32	.45	.35	.38	.21	.22	.29	.21	.25

241

table was to obtain evidence concerning the hypothesis that personality tests predict ratings better than production records and non-personality tests predict production records better than ratings. This hypothesis has frequently been mentioned in psychological circles, presumably stemming from the belief that ratings depend more on personality qualities than do production records. Personality tests did predict ratings better than they predicted production records, but the hypothesis was not con-

TABLE 17.5. *Personality and nonpersonality tests predicting job performance as judged by ratings and production records separated by "ready made" and "tailor made" tests*

r	PERSONALITY TESTS WITH			r	NON-PERSONALITY TESTS WITH						
	Ratings		Prod. Rec.		Ratings		Prod. Records		Ratings & Rec. Com.	
	Ready Made Tests	Tailor Made Tests	Ready Made Tests		Ready Made Tests	Tailor Made Tests	Ready Made Tests	Tailor Made Tests	Ready Made Tests	Tailor Made Tests
.85–.89				.85–.89			1		1	
.80–.84				.80–.84						
.75–.79				.75–.79			2		2	
.70–.74	1	2		.70–.74	2				2	
.65–.69		2		.65–.69			1		1	
.60–.64	2	1*		.60–.64	4	1		1	4	2
.55–.59	1	3		.55–.59	7		1		8	
.50–.54	2	1		.50–.54	1		2		3	
.45–.49	1		2	.45–.49	12	1	1	1	13	2
.40–.44	3		1	.40–.44	3		1	3	4	3
.35–.39	4	1		.35–.39	12	1	4	1	16	2
.30–.34	10		6	.30–.34	10*	3*	4	2	14	5
.25–.29	8		1	.25–.29	9	1	1	2	10*	3
.20–.24	11			.20–.24	6	2	2	8*	8	10*
.15–.19	11		4	.15–.19	10	1	8*	1	18	2
.10–.14	17*		6	.10–.14	9		7	4	16	4
.05–.09	26		4*	.05–.09	7		5	3	12	3
.00–.04	23		17	.00–.04	4		3	7	7	7
Number	120	10	41	Number	96	10	43	33	139	43
Median	.13	.60	.09	Median	.31	.31	.19	.20	.29	.22

sidered substantiated because the non-personality tests did not predict production records better than ratings. Ratings were better predicted by both personality and non-personality tests.

However, one may wish to consider an alternative statement of the above mentioned hypothesis: that personality tests correlated with on-the-job ratings combined with non-personality tests correlated with production records will give higher correlations than personality tests correlated with production records combined with non-personality tests correlated with ratings. To obtain an index of this, an average of the two medians (the correlation of personality tests with ratings and the correlation of non-personality tests with production records) was computed and found to be .23. This was compared with the average of the other two median coefficients (personality tests correlated with production records and non-personality tests against ratings), which was found to be .24. (See bottom of Table 17.2.) This seemed to be additional evidence that the original hypothesis was not substantiated. The average of the two medians was used rather than combining the two distributions and calculating the new median because the number of correlations with one combination (personality tests against ratings and non-personality tests versus production records) would be too highly weighted with personality tests. Furthermore the other combination (personality tests correlated with production records and non-personality tests against ratings) would be too heavily weighted with non-personality tests. This is an important consideration because non-personality tests in general gave higher correlations with job performance than personality tests and the difference found might be evidence of this rather than of the original hypothesis.

Another important finding was the great variation in correlations, a range from .00 to .87. This appears to be further evidence of what psychologists have been advocating for years, that one cannot assume a test to be adequate for predicting performance on a certain job without validating it for that particular job in that particular plant. Another generalization that seems warranted from this table is that ratings are used as a measure of performance more often than production records. This may readily occur because ratings are more easily obtained. The table gives evidence that non-personality tests predict job performance better than personality tests (median correlation of .36 for non-personality tests as compared to .16 for personality tests).

The computations reported in Table 17.3 were made primarily to see whether cross validated tests tended to have lower validities than non-cross validated ones. It was believed that many correlations reported might be spuriously high due to the lack of cross validation of these tests. Among the studies using personality tests, the test had either been previously cross validated or the research reported was the initial cross validation of the test. The number of studies used here was different from the other tables. Whenever it was not possible to determine from the abstract whether the test had been cross validated, the abstract was not used in the tabulation. The only place where a comparison could be made between tests, which were cross validated and those which were not, was in the case of the non-personality tests predicting on-the-job ratings. Here the median correlation was almost the same for cross validated and non-cross validated tests. From this sample of correlations, therefore, there appeared to be little evidence to show that non-personality tests which have not been cross validated have high correlations merely because of the lack of cross validation.

Table 17.4 shows the increase or decrease of validity coefficients as the number of cases is increased. It would have been possible to have found high correlations based on small numbers of cases if the authors had had a tendency to withhold low correlations and report only the high ones. It is to be expected that correlations based on small numbers of cases will fluctuate by chance more than those based on large numbers. There was no consistent trend, however, for the correlations to increase or decrease as the number of cases increased. The median correlation of the personality tests correlated with production records increased as the number of cases increased, but for non-personality tests correlated with production, the correlation tended to decrease as the number of cases increased. When ratings were used as the criterion, there was no trend for the correlations to increase or decrease as the number of cases increased. The same was also true when all tests and performance measures were totalled. While locating the correlations in the literature, it was found that only about four per cent of the studies used more than 120 cases with about 50 as the median number of cases. It is the writer's belief that many of the validation studies did not use enough cases to justify the study. For instance, it is doubtful if those studies employing 10 or 12 cases were worth the cost to management.

Table 17.5 is essentially a comparison of "ready-made" and "tailor-made" tests to see if there is a tendency for one type to result in higher correlations than the other. The tabulations under personality tests cannot be considered to be conclusive because so few personality tests were "tailor-made." The results are quite suggestive, however, that "tailor-made" personality tests may be more satisfactory than the "ready-made" personality tests. This cannot be due to the fact that the "tailor-made" tests were not cross validated while the "ready-made" tests were cross validated. As is evidenced by Table 17.3 all tests in these categories had been cross validated.

More information is included under the non-personality tests because here more "tailor-made" tests were found. Where non-personality tests were used to predict production records the median correlation was about the same for "ready-made" tests ($r = .19$) and for "tailor-made" tests ($r = .20$). Where on-the-job ratings were predicted the median correlations were .31 for both the "ready-made" tests and the "tailor-made" tests. This finding cannot be considered proof that "tailor-made" tests are no better than "ready-made" tests. One reason is that industrial organizations often do not publish the results of their more effective "tailor-made" tests. It is considered by the author, however, as evidence for a need to re-examine the belief that "tailor-made" tests are usually superior. Even if, on the average, the two kinds of tests were equally effective it would not obviate the necessity for a test validation with each job nor would it be evidence that one kind of test would be just as effective as another in any specific situation.

GENERALIZATIONS

The data presented herein seem to warrant the following generalizations:

A. Training records correlated low (median about .20) with on-the-job performance and should not be substituted for on-the-job performance with the belief that they are equivalent, without first determining that they are reasonably so.

B. Care should be used in substituting one criterion for another as the median correlation of job performance criteria with various other criteria is only about .30. These correlations ranged from .00 to .87, however, which would seem to be strong evidence that one should never substitute one criterion for another without first determining if they are reasonably equivalent.

C. The hypothesis that personality tests predict ratings better than production records, and non-personality tests predict production records better than ratings, was not considered to be substantiated.

D. Non-personality tests gave higher predictions for job performance than personality tests, a median of .33 as compared to .15.

E. Only about four per cent of the authors validated their tests with 120 or more cases. The median number of cases in a validation study was about 50.

F. "Ready-made" non-personality tests appeared to be neither better nor poorer in general for predicting job performance than "tailor-made" non-personality tests. However, the evidence is strongly suggestive that "tailor-made" personality tests may be more satisfactory for predicting job performance than "ready-made" personality tests. This is no evidence, however, of the superiority of one kind of test in any specific situation.

REFERENCES

1. BROKAW, L. D. *The Comparative Composite Validities of Batteries of "Short" Versus "Long" Tests.* Human Resources Research Center, Lackland Air Force Base, Research Bulletin, 50–1, January, 1950.
2. DORCUS, R. M. & JONES, M. H. *Handbook of Employee Selection.* New York: McGraw-Hill Book Co., Inc., 1950.

3. Ricciuti, H. N. & French, J. W. *Development of Personality Tests for Naval Officer Selection: I, Analysis of U. S. Naval Academy Criterion of Aptitude for Service.* Technical Report No. 1, Office of Naval Research, Contract 90 onr-98200, Educational Testing Service, Princeton, New Jersey, 1951.

18 Errors in Time-Study Judgments of Industrial Work Pace

KALMAN A. LIFSON

I. INTRODUCTION

Time studies are made to determine how much time should be required to accomplish specified elements of work. One of the steps in a time study is the calculation of the "normal time"—the time which the work element requires when performed at a "normal" pace. In determining the normal time, the time-study man records the amount of time actually used by the operator he is observing, and he also makes a judgment of the work pace of the operator. The actual observed time is adjusted in accord with the judgment of work pace so that the adjusted time is representative of a "normal" performance.

Usually the judgment of work pace is expressed as a percentage of "normal" work pace, and the adjustment is the multiplication of the observed time by this percentage. If, for example, the time-study man believes the observed worker is maintaining a pace that is 30 per cent faster than normal, he rates the performance for the observed work element at 130 (omitting the decimal) and multiplies the observed work time by 1.3.

The judgment is called by various names such as "leveling," "effort rating," "performance rating," "pace rating," or just plain "rating." In this paper the term "rating" will be employed. This rating may be defined as the process of comparing an observed work pace to some concept of a "normal" pace. Time studies are only as reliable and accurate as the ratings on which they are based.

Purpose of Investigation

This study examined the nature of the errors involved in ratings of work pace from several aspects: (a) by determining the magnitude and

From *Psychological Monographs*, 1953, 67, 355. This paper is based upon a thesis (5) submitted to the Graduate School of Purdue University in partial fulfillment of the requirements for the degree of Doctor of Philosophy, August, 1951. The research was done under the committee of Professors E. J. McCormick, chairman, Joseph Tiffin, N. C. Kephart, W. V. Owen, and M. E. Mundel.

assignable causes of errors in pace ratings; (b) by determining the variation among the consistencies of ratings from different sources; and (c) by comparing the relative concepts of "normal pace" of workers with the concepts of the time-study men.

Sources of error. Factors which are the assignable sources of error in pace ratings are evidenced by constant differences in the average level of those ratings which are common to the factor. Specifically: (a) *different observers* may have different general concepts of normal work pace, and tend to rate either consistently high or consistently low; (b) *different jobs* may appear easier to some observers than to others, and this variation may be superimposed on the general high- or low-rating tendency of the observer; (c) *different workers*, maintaining the same tempo of elements per minute on a job, may also be rated differently; and (d) the normal times derived may differ when *different levels of pace* are observed—lower paces may be rated too high, and higher paces may be rated too low.

One of the purposes of this study was to determine the magnitude of the error due to each of these four factors and to their interactions.

Differences in consistency. Besides the differences which may cause some raters to rate higher than others, there may be differences which cause some raters to be more consistent than others. Likewise, some jobs may be rated more consistently than others, and some workers and some paces may be rated more consistently than others.

Consistency is probably more important than the level of rating, since, if a rater is consistently too high, he can be taught to lower his ratings. But, if a rater is not consistent, improvement is not as easy.

A second purpose of this study, then, was to determine if there are real differences among the consistencies of ratings by different raters, on different jobs, on different workers, and on different paces.

Differences between judgments of raters and workers. Workers who are the subjects of time studies, and whose work quota is based on time study, form opinions about the paces they are expected to maintain. Workers may not equate the jobs in the same way as the raters do. To the workers, the raters' idea of normal pace on one job may be more difficult to maintain than the raters' idea of normal pace on another job. Also, what may be a relatively easy normal pace to one worker may be a relatively difficult normal pace to another worker. If this be true, it is probably the cause of many grievances about the time-study system.

A third purpose of this study was to compare the workers' judgments with the observers' pace ratings.

II. PROCEDURE

The general procedure involved the rating, by expert time-study men, of movies of performances of previously established paces. Each of five "workers" performed each of four jobs at each of five paces, and movies were taken of these performances. The workers made an evaluation of each pace on each job. Six time-study men rated twice each of the performances shown on the film; there was an interval of a month between rating sessions.

Workers

The workers were five Purdue students (male) who had been employed at factory jobs where they were either on a piece rate or quota system. They had had no training in time study. They were accustomed to making the kind of judgments about paces that workers usually make.

Jobs Performed

The four jobs were elements of factory tasks. They were simple enough to be learned quickly and to be done in rhythm with a metronome. The jobs are described as follows:

  1. Twisting screws. Twisting a ⅜-inch screw in and out of a threaded hole. The screw was twisted half a turn each beat of the metronome.
  2. Stamping. Stamping boxes with a rubber stamp. The boxes were 3 inches square. They were set in a carton which was 6 inches deep. The boxes were 12 inches from the stamp pad. The box was stamped every other beat and the stamp pad was stamped every other beat.
  3. Twisting bolts. Alternately twisting two ½-inch hexagonal bolt heads placed 30 inches apart, requiring movement of the arm about the shoulder. One bolt was twisted each beat.
  4. Packing. Packing 36 3 × 3 × 2-inch boxes of half-bearings into a carton. The boxes were presented in 6 piles, grasped one at a time with one hand, transferred to the other hand, and placed in the carton in three 3 × 4 layers. When packing, one hand grasped a box and the other hand positioned a box in the carton on the first beat, and the hand-to-hand transfer was done on the second beat.

All workers were apparently able to learn to do these jobs easily in two hours, and after that time apparently they were not bothered by the imposed metronome rhythm. The workers practiced the jobs for six hours before they made their judgments, and the films were taken after that. There was no apparent lack of skill on these performances.

Paces Maintained

The normal pace for each of the four jobs was determined by a preliminary study. For this preliminary study, movies were made of several workers doing the four jobs, and the same six experts used in the actual study rated these preliminary films. Estimates of the tempo that represented normal pace for a job were obtained by dividing the actual tempo (the beats per minute of the performance observed) by the rating for that tempo. These estimates were then averaged for each job to obtain the tempo which the six experts considered the average normal pace.

Each worker performed each job at the tempo corresponding to normal pace, and at 90, 110, 120, and 130 percent of that tempo. The metronome tempo for each pace of each job is given in Table 18.1.

TABLE 18.1. *Metronome settings for paces and jobs.*

Pace	Job 1	Job 2	Job 3	Job 4
90	142	112½	65½	112½
100	158	125	73	125
110	174	137½	80½	137½
120	189½	150	88	150
130	205½	162½	95	162½

Raters

The expert time-study raters were six men who all are making, or have made, time studies in industry. Two were professors on the industrial engineering staff at Purdue. Two were time-study men for a large manufacturing firm, and two were men with several years of experience in time study who had returned to school for advanced degrees.

Film

Movies were taken of each worker on each job at each pace. The film was cut and reassembled in a sequence such that there was no order which the raters could detect.

> Each job was presented once in the first four shots, once in the second four, and so on. Each worker was presented once in the first five shots, once in the second five, and so on. Each pace was presented once in the first five shots, once in the second five, and so on. The order of presentation of jobs, workers, and paces within the groups of four or five was never repeated in the next group. No two shots of the same job were

ever in sequence, and only once was the same worker shown twice consecutively.

Each shot was about 24 seconds of running time. A blank leader, five seconds long, was spliced between each shot. The raters were to write down their ratings while this leader ran through the projector. All of the raters thought that the shots were long enough to rate. The film was put on three reels. Each reel ran about 16 minutes.

When the pictures were taken, the camera was operated by a synchronous motor drive at 1,000 frames per minute. The projector was run at exactly this speed. A strobotac was used to determine the projector speed.

Pace Ratings

Generally, ratings are given in "points," analogous to percentage points. An apparently normal pace is rated as 100 points. A pace 10 per cent slower than normal is rated as 90 points. The measurements of error used in this study are expressed as the number of points in the errors of the ratings.

Two rating sessions were held about a month apart, and all six raters rated on each session. In the second session the order of presentation of the three reels of the film was reversed. A rest pause of about 10 minutes was taken by the raters between reels.

Method of Obtaining Worker Judgments

In order to be able to compare the time-study men's ratings of work paces with the workers' judgments of these paces, it was necessary to quantify the workers' judgments. These judgments represented the workers' relative evaluations of the paces on the four jobs. The quantification was done by having the worker compare, in dollars and cents, his feelings about the four jobs. The worker performed job 2 (stamping) at the normal pace, and was told that be working at that rate he could earn $1.00 an hour. Then he was given another job to perform at one of the five paces. He was asked, "If stamping like that you earned $1.00 an hour, how much should you be earning now?" After answering, he went back to the normal stamping, and then to another job pace to make the next comparison. This process was repeated until he had compared each job at each pace with the standard of stamping at normal pace.

Next, a different job, at a pace that the worker had equated to the normal stamping, by answering "$1.00 an hour" to the question of earnings, was chosen as the standard. The judgment process was repeated, this time using the new standard for comparison.

Finally, a third standard pace, on a third job, was chosen and the process was run again.

Thus, for each pace on each job, the worker made three judgments. The workers were told nothing about the relationship of the paces, or that they were being given the same paces over again. The job paces were presented in a random order.

Statistical Techniques

Analyses of variance (2, pp. 176–190) were made for the 1,200 time-study pace ratings obtained and for the 300 worker judgments. The interpretation of confidence levels was conservative because of the non-homogeneous variances present. An analysis of covariance (2, pp. 333–355) was made betwen worker judgments and time-study pace ratings on each pace of each job.

Reliability of a category of ratings, and of worker judgments, was calculated as the standard deviation of the errors of the ratings in that category, and is expressed as the standard error of the ratings. Significances of differences among standard errors were tested by Bartlett's test (2, pp. 195–197).

III. RESULTS

Reasonably conclusive answers to the questions proposed in the introduction to this study are provided by the data. The interpretation of this summary of results is modified by the following limitations of the study: the time-study men, although they professed the same verbal concept of normal pace, were not from the same plant; in addition, the time-study men may have experienced fatigue from so many ratings; further, the rating on any one shot may have been affected by the preceding shots; the jobs themselves were somewhat simpler than typical jobs;

TABLE 18.2. *Condensed analysis of variance of pace ratings.*

Source	Sum of Squares	Degrees of Freedom	Variance	F*
Jobs	368	3	123	48
Paces	312	4	78	31
Workers	1,456	4	366	142
Raters	4,995	5	999	381
Job×Worker	195	12	16.2	6.4
Job×Rater	559	15	37.3	15
Job×Order	36	3	12	4.7
Pace×Worker	93	16	5.8	2.3
Pace×Rater	562	20	28.1	11
Worker×Rater	155	20	7.8	3.0
Job×Rater×Order	152	15	10.1	4.0
Residual	2,270	889	2.55	
Total	12,151	1,199		

* All significant at .01 level.

and the paces observed did not include some of the extreme values occasionally seen in actual work. Some of these factors would operate to reduce error, others to increase it.

In order to develop the various phases of the results, all of the ratings were converted into "errors" by subtracting from the rating the "correct" rating for that tempo. The correct rating was the ratio of the observed tempo to the normal tempo.

To facilitate handling the data, the errors were coded by dividing them by five. *The analysis-of-variance tables are in terms of this coded error.*

Differences in Level of Rating

To measure the significance of contributions to the total variance, the mean error for each rater, worker, job, pace, order of showing, and interactions was calculated. The differences among means were tested by an analysis of variance. The factors which were significantly different at better than the .01 level of confidence are shown in Table 18.2. Order refers to the first or second rating session.

Differences in mean ratings of raters, workers, paces. Three factors are outstanding in their contribution to total error: differences among raters differences among workers, and differences among paces. The size of the variation among mean values of these groups is shown in Figure 18.1.

Over one-third of the total variance in Table 18.2 is caused by rater-to-rater differences. These differences are very practically significant. For example, on a standard set by rater 6, a worker would have to perform at a pace almost 30 per cent greater than on a standard set by rater 2. These six raters were not all from the same plant, but they were all using the same verbal concept of a normal pace.

The differences in normal times which would result from time studies made on different workers are also of very practical significance. Worker 2, for example, stands out on Figure 18.1 as being rated between 10 and 15 points higher than the others. No reason is advanced for this in terms of his physique. A normal time based on his performance would be 15 per cent slower than one based on worker 4.

The trend to underrate high paces and overrate low paces is also marked, and shows clearly on Figure 18.1. Probably this tendency becomes even more exaggerated at more extreme paces, and forms some basis for workers' preferences to have time studies taken on slow operators. A standard set on an operator working at a pace of 90 would be 7 per cent "looser" than a standard set on an operator working at a pace of 130.

Differences in mean rating of jobs. Had the ratings not changed from the preliminary film to the actual study, no job differences should have occurred. Normal pace for each job was taken as the average of the raters' concepts of normal pace for that job on the preliminary film. The significant difference among job means shown in Table 18.2 is a result

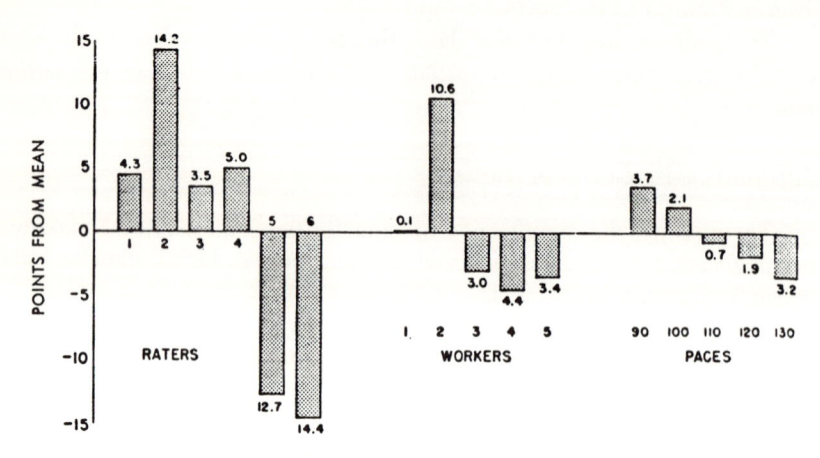

FIGURE 18.1. *Magnitude of variation among different sources.*

of the ratings for job 2 (stamping) being raised about 5 points from the preliminary to the actual study. In the preliminary study the raters saw the stamping from in front of the worker. They saw his hand moving at them. In the actual study the raters saw the worker from the side. This may account for the change, and also indicates that the angle of observation could be a topic for futher investigation.

Interactions of practical significance among pace ratings. The significant job × worker interaction in Table 18.2 reveals a pattern superimposed upon the tendency for some workers to be rated higher than others and the tendency for jobs to be rated differently. When the mean worker ratings are equated and the mean job ratings are equated, there remains a tendency for some workers to be rated higher on some jobs than on others. The size of the standard deviation due to this interaction is about two rating points.

The significant job × rater and worker × rater interactions of Table 18.2 reveal a pattern superimposed upon the tendency for some raters to rate higher than others and the tendencies for jobs and workers to be rated differently. There remain tendencies for some raters to rate some jobs higher than others and to rate some workers higher than others. The sizes of the standard deviations due to these interactions are about 4 and 2 rating points, respectively.

ERRORS IN TIME-STUDY JUDGMENTS 255

Pace × rater interaction of ratings. The pace × rater interaction in Table 18.2 indicates that not all raters underrate the high paces and overrate the low paces. Figure 18.2 shows that raters 2, 5, and 6 exhibit the tendency markedly, while rater 4 does so only slightly, and raters 1 and 3 not at all. The size of the standard deviation due to this interaction is about 5 rating points.

Other interactions of pace ratings. The pace × worker interaction in Table 18.2, which indicates a differential rating of the various workers at different paces, is statistically significant, but the size of the variations

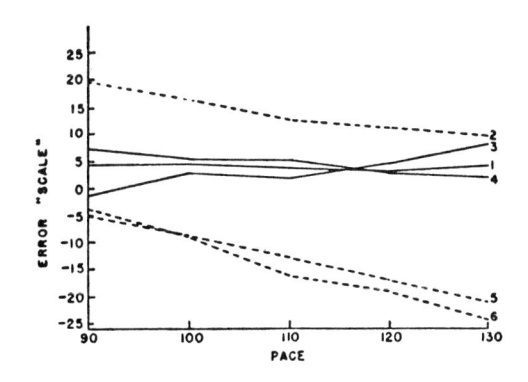

FIGURE 18.2. *Errors of each rater on each pace.*

is small. The interactions involving order are caused by some of the raters changing their concepts of normal on certain jobs. Although statistically significant, the size of the variations is of no practical meaning.

Magnitude of the Standard Errors of Pace Ratings

The standard error of all the ratings is 16 percentage points. This indicates that a normal time obtained from these ratings stands one chance in three of being wrong by ±16 points or greater.

To find the standard error representative of the consistency within a category of ratings, the variance among categories is subtracted from the total variance. The residual standard error, with all known sources of error eliminated, is 7.9 points. This represents the standard error present in any one rater's single rating.

Standard errors for various possible circumstances are shown in Table 18.3. The errors (except for the total) are measures of reliability rather than accuracy. For example, circumstance F might occur when a time-study man attempted to check a standard for a given job by timing several workers. The standard error of the normal times about the average of this rater would be 10.7 percentage points, but this rater's average might differ considerably from the average which other time-study men would get.

Circumstance B might occur in a company having the same job in several plants. The standard error of the normal times about the average would be 15.9 percentage points. Circumstances C, D, and H could occur in checking standards by various methods. Circumstances E and G might occur in a situation designed to test the reliability of raters.

Comparison of Reliability of Pace Ratings

The results of the study have been discussed in terms of errors due to constant differences in levels of ratings and in terms of average standard errors. In addition, real differences in the consistencies of ratings

TABLE 18.3. *Standard errors for various possible circumstances.*

Item	Percentage Points
A. Gross Standard Error	16.0
B. One job, several raters rating different workers at different paces.	15.9
C. One worker on one job, rated by several raters at different paces.	15.1
D. One worker on one job at one pace, rated by several raters.	14.5
E. One rater, rating several workers at different jobs at different paces.	11.2
F. One rater on one job, rating several workers at several paces.	10.7
G. One rater rating one worker, on several jobs at different paces.	9.1
H. One rater rating one worker on one job, at different paces.	8.5
I. One rater rating a worker on a job at one pace.	7.9

within categories do exist. As Table 18.4 shows, some raters are more consistent than others, some jobs can be rated more reliably than others, some workers can be rated more reliably than others, and some paces can be rated more reliably than others.

Differences in reliability of pace ratings of raters, workers, and jobs. Table 18.4 lists the standard error of ratings for each rater, worker, and job. The differences shown are of practical significance. Raters 4, 5, and 6 are much better than rater 3, as indicated in Table 18.4A. Table 18.4B shows that a standard obtained on worker 3 or 4, for

ERRORS IN TIME-STUDY JUDGMENTS

example, would be more reliable than one obtained on worker 2. The standard for job 2 would have to be checked more closely than the standard for job 1, according to Table 18.4C.

Differences in reliability of different paces. Figure 18.3 shows how reliability varies with pace. Normal pace is rated most reliably. The increase in standard error seems steeper at lower paces than higher. The

TABLE 18.4. *Standard errors of pace ratings.*

A. Standard Error in Points for Each Rater

Rater	Standard Error
1	13.2
2	11.8
3	16.2
4	10.6
5	10.4
6	10.1

B. Standard Error in Points of Ratings on Each Worker

Worker	Standard Error
1	14.7
2	17.0
3	14.2
4	14.3
5	15.0

C. Standard Error in Points of Ratings for Each Job

Job	Standard Error
1	12.8
2	17.7
3	15.3
4	16.6

standard error seems to increase proportionally to the increase in pace, about 0.2 per cent every 10 points of pace. While not of great practical significance within the range of paces studied, the trend has importance if extended to extreme paces.

Worker Judgments

The pace judgments of each worker on each job on each pace were subjected to an analysis of variance. As with the pace ratings, these judgments were coded by subtracting the "correct" figure from them, and

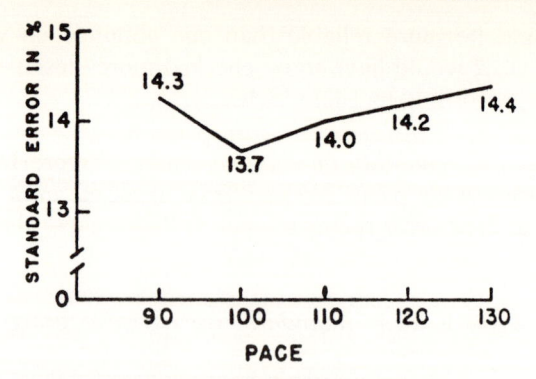

FIGURE 18.3. *Reliability of ratings at various paces.*

dividing this by five. The condensed analysis of variance, listing the factors which were significant at the .01 level of confidence, is presented in Table 18.5.

Worker judgments on jobs. Theoretically, normal times on different work elements or jobs should represent equally difficult levels of performance. The concept of "a fair day's work" should be constant from job-

TABLE 18.5. *Condensed analysis of variance of worker judgments.*

Source	Sum of Squares	D.F.	V	F*
Paces	70	4	17.5	5.37
Jobs	142	3	47.4	22.4
Worker×Job	1,165	16	72.8	14.5
Residual	900	276	3.26	
Total	2,277	299		

* All significant at .001 level.

to-job to both the time-study man and the worker. Other things being equal, a worker paid on an incentive plan should be able to earn as much on one job as on any other.

The results show that the workers do not equate the four jobs as the time-study men do. For example, the workers believe that "normal" on packing (job 4) is worth 12.7 cents an hour more than "normal" on stamping (job 2). Table 18.6 shows the differential, in points, between the workers' judgments and the pace ratings. Because the workers were given a concept of normal, this table does not indicate that the workers' concept of normal, averaged over the jobs, agrees with the raters' con-

ERRORS IN TIME-STUDY JUDGMENTS

TABLE 18.6. *Difference between worker judgments and pace ratings.*

Job	Worker Judgments Minus Pace Ratings, in Points
1	−3.2
2	−6.0
3	+2.5
4	+6.7

cept. It shows that a differential exists to the workers where none exists to the raters.

Worker judgments of different paces. The workers exhibit the same tendency as the raters to overrate low paces and underrate high paces. Table 18.7 lists the mean errors on each pace.

TABLE 18.7. *Mean errors of worker judgments on each pace.*

Pace	Error in Points
90	+2.5
100	+1.9
110	+1.5
120	−2.9
130	−3.0

Worker × job interaction of worker judgments. Not all workers judge the jobs in the same pattern. When the mean worker judgments and the mean job judgments are equated, there remains a tendency for some workers to judge some jobs higher than others. Table 18.8 shows the relative judgment made by each worker on each job. The numbers

TABLE 18.8. *Worker × job interaction of worker judgments (Points deviation from the average for the worker and the job)*

Worker	Job 1	2	3	4
1	−11.8	−6.6	+17.0	+1.5
2	− 0.7	+3.4	− 2.3	−0.4
3	− 1.8	+1.4	− 2.0	+2.3
4	+17.8	+4.0	−21.4	−0.5
5	− 3.5	−2.3	+ 8.6	−2.8

are the points from the average which the worker assigned the job, minus the sum of the points from the average of the job and the worker. The size of these interactions is of practical significance, particularly workers 1 and 4 on jobs 1 and 3. Worker 1 thinks that job 3 is worth much more than job 1, while worker 4 has the reverse opinion. On job 1, worker 1 would be satisfied with a standard time about 30 per cent less than the standard time worker 4 would require. On job 3, worker 1 would look for a standard time about 40 per cent greater than the standard time with which worker 4 would be satisfied.

Standard error of the worker judgments. The standard error of the worker judgments is comparable to the standard error of the pace ratings. The total standard error is 13.8 points, compared to 16.0 for the pace ratings. The residual standard error is 9.0 points, compared to 7.9 for the pace ratings.

Reliability of worker judgments. Real differences in reliability of judgments exist. Some workers are more consistent than others, and some jobs are judged more reliably than others.

Table 18.9 lists the standard error of the judgments of each worker,

TABLE 18.9. *Standard errors of worker judgments.*

A. Standard Error in Points for Each Worker

Worker	Standard Error
1	15.5
2	8.2
3	7.4
4	15.3
5	15.0

B. Standard Error in Points for Each Job

Job	Standard Error
1	15.0
2	8.3
3	18.3
4	9.7

and for each job. The differences shown are of practical significance. Some of the workers are far more reliable than others, as indicated in Table 18.9A. The standard error of workers 2 and 3 is half that of the rest, and compares favorably with the standard error of the time-study men. There is no apparent relation between the worker's being consistent in his judgments and the reliability with which he is rated.

The workers do not agree as well on some jobs as on others. The jobs in Table 18.9B on which the worker judgments are relatively unreliable are not the same jobs on which the pace ratings are relatively unreliable.

The difference in variance among paces is not statistically significant. The standard errors of the judgments seem to increase as pace increases; this was true also of the standard errors of the pace ratings.

Correlation between pace ratings and worker judgments. An analysis of the covariance between ratings of the five workers on the four jobs and the judgments of the workers about the jobs reveals a correlation within the workers and jobs of + .46. The analysis of covariance statistically equates the mean job ratings and worker judgments. The positive correlation indicates that, to the extent indicated by the correlation of .46, a worker will be rated relatively high on a job which he feels *should* be rated relatively high.

IV. PREVIOUS STUDIES OF RATING

Several experimental investigations of time-study rating have been published and are pertinent to the present study. Two have shown that filmed performances are rated the same as live performances. Other studies have attempted to measure the consistency of ratings of work pace, but in general they do not consider the effects of different raters, workers, jobs, paces, and interactions. Some investigators have shown that rating ability is improved by training, and others have been concerned with predicting rating ability. One group of researchers has been interested in the development of aids for rating, in the form of films of known paces.

Use of Film for Rating

The results of the present study would be invalid if performances on movie film are rated differently from live performances. Mundel and Margolin (8) and Barnes (1) have shown that ratings from movies are as consistent and accurate as ratings of actual workers.

Measurements of Consistency

Although a few experimenters report the standard errors of the ratings they have obtained, their data can be manipulated to find the standard errors. Thirteen points represents the mean and the mode of all of the standard errors of ratings of work paces found in the studies cited in the References section. This is compatible with the findings of this study, that the total standard error is 16 points, because the previous studies have measured the reliabilities of single raters, or ratings on single jobs. None of them has had ratings on more than one worker on a job. All but one of the reported standard errors are within the range of from 8 points for residual to 16 points for total standard error reported in the present study.

Training Raters

Several investigations have been made as to whether rating can be improved by training and experience. One of Mundel's students (7) found that raters with over six months' experience had a standard error which was 5/6 the size of that of raters with less experience.

Barnes (1) cites three studies of the rating of walking, wherein the standard error was reduced from 16 points to 12 points following a two-day training session. During a six-month training period, in which a group of raters was trained to rate the specific job on which they were tested, standard error went as low as 3 points. The raters could not be expected to maintain this level of consistency on other jobs.

Lifson (4), with time-study students rating some films of factory jobs, reduced the standard error from 11 to 9 points in an eleven-week training period. He also noted that the raters who were originally most consistent improved the most. Another finding was that the concept of normal pace can be shifted very easily. He changed the level of rating by demonstrating the level of activity which was to be considered as normal, and the ratings shifted as the demonstrated level shifted.

Predicting Rating Ability

Lifson (4) found that ability to rate after training could be predicted from ability to rate before training. The correlation between a consistency measure before and after was +.45. He observed that ability to rate can be predicted even more successfully after the raters have practiced for about two weeks. Holder (3) found no correlation between rating ability and scores in the Purdue Adaptability Test, the Purdue Physical Science Test, the Purdue Mathematics Training Test, the Purdue Placement Test in English, A.C.E., or motion- and time-study tests.

Aids for Rating

In an attempt to objectify the rating procedure, Dr. M. E. Mundel has worked with a system of rating that involves the use of aids in the form of movies of established levels of pace. The rater compares the pace in question to the established standard. He attempts to compare acceleration alone, and later adjusts for job difficulties. A paper by Mundel and his students (7) reports that by using a single standard film, representing a normal pace, the standard error (with no job or worker variance) was reduced from the "unaided" value of 14 points to 13 points. Use of a series of twelve established paces, ranging from 80 to 155, further reduced the standard error to 12 points.

V. IMPLICATIONS

From the pace ratings of experienced time-study men, it was determined that the magnitude of the standard error of these pace ratings is 16 percentage points, and that much of this error is due to differences among raters, workers, jobs, paces, and their interactions.

The residual standard error is 7.9 percentage points. It has also been shown that there are real differences in the reliability of ratings from different sources, that what are two equal paces to time-study men may not feel equal to the workers performing at the paces.

Some further researches and procedures are required to help increase the consistency and accuracy of pace rating. Some specific areas of attention which are suggested by this study are discussed below.

Reliability of Raters

Some raters are more reliable than others. More research is needed in the prediction of reliability, and also in what it is that causes some raters to be reliable. Because of the wide differences in reliability shown among the raters in this study, the need for testing experienced time-study men is revealed. More research is also needed in methods of training time-study men to rate consistently.

Agreement of Raters

Some raters rate higher than others, even when all raters have the same verbal concept of normal pace. Agreement among raters is a major problem. It is apparent that time-study men need concentrated training in recognizing a common concept of normal pace, and frequent checks to assure that their concepts have not changed. Research is needed into methods of objectifying the rating function and into methods of securing agreement among raters.

Averaging of Several Ratings

Consideration should be given to the fact that averages are more accurate and reliable than individual ratings. Although it is expensive to have more ratings made, it is probably less expensive than setting standards which may be 30 per cent off.

Differences in Ratings on Various Workers

Some workers are rated higher than others, even when performing the same jobs in the same time, and some are rated more reliably. No research has been done, though a great deal is needed, into why some workers are rated differently from others. The reliability and level at which different workers are usually rated should be known to time-study men. When there is a choice, they should have as the operator a worker who is rated reliably and at an average level.

Reliability of Different Jobs

Some jobs are rated more reliably than others. Increased reliability may come from knowing why.

Paces Rated Differently

Normal paces are rated most accurately and consistently. When there is a choice, time-study men should avoid timing extremely fast or slow operators. They should look for an operator whose performance is very close to their idea of normal.

Reliability and Accuracy of Worker Judgments

In order for any time-study system to work, paces which the time-study men rate as equal must seem equal to the workers. Time standards are not consistent from job to job unless the workers believe the standards are consistent. This study shows that this belief is not always held.

Much more can be done with worker judgments. They should be used, in some way, as the criterion with which to test the accuracy and consistency of time-study ratings. They should be used to determine adjustments and allowances. This study shows that they are reliable enough to be used for these purposes.

Some of the workers judge more consistently than the time-study men rate. This suggests the possibility of obtaining ratings from certain workers, or of having the time-study men rate while they themselves are performing the jobs.

VI. SUMMARY AND CONCLUSIONS

In a study designed to determine the nature of the errors involved in time-study ratings of work pace, six expert time-study men made ratings of the filmed performances of five workers doing each of four jobs at each of five previously established paces. The variance of the ratings was analyzed to reveal how much of the total error was attributable to differences among the time-study men in their concepts of normal work pace, differences in the way each worker and each job were rated, and differences in the rating errors made at each of the paces. Also, the standard errors of each group of ratings were compared, as a measure of relative reliability.

While the workers were performing the jobs, they evaluated, in relative terms, each pace on each job. Analysis of variance was applied to these judgments to determine the significance of the errors involved. Also, the relative level of the worker judgments on each job was compared with the relative level of the time-study men's pace ratings, to determine the amount of discrepancy.

The following conclusions are presented:

1. Pace ratings involve considerable error. The total standard error of pace ratings from different raters, on different jobs, workers, and paces was 16.0 percentage points. The standard error of one rater rating one worker on a job at a pace was 7.9 points, on the average.

2. Some raters rate higher than others. The highest rater averaged 28 points above the lowest rater.

3. Some raters are more consistent than others. The most consistent rater had a standard error 5/8 the size of the standard error of the least consistent rater. Figure 18.4 shows, for each rater, the spread that would include 19 out of 20 ratings of the average normal pace.

4. Some workers are rated higher than others, even when all perform the same jobs at the same paces. A standard time set on the worker who was rated the highest would have been 15 percent longer than one set on the worker who was rated lowest.

5. Some workers are rated more reliably than others. The standard

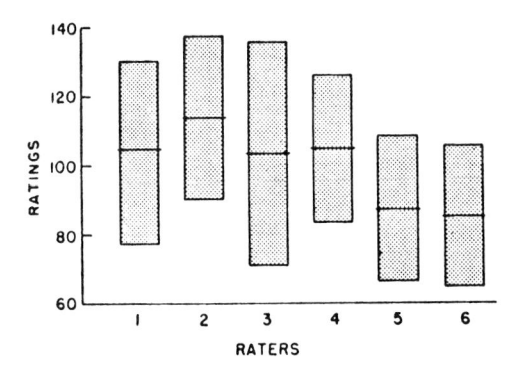

FIGURE 18.4. *Mean and "Range" of ratings by each rater of the average normal pace. (The "range" includes 95 per cent of the ratings by each rater.)*

error of the ratings on the most reliably rated worker was 5/6 the size of the standard error of the ratings on the least reliably rated worker.

6. The raters tend to overrate low paces and underrate high paces. A standard time set on a pace of 90 would have been 7 per cent longer than a standard time set on a pace of 130.

7. Normal pace is rated most reliably. The standard error increased slightly at paces slower or faster than normal.

8. Some jobs are rated more reliably than others. The standard error of the ratings on the most reliably rated job was 3/4 the size of the standard error of the ratings on the least reliably rated job.

9. Interactions are important. Some raters rated some jobs higher than others; some raters rated some workers higher than others; some workers were rated higher on some jobs than on others; and not all raters followed the pattern of underrating high paces and overrating low ones.

10. Workers' judgments on equating the jobs differ from the pace ratings of the time-study men. The workers believed there was as much as a 12 per cent per hour differential between two "normal" paces as established by time-study men.

11. Individual differences among the worker judgments are very important. On the same job there was as much as a 40 per cent difference between two workers' judgments as to what was a normal pace.

12. Some workers can judge more reliably than time-study men can rate. The standard error of the judgments of the two most consistent workers was 3/4 the size of the standard error of the best time-study men.

13. A correlation of +.46 exists between the workers' judgments and the pace ratings of the time-study men. To the extent indicated by this correlation, on a job which a worker judged relatively high, he would be rated relatively high; and on a job which a worker judged relatively low, he would be rated relatively low.

In conclusion, this study has indicated the nature of the errors which are involved in time-study pace ratings, and has indicated some possible approaches to the reduction of these errors.

REFERENCES

1. BARNES, R. M. *Work measurement manual.* (3rd Ed.) Dubuque: Wm. C. Brown Company, 1947.
2. EDWARDS, A. L. *Experimental design in psychological research.* New York: Rinehart, 1950.
3. HOLDER, W. B. Applicability of six standard tests in the prediction of time study rating ability. Unpublished master's thesis, Purdue Univer., 1949.

4. LIFSON, K. A. Performance rating. *Time Study Engr*, 1951, 6 (June), 179–181.
5. LIFSON, K. A. A psychological approach to pace rating. Unpublished doctor's dissertation, Purdue Univer., 1951.
6. LYNCH, H. R. Rating of time studies. In *Proceedings of the 5th annual time study and methods conference.* 1950.
7. MUNDEL, M. E. (Ed.) *Report of the 5th annual motion and time study work session.* Lafayette: Purdue Univer., 1950. (Mimeographed)
8. MUNDEL, M. E. & MARGOLIN, L. *Report of the 4th annual motion and time study work session.* Lafayette: Purdue Univ., 1948. (Mimeographed)
9. SCHELL, H. A. A study on effort rating. *Modern Mgmt*, 1949, 9 (April), 19–20.

IV DIMENSIONS OF PERFORMANCE

The history of psychology is replete with the development of devices to be used for the measurement of individual differences; at present, there are literally hundreds of them. The obvious implications are that the human organism has a high degree of complexity and that adequate measurement requires this profusion of instruments. However, in predicting behavior these same instruments are used to predict a single measurement, usually a rating, and the inference might be that performance, from the complex human organism, is a quite simple and obvious occurrence. Actually, of course, this practice is the result of researchers seizing upon the most available, or apparent, criterion. In effect such usage affirms that behavior is a global characteristic that can be summarized with a relatively simple measure.

An article (in Part I) by Dunnette (1963) elaborates on the implications of using a single, global criterion and presents research results to show the fallacies involved in the practice. In general, the point is made that adequate validation studies require that performance behavior be conceptualized as a complex event that in itself requires study before adequate or even meaningful predictions are possible.

Various attempts, both practical and theoretical, have been made that show the commonly encountered research design of a global measure of performance is inadequate. The article by Flanagan (1949) is the first in a series of efforts to compile information describing performance in all its facets and ramifications. By the collection of "critical incidents" relative to job performance the investigator obtains a wide variety of behaviors that conclusively demonstrate the existence of several behavioral dimensions in even relatively simple tasks and, at the same time, an evaluation of them for criterion purposes; e.g., how effective or ineffective they are in terms of bringing about good or poor performance. In the history of psychology this was the first concerted research effort to examine performance per se *before* attempting its prediction. Subsequent efforts with the technique provide one of the major bodies of evidence to support the thesis of this section—the multi-dimensional nature of performance.

Another approach to the problem has centered around factor analysis as the major investigative technique. The first study by Rush (1953) might be adopted as a model for future research in the area. It consists of carefully constructed training and actual job proficiency criteria for sales work, measures of individual differences in aptitudes, preferences and personality, personal history information, and ratings of performance. A factor analysis showed three separate dimensions of performance which were predicted by different instruments at a significant level. Parenthetically, as related to previous sections, the criteria of actual sales and performance ratings were independent of each other.

The next article, by Ronan (1963), extracted four factors from eleven performance measurements for skilled tradesmen. Two features of note are that a "safety factor" shown as susceptibility to accidents is defined and that it also has a fairly substantial loading on a supervisory-evaluation factor. In effect, this means that employees rated as more competent by their supervisors are likely to be injured more often. This contradictory nature of performance dimensions will be pointed out in some other studies. The most unique feature of the study is that it does demonstrate the usefulness of organizational indices to measure performance probably because of the relatively long time period—ten years—covered by the study.

A much more complex study is that by Wherry, et. al. (1961). A great variety of measurements of both individuals and their performance describe administrative employees and systems and aircraft maintenance mechanics. The general design was to factor criterion information to obtain factor scores against which to validate various predictive information and test scores. Actually several analyses were performed and six meaningful factors extracted. One of the major conclusions is the need for multi-dimensional evaluation of performance. A general summary of the complex research project is, at this point, rather meaningless; it is suggested that it receive close attention from the reader for both methodology and conclusions.

One of the consequent studies reported is that by Turner (1960). The subjects were foremen in two separate plants of the same organization. Five factors were extracted from 20 variables with three factors common to both plants. However, the other two were specific to the separate plants. This is evidence that is also applicable to a later section on the situational determinants of behavior. Three other points brought out by the study deserve comment. The first is that Turner found his performance indices had quite low reliabilities until several months had passed. Second, at least one of his factors shows bipolarity; that is, good foremanship on some aspects precludes good performance on others. The third point is that, as in the Rush study, there is little overlap between objective indices of performance and ratings of the same performance.

The study by Heron (1952), one of the earlier using factor analysis, had criteria of production and ratings by supervisors. In relation to the latter is a rating of "source of concern to his supervisors." The subjects were unskilled workers and four factors were extracted. The most interesting of these was that related to "emotional instability" which showed a substantial relation (negative) with good job adjustment. This is one of the few studies in psychology to report job satisfaction as a criterion and advances an interesting hypothesis as a result; i.e., dissatisfaction with a job results from inability to do the job adequately. In any case the study does show another possible performance dimension and one that can only be evaluated by some sort of rating, "source of concern to their supervisors."

The study by Taylor, et. al. (1965) is representative of the work at the University of Utah concerned with the performance of physicians. This particular study, along with others in this extensive series, conspicuously demonstrates the nature of the problem of concern in this section. From 80 performance measures for general practitioners, 30 factors were extracted to show the possible dimensions involved in evaluating performance in this relatively more complex job. Furthermore, there were no measures of performance directly concerned with the practice of medicine, for example, skill in diagnosis. Undoubtedly the addition of such measures would add further dimensions to those already found and further compound the complexity demonstrated. One of the major conclusions of the investigators has to do with the topic in hand; it is the futility of attempting to assess performance in any complex work with some sort of global measure of performance.

Some further evidence exists regarding the need for developing multi-dimensional measures to assess performance. A number of research studies are available that deal with single criteria or limited aspects of a complex performance. The study by Hilton and Dill (1962) presented here shows the complexities of salary as a criterion.

The general point is supported by Fleishman and Ornstein (1960), who demonstrate the existence of six factors in merely maneuvering an aircraft, a relatively limited part of the job of a pilot being in command of an aircraft. In general, there appear to be some several dimensions for even rather limited aspects of various job performances.

An alternate approach to demonstrating the complexity of job performance is by inference from studies of job functions. The first study, Prien (1965), reports an investigation of functions in clerical work in terms of comparison with previous work. The existence of independent, definable functions identified through factor analysis is rather convincing evidence that criterion development and measurement must be specific and not global if meaningful results are to be expected.

To summarize, what information does exist in the comparatively few attempts to define the dimensions of performance, shows that independent dimensions can be demonstrated and, further, that such dimensions are often negatively related. The implication is in fact that much of our present evidence gathered with limited, "one-shot" studies although of interest is not helpful and may even be misleading when it is applied to understanding performance. For example, a research investigation may show that a given predictive device is quite effective in pinpointing those persons likely to have accidents, but one of the studies presented here illustrates that this may mean a poor worker who does not get hurt because he does relatively little work. It is the authors' position that performance is a quite complex phenomenon and better understanding is directly dependent upon designing studies that use dimensional performance measurements.

REFERENCE

FLANAGAN, J. C. Critical Requirements: A new approach to employee evaluation. *Personnel Psychology,* 1949, 2, 419–425.

19 A Factorial Study of Sales Criteria

CARL H. RUSH, JR.

SUMMARY

In recent years, personnel managers have shown an increasing tendency to use various types of psychometric devices for the selection of potentially successful sales personnel. This trend is partially reflected in the large number of reports on the selection of sales personnel which appear in professional and nonprofessional journals (2, 6). These reports, which range from opinionated hunches to exhaustive tests of predictive efficiency, have perhaps one common denominator—a somewhat perfunctory treatment of the criterion. In those studies which report validation of trial predictors, there is a tendency to emphasize prediction with only slight regard for that which is being predicted. Frequently, the measure of sales success consists of a gross index such as "Sales Volume" or a rating of "Over-all Performance." Use of such global criterion measures assumes that success in selling is unitary; that "good" and "poor" salesmen differ on only one performance dimension. Yet, it is conceivable that a number of relatively independent skills are involved in selling such that any given salesman may be high on one performance characteristic and low on another. Indeed, almost any sales manager can point to a salesman who "knows his product well and can make excellent demonstrations" but who is "weak in closing ability."

If, then, the criterion of sales success is a complex one, it seems reasonable to conclude that the development of effective selection devices will be facilitated by a knowledge of the basic skills involved. Once the criterion dimensions are known, the selection of predictors to be validated may proceed with greater promise of positive results. In addition, it is suggested that perhaps the most fruitful approach to this problem lies in the development of selection tools for the prediction of a "criterion profile" or a weighted composite rather than a single over-all criterion.[1] The present study was an attempt to discover, in a specific selling situa-

From *Personnel Psychology*, 1953, 6, 9–24. The author is indebted to Dr. Roger M. Bellows, Director of the Personnel Research Center, Wayne University for his guidance, and to Mr. Paul Kanold of the Burroughs Adding Machine Company for his cooperation in making this study possible.

[1] For more extensive discussions of this concept, the reader should consult Brodgen and Taylor (1), Fiske (3), Toops (8), and Wherry (9).

tion, the basic factors in sales success and to examine the differential predictive value of a trial set of predictors.

For a sample of 100 salesmen, three types of criterion measures were collected: (1) supervisors' ratings on a number of performance characteristics, (2) sales records, and (3) grades in a technical sales school. In addition, data were gathered for all members of the sample on a series of personal history items and a trial battery of tailor-made tests. Factor analysis of the criterion variables revealed four relatively uncorrelated factors which appeared to represent independent dimensions of performance in this situation. Composite criterion scores were derived for each of the factors against which the trial predictors were validated. Multiple correlations, computed for each of the factors, were sufficiently high to suggest that differential prediction of the multiple criteria of sales success is both feasible and desirable.

THE PROBLEM

This investigation was conducted as part of a program of personnel research in the Marketing Division of the Burroughs Adding Machine Company. This firm, engaged in the production, marketing and maintenance of office machinery, maintains several hundred branch offices throughout the United States and the world. Personnel activities are controlled from the home office in Detroit, Michigan where complete records are available on every member of the sales force. Although branch managers in the field have a large responsibility as regards personnel actions, final authority in selection, remuneration and promotion, as well as some responsibility for training, is vested in the central office. Because recruitment and preliminary screening of applicants are accomplished by the individual branches, management expressed a need for the development of objective devices for the selection and appraisal of sales personnel which would systematize and standardize the personnel functions of branch managers in the field. It was toward this objective that the present study was directed.

TRIAL TEST PREDICTORS

After a careful analysis of the duties and functions of a Burroughs salesman, a trial battery of tests was constructed. These tests were tailor-made for the situation and were developed with a view toward their potential predictive ability. Time limits were established after trial testing sessions with college students. In general the tests were of three main types: (1) verbal facility, (2) numerical facility, and (3) personality. A description of each of the trial tests follows:

Verbal Facility—This test contained 50 multiple choice problems of analogy, inductive and deductive reasoning, and simple definitions. Time limit was 8 minutes.

Numerical Reasoning—Contained 50 multiple choice items designed to measure ability to reason in quantitative terms. Time limit was 16 minutes.

Number Copying—This test consisted of 50 numbers which the subjects were to copy on the reverse side of the test paper. Numbers increased in length, the first being 3 digits and the last number 12 digits. Time limit was 4 minutes.

Number Comparison—This test contained 150 pairs of numbers which the subjects were to compare and indicate whether they were similar or dissimilar. Designed to measure speed and accuracy in checking numbers, this test had a time limit of 6 minutes.

Business Arithmetic—This test consisted of 34 multiple choice items in business arithmetic. Included were problems of discount, fractions, depreciation and interest. Time limit was 16 minutes.

Personal Preferences—This test contained 172 descriptions of people and activities. Subjects were asked to indicate whether they liked, disliked, or were indifferent towards each of these people or activities. There was no time limit.

Personality Inventory—This test contained two parts. The first part consisted of 82 statements concerning behavior or opinion. Subjects were asked to indicate whether or not these statements reflected their usual behavior or opinion. The second part contained 40 multiple choice items dealing with interpersonal relations. Subjects were asked to choose the response which most nearly resembled their usual behavior. Keys for this test were developed through item analysis. There was no time limit.

A team of examiners, trained to accomplish the field testing, visited a number of centrally located branch offices and administered the trial test battery to a total of 352 salesmen, representing 85 branches. In order to partially control length of experience, only those men hired between 1 June 1948 and 1 September 1949 were tested. Established principles of test administration were followed throughout and all tests were returned to the home office for scoring immediately after the testing sessions. This procedure was followed in order to avoid possible contamination of subsequent criterion measures.

While the team of examiners was in the field to administer the trial test battery, an attempt was made to gather tentative criterion data by asking each branch manager and assistant branch manger to rank the men being tested. From the 165 subjects ranked in this fashion, "high" and "low" criterion groups of salesmen were established and a tabulation was made of their responses to the items on the Personality Inventory. Empirical scoring keys were developed using those items which discriminated significantly between the two groups.

NON-TEST PREDICTORS

A group of seven non-test predictors was incorporated into the study in order to determine whether or not these data had predictive value. Items selected for scrutiny were: Age, Marital Status, Number of Dependents, Previous Sales Experience, College Grades, Number of Accounting Courses, and Applicant Index. The first five of these variables are self-explanatory. The last two, however, need some clarification. In the selection of Burroughs salesmen, the majority of whom are college graduates, considerable emphasis has been placed on accounting education on the assumption that some knowledge of accounting principles and terminology is necessary for success in selling Burroughs machines. In order to check on this hypothesis, Number of Accounting Courses was included as a non-test predictor.

The Applicant Index is a rating given each applicant by the central personnel office. When an applicant is recommended for hire by a Branch manager, all pertinent papers are forwarded to the home office in Detroit. These papers, consisting of an application blank, report of physical examination, letters of reference, college transcript, and an interview rating sheet, are assembled and studied by personnel men in the home office. From this scrutiny an over-all rating from 1 to 4 is assigned, based on an estimate of a candidate's potential. This index, essentially a prediction, was included as a non-test predictor.

THE CRITERIA

In an effort to discover available indices of sales success, company forms and records were scrutinized. From this source, three separate sales indices were gathered on all members of the sample for the fiscal year ending 31 December 1949. These were:

> Per Cent of Quota Achieved—When a salesman is assigned a territory he is given a quota toward which to strive. At the end of a given year, his net sales are compared with his quota and a percentage figure is derived.
> Average Monthly Volume—This index was computed by dividing a salesman's net sales (corrected for returns) by the number of months he was in the territory.
> Average Number of Monthly Sales—This index consisted of the average number of sales completed per month. This did not reflect units sold; if a salesman sold five machines on a single order, it was counted as one sale.

At the time of the present study, 100 of the 352 salesmen in the experimental sample had been on their respective territories for more than six months and it was decided to include only these 100 men in the study.

The three sales indices described above were coded in a somewhat unique manner in order to make allowances for differences in opportunity to sell which existed between branches. A crude estimate of these differences was available in the form of the percentage of quota achieved by each branch. Using 1949 sales figures, this index was calculated for each of the branch offices in which members of the sample were working. The branches were then grouped into four categories according to their percentage figures. Group means and standard deviations were computed for each of the indices and standard or z scores were computed for each man relative to his own group. Thus a man's performance was coded in terms of his relative standing when compared with other salesmen operating in branches with equal or near equal opportunity to sell.

As a supplement to the objective variables, a rating device consisting of nine items was developed on the supposition that subjective appraisals might yield additional information as to the relative success or failure of the members of the sample. The rating form consisted of a five interval, forced distribution scale for each of the following characteristics:

1. Technical Knowledge
2. Learning Ability
3. Interest and Enthusiasm
4. Sales Approaches
5. Planning of Work
6. Sales Demonstrations
7. Closing Ability
8. Present Value to Firm
9. Potential Value to Firm

This form was reproduced and mailed to the various branches. Branch managers and supervisors were asked to rate the men in their respective branches in accordance with instructions contained in a separate rating manual. At least two independent ratings were accomplished on each of the 352 members of the original sample even though only 100 men were to be studied in this investigation.

One additional criterion variable was incorporated into the study. Each of the salesmen in the sample had attended a five week sales-training school. This school is conducted at the home office in Detroit and is a vital part of a salesman's training. Instruction is designed to acquaint each man with the full line of Burroughs machines. At the end of each week in the school, a grade was given to each man by his instructor. These grades were qualitative (excellent, good, fair, poor, and failing) but were converted to quantities on a simple 0 to 4 coding system. The total of a man's five school grades constituted his score on this variable.

RELIABILITY OF THE CRITERIA

The reliability of Sales School Grades was determined by means of the conventional odd-even reliability technique. Grades assigned in odd weeks of school were correlated with grades for even weeks and the obtained coefficient, when extended by the Spearman-Brown prophecy formula, was .87.

Reliability checks on the nine rating variables called for a somewhat different technique. Many of the men were rated by three or four raters while others were rated by only two raters. Odd-even methods would have been able to utilize only two of the ratings on all men since that was the lowest common denominator. To meet this problem, a technique recently developed by Horst (4) was used which made it possible to use all the obtained ratings. The nature of the formula allows the use of varying numbers of raters.

The Horst formula was also used to obtain reliability coefficients on two objective sales criteria, Average Monthly Volume and Average Number of Monthly Sales. Again the formula was very useful because a varying number of measures was available on the subjects. Performance records were available for only eight months on some men, 11 months on others, etc. A slight modification was necessary in that number of months was used as a term in the formula rather than number of raters. Per Cent of Quota Achieved did not lend itself to a reliability check. This index was derived at the end of the year by comparing actual sales with quota assigned. No statistical device was available to test the reliability of this kind of an index.

Table 19.1 contains the means, standard deviations and reliability coefficients for the 13 criterion variables. The obtained reliabilities were well within the acceptable range with the exception of Average Monthly Volume (.47).

FACTOR ANALYSIS OF THE CRITERIA

The 13 criterion variables were intercorrelated and the resulting matrix was factored in accordance with the complete centroid method described by Thurstone (7). Four factors were extracted and rotated to what appeared to be a meaningful solution. Table 19.2 contains the original intercorrelations (left of the diagonal), final residuals (right of the diagonal), and the rotated factor loadings. The resulting factors were identified as follows:

Factor I (Objective Achievement)—Interpretation of this factor was relatively simple because of the high loadings on the three objective indices of sales performance: Average Number of Monthly Sales, Per Cent of Quota Achieved, and Average Monthly Volume. All other criterion variables showed non-significant loadings.

Factor II (Learning Aptitude)—Variables with significant loadings on this factor were: Sales School Grades, Technical Knowledge, and Learning Ability. It will be recalled that the first of these variables reflected success in a training situation (instructor grades) while the last two variables were ratings made by branch supervisors. This would suggest that one of the relatively independent sub-criteria of sales success is an ability to learn quickly and efficiently.

Factor III (General Reputation)—All the nine characteristics rated by branch supervisors have significant loadings on this factor. Some research workers would prefer to call this a "halo" or "bias" factor because of the consistent tendency for subjective ratings of various characteristics to intercorrelate highly. This, however, is a negative sort of interpretation which may detract from the usefulness of ratings. In this situation, it was felt that one of the elements of success may well be the general regard in which a salesman is held by his supervisors. In other words, getting along with his boss may be as important a measure of a salesman's success as his ability to sell the product. Hence this factor was assumed to represent the general reputation of salesmen as viewed by their supervisors. It seemed rather significant that ratings of performance failed to correlate highly with measures of actual sales.

TABLE 19.1. *Means, standard deviations and reliability coefficients for 13 criterion variables*

CRITERION VARIABLE	MEAN	STANDARD DEVIATION	RELIABILITY COEFFICIENT
Sales School grades	16.00	2.10	.87
Technical Knowledge	2.30	.68	.68
Learning Ability	2.62	.69	.67
Interest and Enthusiasm	2.69	.84	.79
Planning of Work	2.35	.84	.92
Sales Approaches	2.20	.79	.69
Sales Demonstrations	2.24	.75	.71
Closing Ability	2.16	.87	.79
Present Value to Firm	2.30	.82	.73
Potential Value to Firm	2.64	.82	.79
Average Number of Monthly Sales	4.10	1.73	.75
Per Cent of Quota Achieved	91.12	43.16	—*
Average Monthly Volume	$1443.69	$695.91	.47

* Reliability coefficient not computed.

TABLE 19.2 *Intercorrelations, rotated factor loadings and final residuals for 13 criterion variables**
N = 100

	1	2	3	4	5	6	7	8	9	10	11	12	13	I	II	III	IV	h²
1. Average Number of Monthly Sales		−03	04	00	−01	−01	−02	01	01	04	02	−01	01	73	−07	17	00	57
2. Per Cent of Quota Achieved	46		03	−03	−02	−03	00	03	01	−04	−02	01	02	65	00	10	50	68
3. Average Monthly Volume	62	73		−04	−03	00	01	00	−02	−01	00	01	01	74	−18	14	40	76
4. Sales School Grades	−04	−07	−16		−01	02	−03	−02	02	04	01	−02	03	−03	48	07	−05	24
5. Technical Knowledge	−06	13	00	24		03	03	02	−01	01	−02	04	−03	−15	48	52	40	68
6. Learning Ability	05	22	13	34	72		−01	−02	02	−04	04	−01	01	03	63	47	38	76
7. Interest and Enthusiasm	21	18	20	11	48	46		04	01	−04	−03	02	−04	17	20	72	00	59
8. Planning of Work	29	26	24	14	46	47	63		−05	01	−02	01	−05	25	25	69	00	60
9. Sales Approaches	21	36	33	05	57	56	61	53		03	03	−01	03	09	00	81	42	84
10. Sales Demonstrations	18	23	23	16	61	55	53	57	78		01	−02	−02	03	17	74	35	70
11. Closing Ability	30	40	41	08	53	60	55	56	81	71		−01	−02	22	10	73	40	75
12. Present Value to Firm	28	38	38	10	60	58	65	65	75	69	73		00	24	18	77	28	76
13. Potential Value to Firm	30	36	34	21	60	68	66	66	83	74	77	82		23	28	85	22	90

* Decimals are omitted throughout the table.

Factor IV (Sales Techniques and Achievement)—This is a relatively weak factor which is somewhat difficult to interpret. It is the only factor on which communality is shown between the rating variables and the objective sales indices. Moderate loadings are found on Per Cent of Quota Achieved, Average Monthly Volume, Technical Knowledge, Learning Ability, Sales Approaches, Sales Demonstrations, and Closing Ability. One might conclude that this factor shows the influence of skill in selling techniques (as perceived by supervisors) on actual sales figures.

PREDICTION OF CRITERION COMPOSITES

Having defined the sub-criterion elements of sales success, the next step was to derive a composite of the criterion variables comprising each factor. For this purpose the Wherry-Doolittle test selection method (5) was used to compute beta weights for the maximum prediction of each factor. A slight modification from the usual procedure was necessary in that the rotated factor loadings were used as validity coefficients. Table 19.3 presents the results of this analysis, showing the variables compris-

TABLE 19.3. *Beta weights for variables comprising factor composites*

FACTOR	PREDICTOR	BETA WEIGHT
I. Objective Achievement	Average Number of Monthly Sales	.439
	Average Monthly Volume	.332
	Per Cent of Quota Achieved	.283
	Sales Approaches	−.213
II. Learning Aptitude	Sales School Grades	.218
	Technical Knowledge	.240
	Learning Ability	.679
	Sales Approaches	−.528
III. General Reputation	Planning of Work	.260
	Sales Approaches	.402
	Potential Value to Firm	.594
	Per Cent of Quota Achieved	−.278
	Learning Ability	−.221
IV. Sales Techniques and Achievement	Sales Approaches	.586
	Technical Knowledge	.530
	Per Cent of Quota Achieved	.316
	Average Monthly Volume	.237
	Interest and Enthusiasm	−.282
	Planning of Work	−.221
	Potential Value to Firm	−.446

TABLE 19.4 *Intercorrelations and validity coefficients for 14 predictor variables**
$N = 100$

Predictors	1	2	3	4	5	6	7	8	9	10	11	12	13	14
1. Verbal Facility														
2. Numerical Reasoning	38													
3. Number Copying	25	28												
4. Number Comparison	25	17	35											
5. Business Arithmetic	50	72	44	38										
6. Personal Preferences	−29	−18	03	10	−10									
7. Personality Inventory	−28	−05	12	14	−03	47								
8. Applicant Index	−02	18	06	05	17	10	11							
9. Age	07	08	02	−14	04	−03	−18	−21						
10. Marital Status	08	05	18	00	02	05	12	−15	14					
11. Number of Dependents	08	02	25	12	04	05	10	−09	18	80				
12. Previous Sales Experience	05	00	−05	−20	−13	10	00	03	04	10	02			
13. Number of Accounting Courses	−28	−13	−07	−09	02	04	−04	13	18	−09	−01	−22		
14. College Grades	17	17	20	−10	14	−13	02	33	00	−02	01	12	03	
Criterion Composites														
I. Objective Achievement	06	11	16	02	−08	−01	10	08	−09	07	−03	24	−32	13
II. Learning Aptitude	21	23	18	26	33	−15	01	03	−13	02	10	−20	13	21
III. General Reputation	−09	−14	−15	09	−10	18	31	18	03	−05	06	03	−09	−08
IV. Sales Techniques and Achievement	07	00	02	07	07	05	07	−12	−11	−15	−17	−05	−15	−06

* Decimals are omitted throughout the table.

ing each factor composite and their respective beta weights. It should be noted that, although shrunken multiple correlations were obtained in this analysis, they were of limited significance inasmuch as the primary objective was to obtain beta weights for the optimal combination of the criterion variables.

The 14 trial predictors were correlated against each of the criterion composites by means of the correlation of sums formula.[2] Validity coefficients and intercorrelations of the predictor variables are presented in Table 19.4. From the data in Table 19.4, multiple correlations were computed for the four criterion composites. Again, the Wherry-Doolittle method was used and shrunken multiple r's ranging from .22 to .44 were obtained. Table 19.5 shows, for each criterion composite, the selected predictors in the order in which they were selected, the derived beta weights, and the shrunken multiple correlations. With the exception of Factor IV, all multiple r's are significant, suggesting the use of these prediction equations for the selection of future sales applicants in this company.

It is, perhaps, of more general interest to examine the nature of the predictors which contribute most to the prediction of the first three criterion factors. For Factor I (Objective Achievement), Number of Accounting Courses and Previous Sales Experience are the most significant variables. These two experience items yield a multiple correlation of .35 with the factor composite and the addition of three numerical tests increases the multiple only slightly. It is interesting to note that Number of Accounting Courses correlates negatively with this criterion, a finding which is contrary to Burroughs employment policy.

For Factor II (Learning Aptitude), the predictors which contribute most to the multiple correlation are Business Arithmetic and College Grades. The first of these would probably correlate highly with general intelligence and hence its correlation with academic or educational achievement is not surprising. Similarly, it is reasonable for success in college (College Grades) to correlate with success in other learning situations.

The results for Factor III (General Reputation) also seem reasonable in that the largest single contribution to the multiple correlation is made by the Personality Inventory. Thus, a measure of personality provides the best prediction of superior's ratings, the composite of which we

[2] For the correlation of a single variable with a weighted composite of several variables, the following formula is useful:

$$r_{xy_6} = \frac{\beta_1 r_{x1} + \beta_2 r_{x2} + \ldots + \beta_n r_{xn}}{\sqrt{\beta_1^2 + \beta_2^2 + \ldots + \beta_n^2 + 2\beta_1\beta_2 r_{12} + \ldots + 2\beta_{n-1}\beta_n r_{(n-1)n}}}$$

Where:
x = a predictor variable
y_6 = a criterion composite of n variables
1, 2, 3 = criterion variables

have chosen to call General Reputation. It will be recalled that this predictor was a paper and pencil personality test scored with empirically derived keys. The results obtained for this test represent a cross validation inasmuch as the keys were developed through item analysis of responses given by a separate sample of Burroughs salesmen.

TABLE 19.5. *Selected predictors, beta weights and shrunken multiple correlations for the prediction of four criterion composites*

FACTOR	PREDICTOR	BETA WEIGHT	MULTIPLE r
I. Objective Achievement	Number of Accounting Courses	−.228	.32
	Previous Sales Experience	.156	.35
	Number Copying	.231	.37
	Business Arithmetic	−.349	.39
	Numerical Reasoning	.267	.42
II. Learning Aptitude	Business Arithmetic	.240	.33
	College Grades	.256	.36
	Previous Sales Experience	−.120	.39
	Number Comparison	.176	.40
	Age	−.119	.41
	Number of Accounting Courses	.158	.42
	Applicant Index	−.157	.44
III. General Reputation	Personality Index	.310	.31
	Number Copying	−.225	.35
	Applicant Index	.249	.37
	Age	.209	.38
	Number of Accounting Courses	−.172	.40
	Numerical Reasoning	−.172	.42
	Number Comparison	.156	.43
IV. Sales Techniques and Achievement	Number of Dependents	−.182	.17
	Number of Accounting Courses	−.136	.21
	Applicant Index	−.119	.22

CONCLUSIONS

The findings of this study suggest that prediction of the multiple criteria of sales success is possible to a moderate degree. There is need for caution, however, in the interpretation of these results. Although significant multiple correlations were obtained for three of the four criterion factors, cross validation checks are needed to determine the stability of the findings. Despite the tentative nature of the findings with respect to predictive efficiency, there are several general conclusions to be derived from this study:

1. The criterion of sales success is multi-dimensional rather than unitary and hence the use of global measures of success or failure would seem undesirable. Indeed, the use of such all-encompassing variables in validation studies may obscure the underlying relationships.

2. The development of effective selection devices may be facilitated by a knowledge of the component elements of job criteria. There may be a certain class or type of predictor which is most effective in the prediction of each of the separate skills or dimensions of job performance. In the present study, for example, experience items were the best predictors of objective sales achievement while a measure of personality characteristics was the best single predictor of general reputation. These specific findings may not have universal application but they suggest a possible approach to the development of more effective selection devices.

3. Factor analysis is a useful technique for the study of the complex elements of job criteria. While it cannot be assumed that the factors obtained in this investigation were applicable to sales criteria in other companies, the methods employed may be appropriate for the study of criteria in many types of jobs and companies.

REFERENCES

1. BROGDEN, H. E., & TAYLOR, E. K. Theory and classification of criterion bias. *Educational and Psychological Measurement*, 1950, *10*, 159–186.
2. CLEVELAND, E. Sales personnel research 1935–1945. *Personnel Psychology*, 1948, *1*, 211–256.
3. FISKE, D. W. Values, theory, and the criterion problem. *Personnel Psychology*, 1951, *4*, 93–98.
4. HORST, P. A generalized expression for the reliability of measures. *Psychometrika*, 1949, *14*, 21–28.
5. STEAD, W. H., & SHARTLE, C. L. *Occupational Counseling Techniques.* New York: American Book Co., 1940. Appendix V.
6. SWENSON, W. M., & LINDGREN, E. The use of psychological tests in industry. *Personnel Psychology*, 1952, *5*, 19–23.
7. THURSTONE, L. L. *Multiple Factor Analysis.* Chicago: University of Chicago Press, 1947.
8. TOOPS, H. A. The criterion. *Educational and Psychological Measurement*, 1944, *4*, 271–297.
9. WHERRY, R. J. Criteria and validity. In D. Fryer and E. Henry, (eds.), *Handbook of Applied Psychology I.* New York: Rinehart, 1950. Pp. 170–177.

20 A Factor Analysis of Eleven Job Performance Measures

WILLIAM W. RONAN

INTRODUCTION

The purpose of this study was to establish possible criteria for use in the selection and evaluation of skilled trades apprentices and journeymen. It was assumed that a multiple criterion was desirable both in light of other studies (Balma, *et al.*, 1959, Flanagan, *et al.*, 1953, McQuitty, *et al.*, 1954, Thorndike, 1949) and the complexity of skilled trades work. For these reasons, eleven variables were evaluated.

VARIABLES

The eleven variables studied were:

1. *Shop Rating*—Every six months all apprentices were rated on a twelve-category scale. The scales cover technical competence (four items), learning ability (two items), interest in trade (two items), general attitude (two items), and prediction of potential (two items). During the entire course of an apprenticeship, rating was done by an immediate supervisor. As many as ten different supervisors may have rated one apprentice on a five-point scale varying from 1 "outstanding" through 3 "average" to 5 "very poor." Ratings for this study were averaged to give one over-all measure.

2. *School Rating*—All apprentices were rated every six months by two instructors teaching related trade material in a company-conducted school. Again, rating was the same five-point scale but covered only the six categories of absorbing material (2), quality (1), and quantity (2) of work and interest (1). Again, an average over-all rating was calculated.

3. *Mathematics Grade*—All apprentices were required to complete certain mathematics courses depending upon the particular trade. These ranged from beginning algebra and geometry to beginning calculus. Definite time limits were set and the grade, again 1 through 5, depended upon actual completion date. This criterion was one of the more objective in

From *Personnel Psychology*, 1963, 16, 255–267

that deviations, by months to complete work, were given definite scores. The grade was a single average value given at the completion of apprenticeship.

4. *Absence Index*—This measure was obtained by counting days absent from work on the company "lost time records," dividing by years of service, and arriving at a days absent per year index. There was some question, but little definite evidence one way or the other, of how completely absences were reported. However, it seemed that no systematic error was involved by department or individual, but rather a general under-reporting through "forgetting" or some other reason.

5. *Injury Index*—For this measure, all visits to the company hospital were counted, divided by years of service, and an injury per year index derived. Only the original visit, not visits for redressings, was counted. The term "injury" is somewhat misleading in that employees did visit the hospital for headaches, colds, and similar non-work connected ailments, but they were only a minor part of the total count. Another more serious drawback to the measure was that some employees, in spite of a company rule to do so, did not report injuries. Obviously, such a practice can affect a criterion both in terms of under-reporting of injuries and by biasing on the part of particular individuals. However, the problem is common in all industrial settings and the index was included as a possible criterion measure.

6. *Lost Time Accidents*—A written record was kept of all injuries serious enough for an employee to be unable to report for work on his next scheduled shift. The criterion was a simple count of the injuries dichotomized into "none" ($N = 147$) and "one-or-more" ($N = 52$). Parenthetically, in the particular organization there was no effort to "cover" lost time accidents by allowing an injured man to report for but do no work. In addition, the decision concerning whether or not the employee should report for work is made by a company physician. These two features probably made this measure as objective as is possible with this type of data.

7. *Grievances*—A written record of all grievances was kept, and again a simple count provided the criterion measure. One question that arose in connection with the measure was whether or not grievances were desirable or undesirable from the criterion point-of-view. A respectable case can be made for either side of the question. It was decided to treat them, for the purposes of this study, as undesirable.

8. *Disciplinary Actions*—A written record was kept of these actions. They ranged from written reprimands to outright discharge. Again, however, the problem of under-reporting arose. For instance, one supervisor may report as a disciplinary action an event that another would dismiss with only a verbal warning. Again, no discernible bias was in evidence by department or particular employee, but the measure was probably some-

what distorted by under-reporting or individual idiosyncrasies on the part of the various supervisors.

9. *Promotions*—A written record was kept of all promotions, whether a wage rate change or a change in status. A simple count provided the measure for this study.

10. *Supervisory Ratings*—For this study a special rating form was prepared. It covered quantity of work, quality of work, general attitude, relations with fellow workers, and relations with supervision. Each category was on a five-point scale, with one being the most desirable score. The rating supervisors were carefully instructed in the techniques of ratings, pitfalls were pointed out, and a description of the categories given. A follow-up question and answer period, it is believed, laid the groundwork to obtain measures that were as reliable as possible with this technique. The five ratings were averaged to give a single value for each individual rated.

11. *Personality Disorder*—In the evaluated group there were individuals who had histories of diagnosed personality disorders, and, in some cases, of hospitalization for such ailments. It can of course be argued that others of the group could have been victims of such disorders but that circumstances never put them under psychiatric observation. However, for this study the actual fact of diagnosis was established as the categorizing principle.

Other possible criterion measures were considered for this study but rejected for one reason or another. For example, the company has an incentive bonus system and bonus earnings that might, at first glance, seem a possible criterion. However, time to complete a given unit of work is estimated in total, and completion may require days or even weeks with several different men working on the job. Total bonus payable is computed and paid on a total hours "saved" basis with no attempt to evaluate individual efforts. "Scrapping" jobs was also considered, but the same general objection—isolating individual contribution—applies. Certainly, in light of the discussions by Ghiselli (1956), Ghiselli and Haire (1960), Herzberg, *et al.*, (1957), and Cureton and Katzell (1962), the selected measures barely scratched the surface when one considers the total employee at work in a complex industrial organization. However, they do cover an important work group, a wider range of variables than is usually found and, as described below, an extended time period.

PROCEDURE

For the ten-year period 1947 to 1957, company records were searched for applicants tested for and admitted to apprenticeships with a total of 199 individuals finally reached. At the time of this study, 137 were still working for the company and the other 62 had left company employment. The age range at time of admission to apprenticeship was 18 to 32 and, at the time of this study, 30 to 42. All but ten were high school graduates and were admitted as apprentices to 17 different trades. These trades by Dictionary of Occupational Titles were: Blacksmith (4–86.010), Bricklayer (5–24.010), Carpenter (5–25.830), Coremaker (4–82.010), Electrician (4–97.420), Fitter (5–78.100), Machinist (4–75.010), Millwright (5–78.100), Molder (4–81.030), Patternmaker (5–17.020), Pipefitter (5–30.010), Rigger (5–88.020), Roll Turner (4–78.011), Sheet Metal Worker (4–80.010), Structural Fitter (4–84.010), Template Maker (4–76.210), Toolroom Fitter (5–83.641). In summary, these data cover applicants tested over a ten-year period, who have work histories of five to twenty years and are a fairly homogeneous population.

As previously described, personnel records were searched and the special supervisory rating completed to obtain criterion data. It might be pointed out here that because of missing data in company records, particularly for those employees who had left company service some years previously, certain omissions were inevitable. In addition, no supervisory rating was attempted for those employees who had left company service. For these reasons the correlations are on groups of various sizes, from 125 to 172; in no case could every individual be used. Significance tests of descriptive statistics revealed, however, that no serious distortion resulted for inclusion or failure to include certain individuals in the various groups. In consequence, all groups for this study were treated as having been selected from the same population.

RESULTS

The nature of the collected data dictated three different techniques of estimating correlations. They were product-moment r (as variable 1 vs. 2), point biserial r (as variable 1 vs. 6), or phi coefficient (as variable 6 vs. 7). Guilford's (1950) methods of calculation, as well as evaluating significance, were followed for the latter two techniques. The more common procedures were followed for calculation and evaluating Pearson r's. The different methods required for estimating significance, as well as variation in the size of N, account for the fact that some correlations, larger than those showing significance, are shown as nonsignificant.

Intercorrelations of the 11 criterion variables are shown in Table 20.1.

Using the procedure described by Johnson (1949), the r distribution was tested against a theoretical chance distribution. The chi-square value obtained approaches 80, well over the 1 per cent level value. Thus, even

TABLE 20.1. *Correlations of criterion variables (decimals omitted).*

	2	3	4	5	6	7	8	9	10	11
(1) Shop Rating	−040	278**	085	−010	−046	225**	133*	−094	270**	466**
(2) School Rating		606**	256**	015	−001	122**	294**	−057	−115	211**
(3) Math Grade			208**	−020	−102	160**	221**	103	211*	−028
(4) Absence Index				054	−081	243**	180**	094	517**	697**
(5) Injury Index					787**	−060	−011	−143	085	146*
(6) Lost Time Accidents						083	061	−140*	184**	123
(7) Grievances							083	058	048	150
(8) Disciplinary Action								141*	294**	028
(9) Promotions									325**	−038
(10) Supervisory Rating										104**
(11) Personality Disorder										—

* Significant at 5% level.
** Significant at 1% level.

though 38 of the 55 correlations fall between plus or minus .20, the shape of the distribution is significantly different from the theoretical model of a random sample.

The reliability of the criterion variables could not be adequately tested due to various factors. Most important, some records were incomplete, i.e., lacking indication of which supervisors had rated a given apprentice, of which employees had failed to report injuries, or single administration in the case of the supervisory rating. In any event, the factor analysis provides estimates of reliability.

The correlation matrix was analyzed using Thurstone's Centroid Method (1947). The factors extracted are shown in Table 20.2 and, after orthogonal rotation, in Table 20.3.

Factor extraction was continued through a fifth factor, resulting in

TABLE 20.2. *Factors extracted by centroid method*

Variables	I	II	III	IV	h^2
Shop Rating	341	−080	250	185	219
School Rating	417	285	−485	453	696
Mathematics Grade	495	403	−286	252	553
Absence Index	651	181	391	070	614
Injury Index	359	−671	−365	−224	763
Lost Time Accidents	365	−629	−353	−349	775
Grievances	299	053	122	155	131
Disciplinary Actions	379	243	−116	−125	232
Promotions	127	372	135	−367	307
Supervisory Rating	538	139	234	−427	546
Personality Disorder	564	−306	478	381	785

TABLE 20.3. *Factors after orthogonal rotation*

Variables	I	II	III	IV	h^2
Shop Rating	084	−030	008	459	219
School Rating	161	794	0	201	696
Mathematics Grade	006	651	222	281	552
Absence Index	−068	044	339	700	612
Injury Index	844	110	185	−069	763
Lost Time Accidents	808	−151	298	−113	777
Grievances	−020	099	055	342	131
Disciplinary Actions	010	251	389	134	232
Promotions	−308	−029	460	0	307
Supervisory Rating	−006	−131	655	311	543
Personality Disorder	247	−149	−104	830	783

values ranging from .005 to .043. For this reason, only the four factors were considered.

Factor rotation was continued until it became apparent that the results shown in Table 20.3 were the best that could be achieved. Apparently the variables of Promotions and Personality Disorder have some inherently negative relationships, and the Injury-Lost Time Accident doublet also makes a positive manifold unlikely with these data. The discussion that follows accepts the obtained as the best possible structure.

In addition to the above, the data were analyzed for significant differences between the group of employees still in company employ vs. those who were not. On the eleven variables, only absenteeism showed a significant difference. With an N of 199, the t value found was over 5.0. In fact, only one employee still with the company had a higher absence index than the lowest absence index of any member of the separated group. This finding, that excessive absenteeism indicates that an employee will eventually leave the company, confirms others concerned with the specific problem (Clarke, 1946; Margolius, 1945; Sawatsky, 1951; Young, 1950).

DISCUSSION

The four rotated factors showed three to be of relatively clear-cut interpretation, with Factor IV showing much more complexity.

Factor I

5.	Injury Index	844
6.	Lost Time Accidents	808

This is apparently a "safe worker" factor which probably constitutes one independent aspect of job performance. That this is a predictable aspect of employee performance has been shown by Jenkins (1961) in studies connected with his "Job Attitudes Survey" inventory.

Factor II

2.	School Rating	794
3.	Mathematics Grade	651

This factor, measuring successful school work, would actually be an intermediate criterion of job performance. In addition to an assumed aptitude basis, there may be an "acceptance of authority" component as shown by a small value, .251, in the Disciplinary Action variable. It is of interest to note in the correlation matrix that the Mathematics Grade was slightly, though significantly (.211), related to Supervisory Rating but not significantly related to Promotions (.103). The two School Rating correlations with the same variables were not significant. It appears that the two variables, used as intermediate criteria for some type of administrative action, would necessitate a complex scoring and weighting procedure.

Factor III

9.	Promotions	460
10.	Supervisory Rating	655

This factor appears to measure supervisory evaluation of employee performance. The factor values for Absence and Disciplinary Actions probably are actually negative. The original correlations show that lower absence and fewer disciplinary actions are significantly related to both more promotions and higher supervisory ratings. With these relationships, halo or reputation is an easily surmised basis. However, it should be recalled that these data cover working periods of at least ten years, giving the supervisors a maximum of opportunity to evaluate job performance. In addition, promotions are subject to higher level approval and evaluation so that it would seem there is a more solid basis for the findings as shown previously by Knauft (1955).

The variables of Factor III show some contradictory relationships with those of Factor I. The correlation matrix shows more promotions associated with more lost time accidents, whereas a better supervisory rating is associated with fewer lost time accidents. Thus, if applicants were selected to avoid those more likely to be injured they would be rated as better employees by supervisors but would be less likely to be promotion prospects. Obviously, scoring and evaluating scores on selection instruments would become quite complex under these circumstances.

Factor IV

4.	Absence Index	700
11.	Personality Disorder	830

This appears to be an "adjustment" factor either personal, to the particular organization, or both. It also contains most of the variance of the Shop Rating and Grievances. In the case of the former, the sign should probably be negative since the matrix correlation shows that a better Shop Rating is associated with an absence of personality disorder. In the case of Grievances, the reliability, as estimated by its communality, is so low there is some question of whether any meaningful measurement is being made. However, it is a fairly common opinion in industry that the habitual grievant "can't get along with anybody," as discussed by Heron (1952). If this is so, it probably indicates some more or less serious personality problem that throws it into this "adjustment" factor. Since the original correlation between Grievances and the Absence Index is significantly positive, it would seem they belong in the same factor.

One last point concerns the finding for the Disciplinary Action variable. Again, the reliability, as shown by the communality, is low but the correlation matrix shows six significant correlations. The variance is scattered through three factors, although concentrated mainly in II and III. The raw correlations are all of the nature showing that fewer disciplinary actions are associated with better performance. Possibly it is another type of "adjustment" different from that of Factor IV and more heterogeneous in its effects. This is further confirmed by the fact that the correlation between Grievances and Disciplinary Actions is negative.

LIMITATIONS

Probably the most serious limitation of this study is that it contains no specific measure of job skill; for example, a job performance test. The Supervisory Rating asked for such an evaluation but with other aspects of performance. It is conceivable that such a measure, as shown by Siegel (1954), could have a marked effect on the factor structure found in this study.

Another limitation is the fact that other indices of job performance might be included. For example, morale and attitude survey results or production performance results might be considered along with many others. All those available in the particular organization were included in this study, but inclusion of others might materially change the results.

CONCLUSIONS

It would appear from these data that "over-all job performance" or any single criterion is of limited usefulness in evaluating skilled trades job performance. Here, with a relatively limited number of variables, four distinct factors have appeared. This complexity of job performance in modern organizations has been discussed by Guion (1961), but still comparatively little work has been done on criterion development.

That various criterion measures bear little or no interrelation is shown again in this research as in earlier studies (Adjutant General's Office, 1943; Flanagan, 1948; Rothe & Nye, 1958). However, when conducted on a long-term basis it would appear that many of the relationships found in this study may be stable. A study by Fleishman, *et al.* (1955), with four of these variables, shows results similar to those found here. It appears probable that Factors I, II and IV are all loaded to some substantial extent with personality traits. Since this is the area in which instruments for industrial selection are weakest (Ghiselli & Barthol, 1953), serious selection problems are indicated. To further compound the problem, a complex pattern of positive and negative relationships over several criteria, as appears likely from this study, would make proper selection even more difficult.

If studies resulting in disappointing validity measures are to be avoided, it appears necessary to study performance measures on a wider, longer term basis to determine what it is that is to be predicted. The possibility of using available organization records for this purpose is indicated.

Many other studies (Bechtoldt, 1951; Brogden & Taylor, 1950; Guilford, 1947; Kipnis, 1960; Mosier, 1951) have investigated and discussed the problem of effective prediction in view of criterion complexity. However, little progress has been made in the identification of criterion dimensions and their interrelations. It is suggested that independent dimensions of job performance do exist and that they will have to be more fully described if effective predictions are to be made.

REFERENCES

ADJUTANT GENERAL'S OFFICE, Personnel research in the army, VI, the selection of truck drivers. *Psychological Bulletin*, XL (1943), 499–508.

BALMA, M. J., GHISELLI, E. E., McCORMICK, E. J., PRIMOFF, E. S., & GRIFFIN, C. H. The development of processes for indirect or synthetic validity (a symposium). *Personnel Psychology*, XII (1959), 395–420.

BECHTOLD, H. P. Selection. In *Handbook of Experimental Psychology*, S. S. Stevens (Editor). New York: John Wiley & Sons, 1951.

BROGDEN, H. E., & TAYLOR, E. K. The theory and classification of criterion bias. *Educational and Psychological Measurement*, X (1950), 159–186.

CLARKE, F. R. Labor turnover studies. *Personnel Journal*, XXV (1946), 55–58.

CURETON, E. E., & KATZELL, R. A. A further analysis of the relations among job performance and situational variables. *Journal of Applied Psychology*, XLVI (1962), 230.

FLANAGAN, J. C. (Editor). The aviation psychology program in the Army Air Forces. *Army Air Forces Aviation Psychology Program Research Reports*. Washington, D.C.: U.S. Government Printing Office, 1948.

FLANAGAN, J. C., ET AL. The performance record for hourly employees. Chicago, Illinois: Science Research Associates, 1953.

FLEISHMAN, E. A., HARRIS, E. F., & BURTT, H. E. Leadership and supervision in industry. *Bureau of Education Research Monograph No. 33.* Columbus, Ohio: Ohio State University, 1955.

GHISELLI, E. E., & BARTHOL, R. P. The validity of personality inventories in the selection of employees. *Journal of Applied Psychology*, XXXVII (1953), 18–20.

GHISELLI, E. E. Dimensional problems of criteria. *Journal of Applied Psychology*, XL (1956), 14.

GHISELLI, E. E., & HAIRE, M. The validation of selection tests in the light of the dynamic character of criteria. *Personnel Psychology*, XIII (1960), 225–231.

GUILFORD, J. P. (Editor). Printed classification tests. *Army Air Forces Aviation Psychology Research Report*, No. 5. Washington, D.C.: U.S. Government Printing Office, 1947.

GUILFORD, J. P. *Fundamental Statistics in Psychology and Education*. New York: McGraw-Hill Book Company, 1950.

GUION, R. M. Criterion measurement and personnel judgments. *Personnel Psychology*, XIV (1961), 141–149.

HERON, A. A psychological study of occupational adjustment. *Journal of Applied Psychology*, XXXVI (1952), 385–387.

HERZBERG, F., ET AL. *Job Attitudes—Review of Opinion and Research*. Pittsburgh: Psychological Service of Pittsburgh, 1957.

JENKINS, T. N. Identifying the accident-prone employee. *Personnel*, XXXVIII (1961), 56–62.

JOHNSON, P. O. *Statistical Methods in Research*. New York: Prentice-Hall, Inc., 1949.

KIPNIS, D. Some determinants of supervisory esteem. *Personnel Psychology*, XIII (1960), 377–391.

KNAUFT, E. B. Test validity over a seventeen-year period. *Journal of Applied Psychology*, XXXIX (1955), 382–383.

MARGOLIUS, S. Reducing labor turnover. *Personnel Journal*, XXIV (1945), 22–28.

MCQUITTY, L. L., WRIGLEY, C., & GAIER, E. L. An approach to isolating dimensions of job success. *Journal of Applied Psychology*, XXXVIII (1954), 227–232.

MOSIER, C. I. Batteries and profiles. In *Educational Measurement*, E. F. Lindquist (Editor). Washington, D.C.: American Council on Education, 1951.

ROTHE, H. F., & NYE, C. T. Output rates among coil winders. *Journal of Applied Psychology*, XLII (1958), 182–186.

SAWATSKY, J. C. Psychological factors in industrial organizations affecting employee stability. *Canadian Journal of Psychology*, V (1951), 29–38.

SIEGEL, A. I. The check list as a criterion of proficiency. *Journal of Applied Psychology*, XXXVIII (1954), 93–95.

THORNDIKE, R. L. *Personnel Selection: Test and Measurement Techniques*. New York: John Wiley & Sons, 1949.

THURSTONE, L. L. *Multiple-Factor Analysis: A Development & Expansion of the Vectors of Mind*. Chicago: University of Chicago Press, 1947.

YOUNG, R. J. Reduce excessive turnover costs through proper analysis. *Personnel*, XXVII (1950), 75–79.

21 Dimensions of Foreman Performance: A Factor Analysis of Criterion Measures

WELD W. TURNER

In constructing criteria of job performance, psychologists have become increasingly cognizant of the need to cover all aspects of the job. This point of view has been expressed quite well by Ghiselli's (1956) position that criteria are multidimensional, that the dimensions are unlikely to be equally important and that the dimensions should be differentially weighted by some method that does not assume a general factor of success.

The multidimensionality approach to criterion development was employed in this study through the factor analysis of 20 measures of foreman performance. The purposes of this research were (*a*) to identify criterion factors or dimensions that could be used separately as subcriteria, (*b*) to devise relevance weights that could be used to combine the factors into a composite criterion, (*c*) to determine which criterion factors were inadequately covered by the measures used in the study, and (*d*) to examine the consistency of the factor structure in two plants. The problem of developing factor score equations for reproducing criterion dimensions will not be considered in this paper.

It should be emphasized that there is no assurance that factor analysis will reveal all dimensions of performance unless an exhaustive number of measures have been obtained on all possible aspects of the job. The most obvious omission in this study is an objective measure of quality, which was not available. Nevertheless, the measures utilized here are fairly representative of those typically available for production foremen.

From *Journal of Applied Psychology*, 1960, 44, 216–223. Except for the relevance weighting procedure, the research reported in this paper is part of a PhD thesis submitted to the faculty of Purdue University. The author would like to express his appreciation for the guidance and assistance provided by the thesis committee, composed of Joseph Tiffin, Chairman, E. J. McCormick, B. J. Winer, and W. V. Owen. The author is also indebted to Orlo L. Crissey, Administrative Chairman of Personnel Evaluation Services, General Motors Institute, for making the data available and for contributing staff and clerical time to expedite the processing of the data.

PROCEDURE

Sample

The sample consisted of production foremen (first line supervisors) in two plants of an automobile assembly division of a large corporation. The two plants perform identical production operations and are located in metropolitan areas of the Midwest (Plant X) and East (Plant Y).

In order to insure a nominal level of experience on the part of the foremen used in the study, only those foremen were included in the sample who had at least two monthly scores on one or more of the criterion measures. This provided n's of 102 in Plant X and 104 in Plant Y. Some of these foremen had only one score on certain variables due to vacations, different collection periods for the various measures, and other vagaries of the data collection process.

Objective Measures

Eleven objective measures were constructed from information supplied by the plants at weekly or monthly intervals. The collection period for the objective measures extended from December 1956 to May 1957. The actual number of months for which data were available for any one measure ranged from three to six, varying for different criteria and for the two plants.

The objective measures were Grievances, Turnover (voluntary quits), Absences, Suggestions, Hospital Passes (occupational injuries), Disciplines, Absentee Flexibility (hours spent by the foreman's Utility Trainer in training men on jobs), Scrap, Expense Tools, Expense Processing Supplies, and Efficiency. There was no objective quality data that could be attributed to specific foremen with any degree of certainty. All of the objective measures were based on the performance of a foreman's section as an operating unit. Absences, for example, referred to absences of hourly employees, not foreman absences.

In calculating monthly values for the first six measures (see Table 21.1), frequency counts for a foreman's section were divided by the number of man-days worked during the time period to adjust for differences in section size. The Grievances index was multiplied by the number of employees submitting grievances to reduce the influence of chronic grievers and to increase the index value when dissatisfaction was more widespread. The Scrap index was merely the scrap cost in dollar units. Index values for Expense Tools and Expense Processing Supplies were dollar costs in excess of budget. Efficiency index values were calculated by the Work Standards Department; although the method of computing it differed in the two plants, Efficiency was intended to be a measure of a section's performance relative to standard time allowances.

Ratings

During the six months from January through June of 1957, general foremen provided monthly ratings of the foremen reporting to them. The ratings consisted of alternating rankings of foremen on Overall Performance and eight functional areas of job performance, giving nine separate measures. The eight areas were Quantity, Quality, Cost Control, Organization and Planning, Employee Relations, Cooperation with Other Supervision, Safety, and Housekeeping. Responsibilities for each area were defined on the rating form, with the definitions abstracted from a divisionwide job description for production foremen. The Overall Performance Rating was to include performance on the eight areas plus any other functions that the rater thought important.

Score Transformations

Original scores on the objective variables were transformed to normal distributions because scores on most of the measures were highly skewed, piling up at the low end of the scales where there was a lower limit of zero. It was felt that the abilities underlying the criterion scores could be approximated more closely by the traditional normal curve.

In addition to non-normal distributions, scores on the objective measures were subject to biases in the form of score differences attributable to conditions inherent in different plants, departments, shifts and months. Because of the possibility of biases, adjustments were made to equalize monthly score means within each plant-department-shift unit. This adjustment provided a set of scores generally representative of scores unbiased by plants, departments, shifts, or months.

Score transformations and adjustments on the objective measures were made by ranking the original monthly index values within organizational sub-groups, then converting the ranks to normalized scores (*T*-scores) with a mean of 50 and a standard deviation of 10 (Edwards, 1954, p. 512). In ranking the index values, a rank of 1 always indicated the best performance. On Absentee Flexibility, Suggestions, and Plant Y's Efficiency, better performance was interpreted as higher scores. On the remaining objective measures, lower scores were taken as better performance.

The ratings, received from general foremen as monthly rankings, were also converted to *T*-score, which normalized rating scores within general foremen's areas and equalized score means from general foremen to general foreman. Since a general foreman's area was smaller than a department, rating score means were unbiased (equalized) for months, plants, departments, and shifts, as well as for general foremen.

Besides his monthly T-scores, each foreman was given an overall T-score on every measure by calculating mean T scores for all foremen, converting the mean T-scores to percentile distributions within each plant and transforming the plantwide percentiles for each criterion variable to T scores (Edwards, 1954, p. 511). For those foremen having only one score on a measure, the single score rather than a mean was used in the above procedure.

It should be remembered that although the 20 variables were collected from December through June of one product model year, none of the measures were obtained for all seven months. This created no difficulties in assessing the reliability of monthly scores. However, in intercorrelating the variables there was a choice of either using only the months in common to all of the variables, thereby losing a major part of the sample, or using all of the data available for each measure to get a single, average score representing a foreman's standing on that measure. The latter alternative was chosen because it was felt that more dependable and representative results would be found by using all of the data.

Reliabilities

The monthly T-scores were used in estimating the reliability of the measures across time. Only those foremen receiving two or more monthly scores on a criterion could be used in the reliability estimates. The number of monthly scores on any measure were not the same for all foremen. Reliability estimates were computed from Ebel's (1951) intraclass analysis of variance method for incomplete sets of scores (unequal observations from person to person).

Reliabilities were calculated for both single scores and mean scores for k_0 months (k_0 being an approximation of the harmonic mean of the number of scores for each foreman). Ebels' method of determining the reliability of an average score is equivalent to stepping-up the reliability of a single score k_0 times in the Spearman-Brown formula. The Spearman-Brown formula was used to estimate the reliability of mean scores for three, six, and nine months. The purpose of these latter reliabilities was to gain information regarding the adequacy of reliabilities of criterion data collected for varying numbers of months. All reliability estimates were made separately for the two plants.

Factor Analyses

The overall T-scores for each foreman on the criterion variables were used in obtaining the intercorrelations of the 20 measures. Intercorrelation matrices for Plant X and Plant Y were calculated on an IBM 650 computer.

Factor analyses for the two intercorrelation matrices were run on Purdue's Datatron computer using principal components solutions. Communality estimates were the squared multiple correlations of each variable with the other 19 variables. The computer extracted 20 factors from each matrix. Factors were selected according to the size of their latent roots; enough factors were retained to make the sum of their latent roots roughly equal to the sum of the communality estimates. In Plant X the sum of the communalities was 9.15 and the sum of the five largest latent roots was 9.16. For Plant Y the sum of the first five latent roots was 9.01 compared to 8.92 as the sum of the communality estimates. A high degree of correspondence between the estimated communalities and the obtained communalities indicated that the common-factor variance in the intercorrelation matrices was sufficiently accounted for by the retained factors.

The resulting factors were rotated graphically and orthogonally to approximate simple structure.

Relevance Weights

For the purposes of this research, a criterion was defined as a yardstick for evaluating a foreman's contribution to the success of organizational operations. Some estimate of relevance was desired which would indicate the relative importance of the criterion dimensions to the success of the organization. Basing criterion relevance values on either factor loadings or the proportion of common-factor variance accounted for by a factor was not justified because the domain of total criterion performance was not necessarily completely covered nor proportionally sampled by the 20 measures. Criterion relevance was established from the judgments of production department superintendents, who were one supervisory level higher than the general foremen.

Eight superintendents, four from each plant, were asked (*a*) to rank the criterion measures according to the extent to which they would reflect a foreman's contribution to the success of their department's operations and (*b*) to identify measures that they thought were completely irrelevant. The names and descriptions of the criterion measures were typed on separate cards, which were sorted into four decks. In individual sessions the superintendents ranked the cards in the four decks and collated the decks into an overall rank order.

No superintendent named any measure as being nonrelevant; consequently, it was assumed that all measures embodied some relevance to the effectiveness of production operations within a department. The criterion measures were given relevance scores from each rater by reversing the rank order (the highest ranked variable was given a score of 20, the second highest was given a score of 19, etc.). Interrater agreement reliabilities were computed for mean relevance scores from the superintendents within each plant (.90 in Plant X and .82 in Plant Y) and across both plants (.92) by using Ebel's (1951) method for finding the reliability of complete sets of ratings. As a direct check on the agreement between plants, a rank order correlation between mean criterion relevance scores within the two plants was computed. The between-plant rank order correlation was .74. Because of this rank order correlation and the high reliability for average scores across eight raters, it was decided to use a single relevance score applicable to both plants for each criterion variable. A measure's final relevance score was the mean score from all eight superintendents.

The final relevance score for each criterion measure was distributed among the meaningful factors in proportion to the measure's factor loadings of .20 and higher (an r of .20 with 100 df is significant at the .05 level). One example of the distribution of relevance scores to factors is a measure whose two factor loadings above .20 were .34 and .44: the relevance score was divided between the two factors in the ratio of 3 to 4. Other allocations of relevance scores were made in a similar manner. If a variable had only one factor loading as high as .20, all of the relevance score was given to that factor. All criterion measures had at least one factor loading of .20 or higher, making it possible to assign all of the relevance scores to the factors.

The criterion relevance values assigned to the factors were given the signs of the corresponding factor loadings and summed algebraically for each factor. The total factor relevance values were divided by the number of variables contributing relevance to the factors; this step yielded a mean relevance weight for every factor. A factor's mean relevance weight would be more representative of that factor's relevance than a total value because the latter would be more dependent on the number of different kinds of variables included in the factor analysis. The average factor relevance weights were rounded to the nearest integer to serve as estimates of factor relevance.

The relevance weighting procedure was repeated using two other approaches: once by getting separate factor relevance values for the two plants from relevance judgments pooled within plants instead of across plants, and again by converting relevance ranks to T-scores and assigning to the factors only that portion of a criterion's relevance T-score accounted for by its factor loadings of .20 or higher. All three relevance weighting procedures gave virtually identical results, so only one method is explained here.

RESULTS

Reliabilities

Reliabilities for single monthly scores on the objective measures were quite low. In Plant X they ranged from .03 to .59 with a median of .35; in Plant Y they ranged from .07 to .65 with a median of .27. Reliabilities of single monthly scores on the ratings were higher, ranging from .46 to .69 in Plant X and from .39 to .66 is Plant Y.

When the reliabilities were stepped up by the Spearman-Brown formula for average scores taken across three, six, and nine months, it was found that satisfactory reliability could be obtained for most of the measures by taking averages of several monthly scores. Nearly all of the rating scales in both plants reached a reliability of .70 or higher for an average of three monthly scores. Four measures—Grievances, Turnover, Suggestions, and Disciplines—failed to attain a reliability of .70 in either plant for mean scores from as many as nine months; this was also true for Absentee Flexibility in Plant X.

Table 21.1 gives $r_{\bar{x}\bar{x}}$, the reliability of mean scores from k_0 months, for the 20 criterion measures. This $r_{\bar{x}\bar{x}}$ is the reliability of mean overall scores, which were used in computing the intercorrelations, for those foremen having two or more scores. Intercorrelations and factor analyses were based on the total plant n's of 102 and 104, but the reliability n's were smaller. The difference between the total plant n's and the reliability n's shown in Table 21.1 is the number of foremen who had only one monthly score on a measure. Although $r_{\bar{x}\bar{x}}$ is not the actual reliability of all intercorrelated scores on those variables for which some foremen had only one score, it can be regarded as a close approximation.

Intercorrelations and Factor Analyses

The intercorrelation matrices and principal component factor loadings for the two plants can be found elsewhere (Turner, 1959), so they are not given here. However, some aspects of the intercorrelations bear mentioning. The objective measures in Plant X and Plant Y had low correlations with other objective measures and with the ratings; nearly all of these significant r's were in the .20's. Low correlations resulted in low communalities for the objective measures. Intercorrelations among the rating scales were fairly high (generally in the .50's, .60's, and .70's).

The intercorrelations were examined to determine if objective measures were correlated with ratings that might logically be expected to cover similar kinds of job achievement. The objective cost measures—Scrap, Expense Tools, and Expense Processing Supplies—were not signifi-

		Plant X									Plant Y						
		Reliability		Factor Loadings[a]						Reliability		Factor Loadings[a]				
Criterion Measure	n	k_0	r_{zz}	I	II	III	IV	V		n	k_0	r_{zz}	I	II	III	IV	V
1. Grievances	99	4.5	.28	21	42	−34	−23	23		104	4.9	.30	05	24	07	07	26
2. Turnover	102	5.3	.37	−17	29	−06	36	−06		104	4.9	.28	−10	50	−07	40	−19
3. Absences	102	5.3	.74	01	46	11	00	05		104	5.0	.60	11	56	−02	−02	06
4. Suggestions	102	5.3	.14	−06	19	−28	04	05		104	5.0	.45	05	−12	−44	34	−10
5. Hospital Passes	102	5.3	.86	18	30	−22	−10	−19		90	3.5	.57	09	−28	22	12	39
6. Disciplines	102	5.3	.32	−09	54	−14	−02	33		104	4.9	.39	−15	57	01	−05	−05
7. Absentee Flexibility	90	2.7	.36	−09	14	10	−44	−02		91	3.6	.74	02	−15	−44	−20	−01
8. Scrap	99	5.4	.88	02	12	61	−05	−01		91	3.6	.76	−14	−10	64	01	−05
9. Expense Tools	102	5.3	.79	−04	45	15	04	−14		91	3.6	.87	02	35	35	−06	−27
10. Expense Processing Supplies	102	5.3	.88	10	09	01	−20	−27		91	3.6	.79	−12	−15	−41	−23	−08
11. Efficiency	102	5.3	.86	10	02	−28	25	−02		104	5.0	.68	05	−08	−02	47	−03
12. Quantity Rating	100	5.3	.88	90	−01	−14	−15	−04		97	5.1	.82	69	02	−10	−28	28
13. Quality Rating	100	5.3	.87	87	08	04	06	22		97	5.1	.81	72	08	−07	−22	−03
14. Cooperation Rating	100	5.3	.82	71	04	−08	−09	−11		97	5.1	.82	49	−15	10	11	24
15. Cost Control Rating	100	5.3	.85	80	05	14	06	21		97	5.1	.91	85	00	−04	04	06
16. Organization Rating	100	5.3	.85	87	11	05	−19	08		97	5.1	.86	89	02	−08	06	06
17. Employee Relations Rating	100	5.3	.87	77	20	−05	03	−27		97	5.1	.90	72	29	−04	13	20
18. Safety Rating	100	5.3	.82	60	11	24	25	−11		97	5.1	.77	55	−06	−25	06	−13
19. Housekeeping Rating	100	5.3	.88	54	15	29	25	21		97	5.1	.76	62	−07	04	05	−26
20. Overall Performance Rating	100	5.3	.92	95	00	00	04	01		97	5.1	.87	95	−02	02	01	01

[a] Decimals omitted.

TABLE 21.1. *Reliabilities and rotated factor loadings of criterion measures*

cantly correlated with Cost Control Ratings in either plant. The Employee Relations Rating in Plant Y was significantly correlated (.21) with only one (Absences) of the six (Variables 1 through 6) personnel measures, while Plant X's Employee Relations Ratings were significantly correlated with Grievances (.21) and Hospital Passes (.26). In both plants the objective Efficiency index had near-zero r's with Quantity and Quality Ratings. It is obvious that ratings and objective data are not necessarily equivalent, even when they supposedly measure similar things.

The rotated factor loadings are shown separately for Plant X and Plant Y in Table 21.1. Four interpretable factors were found for each rotated factor matrix. The fifth factors, having only one loading above .30, appear to be residual factors. Factors I and II are the same in both plants, but the third and fourth factors have plant differences.

Dimension I: Job performance reputation. Factor I is a rating dimension on which all of the ratings have high loadings. Factor I accounts for nearly all of the rating communalities and is anchored by the Overall Performance Rating. None of the objective variables have loadings of any consequence on Factor I. Factor I "cross-validated" quite well from Plant X to Plant Y.

The Overall Performance Rating, with Factor I loadings of .95 and zero or near-zero loadings on other factors, is sufficient to identify this dimension. It appears that additional ratings are superfluous.

The low or negligible loadings of the ratings on the remaining factors is a further indication that ratings and objective data are far from interchangeable. Ratings of foreman performance seem to be determined primarily by a general reputation for job performance. This reputation is not necessarily completely divorced from a foreman's actual contribution to the organization. Nevertheless, the low relationship of ratings with other factors and with individual objective measures suggests the possibility that some irrelevant considerations might affect job performance reputation.

Dimension II: Employee relations. Factor II in both plants is characterized by few absences, few disciplines, and a tendency to stay within the budget allotment for expense tools. Of the six objective personnel measures, Hospital Passes and Suggestions do not have consistent positive correlations with this factor. Grievances and Turnover have low to high positive loadings in the two plants. Since Factor II seems to be marked by a good relationship between foremen and their subordinates, it is named Employee Relations.

Dimension III: Scrap vs. organization of production operations. The plant-to-plant similarities on the third factor are high positive loadings for Scrap, negative loadings for Suggestions and evidence of bipolarity.

In Plant X a good showing on Scrap is accompanied by a poor record in Grievances and a little difficulty in meeting production standards (Efficiency). The negative loadings for Variables 1, 4, 5, and 11 cause one to suspect the existence of bipolarity in Plant X's third factor, although the nature of the bipolarity is unclear.

The bipolarity is clarified somewhat in Plant Y by moderate negative loadings for Suggestions, Absentee Flexibility, and Expense Processing Supplies. Foremen in Plant Y who do well on Scrap tend to have fewer suggestions from subordinates, provide less on-the-job training for employees and exceed budget allowances for processing supplies.

High performance on Factor III appears to be made at the expense of activities that, for lack of a better term, might be referred to as organization of production operations. The specific areas on which competence is diminished differ in the two plants. Something other than Scrap performance that is not measured by the 20 variables could also be tied to the high end of Factor III.

Dimension IV. This is another factor for which plant differences exist, but there are some similarities from Plant X to Plant Y. The number of negative loadings, although most are small, suggest the presence of bipolarity in the two plants. Turnover has moderate positive loadings and Expense Processing Supplies has low negative loadings in both plants. The most noticeable plant differences are the sizes of the loadings for Efficiency (.25 in Plant X and .47 in Plant Y) and Absentee Flexibility (−.44 in Plant X and −.20 in Plant Y).

High performance on Plant X's Factor IV consists of providing little on-the-job training for employees, less turnover, and a somewhat better-than-average ability to produce within work standards estimates. Plant X's Factor IV might tentatively be called flexibility vs. stability in job assignments.

Factor IV in Plant Y is typified by producing jobs in less than standard time, receiving relatively more suggestions from subordinates and experiencing fewer voluntary quits among hourly employees. The high end might be called productivity or smoothness of production operations, but the opposite pole is poorly defined by the small negative loadings.

Factor Relevance Weights

The integral factor relevance weights can be seen in Table 21.2. These weights can be interpreted as approximate indexes of the relative importance of the four factors.

Superintendents had more confidence in the general foremen's ratings than in objective measures; Factor I, the rating dimension, is about twice as relevant as Factor II. The first two factors were the same in both plants, so similar relevance weights would be expected for Factors I and II in Plants X and Y. It is surprising, however, to find that the relevance values for Factors III and IV consistently round to zero in spite of their plant differences. The zero relevance weights were obtained because positive and negative loadings on the bipolar factors are counterbalanced in terms of judged relevance. This does not mean that high performance on Factors III and IV contributes nothing to the success of production operations, but that high factor performance is offset by poor performance on the negatively loaded variables. In other words, a low score would be as good as a high score on the third and fourth factors.

The relevance weights shown in Table 21.2 could be used in combining factors into a composite criterion. Because of the failure to establish a preferred end for the bipolar third and fourth factors, these two factors should be omitted from a composite criterion.

CONCLUSIONS AND DISCUSSION

Several rather general conclusions can be made for both plants from the results of this study, and it is the writer's hypothesis that the same conclusions are applicable to other plants in the assembly division. The results also have implications for criterion development that might be undertaken in other organizations.

Single monthly scores on criterion measures tend to have inadequate reliability across time. Averages of several monthly scores are needed to attain a satisfactory level of reliability. Reliability across time would seem important if a criterion score is to be a dependable index of an individual's standing on a measure. A person conducting research should not be surprised if he finds it necessary to collect criterion data for several months.

TABLE 21.2. *Factor relevance weights derived from judgments of superintendents*

Factor	Relevance Weights	
	Plant X	Plant Y
I	12	12
II	5	5
III	0	0
IV	0	0

There is little relationship between objective data and ratings which purportedly cover similar job areas. The equivalence of ratings and objective criterion measures should never be assumed. Moreover, the nine ratings used in this study represent a single criterion dimension which is almost completely defined by the Overall Performance Rating. This factor is comparable to "general" factors found by others from factor analyses of ratings (Creager & Harding, 1958; Grant, 1955). It might be argued that supervisory opinion is a realistic, legitimate criterion. Nevertheless, one might question whether ratings reflect a person's contribution to organizational effectiveness when ratings can be shown to be unrelated to relevant objective records.

The first two dimensions, Job Performance Reputation and Employee Relations, are the same in Plant X and Plant Y, and their counterparts have been identified for foremen in other companies (Creager & Harding, 1958). The third and fourth dimensions, which together comprise the cost-production segment of criterion performance, have plant differences in factor content, but they are consistently bipolar in factor structure and relevance. Additional objective measures directly related to production activities are needed to clarify the content of Dimensions III and IV; an objective measure of quality would be especially desirable.

The bipolarity of Dimensions III and IV is indicative of a loss-gain compensation in which good performance on some aspects of the job is accompanied by diminished proficiency on equally important areas. It appears that there is more than one pattern of foreman success and that it may be unrealistic to expect foremen to do well on all aspects of the job.

SUMMARY

Twenty criterion variables, 9 ratings and 11 objective measures, were collected for production foremen in two automotive assembly plants. Four meaningful dimensions were identified by factor analyzing the measures separately for each plant. Relevance weights for the dimensions were derived from superintendents' relevance rankings of the 20 variables.

The first two dimensions are the same in the two plants. Dimension I, Job Performance Reputation, is a rating factor. Dimension II, Employee Relations, represents objective personnel measures. The third and fourth dimensions, consisting primarily of objective cost and production measures, have plant differences in their specific factor content and are incompletely covered by the available measures. However, Dimensions II and IV are consistent from plant to plant in the bipolarity of both their factor structure and their relevance weights.

REFERENCES

CREAGER, J. A., & HARDING, F. D., JR. A hierarchical factor analysis of foreman behavior. *J. appl. Psychol.*, 1958, 42, 197–203.
EBEL, R. L. Estimation of the reliability of ratings. *Psychometrika*, 1951, 16, 407–424.
EDWARDS, A. L. *Statistical methods for the behavioral sciences.* New York: Rinehart, 1954.
GHISELLI, E. E. Dimensional problems of criteria. *J. appl. Psychol.*, 1956, 40, 1–4.
GRANT, D. L. A factor analysis of managers' ratings. *J. appl. Psychol.*, 1955, 39, 283–286.
TURNER, W. W. Development of a job performance criterion for production foremen. Unpublished doctoral dissertation, Purdue Univer., 1959.

22 A Psychological Study of Occupational Adjustment

ALASTAIR HERON

This paper reports a study of male unskilled factory workers. The aim may be stated as follows: by means mainly of objective psychological tests to study the relationships which may thereby be shown to exist between various aspects of the personalities of a group of unskilled male factory workers, and the extent to which they appear to be meeting the demands of the job situation.

POPULATION STUDIED

The population consisted of an intact section of a basic production department in a medium-sized factory. The 80 men concerned, varying in age from 22 to 64 years, were unskilled operatives on individual piecework who had been in that department for periods ranging from 1 to 30 years, the median falling at 10 years. As raw material accounted for nearly 90 per cent of the cost of the product, the firm offered attractive wage and bonus rates. The job is one which over the years would select men who were in the main physically fit steady workers unlikely to be exceptional in many respects. It is the kind of job in which Russell Fraser (2) found the lowest incidence of neurosis.

Study of the task—pouring molten lead into hand-operated moulds—suggests that only minimal intellectual equipment would be required, and that some obsessionals might adapt well. Beyond that it was not meaningful to hypothesize in terms related to the demands of the job, except insofar as it is generally believed that emotional instability is reflected in poor job adjustment.

From *Journal of Applied Psychology*, 1952, 36, 385–387. This paper was presented in condensed form to the 10th International Congress of Psychotechnics at Gothenburg, Sweden, in July 1951. It is a revision of part of a Ph.D. thesis accepted by the University of London in 1951.

PERSONALITY VARIABLES

A battery of 22 individually administered objective tests was used, designed to cover such aspects of personality as general mental ability, emotional stability, temperament, and dexterity. Full details of the tests, the results obtained and the methods of statistical analysis will be found elsewhere (3). For the present purpose it will suffice to say that, with age partialled out, the matrix of product moment correlations between the tests was factor-analyzed, using Burt's simple summation method. The analysis yielded four significant factors accounting for 30 per cent of the variance. After five orthogonal rotations, three of these factors were readily identified in the light of previous data about the tests concerned.

Factor scores were obtained by simple addition of the individual's normalized percentile scores on the four tests having the highest loadings on the factor in question, in the final rotated solution. In this way *no weight has been given to the actual loadings themselves.* The factor analysis has in effect been used to select small groups of tests which have been shown to be related to one another in a psychologically meaningful way. Its arithmetic is then abandoned, and relationships between the "factor scores" and the criteria are expressed as zero-order coefficients.

CRITERIA OF OCCUPATIONAL ADJUSTMENT

Details of the establishment of these criteria will be found elsewhere (4). In view of their decisive importance, however, a description of each is considered necessary here.

Productivity. This was an index based on the individual's average productivity over a period of 67 weeks, as obtained from shop-floor records. It appeared to be so closely related to actual output (checked for 45 men over 26 weeks on a particular type of casting) as to justify considerable confidence in its use. The principal criticism to which it should be subjected is that it may suffer from artificial limitation of range due to external variables. It is free from the familiar criticism in terms of the unknown effect upon production which can result from direct observation of the worker or the installation of special counting devices. As these men were working on an individual piecework basis, such an index seems to provide a measure of occupational effectiveness in terms of the individual's "ability" to earn his living relative to that of others doing the same work. This does not, however, take into account the incentive differences arising from social, familial and economic pressures. Two men might easily possess the same hypothetical ability to carry out the working-operation at a high average rate, but one might show an actual rate much lower than the other because, for example, his wife was earning and he had no children to support. All but one of the men in the present study were married and a considerable proportion had children under school-leaving age. The latter variable was found to correlate with Productivity + .226 (P = .05), thus illustrating the point under discussion. It seems obvious that no collection of psychological assessments could hope to account among them for more than a small proportion of the variance of this criterion.

Job Adjustment. For this the author obtained a rating on a normally distributed 5-point scale, combined from the independent ratings of six supervisors on each of two occasions five weeks apart. The average consistency coefficient of the raters was .78, and careful statistical analysis established the unidimensionality of the criterion. It may be defined as a measure of *the extent to which a man is a source of concern to his supervisors.*

This criterion differs from a "merit rating" as generally used. The latter is most usually a means whereby men are considered for promotion in status, responsibility or earnings, and the rater's judgments are deliberately oriented in such a way as to maximize the predictive power of the rating for these purposes. In the present situation, no such merit rating system was in existence; the procedure used was to obtain an assessment of the extent to which each man was a source of concern to the supervisor. Further, the role of the investigator as a member of a research unit was already well established, and his independence of management recognized to a very considerable extent. The influence of "halo" resulting from familiarity was not, however, wholly absent; this could not readily be avoided when studying a well-established group whose experience in that department ranged from 1 to 30 years. In general, the criterion may perhaps be regarded with some justification as being satisfactory for the purpose.

RESULTS

In view of the significant correlation with *age* of various tests in each factor score, its effects have been held constant by partial correlation when computing the relationship of each factor score with the Productivity criterion. When the Job Adjustment criterion is involved, both *age* and *experience* in the shop are held constant, as the latter variable correlates +.4 with this criterion.

For the sake of clarity the results are presented in summary form, and only those coefficients are shown which are significant at the .05 level or better. Short titles of tests are provided in order to facilitate reference to details available elsewhere (3).

1. Factor I. "General Mental Ability" (Dominoes Non-verbal + Letter Series + Paper Formboard + Vocabulary) showed no significant relationship with either criterion.

2. Factor II. This factor is not named, but is suggestive of "Hysteric Tendency" or "Neurotic Extraversion" (low Hand Persistence + low Leg Persistence + many Food Aversions + high "neurotic" score on Word Connection List) and also showed no significant relationship with either criterion.

3. Factor III. "Emotional Instability" (many Worries + much Static Ataxia + many Annoyances + many Interests) correlated with Poor Job Adjustment +.45 (P = .001).

4. Factor IV. "Speed of Approach" (Finger Dexterity + Quick Approach to Time Test + Manual Dexterity +Speed on Track Tracer) showed the following relationships: (a) with Productivity, +.25 (P = .05); and (b) with Good Job Adjustment, +.28 (P = .01).

5. An *unweighted* combination of Factor III (reversed) and Factor IV, using the "pooling square" technique, gave a correlation with Good Job Adjustment of + .53.

DISCUSSION

It may be concluded formally that the null hypothesis was confirmed in respect of general mental ability, as assessed by non-verbal, verbal-educational and visuo-spatial tests. In view of the low level of intellectual demand implicit in the actual job, and the number of men employed on it who were shown to be well above average in general mental ability, this finding is of importance. If it were true in this instance, as suggested by Wyatt and Langdon (6), that such men would be handicapped by their excess of unneeded intellectual potential, this should have been reflected in a small negative relationship with one or more criteria of adjustment; no such relationships were found. It may be, of course, that these men exhibit adaptation to other aspects of the total situation which favor them in a way which they had not encountered on jobs apparently more in line with their intellectual potentialities. Conversely, it also seems of some importance that men of extremely low mental ability—equivalent in several cases to that of high-grade mental defectives—appear able to do this job satisfactorily. This supports the conclusion reached by Tizard and O'Connor (5), when considering the employability of high-grade mental defectives, that monotonous work of a relatively simple kind may suit them well.

If the hypothesis be advanced that "emotional instability" as evidenced by objective tests is related systematically to "poor job adjustment" as rated by supervisors, it is sustained by the findings. It is not sustained in respect of productivity. The four tests having the highest loading on this factor are all associated with what has been described as the "dysthymic" rather than the "hysteric" end of the temperament continuum in neurotics (1). This includes the anxiety states, obsessional tendency and reactive depression. It seems that in the sample studied it is this heterogeneous group of relatively unstable men who tend to be a source of concern to their supervisors. Their handicap is not, however, sufficient to affect their productive capacity over a long period.

No hypothesis is required to provide a basis for the unsurprising finding that a tendency to "Speed of Approach to a Task," as measured by the Factor IV score, is related to Productivity. If, as has been suggested, this may be regarded as a characteristic mode of personality, then for a man engaged on individual piecework its deficiency appears to constitute a handicap. At this point we may recollect the attenuating effects on such a relationship of the defects of the criterion; it may well be that a coefficient of .25 represents in this instance a more serious handicap than would appear from its size.

The combination of a high tendency to "emotional instability" of an anxious or depressive type, and a slow characteristic approach to a task, is found to be related to supervisory assessment of job adjustment at a level which, without the aid of weights derived from multiple correlation, is high enough (.53) to be regarded as evidencing a genuine handicap in the situation studied.

SUMMARY

1. This paper reports the relationships found between personality variables and occupational adjustment in a sample of 80 male unskilled factory workers.

2. Personality variables were derived from a factor analysis of the intercorrelations between 22 individually-administered objective tests.

3. Two occupational criteria were specially prepared for the investigation; one was a measure of productivity, the other of the extent to which men were a source of concern to their supervisors.

4. Some significant relationships were found and are discussed briefly from various points of view.

REFERENCES

1. EYSENCK, H. J. *Dimensions of personality.* London: Kegan Paul, 1947.

2. Fraser, R. *The incidence of neurosis among factory workers.* Rep. No. 90, Ind. Hlth. Res. Bd. London: H. M. Stationery Office, 1947.
3. Heron, A. The objective assessment of personality among factory workers. In press.
4. Heron, A. The establishment for research purposes of two criteria of occupational adjustment. *Occup. Psychol.*, 1952, 26, 2, 78–85.
5. Tizard, J., and O'Connor, N. The employability of high-grade mental defectives, II. *Amer. J. ment. Def.*, 1950, 55, 144–157.
6. Wyatt, S., and Langdon, J. N. *Fatigue and boredom in repetitive work.* Rep. No. 77, Ind. Hlth. Res. Bd. London: H. M. Stationery Office, 1937.

23 An Investigation of the Criterion Problem for One Group of Medical Specialists

JAMES M. RICHARDS, JR., CALVIN W. TAYLOR,
PHILIP B. PRICE, and TONY L. JACOBSEN

The sample consisted of 190 Utah physicians fully certified as specialists by an American Board. 80 scores relevant to the performance of these physicians were intercorrelated and factor analyzed using the principal components solution based on eigenvalues and eigenvectors. The 92 factors which had an eigenvalue greater than 1.00 were rotated by the varimax procedure and interpreted. The most important finding was the great criterion complexity for this group of medical specialists. This complexity suggests that one cannot adequately measure physician performance on the basis of a single score or a few scores. Instead, one must obtain a relatively large number of scores. Performance in both premedical and medical education was independent of performance as a physician.

  Over the last 10 years, studies evaluating the procedures used in the selection of medical students, and especially the Medical College Admission Test, have, for the most part, indicated only marginally satisfactory results (Gottheil & Michael, 1957; Ralph & Taylor, 1952; Richards & Taylor, 1961; Taylor, 1950; Wantman, 1953; Wesman, 1959). However, these studies of selection procedures have typically used as a criterion only some measure of performance in medical education, whereas the ultimate goal in selection of medical students is to pick those candidates who will be successful as practicing physicians. Stalnaker (1951) in particular has criticized studies of selection procedures, because the criterion measures lack pertinence to quality of performance as a physician. Although the use of existing selection procedures has sometimes been justified by their presumed relationship to qualities

From *Journal of Applied Psychology*, 1965, 49, 79–90. This research was supported by a contract between the University of Utah and the Cooperative Research Branch, United States Office of Education, Project No. 1551 (Robert Beezer, Monitor). The authors wish to express their gratitude to Theodore M. Yellen, Gary Shirts, Gary Jorgensen, and Sally Merk for their assistance on this project.

desirable in a professional practitioner, very few studies have been made of the relationship between the information used in the selection of medical students and criteria of post-medical school performance. In those studies which have been done, the results have been discouraging (Peterson, Andrews, Spain, & Greenberg, 1956; Richards, Taylor, & Price, 1962). There is, therefore, a great need for studies which do explore the relationship between characteristics of the medical student and his later performance as a physician, in order that selection and education of medical students may be based on appropriate variables.

It is clear that before such studies can be carried out successfully, much research has to be done on the criterion problem itself. The present investigation, therefore, is one of a series of studies aimed at developing performance measures for physicians in various types of practice. The basic assumption of this series of studies is that physician performance is complex and multivariable; accordingly, the basic procedure is based on that used by Taylor and his associates (Taylor, Smith, & Ghiselin, 1963; Taylor, Smith, Ghiselin, & Ellison, 1961) in an investigation of the criterion problem for a group of physical scientists. In the physical-scientist study, more than 50 different measures of on-the-job performance of the scientists were factor analyzed to isolate 14 different aspects of the productivity, creativity, and other contributions of these scientists. Similarly, in the present study, a large number of measures were obtained of the on-the-job performance and accomplishments of physicians practicing in urban areas in Utah who had specialized practices. These measures were then intercorrelated and factor analyzed to yield independent criterion dimensions.

It should be noted that the sort of physician studied in this research, the certified specialist, is increasingly the typical American doctor. Fully half of the private practitioners in the United States today are specialists, compared to only 16 percent in 1931 (Peterson, 1963). Since this trend toward specialization in many respects represents an adjustment to the very rapid expansion of knowledge in medical science and of complex medical technology, there is little reason to suppose that the trend will be reversed in the foreseeable future.

Method

Criterion Measures. Eighty scores relevant to physician performance, including 3 scores measuring performance in education, were obtained from a variety of sources and were analyzed. The first 5 of these scores were based on colleague's opinion; these included 1 score based on other specialists' examinations of the physician as an outstanding contributor to medicine, 1 score based on nominations by other specialists as a preferred consultant, 1 score based on nominations by general practition-

INVESTIGATION OF THE CRITERION PROBLEM   319

ers, 1 score based on nominations by the University of Utah College of Medicine full-time faculty, and a scored based on a rating of "clinical excellence" by the head of the College of Medicine Department corresponding to the individual doctor's field of specialization. The next 6 scores were obtained from medical directories and other compendiums; these included 2 scores concerning residency training, 1 score concerning specialty certification, 1 score concerning current rank, if any, on the University of Utah College of Medicine clinical (i.e., part time) faculty, 1 score based on listings in honorary compendiums such as *Who's Who In America*. The next 57 scores were obtained during an interview with each participating specialist, including 1 score based on income, 2 scores having to do with society memberships, 1 score from a special questionnaire dealing with sources and degrees of occupational satisfaction, 49 scores based on answers to direct questions asked in the course of the interview, and 3 scores dealing with the specialist's "image" of success. The final 12 scores, obtained from heterogeneous sources, included 1 score involving ratings by expert judges of "overall performance" (as indicated by the information represented in the foregoing 68 scores), 3 ratings by the particular project researcher who conducted the interview, 5 "control" scores involving such variables as years of experience, and 3 scores measuring performance in undergraduate and medical education. The exact titles of the 80 variables and the sources from which they were obtained are listed in Table 23.1. Details of the system by which raw scores were derived are presented elsewhere (Price, Taylor, Richards & Jacobsen, 1963).

Subjects. The population under consideration consisted of 332 physicians practicing in the State of Utah who had passed an American Board Specialty Certification examination and who were practicing in the urbanized Ogden-Salt Lake City-Provo complex. Letters signed by the Dean of the University of Utah College of Medicine were sent to these physicians requesting that they participate in this project, which participation primarily required that they grant an interview lasting approximately an hour. A second letter was sent to those doctors who did not respond to the first letter; physicians who did not respond to the second letter were dropped. Ultimately there were 190 physicians who agreed to participate. This smaller group was the sample actually studied in detail in this research.

Since some scores were available for both participating and nonparticipating physicians, it is possible to make a partial check of bias in the sample. The criterion scores which were available for the nonparticipating physicians were the two scores dealing with residency, the score concerning quality of board certification, the two scores concerning nominnations by other specialists, the score based on *Who's Who* listings, the

TABLE 23.1. *Title and source for each variable for urban specialist sample*

	Title	Source
1.	Number of Times Nominated as Outstanding Contributor by Urban Specialist Colleagues	Colleagues
2.	Number of Times Nominated as Preferred Consultant by Urban Specialist Colleagues	Colleagues
3.	Number of Nominations as Outstanding Contributor or Preferred Consultant by General Practitioners	General Practitioners
4.	Number of Times Nominated as Outstanding Contributor by College of Medicine Faculty	Medical Faculty
5.	Rating of "Clinical Excellence" by Medical College Department Head	Department Head
6.	Number of Different Residency Hospitals	Compendiums
7.	Number of Years Spent in Residency	Compendiums
8.	Judged Quality of National Board Certification	Expert Judges
9.	Present College of Medicine Clinical Faculty Rank	Official Records
10.	Mobility Rate in Professional Positions Since Receiving M.D.	Interview and Official Records
11.	Total Number of Listings in Honorary Compendiums	Compendiums
12.	Gross Income from Medical Profession	Interview
13.	Number of Current Memberships in Scientific and Professional Societies	Interview
14.	Average Judged Quality of Societies in Which Membership is Current	Interview and Expert Judges
15.	Overall Occupational Satisfaction	Questionnaire
16.	Number of Times During Career Invited to Serve as Editor of Scientific or Professional Journal	Interview
17.	Number of Times During Career Invited to Serve on Scientific and Professional Advisory Boards	Interview
18.	Average Judged Quality of Scientific and Professional Awards Received During Career	Interview and Expert Judges
19.	Self-Reported Number of Contributions Made to Medicine	Interview

20. Average Judged Quality of Self-Reported Contributions Made to Medicine — Interview and Expert Judges
21. Self-Reported Number of Non-Medical Contributions to Society — Interview
22. Total Number of Papers Presented at Scientific and Professional Meetings During Career — Interview
23. Average Number of Journal Publications Per Year Since Receiving M.D. — Interview and Compendiums
24. Average Level of Contribution to Publications as Indicated by Senior vs. Junior Authorship Status — Interview and Compendiums
25. Number of Research Projects with Which Involved During Career — Interview
26. Number of Scientific and Professional Journals Reviewed Regularly — Interview
27. Number of Subscriptions to Scientific and Professional Journals — Interview
28. Number of Articles in Scientific and Professional Journals Read in Detail Each Month — Interview
29. Average Number of Society Meetings Attended Annually — Interview
30. Number of Postgraduate Courses Taken During Career — Interview
31. Number of Refresher Courses Taken During Career — Interview
32. Physician Evaluation of Usefulness of Drug Detail Men — Interview
33. Extent of Physician's Experimental Use of Drugs Provided by Drug Detail Men — Interview
34. Number of Techniques Other Than Journals, Meetings, and Drug Detail Men Used in Keeping Abreast — Interview
35. Average Number of Formal Medical Consultations Called into Monthly — Interview
36. Average Number of Informal Medical Consultations Called into Monthly — Interview
37. Percentage of Patients on Which Consultations are Required — Interview
38. Number of Patients Seen Per Day — Interview
39. Average Amount of Time Spent with Patients on First Visit — Interview
40. Average Amount of Time Spent in Explaining Diagnoses to Patients — Interview
41. Proportion of Office Patients Treated Without Charge — Interview
42. Proportion of Office Patients That Fail to Pay Physician for Services Rendered — Interview
43. Self-Estimated Average Socioeconomic Level of Patients — Interview

TABLE 23.1. *Title and source for each variable for urban specialist sample—(Cont.)*

Title	Source
44. Degree to Which Physician Adheres to Patient Appointment Schedule	Interview
45. Average Number of House Calls Made Per Week	Interview
46. Degree to Which Physician Considers Psychological Factors in Diagnoses	Interview
47. Average Number of Hours Per Week Devoted to Medical Practice	Interview
48. Average Number of Hospitalized Patients	Interview
49. Number of Hospitals in Which Physician Works	Interview
50. Average Judged Quality of Hospitals in Which Physician Works	Interview and Expert Judge
51. Number of Hospitals in Which Physician Maintains Courtesy Privileges	Interview
52. Average Judged Quality of Hospitals in Which Physician Maintains Courtesy Privileges	Interview and Expert Judges
53. Number of Formal Responsibilities Physician has in Hospitals	Interview
54. Average Judged Quality of Hospital Responsibilities	Interview
55. Self-Estimated Value of Office Equipment	Interview and Expert Judges
56. Number of M.D. Assistants on Physician's Ancillary Staff	Interview
57. Number of Nurses on Physician's Ancillary Staff	Interview
58. Number of Technicians on Physician's Ancillary Staff	Interview
59. Number of Clerical, Administrative, and Janitorial Workers on Physician's Ancillary Staff	Interview
60. Average Number of Speeches on Medical Topics to Laymen Groups Per Year	Interview
61. Average Amount of Vacation Taken Annually	Interview
62. Extent to Which Physician Plans and Maintains Leisure Time Activities	Interview
63. Number of Current Memberships in Social and Avocational Organizations	Interview
64. Number of Current Memberships in Civic and Political Organizations	Interview
65. Characteristics Physician Considers Important for Success in Medicine: Number of "Common" Responses	Interview

66. Characteristics Physician Considers Important for Success in Medicine: Number of "Uncommon" Responses — Interview
67. Characteristics Physician Considers Important for Success in Medicine: "Commonness" of Responses Elicted — Interview
68. Self-Rating of Success in Medicine — Interview
69. Expert Panel Rating of Overall Performance Based on All Available Information — Expert Judges
70. Interviewer Rating of Condition of Physician's Office — Project Interviewer
71. Interviewer Rating of Likeability — Project Interviewer
72. Interviewer Rating of Physician's Involvement in This Project — Project Interviewer
73. Age at Which Received M.D. — Control Variables
74. Number of Years Between Receiving M.D. and Receiving National Board Certification — Control Variables
75. Years of Experience Since Receiving M.D. — Control Variables
76. Individual Practice Rather Than Group, Clinic or Hospital Practice — Control Variables
77. Hospital Practice Rather Than Individual, Group, or Clinic Practice — Control Variables
78. Undergraduate Grade Point Average — Official Transcripts
79. Grade Point Average for First Two Years of Medical School — Official Transcripts
80. Grade Point Average for Last Two Years of Medical School — Official Transcripts

score concerning current rank on the College of Medicine clinical faculty, and the three control scores of years of experience, age at which the MD was obtained, and the number of years between receiving the MD degree and obtaining speciality certification. On these 10 stores, *t*-tests were made comparing the physicians who did not participate with the physicians who did. Only one difference out of the 10 was significant at the 5 percent level; this difference indicated that the nonparticipating physicians held *lower* rank on the College of Medicine clinical faculty. The meaning of this difference is not entirely clear. However, since the other nine differences were not significant, it appears that the sample of 190 participating physicians is not seriously biased.

Procedure. Scores on all variables, with the exception of the two dichotomous control variables dealing with type of practice, were converted to Normalized *T*-scores (Guilford, 1956, pp. 494–501) with a mean of 50 and a standard deviation of 10. The next step in the data analysis was to compute the 3,160 intercorrelations among the 80 scores.[2] The resulting correlation matrix was then factor analyzed, using the principal components solution based on eigenvalue and eigenvector analysis (Harman, 1960). Unity was placed in the diagonal cells of the correlation matrix, and all factors having an eigenvalue greater than 1.00 were extracted. These factors were then rotated to a final solution on the computer, using the varimax analytic orthogonal-rotational solution. The rationale for this method of factoring, including the insertion of unity in the diagonal, and rotating is presented in detail by Kaiser (1960). While it is true that some users of factor analysis might prefer some other estimate of the communalities such as the multiple correlation between each variable and all other variables combined, it should be noted that when the number of variables is large the factor solution is relatively insensitive to different communality estimates.

We have learned that some missing scores are inevitable in large-

TABLE 23.2. *Distribution of missing scores taking each variable as a case*

Percentile	Number of missing scores
10	4.75
25	11.78
50	18.05
75	33.25
90	50.35

[1] All computations for this project were carried out at the Western Data Processing Center, University of California, Los Angeles, California.

scale criterion research of this type. Since the factor analysis computer program used does not allow for missing data, the mean score, or 50, was substituted for all missing scores. On an overall basis, approximately 13 percent of the scores were missing. However, missing scores were not evenly distributed over the 80 variables, and accordingly a more detailed description of the distribution of missing scores over the 80 variables is presented in Table 23.2. It should be emphasized that the percentiles in Table 23.2 refer to the distribution of variables and not to the distribution of physicians. In other words, the tenth percentile in Table 23.2 refers to the 8 variables with the smallest number of missing scores.

The identification number and name of variables falling above the ninetieth percentile and the number of missing scores for those variables are as follows: 12. Gross Income from Medical Profession (67 scores), 40. Average Amount of Time Spent in Explaining Diagnoses to Patients (78 scores), 54. Averaged Judged Quality of Hospital Responsibilities (80 scores), 55. Self-Estimated Value of Office Equipment (55 scores), 74. Number of Years Between Receiving MD and Receiving National Board Certification (68 scores), 78. Undergraduate Grade Point Average (120 scores), 79. Grade Point Average for First 2 Years of Medical School (87 scores); and 80. Grade Point Average for Last 2 Years of Medical School (51 scores).

On a priori basis, it is difficult to evaluate the exact effect of substituting the mean for a fairly substantial number of missing scores, although it can be stated that the general effect of such a substitution is to reduce the correlation between variables, and that this in turn produces a tendency toward lower factor loadings and, in combination with unity in the diagonal, toward unique factors. In order to provide a more specific estimate of the extent to which correlations for the present study were affected by the substitution of the mean for missing scores, the correlations between each of the 3 grade point average variables and the other 77 scores were computed, eliminating from the calculations for each grade point average variable those physicians for whom no grade average was available. When the mean is substituted for missing grade scores, the median correlation between the three grade point averages and the other 77 variables is .03 with a range of correlation from —.17 to .18. When computations are based only on those cases for whom grades are available, the median correlation is still .03, but with a range of correlation from —.21 to .28. The distributions of the correlations both appeared fairly symmetrical, and were highly similar to each other with respect to the pattern of correlations with the other 77 variables. In the opinion of the authors, these results suggest that the results of this study were not materially affected by the substitution of the mean for missing scores.

In most cases, the raw scores on a scale were simply the numbers which the physicians gave in answer to a free-response question. Practical considerations made it impossible to obtain a direct measure of the reliability (and, for that matter, validity) of these responses. An indirect indication of the reliability is provided by the communalities obtained in the factor analysis. From this indirect indication, it would appear that the reliabilities are at least reasonably satisfactory.

RESULTS AND DISCUSSION

A surprisingly large number of factors, namely 29, had an eigenvalue greater than 1.00 and were included in the analysis. The rotated factor matrix[2] is presented in Table 23.3, together with the communality of each variable. These 29 factors are described below.

Factor A has high loadings on all variables involving colleague nominations and the rating of clinical excellence by the department head. Therefore, the most appropriate title for this factor might be *professional recognition for achievements*. High scorers on this variable have also attained higher rank on the clinical faculty, have been slightly more mobile than their lower-scoring colleagues, have read a slightly above average number of papers at scientific and professional society meetings, and have achieved some national recognition in that they have been asked to serve as journal editors. The overall picture presented by this factor is that of a physician who has achieved both a high degree of "visibility" and a good reputation and high status among his medical peers.

Factor B is characterized by loadings which indicate that the high scorer sees fewer patients each day, but spends more time with each patient, both in examination and in explaining his diagnosis. He also makes more use of consultations than the average specialist and relies less on drug salesmen as a source of information about pharmacological developments than does the average specialist. A common thread running through these variables is thoroughness in dealing with the patient and willingness to take as much time with each patient as is necessary. The best title for this factor, therefore, might be *diagnostic thoroughness*. Perhaps because of the smaller volume of patients, high scorers have a lower-than-average income. However, they work in fewer but better quality hospitals and are regarded as outstanding contributors. If this factor is reflected, the loadings suggest a busy, financially successful physician with a large practice who contributes primarily through the *quantity* of people he reaches.

[2] Copies of the complete correlation matrix and the unrotated factor matrix have been deposited with the American Documentation Institute. Order Document No. 8221 from ADI Auxiliary Publications Project, Photoduplication Service, Library of Congress, Washington, D. C. 20540. Remit in advance $1.25 for microfilm or $1.25 for photocopies and make checks payable to: Chief, Photoduplication Service, Library of Congress.

Factor C might best be titled *psychosomatic orientation,* since its highest loading is on the variable measuring the degree to which the physician considers psychological factors in providing care to patients. It is interesting to find that high scorers are more satisfied with their professional activities than is the average specialist in our sample. As might be expected, high scorers tend to be in individual, group, or clinic practices rather than on a full-time hospital staff. Secondary loadings suggest that the higher scorer continues to take, and apparently likes, courses in medical subjects, and is a member of an above-average number of professional societies.

Factor D in many ways appears to involve the traditional "family doctor" pattern in that the most salient feature is the doctor's willingness to make house calls. This interpretation is strengthened by the fact that the high scorer, when asked what his major contributions have been, tends to answer with things that are directly related to medicine, tends to spend an above-average amount of time examining patients on their first visit, makes relatively more use of consultants, and works a slightly above-average number of hours at his practice. Contrary to the findings of other researchers (Anderson & Feldman, 1956; Peterson et al., 1956), in addition to being a family doctor, the high scorer is also a "doctor's doctor," since he is nominated to a greater-than-average degree both by general practitioners and by other specialists, and his contributions are, according to expert medical judgment, of high quality. The characteristics common to many of these contributions seem to be a willingness to go out of his way when necessary to provide care to a patient; therefore, the title proposed for this family doctor factor is *willingness to provide special attention to patients.*

Factor E should be reflected and titled *medical charity work,* since the described physician provides an above-average amount of free medical work, not only intentionally and voluntarily, but also involuntarily through the failure of a significant number of his patients to pay their bills. It could be, of course, that more of his patients do not pay their bills because this doctor is less concerned with payment and therefore does not press bill collecting. However, he does deal with poorer patients. Other loadings portray a physician who is relatively lax about his appointment schedule, who practices in a group or clinic setting, who works in relatively few hospitals, who does not belong to many professional societies, and who takes more than the average amount of course work.

Factor F, which is more clearly interpretable if reflected and which primarily involves the length and variety of residency experience, might best be titled *length of residency.* Doctors with long residencies appear to be the newer doctors, and surprisingly obtain their specialty certification relatively soon after receiving their MD degree. It is interesting to

TABLE 23.3. *Rotated factor matrix and communalities for urban specialist sample*

Variable	A	B	C	D	E	F	G	H	I	J	K	L	M	N	O	P	Q	R	S	T	U	V	W	X	Y	Z	AA	BB	CC	h^2
1	60	21	03	26	−05	05	−10	−01	−01	−04	−07	07	−21	−03	08	−08	−05	00	−15	15	03	−15	−01	−01	−01	05	−13	−06	−15	68
2	50	−08	−12	28	−15	−16	−14	17	03	14	−03	01	−09	−15	00	05	06	35	−12	03	−08	−13	−20	05	06	−03	−07	−16	00	74
3	27	−07	−09	42	05	−03	−01	05	12	−06	−01	−19	04	02	−08	01	−14	13	−22	−24	14	−13	−14	−08	−14	−04	−17	03	−09	69
4	76	12	−01	08	−02	01	−01	00	26	−13	05	08	−16	07	−08	−15	−03	01	−03	09	−03	12	01	01	−01	−10	−13	09	−01	74
5	74	04	02	12	−02	−06	−09	−09	−02	08	05	−03	11	00	11	03	−01	−13	10	−10	08	−04	02	−13	−01	13	−13	−11	−01	74
6	−07	−06	18	06	−21	−70	−22	14	−06	01	10	−02	04	05	−01	07	−04	−05	−03	02	−05	07	01	−06	−06	−05	−02	07	07	69
7	−02	10	−11	03	05	−83	−17	01	10	06	10	−10	−01	01	−05	07	−13	−03	−03	03	−05	−07	−01	−02	−10	−05	−02	07	−03	81
8	14	02	−16	00	−08	−17	−31	03	10	04	−10	11	−05	−01	−01	−13	−04	02	−06	−10	04	−11	00	00	16	00	−13	02	−03	77
9	55	−16	01	−03	−01	35	25	−02	−07	−13	−09	−06	−10	−04	−14	−02	−02	10	−08	−07	04	−08	−13	−05	16	02	15	−04	−12	69
10	25	15	−02	−10	12	−35	−28	06	−18	01	−34	06	07	−06	08	−10	30	−15	−08	−10	03	−07	17	10	08	−13	15	07	10	70
11	33	−07	03	20	07	12	−28	−24	−04	−30	−04	13	−21	11	−05	−22	−11	03	06	00	−08	−10	06	−04	−05	−06	20	−16	07	70
12	03	−25	06	−10	07	−20	−29	23	−03	−15	−04	−07	−10	03	10	06	02	11	−02	11	03	−17	−56	−01	05	−06	−16	−07	10	73
13	01	−13	23	−08	29	04	−36	−01	09	−08	−06	−09	−15	25	05	−36	−08	−22	14	07	03	−05	−15	08	−04	−06	13	−13	05	67
14	18	−03	03	−03	−02	−02	−58	04	09	−27	−06	−07	−01	−08	00	−31	00	00	14	11	09	−04	−01	01	−14	−03	07	−07	−05	65
15	02	03	46	−01	−04	−07	09	−17	00	07	13	−02	−02	−04	12	−15	09	06	14	07	09	−14	−01	−08	08	02	11	08	−22	61
16	25	−15	05	18	−00	02	−15	−27	08	−49	−01	14	−14	−15	18	−10	−05	−01	00	20	−10	07	10	03	−06	17	−01	18	06	69
17	08	−10	14	03	00	12	−03	−02	08	01	−08	56	−04	−05	02	−25	−11	10	−07	10	10	03	01	11	−06	28	−28	−03	06	65
18	12	04	02	05	−09	23	03	02	10	−05	−11	25	−25	−03	04	−26	−09	10	−07	19	28	−25	−04	00	−06	−09	10	14	−15	62
19	04	15	15	45	07	10	−15	15	02	−10	12	21	−09	29	04	02	12	09	03	05	27	−16	−12	−19	−10	19	12	−25	−12	65
20	12	15	−01	22	16	23	−15	02	−10	−10	−03	28	07	77	−06	01	19	10	−08	10	−20	−28	18	−12	−07	09	07	−19	−13	68
21	05	−15	08	04	08	−03	−03	09	−19	07	−03	−11	−13	13	03	−01	−02	06	−08	10	05	09	07	−06	−07	01	−10	−04	09	76
22	25	−07	−10	04	−03	−03	−12	−08	01	10	−06	33	−20	−05	03	−03	19	10	08	−04	01	−05	−10	05	−04	05	−02	03	−08	68
23	11	00	−05	−10	−17	19	−07	−01	06	−19	−07	10	−79	03	02	−03	−06	−07	−03	−02	02	−03	−07	−13	−04	−04	00	−10	−11	81
24	10	05	00	−07	08	07	−12	−08	00	00	−07	33	−83	03	03	−07	04	04	08	−04	02	09	−09	05	04	−04	05	−01	−03	76
25	07	13	−06	−08	−03	02	−07	00	12	−01	−09	71	−19	−07	03	−07	−10	−06	12	−10	04	−03	−07	−13	04	−04	04	01	−10	66
26	08	06	−03	06	00	−08	−13	15	−07	−12	01	15	−06	04	−08	−78	−03	08	−02	14	04	02	−05	04	−10	−02	−02	−03	−14	81
27	06	06	02	−05	−03	−10	−09	09	08	−08	−08	−02	−04	05	−08	−77	04	08	−05	−03	−13	02	−09	−03	−10	04	04	−02	07	68
28	−06	01	02	04	−03	05	−09	04	−10	−01	01	31	06	−17	−21	−46	04	−07	12	−03	−02	−02	13	−25	00	−02	−02	−10	07	61
29	02	−01	−05	02	10	−08	−14	04	01	10	−16	−06	08	03	−02	−08	05	07	−05	80	11	08	00	06	−10	−02	12	−10	−02	80
30	−15	−11	28	09	10	−31	14	−10	10	03	−16	12	08	08	−02	−09	37	04	−27	−05	15	00	−07	06	−27	09	−11	−13	−18	70
31	03	−03	01	05	−11	14	−08	−10	06	−05	−05	01	03	03	−01	−08	65	07	−05	−05	15	07	−01	01	−05	04	08	−13	11	68
32	02	11	12	−08	03	13	−05	02	−03	−06	−05	01	04	10	−01	−08	37	06	−27	−04	−05	07	−01	06	−05	−07	05	05	−18	68
33	02	−36	01	09	03	13	19	−04	25	−06	12	03	04	−03	−10	01	−10	76	−04	05	−03	−09	−01	−12	−11	04	08	05	11	66
34	08	−01	06	09	00	−05	01	03	08	−01	03	04	04	06	−10	−17	−04	44	−81	−03	14	−09	−01	−12	−11	11	27	10	−01	75
35	07	−14	−20	−22	−04	−15	−04	05	13	−42	−28	07	−09	−01	10	10	19	01	−16	−18	06	00	02	01	16	11	−05	−04	−07	68
36	−02	08	02	08	−04	08	−12	23	05	−01	−81	−14	06	01	−08	−07	02	−02	−10	13	06	−12	−08	−07	00	11	00	−05	06	79
37	−04	54	06	26	−08	10	−12	03	05	−21	−02	21	11	18	−08	−12	02	13	−06	05	−03	05	−12	00	11	−04	−05	−15	−15	73
38	−19	−76	−06	17	−03	13	−06	12	−04	−01	−01	11	06	11	10	00	02	−04	−10	09	−05	−04	−10	12	−02	−03	00	06	−09	76
39	10	46	−06	31	−04	−04	10	10	16	04	−11	05	−15	−15	11	−27	13	−06	−06	21	03	−14	−03	06	06	−21	07	12	−16	72
40	00	38	13	15	00	04	17	−01	22	−13	04	19	−12	−01	11	−15	09	18	22	27	03	−14	−03	12	−11	−31	−05	−06	−05	63

328

Variable	A	B	C	D	E	F	G	H	I	J	K	L	M	N	O	P	Q	R	S	T	U	V	W	X	Y	Z	AA	BB	CC	h^2
41	09	01	07	06	-75	-04	04	09	02	-07	-05	-02	11	-01	-02	-02	-15	-01	-06	-07	16	-08	-02	08	04	-07	09	-08	01	70
42	-12	-03	-11	-09	-59	-10	-13	-13	-03	10	-01	04	03	05	-01	-09	02	-09	10	-03	-09	-05	24	-22	-04	15	02	09	17	65
43	-07	-07	20	13	28	09	-13	-28	07	03	-07	-08	07	-18	22	-18	-36	18	04	-23	07	11	-13	-07	-05	-05	04	-11	-17	67
44	15	13	16	-11	25	-01	04	05	31	-16	-07	-09	-07	06	-19	-08	-11	-22	-19	27	07	12	-14	-15	-01	-02	-18	-05	-04	78
45	09	-05	12	82	-13	00	01	02	-02	-02	-03	01	-01	00	01	-06	-10	-06	-05	02	07	14	05	02	-05	-02	-10	00	-04	78
46	-03	16	76	08	01	06	05	04	03	06	-02	-09	05	00	03	03	-05	10	-06	02	12	06	09	-16	-08	-05	07	-01	06	70
47	06	-08	05	22	-17	-03	06	04	-02	06	-01	-13	-05	-08	13	-15	-05	-07	03	-06	-05	-29	-05	-13	-08	-12	02	-01	03	70
48	22	-04	00	16	-06	-03	-30	14	-06	04	05	06	00	-01	13	04	-11	-04	17	01	-04	-56	-05	-16	-06	-04	02	16	02	71
49	20	-31	00	13	15	-28	03	10	03	31	-01	28	-10	-14	10	22	-06	01	-17	01	07	20	25	-14	12	-09	17	-08	16	73
50	02	22	-03	14	20	-02	-02	13	-07	07	00	-16	-04	-09	02	-20	29	04	14	-07	-10	06	-14	13	00	12	-18	36	-16	63
51	14	09	-01	-02	-27	00	-05	09	23	07	-27	-25	09	-14	10	-27	13	19	14	-05	-16	05	07	-36	-10	18	-31	-18	19	74
52	02	04	-02	-05	00	00	-02	09	27	-24	-11	05	17	02	-13	-20	22	-03	-07	-11	-31	05	11	-22	-31	19	-13	07	06	72
53	21	00	-02	-02	-06	-03	-08	66	04	-16	00	05	-07	02	25	-19	05	-03	-05	-02	20	11	11	00	00	08	05	01	-11	74
54	06	-03	-06	04	00	11	-20	-03	78	08	03	-07	-02	-12	-07	04	-09	04	-10	00	00	-04	06	03	-04	-02	05	-07	-02	74
55	-19	-06	05	10	00	16	-07	43	-12	19	04	16	-17	15	-07	-24	-10	-17	-06	-10	15	-03	03	06	-04	03	03	-24	-05	60
56	02	10	-06	02	01	06	15	16	-11	-79	02	-03	-02	-01	-04	-02	-07	-01	-01	09	04	-11	-10	36	-04	-23	11	17	09	71
57	06	-02	15	31	-05	-01	15	07	42	01	-04	11	-10	15	-15	-17	-09	-17	14	02	-22	-11	11	-10	-05	18	05	17	-05	72
58	06	-12	-22	-16	-13	-02	09	26	-14	-24	-41	14	-07	-41	-24	-25	22	02	14	09	-22	07	11	-05	01	-23	01	-23	09	70
59	-16	-18	-21	-23	-07	-03	09	18	-16	-04	00	06	-07	-07	-08	-15	-05	-05	-36	-21	15	07	37	-05	-05	-19	01	-18	-06	73
60	07	04	-11	13	05	-14	17	09	-05	15	00	10	04	-07	03	-13	-08	02	-15	-23	47	-03	-75	-13	-04	-23	-09	15	07	65
61	00	04	-11	13	10	15	-02	-21	-04	06	-04	11	03	10	-01	00	00	-05	-03	-03	00	06	-01	01	03	-11	13	-02	13	77
62	00	-04	02	17	10	12	04	-07	-05	15	-06	-06	-03	40	-07	05	06	-04	00	09	79	04	-03	-04	-04	02	-06	00	-10	71
63	00	-02	04	06	-10	-05	-11	-07	03	06	-06	-06	-03	-06	-07	-18	-16	-11	06	-02	39	68	-03	01	03	11	-03	02	-10	72
64	-04	04	02	42	-10	-05	00	01	15	-00	-05	13	01	40	23	-18	08	02	00	03	02	07	-10	-04	-04	02	06	-04	20	70
65	03	-03	-05	14	-10	02	04	06	03	-07	03	-07	01	-06	-06	04	-12	-11	-08	03	01	-07	-03	00	-78	11	04	01	-05	69
66	-03	-02	-02	-15	01	-08	05	-03	00	00	04	00	00	-02	05	04	-04	02	00	03	-01	-06	04	07	-03	05	05	01	03	69
67	-04	-01	-03	-15	00	-18	06	-03	00	-02	04	00	00	-02	16	-06	08	09	-08	07	-01	01	-06	00	-73	01	07	-01	-14	75
68	-04	-07	11	02	-03	02	-01	11	-04	05	-01	00	-04	-02	83	-06	00	09	-04	07	-01	-06	00	-09	-06	04	-07	-06	-03	67
69	38	11	-11	02	13	07	23	13	10	-01	08	00	-13	13	02	-27	00	-07	-04	-15	10	-16	-14	-13	-18	04	-07	13	-15	73
70	18	-21	26	-13	-09	-14	05	04	-03	-05	-14	28	03	22	-17	00	-04	06	36	19	-12	00	-26	-13	13	00	13	05	-05	67
71	15	14	-08	03	-20	-12	06	13	-10	08	-28	11	-16	15	02	00	-01	01	-05	06	-04	-07	-21	-78	05	00	05	24	-05	73
72	01	-01	03	-10	07	-12	-02	03	01	-11	14	-02	-02	04	08	-02	04	09	-10	06	-06	04	-64	00	05	00	-04	-02	-08	69
73	-13	-04	13	-10	-11	10	-16	13	05	11	05	-05	-07	-08	-05	-04	-15	09	05	14	-07	19	-05	01	-12	09	73	-08	05	72
74	-02	08	03	03	-02	62	-16	-15	09	04	02	-14	-06	06	01	-16	20	-06	-10	07	04	03	-08	01	-16	-16	17	-08	14	68
75	00	-08	11	-10	02	55	-47	13	06	-03	20	-04	-28	-21	-06	09	14	12	05	12	04	12	-16	-04	07	-09	11	03	-10	81
76	-12	03	08	00	02	-20	-11	13	-02	09	19	-02	-23	-01	16	-21	-06	37	-16	04	-04	19	-04	-04	04	15	02	27	24	72
77	-05	-08	-35	02	-03	-02	06	-09	09	01	10	-14	15	-21	06	-06	04	-03	-07	02	04	-06	-03	08	06	-19	-23	-19	-04	67
78	07	10	05	-05	-01	-03	01	-15	05	08	-05	-04	-10	-01	03	-08	07	00	04	12	08	07	-03	-01	02	01	02	-15	-10	70
79	03	09	-01	01	05	-01	-01	00	-02	08	17	00	-06	-12	-04	-08	06	00	03	02	05	00	07	-01	-01	01	-05	-11	-32	78
80	-01	-06	00	07	04	01	-12	05	05	05	-11	10	-08	05	03	00	06	-02	00	00	00	07	04	-08	-02	13	-05	00	-77	70

note that during residency the high-scoring physician tended to move from one hospital to another, but when he completed his residency, he settled into a local practice and has since moved less than the average specialist.

Factor G should be reflected and seems to be *level of medical specialization and attainment*, since its highest loading indicates that the physician is in a high-status specialty. Since passing a high status specialty is a prerequisite to membership in many high-status societies, there is, as expected, a high loading indicating membership in societies of above-average quality. As is also to be expected, the high scorer had a relatively long specialized training. Moreover, the fairly high loading on typical number of hospitalized patients is also probably a function of the physician's level of specialization. In other words, as specialization increases, the seriousness of the diseases treated increases. Secondary loadings appear for income, number of honorary compendium listings, and overall rating by expert judges.

Factor H should be called *quantity of hospital responsibilities*, since it is characterized by a relatively large number of hospital duties. As is to be expected, the high scorer devotes a substantially greater than average amount of time to his medical practice and takes a shorter than average vacation. In spite of working with poorer patients, he has an above-average income and apparently has plowed money back into his practice to equip his office and to provide a nontechnical staff. He is below average in national recognition.

Factor I should be called *quality of hospital responsibilities*, since it is characterized by relatively high-quality hospital duties. In addition to his hospital duties, the high scorer has a sizeable nursing staff to assist him. Perhaps because of this assistance, he is efficient in utilizing his time so that he keeps on schedule. Apparently he has wide contact with general practitioners, who respect him highly. He utilizes the newest drugs available and deals to a slightly above-average extent with the psychological side of patients in that he makes certain his patients understand his diagnoses.

Factor J, which should be reflected, represents a physician who has some younger doctors working under him, who consults, edits, and belongs to higher status societies, and who has achieved some national recognition. He tends to work in relatively few hospitals. Thus the overall impression is that of a doctor who has achieved high status through essentially administrative or supervisory contributions. Therefore, the best title for this factor might be *medical supervisory responsibilities*.

Factor K might be best titled *medical consulting and liaison*, since, if the factor is reflected, the high scorer claims that other physicians frequently ask his judgment on medical problems, especially informally but also on the basis of a formal consultation. He maintains a well-equipped office with a large ancillary technical staff. From this, one might get the impression of well-established medical specialist. However, other secondary loadings show this type of physician is not only younger than most of his colleagues, but also has frequently moved from one professional position to another.

Factor L, which might best be titled *attainment in research*, gives a highly consistent pattern, which can be interpreted as a strong orientation toward science. The high scorer has been involved in medical research which has been of a quality to lead to publication. He also serves on scientific advisory boards, delivers papers at scientific meetings, and keeps up with what other investigators are doing by reading and reviewing the scientific literature. Since he has won both honors and other recognition for his contributions, it appears that his research is significant. Moreover his own self-concept seems to agree with these findings. Specifically, he considers his most important contributions to be those directly related to medicine. In turn, these contributions are regarded as high in quality by expert medical judges.

Factor M, which should be reflected before interpretation, might be called *attainment in publications*, since the two highest loading variables indicate that the high scorer has been productive of publications in which he has tended to be the sole or senior author. As a result of his contributions, he has been recognized as an outstanding contributor both by his colleagues and by the compilers of honorary compendiums, and he has been honored for his accomplishments. He tends to be in individual medical practice.

Factor N is complex and somewhat difficult to interpret. The highest loading indicates that when the high scorer is asked what his most important contributions have been, he tends to give a larger than average number of general contributions to society rather than strictly professional contributions. However, what medical contributions he does list are regarded as important by expert judges. He tends to be practicing in a hospital, which perhaps is less of a drain on his energies than individual, group, or clinic practice would be, thus allowing him more freedom to make contributions as a responsible citizen. This interpretation is supported somewhat by the fact that he is active in community organizations. His overall attainment is considered good by expert judges. All in all, perhaps the best title for this factor would be *self-evaluated contributions to society*.

Factor O clearly involves *self-evaluated overall professional success*, since its only really substantial loading is on the self-rating of success, and since the secondary loadings do not fall into a highly consistent pattern. The most striking thing about this factor is that there is nothing outstanding about high scorers except that they rate themselves as being quite successful. In terms of other tangible evidence, therefore, their self-concept of success seems somewhat exaggerated.

Factor P, which seems to involve primarily the source to which the physician goes to obtain information, should be reflected and titled *keeping abreast of field by journal reading*. This tendency to go to original sources suggests that the high scorer is a cautious, critical-thinking specialist whose self-discipline is such that he exerts extra effort to be thorough in all phases of his medical practice. This impression is supported by the fact that secondary loadings indicate a physician who takes time to make a thorough examination of patients on their first visit, and who works in the better hospitals. He also belongs to more and better societies than the average specialist, has achieved both honors and recognition, and is rated as above average by expert judges. There is thus some suggestion that physicians who use journals as their means of keeping themselves informed display an above-average level of performance in a number of different areas.

Factor Q, another source-of-information factor, specifically relates to postgraduate education and indicates either doctors who take a relatively large number of formal courses for credit and take a relatively small number of refresher courses, or vice versa. The physician taking a large number of *refresher* courses deals with wealthier patients, but has been less mobile and is working in low-status hospitals. An appropriate title for this factor is *keeping abreast by means of refresher courses*.

Factor R, still another information source factor, should be titled *keeping abreast by means of detail men,* since the high scorer on this factor utilized both drug salesmen and the newest drugs provided by them as resources. Secondary loadings suggest that he is a preferred consultant, and he is in either individual or hospital practice rather than group or clinic practice.

Factor S, which should be reflected, might be titled *keeping abreast by means of uncommon techniques,* since the highest loading indicate a doctor who uses less commonly utilized techniques for keeping up with changes in his field. A striking example of such a technique is tape-recorded summaries of new knowledge in a given specialty which the physician can play while he is shaving, driving his car, etc. The high scorer has a less impressive office but more clerical help than average, and contrary to what might be expected, has attained some honors and some recognition among general practitioners.

Factor T clearly involves *participation in professional societies*, since the outstanding characteristic of high scorers is that they go to many society meetings. They also derive satisfaction from their professional activities to a greater than average degree. Secondary loadings indicate that they place value on taking enough time to insure that patients understand their diagnoses, but still maintain their appointment schedule; work with poorer patients; have an average reputation among their specialist colleagues and below-average among general practitioners; and receive some requests to speak and to do editorial work.

Factor U should be called *civic participation*. Its three highest loadings all deal in one way or another with contacts with laymen. Thus, one major contribution of high scorers is that they provide a link between professional medicine and society. Other smaller loadings form a complex pattern and indicate that the high scorer, in a self-report of his contributions, can and will point to many things that are above average, has been honored for his contributions, has courtesy privileges in below average hospitals, has a relatively small staff, and is slightly dissatisfied professionally. Thus, there is a suggestion that the high scorer may be somewhat frustrated in his profession, and perhaps has turned to contacts with laymen as an alternative source of satisfaction.

Factor V represents a physician who organizes his time to provide opportunities for leisure; he thus has a shorter than average workweek. There is some indication that this may be partly due to the fact that he works with less sick patients, who are less likely to require hospitalization The best title for this factor might be *leisure planning*. Contrary to the findings of Peterson, et al. (1956), there is little indication that high scorers are superior physicians.

Factor W, if reflected, presents the picture of a physician who achieved enough financial success to be able to afford long vacations. In view of this, it is somewhat surprising that he has an above-average number of patients who do not pay their bills. However, he does have a relatively impressive office, and has achieved a slightly above-average reputation both among his specialist colleagues and among general practitioners. This factor might best be called *need for long vacations—financial success*.

Factor X, involving mainly the impact the physician had on the person who interviewed him for this research, should probably be titled *interviewer's rating of likeability*. When the factor is reflected, high scorers seem to have better than average social skills and can move easily among people and can become deeply involved in an activity.

Both Factor Y and Factor Z should be reflected, and both involve the doctor's ideas about what constitutes success within his own specialty. Thus, they are perhaps not true criterion factors, although the authors had expected that a physician's expressed ideas about what goes into success would have some relationship to his actual success. Factor Y represents a doctor who is quite typical in such an analysis and might therefore be titled *orthodox success image*. On the other hand, high scorers on Factor Z have unusual ideas about success, so this factor might best be called *unorthodox success image*. Otherwise, there is little that distinguishes high scorers on either factor from other specialists.

Factor AA, which has its highest loading on a control variable, should be titled *late attainment of MD degree*. Smaller loadings show that high scorers on this factor work in relatively few hospitals and have relatively few patients in hospitals at any given time. They use drugs provided by detail men, and are in some form of group practice. They have achieved some national recognition, but are not asked to serve on advisory boards.

Both Factor BB and Factor CC should be reflected. These factors appear to be measures of grade-getting ability, with Factor BB involving *achievement in undergraduate education* and Factor CC involving *achievement in medical education*. In other words, to the extent to which one may generalize from the results of this study, performance in education is essentially independent of performance as a medical specialist. It does *not* appear that this finding is *entirely* due to the large number of missing scores for these variables, since as indicated previously the distribution of correlations for these variables was only slightly affected by the substitution of the mean for missing scores. Nor does it appear that it is an artifact of using an orthogonal rotation procedure, since the hyperplane count for these variables is quite high. It should also be noted that recent research (Lindquist, 1963) indicates that the correlation between grades and other variables is changed very little by elaborate procedures for scaling grades to eliminate differences resulting from varying grading standards at different schools.

A finding that performance in education is not much related to performance as a physician could be justified for undergraduate education on the basis of the traditional liberal arts argument that learning is an important activity in and of itself, but such an argument would hardly seem applicable to professional education such as that provided in medical schools. Therefore, the authors feel that these results indicate a need for further research on the nature of medical education and on medical school grading policies.

Before this investigation was started, the authors discussed it with numerous physicians in order to get their reactions and suggestions. A significant number of these physicians objected to the whole idea of such a study, basing their objection on their view that success as a physician is quite complex. They stated quite strongly that one cannot have a meaningful measurement of physician performance on the basis of a single score or a few scores. The results of this study clearly indicate that such a view is correct, since the single most important finding, perhaps, was the great complexity of the criterion area. The fact that there was not a great deal of overlap generally, between the different measures of physician performance indicates this complexity. Further proof is that one factor was found for approximataly every three scores included in the analysis. In other words, as soon as a large number of measures of performance is obtained, the real complexity of the criterion problem emerges forcefully.

In this connection, it should be pointed out that the present study is probably a conservative estimate of the real complexity of physician performance. In any first study such as this one, ways to insure the maximum cooperation of the group studied must be very strongly considered. Accordingly, in the present study, measures of some sensitive areas were intentionally omitted in the data collection. For example, no attempt was made to obtain patient reaction to individual physicians, and no effort was made to study *directly* the quality of medical care provided by individual physicians through such techniques as the Medical Audit (Mortrud, 1953). While the Medical Audit technique was developed primarily as a way of measuring the effectiveness of medical care provided by hospitals, instruments were developed which could be, and have been, used to evaluate some aspects of the effectiveness of individual physician performance. Since such measures are quite important, and since there is little reason to suppose that they overlap to any great extent with the measures used in the present study, an attempt should be made to include them in any followup studies of the criterion problem for medical specialists.

To summarize, there are many different kinds of contributions to which a medical specialist can devote his energies and efforts. While a physician can focus his efforts toward a larger or smaller number of these kinds of contributions, it is unlikely that an individual can devote very much energy to all of the available kinds of contributions. As a result, the total amount of energy available, the selection of outlets for that energy, and the effectiveness with which one's efforts are expended in those outlets are important in assessing the overall accomplishments and contributions of an individual. All of these considerations should be used in evaluating medical specialists.

REFERENCES

ANDERSON, W. W., & FELDMAN, J. J. *Family medical costs and voluntary health insurance: A nationwide survey.* New York: McGraw-Hill, 1956.

GOTTHEIL, E., & MICHAEL, C. M. Predictor variables employed in research on the selection of medical students. *Journal of Medical Education,* 1957, 32, 131-147.

GUILFORD, J. P. *Fundamental statistics in psychology and education.* New York: McGraw-Hill, 1956.

HARMAN, H. H. *Modern factor analysis.* Chicago: Univer. Chicago Press, 1960.

KAISER, H. F. The application of electronic computers to factor analysis. *Educational and Psychological Measurement,* 1960, 20, 141-151.

LINDQUIST, E. F. An evaluation of a technique for scaling high school grades to improve prediction of college success. *Educational and Psychological Measurement*, 1963, 23, 623-646.

MORTRUD, L. C. The control of professional practice through the Medical Audit. *Hospitals*, 1953, 27, 91-184.

PETERSON, O. L. Medical care in the United States. *Scientific American*, 1963, 209, 19-27.

PETERSON, O. L., ANDREWS, L. P., SPAIN, R. S., & GREENBERG, B. G. An analytic study of North Carolina general practice. *Journal of Medical Education*, 1956, 31, No. 12.

PRICE, P. B., TAYLOR, C. W., RICHARDS, J. M., JR., & JACOBSEN, T. L. *Performance measures of physicians*. Cooperative Research Project, No. 1551, United States Office of Education, 1963.

RALPH, R. B., & TAYLOR, C. W. The role of tests in the medical selection program. *Journal of Applied Psychology*, 1952, 36, 108–111.

RICHARDS, J. M., JR., & TAYLOR, C. W. Predicting academic achievement in a college of medicine from grades, test scores, interviews and ratings. *Educational and Psychological Measurement*, 1961, 21, 987–994.

RICHARDS, J. M., JR., TAYLOR, C. W., & PRICE, P. B. The prediction of medical intern performance. *Journal of Applied Psychology*, 1962, 46, 142-146.

STALNAKER, J. M. Validation of professional aptitude batteries: Tests for medicine. In *Proceedings 1950 Invitational Conference on Testing Problems*. Princeton: Educational Testing Service, 1951.

TAYLOR, C. W. Check studies on the predictive value of the Medical College Admission Test. *Association of American Medical Colleges Journal*, 1950, 25, 33-40.

TAYLOR, C. W., SMITH, W. R., & GHISELIN, B. The creative and other contributions of one sample of research scientists. In C. W. Taylor & F. Barron (Eds.), *Scientific creativity: Its recognition and development*. New York: Wiley, 1963.

TAYLOR, C. W., SMITH, W. R., GHISELIN, B., & ELLISON, R. S. *Explorations in the measurement and prediction of contributions of one sample of scientists*. United States Air Force Air Systems Divisions Technical Report, 1961, No. 61–96.

WANTMAN, M. F. Review of the Medical College Admission Test. In O. K. Buros (Ed.), *Fourth mental measurements yearbook*. Highland Park, N.J.: Gryphon, 1953.

WESMAN, A .G. Review of the Medical College Admission Test. In O. K. Buros (Ed.), *Fifth mental measurements yearbook*. Highland Park, N.J.: Gryphon, 1959.

24 Salary Growth as a Criterion of Career Progress

THOMAS L. HILTON and WILLIAM R. DILL

As a possible improvement on absolute salary as a criterion, the authors computed the annual percentage growth of the salaries of 143 engineering graduates employed in industry. Although 1st-year salaries increased markedly from 1950 to 1955, and 1957 salaries varied with years of service, the growth rates were homogeneous. The rates for different professional groups were different. 1st-year salary and salary growth were unrelated. Growth was related to academic grades, but absolute salary unexpectedly had a stronger relationship. Salary growth has some useful properties, but it is not uniformly applicable.

The shortcomings of salary as a measure of a man's progress are well known (Bechtoldt, 1947; Bellows, 1941; Hilton, 1961; Patterson, 1946; Thorndike, 1957; Toops, 1944). How his salary is set by his superiors may be unrelated to the value of his contribution to the organization. It may, for instance, depend primarily on his years of service, as in the case of most civil servants. His age or educational level may be the major determinant. Or, as Stark (1959) has pointed out in discussing the weaknesses of organization rank as a criterion, prejudices, the chance availability of openings for promotion, sponsorship, and internal politics may strongly influence a man's salary.

In addition, situational factors may preclude his receiving a favorable evaluation. The level of all salaries may be low in his particular branch of industry. His company's ability to pay for professional skills may be depressed and the supply of skilled people high. This paper concerns an effort to correct for several of these factors and describes some of the problems encountered.

Hypotheses. To adjust for differences in absolute level of salary from one company to another and one industry to another an obvious step is to compute the difference between starting salary and current salary. Then one may divide by the number of years of employment to obtain the average annual increment. A criticism of this method, however, is that as a model of the salary setting process it is not consistent with actual practices. The observations of the authors are that in determining the annual increase in an employee's salary the factor which receives the most attention is the amount of the increment relative to the man's current salary. In other words, the adequacy of a salary increase tends to be evaluated in terms of the percentage growth that it represents. An increase of $800, for example, is regarded as a substantially more liberal increase for a man earning $5,000 than for a man earning $20,000. The percentage growth in salary may be psychologically more relevant and significant to an employee as a measure of his success than the absolute salary level or than the summed increments in salary over a period of years. Also it is probably the relative increment which enters into the social comparisons studied recently by Patchen (1961) and earlier by Festinger (1954).

These observations suggested the following hypotheses:

1. For at least the first 6 years of employment, annual salary growth rate is independent of number of years employed. Casual observation indicates that salaries of industrial professional employees do not continue to grow at a constant rate throughout their years of employment and therefore the hypothesis was restricted to the first six years, the time span covered by the data available in this study.

2. In the same way that starting salaries and thereby the first year salaries of graduates of different professional programs (i.e., civil engineering, industrial management, etc.) are different, the annual salary growth rates of these groups will be different.

3. For single individuals salary growth is positively related to first year salary. The thinking here was that to the extent that personal evaluations determine first year salaries they would continue to determine salary growth. The appraisal of a college graduate's ability should influence the salary he is offered for his first year of employment, and *ceteris paribus*, one would expect him to perform in a manner consistent with the initial appraisal or, at least, one would expect later appraisals to be consistent with the first one. Thus, a positive relation should exist between first year salary and salary growth. Since first year salary enters into the computation of salary growth, caution must be exercised in interpreting any correlation obtained between the two measures. This problem will be discussed further shortly.

4. Undergraduate grade average—as a rough measure of each man's ability to perform well in competitive situations—is positively related to salary growth. When the subjects have widely differing years of industrial experience, the correlation between grade average and growth should be stronger than that between grade average and absolute salary level. This is because the correlation between grades and absolute salary tends to be obscured by the correlation between absolute salary and years of experience mentioned earlier.

METHOD

Subjects. Salary data was obtained for a sample of 143 male college graduates selected from a large sample of graduates who were part of another study conducted by the authors. All received BS degrees in engineering from the same eastern college from 1950 to 1955 and were employed by industrial firms. Men who received advanced degrees were not included in the sample. Seven were employed in administrative positions; 93 in construction, maintenance, design, or field work; 29 in research and development; and 14 in production and operations. Seventy-two percent were veterans and 74% were married at the time they completed the questionnaires.

Thus this group is not a representative sample of a typical college class. It might rather be described as a group of young well-educated engineers working in American industry.

Data. The data were obtained from one page of a long questionnaire which was sent to the subjects in May 1958 as part of a larger study. The exact wording of the relevant questions was as follows:

> 1. What was your total basic salary for the calendar year 1957 (If you moved from one position to another or if your rate was changed, please give the actual total received during the year. If employed for less than the whole year, please give the number of months.)
> 2. What was the total of your bonus and/or incentive payments (excluding base salary) during 1957?
> 3. What were the comparable figures for your first year of full-time employment after completing undergraduate work or after military service.
>
> Basic Salary $_____
> Bonus and/or incentive payments $_____
> Calendar year in which salary was received _____
>
> 4. Did you have (in 1957) additional taxable income from other sources in excess of $500?

The subjects were instructed to enclose the page in a small envelope marked "Confidential," to seal it, and to return it in the same envelope as the questionnaire. Note that the authors asked for basic salary and bonuses for the "first year of full-time employment after completing undergraduate work or after military service." This figure is likely to be different from starting salary, a datum which has been used in other studies in this area. Note also that the information was treated as confidential and that unearned income was not included in the reports.

How to handle bonuses was a problem. Are they purely windfalls or are they related to the quality of an individual's performance? In this study it was decided to focus on the sum of salary and bonus, primarily because earlier studies by the authors indicated that for all intents and purposes the bonuses are usually equivalent to salary and should be treated as such. Wherever the word salary is used, therefore, it should be construed to include bonuses.

Salary growth rate was computed by means of the conventional formula for compound interest rate:

$$r = \left(\left[\frac{E_c}{E_s} \right]^{1/n} - 1 \right) \times 100$$

Where: r = annual rate of increase (percentage/year)
E_c = 1957 salary + bonus (dollars)
E_s = first year salary + bonus (dollars)
n = 1957−year in which first salary was received (years)

The distributions for salary growth, first year salary and 1957 salary are given in Figure 24.1. Because of the skewness of the distribution, medians have been used as the measure of central tendency except where noted.

RESULTS

Table 24.1 gives the first year salaries, the 1957 salaries, and the annual growth rate for the graduates arranged in accordance with the calendar year in which the "first year salary" was received. It should be noted that this year in which the first year salary was received is not necessarily the year the subjects completed their undergraduate work for many of them served in the armed services before taking an industrial

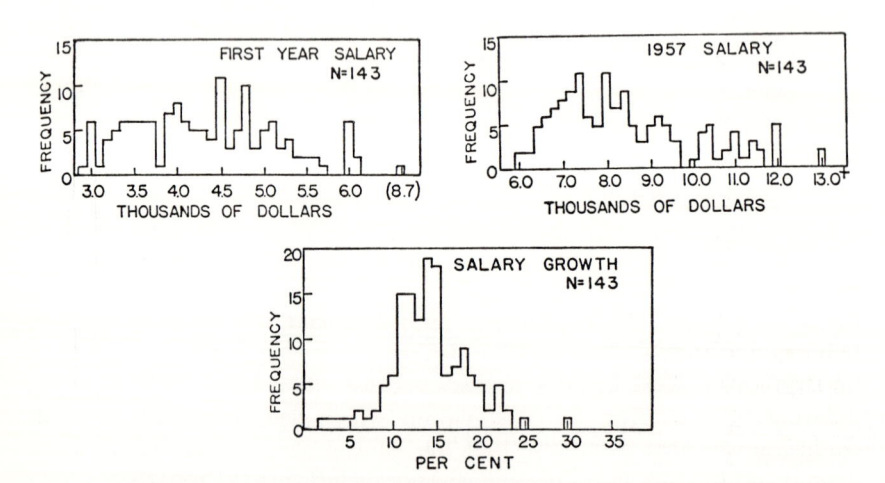

FIGURE 24.1. *Distribution of salaries and salary growth*

position. From Table 24.1 it is clear that salaries received during the first year of employment steadily increased during the 1950-55 period and that the 1957 salaries of the different groups increased with the time which elapsed since the first year in industry. Salary growth, on the other hand, remains fairly constant. When a chi-square test is performed on the number of individual growth rates within each yearly group which are above the grand median and the number below, the growth rates prove to be homogeneous ($p = .72$).

The second hypothesis (about different professional groups) was confirmed, as Table 24.2 shows. Because first year salaries have increased each year, the authors focused attention on a limited time segment, namely, 1950–51. Otherwise both first year salary and 1957 salary largely reflect differences in the average longevity of the members of the groups. The chi-square test indicates that the growth rates of the different professional groups are not homogeneous ($p < .01$).

Hypothesis 3 (about first year salary) was not confirmed, as is most clearly shown by the correlations in Table 24.3. The sample for these correlations is the group of subjects who entered industry in 1950.

As mentioned earlier there is a part-whole problem in interpreting the correlation between first year salary and salary growth. One way to avoid the problem is to examine the correlation between first year salary and 1957 salary for a group of men who entered industry at approximately the same time. If there is a nonspurious correlation between first year salary and growth there will also be a correlation between first year salary and 1957 salary. If there is no correlation between these we can be confident that there is no correlation between first year salary and salary growth. The obtained correlation of zero indicates that even when

TABLE 24.1. *Salaries and growth rate by year in which first year salary was received*

First year in industry	First year salary and bonuses Median	First year salary and bonuses Upper 25%	First year salary and bonuses Lower 25%	1957 salary and bonuses Median	1957 salary and bonuses Upper 25%	1957 salary and bonuses Lower 25%	Annual growth rate (percentage) Median	Annual growth rate (percentage) Upper 25%	Annual growth rate (percentage) Lower 25%
1950 ($N = 35$)	3500	4000	3200	8740	9540	8000	13.1	15.8	12.0
1951 ($N = 34$)	3955	4415	3500	8440	9700	7400	13.5	15.4	11.5
1952 ($N = 23$)	4250	4950	3960	8272	9300	7965	14.2	16.1	12.2
1953 ($N = 21$)	4520	5000	4470	7884	9168	7500	14.7	19.1	11.3
1954 ($N = 17$)	4850	5336	4500	7164	7550	6812	14.8	16.8	11.3
1955 ($N = 13$)	5100	5400	4900	6535	7058	6440	14.3	17.2	13.5

number of years of employment is held constant the 1957 salary of the men cannot be predicted from a knowledge of their first year salary. The high negative correlation between growth and the first year salary will be discussed shortly.

The fourth hypothesis (about undergraduate grades) is given some support by the correlations in Tables 24.3 and 24.4 but is not confirmed entirely by them. Contrary to prediction, the correlation between grades and 1957 salary is larger for the total sample than it is for the 1950 sample alone.

Additional results. In the way of exploration, a number of other categorizations of the total sample were made to check some possible sources of variance in growth rates. None of these splits of the sample revealed any appreciable differences. They included married versus unmarried, whether the man was still with his first employer or not (apparently moving from one employer to another does not on the average accelerate salary growth), activity in various organizations, number of hours worked per week, satisfactions experienced, and problems encountered.

TABLE 24.2. *Median salaries and growth rate by undergraduate major for subjects entering industry in 1950 and 1951*

Undergraduate major	N	First year salary and bonuses	1957 salary and bonuses	Annual growth rate
Chemical engineering	11	3720	7461	13.0
Civil engineering	8	4000	8612	10.3
Electrical engineering	18	3544	8758	16.0
Industrial management	7	3640	8046	12.0
Mechanical engineering	20	3630	9171	14.6
Balance	5	3660	8400	14.0

TABLE 24.3. *Product-moment correlations and related statistics between salary measures and grades for 1950 graduates* (N = 35)

Measure	M	SD	First salary	1957 salary	Salary growth	Grade average
First year salary	3691	687	—	.00	−.78**	.07
1957 salary	8860	1225	.00	—	.62**	.29*
Salary growth	13.5	3.4	−.78**	.62**	—	.22
Grade average	2.9	.5	−.07	.29*	.22	—

* Significant at .05 level of confidence, one-tailed test.
** Significant at .01 level of confidence, one-tailed test.

TABLE 24.4. *Product-moment correlations and related statistics between salary measures and grades for total sample* (N = 143)

Measure	M	SD	First salary	1957 salary	Salary growth	Grade average
First year salary	4372.7	868.6	—	.10	−.25**	−.01
1957 salary	8464.6	1623	.10	—	.53**	.34**
Salary growth	14.23	4.29	−.25**	.53**	—	.15*
Grade average	2.8	.6	−.01	.34**	.15*	—

* Significant at the .05 level of confidence, one-tailed test.
** Significant at the .01 level of confidence, one-tailed test.

DISCUSSION

The fact that median salary growth rates are homogeneous for the subsamples entering employment in different years makes the statistic useful as a criterion when one is dealing with subjects who entered industry at different times. When the subjects all entered industry in the same year a choice has to be made as to which is the better criterion. If one is interested in absolute level of salary regardless of starting salary, then the terminal salary is probably the best index. On the other hand one may wish to assign a high criterion score to subjects who for one reason or another started at low levels, but relative to their base have gained at a high rate, even though they did not reach the same absolute level as the first.

Table 24.5 shows some of the interpretational problems in this area. Individual A started low but relative to this low level received a high increment ($600) giving him the highest growth figure. Apparently the presence in the sample of a group of subjects of this type contributed to the high negative correlation between first year salary and salary growth. Individual B had the highest increment ($640) but because his first year earnings were higher than A's his growth rate is lower. Individual C has the highest salary but the increment was low and similarly the growth rate. It is interesting to note that if the salaries of A and C continue to grow at the present rate, A will overtake C in approximately 5 years.

TABLE 24.5. *Hypothetical salaries and growth rates*

Subject	First year salary	Salary one year later	Growth rate
A	$3000	$3600	20%
B	$4000	$4640	16%
C	$5000	$5500	10%

Why there is no correlation between first year salary and 1957 salary is not obvious. A possible explanation is that first year salaries are influenced primarily by supply and demand in the professional marketplace whereas later salaries are influenced more by the on-the-job performance of the man. But we know that a man's salary is not based entirely on the basis of his performance; for example, the different professional specialties (chemical engineering, civil engineering, etc.) have differing median growth rates as seen in Table 24.2. It is well known that in any year there will be sizable differences in the average starting salaries for different professional specialties. Evidently there are also differences in the rates of salary growth among the groups. These differences are probably attributable to differences in demand among the specialties. If two men are equally competent and at the same salary level, the one who has the professional training which is in higher demand in the general market is likely to receive a higher increase in his salary. Since there are annual fluctuations in the demand for different specialties, market pressures probably diminish any positive correlation between first year salary and salary growth.

The absence of a strong correlation between grades and salary growth is no doubt related to the lack of correlation between starting salary and 1957 salary. Also it appears to have resulted in part from the peculiar numerical properties of salary growth. Inspection of scatter plots of the correlation between growth and grades indicated that there was a substantial number of subjects with high grades whose salary history appeared to be similar to Individual C in the hypothetical example given: their 1957 salary was high but their first year salary was also high resulting in their growth rates being relatively low. One possibility is that high ability men with high grades and high starting salaries are prevented from receiving salary increases consistent with their ability by salary ceilings imposed by the classification systems prevalent in most large American corporations. Since absolute salary levels have also risen rapidly, highly paid young college graduates bump rapidly against informal norms about what are proper salary limits for men of their age and experience.

SUMMARY AND CONCLUSIONS

It would be good if there were a criterion of career progress which was not subject to the shortcomings which salary is, particularly its dependence on longevity and its variation between industries and between professional specialties. In the past the authors have attempted to use peer ratings, supervisory ratings, measures of administrative responsibility (e.g., number of men supervised), and indices of organizational attainment (e.g., level in the organizational hierarchy) to name a few alternatives. But each of these has deficiencies which in the experience of the authors are sufficiently serious to justify the use of salary as an alternative measure despite its ineffectiveness.

The authors designed the salary growth measure as a way of avoiding some of the shortcomings of absolute salary. The finding that the growth figure was independent of number of years of employment for at least the first six years indicates that the authors were to some extent successful. There were differences, however, among the median growth rates when the subjects were grouped according to their undergraduate major. Thus salary growth is an advantageous measure when comparing subjects with differing years of industrial experience but when comparing subjects in different professional specialties it has the same shortcomings as absolute salary.

Obviously the salaries of most men do not continue to grow at constant rates through their years of industrial employment. It would not be meaningful, therefore, to compare the growth rates of men with 25 or 30 years of tenure with those of new employees. Also the fact that growth rates are highly sensitive to differences in first year salaries may make the results deceptive for certain comparisons. These observations suggest that although salary growth rate has some useful properties as a measure it must be used with discretion. Whether it is used in a particular study depends, as with other measures of career progress, on the characteristics of the sample in question and on the precise interests of the investigator.

REFERENCES

BECHTOLDT, H. P. Problems in establishing criterion measures. In D. B. Stuit (Ed.), *Personnel research and test development in the Bureau of Naval Personnel.* Princeton: Princeton Univer. Press, 1947. Ch. 19.

BELLOWS, R. M. Procedures for evaluating vocational criteria. *J. appl. Psychol.*, 1941, 15, 449-513.

FESTINGER, L. A theory of social comparison processes. *Hum. Relat.*, 1954, 7, 117–140.

HILTON, T. L. Executive leadership and development. In B. v. H. Gilmer (Ed.), *Industrial psychology.* New York: McGraw-Hill, 1961. Pp. 175–196.

PATCHEN, M. A conceptual framework and some empirical data regarding comparisons of social rewards. *Sociometry*, 1961, 24, 136 155.

PATTERSON, C. H. On the problem of the criterion in prediction studies. *J. consult. Psychol.*, 1946, 10, 277-280.

STARK, S. Research criteria of executive success. *J. Bus.*, 1959, 32, 1-14.

THORNDIKE, R. L., & HAGEN, E. *Ten thousand careers.* New York: Wiley, 1959.

TOOPS, H. A. The criterion. *Educ. psychol. Measmt.*, 1944, 4, 271–293.

25 An Analysis of Pilot Flying Performance in Terms of Component Abilities

EDWIN A. FLEISHMAN
and GEORGE N. ORNSTEIN

The job of flying an airplane involves one of the most complex perceptual-motor tasks found in practice. In response to a continually changing set of cues, the pilot must manipulate many diverse controls in order to accomplish a specific flight path or set of flight conditions. He achieves this by controlling the movement of the aircraft along and about the vehicle's three axes. In addition, the pilot must monitor and time-share a number of displays, must shift attention frequently, and must actively schedule his future activities. All of these tasks are performed under an essentially forced-pace condition, since he cannot stop and must, in fact, maintain a certain speed or the aircraft will stall.

During World War II and the early postwar period, aviation psychologists were highly successful in developing procedures for selecting people for this complex job. The validity achieved through the use of objective selection tests constitutes one of the major practical accomplishments of psychological methods (Flanagan, 1947; Fleishman, 1953, 1956; Guilford, 1947; Melton, 1947). The criterion of pilot success, which these tests were designed to predict, was whether the pilot trainee passed or failed during the first six months of his training. The limitations of the pass-fail criterion, as a measure of pilot performance, were recognized. Consequently, efforts were made to obtain more analytical information on the *nature* of pilot proficiency as a basis for developing objective measures of flying performance. Initial efforts to obtain more analytical information were based on the analysis of instructor ratings of pilot performance. The subjective nature of these data often resulted in low relia-

From *Journal of Applied Psychology* 1960, 44, 146–155. This research was carried out while the authors were with the Air Force Personnel and Training Research Center. The work was done under ARDC Project No. 7710 in support of the research and development program of the Air Force Personnel and Training Research Center, Lackland Air Force Base, Texas. Permission is granted for reproduction, translation, publication, use and disposal in whole and in part by or for the United States Government. The authors are indepted to Ralph E. Flexman for his invaluable support and many technical contributions during the conduct of the study.

bility or in "halo effect" which made meaningful analyses difficult (Ben-Avi, 1947; Kelly, 1943). A thorough review of developments in measuring pilot performance up to 1952 has been presented by Ericksen (1952a). In the late postwar program considerable progress was made in developing more objective flying performance measures in connection with pilot selection and training studies in the Air Force research program (Boyle & Hagin, 1953; Flexman, Townsend, & Ornstein, 1954; Ornstein, Nichols, & Flexman, 1954; Sutter, Townsend, & Ornstein, 1954). It is from this series of studies that a practical and reliable in-flight performance measure has emerged.

PROBLEM

The present study is concerned with a factor analysis of performance in different flying maneuvers. The attempt is to specify the variance in common between maneuvers which may provide insight into the dimensions of individual differences in this complex task. Essentially this study represents a convergence of two lines of research. One involves the development of analytical objective measures of pilot performance (Boyle & Hagin, 1953; Ericksen, 1952b; Ornstein, Flexman, & Nichols, 1954; Smith, Flexman, & Houston, 1952; Sutter, Townsend, & Ornstein, 1954). The other line of research is represented by laboratory studies of experimental tasks concerned with the isolation of generalizable dimensions of skilled performance (Fleishman, 1953, 1954, 1956, 1957, 1958a, 1958b, 1959; Fleishman & Hempel, 1954a, 1954b, 1955, 1956; Hempel & Fleishman, 1955; Parker & Fleishman, 1959).

METHOD

Subjects

The Ss were 63 graduates of a special Primary Pilot Training Program at Goodfellow Air Force Base, Texas. The Pilot Aptitude Scores for these Ss were distributed normally between 3 and 9 on the 1 to 9 stanine scale of the Aircrew Classification Battery. The hypothesis that there was no difference between the distribution found in this sample, and a normal distribution of the same mean and variance could not be rejected at the 5% level.

Measurement of Performance in the Air

The performance of these pilots was measured in the T-6 aircraft which was the operational training aircraft in use at the time. Daily recordings of student performance were made by each student's instructor on forms called Daily Progress Record Sheets (DPRS). A complete description of the rationale, development, and characteristics of the measuring device may be found elsewhere (Smith, Flexman, & Houston, 1952; Sutter, Townsend, & Ornstein, 1954).

There is a separate DPRS for each maneuver. Each contains items which were determined by extensive analysis of the actual performances required in that maneuver (Houston, Smith, & Flexman, 1954). Each item was designed so that it could be recorded categorically as "correct" or "incorrect." The sum of the incorrect items within a maneuver was taken as a maneuver error score. Table 25.1 presents examples of the items recorded for the maneuver: Power-On Stall. The instructor indicates success or failure of each item with a $\sqrt{}$ or X mark in the box to the right.

In the present analysis a maneuver score for a given S is the sum of the first four *recorded* trials for that S flying that maneuver. For any given maneuver only the first performance (trial) of that maneuver was recorded during any flight, and no instruction on that maneuver was given until after the first performance of the maneuver during that flight. Thus, the four trials summed for a given maneuver were recorded on different (successive) flights.

An estimate of the reliability of performance on each maneuver was obtained as follows. First, the test-retest (i.e., flight-flight) intercorrelation was determined for each successive pair of flights; next, the arithmetic average of these intercorrelations was obtained; and, finally, the average single-ride reliability was adjusted by Spearman-Brown "prophecy-formula" so as to correspond to a test of four times the length of the single trial. While these coefficients cannot be interpreted in traditional reliability terms, they do provide a conservative estimate of maneuver reliability.

Description of Maneuvers

The present analysis is based upon the scores for 24 maneuvers selected from the 33 nonacrobatic maneuvers included in the syllabus of flying instruction for this training program. The nine maneuvers excluded from this analysis were eliminated on the basis of a joint consideration of low reliability, high difficulty, and similarity to other maneuvers included. The 24 remaining maneuvers were considered representative of the original group of maneuvers. These maneuvers all involve "contact flying"; that is cues outside the cockpit were available. Parallel maneuvers in which the S had to rely only on his instruments are not included.

Brief descriptions follow of the 24 maneuvers included in the present analysis. Also included is a reliability estimate for each maneuver.

1. *Straight and level:* The pilot is required to maintain a specified altitude and heading. When deviations occur he makes small and frequent corrections in bank and small but temporally more extensive corrections in pitch. (Reliability = .47)

2. *90° Climbing turn:* The pilot establishes and maintains a specified bank, air speed, rate of turn, and power setting until the appropriate recovery point. A highly controlled blending of stick and rudder pressures is required continuously throughout the maneuver. ($r = .60$)

3. *Level-off from climbing turn:* The pilot attempts to achieve a level flight attitude as he reaches a specified altitude and heading. An anticipatory response is required utilizing coordinated elevator, aileron, and rudder pressures. This coordination may nor may not be simultaneous in all three dimensions. ($r = .52$)

4. *Gliding turn:* The pilot executes several preparatory procedural items and establishes certain specific flight conditions (including reduction of power) prior to initiating the bank and turn. This maneuver requires the proper anticipation of control pressure changes and a threefold coordination of elevator, aileron, and rudder. Relatively gross movements are used compared to those used during power-on maneuvers. ($r = .58$)

5. *Level-off from gliding turn:* The pilot attempts to achieve a level flight attitude as he reaches a specified altitude and heading. Consider-

TABLE 25.1. *Example of items in the daily performance record for the maneuver: power-on stall*

Entry

Gyros Caged
Looks
Two Clearing Turns
Direction (±5°)
Torque
Pitch Proper

Recovery

Direction (±5°)
Recovery at Stall
Stick & Throttle Together
Throttle to Sea-Level Stop
Aileron Usage
Torque Correction
Pitch Control Proper
M.P. Reduced to 25"

able coordination in the alternative manipulation of throttle, elevator, rudder, and aileron controls is required. ($r = .57$)

6. *Take-off:* The pilot is required to maintain a specific track and establish a proper climb attitude while accomplishing a large number of procedural items. Rapid and small, sensitive, rudder corrections, and the application of continuously changing elevator pressures are called for. ($r = .34$)

7. *Coordination exercise:* The pilot is required to make several consecutive turns during which he maintains a specified bank, turns a given number of degrees, and holds his entry altitude. Continuous and precise coordination and timing of elevator, rudder, and aileron pressures are required. ($r = .28$)

8. *Straight and level gear check:* The pilot is to maintain a specified heading and altitude while accomplishing a large number of procedure-type actions. Considerable sharing of attention is required as well as the ability to anticipate the resultant effect of the procedures upon aircraft performance. Frequent elevator corrections are normally needed to keep the aircraft stable. ($r = .48$)

9. *Traffic pattern at auxiliary fields:* The pilot is required to execute a large number of procedural items while flying a predetermined pattern over the ground. Specific procedures must be accomplished in a given sequence and with timing such that the predetermined flight path is accomplished. (r: no estimate)

10. *Rectangular pattern:* This maneuver is similar to Maneuver 9—differing primarily with respect to the magnitude of the planning requirements. Here, the pilot, in addition to the requirements of Maneuver 9, must locate some field upon which he may land the aircraft safely, and must fly the maneuver under less familiar conditions. (r: no estimate)

11. *Three-point landing:* This is one of the most difficult maneuvers to learn. Proper performance requires precise timing of changes in pitch attitude, the planning of ground track and position, and, at times, an unusual correction of aileron and rudder to account for wind. Both fine and relatively large and abrupt control movements may be required on all controls. ($r = .39$)

12. *Climbing turn from level:* The pilot establishes proper pitch and bank attitude by integrating application of power with coordination of elevator, rudder, and aileron. ($r = .62$)

13. *Landing characteristic stalls:* This maneuver integrates Maneuvers 4 and 11. It differs from 11 in that no ground path must be maintained and less "timing" is required when changing pitch. The recovery from the stall requires rather abrupt, but not overcontrolled, use of controls and, hence, implies only crude coordination requirements. ($r = .62$)

14. *Power-on stall:* The pilot is required to establish and maintain a

specific pitch attitude until a stall occurs. He is then to effect an immediate recovery. Specific but changing pressures must be applied to the various controls until the stall occurs. Then, brisk throttle and control movements must be executed in a coordinated but mechanical fashion. ($r = .52$)

15. *Approach to stall:* The pilot is required to perform as in Maneuver 14 except that he does not quite permit the aircraft to stall. Throughout the maneuver fine, sensitive, control pressures are applied and at no time are the brisk large movements used. ($r = .70$)

16. *Power-off stall:* This maneuver is performed from a normal glide. The pilot establishes and maintains a specific pitch attitude until the stall occurs. The maneuver emphasizes the recovery from the stall—a recovery wherein rather gross control movements are used. ($r = .72$)

17. *Steep turn (360°):* The pilot is required to establish and maintain a steep bank, to maintain a specific altitude, and to *time* his recovery so as to turn exactly 360°. Extremely fine elevator pressure changes must be made during the maneuver, as well as fine aileron and rudder movements. ($r = .52$)

18. *Maximum performance climbing turn:* The pilot is required to initiate a steep climbing turn from level flight. No requirement exists for either specific bank, altitude, or degree of turn. This maneuver is a preparatory exercise for a more advanced maneuver. Coordination and timing is not emphasized. ($r = .31$)

19. *Spin:* The pilot is required to stall the aircraft from a power-off flight condition. He then must abruptly apply rudder movement in order to cause the spin. During the spin the pilot must maintain his orientation with respect to the earth so as to properly time the application of a sequence of abrupt control movements designed to effect recovery from the spin. ($r = .45$)

20. *Rudder control stall:* The pilot is required to initiate the maneuver as in Maneuver 14. However, after the stall occurs he keeps the aircraft in the stalled condition, wings level, until a level flight attitude is attained. He then recovers. Critical to good performance is the extremely fine rudder control used to keep wings level. ($r = .65$)

21. *Slow-flight turn:* The pilot initiates the maneuver from straight and level slow flight. Maintaining altitude, he enters and holds a shallow bank and turns a specified number of degrees. The rudder is the primary control in correcting for the high torque condition. Small rudder, aileron, and elevator pressure coordinations are required throughout. ($r = .63$)

22. *Slow-flight recovery:* The pilot returns from straight and level slow flight to a normal cruise condition while maintaining both altitude and direction. Primary coordination is between the throttle and rudder. Gradual changes in elevator pressure are required as airspeed builds up. ($r = .61$)

23. *Forced landing:* From any attitude and location the pilot is

TABLE 25.2. Intercorrelations among maneuvers[a]

Maneuver	1	2	3	4	5	6	7	8	9	10	11	12	13	14	15	16	17	18	19	20	21	22	23	24
1. Straight and level	—	51	19	44	48	41	44	20	40	22	29	32	36	56	30	59	47	04	34	32	45	35	19	34
2. 90° Climbing Turn	51	—	51	59	33	58	51	28	42	59	44	35	64	39	47	42	46	14	29	42	47	53	56	20
3. Level-Off from Climbing Turn	19	51	—	58	32	42	20	40	38	34	21	44	39	45	37	35	44	02	39	47	39	49	60	34
4. Gliding Turn	44	59	58	—	52	39	53	39	35	48	21	48	51	58	52	60	41	02	41	51	37	49	63	49
5. Level-Off from Gliding Turn	48	33	32	52	—	33	38	25	38	34	18	38	35	44	38	55	19	14	32	35	51	50	48	47
6. Take-Off	41	58	42	39	33	—	60	27	17	20	40	39	44	37	42	43	37	07	25	46	39	44	46	40
7. Coordination Exercise	44	51	44	53	38	60	—	15	16	36	26	42	48	37	51	39	35	02	22	36	44	43	34	42
8. Straight and Level Gear Check	20	28	40	39	25	27	15	—	31	23	32	25	35	29	29	19	29	−08	26	26	20	43	38	45
9. Traffic Pattern at Auxiliary Field	40	42	38	35	38	17	16	31	—	47	10	19	32	38	25	36	24	13	33	44	32	41	37	44
10. Rectangular Pattern	22	59	34	48	34	20	36	23	47	—	10	34	41	37	45	43	32	23	34	36	36	49	39	54
11. Three-Point Landing	29	44	21	21	18	26	26	32	10	10	—	26	48	10	30	04	04	04	19	24	30	31	18	42
12. Climbing Turn from Level	32	35	44	48	38	39	42	32	19	34	26	—	34	51	56	52	43	08	24	42	56	62	50	53
13. Landing Characteristic Stall	36	64	39	51	35	44	48	35	32	41	48	34	—	39	62	66	51	06	51	59	42	58	46	42
14. Power-On Stall	56	39	45	58	40	37	37	29	38	37	10	51	39	—	48	64	36	11	43	37	47	49	42	41
15. Approach to Stall	30	47	37	52	38	42	51	29	25	45	30	56	62	48	—	64	48	13	52	45	66	50	51	51
16. Power-Off Stall	59	42	35	60	55	43	39	19	36	43	25	52	66	64	64	—	42	15	44	56	52	54	52	53
17. Steep Turn (360°)	47	46	44	41	19	37	35	29	13	32	43	32	48	36	48	42	—	00	41	39	40	38	34	30
18. Maximum Performance Climbing Turn	04	14	02	02	14	07	02	−08	13	23	04	08	06	11	13	15	00	—	04	13	03	27	15	34
19. Spin	34	29	39	41	32	25	22	26	33	34	19	24	51	43	52	44	41	04	—	46	38	35	17	37
20. Rudder Control Stall	32	42	47	51	35	46	36	26	44	36	24	42	59	37	45	56	39	13	46	—	47	51	53	41
21. Slow-Flight Turn	45	47	39	37	51	39	44	20	32	36	30	56	42	47	66	52	40	03	38	47	—	58	37	37
22. Slow-Flight Recovery	35	53	49	49	50	44	43	43	41	49	31	62	58	49	50	54	38	27	35	51	58	—	56	58
23. Forced Landing	19	56	60	63	48	46	34	38	37	39	18	50	46	42	51	52	34	15	17	53	37	56	—	52
24. Traffic Pattern at Home Field	34	20	34	49	47	40	42	45	44	54	42	53	42	41	51	53	30	24	34	37	41	58	52	—

[a] Rounded to two places and decimals omitted.

352

ANALYSIS OF PILOT FLYING PERFORMANCE

required to select an emergency landing area, to accomplish certain procedures and to plan and accomplish a flight pattern that will enable him to land in the selected area. The primary requirement is the effective planning and accomplishing of procedures while maintaining control of aircraft and orientation with respect to the ground. ($r = .56$)

24. *Traffic pattern at home field:* This maneuver is very similar to Maneuvers 9 and 10 in that the student must attend and respond to cues outside of the aircraft in coordinating and choosing his control movements. However, the cues here are more familiar. ($r = .75$)

Data Analysis Procedures

The correlations among these maneuver scores were obtained and are presented in Table 25.2. Table 25.3 presents the centroid factors extracted by the Thurstone Method (Thurstone, 1947). Orthogonal rotations to simple structure were made "blind" by an analytical procedure programmed for an IBM 650. Table 25.4 presents the rotated factor matrix.

TABLE 25.3. *Centroid factor loadings*[a]

Maneuver	I	II	III	IV	V	VI
1. Straight and Level	59	−22	26	08	−17	−28
2. 90° Climbing Turn	72	−17	−29	−20	−18	24
3. Level-Off from Climbing Turn	64	15	−18	−32	32	−06
4. Gliding Turn	75	13	06	−17	29	05
5. Level-Off from Gliding Turn	61	15	25	13	−13	−03
6. Take-Off	62	−25	06	−31	−15	07
7. Coordination Exercise	62	−19	26	−24	−17	14
8. Straight and Level Gear Check	46	19	−19	−17	08	−28
9. Traffic Pattern at Auxiliary Field	54	18	−25	25	−19	−25
10. Rectangular Pattern	60	20	−14	17	−14	14
11. Three-Point Landing	45	−25	−18	−15	−24	−23
12. Climbing Turn from Level	65	12	27	−09	06	10
13. Landing Characteristic Stall	74	−32	−27	11	13	14
14. Power-On Stall	67	10	26	08	18	−16
15. Approach to Stall	74	−17	11	08	20	18
16. Power-Off Stall	76	−07	23	30	19	10
17. Steep Turn (360°)	59	−29	−17	−08	12	−22
18. Maximum Performance Climbing Turn	16	16	−06	25	−21	17
19. Spin	55	−14	−07	29	26	−21
20. Rudder Control Stall	67	−05	−14	07	15	12
21. Slow-Flight Turn	68	−13	20	12	−05	04
22. Slow-Flight Recovery	77	21	−07	05	−09	16
23. Forced Landing	69	31	−05	−24	14	27
24. Traffic Pattern at Home Field	69	33	10	08	−15	−13

[a] Rounded to two places with decimals omitted.

RESULTS

The factor interpretations follow. We have listed loadings above .30.

Factor Interpretations

Factor I is best measured by those maneuvers which place a premium on highly controlled, but not overcontrolled, muscular movements. Many of these maneuvers emphasize a sensitive touch on the rudder controls, but hand-arm control movements are also involved. This factor seems highly similar to one previously identified as general to a variety of psychomotor tests emphasizing highly controlled movements (Fleishman 1957a, 1958b; Fleishman & Hempel, 1956). Originally this factor was called Psychomotor Coordination I or Fine Control Sensitivity. As the nature of this factor became better understood through subsequent research, the name *Control Precision* was introduced as more appropriately descriptive (Parker & Fleishman, 1959).

Variable No.	Maneuver	Loading
13	Landing characteristic stall	.68
2	90° climbing turn	.68
6	Take-off	.54
17	Steep turn (360°)	.47
15	Approach to stall	.45
11	Three-point landing	.42
20	Rudder control stall	.41
7	Coordination exercise	.41
21	Slow flight turn	.31

Factor II seems best defined by maneuvers which emphasize *Spatial Orientation* (see Michael, Guilford, Fruchter, & Zimmerman, 1957). Judgments about one's location in three-dimensional space seem especially critical in maneuvers such as Forced Landings, Flying Traffic Patterns, Climbs, and Turns. A number of the maneuvers loading on this

Variable No.	Maneuver	Loading
23	Forced landing	.53
3	Level-off from climbing turn	.52
22	Slow flight recovery	.47
8	Straight and level gear check	.47
9	Traffic pattern at auxilliary field	.46
10	Rectangular pattern	.43
2	90° climbing turn	.41
24	Traffic pattern at home field	.39
4	Gliding turn	.38
20	Rudder control stall	.31

ANALYSIS OF PILOT FLYING PERFORMANCE 355

factor also emphasize knowledge and integration of rules and procedures, but the Spatial aspect seems the more general feature.

Factor III includes maneuvers which emphasize the coordinated use of multiple limbs: two hands, two feet, or combinations of feet and

Variable No.	Maneuver	Loading
7	Coordination exercise	.60
12	Climbing turn from level	.56
4	Gliding turn	.51
6	Take-off	.50
23	Forced landing	.49
14	Power-on stall	.45
24	Traffic pattern at home field	.43
5	Level-off from gliding turn	.42
3	Level-off from climbing turn	.39
1	Straight and level	.38
21	Slow flight turn	.37
22	Slow flight recovery	.36
15	Approach to stall	.34
16	Power-off stall	.33

TABLE 25.4. *Rotated factor loadings*[a]

Maneuver	I CP	II SO	III MLC	IV RO	V RC	VI KD	h^2
1. Straight and Level	23	−08	38	42	41	07	56
2. 90° Climbing Turn	68	41	29	21	−01	06	76
3. Level-Off from Climbing Turn	25	52	39	−16	22	32	66
4. Gliding Turn	24	38	51	05	17	46	70
5. Level-Off from Gliding Turn	08	16	42	48	06	24	49
6. Take-Off	54	11	50	13	11	00	58
7. Coordination Exercise	41	00	60	23	01	07	59
8. Straight and Level Gear Check	07	47	23	02	34	07	40
9. Traffic Pattern at Auxiliary Field	09	46	00	49	31	06	56
10. Rectangular Pattern	20	43	15	45	−03	22	50
11. Three-Point Landing	42	17	18	18	35	−18	43
12. Climbing Turn from Level	15	16	56	23	04	33	53
13. Landing Characteristic Stall	68	23	07	24	19	38	76
14. Power-On Stall	05	14	45	29	33	43	60
15. Approach to Stall	45	09	34	25	12	51	66
16. Power-Off Stall	27	05	33	43	16	61	77
17. Steep Turn (360°)	47	15	19	09	46	16	53
18. Maximum Performance Climbing Turn	01	15	−05	37	−17	05	20
19. Spin	22	13	02	24	43	43	50
20. Rudder Control Stall	41	31	19	21	12	40	58
21. Slow-Flight Turn	31	03	37	41	16	30	57
22. Slow-Flight Recovery	26	47	36	41	−02	27	66
23. Forced Landing	23	53	49	06	−11	37	72
24. Traffic Pattern at Home Field	−01	39	43	48	17	18	63

[a] Rounded to two places with decimals omitted.
[b] Factors are interpreted as I, Control Precision; II, Spatial Orientation; III, Multilimb Coordination; IV, Response Orientation V, Rate Control; and VI, Kinesthetic Discrimination.

hands. This corresponds to the factor called *Multilimb Coordination* in certain laboratory research (Fleishman, 1958b; Parker & Fleishman, 1959). In one study it was called Psychomotor Coordination II (Fleishman & Hempel, 1956). This factor and Factor I apparently are components of the Psychomotor Coordination factor found valid for pilot selection during World War II (Fleishman, 1953; Guilford, 1947). Both of these components have been found valid in subsequent studies (Fleishman, 1956b; Fleishman & Hempel, 1956).

Factor IV contains many of the same maneuvers as those loading on Factor II. For example, the traffic pattern maneuvers appear prominent. A tentative interpretation is that this factor corresponds to the *Response Orientation* factor previously identified (Fleishman, 1956b, 1957a, 1957b, 1958b; Fleishman & Hempel, 1956; Parker & Fleishman, 1959). The essential feature of this factor is the ability to make rapid response decisions under rapidly changing stimulus conditions. The rapid selection of controls and their proper directional manipulation in response to cues which change from moment to moment is critical. An alternative hypothesis is that this factor represents procedural integration of some kind.

Variable No.	Maneuver	Loading
9	Traffic pattern at auxilliary field	.49
24	Traffic pattern at home field	.48
5	Level-off from gliding turn	.48
10	Rectangular pattern	.45
16	Power-off stall	.43
1	Straight and level	.42
21	Slow-flight turn	.41
22	Slow-flight recovery	.41

Factor V is confined to fewer maneuvers, but there appears to be a feature common to those maneuvers with the highest loadings. In these maneuvers responses are made in relation to anticipations of velocity and rate changes. Moreover, these judgments are based on visual feedback from the outside environment (e.g., the horizon) rather than from the feel of the controls or from instrument data. If this tentative interpretation is correct then this factor corresponds to a factor which has been

Variable No.	Maneuver	Loading
17	Steep turn (360°)	.46
19	Spin	.43
1	Straight and level	.41
11	Three-point landing	.35
8	Straight and level gear check	.34
14	Power-on stall	.33
9	Traffic pattern at auxilliary field	.31

called *Rate Control* in analyses of laboratory psychomotor tasks (Fleishman, 1958b; Fleishman & Hempel, 1955, 1956).

Factor VI groups most of the maneuvers which emphasize "stalls" and slow movements of the aircraft. Pilots often describe the control characteristics of these maneuvers as "muddy" or "soft"; that is, there is increased lag in the response of the aircraft to the control movements made—there is a "mushiness" in the controls. It thus appears that these maneuvers emphasize "kinesthetic feedback." There is no direct counter-

Variable No.	Maneuver	Loading
16	Power-off stall	.61
4	Gliding turn	.46
15	Approach to stall	.51
19	Spin	.43
14	Power on stall	.43
20	Rudder control stall	.40
13	Landing characteristic stall	.38
23	Forced landing	.37
12	Climbing turn from level	.33
3	Level-off from climbing turn	.32
21	Slow-flight turn	.30

part to this factor encountered in the laboratory research unless it is the "Postural Discrimination" factor previously identified (Fleishman, 1954). One is tempted to identify the present factor with the "flying by the seat-of-one's pants" ability to which pilots often refer. For the present, however, we shall employ the tentative name of *Kinesthetic Discrimination*.

DISCUSSION

A word about the interpretation of the factors is relevant here. The authors are aware of the limitations and hazards involved in the factor interpretation procedure used. Assigning meaning to factors always involves a certain amount of arbitrary decision making wherein the decision rules are not easy to spell out. In the present instance, interpretations were made with the assistance of a psychologist who was also a skilled pilot and thoroughly familiar with the maneuvers involved. In a sense, one might say that he "flew" the factors, or at least he "empathized" the operations of the pilot and aircraft while performing the maneuvers. In going about the interpretations it was at first thought the factors might be interpretable in terms of common subtask operations or requirements. Alternative possibilities included common control movements, or control-display relationships. The fact that most maneuvers were factorially complex did not make interpretation any easier. Initially, the pilot-psychologist looked for such evidence of commonality as Do the maneuvers on this factor all involve application of power? or Do they all involve lining up ground reference points?

The important point is that there was no explicit objective or attempt, initially, to define these factors in terms of more basic ability constructs. However, after repeated failure to "make sense" out of the blind rotations, descriptions in terms of ability factors were attempted. It appeared that this level of description best fitted the data. In other words, the ability model developed from experimental-correlational analyses of laboratory tasks seemed most adequate for describing the common requirements of these aircraft maneuvers.

In support of this factor, interpretation reference is made to an earlier report of a cluster analysis of measures obtained from an instrument flight check battery (Butler, Banford, Kautz, & Ornstein, 1954). The measures were 77 individual items (i.e., parts of maneuvers) and they were clustered through 14 successive iterations in a modified Tryon analysis. As the result, 5 clusters and 23 residuals were produced. Attempts to identify the clusters "in terms of constructs meaningful to the psychologist and/or pilot" at that time were unsuccessful. The authors, in fact, stated that "this approach was abandoned as fruitless." After the completion of the present study an inspection was made of this earlier work. Indications were that each of these five clusters was readily identifiable with one of the six factors resulting from the present analysis. The factor having no counterpart in the previous study is the one termed Kinesthetic Discrimination. This is hardly surprising in view of the fact that the cluster analysis was performed on items from a set of *instrument flying* maneuvers which did not include any of the stall series—here found to be the defining maneuvers in the Kinesthetic Discrimination factor.

It would have been ideal if the same student pilots in our study had also taken the reference battery of ability tests which originally identified the factors described. This, of course, was not possible. However, Ornstein (1954) correlated the "Pilot Aptitude Index" composite of the Aircrew Classification Battery with performance on the maneuvers in the present study. This Aptitude Index is a weighted composite of eight aptitude tests, and at that time 60% of the weighting comprised psychomotor test scores. The tests in use are known to measure the Control Precision and Multilimb Coordination factors (Fleishman, 1956b). These results showed that of the seven Aptitude Index-Maneuver correlations greater than .50 (corrected for maneuver reliability), four of the maneuvers are loaded on our Factor I (Control Precision) and four on our Factor III (multilimb Coordination). (One maneuver appears in both factors.) Thus, we find further support of the present interpretations.

More than 13 years ago Neal Miller summarized the wartime

research on pilot training and proficiency measurement (Miller, 1947). At that time, Miller stated:

> It may be that attempts to make a more penetrating analysis of flying skill will not be profitable until knowledge of simpler psycho-motor skills, in situations which are easier to control, has been increased and a clearer idea is developed of the general structure of human perceptual, motor, and intellectual abilities.

This prediction is especially interesting in view of our results. Information about the general structure of perceptual-motor abilities was not available in 1947. Much of the basic research has been done within the last eight years. While there are obvious limitations in our conclusions, we would have been at a loss to interpret our factors meaningfully without the ability concepts developed from this basic laboratory research. Thus, this study provides additional evidence of the usefulness of this ability framework in describing complex operational skills.

SUMMARY

Measures of flying proficiency in 24 separate maneuvers were obtained on a sample of student pilots. The intercorrelations among these maneuver performances were subjected to factor analytic study. The interrelationships were best interpreted in terms of ability factors, most of which had been identified previously in laboratory studies of experimental perceptual-motor tasks. The factors were identified as Control Precision, Spatial Orientation, Multilimb Coordination, Response Orientation, Rate Control, and Kinesthetic Discrimination. The results seem to indicate the usefulness of such ability categories in describing complex skills. Similar analyses of the interrelationships among component performance measures of other complex jobs may provide one way of defining the ability requirements underlying proficiency in those jobs.

REFERENCES

Ben-Avi, A. H. Studies of subjective measures of flying proficiency. In N. E. Miller (Ed.), *Psychological research on pilot training*. Washington: U. S. Government Printing Office, 1947. (*AAF Aviat. Psychol. Prog. Res. Rep.* No. 8)

Boyle, D. J., & Hagin, W. V. The light plane as a pre-primary selection and training device: I. Analysis of operational data. *USAF Hum. Resour. Res. Cent. Tech. Rep.*, 1953, No. 5333.

Butler, R. G., Bamford, H. E., Kautz, R. L., & Ornstein, G. N. Cluster analysis of pilot proficiency measures: IV. The instrument flight check battery. *USAF Personnel Train. Res. Cent.*, 1954. (Proj. 7710, task 77166; unpublished draft)

Ericksen, S. C. A review of the literature on methods of measuring pilot proficiency. *USAF Hum. Resour. Res. Cent. Bull.*, 1952, No. 52–25. (a)

Ericksen, S. C. Development of a light plane proficiency check to predict military flying success. *USAF Hum. Resour. Res. Cent. Tech. Rep.*, 1952, No. 52–6. (b)

Flanagan, J. C. The aviation psychology program in the Army Air Forces. Washington: U.S. Government Printing Office, 1947. (AAF *Aviat. Psychol. Prog. Res. Rep.* No. 1)

Fleishman, E. A. Testing for psychomotor abilities by means of apparatus tests. *Psychol. Bull.*, 1953, 50, 241–262.

Fleishman, E. A. Dimensional analysis of psychomotor abilities. *J. exp. Psychol.*, 1954, 48, 437–454.

Fleishman, E. A. Predicting advanced levels of proficiency in psychomotor skill. In G. Finch & F. Cameron (Eds.), *Symposium on Air Force human engineering, personnel, and training research.* Washington: National Academy of Sciences–National Research Council, Pub. 455, 1956. (a)

Fleishman, E. A. Psychomotor selection tests: research and application in the U.S. Air Force. *Personnel Psychol.*, 1956, 9, 449–467. (b)

Fleishman E. A. A comparative study of aptitude patterns in unskilled and skilled psychomotor performances. *J. appl. Psychol.*, 1957, 41, 263–272. (a)

Fleishman, E. A. Factor structure in relation to task difficulty in psychomotor performance. *Edu. psychol. Measmt.*, 197, 17, 522–532. (b)

Fleishman, E. A. Analysis of positioning movements and static reactions. *J. exp. Psychol.*, 1958, 55, 13–24. (a)

Fleishman, E. A. Dimensional analysis of movement reactions. *J. exp. Psychol.*, 1958, 55, 430–453. (b)

Fleishman, E. A. Le Propostic des niveaux éléves d'aptitude de des taches complexes. (The prediction of high levels of proficiency in complex tasks.) Bulletin de L'Association Internationale de Psychologie Appliquée, 1959, 8, 27–43.

Fleishman, E. A., & Hempel, W. E. A factor analysis of dexterity tests. *Personnel Psychol.*, 1954, 7, 15–32. (a)

Fleishman, E. A., & Hempel, W. E. Changes in factor structure of a complex psychomotor test as a function of practice. *Psychometrika*, 1954, 19, 239–252. (b)

FLEISHMAN, E. A. & HEMPEL, W. E. The relation between abilities and improvement with practice in a visual discrimination reaction task. *J. exp. Psychol.*, 1955, 49, 301–310.

FLEISHMAN, E. A. & HEMPEL, W. E. Factorial analysis of complex psychomotor performance and related skills. *J. appl. Psychol.*, 1956, 40, 96–104.

FLEXMAN, R. E., TOWNSEND, J. C. & ORNSTEIN, G. N. Evaluation of a contact flight simulator when used in an Air Force Primary Pilot training program: Part I. Over-all effectiveness. *USAF Personnel Train. Res. Cent., Tech. Rep.*, 1954. (AFPTRC-TR-54-38)

GUILFORD, J. P., & LACEY, J. I. (Eds.) *Printed classification tests.* Washington: U. S. Government Printing Office, 1947. (*AAF Aviat. Psychol. Prog. Res. Rep.* No. 5)

HEMPEL, W. E., & FLEISHMAN, E. A. Factor analysis of physical proficiency and manipulative skill. *J. appl. Psychol.*, 1955, 39, 12–16.

HOUSTON, R. C., SMITH, J. F., & FLEXMAN, R. E. Performance of student pilots flying the T-6 aircraft in primary pilot training. *USAF Personnel Train. Res. Cent., Tech. Rep.*, 1954. (AFPTRC-TR-54-109)

KELLY, E. L. *The development of a scale for rating pilot competence.* 1943, CAA Division of Res. Rep. No. 18.

MELTON, A. W. (Ed.) *Apparatus tests.* Washington: U. S. Government Printing Office, 1947. (*AAF Aviat. Psychol. Prog. Res. Rep.* No. 4)

MICHAEL, W. B., GUILFORD, J. P., FRUCHTER, B., & ZIMMERMAN, W. S. The description of spatial-visualization abilities. *Educ. psychol. Measmt.*, 1957, 17, 185–199.

MILLER, N. E. (Ed.) *Psychological research on pilot training.* Washington: U. S. Government Printing Office, 1947. (*AAF Psychol. Prog. Res. Rep.* No. 8)

ORNSTEIN, G. N. Stanine as a predictor of pilot performance on specific maneuvers. *USAF Personnel Train. Res. Cent.*, 1954. (Project 7710, task 77166; unpublished draft)

ORNSTEIN, G. N., NICHOLS, I. A., & FLEXMAN, R. E. Evaluation of a contact flight simulator when used in an Air Force Primary Pilot training program: Part II. Effectiveness of training on component skills. *USAF Personnel Train. Res. Cent., Tech. Rep.*, 1954. (AFPTRC-TR-54-110)

PARKER, J. F., & FLEISHMAN, E. A. *Prediction of advanced levels of proficiency in a complex tracking task.* Arlington, Va.: Psychological Res. Ass., 1959.

SMITH, J. F., FLEXMAN, R. E., & HOUSTON, R. C. Development of an objective method of recording flight performance. *USAF Hum. Resour. Res. Cent., Tech. Rep.*, 1952, No. 52–15.

Sutter, E. L., Townsend, J. C., & Ornstein, G. N. The light plane as a pre-primary selection and training device: II. Analysis of training data. *USAF Personnel Train. Res. Cent., Tech. Rep.,* 1954. (AFPTRC-TR-54-35)

Thurstone, L. L. *Multiple-factor analysis.* Chicago: Univer. Chicago Press, 1947.

26 Development of a Clerical Position Description Questionnaire

ERICH P. PRIEN

Research on the questionnaire method of developing position descriptions has been directed to the solution of two general objectives. The first and most common objective has been to provide information on characteristic job acts and psychological requirements in combination, within a criterion-development program. The attempt is to generate results immediately applicable to selection, placement, and performance-evaluation of the objectively-defined functions. Work by Thomas (1952), Turner (1960), and Chalupsky (1962) illustrates this general approach. The second approach is illustrated by the work of Hemphill (1960), Prien (1963), and Dudek (1948) and is characterized by the development of instruments, without respect to a specific purpose, solely for the generation of a precise description of a type of occupational activity. The application of results of the latter studies, of course, requires additional research and development.

This study was conducted to develop an instrument applicable across companies but limited to clearly defined job clusters. The specific objective was to develop an instrument which would provide a relatively precise description of clerical functions.

METHOD AND PROCEDURE

A check list of clerical functions was developed using conventional job description information of a wide variety of positions and the knowledge of clerical positions obtained through experience in job analysis. Eighty items (which appeared to reflect a single job act) were retained from an initial list in excess of 200. Items rejected in this initial screening were those which appeared to overlap or involve a combination of job acts. Items were retained which were fairly specific, and thus should load on only one factor, but sufficiently general so that they would not be unique to any one company.

From *Personnel Psychology*, 1965, 18, 91–98.

Sample of Jobs

Printed questionnaires were distributed to 126 clerical workers employed in a variety of positions ranging from a highly specific IBM Keypunch Operator to the rather general and complex position of Administrative Secretary, which included some elements of supervision. Respondents were obtained from eleven departments of six different companies representing the major industrial functions. Written instructions were provided each respondent, directing them to complete the questionnaire describing their current position as they performed it. In addition, written descriptions based on a job interview were available for all respondents, which were used as an informal content check of each questionnaire. The purpose of this verification was to insure that respondents had conscientiously completed the questionnaires and had not entered random responses. The check was not considered a reconciliation or validation of the check list of responses since it was assumed that the respondents' judgment would be the most accurate reflection of what was actually done on the job.

Data Analysis

Product-moment correlations were computed between all items for the sample of 126 respondents. The item intercorrelations were factor analyzed by the principal components method. Communalities were estimated, the multiple correlation of each item with all others being used in preference to unity. Fifty-eight factors were extracted—fewer than the number of variables but still including many which account for only a very minor portion of total variance. A plotting of both the Eigen values and the proportion of variance accounted for by each factor in the order extracted suggested that only the first twelve factors would warrant attempted interpretation.

RESULTS AND DISCUSSION

The proportion of variance accounted for by each factor and the respective Eigen values appear in Table 26.1. The column on the right of Table 26.1 shows the cumulative proportion of variance accounted for by the factors as extracted. Although the table shows twenty factors, interpretation was attempted for only the first twelve. Examination of the table shows that the proportion variance accounted for by any one factor begins to drop off after factor eleven. Also, attempted interpretations of additional factors were not fruitful and did not seem to warrant inclusion.

The factors are defined as follows:

TABLE 26.1. *Proportion of variance and Eigen values for each factor*

Factor	Eigen Value	Proportion of Variance	Cumulative Proportion of Variance
1	10.376	15.0	15.0
2	7.163	10.3	25.3
3	4.525	6.5	31.8
4	3.639	5.3	37.1
5	3.363	4.8	41.9
6	2.895	4.2	46.1
7	2.710	3.9	50.0
8	2.469	3.5	53.5
9	2.166	3.2	56.7
10	2.024	2.9	59.6
11	1.921	2.8	62.4
12	1.701	2.4	64.8
13	1.583	2.3	67.1
14	1.437	2.1	69.2
15	1.407	2.0	71.2
16	1.349	1.9	73.1
17	1.293	1.9	75.0
18	1.217	1.8	76.8
19	1.102	1.5	78.3
20	1.016	1.5	79.8

Factor 1 This factor involves items which reflect a variety of typing acts, in terms of the source of material from which the typing is done and the potential use of the material after it is typed. The sources are from copy, shorthand notes, dictation, recording tape and so forth. The use of the material is in terms of typing for photo reproduction, final copy, statistical tables or mats, and masters for automatic reproduction equipment. In addition, several items involved the handling, preparation, and distribution of the reproduced materials. The factor is best described as: Responsibility for Typing and Processing and Distribution of Written Material.

Factor 2 This factor is identified by items with a major emphasis on the evaluation and supervision of clerical employees. Such functions as evaluating, supervising, making decisions about selection, checking, and distribution of routine work assignments, as well as development of work procedures, are involved. The content of this factor clearly indicates the appropriate title. The factor is named: Responsibility for the Supervision of Clerical Employees.

Factor 3 Items which have a high loading on this factor involve the verification of work, keeping a running balance of an account, handling of figures in terms of transferring or recording to specific accounts, preparation of specific payrolls, performing arithmetic computations, the accumulation of data, and working to deadlines. The responsibility involved in the performance of this work is clearly in the area of bookkeeping and accounting, although the accounting is of less than a professional level. The factor is titled: Responsibility for Bookkeeping and Clerical Accounting.

Factor 4 The items which have significant loading on this factor involve the filing of materials, checking of invoices, maintaining of supply inventory, preparing filing procedures, and the location and retrieval of filed material. The factor is titled: Responsibility for Filing and Retrieval of Business Information and Documents.

Factor 5 The items which load significantly on this factor involve the preparation, set-up, and operation of data processing equipment. Such things as operating an interpreter, reproducer, key-punch, and other punch card equipment are involved. This factor is clearly titled: The Responsibility for the Operation of Data Processing Equipment.

Factor 6 The items which load significantly on this factor involve the calculation of formulas, processing of data, analysis of accounting-type data, and the preparation of reports or correspondence reflecting the analysis or interpretation of the data. The title of this factor is: Responsibility for the Analysis, and the Reporting of Analysis and Interpretation of Business Data.

Factor 7 The items which load significantly on this factor involve issuing checks, verification of expense accounts, keeping petty cash, and approving payment of company bills. While this factor involves responsibility for the use of money, the funds are not included in the principal operating expense of the organization. This factor is titled: Responsibility for Cash Operating Accounts.

Factor 8 Items which load significantly on this factor reflect activities dealing with hiring of personnel and the maintenance and use of personnel records. A tentative title for this factor is: Manpower Records Maintenance.

Factor 9 The items which load significantly on this factor reflect activities performed specifically for a high level executive. Such things as maintenance of the supervisor's schedule book, working overtime, making personal concessions regarding the work schedule, preparing a confidential part-time employee payroll, and scheduling of appointments suggest that the activities are carried on with reference to the time and schedule of another person. The tentative title of this factor is: Executive Secretarial Assistance.

Factor 10 The items which load significantly on this factor involve the handling of company mail and the use and maintenance of mail room equipment. It is titled: Responsibility for Processing Company Mail.

Factor 11 The items which load significantly on this factor involve representing the company to outsiders for the purpose of conducting specific business transactions and implementing company programs. Planning and conducting community projects, handling the bulletin board, paying company bills, recommending the purchase of office equipment, and completing transactions with outside personnel are involved. The content of the items which load significantly on this factor suggest the tentative title of: Communication and Public Relations.

Factor 12 The items which load significantly on this factor involve the receiving and routing of company visitors, handling of outside tele-

TABLE 26.2. *Comparison of factors obtained in three studies of clerical work*

Prien	Thomas	Chalupsky
1. Typing, processing, and distribution of written material	I. Typing	Typing and general clerical
2. Supervision of clerical workers	IV. Planning and supervision	B. Supervision
3. Bookkeeping and clerical accounting	II. Listing and compiling	A. Inventory and stockkeeping
4. Filing and retrieval of material	V. Filing	
5. Operation of data processing equipment		
6. Analysis and reporting of business data	VIII. Calculation	C. Computation and bookkeeping
7. Cash operating accounts		
8. Manpower records maintenance		
9. Executive secretarial assistance		
10. Mailing	VI. Stock handling	
11. Communication and public relations	III. Communication	D. Communication and public relations
12. Receptionist		

phone calls, and providing information, directions, and completing general communications with people outside of the organization. The nature of the items very clearly suggests the title of: The Receptionist's Responsibility.

A comparison of the results of this study with those obtained by Thomas and Chalupsky indicates that most of the factors accounted for by the latter two studies are apparently contained in this study. The exception is the factor defined by Thomas as Routine Clerical Work. In the author's study it is combined with Factor 1, Typing and General Clerical Work. Thomas has a typing factor in addition to the separate routine clerical factor. Table 26.2 shows a comparison of the factors obtained in these three separate studies.

Unlike the Thomas and Chalupsky research, the procedure in this project did not include provision for eliminating items because of low response frequency. Possibly as a result of this, or as a result of recent automation, factors involving the use of automatic business equipment and data processing equipment do appear here (Factor 5, which is entitled *The Responsibility for the Operation of Data Processing Equipment*). The appearance of additional factors which are unique to this study is attributed partially to the selection of jobs to be included and to the method of analysis. While the problems involved in sampling are obvious, the differences in results as related to methods warrant some comment. First, Thomas used a clustering method to identify factors and might, therefore, have overlooked several relationships. Chalupsky. on the other hand, did not use incumbents to provide job information, but had judges complete the check list based on their reading of a USES job description. Finally, unlike both the Thomas and Chalupsky studies, items were eliminated in this study only following the factor analysis, the assumption being that in this study items which are highly unique or highly ambiguous and thus unreliable would account for a very small proportion of the variance.

While comparison with previous studies must be limited to the comparison of content, the additional factors defined in this study suggest greater variety in clerical work than has been heretofore indicated. Of the five factors which appear unique to this study, three involve dealing with the human element in industry or at least face-to-face relationships. Perhaps clerical jobs are changing somewhat over the years, and in the direction suggested by current social scientists. The value of interpersonal relations, or at least the opportunity to maintain contact with other people and for the company or organization to maintain contact with either individuals or other organizations' representatives, is a matter not to be dismissed lightly. The contribution of an opportunity to maintain personal relations to employee morale has been well demonstrated. Also, while not as well demonstrated, the personal touch afforded by face-to-face relationships is acknowledged as a contributor to organization effectiveness, particularly in the marketing and merchandising field.

Finally, the results of this study indicate that what is considered clerical work today includes something more than typing, filing, and semi-skilled white-collar labor. As competition increases, and as industries become more complex, the role and presumably the importance of clerical functions will change.

REFERENCES

BIMED 17. Factor analysis and varimax rotation, *Behavioral Science*, April, 1962, 266.

CHALUPSKY, ALBERT B. Comparative factor analyses of clerical jobs. *Journal of Applied Psychology*, XLVI (1962), 62-66.

DUDEK, E. E. An operational approach to the evaluation of office jobs. Unpublished Ph.D. thesis, Purdue University, 1948.

HEMPHILL, J. K. Dimensions of executive positions. *Ohio State University Bureau of Educational Research Monograph*, 1961, No. 98.

MCCORMICK, E. J., FINN, R. H., & SCHEIPS, C. D. Patterns of job requirements. *Journal of Applied Psychology*, XLI (1957), 358-364.

PALMER, GEORGE J. & MCCORMICK, E. J. A factor analysis of job activities. *Journal of Applied Psychology*, XLV (1961), 289-294.

PRIEN, ERICH P. Development of a supervisor position description questionnaire. *Journal of Applied Psychology*, XLVII (1963), 10-14.

THOMAS, L. L. A cluster analysis of office operations. *Journal of Applied Psychology*, XXXVI (1952), 62-66.

TURNER, W. W. Dimensions of foreman performance: A factor analysis of criterion measures. *Journal of Applied Psychology*, XLIV (1960), 216-223.

V PERFORMANCE AND EXTRA-INDIVIDUAL CONDITIONS

In contrast to some of the other parts, the problem here was to select emphases from a most variegated body of research studies. The attempt has been to indicate the pervasiveness of the problem or problems involved in studying performance context with (it is hoped) representative studies.

The fact that level of performance may be affected by conditions surrounding the performance has received recognition but relatively little actual research attention. The first article presented, from a publication edited by Horst (1942), discusses the problem in general terms and points out that "contingency factors" are one of the major reasons why performance prediction has not been more accurate. The need to adjust criteria to compensate for the influence of contingency factors is mentioned as are the facts that such factors may be used as predictors or themselves be predicted. Such factors are in any research design regardless of the amount of recognition given them, but there have been few attempts to assess their effects on performance variability.

A research investigation that did recognize some of the contingency sources of variance in performance is that presented by Dorcus (1940). The job in question, door-to-door sales of bakery products, is a relatively simple one and yet, as Dorcus shows, there are many possible sources of bias in the performance of the job. Dorcus even went to the length of constructing economic maps of the city, based upon rental value of homes, to estimate the effects of the sales territory on sales volume. This study, completed over twenty-five years ago, *could* serve as a model of thoroughness in constructing performance criteria, but it has not; most studies continue to use limited criteria of performance.

In contrast to the complexity of the Dorcus study, that by Ferguson (1951) made a relatively simple investigation that showed an important source of bias in a performance evaluation. The investigation involved comparing validity coefficients for the Life Insurance Aptitude Index using district or agency manager performance ratings as criteria. Their averages and distributions of ratings were about equal, but there was a wide variation in the size of the validity coefficients. The author concludes that validity is as much a result of the quality of district and agency management as it is of performance.

The research attention devoted to isolating situational sources of performance variance has proceeded from rather limited studies to designs of more and more complexity as the next study by Stogdill et. al. (1955), concerned with the "administrative behavior" of Naval Officers. The study covered a wide range of job duties in technical and professional areas, operations, service as public information, construction, and maintenance; in general, the varied duties that are found in a large and complex organization. Descriptions of job behaviors were obtained from incumbents, peers, and supervisors and were factor analyzed to yield eight factors which categorized persons by the type of position they held, whether sea or shore duty, or large or small installation. In general, the results indicated that performance is at least partially determined by the specific job and place. In other words, persons in similar assignments tend to exhibit similar patterns of behavior.

The next study, by Cureton and Katzell (1962), was based upon data from seventy-two divisions of a company with five measures of divisional performance and five variables descriptive of the location of the performance. Two factors were extracted from the data showing performance differences in an urban as opposed to non-urban location.

Two more recent and much more complex studies are by Dunteman (1966) and Friedlander (1966). The former, presented here, analyzed the relationship among eighty-four characteristics of organizations, management and workers, incentive conditions and personnel performance in 234 manufacturing organizations. The data were obtained by questionnaire and are somewhat suspect as to accuracy, but this is one of the first comprehensive studies attempting to isolate variables in this highly complex area. The data were factor analyzed and fourteen factors were extracted to describe organizations and various behaviors in relation to the organizations. The results open quite serious questions regarding some of the dogma about organizations and performance. For example, neither the size nor age of the organization showed relationships with measures of personnel performance or organization functioning. Actually the most likely value of this study is to show the complexity of the relationships among variables that can be studied and, as specifically pointed out, the addition of more variables for study is likely to alter relationships or, more pointedly, our conceptions of situational influences on performance.

The Friedlander study was concerned with the effectiveness of work groups which functioned as both policy-making and planning committees in the organization studies. A special questionnaire was carefully constructed and group members were asked their opinions concerning their particular group as to the adequacy and effectiveness of meetings. The data were factor analyzed and nine factors extracted. The factor accounting for the major portion of the variance was "Group Effectiveness" as this relates to actual problem-solving effectiveness. The other eight factors had to do with group leadership, involvement, personal relationships, and other characteristics not seen as directly related to group effectiveness. Here it is likely that an individual's performance could be affected as he sees himself a member of a more or less effective group. This study, along with that preceding it, does recognize the fact that performance behavior can be varied by the context of the performance of interest and, of particular note, both give some idea of the complexity of the full performance situation.

There is one situational consideration surrounding research studies that has been neglected, usually of necessity, but which seems to have a quite marked effect on the prediction of performance. The consideration is the length of time elapsing between measurements of individual characteristics and the measurement of performance which the characteristics might predict. The two studies presented, by Ball (1938) and Knauft (1955), show surprisingly high relationships between comparatively simple measures of mental ability and performance, as measured by the occupational level attained. The correlations are much higher than are usually found in predictive studies and are likely even higher in actuality, because in neither case is there correction for restriction of range. In these studies it is obvious that quite limited measures of individual ability give good predictions of at least one dimension of performance, the question is why these same predictors cannot be shown to have such substantial relationship over more limited time periods? The authors believe that the rather disappointing success for prediction over shorter time periods is because performance behavior is not well understood and very likely wrong or too limited measures have been used in the past. The contention is that the plentitude of predictors are probably adequate if it is known what to predict.

REFERENCE

FRIEDLANDER, F. Performance and interactional dimensions of organizational work groups, *Journal of Applied Psychology*, 1966, 50, 257–265.

27 Contingency Factors

Contingency factors are among the most frequent sources of inaccuracy of prediction and are also among the most difficult to control. They comprise those personal and situational factors which affect level of performance but for which the probability of subsequent presence or absence is not known at the time the prediction is made. Even though it is not known in advance whether certain conditions will arise, the direction of their influence in the event that they do arise can be established. In making a prediction it can then be indicated that the prediction is contingent upon the operation of these factors.[1] For example, a person's chances of successful marital adjustment may be predicted as contingent upon whether or not the mother-in-law will live with the couple. The success of a parolee may be predicted as contingent upon the type of neighborhood to which he returns, or the potential scholastic success of a prospective college student may be regarded as contingent upon the amount of outside employment he is forced to take. In the vocational field, success may depend not only on the specific aptitudes and abilities of the person, but also, let us say, on whether or not he gets married.

While situational factors are most frequently considered in this connection, personal factors may by no means be eliminated. For example, the contingency may involve directly some aspect of the personality of the individual; he may, for example, receive psychotherapy and, as a result, become less aggressive than he was at the time the prediction for him was made. It should be realized then that in making predictions for individuals one is dealing not only with external conditions which are subject to change, but also with persons who are themselves flexible and subject to modification.

The problem of contingent prediction is implicit in most prediction studies. One of the chief reasons why many prediction procedures have not attained a higher level of accuracy has been their failure to take into account contingency factors. In this chapter three ways of dealing with such factors are discussed: (1) the criterion score may be adjusted for the contingency; (2) the contingency factor may be treated as one of the predictive elements; or (3) the contingency factor itself may be predicted.

From Chapter V, *The Prediction of Personal Adjustment*, Paul Horst (Ed.). New York, New York. Social Science Research Council, 1951.

[1] For a discussion of contingency factors in the prediction of marital success, see Burgess, E. W. and Cottrell, Leonard S., Jr. "Contingency Factors: Stability and Security." *Predicting Success or Failure in Marriage.* New York: Prentice-Hall, Inc. 1939. Chap. XIII

CONTINGENT PREDICTION AND SPECIFICITY OF THE CRITERION

One approach to the problem of contingent prediction is to consider the contingency a part of the activity situation; in other words, one predicts not merely success in marriage, but success in marriage when the mother-in-law is to live with the couple. Instead of a general prediction of an individual's success as a salesman, specific predictions of success in a southern territory or success in a large metropolitan territory may be made. Instead of predicting an individual's success as a student, one predicts his success as a student who works half-time on an outside job.

This approach may be viewed as requiring adjustment of the criterion measure for the specific factors which are called contingencies. It may be known, for example, that under certain circumstances living with in-laws is a hazard to marital success. In this case, a successful adjustment when the in-laws are with the couple surpasses the level of an otherwise equally successful adjustment where in-laws are not present. The former adjustment would therefore be given a higher rating on the criterion measure. This is analogous to saying, to cite another example, that of two men selling equal volumes, the one who sells in the territory having the keenest competition is doing the better job, and therefore should receive the higher score. In one sense, then, the contingency problem may be thought of as a matter of adjusting the criterion score for the contingency.

THE CONTINGENCY FACTOR AS A PREDICTIVE ELEMENT

On the other hand, the contingency factor may be treated as itself a predictive element, to be combined with other factors used in predicting success in the activity.[2] For example, the respective weights to be given "absence of mother-in-law" and "presence of mother-in-law" in the marriage prediction equation may be determined, or weights may be assigned for given amounts of time spent in outside work in the case of predicting scholastic success. It would be necessary, however, to wait until the contingency factors have operated and until the original group, on whom the prediction formula is worked out, has had time to demon-

---

[2] For a statement of the problem of contingency factors in school prediction, see Blair, J. L. "Significant Factors in the Prediction of the Success of College Freshmen." (Unpublished PhD. thesis, University of Chicago, 1931). Pp. 181–182. See also Williamson, E. G. "The Decreasing Accuracy of Scholastic Predictions." *Journal of Educational Psychology*. 28: 15–16. 1937

strate degree of success in the activity before the appropriate weights for the contingency factors could be determined.

Perhaps the essential difference in the two ways of looking at the contingency problem is in the purposes to be served. If primary interest is in ascertaining under what circumstances success in the activity would be at a maximum, the contingency element should be considered as a prediction factor whose value in order to give the greatest success as measured by the criterion may be established. Attention is then focused, not on how good a job a man is doing under given circumstances, but rather on what factors must be introduced if he is to do a better job.

PREDICTION OF CONTINGENCY FACTORS

Still another way of taking into account contingency factors is to predict them directly. For example, if amount of income is a contingency factor with reference to a man's martial adjustment—the marriage, let us say, will not be successful unless the man makes a fairly good income—one may predict directly the probability of his having a good income. By predicting the contingency factor, it may be possible to make a more accurate unqualified prediction of the man's success in marriage. Factors related to the man's future income may be included in the marriage prediction equation, and since marital adjustment would be a function of income, these factors would help to predict success in the marriage relationship. If it were known that the success of a given salesman depended on whether or not he would get married, since a home and family would be an incentive to harder efforts, it might be possible to include in the prediction formula factors related to behavior leading to marriage, such as social aggressiveness, need for affection, desire for children, etc. The inclusion of such factors to predict the contingency, marriage, would at the same time improve the prediction of performance in the activity, selling.

In attempting to evaluate possible alternate configurations of factors in prediction the relative flexibility of case study methods is extremely valuable. By the use of the case study one may attempt to evaluate not merely static combinations but processes involved in shifting situational configurations.

Thus there are three general ways of dealing with the sometimes troublesome problem of contingency factors. Whether such factors are adjusted in the criterion score, whether they are treated as predictive elements, or whether they are themselves predicted will depend upon the nature of the particular problem under consideration. Whatever the procedure, it should be recognized that contingency factors must be accounted for in some way in almost any prediction study if it is to achieve a satisfactory level of accuracy.

28 Methods of Evaluating the Efficiency of Door-to-Door Salesmen of Bakery Products

ROY M. DORCUS

In the scientific selection of men for employment for specific jobs, we are faced with a problem to which insufficient attention has been given; namely, that of determining what constitutes a good employee and what his characteristics are. Theoretically job analysis should answer this question, but very often the characteristics which are thought to be essential for the job do not turn out to be of major importance. We have only to turn to the selection of automobile drivers to illustrate the point in question. In the beginning, it was assumed that quick reaction time, certain qualities of sensory function, a given level of intelligence, and ability to maintain attention would be necessary for a good driver. Most of these criteria have failed to separate satisfactorily the poor drivers from the good drivers. If, therefore, these assumed attributes of the good driver are no longer valid, what are the attributes of a good driver? We have to conclude that we do not know. Many other occupations have been assumed to require obvious traits or characteristics, and we have proceeded to select individuals that have these assumed characteristics without properly ascertaining whether the assumed characteristics actually are essential to the occupation.[1]

When I attempted to select door-to-door salesmen for a large baking organization, I was confronted with the problem of what constituted a good salesman. Now it is perfectly clear that the selection of a salesman of this type or any other type, by test procedure, will be no more reliable than the reliability of the criteria against which we match the results of test selection. It was necessary first to determine the standards to be applied to salesmen already in the company's employment.

The first method which normally suggests itself is that of volume of

From *Journal of Applied Psychology*, 1940, 24, 587–594.

[1] Some of the figures presented in this paper are altered to a certain extent, since the actual figures would furnish information of a private nature to the general public. These alterations are always representative, however, of the directional trends and for discussion purposes suffice for the true figures.

business secured by each salesman. Since maintenance of the company or organization depends upon financial returns, this would seem to be an adequate criterion. In other words, if the company could hire salesmen whom they could predict would secure, for example, a minimum of $250 worth of business per week, they would be assured of a profit as a result of these efforts. Unfortunately the problem is not that simple. The salesman who actually produces the most business may be the least efficient in the company and the reverse may also be true; namely that the salesman who produces the least volume of business may be doing the best job of selling. Standard practices in setting up routes have a decided bearing on this matter. The number of houses, and hence potential business, may vary from 300 to 4000 or even more per route depending upon the Sales Manager's opinion of the potentialities of the territory. Of course, if these opinions were accurate, then the problem of evaluating the salesman would not be so difficult. It has been found from practical experience that two men may produce different results from the same territory but that it is undesirable to shift men from territory to territory to determine the actual status of the territory involved. This notion is based on the contention that the salesman builds up personal contacts with customers which are disrupted with each shift of the man. The sales manager, therefore, has had to rely on personal judgment of the territory in deciding whether the salesman is producing a satisfactory volume of business in a given territory. As will be shown later, this judgment is fairly often erroneous.

Let us now return to my earlier statement, that a high volume producer may be inefficient and that a low volume producer may be efficient. Let us assume that a salesman produces $400.00 worth of business from a territory of 4000 homes. He may, nevertheless, be only skimming the territory, whereas the salesman who produces $200.00 worth of business from a territory containing 1000 homes is selling twice the percentage of available customers. You may say that this indicates that the routes are poorly laid out and I would agree. The judgment of whether the salesman is good or poor, however, is influenced by such factors and selection by test will in turn be influenced by such factors. Further, no satisfactory method of evaluating territory has been worked out previous to this investigation. More will be said of this later.

A second method of evaluating salesmen is by the well-known rating technique. Under these circumstances various supervisors are asked to throw the men, on a basis of efficiency, into two or more groups. While there is a fair degree of correlation in rating, considerable disagreement is found and the supervisors cannot divorce their judgments from volume of business obtained.

The third method consists of a job analysis in which the supposed characteristics of good salesmen are checked against the supposed possession of the characteristics. This method has two faults: (1) The supposed traits may be relevant or they may not be relevant. (2) The judgment of whether the individual possesses the trait may or may not be accurate. Although we have collected considerable data on these two points, no attempt to present this material will be made in this paper.

After considerable consultation with the sales manager, sales supervisors and other officials of the organization, it was decided that the most profitable approach to the selection problem could be made after careful evaluation of the route set up. We attempted, therefore, to develop a yardstick that could be applied to each route. Certain information was already available as a basis on which to begin this task. The department of commerce and the publishers of the *Saturday Evening Post* were able to supply data from which economic maps of the city could be constructed. For classification purposes the city was then divided into areas on a basis of relative rental values of homes. For convenience of designation we shall refer to these areas as red, yellow, green and blue. The red areas were those in which the highest wage level prevailed, and the blue, those areas in which the lowest wage level obtained. It so happens that the size of families and consumption of bread per member of the family is not in direct ratio to economic status. From sampling data obtained by the firm, it was ascertained that the consumption of bread and baking products per family was highest in the green area and lowest in the red area. The blue area which is the lowest economic area and highest in members per family, consumed slightly less bread per family than the green area. This can be explained on a basis of low income from which other necessities must be bought, and of these necessities, certain other food products are somewhat cheaper than bread. The people of the high income area (red) consume less bread per member of the family because other more expensive bakery products and other more expensive non-bakery products can be afforded to supplement the diet. The differential in buying power introduces still another factor; namely, that the various economic levels purchase in varying percentages from door-to-door salesmen. Since the cost of bakery products is somewhat higher when delivered to the door, we find that the higher the income level the greater the patronage of house delivered products. In the blue area, (the lowest economic level) very little door-to-door selling is done because these areas are supplied with stale stores and cheap bakery products. The percentage of buyers from door-to-door bakery salesmen varies from almost 0 in the lowest economic areas to about 75 per cent in the highest areas. With the foregoing information available we are in a position to determine what potential business might be expected from a given route, provided there were no competitors. If we count the number of houses or families on a route; multiply the number by the percentages of families that buy home delivered products in the type of area involved; then multiply, by the number of loaves of bread consumed per family; and finally by the price per loaf, we can fairly accurately estimate the business that may be expected. Since competitors will secure some of this potential business, we have to ascertain the average business done by each organization. Sampling techniques again supply the information. The well managed organizations obtain approximately the same percentage of the total business and the relative volume is fairly constant for all economic areas. We can therefore substitute in the formula previously given, the percentage of customers buying from the bakery in question, for the percentage buying from door-to-door delivery. If then the route fails to produce the expected business we may look into the sales ability of the man on the route. As soon as we begin to investigate salesmen from this angle, we find that there are at least two phases of the selling problem: first, that of obtaining customers and second, that of selling the necessary quantity of the products to each customer. These two factors do not appear to go hand in hand. Some salesmen seem to be excellent solicitors but are unable to persuade the customer to buy in any quantity, others seem to be able to sell their customers but are unable to secure them initially.

The routes were analyzed next to determine whether the salesman was at fault or whether the route was improperly laid out. If we take a few illustrations of the points made earlier we can see how the system works out. One route showed a sales volume of $190.00 per week. The sales per customer was the average for that type of territory; the salesman was actually selling 45 per cent of the homes on the route; nevertheless, if judged on volume of business obtained, he was a poorer salesman that the one whom I will now describe. The salesman produced a total of $235.00 worth of business. His sales per customer were average for the type of territory in question yet he was selling only 20 per cent of the homes on his route. This man was doing a successful job from every angle, since the company only expected to secure 20 per cent of the potential business in this territory. The first salesman was the superior salesman, in view of the fact that he secured almost double the anticipated number of customers. A third salesman who produced a satisfactory volume of business was actually selling only 12 per cent of the homes on his route. This man was a poor salesman. He apparently was satisfied with his earnings and was unwilling to exert extra effort to increase his earnings. There is a high probability that his territory would have supported two routes instead of one.

In a part of the survey 70 salesmen were analyzed by the sales manager and by our yardstick. We found that there was a serious discrepancy between his estimates and our yardstick in 20 of the 70 cases. Later in a conference we attempted to account for these discrepancies. This brought to light certain fallacies that had existed in the minds of the sales supervisors. One of the fallacies was the belief that territories containing a high percentage of Jewish homes were poor territory because Jewish people are supposed to buy chiefly from Jewish bakeries. Consequently, certain salesmen were rated as good salesmen by their supervisors, largely because they were doing a satisfactory volume of business in what the supervisors thought was poor territory. On a basis of the following illustrations we can see that this belief is actually without much foundation.

All four of these men produced a satisfactory volume of business. Of the four, the salesman on route B produced the highest volume of business, yet he was rated as only fair by the supervisor and poor by me. When we examine the data carefully we find that on route A, 12 per cent of the homes were sold; on B, 16 per cent of the homes; on C, 8 per cent of the homes; and on D, 13 per cent of the homes. If high Jewish population were the controlling factor, then we should have expected route D which is 75 per cent Jewish to be lowest in percentage of homes sold and routes A and B to be higher. Route C which is intermediate in this factor shows the lowest percentage of homes sold, yet the salesman on this

Route	Supervisors' comment	Comment made on basis of proposed yardstick
A	Good salesman, good canvasser, good territory, 25% Jewish.	Poor canvasser, sales per customer low, route too large.
B	Fair salesman, poor canvasser, good territory, 25% Jewish.	Poor canvasser, sales per customer low, route too large.
C	Good salesman, territory poor, 50% Jewish.	Poor canvasser, sales per customer low.
D	Good salesman, territory poor, 75% Jewish.	Poor canvasser, sales per customer low.

route has been rated as good by the supervisors. It would be impossible to present an analysis of each route and salesman in this paper, but it will suffice to state that more careful consideration was given to the rating of the salesmen and to the route structure as a result of this analysis. We finally came to rather close agreement about the various salesmen. In some instances, the yardstick was ineffective, particularly in evaluating country routes. Special circumstances operated which influenced other routes and if these special circumstances could not be discounted, the yardstick was not applied.

This method of determining the efficiency of the route salesmen is effective only when applied to men who have been on the job for a period of several months. Any change in the man on the route usually results in a slight loss in the number of old customers. What happens after this initial loss depends largely upon the ability of the man. Customers may gradually drift away or new customers may be added. The best technique of selection will not eliminate all of the inferior men, hence a certain percentage of poor salesmen who subsequently have to be eliminated find their way into the organization. All we can hope to accomplish is to reduce the number of such men to a minimum and to detect these inferior men as soon as possible. The cost of labor turnover in door-to-door selling is high. The men are paid during the training period and the intangible costs in form of lost good will cannot be accurately estimated. It may run as high or even higher than $200.00 per man.

The sales of bakery products is seasonal; is influenced by short period weather changes; and is subject to change with vacation periods and other holiday periods. It is difficult, therefore, in a short interval of time to estimate whether the individual salesman is good or poor. If he takes over a route which has been furnishing a given amount of business for the previous weeks, we may find that the level has suddenly risen or dropped. Is this drop or rise due to the new salesman? If he took the route over at the beginning of a very warm period, the returns may show a drop which reflects nothing more than the short seasonal variation; if he took it over just at the beginning of a cool or cold period, the resulting rise may not be due to the salesman's efforts. It is desirable to eliminate guess work in this situation. If an average weekly sales curve is plotted for all of the employees in the organization, these fluctuations can readily be spotted. Now, if the new salesman shows a disproportionate change to the average weekly level, we can detect whether he is improving or declining in relative sales volume and thereby take measures to correct the difficulty before the cost becomes too high.

In summarizing, we may say that the formulae proposed for determining individual efficiency are of decided value in checking on the subjective estimates of door-to-door salesmen and make it possible to eliminate inferior men at an earlier period than has heretofore been possible.

# 29 Management Quality and Its Effect on Selection Test Validity

LEONARD W. FERGUSON (Assisted by
JOHN J. HOPKINS)

The most widely used measure of sales aptitude in the field of life insurance is a test published by the Life Insurance Agency Management Association. This test is known as the Aptitude Index.

The Aptitude Index has had a long and honorable history. It had its beginnings in 1919 in a weighted application blank devised by Miss G. V. Cope of the Sales Research Department of the Phoenix Mutual Life Insurance Company. Shortly thereafter, Miss Grace Manson, then a graduate student at the Carnegie Institute of Technology, expanded on this work for her doctoral dissertation. Later, Dr. Arthur Kornhauser added a personality section, and, finally, Dr. Albert Kurtz revised the test and subjected both of its component parts to thorough and extensive validation. Kurtz completed his work in 1938, and since that time more than one million prospective agents have had their fate decided in part by the marks they have secured on the Aptitude Index.

Kurtz used as criteria both production and survival. He assigned item or scoring weights such that the Aptitude Index makes possible valid predictions of survival for one year, or for two years, and of production for either of these periods of time. Subsequent to Kurtz' work, many member companies of the Life Insurance Agency Management Association have conducted revalidation studies, and in general, whenever appropriate criteria have been employed, these companies have been able to reaffirm the basic validity of the Aptitude Index. There is no question but what this test has been, and is, of great service in increasing the effectiveness of the process by which insurance agents in this country and in Canada have been, and are being, selected.

In spite of the long and honorable history of the Aptitude Index, and in spite of its basic validity, it is a truism that the Aptitude Index does not make possible perfect predictions. The reasons for this are many and are well known, so we need not recite them here. Our task in this paper

From *Personnel Psychology*, 1951, *4*, 141–150. Presented at the Brooklyn meetings of the Eastern Psychological Association, March 30, 1951.

is to examine the operation of a factor often said to be a determinant of success in the life insurance business, and one which is frequently alleged to have a differentiating effect upon the validity of the predictions made from the Aptitude Index. This factor is the quality of district or agency management.

It seems natural for us to suppose that when quality of district or agency management is high, agents should be more successful than when quality of district or agency management is low. In addition, it would also seem logical for us to assume that variations in quality of district or agency management should affect the accuracy of the predictions we can make from the scores on the Aptitude Index.

Management quality is, at best, a vague term. But, in this instance, we have in mind an index based upon a number of factors considered important in the management of the district offices of the Metropolitan Life Insurance Company. We need not review all of the elements comprising this index (there are 15 of them) but in general we may state that they are designed to reflect district production, conservation of business, and the quality of personnel—this last factor being measured by the number of promotions, the number of agents qualified for various honors and the number of (presumably) avoidable terminations. It can be argued, of course, that factors other than quality of district or agency management can cause variations in these items. However, it seems legitimate for us to assume that quality of district or agency management can and does play a significant part in the variations which are involved.

THREE PROBLEMS

We have in this paper a three-fold task. First, we must determine the extent to which agent performance is related to the quality of district or agency management. Second, we must determine the extent to which agent performance is related to agent aptitude. And third, we must determine the extent to which this latter relation can be affected by variations in the quality of district or agency management.

In order to answer our first question, we have divided 524 agents into three groups according to whether they worked in districts classified above average, average or below average in management quality. Then for each of these groups we have determined the per cent of agents falling into above average, average or below average criterion or performance groups—these groups being divided according to production and income.

We find (see Table 29.1) that 23 per cent of the agents working in districts above average in management quality, 20 per cent of the agents working in districts average in management quality, and 9 per cent of the agents working in districts below average in management quality made an above average income during their first two years in the life insurance business. These figures give odds approximately 5 to 2 in favor of agents working in districts above average in management quality. Conversely, (see Table 29.1 again), we find that 12 per cent of the agents working in districts above average in management quality, 24 per cent of the agents working in districts average in management quality, and 35 per cent of the agents working in districts below average in management quality made a below average income during their first two years in the life insurance business. Here the pertinent odds are approximately 3 to 1

TABLE 29.1. *Agent's income in relation to management quality and aptitude index scores*

ROW NO.		NUMBER	Below Average, Per Cent	Average, Per Cent	Above Average, Per Cent	Total, Per Cent
	Management Quality					
1	Above Average	82	12	65	23	100
2	Average	298	24	56	20	100
3	Below Average	144	35	56	9	100
	Total	524				
	Aptitude Index					
4	Above Average	191	23	53	24	100
5	Average	266	26	58	16	100
6	Below Average	67	33	61	6	100
	Total	524				
	Management Quality and Aptitude Index					
	Management Quality: Above Average					
7	Aptitude Index: Above Average	32	12	54	34	100
8	Aptitude Index: Average	43	16	65	19	100
9	Aptitude Index: Below Average	7	14	86	0	100
	Management Quality: Average					
10	Aptitude Index: Above Average	104	41	33	26	100
11	Aptitude Index: Average	147	26	54	20	100
12	Aptitude Index: Below Average	47	34	57	9	100
	Management Quality: Below Average					
13	Aptitude Index: Above Average	55	42	43	15	100
14	Aptitude Index: Average	76	29	64	7	100
15	Aptitude Index: Below Average	13	38	62	0	100
	Total	524				

against agents working in districts below average in management quality. A correlational summary of these results, as well as of those for our two production criteria, is given in row 1 of Table 29.4. (See, however, rows 1 to 3 in Tables 29.2 and 29.3 for additional details.) We can say with confidence that quality of district management is related to agent performance.

To find the answer to our second question, "Is agent performance related to agent aptitude?" we divided our 524 agents into three groups according to whether they had received above average, average or below

TABLE 29.2. *Ordinary production in relation to management quality and aptitude index scores*

ROW NO.		NUMBER	Below Average, Per Cent	Average, Per Cent	Above Average, Per Cent	Total, Per Cent
	Management Quality					
1	Above Average	82	20	54	26	100
2	Average	298	28	53	19	100
3	Below Average	144	33	54	13	100
	Total	524				
	Aptitude Index					
4	Above Average	191	22	53	25	100
5	Average	266	30	55	15	100
6	Below Average	67	33	55	12	100
	Total	524				
	Management Quality and Aptitude Index					
	Management Quality: Above Average					
7	Aptitude Index: Above Average	32	*6*	60	*34*	100
8	Aptitude Index: Average	43	28	51	21	100
9	Aptitude Index: Below Average	7	29	57	14	100
	Management Quality: Average					
10	Aptitude Index: Above Average	104	19	55	26	100
11	Aptitude Index: Average	147	*31*	*54*	*15*	100
12	Aptitude Index: Below Average	47	36	49	15	100
	Management Quality: Below Average					
13	Aptitude Index: Above Average	55	36	48	16	100
14	Aptitude Index: Average	76	32	55	13	100
15	Aptitude Index: Below Average	13	*23*	77	0	100
	Total	524				

SELECTION TEST VALIDITY

average Aptitude Index scores. Then for each of these groups, we determined the per cent of agents falling into above average, average or below average criterion performance groups.

Table 29.1 (rows 4 to 6) shows that 24 per cent of the agents with Aptitude Index scores above average, 16 percent of those with average Aptitude Index scores, and 6 per cent of those with Aptitude Index scores below average made an above average income during their first two years in the life insurance business. The pertinent odds are approximately 4 to 1 in favor of agents with Aptitude Index scores above average. Table

TABLE 29.3. *Industrial production in relation to management quality and aptitude index scores*

ROW NO.		NUMBER	Below Average, Per Cent	Average, Per Cent	Above Average, Per Cent	Total, Per Cent
	Management Quality					
1	Above Average	82	10	69	21	100
2	Average	298	21	60	19	100
3	Below Average	144	28	62	10	100
	Total	524				
	Aptitude Index					
4	Above Average	191	18	58	24	100
5	Average	266	23	63	14	100
6	Below Average	67	24	67	9	100
	Total	524				
	Management Quality and Aptitude Index					
	Management Quality: Above Average					
7	Aptitude Index: Above Average	32	*3*	*72*	*25*	100
8	Aptitude Index: Average	43	14	65	21	100
9	Aptitude Index: Below Average	7	12	86	0	100
	Management Quality: Average					
10	Aptitude Index: Above Average	104	13	63	24	100
11	Aptitude Index: Average	147	*23*	*59*	*18*	100
12	Aptitude Index: Below Average	47	30	59	11	100
	Management Quality: Below Average					
13	Aptitude Index: Above Average	55	35	41	24	100
14	Aptitude Index: Average	76	28	71	1	100
15	Aptitude Index: Below Average	13	*8*	*84*	*8*	100
	Total	524				

29.1 (rows 4 to 6) shows, also, that 23 per cent of the agents with Aptitude Index scores above average, 26 per cent of the agents with average Aptitude Index scores, and 33 per cent of the agents with Aptitude Index scores below average made a below average income during their first two years in the life insurance business. We see that the appropriate odds are approximately 3 to 2 against agents with low scores on the Aptitude Index. Our correlational summary of these results, and of those for our production criteria, is given in row 2 of Table 29.4. (See rows 4 to 6 in Tables 29.2 and 29.3 for additional details.)

And now, what about agents' performance in relation to district

TABLE 29.4. *Selection test validity as affected by management quality**

ROW NO.		NUMBER			CORRELATION	
		Districts	Agents	Income	Ordinary	Industrial
	(Management Quality and Aptitude Index versus Agent Performance)					
1	Management quality	340	524	.22	.22	.20
2	Aptitude Index	340	524	.22	.21	.11
3	Management quality and Aptitude Index	340	524	.31	.31	.23
	(Aptitude Index versus Criteria)					
4	Management quality: Above Average	58	82	.35	.34	.11
5	Management quality: Average	196	298	.24	.25	.15
6	Management quality: Below Average	86	144	.08	.03	.01
	(Criterion Reliability)					
7	First year versus second year	340	524	.69	.60	.56
8	Estimated Spearman-Brown reliability for two years	340	524	.82	.75	.72
	(Management Quality and Aptitude Index versus Agent Performance—Corrected Coefficients)					
9	Management quality	340	524	.24	.25	.24
10	Aptitude Index	340	524	.24	.24	.13
11	Management quality and Aptitude Index	340	524	.34	.36	.27
	(Aptitude Index versus Criteria—Corrected Coefficients)					
12	Management quality: Above Average	58	82	.38	.39	.13
13	Management quality: Average	196	298	.26	.29	.18
14	Management quality: Below Average	86	144	.09	.03	.01

management quality and Aptitude Index scores jointly considered? We find (see row 7 in Table 29.1) that 34 per cent of the agents working in districts above average in management quality and who also have Aptitude Index scores above average made an above average income during their first two years in the life insurance business. The corresponding figure for agents working in districts average in management quality and who also have average Aptitude Index scores (see row 11 in Table 29.1) is 20 per cent. Finally, the per cent is zero (see row 15 in Table 29.1) for agents working in districts below average in management quality and who also have Aptitude Index scores below average. The odds in favor of agents with Aptitude Index scores above average and who work under superior management are indeterminate, but they are obviously high.

We also find (refer, again, to rows 7, 11 and 15 in Table 29.1) that 12 per cent of the agents with high Aptitude Index scores who work under superior management, 26 per cent of the agents with average Aptitude Index scores who work under middling managment, and 38 per cent of the agents with Aptitude Index scores below average who work under inferior management made a below average income during their first two years in the life insurance business. Here the odds (in a ratio of over 5 to 1) are clearly against agents with low scores on the Aptitude Index who must also work under inferior management. Our correlational summary for these figures, as well as for our production criteria, is given in row 3 of Table 29.4. (See rows 7 to 15 in Tables 29.2 and 29.3 for additional details.)

Let us now consider our last question. "Does quality of district management have any effect upon, or relation to, the accuracy with which we can predict agent performance from a knowledge of Aptitude Index scores?" In other words, is the accuracy of a prediction of agent performance (from a knowledge of an Aptitude Index score) contingent upon the quality of district management? Our answer is, "yes," as the correlational data in rows 4 to 6 of Table 29.4 clearly show. The better the quality of district management, the more accurate our predictions.

TREND REVEALED

These are interesting correlations and the trend they reveal is most provocative. It is not caused by artifacts in the distributions (either test score or criterion) as all these distributions are reasonably normal. Furthermore, the average Aptitude Index score is the same for all three groups of districts. And the spread of all criterion distributions remains constant. Therefore, we are forced to the conclusion that there is a substantial and significant change in test score validity according to quality of district or agency management.

At the moment, our rationalization of this result is to the effect that agent performance will fall most nearly in line with agent aptitude in those districts having a management capable of getting agents to perform at or near maximum capacity. In districts poorly or inadequately managed, agent performance is, in many instances, much less than that of maximum capacity. So the relation between capacity and performance is, in these latter districts, much attenuated.

You will have noted that we have placed more emphasis upon our income criterion than upon our two production criteria. And you will probably have decided that we have done this because it is with this criterion that we most frequently achieve our most clear-cut results. While this may be true, an additional reason for our emphasis upon income is that it is our most reliable criterion. Measured by the correlations between first and second year performance, the reliabilities of our criterion variables can be said to be in the neighborhood of the figures given in row 8 of Table 29.4. And by the way, if these reliability figures are used to correct our test-criterion correlations in rows 1 to 6, we secure the unattenuated correlations given in rows 9 to 14.

CONCLUSION

In conclusion, we believe we have demonstrated, again, that agent performance, as measured by production or income, can be predicted with a substantial degree of validity from the scores on the Aptitude Index. Second, that the accuracy of these predictions is materially affected by, or related to, quality of district or agency management—which is itself and in its own right, a valid predictor of agent performance. And third, that in making predictions of agent performance, we should give joint, simultaneous and, incidentally, equal consideration to the two factors of agent aptitude and quality of district management.

30 A Factorial Study of Administrative Behavior

RALPH M. STOGDILL, CARROLL L. SHARTLE,
ROBERT J. WHERRY, and WILLIAM E. JAYNES

SUMMARY

The present paper describes a study of 470 Navy officers who occupied 45 different types of positions in 47 different organizations. These officers were divided into 120 groups. Each group consisted of all the officers in the same specialty in the same type of organization. In order to avoid the computation of intercorrelations among the 120 groups, an iterative method of factor analysis was employed. Eight factors emerged. The factors isolate those groups of officers who exhibit similar patterns of performance. It is found that groups of persons occupying the same type of position tend to fall in the same factor. The factors also reflect differences in organizations, in that some types of positions isolated by the factors are found almost exclusively either in large or in small organizations, or either on ships or in units ashore.

INTRODUCTION

The present research was designed to test the hypothesis that groups of persons occupying similar administrative and executive positions will exhibit similar patterns of behavior, even though the groups are found in different types of organizations. This hypothesis carries the implication that patterns of administrative behavior will be highly determined by the demands of the job. It does not imply that job demands are the only factors that determine performance.

There are several reasons why it is important to test this hypothesis. First, in spite of four decades of research since World War I the methods available for the selection and evaluation of persons for high level execu-

From *Personnel Psychology*, 1958, 8, 165–180. A cooperative contribution of the Office of Naval Research (Contract N6ori-17 T. O. III N R 171 123) and The Ohio State University Research Foundation.

tive positions have been shown to have very low validities from one sample to another. Various tests of intelligence and personality are widely used for screening purposes. But, given an effective initial screening program, there remains the problem of the differential selection and assignment of personnel in groups that are relatively homogeneous in intelligence and, perhaps, also in training, personality, and other factors. This is the problem confronting industry and the armed services in the appointment and assignment of men to high level positions.

Second, the majority of studies in military and industrial personnel appear to have been conducted on the assumption of a general criterion of effective leadership or executive performance which should be equally valid for all types of positions in all types of situations. However, if it can be shown that patterns of behavior vary from one type of position to another, it might be possible to develop methods and criteria which are specific to particular families of positions. If administrative performance is determined by job demands, it seems reasonable to believe that selection and assignment might be improved by taking these factors, as well as the characteristics of individuals, into account.

It is the purpose of this study, not to develop complete and usable instruments for the selection of administrative personnel, but to determine whether patterns of behavior can be isolated which are related to specific types or families of positions.

METHODS AND PROCEDURES

The subjects of this study are commissioned officers in the United States Navy. The data were collected by means of interviews and prepared scales and forms. The development, reliability and validity of the methods are described in detail by Shartle and Stogdill (2). The measures include: (1) *a priori* scales of level in the vertical organization hierarchy and military rank; (2) sociometric score (number of nominations received as work partner); (3) self-descriptions of level of responsibility, authority and delegation made on items scaled by the method of equal appearing intervals; (4) per cent of time spent in various kinds of working contacts with persons (10 items including attending meetings, interviewing outside persons, conferring with assistants, etc.); (5) per cent of time spent in various kinds of individual effort (10 items including reading and answering mail, writing reports, mathematical computation, etc.); (6) per cent of time spent in major responsibilities (14 items including planning, coordination, public relations, etc.); (7) self-descriptions of leader behavior (5 scores obtained from items describing communicative behavior, integrative behavior, acting as group representative, etc.).

Those measures provided data on 46 different variables of behavior and status. The data for each variable were coded on a scale ranging from zero to nine (0 to 9). This method of coding preserved the integrity of the original distribution of raw scores, except that the zero (0) and nine (9) codes brought extremely deviant scores closer to the mean than in the raw score distributions. No attempt was made to force a normalized distribution for each variable, as is required by Stephenson's (3) method of correlating persons with persons. It is believed that the skewness of the distributions for some of the variables is not sufficient to affect the results to any undue degree.

The 470 officers who were subjects of this study ranged in rank from admiral to ensign. They occupied 45 differentiated positions or billets in 47 Naval organizations. The organizations were of the following numbers and types: 4 units under the Secretary of Defense an dthe Chief of Naval Operations, 1 naval bureau (selected units), 2 naval district command staffs, 6 command staffs, 1 naval air station, 2 hydrographic units, 2 cruisers, 10 submarines, 4 destroyers, 3 mine ships, 3 landing ships and supply ships combined as a group, and 9 landing ships (LST, LSM). This classification results in 12 types of organizations with multiple representation in each type except naval bureaus and air stations.

The 45 types of billets are thus located in 12 types of organizations. Nine of the billets are found in only a single type of organization. One billet, operations officer, is found in nine different types of organizations. The remaining billets are located in two to seven types of organizations. This multiple representation of billets and organizations results in 105 groups, each group composed of all the officers in the same type of billet in the same type of organization. Fifteen additional groups were formed, representing combinations of officers in the same type of specialty but from different types of organizations. These combinations were made to avoid a large number of unreliable groups represented by a single individual. The average number of persons per group was 3.92. Two groups were composed of one person each. The largest group was composed of 20 persons.

The grouping of persons in the same specialty and in the same type of organization makes it possible to test the additional hypothesis that persons in similar types of organizations will exhibit similar patterns of behavior even though they are in different types of positions. We might also have hypothesized that different persons will show somewhat different patterns of behavior even though they are in the same type of billet and in the same type of organization, but we are not interested in testing this hypothesis. Rather, we seek to control any such possible effect of individual variance in the present study by combining the scores of two or more persons within a given specialty in the same type of organization. This will remove such random variability which might tend to obscure differences between specialties and/or organizations, thus securing more reliable measures to satisfy our main purpose.

It will be noted, then, that this study is based on 46 different measures for each of 120 groups representing 47 organizations of 12 types (plus a combined group), 45 types of billets, and a total of 470 officers. It is this matrix of data which this report analyzes and seeks to explain.

THE FACTOR ANALYSIS

The scores of all the officers in each of the 120 groups were combined and averaged for each of the 46 variables. Since the scores for each variable were reduced to a scale ranging from 0 to 9, it is possible to use these scores in order to correlate each group with every other group. This, however, is a very time consuming and laborious process.

Fortunately, Wherry and Winer (6) have developed an iterative method of factor analysis which does not require the computation of the complete table of intercorrelations among the 120 groups. This approach is an improved modification of an earlier method developed by Wherry and Gaylord. Wherry, Campbell, and Perloff (5) have demonstrated that the Wherry-Gaylord procedure and the Thurstone multiple group analysis of subtests result in the same factors. Winer (7) has shown that the new Wherry-Winer method gives results nearly identical with an analysis based upon the actual intercorrelation of the items themselves.

The Wherry-Winer method requires the preparation of a set of reference keys which hypothetically represent the different patterns of performance that might be expected to emerge from the analysis. The number of reference keys must exceed the number of dimensions present in the data to be analyzed. Thirteen such reference keys were prepared.

The first step in the factor analysis consisted of computing the intercorrelations among the 13 reference keys. A modified Doolittle method was next used to determine (a) the number of dimensions necessary to determine and describe the thirteen reference keys, (b) which selection of the original set of keys would best reflect those dimensions, and (c) a set of weights which could be used to change Group-Key Correlations into Group-Independent Factor Correlations. The Doolittle solution resulted in the selection of eight keys.

The next step consisted of computing the correlations between each of the eight selected reference keys and each of the 120 groups. These coefficients represent the projections of the various groups upon the oblique (correlated) reference keys (axes). These oblique factor loadings were next converted to projections (loadings) of the groups upon the orthogonal (independent) factors by means of the transformation weights obtained from the Doolittle solution. Eight factors emerged.

The next step was the rotation of these orthogonal axes to maximize meaningfulness. The complete tables of coded data and of the various

STUDY OF ADMINISTRATIVE BEHAVIOR 395

stages of the factor analysis are reported elsewhere by Stogdill, Wherry and Jaynes (4).

An examination of the h^2 values for the 120 groups indicated that on the average the factors explain about 60 per cent of the variance for a particular group. For approximately one out of eight this value exceeded 75 per cent, while it fell below 30 per cent in less than 2 per cent of the cases. It can be concluded that the eight factors explain a large part of the non-error portion of the profile variation.

THE IDENTIFICATION OF THE FACTORS

A factor is defined or identified by the variables (or in the present case, by the groups) with high loadings on the factor. Since each group in this study was represented by scores on a great diversity of variables, it seemed desirable to utilize the profiles of these scores as a further aid in identifying the factor. The profiles of scores of those groups with the highest loadings on a factor were compared with a profile of the average scores of the 470 officers combined. When the profile points of the specialty groups deviated markedly from a corresponding profile point for the combined total group, this deviation identified a variable which might be regarded as uniquely characteristic of the groups with high loadings on the factor.

In the following tables, the groups are arranged in order of their l^2/h^2 values. The value, l^2/h^2, is an index which indicates the proportion of the common factor variance which is accounted for by the factor in question.

The groups with the highest loadings on Factor I are public information officers. Comparison of the score profiles of these groups with the average profile of all officers combined indicates that groups with high loadings on Factor I exceed the average in writing for publication, con-

TABLE 30.1. *Public relations representatives*
Groups with Highest Loadings (1) on Factor I

Specialty	Organization	l	h^2	l^2/h^2
Public Information	Combined	.64	.69	.59
Public Information	Nav. District	.62	.69	.55
Training (Spec.)	Air Station	.45	.57	.36
Dental	Nav. District	.36	.63	.21
Public Information	Ch. Nav. Op.	.34	.62	.19
Training (Gen.)	Combined	.34	.64	.18
Operations	LST	.31	.53	.18

sulting outsiders, reflection, and representation (leader behavior); but are below average in consulting juniors, inspection, examining reports and personnel functions. Both the billet titles and the characteristic performances point to an out-of-organization orientation with writing for release, consulation with outside persons and speaking as group representative constituting the major responsibilities. We feel quite safe therefore in identifying this factor as a group of *Public Relations Representatives*. There is a trend for persons engaged in these performances to be located in the larger, shore based organizations.

TABLE 30.2. *Professional consultants*
Groups with Highest Loadings on Factor II

Specialty	Organization	l	h^2	l^2/h^2
Legal	Combined	.60	.62	.59
Accounting	Nav. District	.62	.68	.56
Commanding	Cruisers	.61	.72	.52
Publications	Combined	.58	.69	.49
Hydrographer	Hydr.	.47	.46	.48
Public Works	Nav. District	.58	.75	.45
Chaplain	Combined	.47	.53	.42
First Lieut.	Command Staff	.36	.31	.42
Supply	LST	.53	.72	.39
Accounting	Command Staff	.42	.45	.39
Navigation	Land & Supply	.34	.30	.39
Accounting	Air St.	.43	.55	.33
Supply	Destroyers	.41	.51	.33
Supply	Command Staff	.49	.74	.32
Dental	Nav. District	.45	.63	.32
Supply	Subs	.46	.68	.31
Dental	Combined	.42	.57	.31
Accounting	C.N.O.	.28	.37	.21

The groups with high loadings on Factor II consist largely of those billets requiring professionally trained persons such as lawyers, ministers, dentists, accountants, supply officers, and scientists (hydrographers, navigators). The deviant points in their profiles of scores indicate that they spend comparatively large portions of their time in interpretation and consultation of a professional nature. We feel quite safe therefore in identifying them as *Professional Consultants*. Again there appears to be a trend for such personnel to be attached to the larger, higher echelon units, although some appear aboard ship.

The specialty titles with high loadings on Factor III suggest the idea of personnel activities. The deviant profile points indicate that these groups exceed the average in authority, attending meetings, planning and interviewing personnel, and suggest that they function at a rather high level. This interpretation is further reinforced by the fact that all groups represent personnel at the larger, shore based units of organization. The combination of these considerations enables us to identify this factor as *Personnel Administrators*.

Factor IV contains more groups with significant loadings than does any other factor. The l^2/h^2 values for 37 of these groups are above .30. Due to considerations of space, only those groups with l^2/h^2 values above .45 are reported here.

TABLE 30.3. *Personnel administrators*
Groups with High Loadings on Factor III

Specialty	Organization	l	h^2	l^2/h^2
Personnel (Spec.)	Air St.	.60	.59	.61
Training (Gen.)	Bureau	.48	.50	.46
Nav. Reserve	Combined	.47	.52	.43
Medical	Air St.	.51	.61	.43
Training (Spec.)	Air St.	.48	.57	.40
Supply	Air St.	.50	.66	.38
Research	Combined	.44	.57	.34
Education	Bureau	.47	.65	.34
Personnel (Gen.)	C. S.	.47	.68	.32
Communication	N. D.	.37	.43	.32
Type Training	Air St.	.43	.59	.31
Personnel (Gen.)	Bureau	.38	.49	.29
Personnel (Gen.)	N. D.	.41	.67	.25

The billet titles (electrical, electronics, engines, gunnery, navigation, engineering, communication, medical, etc.) have a generally technical sound. This technical aspect is reinforced when we find use of machines, mathematical computation, and technical performance among the differentiating performances. The fact that they are officers, plus the presence of teaching, supervision, and speechmaking (in) among the differentiating performances mark these men as supervisors. They tend to appear largely on ships (cruisers, destroyers, submarines, LSTs, mine ships, landing and supply ships) or in some technical operating group located at a larger shore center (air station, beach group, command staff). We can clearly then identify this group as *Technical Supervisors*.

The officers in Factor V are mostly billeted as operations officers. It appears that they prepare schedules and procedures after reading technical publications and interviewing and consulting peers. They regard their work as reflecting high level and authority yet have relatively low military rank. We therefore identify this group as *Schedule-Procedure Makers*. They tend to be associated predominantly with ships.

The billets (public works, damage control) in Factor VI tend to suggest construction and maintenance performances with some hint of contracting financial outlay for these purposes. Such performances as use of machines, mathematical computation, preparation of charts, and technical performance again reinforce the technical and numerical interpreta-

TABLE 30.4. *Technical supervisors*
Groups with High Loadings on Factor IV

Specialty	Organization	l	h^2	l^2/h^2
Electrical	Cruisers	.73	.65	.82
Electrical	Land & Supply	.61	.49	.76
Electronics	Destroyer	.62	.53	.72
Main Engines	Cruisers	.66	.62	.70
Electronics	Combined	.71	.73	.69
Gunnery	Cruisers	.71	.75	.67
Navigation	Cruisers	.55	.45	.67
Communications	Destroyer	.62	.59	.65
Communications	Cruisers	.71	.82	.62
Aircraft Maint.	Air St.	.59	.59	.59
Electronics	Subs	.63	.69	.57
Gunnery	Land & Supply	.58	.62	.55
Gunnery	Mine	.48	.42	.55
Medical	Cruisers	.46	.38	.55
Commissary	Combined	.56	.59	.53
Engineering	Subs	.52	.51	.53
Gunnery	LST	.55	.60	.50
Operations	Subs	.58	.69	.49
Engineering	LST	.52	.57	.48
Engineering	Destroyers	.58	.72	.47
Bttn. Cdr.	(Beach Group)	.49	.54	.45

tion. The further activities such as professional consultation, interpretation, and the attending of meetings point to the planning and administrative nature of their work. This group is therefore identified as *Maintenance Administrators*. In civilian life, such men might be called

TABLE 30.5. *Schedule-procedure makers*
Groups with High Loadings on Factor V

Specialty	Organization	l	h^2	l^2/h^2
Operations	Land & Supply	.52	.66	.41
Operations	Mine	.40	.50	.32
Operations	Cruisers	.49	.84	.29
Gunnery	Destroyers	.30	.44	.21
Planning	N. D.	.33	.57	.19
Operations	Destroyers	.28	.42	.19

contractors or *purchasing agents.* They are located both at larger shore installations and on ships.

The billet designations suggest that there are two groups of specialties measured by Factor VII. These are as follows:

(a) Commanders (commander, commanding officer, deck officer,

TABLE 30.6. *Maintenance administrators*
Groups with High Loadings on Factor VI

Specialty	Organization	l	h^2	l^2/h^2
Public Works	C. S.	.35	.26	.48
Damage Control	Destroyers	.34	.31	.38
Ship's Store	Combined	.44	.62	.31
Operations	Air St.	.42	.59	.30
Public Works	Air St.	.43	.67	.27
Public Works	N. D.	.43	.75	.25
Gunnery	Subs	.44	.76	.25
Supply	Subs	.40	.68	.24
Supply	Destroyers	.35	.51	.24

first lieutenant) who may be located either in a high echelon organization (command staff) or on a ship (land & supply, destroyer).

(b) Program Directors (medical, intelligence, welfare, training, chaplain, and planning) almost always found at a high echelon organization (naval district, command staff, or combinations including such levels).

TABLE 30.7. *Directors or decision makers*
Groups with High Loadings on Factor VII

Specialty	Organization	l	h^2	l^2/h^2
Medical	N. D.	.55	.64	.47
Medical	C. S.	.55	.70	.43
Commander	C. S.	.50	.65	.38
First Lieut.	Land & Supply	.48	.60	.38
Intelligence	Combined	.41	.46	.37
Welfare	N. D.	.41	.51	.33
Training	Combined	.41	.55	.31
Administrative O.	N. D.	.35	.45	.27
Planning	C. S.	.30	.38	.24
Planning	N. D.	.36	.57	.23
Chaplain	Combined	.35	.53	.23
Deck Officer	Land & Supply	.36	.60	.22
Commanding Officer	Destroyer	.35	.60	.20

Inspection of the profiles indicates that these groups are unique in four performances: inspection, integrative behavior delegation, and making speeches outside the organization. These functions clearly suggest a person in complete authority over some group or program. Other differentiatingly high profile points for representation, cordial relations with juniors, preparing procedures, examining reports and holding high military rank also point to the relatively high standing of these people in these organizations. The absence of technical performance and lack of peers to consult (low profile points) also point to their high status.

It is clear from the differentiating duties that representatives of the groups of Program Directors are not engaging in the actual professional or technical performances of their professions, but are instead directing or heading up programs in these professional areas. They too, in this

TABLE 30.8. *Coordinators*
Groups with High Loadings on Factor VIII

Specialty	Organization	l	h^2	l^2/h^2
Executive O.	Destroyers	.61	.64	.58
Executive O.	Cruisers	.61	.67	.56
Engineering	Cruisers	.67	.80	.56
Operations	C. S.	.61	.69	.54
Aide	Combined	.49	.51	.47
Commander	Mine	.50	.54	.46
Chief of Staff	N. D.	.57	.72	.45
Executive	Mine	.56	.71	.44
Personnel (Spe.)	N. D.	.55	.69	.44
Aircraft Maint.	C. S.	.48	.52	.44
First Lieut.	Cruisers	.55	.69	.44
Engineering	Mine	.42	.40	.44
Executive	Land & Supply	.54	.68	.43
Chief Staff O.	C. S.	.53	.66	.42
Base Maint.	C. N. O.	.41	.41	.41
Logistics	N. D.	.47	.55	.40

sense, exercise the command function over their subordinates in their professions. In the business world we would call these persons top management officers or executives. (We avoid the term here because of the billet title Executive Officer). We therefore will identify this group as *Directors* or *Decision Makers*.

Factor VIII was the second most numerous in the number of groups for which it was important. Twenty nine groups obtained l^2/h^2 values above .20. Only groups with l^2/h^2 values above .39 are listed here.

Among the billets with high loading on Factor VIII, we find such titles as executive officer, chief of staff, chief staff officer, aide, administration officer, and administrative assistant. The presence of commanding officers of small ships and of shore units suggests that while they have decision making functions in their own units, they also have the function of executing and carrying out orders from commanders of higher units of organization.

The differentiating profile points for these groups indicate that while operating at a high level and holding high military rank they, nevertheless, consult juniors, carry out personnel functions, and engage in direct supervision. They also spend considerable portions of their time in scheduling and in reading reports. They are not engaged in technical performances and spend little time in reading technical publications. These men appear to be the coordinators who execute and coordinate the decisions of the directors. In business organizations they would be called intermediate management officials. We choose to identify them as *Coordinators*.

DISCUSSION

The results of this research lend considerable support to the hypothesis that groups of persons in similar specialties in different kinds of organizations will exhibit similar patterns of performance. The study also yields the encouraging finding that the number of unique patterns of performance is not as great as the number of billets. Eight independent dimensions have been found along which administrative behavior can be described, and these eight dimensions enable us to predict on the average nearly 60 per cent of the variability among 46 types of performance for a given group. This percentage increases as the number of persons representing the group increases.

The factors adequately account for from 40 per cent to 89 per cent of the variance for 111 of the 120 groups. The nine groups with h^2 values below .40 have one thing in common: all except one of the groups is composed of two persons each. The ninth group is composed of four cases. A possible explanation of the poor prediction for the unexplained groups may be simply one of unreliability due to inadequate sampling.

It should be pointed out that many of the groups received high loadings on more than one factor, indicating that their work is complex in nature and can be adequately described only in terms of the performances represented by two or more factors. When the profiles of factor loadings for groups in similar specialties were compared, some specialties showed closely similar profiles for all the groups represented. Almost identical profiles were found for groups in the following positions: chief of staff, planning officer, public information officer, beach group commander, dental officer, first lieutenant aboard ship, communications officer aboard ship, electrical officer and electronics officer aboard ship. Specialties in which the factor profiles of different groups were not well matched consisted of operations officers, navigators, and damage control officers, suggesting that the status and/or duties of these positions may not be well standardized from one organization to another.

Some of the specialties showed distinct sub-group factor profiles which reflected differences in type of organization. These included (a) more Technical Supervision by executive officers when aboard ship than when ashore, (b) more Personnel Administration and Less Technical Supervision by operations officers when at large shore establishments than when aboard small ships, (c) more Technical Supervision and Coordination by first lieutenants when aboard ship than when ashore, (d) more Technical Supervision and less Personnel Management by communications officers when aboard ship than when ashore, and (e) more Personnel Management and Decision Making and less Technical Supervision by medical officers when located in naval districts or command staffs than when aboard ship. These findings lend some support to the hypothesis that performance will vary according to type of organization.

There remains the question as to whether a type of analysis which places such diverse specialties as Electronics Officer, Gunnery Officer, Medical Officer and Commissary Officer in the same factor represents any theoretical or practical advance. The unique performances of specialties with high loadings on Factor IV include use of machines, mathematical computations, and technical performances, as well as supervision and teaching. It is obvious that they do not know the same specialized branches of mathematics or science, substitute in the same equations, utilize the same professional techniques or operate the same equipment. Can they rightly, then, be regarded as similar in patterns of performance? Except for Medical Officers aboard ship, these officers engage very little in the actual technical performances of their specialties. The technical work is done mostly by the subordinates whom they supervise. They can and do supervise one of these specialties (except medicine) as readily as another. Reference to the interview data indicates that some officers who have technical knowledge of the specialty being supervised feel it to be an advantage in that they are better respected by the people supervised. Those who have little technical knowledge of the specialty being supervised report that it may be an advantage, since they tend to interfere less with the people who are doing the technical work. The results of the present research do not discredit the opinion of the latter group.

A further question remains as to the significance of these findings for the field of personnel selection and assignment. Is there any advantage in knowing that the 47 specialties can be described in terms of 8 rather than 47 different patterns of performance and that persons in similar positions tend to exhibit similar patterns of behavior? These findings would appear to offer considerable encouragement for the differential selection and assignment of personnel for administrative and supervisory positions. It would appear feasible to match persistent personal patterns of administrative behavior with the performance patterns required by the job. This procedure might represent a considerable advance over present methods of selection based on considerations of such general characteristics as initiative, judgement, dependability, and the like. However, much further research will need to be done in order to put this hypothesis to a convincing test.

REFERENCES

1. Jaynes, W. E. *An analysis of differences among navy officer specialties and among navy organizations.* Columbus: The Ohio State University Research Foundation, 1952.
2. Shartle, C. L., & Stogdill, R. M. *Studies in naval leadership: methods and applications, final technical report.* Columbus: The Ohio State University Research Foundation, 1953.
3. Stephenson, W. Correlating persons instead of tests. *Character and Personality*, 1953, *4*, 17–24.
4. Stogdill, R. M., Wherry, R. J., & Jaynes, W. E. *Patterns of leader behavior: a factorial study of navy officer performance.* Columbus: The Ohio State University Research Foundation, 1953.
5. Wherry, R. J., Campbell, J. T., & Perloff, R. An empirical verification of the Wherry-Gaylord iterative factor analysis procedure. *Psychometrika*, 1951, *16*, 67–74.
6. Wherry, R. J., & Winer, B. J. The direct method of factoring items. Unpublished manuscript, 1952.
7. Winer, B. J. *Iterative factor analysis: Its psychological and mathematical bases and limits.* Columbus: The Ohio State University Library. Unpublished doctoral dissertation, 1952.

31 A Further Analysis of the Relations Among Job Performance and Situational Variables

EDWARD E. CURETON and
RAYMOND A. KATZELL

In connection with an investigation of the relationships among employee attitudes, performance, and characteristics of the situation data were collected from 72 divisions of a company. The variables included 5 measures of divisional performance and 5 descriptives of the situation. An oblique-factor analysis of these variables results in 2 positively correlated factors. The first factor is associated negatively with divisional and community size, and positively with productivity and profitability. The second is associated inversely with wage rate, unionization, and proportion of male employees, and positively with turnover. These results, in combination with some previously reported, indicate that performance is related to 2 aspects of the degree of urbanization of the situation.

This paper reports the results of an oblique factor analysis of the correlations presented in Table 1 of the article by Katzell, Barrett, and Parker (1961, p. 67). That table listed the intercorrelations among five measures of job performance and five situational characteristics in a sample of 72 warehousing divisions of a pharmaceutical company. Table 31.1, below, shows the loadings of these variables on the two resulting centroids when rotated to an oblique solution. The two factors are positively correlated, the cosine of the angle between the reference vectors being —.44.

Factor I is associated positively with productivity and inversely with size variables; Factor II is associated positively with turnover and inversely with three other situational variables; it may possibly constitute a female-employee syndrome.

It is of interest to compare these results with those yielded by the orthogonal factor analysis reported in the original article. There, Factor I emerged as a nearly general one, characterized by positive loadings on

From *Journal of Applied Psychology*, 1962, 46, 230

TABLE 31.1. *Rotated oblique factor loadings* (N = 72)

Variable	Factor I	Factor II
Performance variables		
Quantity	.49	.01
Quality	−.09	.14
Profitability	.51	.20
Product-value	.78	−.23
Turnover	−.13	.39
Situational characteristics		
Size of work-force	−.53	−.01
City size	−.60	−.02
Wage rate	.01	−.85
Unionization	−.27	−.44
Percentage male	.05	−.46

the productivity variables and negative loadings on the five situational characteristics. It was interpreted as portraying a small town or nonurban culture pattern. (Turnover was erroneously listed in Table 2 of that article as having a loading of —.32; a recheck prompted by the present results showed that it has virtually no loading on this factor.) Factor II, which was not discussed there because it was both dim and not particularly relevant to the theoretical issue under discussion, generally resembled Factor II as described in the present study.

In summary, the oblique factor solution indicates that the nonurban culture pattern previously reported may be thought of as comprising two positively correlated facets: one reflects small size of plant and community and is associated with relatively high productivity and profitability; the other reflects relatively low wages, proportionately few male employees and the absence of a union, and is associated with relatively high turnover.

REFERENCE

KATZELL, R. A., BARRETT, R. S., & PARKER, T. C. Job satisfaction, job performance, and situational characteristics. *J. appl. Psychol.*, 1961, 45, 65–72.

32 Organizational Conditions and Behavior in 234 Industrial Manufacturing Organizations

GEORGE H. DUNTEMAN

This study was to explore some of the interrelations among 84 variables pertaining to company and formal organization characteristics, management attributes, incentive conditions, worker characteristics, personnel performance, and organizational functions in a sample of 234 manufacturing firms. The data were obtained by an 84-item multiple-choice questionnaire sent to a representative sample of 2,938 manufacturing firms located throughout the United States. The correlations among the 84 variables were factor analyzed and the factors rotated to a simple structure. Fourteen dimensions of organizational attributes and behavior were isolated and interpreted. Among the significant findings was the relatively high independence of organizational attributes and behavior as evidenced by their being defined by separate sets of factors.

In recent years much theory and consequent research on organizational behavior has been evident. However, March and Simon (1958) point out that the writings about organizations are scattered and diverse, and that the literature discloses large discrepancies between hypotheses and evidence. The literature contains many assertions, often with little data to back them up. Research on this topic has traditionally been carried out through laboratory investigations, field experiments, and the intraorganizational approach. Although little laboratory research has been directed toward the investigation of industrial organizations per se, much laboratory research which has been conducted on small groups may be considered to have relevance to the process and perhaps particularly the unprogramed activities of groups that occur in formal organizations (Bass, 1960; Cartwright & Zander, 1960).

Field experiments are characterized by the actual manipulation of variables rather than just by survey and correlational analysis. Coch and

From *Journal of Applied Psychology*, 1966, 50, 300–305. This article is based on the author's doctoral dissertation while at Louisiana State University, prepared under the direction of George J. Palmer, Jr. This study was partially supported by the Office of Naval Research, Contract Nonr 1575(05), Project NR 170-478.

French (1948) have carried out field experiments involving the effect of various types of supervision on worker performance. In general, field experiments involving organizations, especially those involving the manipulation of major variables, are quite scarce for the obvious reason of interference in organizational procedure.

The intraorganizational approach has been utilized by Shartle (1956), McGregor (1960), Rubenstein (1960), Argyris (1960), and others. These researchers attempted to support their hypotheses by survey and correlational analysis of personnel variables within organizations, analysis of unit (e.g., departmental) operations, participant observation, and interview findings.

Most of the current literature of research on real-life organizations has been provided by the intraorganizational approach. Such research typically involves the investigation of one or a small number of firms. The possibility of generalizing from such studies has been necessarily curtailed because there has been no sampling of organizations, of time periods, or control over the relevant organizational variables which would explain the circumstances under which relationships do or do not occur.

An approach which is considered more appropriate for the objectives of organizational study and which overcomes many of the mentioned limitations involves the use of sampling surveys whereby data can be gathered from a large number of organizations. Palmer (1961) examined 35 organizational survey variables pertaining to organizational conditions and personnel performance for a sample of 188 manufacturing firms in a southern metropolitan region. An analysis resulted in eight orthogonal rotated factors. The factors were identified as follows: Retirement Welfare, Cooperation with Survey, Size of Work Force, Thrift Benefits, Cost of Sickness versus Use of Machinery, Job Aversion (e.g., lates, turnover, grievances, and complaints), Insurance Benefits, and finally Product Theft versus Discounts on Product.

Examination of the rotated factors indicated no support for Revans' (1958) notion that less favorable performance is associated with larger firms. Palmer's (1961) analysis also disclosed that productivity, job aversion, and theft were mutually independent behaviors and further that job-aversion behavior was unrelated to any positive incentive conditions investigated. Each of these independent behaviors was found to be related to different organizational conditions.

The purposes of the present study were as follows:

1. The isolation of various independent dimensions of organizational behavior and attributes (the indentification of major sources of variance among companies);

2. Examining the relationships between organization effectiveness, personnel performance, and the extracted factors; determining the char-

acteristics of the factors related to personnel performance and organizational effectiveness.

METHOD

The present investigation was concerned with a factor analysis of a limited number of variables. The areas investigated were as follows: company and formal organization characteristics (e.g., size of firm), management attributes (e.g., average management tenure), incentive conditions (e.g., presence of pension programs), worker characteristics (e.g., percentage of workers who are high school graduates), personnel performance (e.g., turnover), and organizational effectiveness (e.g., number of jobs eliminated by laborsaving devices).

In general, the criteria for selecting these variables were as follows: (*a*) relevance or importance as indicated by current theory and research, (*b*) facilitating factor identification by including Palmer's (1961) factor markers, (*c*) accessibility of the information, and (*d*) objectivity of recording the data. It is important to realize that not all the variables considered in this study were selected to define factors and provide factor saturations, but that some of them were included as controls so that specified influences such as size and age of firm could be recognized and partialed out.

Questionnaire

A multiple-choice questionnaire containing 84 items pertaining to the six areas of organizational attributes and behavior discussed previously was developed and pretested on a sample of local manufacturers.

Sample Survey

A representative list of 2,938 manufacturing firms residing throughout the continental United States was developed. The number of firms selected from each state was based on the proportion of manufacturing in the respective states according to the 1961 United States Statistical Abstracts. However, within each state the firms were drawn at random from the appropriate state directory of manufacturers. The questionnaires were addressed to the personnel managers of the various organizations. It is presumed that either the personnel manager or someone "qualified" in the personnel department answered the questionnaire. It could be that some of the answers are based on estimates. However, the options for most of the items are written so that an exact answer is not necessary, for example, 10–20%. With each questionnaire was sent an explanatory covering letter, a postage-paid return envelope, and two IBM mark-sense cards for recording answers. Each company was offered a free summary report if they desired one. The participating firms were assured that all information would be kept confidential.

Data Analysis

Pearson linear product-moment correlations were utilized to compute the intercorrelations between the 84 variables. Where some respondents reported no information for some questions, correlations among the variables were based upon the number of cases common to each pair of variables. The N for the correlations ranged from 66 to 232. However, the majority of the correlations were based on an N of 180 or more and in only four instances were the correlations based on an N of less than 100.

The 3,486 correlations were subjected to a principal components analysis (unities were placed in the principal diagonal) and rotated to nearly orthogonal, simple structure by the varimax method (Kaiser, 1958).[1] The decision to stop factoring was based upon the diminishing contributions to the total variance of the successively extracted factors.

RESULTS

Returns

Eight percent (234) of the 2,938 questionnaires were returned. The low percentage of returns is attributed in part to the length of the questionnaire, the reluctance to reveal certain information, and the low pulling power of a general appeal by letter. Because of the small number of returns and the consequent possibility of bias, the results of this study must be interpreted with caution. However, the bias, while probably affecting the item means of the questionnaire, might not have appreciably affected the pattern of intercorrelations.

The first 14 unrotated factors extracted accounted for 54% of the total variance. In general, the examination of the 84 lambdas suggested much specificity in the original intercorrelation matrix. After these 14 factors were rotated, it was found that Factor I accounted for 26.7% of the common variance while the remaining 13 factors contributed from 7.9 to 3.8% of the common variance. The rotated factors were nearly orthogonal, the correlations between factors ranging from .00 to .35. However,

[1] A list of the 84 items comprising the questionnaire and the rotated factor loadings of these items has been deposited with the American Documentation Institute. Order Document No. 8896 from ADI Auxiliary Publications Project, Photoduplication Service, Library of Congress, Washington, D. C. 20540. Remit in advance $1.75 for microfilm or $2.50 for photocopies and make checks payable to: Chief, Photoduplication Service, Library of Congress.

only 2 of the 91 intercorrelations were above .20. The majority of the items were defined in terms of either absolute numbers or percentages. Therefore, in most instances, only measures based on percentages can be meaningfully related to size and other variables associated with size. It was expected, for example, that larger firms would have a greater number of absentees.

Factor I: Size of Organization. The variables that load significantly on Factor I seem to be indicative of the size of the organization. Larger firms are able to offer more in the way of recreation, retirement, and insurance programs than smaller firms. Furthermore, larger firms offer more opportunities for promotions and pay increases.

The volume of personnel behaviors such as absenteeism, accidents, discharges, behavior problems, and theft is highly related to size as would be expected on the basis of item definitions. However, there is no evidence to indicate that these performance measures are disproportionately related to size, lending no support to Revans' (1958) conclusion that generally less favorable preformance is associated with size. Job-aversion behaviors such as lates and turnover were completely independent of size.

Larger firms experience more strikes, etc., and a higher percentage of worker grievances than do smaller firms. A partial explanation for this relationship might be found in the increased union activity in the larger firms.

The structure of this factor also suggests that larger firms tend to be more attractive to job seekers as indicated by the percentage increase in applicants loading on this factor. This observation lends support to March and Simon (1958) who contend that larger firms are more visible and therefore more likely to attract applicants.

Factor II: Economic Growth. This factor is characterized by growth primarily in the economic sphere of industrial functioning. It is important to note that organizational growth is independent of size, management education and experience, employee skills and performance, and all the other organizational variables considered. It would seem highly probable, because of the many internal conditions examined here, that conditions external to the organization play a substantial role in the organizational growth of a business enterprise.

Factor III: Tardiness versus Family Responsibility. The positive pole of Factor III is substantially related to the incidence of morning and afternoon lates and the negative pole moderately related to the percentage of employees who are married with two or more children. This observation suggests that workers with family responsibilities are less likely to exhibit irresponsibility on the job at least in respect to reporting late.

Factor IV: Pay-Skill Level. Various incentive conditions (primarily pay level) and worker characteristics (skill, sex, and education) covary together, contributing essentially all of the factorial variance to this factor. This factor exemplifies the common observation that jobs requiring education and skill are more highly rewarded than those that do not. An implication here is that money buys skills, but not necessarily better performance.

Factor V: Personnel Tenure. Both management and worker tenure are highly interdependent. This supports the notion that, in general, firms have attractions which transcend all levels of employment. Besides the expected inverse relationship with turnover, tenure is conspicuously independent of all other considerations. Of particular interest is the fact that tenure is independent of incentive conditions, particularly those involving retirement benefits which would be expected to be especially effective in prolonging tenure.

Factor VI: Ownership and Concern for Organizational Interests. The negative pole of this factor reflects dissatisfaction with pay, lack of concern for plant and equipment, and customer dissatisfaction, while the positive pole reflects personal involvement of both management and employees as evidenced by stock ownership. The significant result here is that stock ownership is related to those performance measures that involve direct cost reduction or maintaining the goodwill of the clientele. A possible conclusion to be drawn from this factor is that employees with ownership roles cooperate toward some important goals by essentially protecting their own investemnts.

Factor VII: Work-Force Reduction and Job Mechanization. This factor suggests that firms manufacturing for inventory are more likely to reduce their work force and number of jobs as a consequence of automation or mechanization.

Factor VIII: Technical Personnel and Controls versus Protection against Human Liabilities. One pole of this factor emphasizes the use of technical specialists and procedures while the other pole indicates the presence of group insurance programs. The interpretation of this factor is not clear-cut. One interpretation might be that organizations attempt to insure themselves against contingencies that cannot be coped with by technological specialists.

Factor IX: Minority-Group Composition. This factor primarily reflects the presence of minority groups in the working force.

Factor X: Improvement of Working Conditions. Improvement of working conditions loads substantially on this factor while substandard production and the number of people involved in research and development load slightly in the same direction. This factor pattern is not clear-cut, but it is possible that the existence of substandard production has in part prompted research and development and the improvement of working conditions.

Factor XI: Retail Sales Personnel and Authority-Conflict Behaviors. The incidence of theft and superior-subordinate conflict is more frequent in those firms characterized by larger retail sales forces and local product distribution. It is quite possible that a large number of superior-subordinate conflicts revolve around theft situations. Palmer's (1961) finding that amount of product discount was inversely related to the incidence of theft was not disclosed in the present analysis, but his finding that theft was an independent dimension of behavior was confirmed.

Factor XII: Community and Employee Support versus Work-Output Restriction. The general picture is that of an organization which offers benefits to employees through recreation and savings-investment programs, and to the local community through monetary contributions and management participation in charitable and civic organizations. Organizations fulfilling this description experience fewer work stoppages and less substandard production relative to other firms. Such organizations are also more likely to experience an increased percentage of applicants. This factor is interesting because it is one of the few factors to suggest a direct relation between personnel benefits and productivity, although the magnitude of the relationship is low.

Factor XIII: Employee Selectivity. The implication here is that firms paying better wages enjoy a more favorable selection ratio.

Factor XIV: Allocations to Labor versus Product Development. Firms that are composed of hourly workers are more likely to grant pay increases and less likely to introduce new products in their product line. Although the meaning of this factor is not clear, one suggestion is that investment is made in worker wages rather than in the development of new products.

DISCUSSION

Neither size nor age was appreciably related to measures of personnel performance and organizational functioning. Personnel performance and organizational functioning varied with factors that could be controlled (e.g., recreation and savings-investment programs) rather than with the enduring and unalterable conditions of an organization such as size and age.

Management tenure and experience were completely independent of other management characteristics such as age, education, pay level, and incidence of promotions. Most important, management tenure and experience were conspicuously independent of other variables, especially those involving personnel performance and organizational functioning.

One would not suspect that incentive conditions, benefits, and programs are so far removed from being unidimensional in nature. That they are not unidimensional is attested by their breaking up and scattering over nine different factors.

Pay level tends to be related to worker characteristics pertaining to skill and education, and is independent of personnel performance and organizational functioning. Quite the opposite holds true for recreation and savings-investment benefits which are essentially independent of worker characteristics, but related to a number of personnel performance (substandard production, incidence of strikes, work stoppages, etc.) and organizational effectiveness (monetary civic support, management office holders, and increase in applicants) variables in the expected manner. Consequently, the importance of fringe benefits in the maintenance of performance is given some support.

Following the pattern of management attributes, employee tenure was independent of other worker characteristics, especially those involving skill and education. In both cases, tenure was unrelated to any identifiable organization attributes or conditions.

The present finding that productivity, job aversion, and theft are mutually independent behaviors is in agreement with Palmer (1961). However, Palmer (1961) found job-aversion behaviors to be rather unitary while in the present study aversive behaviors split into a number of independent components. For example, strikes, lates, and turnover were found to be independent of each other. These are distinct ways of avoiding the job and each seems to be related to unique conditions within the organization. Strikes are related to the presence of unions; turnover is associated with employee age and tenure; and tardiness covaries with family responsibility.

Productivity loads slightly on three different factors and has no simple relationships with other variables. Theft, on the other hand, seems simply to be related to the presence of a retail sales force where opportunities for theft would seem to best present themselves.

Like personnel performance, organizational functioning was multidimensional in nature. The interdependence of personnel performance and organizational functioning is noticeably absent in many respects.

Probably the most significant aspect of this investigation is its demonstration of the complex relationships that can be expected to exist between various organizational attributes and behaviors. Typically, investigations have been concerned with a relatively few number of variables such that complex relationships were automatically ruled out. As more variables are taken into consideration, relationships among the original variables become altered and take on new significance. This is partially exemplified by comparing the results of the present investigation with those of Palmer's (1961).

REFERENCES

Argyris, C. *Understanding organizational behavior.* Homewood, Ill.: Dorsey Press 1960.

Bass, B. M. *Leadership psychology and organizational behavior.* New York: Harper, 1960.

Cartwright, D., & Zander, A. F. (Eds.), *Group dynamics: Research and theory.* Evanston, Ill.: Row, Peterson, 1960.

Coch, L., & French, J. R. Overcoming resistance to change. *Human Relations,* 1948, 1, 512-532.

Kaiser, H. F. The varimax criterion for analytic rotation in factor analysis. *Psychometrika,* 1958, 23, 187–200.

March, J. G., & Simon, H. A. *Organizations.* New York: McGraw-Hill, 1958.

McGregor, D. *The human side of enterprise.* New York: McGraw-Hill, 1960.

Palmer, G. J., Jr. Incentive conditions and behavior in 188 industrial manufacturing organizations. Technical Report No. 3, 1961, Project NR 170–478, Tulane University, Contract Nonr 475(08), Office of Naval Research.

Revans, R. W. Human relations, management, and size. In E. M. Hugh-Jones (Ed.), *Human relations and modern management.* Amsterdam, Netherlands: North Holland, 1958. Pp. 177–220.

Rubenstein, A. H., & Haberstroh, C. J. (Eds.), *Some theories of organization.* Homewood, Ill.: Irwin, 1960.

Shartle, C. L. *Executive performance and leadership.* Englewood Cliffs, N. J.: Prentice-Hall, 1956.

33 The Predictability of Occupational Level from Intelligence

RICHARD S. BALL

In 1918 and again in 1923, Dr. S. L. Pressey administered his Mental Survey Test, Schedule D, to children in grades two to ten of the Bloomington, Indiana, public schools. These test blanks were preserved in the Psychological Clinic of Indiana University. The availability of records some fifteen to twenty years old provided an excellent opportunity to check on the much discussed problem of the predictability of occupational attainment from intelligence. With the consent and cooperation of Dr. Pressey and under the direction of Dr. C. M. Louttit, this problem was undertaken.

Combining the records of both years, 1918 and 1923, there were 559 cases available. The total raw score for the ten sections of the test was divided by the chronological age (to the nearest year) of the person at the time the test was taken, the resulting quotient being taken as the measure of intelligence, and as roughly analogous to the intelligence quotient of the Stanford-Binet. Our justification for this method of establishing the measure lies in the fact that Pressey's median scores for each age plotted against age reveal a perfect linear relation. Since equal increments in age accompany equal increments in score this procedure, we believe, is satisfactory. Hereinafter we shall refer to this value as the "Mental Survey Quotient," abbreviated M. S. Q.

Casual inspection of the test suggests that it would measure intelligence in much the same manner as other tests, since it is quite similar to them in general form and content. Furthermore, there is empirical evidence to this effect. The 559 cases distribute themselves rather normally. Seventeen cases who had been tested in 1918 were re-examined in 1923. The rank-difference correlation for these 17 overlapping cases was computed at .84, ±.048. There were 49 cases out of the total number who had also been given the Stanford-Binet in the University Psychological Clinic. A rank-difference correlation between the Binet I. Q. and the Pressey M. S. Q. was computed for these 49 cases at .61, ±.06.

The current occupational status (as of March-April, 1937) of the

From *Journal of Consulting Psychology*, 1938, 2, 184–186. Publications, Indiana University Psychological Clinics, Series II, Number 18.

cases was traced primarily through the Bloomington City Directory whenever it gave sufficiently reliable and detailed information. In equivocal cases this was refined either by telephone or personal interview. Some additional cases were traced by more or less fortuitous information received from townspeople who were well acquainted with the particular individual. The criterion of "success" was one simply of the actual type of work in which the person was engaged. No use was made of earnings, satisfying quality of the job, or length of hire, as has been the case in other studies. Hence the criterion was not so much "success" within any one occupation as merely the level of occupation attained. Thus this study differs fundamentally from so many others which have investigated intelligence in relation to occupational success with very restricted ranges of employment.

Each case was assigned its proper Barr Scale value, dependent on the occupational status as determined. At an early stage of the investigation (129 cases), the Pearson correlation between the Barr values and the test scores for the two year groups (1918 and 1923) combined was computed at .57, ±.04. At this same early stage, using the Taussig 5-point scale of occupational classification instead of the Barr, almost identical results were obtained.

We have been able at this writing to secure what we believe is a fairly reliable description of the occupations of 60 cases (32%) of the children tested in 1918, and of 159 (39%) of those tested in 1923. That the traced cases are a representative sample of the total number is indicated by the fact that the distribution curve of M. S. Q.'s for the total group, the traced cases, and the untraced are all similar and approximately normal.

In the 1918 group, there have not been traced proportionally as many cases in two ranges of occupation as would be theoretically expected, ranges which correspond to Barr Scale values of approximately 6 to 10, and 12 to 14. There is evident shortening at the extremes, also. The same trend, though less pronounced, appears in the cases traced in the 1923 group. The failure to trace low cases is probably due to the same factors which Proctor suggests (mobility, reluctance, etc.). As for the highest levels, two factors might be operating. Most of the cases are still too young to have achieved the high values of the Barr Scale, and secondly, a relatively small town such as Bloomington provides little opportunity for such eminence. For the variations in the central ranges there is as yet no complete explanation.

The Pearson product-moment correlation of occupational status with the M. S. Q. was computed at .57, ±.035 for the year group 1923. By this same method, the correlation for the 1918 group is .71, ±.04.

From the 1918 correlation, the prediction value in score units was computed. If, for example, we take a M. S. Q. of 8, the best estimate of occupational status on the Barr Scale will be 8.88, ±1.35 (68 chances in 100). This corresponds in terms of actual occupations to such vocations as steel-worker, policeman, brakeman, or telephone lineman at the lower value, on up to undertaker, station agent, or telegrapher at the higher value. Thus is established a rather narrow range of occupations within which we might reasonably expect success from a person with such test performance.

DISCUSSION

It may be objected that we have not measured the relation between intelligence and occupational level, since our measurement of the latter was in terms of the Barr Scale which ranks the occupations according to the intelligence required. However, the same ranking would presumably result if the criterion were that of difficulty; and in any case, we can at least demonstrate that there is a differential relation of intelligence to certain occupational classifications, whether those classes are arrived at descriptively (professional, semi-skilled, etc.), or by estimates as in the Barr Scale. Since the Barr Scale is essentially an elaboration and refinement of the traditional five basic classes, this criticism is of small consequence.

The corollary of our original hypothesis concerning the relation of intelligence to occupational status was, that as time elapsed, an increasing adjustment would occur such that the correlation would increase as the time between the determination of intelligence and the determination of occupational status increased. It was supposed that those low in intelligence would commence at relatively low occupational levels and tend to remain there more or less for life. Those of the higher intelligence, on the other hand, would probably also begin relatively low, and then with experience and increasing efficiency, their promotion to higher jobs would take place. Such a condition would tend to increase the positive relationship.

This is precisely what the results indicate. The difference of .14 between the two correlations has a P. E. of ±.053, hence 96 chances in 100 that there is a true difference in this direction. The coefficient of determination for year 1923 is .33 and for 1918 .50. Because of the psychological nature of the correlated variables, this cannot be interpreted to mean that so much of occupational status is determined, or caused, by intelligence. It does, however, argue for a substantial participation of the latter in the former, and that this undergoes an increment with the passage of time, during which we postulate an increasing adjustment of intelligence and level of occupation. If this be the case, perhaps herein lies the reason for the lower correlations heretofore found. In previous studies the cases traced had not apparently had sufficient time in which to reach their ultimate level. Most of the present cases have not either, of course, but they have generally more nearly approached it. In this light, a follow-up after another decade or so should prove most interesting.

Why these findings so disagree with those of Thorndike and complement those of Proctor is answered by the fundamental differences and likenesses of the studies in question. From our results it appears that Thorndike failed to find any significant predictability simple because: (1) the cases were too "young" occupationally to have reached any stable level of employment; (2) there was too short a time (only 6 to 8 years) between measurements to allow this adjustment to take place; (3) the ranges of occupation defined were so narrow that other factors than intelligence played the dominant role in determining success in terms of his criteria. This was only to be expected since from the time of the Army testing, the wide range of ability within any one occupation has been clearly recognized; (4) in terms of the problem as usually conceived, the tests were too simple to adequately sample intellectual dispositions to complex jobs.

SUMMARY AND CONCLUSIONS

The occupational status of 219 Bloomington public school children who were given the Pressey Mental Survey Tests, Schedule D, in 1918, and in 1923, was determined. Correlations for each year group were computed between intelligence and occupational status. For 1923 the correlation was .57, for 1918, .71. These coefficients indicate a substantial conditioning of occupational level by intelligence, such that, even granting the important role of other factors (*e.g.*, special tuition, traits of character and personality, chance opportunities, and favoritisms), practical use may be made of intelligence scores in vocational guidance work. This holds, of course, only for grosser distinctions in level of occupation, since it is patent enough that adjustment to finer distinctions of occupations is most significantly determined by other than intellectual factors.

That the correlation increases as the time between measurements increases, is interpreted to mean that an increasing adjustment of the two variables is taking place. This would account for the fact that cross-sectional studies on young persons and short-interval longitudinal studies generally yield low correlations, whereas cross-sectional studies of mature persons and long-interval longitudinal studies yield higher correlations.

34 Test Validity Over a Seventeen-Year Period

E. B. KNAUFT

A 15-minute general mental ability test, known as LOMA-1, has been administered to applicants in the home office of the Ætna Life Affiliated Companies since 1937. The most recent validity study of this test, although generally confirming previous studies, was felt to be of interest because it covers a period of 17 years.

The principal finding concerns the relationship between test score and job level the employee has attained over a period of years. The analysis was based on 692 persons hired between 1937 and 1949 and still employed by the company on March 1, 1954. These persons were tested at the time they were employed. A product-moment correlation of + .60 was obtained between LOMA test score and present job classification of the 692 employees. The classification system for these jobs includes seven grades or classes ranging from simple clerical jobs such as file clerk to complicated decision-making jobs such as senior underwriter and senior claim examiner. The great majority of these employees started in one of the bottom three classes. The company adheres to a policy of promotion from within, and it is very unusual for anyone to be initially employed on a job above the third class from the bottom. The correlation of + .60

TABLE 34.1. *Relationship between job class and LOMA score*

| | \multicolumn{6}{c}{LOMA Score} | |
| | 0–99 | | 100–119 | | 120 and Over | | |
Job Class	N	%	N	%	N	%	Mean Score
Decision-making 3	0	0	1	1	6	3	148.6
Decision-making 2	4	1	8	5	58	25	133.7
Decision-making 1	10	4	23	13	60	26	123.9
Complicated clerical 2	61	21	59	34	57	24	105.7
Complicated clerical 1	87	31	56	32	38	16	94.8
Simple clerical 2	100	35	23	13	11	5	79.2
Simple clerical 1	24	8	3	2	3	1	70.0
Total	286	100	173	100	233	100	

From *Journal of Applied Psychology*, 1955, 39, 382–383.

thus indicates that the LOMA test score is a fairly good predictor of the extent to which an employee will be promoted over a period of years.

Table 34.1 summarizes the relationship between job class attained and LOMA score. The number and percentage of persons falling in each job class are given for each of three score categories.

A second criterion for evaluating the effectiveness of the LOMA test is the individual's present job performance. In several departments production records were available for simple and complicated clerical jobs which are on a wage incentive plan. The criterion used was the mean of 14-weeks bonus efficiencies of employees who had been on the job long enough to be producing at a relatively constant rate. The bonus efficiency represents net production with allowances for time on "non-bonus" activities. Results obtained from four departments used in this study are summarized in Table 34.2. Criterion reliabilities are based on a correlation

TABLE 34.2. *Relationship between LOMA score and production*

Department	No. Cases	Criterion Reliability	Validity Coefficient
A	36	.92	.40*
B	23	.91	.48*
C	14	.94	.29
D	19	.87	.32

* Significant at 5% level of confidence.

between odd and even weeks for 16 weeks. Validity coefficients are product-moment correlations between the production criterion and LOMA score.

Although the LOMA test appears to be most effective as an aid to prediction of job class eventually attained, indications from four small samples suggest that at least in some instances it is also effective as a partial predictor of performance on various kinds of clerical jobs.

VI ORGANIZATION PERFORMANCE

The questions raised by the papers in this part are on the existence and the nature of organization performance, and their effects, if any, on individual performance. Some recent efforts suggest focusing on the organization as the unit of study as well as the individuals who are members of the organization. There seems to be little question in the thinking of some of the writers that organizations "perform" in much the same way as individuals "perform."

To cite only a few, writers such as Bass (1952 represented here), Caplow (1953), and Seashore, Indik, and Georgopoulos (1964) imply that organizations perform in a manner that is not directly a derivative of individual performance. There seems, however, to be some middle-of-the-road thought on the point suggesting that organization performance is an interaction between situational factors and the performance of the individuals who make up the organization. (We refer here to organizations as intact groups of individuals. Generally, however, we would restrict our concern to those situations in which a power hierarchy exists and in which two or more groups would interact with a leader.)

The basic question of whether an organization is anything more than the sum of its members appears to be meaningless. The basis for this statement is the lack of formal definitive studies in contrast to the existence of a taxonomic structure of information derived from individuals or from sources describing organizations as a whole. Barton (1961) points out three external characteristics of organizations: input, output, and environment. Also, there are three types of internal characteristics: social structure, attitudes, and activities. The analysis of existing data according to the above classification scheme raises a question, but, at the same time, lends some support to the concept of the organization being something more than the aggregate of its members. Unfortunately, Barton does not include in his purpose the derivation of principles or the formulation of a theory of organization. The emphasis is on measurement of organizational environments to facilitate the study and comparison of organizations.

If the amount of effort already invested is indicative of the eventual results, then can we assume that something substantive does exist? This is a dangerous assumption, to say the least.

The focus on the organization as a social-economic system is represented by the reports of empirical research by Merrihue and Katzell (1955) and Likert (1958). The first study reports an attempt to construct a global index of employee relations organizational effectiveness but concludes that the elements of the index do not represent a single continuum. The second article reports data for several questions regarding the relationship of leadership and productivity of work groups. A compilation of the assumptions and results of the two studies lends little clarification to the question of importance of individual variables, such as leadership, in determining organization performance.

A more recent statement by Seashore (1964) (1965 reprinted here) suggests the idea that the approach to the study of organizations might utilize a set of "core variables," behavioral variables of sufficient generality to occur and be available for measurement in the majority of study situations. The emphasis is on human responses although in an earlier study Georgopoulos, Indik, and Seashore (1960) incorporated impersonal indices in deriving and testing these models or organization effectiveness. Three models are presented. The first assumption that organizations attempt to achieve specified objectives (maximum output); the second to optimize output relative to input (efficiency); and the third does not involve assumptions being an explanatory approach using factor analysis. The authors conclude that their data support each model as having advantages for the study of organizations.

An empirical study by Palmer and Schroeder (1961 reprinted here) reports a factor analysis of organization conditions and behaviors in 188 organizations which yielded eight factors. The authors concluded that organization conditions tend to be linked with the individual behaviors of productivity, job aversion, and theft. A casual relation is inferred as in other studies but not tested although this would seem to be a logical conclusion.

Contemporary empirical studies using the factor analytic model are represented by Seashore and Yuchtman (1967), Indik (1966), and Prien and Ronan (1970).

The first study, by Seashore and Yuchtman, reports the analysis of criteria of organization performance at different levels and compares the results of three separate analyses of the same organization at five-year intervals. While some stability of structure is evident, differences are evident as well. Indik reports comparative analyses of the often reworked data of the package delivery stations, insurance agencies, and automobile dealers. Again, some consistency is reported of the dimensionality of organizational effectiveness criteria. The final study in this set, by Prien and Ronan (1970), reports on analysis of combined input and output data from small firms and the comparison of results with other studies.

It seems evident that there are causal relations between organizational conditions or characteristics in terms of the single or cumulative performance behaviors of the people who constitute the "organization." It seems evident, however, that the concept of organization *effectiveness* which implies criterion dimensions independent of the performance of single individuals or the cumulative performance of all involved individuals is erroneous and misleading. What exists is more appropriately considered under the rubric of "organization effects," extra-individual conditions which moderate or which interact in some probably complex manner with individual performance behavior.

REFERENCES

BARTON, A. H. Organization measurement and its bearing on the study of college environments. New York, N.Y. *Columbia University Press*, 1961.

CAPLOW, T. The criteria of organization success. *Social Forces*, 1953, 32, 1–9.

GEORGOPOULOS, B. S., INDIK, B. P., & SEASHORE, S. E. *Some models of organizational effectiveness.* Ann Arbor, Mich. Institute for Social Research, 1960 (unpublished).

LIKERT, R. Measuring organization performance. *Harvard Business Review*, 1958, 36, 41–50.

MERRIHUE, W. V. & KATZELL, R. A. ERI—Yardstick for Human Relations *Harvard Business Review*, 1955, 33, 62–71.

SEASHORE, S. E., INDIK, B. P. & GEORGOPOULOS, B. S. Relationship among criteria of job performance. *Journal of Applied Psychology*, 1960, 44, 195–202.

35 Ultimate Criteria of Organizational Worth

BERNARD M. BASS

SUMMARY

The purpose of this article is to suggest that the ultimate criteria of organizational worth be expanded.

Instead of evaulating the success of programs for improving selection, placement, training, job methods and human relations in an industrial organization solely in terms of the extent to which they serve to increase the company's productivity, profits and efficiency, it has been proposed that they also be evaluated on the extent to which they increase the worth of the organization to its members and society as a whole. It is felt that this proposal is consonant with the philosophical principles underlying certain aspects of labor legislation, labor relations, military organization, and industrial organization. It is probably much more acceptable to the trade unionist than the present approach to evaluation and may have more support from management than might be apparent at first—although the verification of this last hypothesis will have to await research on the subject.

DISCUSSION

Fiske (7) in a recent article suggested that the need to judge the worth of individual workers within an organization could be minimized by developing general principles concerning the relationships between the worth of the organization of the individual worker interacting with others and the success with which the organization attained its goals. If such relationships were known, then value judgments would have to be made only about the success of the organization as a whole; criteria of success or worth of individual employees would be empirical functions of organizational success.

The concept of organization success or goal attainment is a valuable one and the uses Fiske proposes to make of it appear more fruitful. How-

From *Personnel Psychology*, 1952, 5, 156–173.

ever, a thorough examination of the meaning of organizational success appears in order.

Upon What Ultimate Criteria Should Organizational Success Be Evaluated?

The criterion question may be expanded further by considering the bases upon which organizational success or degree of goal attainment should be evaluated. The present tendency of personnel psychologists is to accept as ultimate criteria[1] of organizational success—organizational productivity, net profits, success with which the organization maintains or expands itself, and the degree to which the organization accomplishes its missions as assigned by higher authority.

Following Fiske's suggestions, one would evaluate the individual employee in terms of the degree to which his performance increases the worth of the organization as estimated by the above indices. Likewise, the adequacy or success of new personnel programs of selection, training, counseling and so forth would be evaluated in terms of these same indices.

The purpose of this article is to try to broaden the bases for evaluating the success of an organization and also therefore, the success of the individual employee and the individual personnel program. It is felt that two additional indices of value should be introduced formally into the final evaluations of organizations, and their dependent employees and programs. The proposal is that in addition to the previously cited indices of organizational success, there be included as measures of organizational value, *the worth of the organization to the individual members and the worth of both individual members and the organization to society.* It is suggested, therefore, than an organization be evaluated in terms of: (1) the degree to which it is productive, profitable, self-maintaining and so forth; (2) the degree to which it is of value to its members; and (3) the degree to which it and its members are of value to society. Since there will be little quarrel with ultimate criterion No. 1., we shall concentrtae our efforts on supporting the introduction of criteria 2 and 3 into the formal evaluation of organizational success.

Nothing really new has been suggested. Rather, what has been suggested is that the goals and objectives which the industrial psychologist has recognized informally be integrated formally into his methods of evaluating the success of his own work.

Two Alternatives

The nature of the argument necessary to support the introduction of criteria 2 and 3 will depend on the extent of the correlation between (1)

---

[1] For a discussion of the distinction between immediate, intermediate and ultimate criteria, the reader is referred to R. L. Thorndike, Personnel Selection: Test and Measurement Techniques. New York: Wiley, 1949, pp. 121–124.

the "material" criteria of profits, productivity and self-maintenance and (2) and (3) the "social" criteria of worth of the organization to the individual members and both to society. In the absence of systematic quantitative evidence, the amount of the correlation is a matter for conjecture. At least two hypotheses concerning this correlation appear tenable. The first hypothesis is that the three criteria are so highly interrelated that a company which scores highly on any one always tends to score highly on the others. The second hypothesis is that the three criteria may tend to be related either to a small extent or not at all, or may be highly related only if a number of other conditions are present. For the sake of argument, these two possibilities have been labeled Hypothesis A—a high positive correlation always exists among the three criteria and Hypothesis B—a high positive correlation does not always exist among the three criteria.

Hypothesis A—The Ultimate Criteria are Always Highly Correlated

A number of personnel psychologists have suggested this hypothesis. Thus, Blum (3) introduces the student to the purpose of industrial psychology by declaring: "(The) goal of (industrial psychology) should be the satisfaction of man, not of any one man to the disadvantage of others, or of one group over the other. Men must be free to express their feelings, to reach goals, to produce, and to develop as secure individuals. These and other freedoms are possible ... in an industrial system operating in a democracy." But, he finds it necessary to add: "Efficiency then follows as a necessary accompaniment." (3, p. 1.)

Similarly Ghiselli and Brown (8), point out that whenever management—whatever the motive—introduces programs to increase worker comfort, safety and satisfaction, such programs in the long run lead to higher profits. In other words, they suggest that a high correlation exists among the ultimate criteria 1, 2 and 3 formulated in this article. This same view is expressed by V. J. Bentz, of Sears, Roebuck & Company, who asks the question. "Can an organization survive and perpetuate itself solely on goals of profit and productivity?" Again, W. V. Bingham observes in a letter to the author:

> To my mind, one of the outstanding characteristics of the American enterprise system is that, by and large, two spectacularly dissimilar goals of organizational success namely (a) corporate profits in the long run and (b) worth of the enterprise to the community and to the individual worker, lie so nearly in the same general direction that steady advance toward either goal commonly means progress toward the other.
> I do not happen to be acquainted with *any* wise, able, successful employer who defines his business goals solely in economic terms,

namely profits . . . nor (anyone) whose goal of organizational success is defined in such very broad social terms that it fails to include the financial interests of . . . the . . . investors who have saved and supplied the indispensable capital requirements.

Bingham goes on to cite the attitude toward this issue of two European industrial psychologists, Walther and Poppelreuter. Walther insisted that he was completely disinterested in profits or anything concerned with money. Poppelreuter declared, "I touch nothing that does not mean profit for the employer." Both used the immediate criterion of more productivity with less expenditure of energy; both introduced into various industrial concerns almost the same identical programs of job analysis, work simplification, selection and training!

To sum up his opinion concerning the correlation between the material and social organization goals, Dr. Bingham concludes:

> Standing between two enormous cauldrons of chocolate, I had bluntly asked the President of Suchards's, 'Why do you have in your staff a psychologist like Dr. Walther?' His prompt reply was 'I find that it pays'.

If Hypothesis A is tenable, then psychologists can feel free to expand the ultimate criteria of organizational success as suggested in this article and to use the three criteria interchangeably. Criteria 2 and 3 could be used where more easily obtainable than criterion 1, and where it was pertinent to demonstrate to the public, to legislatures, to employees, or to other interest groups the value of the company to society. In a certain sense, the validity or reliability of any one of the measures could be checked by obtaining any one of the others. It is difficult to see any particular objections or disadvantages to expanding the ultimate criteria of organizational worth, *if Hypothesis A is tenable.*

Hypothesis B—The Ultimate Criteria Are Not Always Highly Correlated

It is the writer's conviction that Hypothesis B is far more tenable. The validity of Hypothesis B is suggested by the following:
1. MacGregor (*10*) has pointed out that supervisors can motivate workers to perform well in two ways. Supervisors can serve as potential aids to the workers' attainment of material and psychological rewards or they can serve as potential barriers or threats to the workers' attainment of such rewards. The positive or "augmentation" approach is favored over the negative one because although the supervisor can energize the workers by means of threats, there is no guarantee that the worker will be motivated in the direction desired by the supervisor. It is possible to use

the negative or punishment approach only where rigid controls and restrictions can be exerted on the workers' behavior. Thus, if a rider whips a horse, it will run, but not necessarily in the direction desired by the rider. However, the horse *will* run in the direction desired by the rider if the reins are held tightly while the horse is being whipped. In other words, where most of the possible behavior of the workers can be controlled—such as in Nazi, Soviet or other slave-worker situations—high productivity may be maintained by force and threat, despite the ensuing low morale and job dissatisfaction.

2. High productivity appears to occur along with low morale in many work situations in the United States. The reverse is also true. For example, 156 respondents each were able to describe at least one efficient but unpleasant work group. Similarly 344 each were able to describe at least one inefficient but pleasant work group (2).

From the above considerations it is inferred that although satisfied and secure workers will tend to be more productive, there are many situations where such is not the case.

If Hypothesis B is tenable—and the writer would be inclined to accept this alternative—then a series of arguments must be marshalled to justify the inclusion of criteria 2 and 3 as ultimate objectives of business and industrial organizations.

The Thesis

It is proposed that the worth of the organization to the individual worker and the worth of both individual and organization to society should be used as ultimate criteria of organizational success apart from any consideration of the effect these two criteria may or may not have on the ultimate criterion of profits, productivity and self-maintenance. This proposition is presented as an axiom. It cannot be proved or disproved. The acceptance by industrial psychology of the proposition as axiomatic will depend on whether it can be demonstrated: 1. that the proposition is self-evident, or; 2. that it is an established principle, which although unverified and unverifiable is accepted widely especially by those disciplines whose areas of study overlap in content with those of industrial psychology. Since the writer knows of no way of demonstrating the self-evident nature of the axiom, he will be content to emphasize the established nature of the axiom. If it can be shown that the proposition is accepted as an axiom by fields close to industrial psychology, then acceptance of this axiom by industrial psychologists will be profitable. It will enable the derived principles of industrial psychology to be consistent with and to be integrated with a larger framework of consistent knowledge.

A series of briefs follow to show that the proposed axiom has been accepted as fundamental in the fields of jurisprudence, military management, industrial management and labor relations. The briefs are intended to be illustrative rather than expository.

Organizational Worth and the Law

The worth of the organization to the individual and the worth of both organization and individual to society have been recognized matters requiring control by both federal and state legislation. This legislation has tended to regard labor as a natural resource to be protected and conserved—and more recently, as a group of human beings with certain absolute rights. Legislative control of organizational worth to the individual has been covered by state legislation concerning the "mental and moral" health of women workers since 1842; by Congressional action concerning hours of work since 1869; by state legislation concerning industrial safety since 1903, and by many other city, state and national legislative enactments, court decisions, and executive orders (14). Antitrust legislation illustrates the kind of legislative attempts which have been made to control the worth of the organization to society.

Organizational Worth and the Armed Forces

In the military organizations of democracies today, organizational worth to the individual is considered of basic importance. For example, the Armed Forces medical programs are not evaluated solely against such ultimate criteria as the degree to which they raise morale and indirectly help to win battles but also in terms of the deaths and disabling handicaps they can help to avoid among members of the Armed Forces in the course of the members' training and combat activities. Saving lives wherever possible is regarded by those that justify the expense and effort of the medical programs as an important, if not most important value of the programs. Maintaining a maximum of combat effectiveness, preventing disease, lowering loss of trained veterans and keeping morale high are all important indications of the worth of the medical corps, but it is probable that the degree to which the medical programs aid the Armed Forces to be of maximum help to their wounded, injured and diseased members, is regarded by a nation which values the life of the individual highly, as an extremely important index of the success of the Armed Forces and their medical programs.

Witness the following two excerpts from *The Senior R.O.T.C. Manual*, Vol. II, prepared in 1948 under the direction of the office, chief, Army Field Forces, United States Army:

Our current democratic ideals shun all concepts which tend to cheapen human life. These ideals are reflected in our military principles and operations to the extent that during World War II, our leaders often revised strategic plans to save lives." (*18*, p. 484–485.)

The public (during World War II) expected that every effort would be made to keep the American soldier in perfect health; that safety devices would be devised for his benefit or convenience. (*18*, p. 487.)

While the primary objective of the American Armed Forces is to win wars, other objectives more closely related to criteria 2 and 3 are present which may or may not necessarily be related to the primary objective. In fact, the attainment of these "social" objectives may actually, at times, be detrimental to the attainment of the primary objective.

Organizational Worth and Principles of Industrial Organization and Labor Relations

The essence of the thesis advanced in this article suggesting the expansion of the ultimate criteria of organizational worth is manifest in Davis' (*6*), "Industrial Organization and Management" which probably can be considered a representative text in this area. Davis states:

> Business objectives ... those values which a company must preserve, acquire, create or distribute to justify its right to exist ... include the broad social values which it must contribute to society, the economic values with which it must serve the public, and the personnel values that it must supply its own personnel. (*6*, p. 20.)

In a more detailed statement of the business organization's social objectives—defined as broad, general values necessary to the well-being of society that are affected by business activity—Davis points out that a business organization cannot employ child labor in a manner detrimental to the child's well-being and development, since the public interest is more important than the interests of any group. Social security for employees is another social objective of a business organization.

> Any intelligent employer has a direct and immediate interest in the economic security of his employees, and within the limits of his ability and his understanding of his obligations, he attempts to provide this security to a reasonable degree. On the other hand, employers are not in the general business of providing economic security. Nevertheless, our society has decided to attempt this, and the Social Security Act has been passed. The Act requires a business organization to maintain extensive and expensive records, and to pay taxes to the state and federal govern-

ment for the purposes of the Act. The values growing out of social security also have become collateral social objectives of business. Business organizations stand in the position of an agency of the government, in that they collect money from the public in the form of taxes to be used for various social purposes. The collateral social objectives of business are closely related to fair-practice standards and business ethics, and today are given careful consideration by executive leaders. (6, p. 27.)

Scott, Clothier et al. (13) echo similar sentiments in more emphatic form:

> But the tenet of this new doctrine (the human conception of labor) that left many of the old school executives gasping for breath, was that *the workers had certain "inalienable" rights as human beings, that these rights were as important as the rights of other persons with whom they had dealings, and that it was industry's duty to recognize these rights* . . . In short, *this doctrine stated brazenly that industrial concerns have three obligations—to their stockholders, to their customers and the public, and to their employees.*
>
> Whereas some years ago the employers who entertained such enlightened views were in the great minority, it is now true that industry generally is adopting their beliefs. (13, p. 5–6.)

Writing similarly of labor relations, Yoder (15) emphasizes the widespread interest and concern of the public in social problems that arise from industrial relations.

> Among the problems that are of greatest importance to our society in the United States are those of industrial unrest, notably strike and lockouts, economic insecurity, unemployment, old age and disability dependency, sub-standard wages, long hours, discrimination on the basis of race, color, nationality, or religion, health hazards in industry; the under-utilization of skills and monopolistic tendencies inherent in over-zealous or unscrupulous combinations of employers and unions. (15, p. 67.)

Numerous other authorities in this area of personnel and industrial management could be cited to illustrate similar viewpoints.[2]

---

[2] For further illustrations, the reader is referred to: E. Peterson and E. G. Plowman. Business organization and management. Chicago: Irwin, 1949, pp. 40–41; C. C. Balderston, R. P. Brecht, et al. Management of enterprise. New York: Prentice-Hall, 1949, pp. 3, 4, 8, 9; B. E. Goetz, Management planning and control: a managerial approach to industrial accounting. New York: McGraw-Hill, 1949, pp. 21, 25; P. Pigors, L. C. McKenney and T. O. Armstrong. Social problems in labor relations. New York: McGraw-Hill, 1939, pp. V–XI (Foreword written by P. Cabot); H. P. Dutton, Business organization and management. New York: McGraw-Hill, 1935, pp. 18–21.

Where Does the Personnel Psychologist Fit In?

If a personnel psychologist comes along and is able to mitigate some of the above ills, should this work not be judged a worthwhile contribution? If an industry creates these problems, should not, as Davis suggests, one of its objectives be to solve the problems or reduce their effects as much as possible? If an industry, in attaining its production goals contaminates the air surrounding the plant, society can act quickly to force the industry to correct this difficulty. The engineer who prevents further contamination is regarded by the company as a serviceable individual who is helping the company to attain one of its objectives—namely, keeping the air clean around it. If a personnel worker reduces psychological contamination in the area surrounding a plant, should not that likewise be considered a service which is helping the company to attain its social objectives?

Advantages of Accepting the Proposed Axiom

In addition to increasing the consistency and integration of the principles of industrial psychology with available knowledge gathered by other disciplines interested in business, industrial and military personnel, three other advantages should accrue from accepting the axiom that the worth of the organization to the individual worker and the worth of both to society are as relevant ultimate criteria as organization productivity, profits and self-maintenance.

First, much of the work of the industrial psychologist is most directly concerned with improving the job situation for the employee although the psychologist attempts to justify this professional activity mainly by trying to demonstrate how it will ultimately increase organizational productivity and profits. The immediate criteria of morale, job satisfaction, fatigue, safety, health and energy required of the worker become much more relevant or valid as indices of the value of personnel and industrial procedures and innovations if they are related to ultimate criteria such as the worth of the organization to the individual, of both to society as well as to ultimate criteria such as organizational productivity and profits. For example, the success with which a psychologist matches employees to jobs may not be gauged merely by the serviceability of the employees to the organization while performing these jobs, but also on the basis of the satisfaction that accrues to the employees by being placed on the given jobs—not because this increased satisfaction necessarily will lead to increased productivity and lower turnover within the organization, but because worker satisfaction is considered an intrinsic value—desirable in its own right.

Suppose a marginal coal mine, where job satisfaction has been low because of the accident hazards and the instability of employment, improves its safety and employment security. The change in conditions may not only be evaluated ultimately in terms of the degree to which profits and productivity are increased but also in terms of the degree to which worker dissatisfaction is decreased; the degree to which less widows and orphans are created; and the degree to which the more contented workers become better heads of families and better citizens. In addition, account can be taken of the fact that hazardous conditions which lead to accidental deaths and injuries, besides being inherently and intrinsically undesirable, represent economic losses to society as a whole.

A second advantage of the broadened approach to evaluation of personnel innovations is that it should provide an additional argument for enabling the personnel technician to enlist the very essential support of labor in studying and making the changes he wishes to evaluate or introduce. The past history of the "speed up" system, the feelings of the worker and organized labor that what benefits management does *not* necessarily benefit them, and the personal reticence to be a human guinea pig make it often difficult if not impossible for industrial psychologists to collect satisfactory immediate criteria of worker performance. If the viewpoint suggested by this article were accepted and followed, it seems reasonable that the cooperation of organized labor and the individual worker would be easier to secure.[3]

A third advantage of adopting the value judgment proposed is that it may help to merge the role played by the psychologist in industry with his stated ethics concerning his roles in industry and elsewhere.[4] For the psychologist, as a scientist, has professed objectivity and impartiality towards management and worker and yet worked mainly for the benefit of the former, assuming that what was good for management was good for the worker—even where he was not financed by management—*because the problems have been defined for him in a way which forced him to do so.*

It is not meant to suggest that the personnel psychologist has not heretofore been interested in improving the employee's working situation; but what is being suggested is that too often these improvements have been justified or evaluated on the basis of their ability to increase indirectly the worth of the employee to the company. The argument is

---

[3] For a discussion of the trade unionist's attitude towards management personnel philosophy, the reader is referred to Barkin (*1*).

[4] A tentative formulation by the Committee on Ethical Standards for Psychology of the American Psychological Association of ethical standards with reference to the public responsibility includes Principle 1.21-1, which reads as follows:

> The psychologist's ultimate allegiance is to society, and his professional behavior should demonstrate an awareness of his social responsibilities ... (*16*, p. 632).

that personnel practices leading to improved working conditions should also be evaluated against a measure of the extent to which the conditions benefit the worker—and this measure should be considered as ultimate a criterion as any measure of increased worth of the individual to the organization.

Although the point of view expressed is in itself a value judgment, subject to arbitrary acceptance or rejection, it is consonant with the legal and philosophical attitude which has enabled capitalism to survive as a productive, progressive economic system in this country. It is also consonant with the humanistic and moral attitudes towards the individual which prevail here. Thus, acceptance of the proposed axiom will enable the industrial psychologist formally to adopt some of the values about the individual the great majority of the nation holds—which the psychologist as a private citizen does consider, but which he has not incorporated into his evaluation of his own professional services.

What Is Management's Attitude Towards Ultimate Criteria of Organizational Success?

The reader may well agree with what has been said. Yet, he may raise the very fair question, "This is all very well and good in theory but in practice will management be interested in financing a personnel research program which at the outset does not have as its sole ultimate goal the increase of company profits or productivity?"

Before an adequate answer to this question can be obtained it will be necessary to poll a representative sample of top management throughout the country. No doubt, wide variations in management's responses are to be expected. It is probable that some of these variations will be accounted for by the size of the company concerned, its past history of relations with labor, and whether the company is a relatively new, expanding concern, or an old well-established institution. It is also probable that the final answer will have to be in terms of the extent to which management accepts its obligations to workers and society rather than whether or not it recognizes these obligations.

However, there are some indications available as to what some management representatives' attitudes may be. For example, one answer is suggested by Browne (4) when he reports the goals which 23 executives perceived in the planning of top management of a tire manufacturing concern. A summary of the 17 types of goals enumerated included "To develop a better community and help the general prosperity of the city" (Rank 15); "To promote good labor relations and have satisfied workers" (Rank 4) and "To provide good working conditions and good living standards for employees" (Rank 8). By way of contrast, the goal "To make as much money as possible for the stockholders" was ranked thirteenth!

An answer is also suggested by the program of the Esso Standard Oil Company for preparing employees for retirement. In its approach to the problem of retirement, the company appears motivated by the three ultimate goals we have suggested. In the case of Esso, *these* three goals appear as follows: 1. increasing industrial efficiency, prestige, worker satisfaction, reducing costs, and increasing public good-will; 2. aiding the nation and community to solve problems of the aged; 3. helping the worker to be well adjusted in retirement.

> Industry has accepted its share of the responsibility for finding the economic solution to this problem by providing retirement income for employees that is in most cases based on the productivity of the person's working career. Our government's Social Security program has the same basis. This type of retirement income, in the form of an earned annuity, is an approach toward the problem that recognizes the dignity and independence of the individual. It is not a handout.
>
> In the sociological field, the same type of approach is needed in stimulating and helping retired employees to seek a retirement that will be active, fruitful and constructive, one that will combat frustration. Here again, industry must not be guilty of paternalism, the sociological equivalent of a handout. Rather it should strive to give real help and counsel to the individual in thinking through his problem. By such action, industry can contribute to the solution of the national and community problems in addition to deriving obvious direct benefits. (*17*, p. 6–7.)

An answer is also suggested by a cursory examination of a few recent issues of *Advanced Management,* the official publication of the Society for the Advancement of Management which revealed numerous illustrations of where representatives of management showed recognition of industrial objectives other than profits and productivity alone. For example:

> The motivating factors which caused the businessmen of Worcester (Mass.) to catapult their Chamber of Commerce into the field of industrial management are basic to any community. In 1945, a local committee for Economic Development decided that Worcestor's economic progress would be thwarted by a post-war recession. The best approach to offset resulting unemployment would be the development of new and existing Worcester companies. . . . The committee not only recommended, but sold a program to hire four consultants working at this community level under the auspices of the Worcester Chamber of Commerce. . . .

> Since the program is financially supported by the larger businesses ... (it) demonstrates greatly that the Worcester business community recognizes its spiritual as well as economic responsibilities (5, pp. 2–5).

In this same journal, a company president writes:

> Business leaders today who are outstanding in their field are making their decisions on a far broader basis than at any time in the past.
> They are realizing that they have a responsibility, not merely to their stockholders, but to their employees and to the public and to their community and to their nation.
> Unless his decisions can stand up under these tests, a true business leader is failing in his responsibilities. (11, p. 6)

Although writing to oppose present management attitudes towards personnel programs, the criticisms of the following author incidentally expose the bases upon which personnel work has been accepted in many organizations.

> ... Too many personnel departments ... seem to be engaged with activities on the periphery of operating realities ... (Personnel executives)—and their presidents, too—act as if they do not understand the profit making nature of the personnel function. ... The (personnel executive) can no longer be thought of as the 'professional do-gooder,' dealing only in a colorful array of fancy 'programs' which in themselves don't contribute to the profitability of the enterprise. (9, 20, 21).

Ghiselli and Brown (8) describe what they believe to be a trend in management thinking towards the concept of efficiency. This trend is also suggestive of management attitudes toward proposed ultimate criteria 2 and 3.

> In the beginning, with narrowed vision, management evaluated most (efforts to streamline production) in terms of the profit motive. In recent years, with wider vision, interests have broadened to include the ... criterion of workers' comfort and safety in conjunction with that of profits. ...
> ... changes (have been) introduced solely on the criterion of the worker's improvement. At the present time there is a further broadening of management's perspective, which is leading it to include other kinds of worker adjustments as necessary criteria to be used in the evaluation of industrial work. (8, p. 219–220).

Of course, one reason management may evidence interest in the value of the organization to its workers or to the community is that they accept Hypothesis A—namely that the attainment of social objectives will lead in the long run to increased profits, productivity and company security, as suggested earlier by Blum, Ghiselli and Brown, Bentz and Bingham. However, it is difficult to determine to what extent management recognizes or is aware of this correlation when it subscribes to the non-material or social ultimate criteria of organizational success.

REFERENCES

1. BARKIN, S. A trade unionist appraises management personnel philosophy. *Harv. Bus. Rev.*, 1950, 28(5), 59–64.
2. BASS, B. M. Feelings of pleasantness and work group efficiency *Personnel Psychol.* (In Press)
3. BLUM, M. L. *Industrial psychology and its social foundations.* New York: Harper, 1949.
4. BROWNE, C. G. Study of executive leadership in business. III. Goal and achievement index. *J. appl. Psychol.*, 1950, 34, 82–87.
5. CLEAVER, J. P. The Worcester story. *Adv. Mgmt.*, 1951, 16, (8), 2–5.
6. DAVIS, R. C. *Industrial organization and management.* New York: Harper, 1940.
7. FISKE, D. W. Values, theory and the criterion problem. *Personnel Psychol.*, 1951, 4, 93–98.
8. GHISELLI, E. E. & BROWN, C. W. *Personnel and industrial psychology.* New York: McGraw-Hill, 1948.
9. MACCULLOUGH, A. V. Off the fringe and onto the first team. *Adv. Mgmt.*, 1951, 16, (9), 19–21.
10. MACGREGOR, D. The staff function in human relations. *J. Soc. Issues*, 1948, 4, 10–13.
11. RICH, R. H. Management and the community—the human factors of management. *Adv. Mgmt.*, 1952, 16, (2), 5–6.
12. RYAN, T. A. *Work and effort.* New York: Ronald, 1947.
13. SCOTT, W. D., CLOTHIER, R. C. et al. *Personnel Management.* New York: McGraw-Hill, 1941.
14. TAFT, P. *Economics and problems of labor.* Harrisburg: Stackpole Sons, 1942.
15. YODER, D. *Personnel management and industrial relations.* New York: Prentice-Hall, 1948.
16. Committee on Ethical Standards for Psychology, Ethical standards and public responsibility. *Amer. Psychol.*, 1951, 6, 626–649.
17. Esso Standard Oil Company, *Preparation for retirement. A study of post-employment adjustment.* New York: Esso, 1951.
18. Office of the Chief, Army Field Forces, U.S.A. *The senior R.O.T.C. Manual, Vol. II.* Washington, D.C., June 1, 1948.

36 Criteria of Organizational Effectiveness

STANLEY E. SEASHORE

Summary: Most organizations have many goals, not one. These goals are of unlike importance and their relative importance changes. Problems arise because these goals are sometimes competing (i.e., have trade-off value), and sometimes incompatible (negatively correlated). A strategy of optimal realization of goals cannot be determined unless there exists some conception of the dimensions of performance, their relative importance, and their relationships with one another. These relationships may be one of causation, of simple correlation, of interaction; they may be linear and compensatory or non-linear and non-compensatory. A framework is proposed for conceptualizing organizational performance, with distinctions among several different classes of performance dimensions and with consideration for several types of relationships among them.

MULTIPLE, CONFLICTING, GOALS

The aim of the following discussion is to outline a way of viewing the relationships among the numerous criteria that might be considered in the evaluation of the performance of an organization. To understand such relationships we shall need to make some distinctions between different kinds of criterion measures. We shall need to create some encompassing conceptions that serve to aid the evaluation of performance when some desired measures are not available, or when the number of measures is inconveniently large.

The issues taken up here arise because most organizations have multiple goals rather than a single goal, and goal achievement may not be directly measurable. The formal objectives of the organization may themselves be multiple and, in any case, there are multiple short-run goals and subgoals that need to be examined. The matter would be simple if the

From *Michigan Business Review*, 1965, 17, 26–30. This article is adapted and enlarged from Chapter 7 of the book, *Assessing Organization Performance with Behavioral Measurements*, published by the Foundation for Research on Human Behavior, Ann Arbor, Michigan, 1964. Support for this work from the National Science Foundation (Grant GS-70) is gratefully acknowledged by the author.

various goals were all of similar priority and combinable in some simple additive way; but this is not the situation. The manager making decisions that rest upon multivariate assessments of the performance of his organization has to calculate the weights and the correlation values that he will apply when estimating the net outcome of a course of action.

A typical example would be the case of a manager who wishes his firm to obtain a substantial profit, and at the same time to grow in size, to insure future profit by product improvements, to avoid financial risk, to pay a substantial annual dividend to his investors, to have satisfied employees, and to have his firm respected in the community. He cannot maximize all of these simultaneously, as increasing one (e.g. dividends or risk avoidance) may imply reduced achievement on another (e.g. growth, product research). He must consider their "trade-off" value, their contingencies, and the presence of negative correlations among them. To estimate an optimum course of action he has to evaluate the dependability and relevance of the various measures and then estimate the way in which they combine to provide an overall evaluation of performance or a prediction of future change in performance. This task will be easier when we have for his use a theory to describe the performance of organizations. The following suggestions are a step in that direction.

CRITERIA AND THEIR USES

To begin with we need to make some distinctions among different kinds of criteria and their uses.

1. *Ends vs. means.* Some criteria are close to the formal objectives of the organization in the sense that they represent ends or goals that are valued in themselves; others have value mainly or only because they are thought to be necessary means or conditions for achieving the main goals of the organization. Substantial profit, for example, may be a goal sought by a business organization, while employee satisfaction may be valued because it is thought to be an aid in reaching the goal of substantial profit.

2. *Time reference.* Some criterion measures refer to a past time period (profit for the past year), others to current states (net worth), and still others to anticipated future periods (projected growth). Whatever their time reference, all may be used for drawing inferences about past or future conditions or changes.

3. *Long vs. short run.* Some criterion measures refer to a relatively short period of time, others to a longer period; they may refer to performances that are relatively stable (do not change much in the short

run) or relatively unstable (erratic or highly variable in the short run). The usefulness of a criterion measure is limited if the period covered is not appropriate to the usual or potential rate of change in the variable.[1]

4. *"Hard" vs. "soft."* Some criteria are measured by the characteristics of, or number or frequency of, physical objects and events, while others are measured by qualitative observation of behavior or by evaluative questions put to people. Dollar measures, for example, or tons of scrap, or number of grievances, are "hard" measures; while employee satisfaction, motivation to work, and cooperation, product quality, customer loyalty, and many others are usually "soft." *The distinction is useful, but it contains a trap,* for we commonly think of the hard variables as being in some way inherently more valid, more reliable, and more relevant to the performance evaluation problem, when this is not necessarily true. Profit rate, for example—a popular hard variable—is a rather vague concept to begin with (accountants dispute about definition and about conventions for measurement) and it is often in the short run unreliable as a performance and thus quite irrelevant to the evaluation problem, even for an organization whose long-run goals include making a profit. Similarly, a soft variable, such as one representing the intentions of key executives to stay with the organization, may be measured with high reliability in some circumstances and may be vital in the assessment of the organization's performance.

5. *Values.* Some variables appear to have a linear value scale (more is always better than less), while others have a curvi-linear scale (some optimum is desired; more and less are both to be avoided). The shape of the curves determines in part the trade-off relationships among assessment variables under conditions where simultaneous optimization is not possible. Examples: profit rate is usually linear in value in the sense that more is better than less; maintenance costs, by contrast, are usually curvilinear in value in the sense that either excessively high or low costs may be judged to diminish overall firm performance.

THE HIERARCHY OF CRITERIA

A full accounting for the performance of an organization requires consideration for (1) achievement of the organization's main goals over a

[1] Many firms' current operating and financial statistics, although appropriate for control and accounting purposes, prove to be of little value for performance evaluation for the reason that they are short-period measures of unstable performances Monthly plant maintenance costs, for example, may be extremely variable (perhaps seasonal) and may be useful as a performance criterion measure only when applied to longer periods of time. In the short run, apart from other considerations, low maintenance costs may or may not be a favorable indicator.

long span of time, (2) performance over shorter periods on each of those criteria that represent ends valued in themselves, and which, jointly, as a set, determine the net ultimate performance, and (3) performance on each of a number of subsidiary criteria that provide an immediate or current indication of the progress toward, or probability of achieving, success on end-result variables. The network of criteria of performance can be viewed as a pyramid-shaped hierarchy:

1. *At the top* is the "ultimate criterion"—some conception of the net performance of the organization over a long span of time in achieving its formal objectives, whatever they may be, with optimum use of the organization's environmental resources and opportunities. The ultimate criterion is never measured (Except possibly by historians); yet some concept of this kind is the basis for evaluation of lesser criteria of performance.

2. *In the middle* are the penultimate criteria. These are shorter run performance factors or dimensions comprised by the ultimate criterion. They are "output" or "results" criteria: things sought for their own value and having trade-off value[2] in relation to each other. Their sum, in some weighted mixture, determines the ultimate criterion. Typical variables of this class for business organizations are: sales volume, productive efficiency, growth rate, profit rate, and the like. There may be included some "soft" (usually behavioral) variables such as employee satisfaction or customer satisfaction. In the case of some non-business organizations these penultimate criteria might be predominantly of the behavioral kind, as in the case of a school whose output is judged in terms of learning rates, proportion of students reaching some standard of personal growth or development, etc.[3].

3. *At the bottom* of the hierarchy of assessment criteria are measures of the current organizational functioning according to some theory or some empirical system concerning the conditions associated with high achievement on each of the penultimate criteria. These variables include those descriptive of the organization as a system and also those representing subgoals or means associated with penultimate criteria. The number of criteria in this class is very large (over 200 have been used in some studies without showing that the limits were being approached), and they are interrelated in a complex network that includes causal, interactional, and modifier types of relationships. Included are some criteria that are not valued at all except for their power to reduce the amount of uncontrolled variance in the network. Among the "hard" crite-

[2] By trade-off value we mean only that an amount of one kind of performance may be substituted for an amount of another: for example, an increase in sales volume may be judged to offset a decline in profit rate per sales unit.

[3] One large U.S. firm has published what appears to be a carefully considered formulation of its own roster of assessment criteria at this penultimate level. It includes one behavioral category, "employee attitudes," which is further defined in operational terms in a manner compatible with the system outlined here.

ria at this level, for a business organization, might be such as: scrappage, short-run profit, productivity against standards, meeting of production schedules, machine downtime, ratio of overtime to regular time, product return rate, rate of technological innovation, and the like. Among the "soft" criteria at this level may be such as these: employee morale, credit rating, communication effectiveness, absenteeism, turnover, group cohesiveness, customer loyalty, pride in firm, level of performance motivation, and others.

CHARACTERISTICS OF BEHAVIORAL CRITERIA

Such a model locates the behavioral criteria—those descriptive of the members (in this context, customers and clients are also "members") of the organization and of their values, attitudes, relationships, and activities—mainly in the lower regions of the network of assessment criteria, distant and perhaps only indirectly related to the ultimate goals by which the organization is eventually judged.

If behavioral criteria appear near the top of the network, it is because they are valued in themselves and have trade-off value in relation to other priority goals of the organization. In general, however, the hard—non-behavioral—criteria are the preferred ones for most business organizations for the good reason that they are more relevant to the formal objectives of the organization.

The behavioral measures are presumed to have some stable relationships to the various non-behavioral measures; these relationships may be causal, interactional, or merely one of co-variance. It is further presumed that the criteria and their relationships are not entirely unique to each organization, nor transient, but are to some degree stable and to some extent common to all or many organizations. These presumptions appear to have some partial confirmation from analyses performed so far[4].

We come now to the question of the role of behavioral criteria in the light of this broader conception of the evaluation of organizational performance. It appears that behavioral criteria are not likely, for most business organizations, to have a prominent place in the roster of penultimate criteria although they may and do appear there. Their chief role will arise from their power to improve the prediction of future changes in the

[4] See "Applying Modern Management Principles to Sales Organizations," Foundation for Research on Human Behavior seminar report, 1963, for an illustration of the similarity across three sales organizations in the relevance of behavioral measures to hard penultimate criteria of organizational performance. Also, "Models of Organization Performance," an unpublished MS by Basil Georgopoulos, Stanley Seashore, and Bernard Indik; and "Relationships Among Criteria of Job Performance," by Stanley Seashore, Bernard Indik, and Basil Georgopoulos, *Journal of Applied Psychology*, 44, 1960, 195–202.

preferred "hard" criteria, i.e., their power to give advance signals of impending problems or opportunities.

A second use that they may commonly have is to complement the available hard criteria in such a way as to give the manager a more balanced and more inclusive informational basis for his decisions in the case where the hard variable measures are incomplete or not reliable for short-run evaluation.[5]

In some rare instances, the behavioral criteria have to be used exclusively instead of the preferred hard criteria of organizational performance for the reason that measurements of hard criteria are not available at all or not at reasonable cost.

There are three basic strategies that may be applied in formulating a unique version of this general scheme that may be appropriate for a particular organization.

   1. There exist several partially-developed general theories concerning the survival requirements of organizations. These assumed requirements may be defined in performance terms and posited as the roster of penultimate criteria or organizational goals. From this starting point, a set of subsidiary goals and performance criteria may be constructed on empirical grounds, on theoretical grounds, or on some combination of the two.

   2. The existing personal values of the owners of a firm, or of the managers as representatives, may be pooled to form an agreed-upon roster of penultimate criteria together with their corresponding performance indicators, and from this starting point the set of subsidiary goals and performance criteria can be constructed.

   3. Comparative empirical study can be made of the performance characteristics of a set of organizations assumed to share the same ultimate criterion but clearly differing in their overall success as judged by competent observers (for example, such a study might be made of a set of insurance sales agencies, some clearly prospering and others clearly headed for business failure). Using factorial analysis methods and actual performance data to identify the sets of lower-order performance criteria, and using trend and correlational analyses to detect the relationships among these sets of criteria over time, one can, in principle, draw conclusions about the penultimate components of performance that bear upon organizational survival or failure in that particular line of business.

ALTERNATIVE THEORETICAL APPROACHES

These three approaches can and do produce strikingly different sys-

[5] An example, a decision to raise prices is likely to rest not only upon estimates of hard performances, past and future, but also upon estimates of political and economic climate, of customer loyalty, of the feasibility of alternatives such as employee collaboration in cost reduction, etc.

tems for describing the network of criteria to be used in evaluating organizational performance. One of the general theories, for example, proposes that there are nine basic requirements to be met, or problems to be continuously solved, for an organization to achieve its long run goals; these include such requirements as adequate input of resources, adequate normative integration, adequate means of moderation of organizational strain, adequate coordination among parts of the organization, etc. Theories of this kind are produced mainly by general organizational sociologists and stem from the view that an organization is a living system with intrinsic goals and requirements that may be unlike those of individual members. By contrast, the second mentioned approach stems from the personal values of managers. The resulting networks of criteria are different.[6]

A start has been made at the Institute for Social Research in exploring such alternative strategies. With respect to the first approach, two theoretical models have been tested against empirical data from a set of organizations in a service industry, using executive judgments of unit overall effectiveness as the ultimate criterion. Both models proved to be about equally valid, but of limited utility in explaining variance on the ultimate criterion; each "accounted for" about half of the ultimate criterion variance, with the unexplained portion arising from measurement errors and/or faulty theory. An attempt to apply the wholly-empirical approach to the same set of data proved to be a failure in the sense that it was no more powerful in explaining variance on the ultimate criterion than were the simpler, theory-based models, and furthermore the resulting roster of performance dimensions was not very satisfactory in common-sense terms.

A third effort is now in progress, using objective data about the performance of a set of insurance sales agencies over a span of twelve years; the early results look very promising on first examination. It appears that there will be identified a roster of about ten penultimate criteria of agency performance, each independent of the others and of varying weight in relation to ultimate performance, and each associated with a roster of subsidiary criteria of kinds that lend themselves to ready measurement and statistical combination. It remains to be seen whether these criteria are unique to this particular line of business, or have some applicability to other kinds of organizations.

[6] To illustrate, take the criterion of profit: in one case, profit is likely to be treated as one of a few penultimate criteria (ends valued in their own right) while in the other case profit is relegated to a subsidiary role as one of several alternative means for insuring adequate input of resources. If this seems implausible, note that some organizations—government, educational, and religious organizations, for example—have survived and prospered without profit from their own activities.

37 Incentive Conditions and Behavior in 188 Industrial Manufacturing Organizations

GEORGE J. PALMER, JR.
and RONALD H. SCHROEDER

What are the relationships between organizational conditions and behavior? The question has motivated extensive speculation, research, and, nowadays, theories of organization (Bass, 1960; March and Simon, 1958). Answers are as important for effective practice as for science, as most management techniques now in use are largely untested (Yoder, Heneman, Turnbull, and Stone, 1958).

Tentative answers have been given by experimental studies (Bavelas, 1950; Leavitt, 1951), by field experiments (Coch and French, 1948), and by use of simulation to create "environmentally rich" organization laboratories (Chapman and Kennedy, 1955). The larger portion of reported studies have been based on observation within one or a small number of real life organizations. Examples are studies by Likert (1959) on supervision, by Baumgartel and Sobol (1959) on absenteeism, and by Kerr (1950) on accidents.

Some writers maintain that these intraorganizational investigations are the most valuable type, because they permit study of organizations "in depth" (Rubenstein and Haberstroh, 1960). This approach provides essentially clinical case studies, valuable no doubt for understanding the problems of particular organizations; but it provides no basis for making generalizations about organizations.

Vroom and Maier (1961) mention the need for, and the difficulty of, collecting data in multiorganization studies. Comrey's (1960) project, for example, comparing the effectiveness, in one instance, of 18 U.S. Forest organizations is a step in the right direction. But in terms of sampling, these are still small numbers for statistically reliable conclusions.

An alternative approach to study of real life organizations used in this study is provided by sampling survey procedures. Their potential

From *Office of Naval Research Technical Report No. 3*, 1961. This work was supported in part by a contract between the Office of Naval Research (Group Psychology Branch) and Tulane University.

advantages in terms of extensive sampling of organizations and more comprehensive coverage of variates have perhaps not been sufficiently exploited. The investigators take the position that the proper sampling unit for many (but not all) organization research questions is the whole organization.

The purpose of this study was to examine the interrelationships among characteristics of organizations and personnel performance. The main questions of interest were related to, first, the dimensionality of behavior in organizations, second, the conditions associated with independent behaviors and, third, the role of size of organization. It was expected that there would be at least two dimensions of performance, one related primarily to productivity, and the other related to turnover and other behaviors. It was expected, too, as something of a corollary, that distinctly different and independent conditions would be related to the independent behaviors. Finally, it was desired to test the hypothesis prevalent in the literature that larger organizations would have generally less favorable personnel performance. As will be seen, the first two hypotheses tended on the whole to be confirmed, but the third was not sustained.

PROCEDURE

Questionnaire

A 29 item, multiple choice, pencil-and-paper questionnaire, containing 9 items relating to personnel performance and 20 items relating to organizational conditions, was developed and pretested on a sample of judges and companies. Six additional items were pre- or post-coded for classifications of companies and survey returns. The 35 variables are presented in Table 37.2.

Survey

A comprehensive list of 584 manufacturing establishments of a southern metropolitan region was developed. To each establishment was sent a questionnaire, together with an explanatory covering letter and a return address, postal-permit envelope. Each company was offered a free summary report of tabulated results, if desired. Companies were assured that all information would be confidential and that no companies would be identified in any publication of results.

Consistency of Reports

A sample of 23 companies, randomly selected from among the respondents, was retested in order to check the consistency of answering the questionnaire. This second request, conducted by telephone interview, asked companies to help in verifying the accuracy of certain records.

Nonresponse

A random sample of 50 nonrespondents was called back and requestioned in personal or telephone interviews. Differences between proportions of companies (follow-up vs. original respondents) answering in a specified manner to each item indicated the direction of "nonresponse" bias. The differences in proportions served as the basis for a "bias scale." The bias scale was correlated with the loadings of each factor, as a measure of the extent to which each factor was related to nonresponse. Statistical significance of differences between proportions were evaluated graphically by abac (Walker and Lev, 1953).

The samples for consistency and nonresponse checks provided useful approximations for reporting and nonresponse errors, though they are small samples, due to the limited resources available for this study.

Data Analysis

Frequency distributions for each item were divided, insofar as classes permitted, near the median; and phi correlations for 2 x 2 tables were computed.[1] Linearity of regressions among quantitative variables was checked graphically and was found to be reasonably well satisfied in the ranges of the variables present in these data.

The 595 correlations were subjected to a complete centroid factor analysis (Thurstone, 1947) and the factors were then rotated to an orthogonal simple structure by the varimax method (Kaiser, 1958). Communalities were based on iterated values. The decision to stop factoring was based on the residuals.

DISCUSSION OF RESULTS

Returns

Thirty-two per cent of the 584 questionnaires were returned. The distribution of returns according to industrial product classification and for the 35 items are shown in Tables 37.1 and 37.2.

Consistency of Reports

The agreement upon retest is presented in Table 37.3. In general, the agreement was quite high. Only for Item 3, Lates (a.m.), was the pro-

[1] Phi was considered the most suitable correlation for these reasons: to provide a consistent index of correlation for mixed quantitative and qualitative variables; to avoid assumptions about distributions; and to provide a favorable (Gramian) matrix for factor analysis.

portion agreement less than .90. The average agreement per item expressed as correlation was .95. Under Spearman-Brown assumptions for a sample approximately 8 times as large, the average consistency of reporting was over .99, a very high degree of consistency. This figure does not indicate the stability of phenomena themselves; this information was not available.

Nonresponse Bias

It was possible to obtain information from 23 (46 per cent) of the 50 nonrespondent companies in the call-back sample. The 27 companies that refused gave these reasons: lack of interest; lack of time; unwillingness

TABLE 37.1. *Returns by product classification*[a]
($N = 188$)

Product Class	Proportion
Food	.29
Printing and Publishing	.11
Chemical and Allied	.09
Stone, Clay, and Glass	.09
Fabricated Metals	.07
Apparel	.05
Transportation Equipment	.05
Lumber	.04
Miscellaneous	.04
Leather; Electrical Machinery; Paper and Allied; Petroleum; Primary Metals; Professional, Scientific & Control Instruments; Textiles; Tobacco[b]	.11
Total	1.00

[a] This is the standard industrial classification as given by the Bureau of the Budget (1957).
[b] Each of these classes, here pooled, contained two per cent or less.

to reveal information. Table 37.3 compares the 23 responding companies with the original returns. Proportions are based on the same cuts used for phi correlations. Except for Item 18, Eating Facilities, original respondents generally tended to have more favorable reports to give with respect to personnel benefits and services, but approximately equally favorable reports with respect to personnel performance.

TABLE 37.2. *Item distributions*

1. What is your approximate yearly employee turnover? (Consider only unfavorable reasons for terminations. Exclude such reasons as retirement, death, company transfers and the like.) (N=178)

Bi-nary	% Turnover	Per Cent
0	0-1%	36.4
0	2-4%	20.1
1	5-7%	15.6
1	8-10%	12.3
1	11-15%	3.9
1	16-20%	5.0
1	21-25%	2.2
1	26-30%	1.7
1	31-40%	0.0
1	Over 40%	2.8

2. On an average day, about what percentage of your employees return to work late after the lunch period? (N=177)

Bi-nary	% Late (p.m.)	Per Cent
0	0-1%	77.8
1	2-4%	10.5
1	5-7%	4.5
1	8-10%	3.9
1	11-15%	1.1
1	16-20%	0.0
1	21-25%	0.0
1	26-30%	0.0
1	31-40%	0.0
1	Over 40%	2.2

3. On an average day, about what percentage of your employees report late at the start of the workday? (N=177)

Bi-nary	% Late (a.m.)	Per Cent
0	0-1%	67.1
1	2-4%	23.2
1	5-7%	5.1
1	8-10%	4.0
1	11-15%	0.0
1	16-20%	0.6
1	21-25%	0.0
1	26-30%	0.0
1	31-40%	0.0
1	Over 40%	0.0

4. In one year, about how many requests do you receive asking for assistance to collect a bill unpaid by an employee (including garnishments)? (N=177)

Bi-nary	Number of Requests	Per Cent
0	0-1	34.5
0	2-4	21.5
1	5-7	5.1
1	8-10	8.4
1	11-20	11.3
1	21-40	5.6
1	41-60	5.6
1	61-99	2.3
1	100-399	5.1
1	400 or more	0.6

5. Approximately what percentage of the job applications that you receive give your own employees as references? (N=175)

Bi-nary	% Applications	Per Cent
0	0-1%	41.7
0	2-4%	10.2
1	5-7%	4.5
1	8-10%	11.4
1	11-15%	2.9
1	16-20%	6.9
1	21-30%	6.3
1	31-55%	6.9
1	56-80%	6.3
1	81-100%	2.9

6. About what percentage of scheduled man-hours of work is lost due to unexcused absences? (N=176)

Bi-nary	% Man Hours	Per Cent
0	0-½%	46.7
1	½-1%	25.0
1	1-1½%	5.1
1	1½-2%	5.1
1	2-2½%	4.0
1	2½-3%	2.8
1	3-4%	4.5
1	Over 4%	6.8

TABLE 37.2. (continued)

7. About what percentage of your overall production do you reject as being below your acceptable standards? (N=172)

Binary	% Production	Per Cent
1	0-1%	59.2
0	2-3%	23.3
0	4-5%	10.5
0	6-7%	3.5
0	8-9%	0.0
0	10-11%	2.3
0	12-13%	0.0
0	14-16%	0.6
0	17-19%	0.0
0	20% or more	0.6

8. During a year, from about what percentage of your employees do you receive grievances or complaints? (N=177)

Binary	% Employees	Per Cent
0	0-1%	76.8
1	2-4%	8.4
1	5-7%	3.4
1	8-10%	0.6
1	11-15%	3.4
1	16-20%	3.4
1	21-25%	1.1
1	26-30%	0.6
1	31-40%	0.6
1	Over 40%	1.7

9. About how many instances of theft of company property by employees do you receive a year? (N=178)

Binary	Number of Thefts	Per Cent
1	0-1	81.4
0	2-4	13.5
0	5-7	2.8
0	8-10	1.1
0	11-20	0.6
0	21-40	0.6
0	41-60	0.0
0	61-99	0.0
0	100-399	0.0
0	400 or more	0.0

10. About what percentage of employees participate in voluntary company functions such as picnics, dances, parties, and the like? (N=174)

Binary	% Employees	Per Cent
1	1-3%	6.9
1	4-7%	1.1
1	8-15%	1.7
1	16-25%	1.7
1	26-35%	1.7
1	36-45%	2.3
1	46-60%	4.0
1	61-80%	10.9
1	81-100%	14.9
0	None given	54.8

11. How long must an employee be with your company to receive a paid vacation? (N=178)

Binary	Time	Per Cent
0	At least six months	23.0
1	At least one year	64.7
0	Others (less than 1 year)	12.3

12. What is your compulsory retirement age for men? (N=178)

Binary	Age	Per Cent
0	None	70.8
1	55 yrs.	0.0
1	60 yrs.	0.0
1	65 yrs.	22.5
1	Other	6.7

13. What is your compulsory retirement age for women? (N=178)

Binary	Age	Per Cent
0	None	75.3
1	55 yrs.	0.0
1	60 yrs.	2.8
1	65 yrs.	14.6
1	Other	7.3

TABLE 37.2. (continued)

14. In computing pension benefits, what is the maximum number of years of service for which you give credit? (N=177)

Binary	Years	Per Cent
1	20	1.7
1	25	2.8
1	30	3.4
1	35	4.5
1	40	2.3
1	All years	19.8
1	Other	4.0
0	No pension	61.5

15. How many paid holidays do you customarily observe? (N=178)

Binary	Number of Days	Per Cent
0	0-4	21.9
0	5	10.7
1	6	27.5
1	7	23.0
1	8	14.0
1	9	1.7
1	10	0.6
1	11 or more	0.6

16. Approximately what percentage of your employees subscribe to company offered group insurance such as life, hospitalization, and the like? (N=178)

Binary	% Employees	Per Cent
0	1-15%	5.1
0	16-30%	4.5
0	31-45%	1.7
0	46-60%	5.6
0	61-75%	8.4
0	76-90%	12.4
1	91-100%	40.4
0	None offered	21.9

17. At this time, to about how many retired employees are you paying a pension? (N=178)

Binary	Number of Employees	Per Cent
0	0-1	76.8
1	2-4	8.4
1	5-7	3.4
1	8-10	0.6
1	11-20	3.4
1	21-40	3.4
1	41-60	1.1
1	61-99	0.6
1	100-399	0.6
1	400 or more	1.7

18. During regular working hours, what eating arrangements are provided employees? (N=179)

Binary	Eating	Per Cent
1	Free meals	0.0
1	Meals at reduced prices	5.6
1	Meals at regular prices	5.0
1	A place for employees to eat meals which they provide for themselves	32.4
0	No arrangements of any kind	57.0

19. What is your policy in granting time off to an employee to take National Guard or Reserve training? (N=177)

Binary	Policy	Per Cent
0	Must take training during vacation	14.6
0	Given training time off without pay, but also given paid vacation	34.5
1	Given training time off with full or difference of pay, and given paid vacation also.	18.1
1	Paid double if both training and vacation taken at same time	0.6
1	Each case decided separately	32.2

TABLE 37.2. (continued)

20. When may an employee withdraw his contributions from a company-sponsored savings or investment plan? (N=177)

Bi-nary	Plan	Per Cent
0	No such plan	78.6
1	Only at retirement or termination	4.5
1	Any time	14.1
1	At specified intervals	2.8

21. As a percentage of payroll, approximately how much does your benefit program cost? (N=167)

Bi-nary	% Payroll	Per Cent
0	0-1%	47.2
1	2-3%	11.4
1	4-5%	10.2
1	6-7%	4.2
1	8-9%	1.2
1	10-11%	6.6
1	12-13%	3.0
1	14-16%	4.8
1	17-19%	1.8
1	20% or more	9.6

22. For what period of time do you pay a salaried employee absent due to a non-occupational injury or sickness? (N=178)

Bi-nary	Time	Per Cent
0	Length of period depends on length of service	56.2
1	Paid for full period regardless of service	12.4
1	A fixed period regardless of service	9.0
1	Not paid for such absences	14.0
1	Other	8.4

23. For what period of time do you pay an hourly employee absent due to a non-occupational injury or sickness? (N=175)

Bi-nary	Time	Per Cent
1	Length of period depends on length of service	22.3
1	Paid for full period regardless of service	0.6
1	A fixed period regardless of service	11.4
0	Not paid for such absences	58.3
1	Other	7.4

24. Approximately what percentage of your employees make use of financial assistance for education offered by your company? (N=177)

Bi-nary	% Employees	Per Cent
0	None offered	82.5
1	0-1%	9.0
1	2-3%	3.4
1	4-5%	2.8
1	6-8%	1.1
1	9-11%	0.6
1	12-14%	0.6
1	15-17%	0.0
1	18-20%	0.0
1	Over 20%	0.0

25. What parking provisions (on company or commercial property) do you have for employees? (N=179)

Bi-nary	Parking	Per Cent
1	Free parking	57.5
0	Parking at reduced rates	0.6
0	Parking at regular rates	0.6
0	No provisions	41.3

TABLE 37.2. (continued)

26. How is production quality controlled? (N=176)

Binary	Method	Per Cent
0	Judgment of an inspector	45.5
1	Mechanically or electronically	2.8
1	Statistical methods	1.1
1	Combination of above methods	43.8
1	Other	6.8

27. What type diversions or recreation opportunities are offered to employees? (N=178)

Binary	Activity	Per Cent
1	Company sponsored activities only	13.5
1	Company provided facilities only	1.1
1	Both company sponsored activities and provided facilities	13.5
0	None	71.9

28. Approximately what discount do you allow employees on purchases of company product? (N=177)

Binary	Discount	Per Cent
0	1-5%	22.5
0	6-10%	6.1
0	11-15%	3.8
1	16-20%	9.5
1	25% or more	31.5
0	Product is of "unfinished" nature and not ready for consumer use	26.6

29. What union represents your employees? (N=179)

Binary	Union	Per Cent
0	No union	60.4
1	Independent union	3.3
1	Company union	0.6
1	AFL-CIO	35.7

30. If you would like to receive a synopsis of the findings, please indicate below: (N=178)

Binary		Per Cent
1	Yes, send a synopsis	78.2
0	No, do not send a synopsis	21.8

Note: The following questions did not appear on the questionnaire. Questions 31, 32, 33, and 35 were used to classify returns. Question 34, Number of Employees, was pre-coded.

31. Company signature affixed on completed questionnaire? (N=178)

Binary		Per Cent
1	Yes	92.7
0	No	7.3

32. Name and title of person (company officer) affixed to returned questionnaire? (N=178)

Binary		Per Cent
1	Yes	89.0
0	No	11.0

TABLE 37.2. (continued)

33. Number of questions on questionnaire answered by company? (N=188)

Binary	Number of Questions	Per Cent
1	All	88.2
0	27	8.4
0	26	2.2
0	25	0.6
0	Less than 25	0.6

34. Number of employees in the firm? (N=188)

Binary	Number of Employees	Per Cent
0	Less than 10	20
0	10-24	24
0	25-49	16
1	50-99	11
1	100-199	14
1	200-399	08
1	400-999	05
1	1000 or more	02

35. Number of days taken by company to return completed questionnaire. (N=188)

Binary	Days	Per Cent
1	1	53.5
0	2	11.2
0	3	6.1
0	4	4.5
0	5	4.0
0	6	0.6
0	7	7.2
0	8	4.5
0	9	1.7
0	10 or more	6.7

Correlation and Factor Analysis

The original correlations and eighth factor residuals are shown in Table 37.4. The results of the factor analysis and rotation are shown in Table 37.5. For purposes of discussion, a summary of the significant loadings (.30 or greater) is presented in Table 37.6. Some of the factors from Table 37.5 are reflected in Table 37.6. The factors are presented in descending order of common factor variance accounted for.

For discussion of the factors certain points should be kept in mind. The units of study were whole organizations, as mentioned before; the data were therefore normative, involving differences between companies. It was not to be expected that the results would necessarily agree with studies conducted within companies. In addition, allowance should also

TABLE 37.3. *Survey results for original returns, consistency of reports, and sample of nonrespondents*

	Variable	Returns	Proportion[a] Consistency	Nonrespondents
1.	Turnover	44	100	56
2.	Lates (p.m.)	22	92	26
3.	Lates (a.m.)	33	83	35
4.	Bill Collection Requests	44	96	48
5.	Applicants Nominated	48	92	13*
6.	Absences	47	100	26
7.	Production, Substandard	59	92	35
8.	Grievances	23	100	48
9.	Thefts	82	100	82
10.	Social Functions	45	96	09*
11.	Vacation, Tenure for	65	100	00
12.	Retirement, Men	29	100	00*
13.	Retirement, Women	25	100	00
14.	Pension Plan	39	96	00*
15.	Holidays, Paid	40	100	13*
16.	Insurance	53	100	26
17.	Retirees	23	100	00*
18.	Eating Facilities	43	100	83*
19.	Military Training Leave Pay	51	100	52
20.	Savings-Investment Plan	21	100	00*
21.	Cost of Benefits	53	100	17*
22.	Sick Pay, Salaried	44	96	30
23.	Sick Pay, Hourly	42	92	26
24.	Educational Aid	17	100	00*
25.	Parking Facilities	57	100	32
26.	Quality Control Methods	55	96	50
27.	Recreation Facilities	28	100	00*
28.	Discount	52	100	41
29.	Unions	40	100	29
30.	Synopsis Desired	78	96	57
31.	Company Signature on Quest.	93	na	na
32.	Company Officer's Signature	89	na	na
33.	Questions Answered, Number	88	96	91
34.	Employees, Number	40	100	17
35.	Working Days to Return Quest.	54	na	na

[a] Decimals omitted.
* The difference between this figure and that for Returns is significantly different, p less than .05, 2-tailed test.

be made for geographic limitations in the sample. Characteristics of the form of analysis should also be taken into account. In particular, it should be noted that, while the factors were orthogonal, some of the variables representing the factors were substantially correlated.

In interpreting the factors it will be noted that the relationships imply the coexistence of organizational conditions and behaviors; that is, those characteristics that tended to hang together in organizations. No answer is possible on the chicken-or-egg question pertaining to temporal or causal orders among the variables. On the internal evidence of the study alone, no real dependence is necessarily implied, although on other grounds dependency other than a merely statistical one may occasionally be reasonable.

Factors

Factor I. Retirement Welfare. Although the factor has been named for pension and retirement benefits with which it is most closely associated, the factor suggests employee welfare beyond the job site. There are, however, some other factors which also carry considerable welfare implications.

Factor II. Cooperation With Survey. Factor II seems to reflect primarily willingness to release company data.

Factor III. Size of Workforce. This factor presents the remarkable result that the most distinctive correlates of size are opportunities for participation in social and personal relationships. No information is available as to what extent social and recreational activities are utilized, or to what extent they are successful, in fostering social relationships.

Social and recreation activities would appear to be one way to increase interaction potential, thereby reducing some consequences of distance and complexity of relationships in large organization. Along with emphasis on social interaction, the factor contains the suggestion that in large organization even the occasions for social relationships get organized. More generally, the factor suggests the problems and costs of communication and organization that may hinder or disable the organization of "excessive" size—the brontosaurus principle.

It should be pointed out, too, that larger organizations enjoy certain economies of scale; because of existing facilities, e.g., Eating Facilities, social activities may be provided at little additional cost. In addition, larger organizations are influenced more by trends in fads and innovations; industrial recreation and human relations are among these.

Size of organization has been used to explain so many results in the literature that one would expect it to be a general factor. The present

TABLE 37.4. Correlations and eighth residuals[a,b]

Variable	1	2	3	4	5	6	7	8	9	10	11	12	13	14	15	16	17	18	19
1 Turnover	(28)	09	11	-01	04	-03	-06	-06	00	02	-07	-03	-06	-09	06	09	-06	02	-03
2 Lates (p.m.)	30	(42)	-10	02	02	-06	03	04	-16	03	08	-09	07	01	-12	08	-19	-08	-06
3 Lates (a.m.)	43	-15	(48)	-02	11	-09	19	01	-17	02	07	-05	02	-10	-06	-08	-10	-04	14
4 Collections	21	13	18	(38)	00	05	07	-01	08	-05	-05	-02	02	-09	-12	-01	-07	-01	00
5 Applicants	20	17	17	34	(36)	-01	04	-08	02	07	-08	-04	03	-13	-08	00	-09	-04	04
6 Absences	20	15	17	26	15	(24)	-08	-08	18	-02	-12	01	05	-02	06	-15	09	-02	-04
7 Production, Substd.	-17	07	21	07	-05	-14	(40)	03	02	-20	-17	-05	15	-05	-06	-11	-03	24	-01
8 Grievances	18	21	25	29	20	17	-13	(33)	04	-07	03	01	-09	-01	-02	15	00	03	16
9 Thefts	12	-13	09	20	14	25	-16	25	(59)	01	-04	-05	12	01	20	02	-12	-01	04
10 Social Functions	01	08	-05	18	29	11	-11	09	04	(57)	03	-21	-31	16	-01	-04	06	04	-05
11 Vacation	00	06	02	02	07	-07	-41	17	08	08	(16)	13	-01	13	-19	-08	07	-03	05
12 Retirement, Men	-14	06	-14	25	26	05	22	12	04	27	09	(80)	37	08	07	-22	-06	-09	01
13 Retirement, Women	-02	02	00	29	33	03	09	05	24	-30	10	57	(63)	-07	10	-16	-02	00	04
14 Pension Plan	-01	12	04	33	22	05	19	16	04	31	06	62	34	(89)	00	15	01	-14	11
15 Holidays	15	10	-09	13	21	15	16	10	03	14	-09	41	30	43	(53)	-04	04	07	-03
16 Insurance	20	-07	-20	14	20	-23	-32	05	-13	-21	08	-48	26	43	22	(84)	09	02	-19
17 Retirees, No.	01	-15	-01	-19	08	13	15	07	-10	22	02	21	19	39	22	18	(35)	-05	-02
18 Eating Facilities	01	-19	-03	25	21	-02	27	15	07	29	05	25	25	21	25	18	17	(35)	02
19 Military Trng Pay	-05	20	26	03	-03	-13	10	08	03	-29	-07	-08	19	40	-03	04	06	03	(34)
20 Savings Plan	-07	-40	-60	23	28	01	05	08	-13	23	11	30	22	-16	26	15	-13	29	-13
21 Cost of Benefits	-01	12	12	27	41	10	-11	25	11	21	12	43	42	57	22	42	29	30	01
22 Sick Pay, Salaried	-01	08	05	18	19	08	02	20	-20	08	01	27	-36	30	14	21	22	20	-14
23 Sick Pay, Hourly	-01	01	-06	02	14	-08	08	18	-08	15	14	07	14	08	-01	07	15	04	-04
24 Educational Aid	-04	-23	04	19	23	03	-05	04	-09	35	07	25	20	22	22	24	06	29	17
25 Parking	-02	15	-10	17	29	01	07	16	-21	13	08	25	24	33	25	31	15	24	25
26 Quality Control	-03	-07	-12	19	12	-24	03	12	10	16	-03	26	22	27	-37	16	26	19	01
27 Recreation Facilit.	-06	-01	-03	24	32	04	-17	09	12	52	04	30	24	45	26	19	19	35	-24

TABLE 37.4. (continued)

Variable	1	2	3	4	5	6	7	8	9	10	11	12	13	14	15	16	17	18	19
28 Discounts	05	17	17	-10	02	01	-13	04	60	-03	00	08	03	08	06	-03	-02	02	-07
29 Unions	-07	05	-06	25	16	12	-02	01	12	04	07	34	29	37	31	23	16	22	-04
30 Synopsis	07	15	18	17	14	21	-08	07	11	11	07	12	27	18	17	07	24	18	-20
31 Co. Sign	-13	19	07	01	-01	-15	23	-03	14	-07	-04	17	10	10	07	-03	24	-04	-04
32 Person Sign	05	14	04	-02	01	-15	24	-08	18	-05	-07	15	09	07	08	-10	23	01	-05
33 Questions Ans'd	09	17	15	-11	09	03	00	-06	20	-01	-04	03	-01	-08	-13	-03	09	09	-11
34 Employees, No.	09	-02	02	43	19	11	07	18	08	21	20	39	32	48	28	27	45	40	-04
35 Days to Return Quest.	02	06	-86	01	-04	-20	12	-27	10	-08	-05	10	-06	11	-04	20	03	-11	12

Variable	20	21	22	23	24	25	26	27	28	29	30	31	32	33	34	35
1 Turnover	11	-10	-11	00	-06	-02	11	-01	-01	00	-10	-13	04	09	-06	09
2 Lates (p.m.)	-28	04	-11	09	-15	04	19	01	11	-06	-05	01	-11	14	15	21
3 Lates (a.m.)	-13	17	-02	01	00	-07	-09	13	03	03	-03	06	-03	14	00	02
4 Collections	17	-08	11	-10	00	00	06	-02	-13	14	-04	03	03	-09	01	01
5 Applicants	07	-01	11	03	06	07	06	02	-07	-05	-07	-03	01	11	-10	-03
6 Absences	11	03	00	-10	04	03	-12	04	-02	07	13	-03	-06	07	-01	-07
7 Production, Substd.	13	-01	-09	11	-12	-04	-09	-21	02	-07	-09	04	05	-06	05	02
8 Grievances	09	01	16	11	00	12	13	-02	-08	-03	-05	11	04	-01	-03	-14
9 Thefts	02	-05	-14	-05	-12	-16	-11	09	15	00	04	09	08	11	06	15
10 Social Functions	-07	01	02	01	20	09	04	20	03	01	02	-04	00	-03	-15	-02
11 Vacation	-05	-04	06	08	05	10	00	-04	-09	04	00	02	00	-02	10	00
12 Retirement, Men	-04	01	11	-02	05	-07	00	-13	-02	03	04	06	03	-02	20	08
13 Retirement, Women	08	04	-13	-03	02	-05	-13	-13	02	-08	04	-02	00	08	13	-12
14 Pension Plan	-23	08	07	02	-05	-12	03	14	00	04	05	03	03	-08	16	-05
15 Holidays	05	-14	-10	-05	09	-06	-28	03	12	07	02	00	03	-13	11	-09
16 Insurance	-01	07	15	01	07	06	23	10	01	09	-08	-05	-02	-01	00	-04
17 Retirees, No.	-16	10	15	08	-16	-03	06	-06	03	06	-01	00	03	01	10	-09

458

Variable	20	21	22	23	24	25	26	27	28	29	30	31	32	33	34	35
18 Eating Facilities	02	-05	14	-08	04	08	04	04	-02	11	06	06	05	04	03	23
19 Military Trng Pay	09	00	-12	07	13	14	-15	-14	-08	-10	-08	04	15	-07	-02	-02
20 Savings Plan	(61)	01	06	-07	-10	03	15	-12	-03	08	-01	14	20	08	09	-04
21 Cost of Benefits	36	(62)	09	12	-11	-12	-06	-01	02	-02	-02	04	00	-14	08	08
22 Sick Pay, Salaried	13	28	(80)	-08	14	11	-06	-25	08	-14	12	-03	13	-12	-12	-14
23 Sick Pay, Hourly	05	20	-29	(18)	-01	-02	-07	-10	01	-12	01	-08	-04	00	-01	09
24 Educational Aid	05	11	24	06	(25)	01	01	05	06	-03	-02	08	16	01	-10	-05
25 Parking	17	21	20	02	12	(30)	18	05	-01	-11	-06	04	-04	06	-23	12
26 Quality Control	17	03	-46	11	18	27	(48)	-15	02	-06	-03	03	-06	-11	-02	12
27 Recreation Facilit.	22	32	43	12	27	27	18	(59)	07	-04	-12	-02	-10	11	02	12
28 Discounts	-04	23	32	-13	07	01	-02	05	(40)	-09	10	-04	-07	-21	05	01
29 Unions	23	26	-33	-01	-01	20	16	27	-10	(42)	06	-03	-06	14	-13	00
30 Synopsis	02	13	04	10	16	06	07	19	01	19	(51)	05	03	-35	12	18
31 Co. Sign	13	04	-04	-11	25	17	15	20	-08	11	63	(81)	-03	04	11	-21
32 Person Sign	13	-04	08	-09	26	07	05	22	-08	11	59	84	(96)	02	-20	-19
33 Questions Ans'd	11	-11	13	-10	12	06	-17	09	-06	03	-24	30	27	(24)	03	09
34 Employees, No.	33	39	07	15	30	-18	14	34	-04	-20	40	18	-27	16	(86)	10
35 Days to Return Quest.	04	16	04	05	11	21	17	15	04	-04	22	-05	-10	23	31	(21)

a Values rounded to two figures; decimals omitted.
b Entries below the main diagonal are original correlations. Entries above are eighth residuals. Diagonals are communalities.

findings indicate that the effects of size have resulted largely from failure to take account of relevant variables.[2] For example, we find no support for Revans' (1958) conclusions that generally less favorable performance is associated with size. The present results suggest that organization conditions as such (e.g., incentives, programs, management policies), rather than size, are related to personnel functioning. Incidentally, this conclusion should permit us to be somewhat more optimistic about the possibility of constructing favorable organization environments. The variables here found to be related to performance tend to be controllable conditions, rather than size, which under many circumstances is largely uncontrollable.

Factor IV. Thrift Benefits. Factor IV seems to indicate ways in which companies encourage savings either by investing funds or by saving employees' expenses. Not enough is known about these thrift measures to explain the negative relationship with lateness in the morning. The industrial practice of contributing docked pay to recreation funds may provide a partial explanation.

Factor V. Costs of Sickness vs. Use of Machinery. The positive pole is related to provisions for health, recreation, or superannuation of personnel. The variables smack of repairs and maintenance costs for manpower, as opposed to machine power.

Factor VI. Job Aversion. The general picture is of avoidance, escape, discontent, and partial or total withdrawal. Item 4, Bill Collection Requests, may refer to one reason for discharge under company rules; or possibly, it may indicate financial hardship and low pay, and consequent search for other employment. Item 5, Applicants Nominated by Present Employees, may be a partial cause or result of Job Aversion, depending on the quality and use of this source of employees.

The factor has much in common with a number of analyses of objective measures of morale and personnel performance (Giese and Ruter, 1949; Merrihue and Katzell, 1955; Seashore, Indik, and Georgopoulos, 1960; Turner, 1960).

Job Aversion is unrelated to productivity measures; these are related only to Factors I and VII. If Factor VI is identified with job satisfaction, these findings support the conclusions of Brayfield and Crockett (1955) about the independence of productivity and satisfaction. It will be noted

[2] The absence of a general factor does not appear to be an artifact of the method of analysis. Although the varimax method tends to avoid general factors, the data were also rotated by the quartimax method, which tends toward general factors if any exist. The results by the two methods differed only by a point or two in the second or third decimal places. The absence of a general factor is equally convincing from inspection of the correlation matrix.

that our results give no hint of what conditions if any may be related to Job Aversion. Factor VI reflects the "decision to participate," as discussed by March and Simon (1958). However, Job Aversion is concerned more with the decision *not* to participate, which is associated with exit rather than entry. In general, it is supposed that these two decisions are subject to quite different conditions and are therefore not simply opposites.

Factor VII. Insurance Benefits. Like Retirement Welfare, Insurance Benefits are among the few conditions found to be related to productivity measures.

Factor VIII. Theft vs. Discounts. This is a relationship which, to our knowledge, has not appeared before in the published literature. As discounts increase, the probability of theft declines. The relationship suggests a balancing of the advantages of theft with the risk of penalty. Where the product is "of unfinished nature and not ready for consumer use" (one alternative on Item 28, Discount on Company Product) the probability of theft is lowest but not zero. The relationship is presented for clarity in the form of an expectancy chart in Table 37.7.

Theft is a third kind of independent behavior, unrelated to productivity or aversive behaviors. This finding is somewhat at variance with the view that theft, like sabotage or accidents, is an aggressive behavior related to discontent. On this view theft would be related to Factor VI; this is not supported by our results.

Factor VIII indicates a feature of the product "transactions" between employees and companies. In this case, employees are both producers and consumers; a compromise in price is then expected or exacted. The relationship may be important for the March and Simon (1958) analysis; persons who occupy multiple roles in the organization may expect, or engage in, special modes of participation.

Factors and Nonresponse Bias

The relationships of the factors with nonresponse bias (bottom Table 5) indicate the extent to which the factors were representative of the whole population. When allowance is made for the direction of scoring of items and for the sign patterns of factor loadings, it is seen that Factor VII and Factor I (Insurance and Retirement) were less typical of the whole. Factor VI, Job Aversion, is slightly related to nonresponse; aversive behaviors are probably somewhat more typical in uncooperative companies. The correlations with nonresponse bias are generally low; the factors can be retained for the population, although the magnitude of variances accounted for would be somewhat altered.

TABLE 37.5. *Rotated orthogonal factors*

No.	Variable	Direction Scored +	I	II	III	IV	V	VI	VII	VIII	h^2
1	Turnover	Over 4%	-05	-02	-13	20	-05	-42	-08	-16	28
2	Lates (noon)	Over 1%	00	-23	04	10	-20	-55	01	09	42
3	Lates (A.M.)	Over 1%	04	-05	-05	49	00	-34	13	-30	48
4	Requests for Coll'ns	Over 4%	37	03	-29	-07	04	-33	04	-18	38
5	Applications	Over 4%	28	-02	-19	-27	-02	-33	-12	-20	36
6	Absences	Over ½%	03	10	-05	06	-12	-39	14	-14	24
7	Prod'n, Substd.	Less than 1%	34	-18	03	16	-13	14	35	24	40
8	Grievances	Over 1%	19	13	-10	01	04	-45	-02	-21	33
9	Thefts	Less than 2%	02	-08	-03	04	04	-07	06	-75	59
10	Social Functions	Yes	-00	06	-54	-39	-05	-17	25	10	57
11	Vacation, Tenure for	1 Year or more	-06	11	-11	-10	16	-12	-25	-11	16
12	Retirement Age, Men	Yes	76	-11	-11	-32	-07	01	28	-04	80
13	Retirement Age, Women	Yes	58	-08	06	-08	37	-06	-26	-22	63
14	Pension Plan	Yes	83	-03	-33	12	-08	02	-21	03	89
15	Holidays Paid	Over 6%	48	-08	03	-18	-30	-19	-27	22	53
16	Insurance, Per Cent Covered	Over 75%	10	-03	-14	-06	00	03	-89	04	84
17	Retirees, No. of	2% or more	37	-16	-37	13	-01	-03	-04	13	35
18	Eating Facilities	Eating spaces and/or meals	33	02	-32	-36	-03	02	03	-03	35
19	Military Train'g Pay	Full or partial pay	32	07	15	29	18	24	-08	-08	34

No.	Variable	Scored +	I	II	III	IV	V	VI	VII	VIII	h²
20	Savings Plan	Yes	14	-01	02	-75	-04	06	-12	-01	61
21	Cost of Benefits	2% or more	49	09	-22	-27	-10	-19	-37	-23	62
22	Sick Pay (Salaried)	No variation with tenure	14	00	-08	-04	-87	-03	01	-04	80
23	Sick Pay (Hourly)	Yes	08	09	-18	-03	23	-11	-14	20	18
24	Educational Aid	Yes	19	-17	-35	-13	-04	16	-06	-08	25
25	Parking	Free	43	-13	04	-27	02	-07	-05	06	30
26	Qual. Control Method	Mech. & Electronic	23	-10	-27	-12	51	13	18	-05	48
27	Recreation Facilities	Yes	16	-18	-44	-45	32	-06	-10	-01	59
28	Discounts	Over 15%	06	06	03	00	-30	03	-07	-53	40
29	Unions	Yes	40	-15	19	-32	26	-13	-01	04	42
30	Synopsis Desired	Yes	09	-54	-27	00	10	-32	-12	04	51
31	Co. Signature	Yes	07	-89	-05	-01	05	02	00	-01	81
32	Person Sign.	Yes	03	-97	07	00	-01	00	00	-02	96
33	Questions Ansd, No.	All	-10	-30	-14	-04	-19	17	-02	-21	24
34	Employees, No.	Over 49%	26	02	-85	-05	-05	00	-21	-05	86
35	Work-Days to Return Quest.	Over 1%	07	-14	-23	01	-05	32	-16	00	21
	Percentage Variance		20	15	13	12	11	10	10	09	100
	Correlation of Factor with Bias[b]		-31	08	-06	08	-04	-17	41*	-12	

[a] Decimals omitted.
[b] Data for variables 31, 32, and 35 were not appropriate for follow-up conditions and were omitted in these correlations.
* For 30 df, significant at .05 level.

TABLE 37.6. *Summary of factor loadings*

Factor I. Retirement Welfare

No.	Direction +	Variable	Loading
14	Yes	Pension Plan	.83
12	Yes	Retirement, Men, Compulsory	.76
13	Yes	Retirement, Women	.58
21	2% or more	Cost of Benefits (% of payroll)	.49
15	Over 6	Holidays, Paid	.48
25	Free	Parking	.43
29	Yes	Union	.40
17	2 or more	Retirees, Number	.37
4	Over 4	Bill Collection Requests	.37
7	Less than 2%	Production, Substandard	.34
18	Spaces-Meals	Eating Facilities	.33
19	Partial or Full	Military Training Leave Pay	.32

Factor II. Cooperation With Survey

No.	Direction +	Variable	Loading
32	Yes	Signature of Company Officer on Questionnaire	.97
31	Yes	Company Signature on Questionnaire	.89
30	Yes	Synopsis Desired	.54

Factor III. Size of Workforce

No.	Direction +	Variable	Loading
34	Over 49	Employees, Number	.85
10	Yes	Social Functions, Company Sponsored	.54
27	Yes	Recreation Facilities	.44
17	2 or more	Retirees, Number	.37
24	Yes	Educational Assistance	.35
14	Yes	Pension Plan	.33
18	Spaces-Meals	Eating Facilities	.32
4	Over 4	Bill Collection Requests	.30

Factor IV. Thrift Benefits

No.	Direction +	Variable	Loading
20	Yes	Savings-Investment Plan	.75
27	Yes	Recreation Facilities	.45
10	Yes	Social Functions, Company Sponsored	.39
18	Spaces-Meals	Eating Facilities	.36
29	Yes	Union	.32
12	Yes	Retirement, Men, Compulsory	.32
3	Over 1%	Lates (a.m.)	-.49

Factor V. Costs of Sickness vs. Use of Machinery

No.	Direction +	Variable	Loading
22	Not based on tenure	Sick Pay, Salaried	.87
28	Over 15%	Discount on Company Product	.30
15	Over 6	Holidays, Paid	.30
27	Yes	Recreation Facilities	-.32
13	Yes	Retirement, Women	-.37
26	Mechanical	Quality Control Methods	-.51

TABLE 37.6. (*Cont.*)

Factor VI. Job Aversion

2	Over 1%	Lates (p.m.)	.55
8	Over 1%	Grievances and Complaints	.45
1	Over 4%	Turnover	.42
6	Over ½%	Absences	.39
3	Over 1%	Lates (a.m.)	.34
5	Over 4%	Applicants Nominated by Present Employees	.33
4	Over 4	Bill Collection Requests	.33

Factor VII. Insurance Benefits

16	Over 75%	Group Insurance, Employees Covered	.89
21	2% or more	Cost of Benefits (% of payroll)	.37
7	Less than 2%	Production, Substandard	-.35

Factor VIII. Theft vs. Discounts

9	Less than 2	Theft of Company Product	.75
28	Over 15%	Discount on Company Product	.53
3	Over 1%	Lates (a.m.)	.30

Discussion

Productivity, Job Aversion, and Theft are mutually independent behaviors. Productivity and Theft, as well as Lates (a.m.) and Bill Collection Requests, have partial relations with one or another benefit conditions. Factor VI which consists of lates, absences, turnover and other aversive behaviors is unrelated to any positive incentive conditions. These findings generally tend to support the hypothesis that there are positive incentives (satisfiers) which promote favorable performance, and negative incentives (dissatisfiers) which account for unfavorable performance (Herzberg, Mausner, Snyderman, 1959). Two qualifications should be made, however. First, no negative incentives have been identified; second, some behaviors, such as Lates (a.m.), are explained in part by positive incentives and presumably in part by negative incentives.

The union has a role in Factors I and IV, but it is independent of other factors. As expected, benefits are not the exclusive possession of unionized plants. But this implies no denial of union claims of bargaining leadership. For example, it would be simultaneously consistent with union claims and the present results that unions initiate trends which, once launched, spread beyond the companies of origin. It is worth noting, however, that the lack of relationship between unions and Job Aversion does not support the view that unions serve to sublimate discontent into union activity (Chapple and Sayles, 1961).

The factors related to benefit conditions suggest considerable diversity among companies in emphasizing various incentive programs and

TABLE 37.7. *The relationship between discounts and theft*[a]

Per Cent Discount on Company Products	Instances of Theft Percentages of Companies Reporting Two or More Per Year
0-5	29
6-15	23
16-20	20
Over 20	17
Product is "unfinished", not ready for consumer use	13

[a] Certain categories on Item 28, Discounts, were combined in order to clarify this presentation.

services for employees. A general welfare factor is notably absent. The combinations of conditions found in companies are probably related to different "philosophies" or "climates" of employment relations. Whether it will be helpful to use results such as ours in further study of organizations in terms of various "traits" of climate, or policy, or other, is at present somewhat uncertain. One objective of this study will have been accomplished, however, if it calls attention to the importance of general organizational conditions for the study of behavior.

SUMMARY AND CONCLUSIONS

Relationships among organizational conditions and personnel behaviors have been investigated for a sample of 188 industrial manufacturing establishments. The relationships were resolved into the following orthogonal rotated factors: I. Retirement Welfare; II. Cooperation With Survey; III. Size of Workforce; IV. Thrift Benefits; V. Costs of Sickness vs. Use of Machinery; VI. Job Aversion; VII. Insurance Benefits; VIII. Theft vs. Discounts.

The results tended to support the following general conclusions:

1. Organizational behavior consists of a number of independent classes of behavior, three of which have been identified as related to productivity, job aversion, and theft.

2. These behaviors tend to be linked with quite different organizational conditions. Productivity is generally related to "positive incentives," retirement and insurance benefits having been identified. On the other hand, theft is uniquely related to discounts. But conditions associated with Job Aversion have not been identified.

3. Size of organization as such has no relation to performance. Size is associated with problems of interaction among personnel, and with increased organization and coordination.

In general, organizations are a complex of multidimensional conditions and performance, in which the linkages between conditions and behaviors tend to be unique, and in which independent behaviors are related to distinctly different organization conditions.

REFERENCES

Bass, B. M. *Leadership, psychology, and organizational behavior.* New York: Harper, 1960.

Baumgartel, H. & Sobol, R. Background and organizational factors in absenteeism. *Personnel Psychol.*, 1959, *12*, 431–443.

Bavelas, A. Communications patterns in task oriented groups. *J. acoust. Soc. Amer.*, 1950, *22*, 725–730.

Brayfield, A. H. & Crockett, W. H. Employee attitudes and performance. *Psychol. Bull.*, 1955, 52, 396–428.

Bureau of the Budget. *Standard industrial classification manual.* Washington, D.C.: U. S. Government Printing Office, 1957.

Coch, L. & French, J. R. P., Jr. Overcoming resistance to change. *Human Relat.*, 1948, *1*, 512–532.

Comrey, A. L. A research plan for the study of organization effectiveness. In Rubenstein, A. H. & Haberstroh, C. J. (Eds.) *Some theories of organization.* Homewood, Ill.: Irwin-Dorsey, 1960.

Chapman, R. L. & Kennedy, J. L. The background and implications of the Rand Corporation systems research laboratory studies. In Rubenstein, A. H. & Haberstroh, C. J. (Eds.) *Some theories of organization.* Homewood, Ill.: Irwin-Dorsey, 1960.

Chapple, E. D. & Sayles, L. R. *The measure of management.* New York: Macmillan, 1961.

Giese, W. J. & Ruter, H. W. An objective analysis of morale. *J. appl. Psychol.*, 1949, 33, 421–427.

Herzberg, F., Mausner, B., & Snyderman, Barbara. *The motivation to work.* New York: Wiley, 1959.

Kaiser, H. F. The varimax criterion for analytic rotation in factor analysis. *Psychometrika*, 1958, *23*, 187–200.

Kerr, W. A. Accident proneness of factory departments. *J. appl. Psychol.*, 1950, 34, 162–170.

Leavitt, H. J., Some effects of certain communication patterns on group performance. *J. abn. soc. Psychol.*, 1951, *46*, 38–50.

March, J. G. & Simon, H. A. *Organizations.* New York: Wiley, 1958.

Merrihue, W. V. & Katzell, R. B. ERI—yardstick of employee relations. *Harvard Business Review*, 1955, 33, 91–99.

Revans, R. W. Human relations, management and size. In Hugh-Jones, E. M. (Ed.) *Human relations and modern management.* Amsterdam, Netherlands: North Holland, 1958.

Rubenstein, A. H. & Haberstroh, C. J. (Eds.) *Some theories of organization.* Homewood, Ill.: Irwin-Dorsey, 1960.

Seashore, E. E., Indik, B. P., & Georgopoulos, B. S. Relationships among criteria of job performance. *J. appl. Psychol.*, 1960, 44, 195–202.

Thurstone, L. L. *Multiple factor analysis.* Chicago: Univer. Chicago Press, 1947.

Turner, W. W. Dimensions of foreman performance: a factor analysis of criterion measures. *J. app. Psychol.*, 1960, 44, 216–223.

Vroom, V. H. & Maier, N. R. F. Industrial social psychology. In Farnsworth, P. R. (Ed.) *Annu. Rev. Psychol.* Palo Alto, Calif.: Annual Review, 1961.

Walker, H. M. & Lev, J. *Statistical inference.* New York: Holt, 1953.

Yoder, D., Heneman, H. G., Jr., Turnbull, J. G., & Stone, C. H. *Handbook of personnel management and labor relations.* New York: McGraw-Hill, 1958.

38 Factorial Analysis of Organizational Performance

STANLEY E. SEASHORE
and EPHRAIM YUCHTMAN

In 1964 there was proposed a conceptual framework for the assessment of organizational performance.[1] This proposal was developed in response to the repeated failure of managers in forming reliable and valid estimates of their own organizations' performance and the repeated failure of researchers in their attempts to locate stable and generally applicable relationships between predictor variables, on the one hand, and single organizational performance variables on the other. This conceptual scheme also was a response to the fact, often noted by others, that organizations seem to have many goals, not one, and that these goals are often conflicting, incompatible with one another, changing in priorities and in realizations over time. The objective in this formulation was to seek some way to find order, and perhaps simplicity of order, among the numerous and miscellaneous variables that are used by managers, researchers, and the general public when they attempt to define and evaluate the performance of an organization.

The proposed conceptual framework assumed that variables descriptive of organizational performance could be ordered into a hierarchical network based upon the distinction between longer-term output variables, on the one hand, and on the other shorter-term variables descriptive of output behavior and of various organizational states and processes. We conceived of a hierarchical model having the following characteristics:

1. At the top of the hierarchy is the "ultimate criterion"—some conception of the net output performance of the organization over a long span

From *Administrative Science Quarterly*, 1967, *12*, 377–395. The authors are with the Survey Research Center of the Institute for Social Research, The University of Michigan. This investigation has been supported by the National Science Foundation (Grant GS-70), and by the anonymous firm that provided, at considerable expense to itself, the data used in the investigation.

[1] "Criteria of Organizational Effectiveness" by Stanley E. Seashore. *Michigan Business Review*, 17, 4 July 1965, 26–30.

of time in achieving its formal objectives, whatever they may be, with optimum use of environmental resources and opportunities. Such an ultimate criterion may never be measured, except possibly by historians, yet some concept of this kind is the basis for evaluation of lesser criteria.

2. Below the ultimate criterion there may be a roster of penultimate criteria having the following characteristics: they are relatively few in number, they are "output" or "results" criteria referring to things sought for their own value; they have trade-off value in relation to one another; they are in turn wholly caused by partially independent sets of lesser performance variables; their sum in some weighted mixture over time wholly determines the ultimate criterion. We suggested that these criteria would be factorially independent of one another, although probably correlated in observed performances, and that some of the component variables would be universal, others unique to certain classes of organizations.

3. Below this roster of key criterion variables, we conceived there to be subsidiary levels, with the following characteristics: there would be a large number of subsidiary variables; some would refer to sub-goals or means for achieving goals while others would refer to organizational states and processes; they would have interrelationships of many kinds (independence, positive or negative correlation, causation, covariance, interaction, modification, etc.); they would comprise distinguishable but overlapping subsets with each subset containing a full determination (causation) of its own penultimate criterion of organizational performance. The variables in the lower levels of the hierarchy would represent relatively short-term performances, and transitory states and processes of organizational life, responsive to environmental changes and to phases of organizational development. They would, accordingly, present complex time-related changes often of a phasic or cyclic type.

The merits of such a conceptual scheme, whatever its defects, are considerable. The scheme emphasizes that no *one* criterion (except the unmeasurable ultimate criterion) can reasonably be used alone to represent organizational performance; at the very least, account must be taken of the full roster of penultimate criterion variables. The scheme emphasizes that organizational performance is complex, involving, probably, hundreds of variables. The scheme allows for both elements of universality and elements of uniqueness. The scheme acknowledges the elementary but notably ignored fact that organizational performances fluctuate with time and that few single variables if any can be expected to reveal much constancy over time even though the network may have stable features.

Ideally, we should like to measure directly performance in relation to the ultimate criterion. Traditional treatments of the criterion problem have led to the choice of some one measurable criterion to represent this ultimate criterion. The present scheme, however, suggests that we must start with a large number of variables describing the performances of organizations and then examine the pattern of relationships among them in order to infer from this pattern the underlying dimensions of performance. These underlying dimensions could then be interpreted to be the penultimate "goals" of the organizations. These goals would be inferred from the actual behavior of the organizations, not from ideal states, norms, or cultural entities. Given the assumption that the ultimate goal is not a part of actual processes of current organizational life and is thus an unmeasurable construct, it follows that effectiveness can be assessed only in terms of the position of an organization on all of the penultimate dimensions. In line with this thinking, we undertook an empirical investigation. Given a set of data descriptive of many aspects of performance for a set of organizations over a span of time, we could then by statistical tests investigate:

1. Whether there is a set of penultimate performance variables, factorially pure, that account for much of the total variance in performances?
2. Whether the factors are strongly correlated with, and therefore potentially caused by, sets of subsidiary variables representing organizational states and processes but not goals?
3. Whether this set of factors is constant across a number of similar organizations (not tested in our analysis)?
4. Whether this set of factors is constant over some span of time?
5. Whether the performance of a single organization is variable over time within the set of constant factors?
6. Whether the conceptual content of the factors suggests that some of them may be "universals," others "uniques"?

Such an analysis leads to an assessment of whether it now seems reasonable to hope that there might be identified a roster of conceptual variables, limited in number, discrete in meaning, comprehensive in coverage, partially universal in applicability, that can be the taxonomic framework for comparative organizational studies. Such an analysis has been largely completed, and some of the results will be presented next.

The data refer to 75 independently owned and managed life insurance sales agencies located in different communities throughout the United States. They range in size from about 10 to 60 salesman members plus supporting staff, and are thus technically small business organizations although considerably larger than the average business enterprise in dollar volume. All have been in business for a number of years and none have had a recent disruption such as change of territory or of ownership. The data are all from firm records and, although more elaborate than is usual, are of kinds normally kept by business firms. An eleven year span of time is encompassed, the earliest data being for 1952, the latest for 1962. The analyzed performance variables, 76 in number, were selected from an initial roster of over 200 variables; elimination was on grounds of duplication (statistical identity), unreliability of measurement, insufficient variance, dubious accuracy, and similar statistical quality reasons. We think this is an extraordinary set of uniform comparative organizational data, for most smaller firms are hard pressed to find in their records even a dozen performance indicators of statistical quality suitable for analysis. The data, however, are highly restricted: they refer to organizations of rather uniform size, all sharing similar formal business goals, all employing similar methods and resources, and all data refer to "hard" indexes of performance computed in standard ways.

ORGANIZATIONAL PERFORMANCE FACTORS

The empirical design that is implied by the conceptual framework, and the rather complex set of data associated with it, both call for factor analysis as an appropriate statistical model for our purpose. Accordingly, the selected 76 performance variables were factor-analyzed, using the principal component solution, and later rotated according to the varimax method. This yielded about 15 factors that account for over 90% of the total variance. Out of these we have succeeded to label, or to give meaningful identification to, the 10 factors listed in Table 38.1. They account altogether for about 70% of the total variance. The kinds of variables contributing to each of these factors are suggested also by Table 38.1.[2]

Table 38.2 shows (for 1952) the factor loadings upon each of the ten factors for those variables we chose to use as factor indicator variables. With a few marginal exceptions, easily visible to the eye, each of the selected indicator variables loads strongly on one and only one factor, with nonsignificant loadings on all other factors; the only instances of significantly shared loadings occur for variables having a loading on the Factor I, Volume, in addition to their factor of main loading. This is, of course, a simplified table. Among the 53 variables not represented are some with no significant loadings and some with significant loadings on two or more of the factors. The indicator variables were used to calculate factor scores for each of the organizations.

[2] The technical information is not complete here, but will be published in considerable detail early in 1967. The following points, however, may be useful in the present context. The "final" matrices for analysis include, with a few unavoidable exceptions, only items having equal-unit scalar properties and either normal or rectangular distributions. Preliminary factor analyses limited to data of various statistical properties (i.e., omitting ratio scales, omitting items so that no more than one came from each source of basic data, etc.) produced factor structures of such similarity that we feel assured that no serious distortions arise from such causes. Orthogonal rotation was required because the matrix included a large number of high inter-item correlations and the factor structure is complex; the unrotated factors were, in our judgment, uninterpretable.

ANALYSIS OF ORGANIZATIONAL PERFORMANCE

TABLE 38.1. *Performance factors—insurance agency organizations*

Factor	Assigned Name		Indicator Variables
I.	Business volume (Including both accumulated volume and current increment in volume)	4.* 5. 10. 17. 26.	Number of policies in force, year end New insurance sold, dollar volume Renewal premiums collected, dollars Number of lives insured, year end Agency manpower, number of agents
II.	Production Cost	61. 62. 63.	Production cost per new policy Production cost per $1,000 of insurance Production cost per $100 of premium
III.	New Member Productivity	35. 36.	Average productivity per new agent Ratio of new agent vs. old agent productivity ("New agent": less than 5 years service)
IV.	Youthfulness of Members	45. 46.	Ratio of younger (under 35) to total membership Ratio of productivity of younger members to agency total
V.	Business Mix (Many low-value transaction vs. fewer high-value transactions)	13. 14. 76.	Average premium per $1,000 Per cent of new policies with quarterly payments Per cent of business in employee trust
VI.	Manpower growth	27. 28.	Net change in manpower during year Ratio of net change to initial manpower
VII.	Management emphasis	52.	Manager's personal commissions
VIII.	Maintenance cost (Refers to maintenance of accounts, not of physical facilities)	64. 65. 47.	Maintenance cost per collection Maintenance cost per $100 premium collected Average new business volume per agent
IX.	Member productivity	16.	Insurance in force per capita
X.	Market penetration	19.	Number of lives covered per 1,000 insurables

* These are variable identification (serial) numbers included to aid cross-reference between tables.

The point to note from Tables 38.1 and 38.2 is that there is a set of factors that satisfy ordinary hopes and requirements with respect to (1) having identifiable factors that plausibly can be described in ordinary business language, (2) having for each factor one or more variables that

TABLE 38.2. *Factor loadings for selected indicator variables**

Indicator Variables	I	II	III	IV	V	VI	VII	VIII	IX	X
4. Policies in force	86	–	–	–	–	–	–	–	–	–
5. New sales	88	–	–	–	–	–	–	–	–	–
10. Renewal premiums	92	–	–	–	–	–	–	–	–	–
17. Lives insured	83	–	–	–	–	–	–	–	–	–
26. Manpower	87	–	–	–	–	–	–	–	–	–
61. Cost per sale	–	72	–	–	–	–	–	–	–	–
62. Cost per $1,000	–	91	–	–	–	–	–	–	–	–
63. Cost per $100 prem.	–	82	–	–	–	–	–	–	–	–
35. Prod. per new agent	–	–	73	–	–	–	–	–	–	–
36. Ratio new/old prod.	–	–	89	–	–	–	–	–	–	–
45. Ratio young/old agents	–	–	–	86	–	–	–	–	–	–
46. Ratio young/old prod.	–	–	–	89	–	–	–	–	–	–
13. Premium per $1,000	41	–	–	–	79	–	–	–	–	–
14. % quarterly payments	–	–	–	–	69	–	–	–	–	–
76. % employee trust	47	–	–	–	80	–	–	–	–	–
27. Manpower increase	–	–	–	–	–	84	–	–	–	–
28. Ratio increase to total	–	–	–	–	–	82	–	–	–	–
52. Manager's commissions	–	–	–	–	–	–	89	–	–	–
64. Cost per collection	–	–	–	–	–	–	–	86	–	–
65. Cost per $100 premium	52	–	–	–	–	–	–	74	–	–
47. New business per agent	–	–	–	–	–	–	–	–	93	–
16. Insurance per capita	40	–	–	–	–	–	–	–	–	83
19. Lives per 1,000 insurable	–	–	–	–	–	–	–	–	–	82

*Decimals omitted; loadings under .40 omitted. Data are for the year 1952. N = 75 organizations.

have highly discriminating factor loadings and which thus can be used as indicator variables, (3) having a set of factors comprehensive enough to leave a relatively small residual variance.

STABILITY OF FACTOR STRUCTURE

Factor analytic studies frequently have been attacked on different grounds. Some of the criticisms have to do with the fact that most of these studies are based on data collected from some population at one point of time. This raises the problem of the stability of the factor structure over time. It makes, obviously, little sense to work with factors, even

TABLE 38.3. *Factor loadings for indicator variables 1952, 1957 and 1961**

Variable Numbers	I 52 57 61	II 52 57 61	III 52 57 61	IV 52 57 61	V 52 57 61	VI 52 57 61	VII 52 57 61	VIII 52 57 61	IX 52 57 61	X 52 57 61
4	86 86 86	— — —	— — —	— — —	— — —	— — —	— — —	— — —	— — —	— — —
5	88 91 86	— — —	— — —	— — —	— — —	— — —	— — —	— — —	— — —	— — —
10	92 95 94	— — —	— — —	— — —	— — —	— — —	— — —	— — —	— — —	— — —
17	83 89 82	— — —	— — —	— — —	— — —	— — —	— — —	— — —	— — —	— — —
26	87 85 80	— — —	— — —	— — —	— — —	— — —	— — —	— — —	— — —	— — —
61	— — —	72 82 82	— — —	— — —	— — —	— — —	— — —	— — —	— — —	— — —
62	— — —	91 94 90	— — —	— — —	— — —	— — —	— — —	— — —	— — —	— — —
63	— — —	82 90 89	— — —	— — —	— — —	— — —	— — —	— — —	— — —	— — —
35	— — —	— — —	73 79 74	— — —	— — —	— — —	— — —	— — —	— — —	— — —
36	— — —	— — —	89 94 88	— — —	— — —	— — —	— — —	— — —	— — —	— — —
45	— — —	— — —	— — —	86 91 78	— — —	— — —	— — —	— — —	— — —	— — —
46	— — —	— — —	— — —	89 92 89	— — —	— — —	— — —	— — —	— — —	— — —
13	41 42 42	— — —	— — —	— — —	79 76 70	— — —	— — —	— — —	— — —	— — —
14	— 56 42	— — —	— — —	— — —	69 42 69	— — —	— — —	— — —	— — —	— — —
76	47 50 43	— — —	— — —	— — —	80 52 73	— — —	— — —	— — —	— — —	— — —
27	— — —	— — —	— — —	— — —	— — —	84 92 91	— — —	— — —	— — —	— — —
28	— — —	— — —	— — —	— — —	— — —	82 90 89	— — —	— — —	— — —	— — —
52	— — —	— — —	— — —	— — —	— — —	— — —	89 88 87	— — —	— — —	— — —
64	52 55 —	— — —	— — —	— — —	— — —	— — —	— — —	86 81 74	— — —	— — —
65	— — —	— — —	— — —	— — —	— — —	— — —	— — —	74 68 86	— — —	— — —
47	— — —	— — —	— — —	— — —	— — —	— — —	— — —	— — —	93 86 81	— — —
16	40 — —	— — —	— — —	— — —	— — —	— — —	— — —	— — —	— — —	83 86 82
19	— — —	— — —	— — —	— — —	— — —	— — —	— — —	— — —	— — —	82 85 83

*Decimals omitted; loadings under .40 omitted. N = 75 organizations.

475

TABLE 38.4. *Stability of agency factor scores—ten-year period**

Period	I	II	III	IV	V	VI	VII	VIII	IX	X
Five Years 1952–1957	96	41	−13	21	67	15	36	60	71	91
Five Years 1957–1961	95	67	15	30	82	22	67	33	71	89
Ten Years 1952–1961	91	33	02	16	63	05	28	24	53	82

*Factor scores for each organization were computed using the indicator variables shown in Table 2 with equal weights. Figures above are similar to "retest reliability" coefficients. Decimals omitted. N = 75 organizations.

as merely statistical artifacts, if they fail to reappear upon successive analyses of the same kind of data over the same population. A successful replication of a given factor structure, however, tells us at least that regardless of some possible changes in the specific relationships within the pattern of the correlation matrix, the major dimensions underlying that pattern remain, more or less, the same. This should give more confidence in working with such factors similarly to the way personality theorists work with individual traits.

The data available in the present study made it possible to perform factor-analyses for three different points of time: 1952, 1957 and 1961. The high degree of similarity among the three factor structures over the ten-year period is suggested by Table 38.3. This table shows the factor loadings for the indicator variables for each of the three different years. It will be noted that the results are so similar that figures for any one year may be substituted for any other year. This reemergence of the factor structure is taken by us to support the fruitfulness of working with these factors as hypothetical constructs.[3]

STABILITY OF ORGANIZATION PERFORMANCE

The stability of the factor structure over a span of ten years does not arise from stable performances on the part of the individual agencies.

[3] It seems worthwhile to note that our data were also subjected to a different multivariate method of analysis that has been developed by Guttman and his associates in Israel and Ann Arbor. (L. Guttman, "A general nonmetric technique for finding the smallest Euclidean space for a configuration of points," *Psychometrika*, in press.) This nonmetric method is known as "the smallest space analysis." The application of this technique to our data produced a striking confirmation of our factor structure. Each of the relatively distinct clusters of points comprising the Euclidean space is readily identifiable as one of our factors. This adds assurance that our factors are not wholly artifacts of some specific analytic technique.

TABLE 38.5. *Correlations between representative structure/process variables and factor scores 1961 and 1962*

Factors	Manager's Supportiveness 1961 1962	Upward Communication 1961 1962	Manager's Expert 1961 1962	Manager's Power Reward 1961 1962	Total Control 1961 1962
I. Volume	35 37	20 25	34 41	25 31	27 31
II. Production Cost	— —	— -21	— —	-41 -49	— -30
III. New Manpower Prod.	27 20	30 56	— —	— 20	— 30
IV. Youthfulness	34 50	— —	36 36	— 25	26 33
V. Business Mix	— —	— —	— —	-30 —	-28 -22
VI. Manpower Growth	— 45	— —	30 25	— 22	— 30
VII. Managm't Emphasis	— —	— —	23 24	— —	— —
VIII. Maintenance Costs	— 23	— 22	— —	-46 -31	— —
IX. Average Production	— -49	— —	— —	— —	— —
X. Market Penetration	33 33	32 32	— —	44 48	58 61

Correlations less than r=.20 omitted; decimals omitted. Data are for 33 insurance sales agencies. Factor scores are computed from indicator variables shown in Table 2, with equal weights. Organizational structural/process variables are based on member questionnaire responses obtained in 1961. Correlations of .32 are significant at the p=.05 level.

477

Table 38.4 represents this conclusion in the form of correlations between each factor score and itself for each of three time periods, 1952–1957, 1957–1961, and then a ten-year interval, 1952–1961. These correlations, which may be considered as reflecting the reliability of relative performance among these organizations, are not uniform in magnitude.

Factor I (Volume) represents an aspect of organizational performance that is highly stable over time. Over a period of ten years during which the average volume of business rose very substantially (more than two standard deviation units from the starting distribution in 1952) the several organizations maintained virtually the same relative positions. Factor X (Market Penetration) is another factor of performance displaying high interorganizational stability over a time of great change in absolute level of market penetration. Factor V (Business Mix) can also be regarded as a relatively stable aspect of organizational performance. These three factors are stable in part because they are accumulative performances. Volume, for example, begets further volume for the reason that a life policy once sold continues to produce income for some years and for the reason that new customers once sold tend to buy more insurance themselves and to recruit friends as new customers; market extension begets further market extension for the same reasons; a choice of market strategy tends to perpetuate itself as continuation and new business is generated by the old in like kind. In short, these are in part *self-caused* performances and therefore perpetuate themselves, with the result that major changes in relative performance among the organizations come about only over some rather long time period. The stability of these factors no doubt arises as well from the persistence of those subsidiary (causal?) performances which originally gave rise to relatively high or low volume increment rates.

Factor III (Productivity of New Members) is a rather different class of organizational performance with respect to stability over time. The "reliability" of this performance over a five- or ten-year period is virtually zero. The negative correlation for one five-year time interval is nonsignificant in this instance, but represents a possible cyclic or phasic phenomenon: organizations that take on and train many new members in one time period may take on few in the succeeding period. If all these organizations have the same periodicity (a fact not yet determined) and if they are randomly phased, then we may expect very large negative factor score correlations for time intervals matched to the periodicity. If substantiated this would again be an instance of an organizational performance "causing" itself, but in a negative manner.

Factor IV (Youthfulness) may similarly be a phasic or else cyclic organizational performance, as is Factor VI (Rate of Manpower Growth). These two factors share with Factor III a reference to membership maintenance, development and growth. The instability shown for five-year intervals is probably phasic, and may have a periodicity that is not uniform for all organizations nor for all three factors of performance or all initial sizes of organizations.

The remaining factors, II (Production Costs), VII (Management Emphasis) and VIII (Maintenance Costs) are intermediate in their stability over time. It may be that these aspects of performance, along with the performances presumed to be phasic or cyclic, have the burden of adaptation in organizational life—i.e., to sustain growth in volume and in market penetration, or to modify the character of the organization's business strategy, in response to environmental demands and opportunities. One may propose that these internal performances in the case of selling organizations become modified over short-time intervals in service of the longer-term improvement of the market position.

It should be noted that Factor VII (Management Emphasis) is, first, a dubious factor, being defined by a single variable and, second, it may be a factor unique to owner-managed small sales organizations.

"PREDICTABILITY" OF THE FACTOR SCORES

Before relating the meanings of these factors to our conceptual scheme, we now turn to a supplementary set of data: in 1961 a questionnaire survey of all members of 33 of these organizations provided a number of indexes representing various internal states and processes of their organizational lives. These permit us to explore the predictability of our several factors of performance from variables of kinds not ordinarily treated themselves as performance variables. Table 38.5 represents a selected few of these variables and their correlations with the ten performance factors for the year 1961 (the year of the questionnaire survey) and for the subsequent year, 1962. We shall remark upon only a few of the features of this material.

One point to note is not very evident to the eye, but is statistically verified: the survey data correlate more strongly with performances in the following year than they do with performance concurrently with the survey. Out of 14 pairs of correlations in this table, of which at least one of the pair is statistically significant (a correlation of .32 is significant at the .05 level), there are 10 where the correlation for 1962 is higher than the correlation for 1961, 3 are the same, and 1 is lower. While most of the differences within the pairs are statistically non-significant the between-year difference for the total set is highly significant. Such a trend suggests the presence of a causal, rather than merely a covariance, relationship between the "predictions" and the criteria. With time-series performance data, we can determine some of the features of managerial and member behavior that plausibly can be said to be causal in relationship to organizational performances. This trend highlights, in addition, the limitations inherent in data collected at one point of time, on which many studies are based. If we had at our disposal the correlation matrix for 1961 only, we would have to conclude that most of the social-psychological variables treated here have very little to do with dimensions of organizational performance. The results obtained for 1962, however, indicate that a significant portion of the variance in performance is accounted for by such social-psychological variables. One may ask if the relationships are still more strong by the third year, or if each predictor has its own characteristic period of effect.

Second, it may be noted that each of the ten performance factors is significantly related to some of our selected predictors, not significantly related to others. This selectivity in correlation suggests that our hypothesized network of lower-order performance variables (examples here treated as predictors) may in fact assort itself into subsets, each subset having potentially a causal relationship to one of the higher-order performances. For example, "Supportiveness" (on the part of the owner-manager as seen by the members) is significantly related to business volume, productivity of youthful agents, manpower growth, and market penetration, but is *not* related to production cost performance, business mix, owners' devotion to management.

Third, we note that some organizational processes and states have strongly favorable relationships (presumed to be causal) with certain of the performance factors and strongly unfavorable relationships with others. One example again is "Supportiveness" on the part of the owner-manager: high support appears to be associated in the succeeding year with such desirable outcomes as high business volume, high acquisition and retention of manpower, high market penetration, having a relatively youthful force; at the same time supportiveness by the manager is associated strongly with low average productivity per agent. The covariance among these factorially independent variables is evident. A managerial practice (supportiveness) may affect some aspects of organizational performance favorably, others unfavorably. The set of performance factors therefore *must* be treated as an intact set if one is to make reasonable interpretations. Had we been adhering to the usual past practice of examining single pairs of predictors and performance criteria—e.g., support and average agent productivity—for a single time we would have come to the false conclusion that managerial support strongly diminishes individual agent performance. With data for even two years, we are enabled to see better the trade-off relationships among the ten factors of performance.

We suggest that much of the confusion and contradiction in past studies of managerial and organizational practices associated with performance arises from reliance upon single indicators of performance rather than upon a coherent and comprehensive set of criterion variables. There is no future for us in pursuing odd pairs of variables; we must treat comprehensive sets and networks of variables in order to understand these events, for they comprise an intact system of variables.

CONCEPTUAL FRAMEWORK RECONSIDERED

The foregoing fragmentary and perhaps tedious exploration of empirical results has now been carried far enough for our purpose. We have indicated several points of strong support for a conceptual framework of the kind initially outlined, and have pointed to compelling kinds of evidence that forbid further work with conceptions of lesser scope. On one vital point, however, our empirical results flatly contradict our opening propositions and force us to a reconsideration of them.

The moment of insight occurred while we were considering whether our ten performance factors could plausibly be described within the specifications of our conceptual framework. One of these specifications—a crucial one, we thought—was that the penultimate performances would have the character of autonomous "*goals*," things sought for their own value, things valued in themselves, "goals" of kinds that allow one to say that their achievement justifies the creation, existence and continuation of the organization.

Some of the resulting performance factors do indeed seem to have this character. High volume of business, low production costs, high market penetration, and some others can readily be accepted as expressing the central values and purposes of the key people in a sales organization. Others of our factors, however, cannot be so interpreted. Is it a *goal* of a sales organization to have a relatively large part of its productivity coming from youthful members? Is it a *goal* of these organizations to have a relatively high proportion of new members? Even more oddly, how can we say that some choice as to preferred type of business is a goal of these organizations, when the people themselves do not agree on whether one end of the scale is "better" or "worse" than the other?[4]

Even the dimensions that can plausibly be described as "goals" present a problem in theory, for we have difficulty showing that they are in fact goals of the organizations. Neither we, nor others concerned with similar problems, have provided a sound rationale for demonstrating that such "goals" are in fact properties of the organization. If the proposed

[4] The Business Mix factor refers, roughly, to the choice of emphasis upon selling many policies of relatively low unit value as against selling fewer policies of high unit value. While a high-value unit of sale is obviously advantageous in itself, the net goodness of one emphasis or the other, or some intermediate balance, depends upon which strategy best utilizes the existing staff and accessible market toward the end of optimal resource-getting.

"goals" do not, in some sense, belong to the organizations, then it is rather arbitrary to assess organizational effectiveness in reference to such goals. We must show that such "goals" belong to the organizations and that they are not merely transient goals adopted by various interested persons or groups, or by the investigators themselves. Parsons, for example, attempted to escape from this problem by proposing a functional analysis that also fails to adhere to the organizational frame of reference; for Parsons, organizational effectiveness in the final analysis lies in the functional contribution of the organization to meeting the needs of the larger society. This solution is not tenable, for it merely shifts the same problem to a higher level of social organization. Others, Etzioni for example, have tried to retain the effectiveness concept while remaining within the organizational frame of reference, but have then found it impossible to provide an operational means for identifying criteria that correspond to their theoretical definitions of effectiveness.[5]

The solution we offer to this problem is advanced with some trepidation, for if our reasoning is correct, then we shall disturb the thinking and language habits of many people in all kinds of organizations. The solution arose from the task of discovering what it is, if anything, that our ten factorial dimensions have in common. What they have in common is that, without exception, they represent the getting of resources for organizational functioning from the organizations' environments.[6]

The Volume factor, for example, indicates the extent to which the agencies have acquired money, clients and manpower, all of which are scarce and valued resources needed by the organization. The cost factors reflect the efficiency of the agencies in conservation of available resources, i.e., prevention of unnecessary waste. Average member productivity can be viewed as a measure of the agencies' success in extracting resources (selling effort, selling ability) from the members.

This perspective on organizational performance is consistent with the system concept of organizations. According to that concept, organizations as systems are continuously engaged in processes of exchange with their environments. Much of the stuff that is exchanged in these transac-

---

[5] T. Parsons, "Suggestions for a sociological approach to a theory of organizations—I," *Administrative Science Quarterly*, 1, 1, 1956, 63–85.
A. Etzioni, "Two approaches to organizational analysis: a critique and a suggestion," *Administrative Science Quarterly*, 5, 2, 1960, 257–278.

[6] "Environments" is in the plural form to indicate that the proposed conception of organizational effectiveness will require the differentiation of environment into types or classes with respect to the nature of resources involved and the means for organizations to realize these resources. An example is the case of members of an organization who we view as an integral part of the organization with respect to their role defining and role carrying activities, but as part of the organization's environment with respect to abilities, motives, other memberships, and other characteristics that are potentially useful but not utilized by the organization in role performance. An effective organization will incorporate more of the individual member's personality into the organizational system, thus acquiring additional resources from this part of its environment.

tions falls into the category of scarce and valued resources of kinds potentially useful to other social systems as well. There is thus competition for these resources, and under competitive conditions the ability to secure and use resources reflects the relative effectiveness of the organization vis-a-vis other social structures. The significant outcomes of organizational behavior, whether anticipated or not, whether voluntary or constrained, are always influenced by and lead to changes in the ability of the organization to mobilize resources from the environments. Effectiveness in organizations can thus be viewed as the relative bargaining position of organizations in relation to resources over whch there is competition. We define the effectiveness of an organization as its *ability to exploit its environments in the acquisition of scarce and valued resources to sustain its own functioning*.

This general definition must be qualified in two ways. Some organizations exist in relatively rich environments, others in poor environments; we must therefore assess effectiveness in relation to environmental potential. The second qualification is that the *ability* to exploit the organization's environment cannot be equated with *maximum use* of this ability in the short run, for an organization might then destroy its environment and reduce its longer-run potential for favorable transactions. We must invoke an *optimization* concept.

An interpretation of our ten performance factors for sales organizations can illustrate these ideas: these sales organizations are maximizing their ability to get resources when they *optimize*, as an interdependent set, the ten performance factors we have isolated. This optimizing process involves balancing off some exploitative strategies against others, e.g., increased market penetration against temporarily higher production costs; short-run gains against deferred gains; exploiting the manager for current sales as against exploiting him for staff growth and development. The optimum pattern of performance for each of the organizations may be unique to the extent that their histories and environments differ, and they may fall into a limited number of types of alternative general strategies that are equally effective so long as each type maintains its own internal balancing principle. Non-optimization of performance would occur to the extent that some performance factors were under- or over-realized in relation to the others. A gross imbalance could result in the extinction of the organization, i.e., total loss of its ability to derive resources from its environment.[7]

This conception of organizational effectiveness has escaped attention because of our traditional preoccupation with the concept of "goal." We have thought too simplistically that organizations have goals that can be identified and that become the yardstick for assessing organizational effectiveness. This imputation of purposiveness to organizations has

[7] We are aware that this is a very sketchy outline of the conceptual position we are advancing. A more detailed and better documented statement is in preparation.

misled us. While profitability, for example, or growth, or productivity, seem attractive and superficially plausible as goals of an organization, it is apparent from empirical studies, our own included, that in persisting organizations profit is never safely maximized, growth is never safely maximized, and productivity is never safely maximized; as "goals" they become destructive when approached, and they therefore are goals only (a) with reference to certain classes of interested persons (owners, customers, employees, etc.) or (b) with reference to society at large (which must exploit the organization as best it can if it needs the output without destroying the organization), or (c) with reference to some particular limited time span or phase of the organization's life (i.e., a temporary concentration of effort toward restoring balance among the total roster of necessary performances—a transient goal to be moved toward, but not actually reached).

Returning now to the main theme of this conference—that of exploring the possibilities of developing a meaningful and useful system of concepts for describing and comparing organizations—we can conclude by saying that in describing organizational performance or effectiveness, we must first of all reject conceptual schemes that link organizational effectiveness solely to the values of some one or another element in the environment of organizations; instead the standards of effectiveness are to be sought with reference to the organization itself. Second, we require that our ultimate conceptual scheme avoid the trap of imputing goals, or other expressions of the teleological principle, to organizations, for they are not "trying" to do anything—they merely exist and function.

We note that botanists can classify and describe flowers very well in terms of accommodations to environmental resources and internal processes, without imputing goals to flowers. Similarly, zoologists can deal taxonomically with living systems within their domain. Similarly, psychologists are coming to conceive of human effectiveness in terms of "adjustment" and "self-realization," not goal attainment. The suggestions we have offered here appear to follow a well-trodden path laid out by the more advanced discipline relating to the behavior of open systems.

We do not propose that our ten factorial dimensions for these sales organizations constitute a universal roster of such dimensions applicable to all kinds of organizations. It does seem possible, however, that several of them have this universal meaning while others may be unique to these and similar organizations. It is the next task to apply similar procedures to other populations of organizations in an effort to find those dimensions that may confidently be used to compare organizations.

39 The Study of Organizational and Relevant Small Group and Individual Dimensions

BERNARD P. INDIK

ABSTRACT

This report attempts to develop a taxonomy that will be useful in developing an approach to the integration of studies of individuals in groups which are embedded in organizational settings which themselves are in a sociocultural environment.

A classificatory framework is presented which develops seven panels of variables that should be considered. They include two organization level panels—organization structure variables and organization process and function variables; two small group panels—small-group structure variables and small-group process variables; two individual level panels—organizationally relevant individual attitudes, perceptions, abilities, temperaments and motivations and relevant individual behavior variables, and finally, a panel of variables that is descriptive of the organizational environment. Each of these panels is defined and the variables within each panel are described in detail in order to attempt to approximate a set of classificatory variables that are consistent within each panel. Further, an attempt was made to have each panel be a set of mutually exclusive variables so that they would be clearly discriminable from each other. This was not always possible given our present knowledge.

This classificatory schema also suggests many hypotheses about relationships between variables in adjacent panels and, as well, suggests what categories of variables should be considered relevant in prediction studies of various organizationally relevant behavorial outcomes. Further, this theoretical scheme is very helpful in organizing presently available studies of organizational behavior and in suggesting significant questions for future research.

Technical Report 13, December, 1963. Contract Nonr-404(10). Group Psychology Branch, Office of Naval Research, Department of Defense, Washington, D.C.

INTRODUCTION

Only recently have some few authors (Sells, 1963; Inkeles and Levinson, 1963) turned to some of the basic problems we face in developing an understanding of a social psychology of organizations. They have attempted to attack the basic taxonomic type of problems such as what are the appropriate classes of variables to be included for theoretical consideration and within these classifications what are the appropriate variables to be considered.

While there has been a good deal of social psychological research in the study of organizations, students in the field have had very considerable difficulty synthesizing our knowledge in a systematic fashion due to the lack of clear taxonomic work underlying the proliferation of terms, variables, attributes and relationships as well as the complexity of the basic problems. By and large, systematic studies of individuals in organizational settings have been limited to specific subareas of interest to the particular investigator (i.e. communication, control, effectiveness, the fusion process, etc.) with little regard for the view of how these variables fit into a larger, more genotypic schema.

Sells (1963) seems to take the position that all measurable variables belong in the initial exploratory set of variables to be considered. Then using the devices of factor analysis one may sift out the genotypic variables from the more manifest "hodge podge" of measurements. This approach has two major problems: first, there is little guide as to what to include or what to exclude from consideration, second, there is little or no rationale to guide the development of measures of those important variables that are either less accessible to measurement or less tangible and have as yet not been measured. What is necessary is some set of criteria by which one may include or exclude a class of variables from consideration and a set of criteria that will be able to guide the investigator in dividing up the particular class of variables into the variables that should be considered within one class.

Inkeles and Levinson (1963) approach the problem from another point of view. They maintain the rather formalistic division of the disciplines of sociology and psychology and attempt to divide and classify variables at each of the two levels of discourse without attempting to allow for the attack on the central problem of how are the two sets of variables related to each other than by a vague sort of isomorphism.

The present approach will attempt to take advantage of the benefits of these two approaches and as well try to deal with the problems that seem to be implicitly overlooked in the above attacks on the problems. We will attempt to develop a theoretical orientation toward the taxonomic problems presently apparent and develop a simplified classification scheme for the purpose of synthesizing our knowledge of social organizations and their relations to their members.

Such a taxonomic schemata should enable us to specify the genotypic variables relevant to the behavior of both organizations, their groups and their members. It should enable us to specify the concepts necessary to describe the organizations, groups and individuals under consideration. Further this schemata should denote how such variables should be classified, how they are related and which of these variables should be considered when analysis questions for specific problems of organizational behavior are studied. This schema should consider the interrelationship of variables at several levels of analysis i.e. organizations, groups imbedded in organizations, and individuals imbedded in groups and organizations. The classification system ideally should contain classes of mutually exclusive genotypic concepts at each of the three levels of analysis. The schema should also provide for the expectation of interrelationships among the concepts but need not prespecify exact direction and size of relations but should specify which sub-class or sub-classes of variables should theoretically be involved. The schema should also predict where and what variety of variables; their interrelationship and classes of organizational systems not as yet present, could exist in the same manner that Mendeleev's Periodic Table provided direction to the discovery of missing elements in early research in chemistry. This kind of taxonomic device would then also provide considerable payoff in organizing in a systematic fashion the now chaotic state of present fragmentary studies in this area of interest.

Systems, Organizations, Groups and Individuals refer to the collection of interrelated individuals, processes and events encompassed by a recognizable boundary. This boundary may be permeable but not nonexistent. It should allow specification of who or what is in the system and who or what is outside the system. Organizations, groups and individuals are more easily distinguishable in a physical sense though in a psychological sense their life space may to some degree be indeterminate at any given time. We will, however, attempt to define all three types of systems.

An *individual* for our purposes is a human being functioning in a group and/or organizational setting. A *group* is a set of two or more individuals who have some systematic relation to each other and who have some common goal, and some common perceptual basis, for their association with each other. An organization is a set of two or more interrelated groups containing a common status and control hierarchy, and devoted primarily to the attainment of specific goals. It is clear from the above that individual, group and organization are progressively larger concepts of systems. It is also apparent that individuals, groups and organizations are imbedded in an environment, the attributes of which influence the degree, manner and nature of the relationships that exist among these individuals, groups and organizations.

An Approximate Classification Scheme

The initial question to be faced is what are the criteria for designating a set of variables as a class or panel of variables to be included in the classification scheme to be used here.

Criteria

1. Each class of variables should be relevant to the study of individuals in small groups imbedded in organizations which are imbedded in their socioeconomic environments.
2. Each class of variables should be definitionally mutually exclusive from any other class of variables in the taxonomic schema.
3. Each class of variables should be related in specifiable ways to each of the other classes of variables.
4. Each class of variables should contain variables which are homogeneous in the characteristic(s) under which they are classified.

The next question to be answered is specifically what should be the classes of variables to be considered. Inkeles and Levinson (1963) seem to take the position that there are two levels of analysis that are appropriate, the sociocultural system and the personality system, and that the analysis of their interrelationships can be made through the testing of hypotheses as to their isomorphisms. While this looks to be a fruitful approach it is rather limited in its power to organize knowledge since their system cannot deal with how the classes of variables that they consider classes at either level of analysis are related to each other class; that is, with relations other than isomorphisms that may exist between the specific variables of one level of analysis with the comparable variable of the other level of analysis.

Further, the Inkeles-Levinson approach cannot as yet deal with the fact that individuals in organizational settings are imbedded in small groups which are in turn imbedded in organizations which are imbedded in their organizational environments.

The system of classes of variables to be considered should reflect the complex nature of the phenomena to be described and should as well be inclusive of as much of this complexity as can systematically be considered. Sells, 1962, takes a more expansive view:

> The multidimensional model for an organizational taxonomy presented here is based on the following assumptions:
> 1. Organizations are behaving organisms whose behavior is represented

by the coordinated, composite action of their members functioning in their roles as organizational members.

2. The behavior of organizations with respect to any task or index is a predictable function of three major sources of variance, discussed below, which may be referred to as (1) characteristics of individuals participating (abilities, motivational and stylistic personality traits, background, past experience and training, ethnic factors, etc.), (2) organizational characteristics (goals, tasks, group structure, facilities, procedures, etc.), and (3) characteristics of the physical and social environment. It is assumed that significant portions of the variance of behavioral criteria will be accounted for by factors representing these separate sources as well as by other factors representing interactions of these sources.

3. The universes of variables representing persons, organizations, and external environment can be represented by factored dimensions (or common factors) which order the myriad of specific observable characteristics in terms of generalized composites that are both more stable and less redundant, for multivariate prediction, than the specifics by which they are defined.

4. The total variance of any criteria of organizational behavior can be accounted for by weighted combinations of the universe of dimensions of persons, organizations, and environment, within the limits of measurement error. Multiple regression equations, discriminant functions, or other appropriate multivariate techniques are applicable to the prediction problem, but the development of predictor factors for each of the major sources of organizational behavior, and of suitable criteria, are issues of prior importance.

5. The dimensions of the taxonomy of organizations will be indicated by the differential patterns of predictive weights obtained for various combinations of factors.

His general view follows the notion that the stimulus situation in its complexity and the individual in his complexity interact such as to explain the variance in the behavior of that individual. Both the individual variables and the environmental variables and their interaction affect behavior variance. Sells (1963) then deals with taxonomic problems in these areas.

Our problem focus will deal mainly with those individual variables (environmental and interactional) and those group and organizational variables that seem appropriate to explain the behavior variance (individuals' behavior in small groups in organizations) under discussion here. The present study will use seven classes of variables. These include the following panels:

1. Organization Structure;
2. Organization Process and Function;
3. Small Group Structure;
4. Small Group Process;

5. Organizationally Relevant Individual Attitudes, Perceptions, Abilities, Temperaments and Motivations;
6. Organizationally Relevant Individual Behaviors;
7. Organizational Environment.

Panel One: Organizational Structure Variables

This domain is concerned with those attributes of organizations that are relatively static in time. Such variables as the following are considered as being in this category.

A. *Size*—The number of individuals who are members of the organization by organizational criteria.
B. *Span of Control*—The average number of individuals who are responsible to a supervisor.
C. *The Number of Hierarchical Levels in the Organization*—The number of layers of authority between the highest and the lowest member of the organization.
D. *The Authority Structure*—The pattern of influence present in the organization with reference to organizational activities.
E. *The Communication Structure*—The pattern of one way and two way information passing connections between individuals.
F. *The Degree of Task Specification*—The extent to which the roles and tasks within the organization are described and formalized.
G. *The Degree of Task Interdependence*—The extent to which the tasks of the different roles are interrelated to each other.
H. *Task Specialization*—The extent to which jobs are fragmented and made smaller parts of the whole function of the organization.
I. *The Status and Prestige Structure*—The distribution pattern of status and prestige attributed to role occupants in the organization.
J. *The Psychological Distance Between the Decision Makers and the Operating Level in the Organization.*

Panel Two: Organizational Function or Processes

A. *Communication*—The process by which individuals send and receive information to and from other individuals within the organization.
1. The average amount of communication interaction within the organization.
2. The distribution of communication interaction within the organization.
B. *Control*—The process by which individuals or groups influence each other within the organizational setting.
1. The average amount of influence exerted by members in the organization.
2. The distribution of influence exerted by members in the organization.

3. The discrepancy between the actual distribution of influence and the desired distribution of influence in the organization.

C. *Coordination*—The process by which the parts of the organization are geared and articulated toward the objectives of the whole organization.

1. The extent to which parts of the organization are geared and articulated toward organizational objectives.

D. *Organizational Socialization Processes*—The processes by which the organization provides members to replace and increase its size and adapt these members to the needs of the organization. These processes include those processes that reinforce the needs of the organization by rewarding the members for behavior valuable to the system by differential reward values such as pay, promotions and status.

1. *Recruitment Process*—The process by which, and the extent to which members are selected from the population available and placed in the roles allocated by the organizational system.

2. *Orientation and Adaptation Process*—The process by which and the extent to which members are oriented (and/or conditioned) to the needs of the organization.

3. *Reward Process*—The process by which and the extent to which members are rewarded (with pay, status and promotions) for attitudes and behavior desired by the organization.

E. *Supervision*—The process by which and the extent to which managers facilitate the objectives of the organization through the use of their administrative, human relations and technical skills.

1. *Initiating Structure*—The extent to which supervision facilitates task performance by allocating tasks clearly and understandably.

2. *Consideration*—The extent to which supervision facilitates socioemotional needs of the members.

3. *Leadership Style*—The extent to which the approach of supervision is distributed closer to the authoritarian or democratic (participative) end of the continuum (or possibly the "laissez-faire" corner) if the continuum should be considered a triangle.

4. *Supervisory Skill Mix*—The distribution of supervisory skills (administrative, human relations and technical) operating in the organization.

F. *Adaptability to Change*—The extent to which the organization and its members can adjust to internal and external changes in a manner that promotes the survival and development of the organization.

1. *Adaptability to Internal Changes*
2. *Adaptability to External Changes That are Relevant to the Organization.*
3. *Rate of Change*

G. *Conflict Control Process*—The extent to which conflicts of needs or

interests are resolved toward the more effective operation of the organization toward its objectives.
1. *The Amount of Tension and Conflict*
2. *The Amount of Conflict Resolution and Tension Reduction*
3. *The Discrepancy between G1 and G2*

H. *The Mutual Understanding of Reciprocal Role Relations*—The degree to which role expectations in the organization are clear to those who are interdependent in their relationships.

I. *The Degree of Bureaucracy*—The proportion of behavior that is controlled by specified rules and regulations of the organizations.

J (1). *Amount of Communication Interaction by Members of the Organization with Non Members for Organizational Purposes*

J (2). *Distribution of Communication Interaction by Members of the Organization with Non Members for Organizational Purposes*—It can be seen from the above listings of variables within these first two panels of variables that they are not sets of mutually exclusive variables. Ideally they should be such; however, the present state of the field only allows us the possibility to enumerate a wide range (possibly not inclusive enough) of variables within the two organizational panels. It remains for our future research ventures to adequately measure these variables in these domains and clarify and indicate which are the genotypic categories that should be used in our research schema. The same problems exist to a greater or lesser degree in all seven of the panels under study here.

Panel Three: Small Group Structure

This domain is concerned with those variables of groups that are relatively static in time. Such variables as the following are seen as being in this category.

A. *Size of the Group*—The number of individuals who are members of the group by the group's criteria of membership.

B. *The Authority and Influence Structure of the Group*—The pattern of interpersonal control present in the group with reference to group activities.

C. *The Communication Structure of the Group*—The pattern of one way and two way information passing connections between individuals in the group.

D. *The Degree of Task Specification*—The extent to which the roles and tasks within the group are proscribed and formalized.

E. *The Degree of Task Interdependence*—The extent to which the tasks of the different roles are interrelated with each other.

F. *The Degree of Task Specialization*—The extent to which jobs are fragmented and made smaller parts of the whole function of the group.

G. *The Status and Prestige Structure of the Group*—The distribution pattern of status and prestige attributed to role occupants in the organization.

H. *The Psychological Distance Between the Leader(s) of the Group and the Rest of Its Members.*

Panel Four: Group Function or Process

A. *Communication*—The process by which individuals send and receive information to and from each other within the group.
1. The average amount of communication interaction within the group.
2. The distribution of communication interaction within the group.
3. The proportion of socioemotional negative communications in the group.
4. The proportion of socioemotional positive communications in the group.
5. The proportion of "ask for information" communications in the group.
6. The proportion of "giving information" communications in the group.
7. The amount and distribution of communications with the larger system in the organization.
8. The amount and proportion and distribution of communication interaction by members of the group with non-members of the organization.

B. *Control*—The process by which individuals influence each other within groups.
1. The average amount of influence exerted by members in the group.
2. The distribution of influence exerted by members in the group.
3. The discrepancy between the actual distribution of influence and the desired distribution of influence in the group.
4. The amount of influence from the larger system.

C. *Coordination*—The process by which the parts of the group are geared and articulated toward the objectives of the whole organization.
1. The extent to which parts of the group are geared and articulated toward the objectives of the group.
2. The clarity of understanding of the goals of the group by the members.
3. The extent to which the parts of the group are articulated to the objectives of the larger organization.

D. *Group Socialization Processes*—The processes that provide for the needs of the group by bringing in members and developing norms and rewarding the members for behavior valuable to the system by differential reward values such as pay, promotions and status.
1. *Recruitment Process*—The process by which and the extent to which

members of the group are selected from the population available and placed in the roles allocated by the organizational system.

2. *Orientation and Adaptation Process*—The process by which and the extent to which members of the group are oriented (trained and/or conditioned) to the needs of the group.

3. *Reward Process*—The process by which and the extent to which members are rewarded (with pay, status and promotions) and attitudes and behavior desired by the group.

E. *Supervision*—The process by which and the extent to which supervisors (leaders) of groups facilitate the objectives of the group through the use of their administrative, human relations and technical skills.

1. *Initiating Structure*—The extent to which supervision (leaders) facilitates task performance by allocating tasks clearly and understandably.

2. *Consideration*—The extent to which supervision (leaders) facilitates the socioemotional needs of the group members.

3. *Leadership Style*—The extent to which the approach of supervision (leadership) is distributed closer to the authoritarian or democratic (participative) end of the continuum (or possibly the "laissez-faire" corner) if the continuum should be considered a triangle.

4. *Supervisory Skill Mix*—The distribution of supervisory (leadership) skills (administrative, human relations and technical) operating in the group.

F. *Adaptability to Change*—The extent to which the group and its members can adjust to internal and external changes in a manner that promotes the survival and development of the group.

1. *Adaptability to Internal Changes*
2. *Adaptability to External Changes That Are Relevant to the Group*
3. *Rate of Change*

G. *Conflict Control Processes*—The extent to which conflicts of needs or interests are resolved toward the more effective operation of the group toward its goals.

1. *The Amount of Tension and Conflict*
2. *The Amount of Conflict Resolution and Tension Reduction*
3. *The Discrepancy Between G1 and G2.*

H. *The Mutual Understanding of Reciprocal Role Relations*—The degree to which role expectations in the group are clear to those who are interdependent in their relationships.

I. *The Degree of Bureaucracy*—The proportion of behavior that is controlled by specified rules and regulations of the group.

J(1). *Amount of Communication Interaction by Members of the Group With Non Members for Organizational Purposes.*

J(2). *Distribution of Communication Interaction by Members of the Group With Non-Members for Organizational Purposes.*

It can be seen from the above listings of variables within these two panels of variables that they are not sets of mutually exclusive variables. Ideally they should be such; however the present state of the field only allows us the possibility to enumerate a wide range (possibly not inclusive enough) of variables within the two small group panels. It remains for our future research ventures to adequately measure these variables in these domains and clarify and indicate which are the genotypic and which are the phenotypic categories that should be used in our research schema. The same problems exist to a greater or lesser degree in all seven of the panels under study here.

Panel Five: Organizationally and Group Relevant (Nonbehavioral) Individual Variables

In this panel we are going to attempt to place those nonbehavioral psychological variables that have relevance to, and mediate between, the organizational variables and individual behavior in these organizational and small group settings. While any arbitrary set of variables considered might be inexhaustive of this domain, our intention will be to include as many separable and relevant variables as seem appropriate. We will let subsequent empirical analysis and present conceptual criteria govern our choices.

A. *Motivational Variables*—This sub-category of variables will reflect the forces that impel responses toward or away from a class of goal objects, persons or ideas generally found in small group and organizational settings.

1. *Need for Achievement*—The degree to which an individual wants to perform at a high degree of excellence.
2. *Need for Affiliation*—The degree to which an individual wants to be included and feel that he belongs in a group or organization. The converse of this is the need for independence, i.e. the degree to which he wants to be autonomous.
3. *Need for Power*—The degree to which an individual desires to control others and the converse, i.e. to be controlled by others. This is related to authoritarianism.
4. *Need for Ego Support, Status and Recognition*—The degree to which the individual wants to be appreciated and receive positive evaluations of himself in the group and organizational setting.
5. *Need for Affection*—The degree to which an individual wants to like and be liked by others.
6. *Need for Acquisition*—The degree to which an individual wants material things, i.e. money, etc.

B. *Attitudinal Variables*—An enduring system of positive or negative evaluations, emotional feelings, and pro or con action tendencies with respect to a social object, position, person or system. (Krech, Crutchfield and Ballachey, 1962)

1. *Attitude Toward the Organization*—The enduring system of positive or negative evaluations, emotional feelings and pro or con action tendencies with respect to the work organization and its top management.
2. *Attitude Toward Supervision*—The enduring system of positive or negative evaluations, emotional feelings and pro or con action tendencies with respect to his immediate supervisors or superiors.
3. *Attitude Toward the Work Group*—The enduring system of positive or negative evaluations, emotional feelings and pro or con action tendencies with respect to the work group in which the individual finds himself.
4. *Attitude Toward the Job*—The enduring system of positive or negative evaluations, emotional feelings and pro or con action tendencies with respect to the work position the individual fills in the organization.

    a) *Intrinsic Job Satisfaction*—The degree to which an individual feels his needs satisfied by the activities performed on his job.

    b) *Extrinsic Job Satisfaction*—The degree to which an individual feels his needs satisfied by the rewards and punishments associated with his job performance.

5. *Attitude Toward Local Union or Local Union-like Organization*—The enduring system of positive or negative evaluations, emotional feelings and pro or con action tendencies with respect to the local union or union-like organization.

C. *Perceptual Role Relations Variables*—Variables in this category are considered as a sub-category under organizationally relevant (non-behavioral) individual variables. This category of variables includes those variables reflecting aspects of the organizational environment that impinge on the individual and are perceived by the individual but that have not been covered in the other categories so far.

1. *Discrepancies* between the organizationally relevant expectations of the individual and his experiences as he sees them.
2. *Job Related Stress*—a set of forces that impinge on an individual on the job as seen by the individual.
3. *Role Conflict*—(taken from Wolfe and Snoek, 1962)—when two or more sets of role pressures are logically incompatible with each other.

D. *Aptitude Variables*—The variables in this sub-category reflect the capacities of the individuals to perform organizationally relevant behaviors and in this sense form upper and lower limits on their behavioral tendencies. A capacity can only be exercised to the degree it is present.

1. *Perceptual*—The senses of vision audition and kinesthesis and the sense associated with the semicircular canals are considered in this category.

a. *Color Sensitivity*
   b. *Attention*
   c. *Length Estimation*
   d. *Sensitivity to Visual Movement*
   e. *Auditory Sensitivity*—range of frequencies
   f. *Pitch Discrimination*
   g. *Loudness Discrimination*
   h. *Auditory Integral*—Tone duration discrimination
   i. *Kinesthetic Sensitivity*
   j. *Balance Control*
2. *Psychomotor Dimensions* (Guilford, 1959)
   a. *Strength*
      1) *General Strength*
      2) *Trunk Strength*
      3) *Limb Strength*
   b. *Impulsion*—includes reaction times, limb thrust, tapping and articulation speed.
      1) *General Reaction Time*
      2) *Limb Thrust*
      3) *Tapping*
      4) *Articulation Speed*
   c. *Motor-Speed*—This sub-category can be distinguished from the impulsion sub-category by the fact that the motor-speed sub-category tends to emphasize the rate of movement after it has been initiated.
      1) *Arm Speed*
      2) *Hand Speed*
      3) *Finger Speed*
   d. *Static—Precision*
      1) *Static—Balance*
      2) *Arm Steadiness*
   e. *Dynamic Precision*
      1) *Dynamic Balance*
      2) *Arm Aiming*
      3) *Hand Aiming*
   f. *Coordination*—The variables in this sub-category involve the use of patterns of muscles in combination and in sequence.
      1) *Gross Body Coordination*
      2) *Hand Dexterity*
      3) *Finger Dexterity*
   g. *Flexibility*—This sub-category includes variables reflecting upon the looseness of the joints and determines the range of movement of parts associated with those joints.
      1) *Trunk Flexibility*
      2) *Leg Flexibility*

3. *Intellectual Abilities* (Guilford, 1959)—The abilities included in this category include a group of memory abilities and a larger group of thinking abilities.
   a. *Memory Variables*
      1) *Substance—Memory Variables*
         a) *Visual Memory*
         b) *Auditory Memory*
         c) *Memory Span*
         d) *Memory for Ideas*
      2) *Associative Memory Variables*
         a) *Rote Memory*
         b) *Meaningful Memory*
      3) *Memory for Systems Variables*
         a) *Memory for Spatial Position*
         b) *Memory for Temporal Order*
   b. *Cognitive Factors*
      1) *Factors for Knowing Units*
         a) *Visual Cognition*
         b) *Auditory Cognition*
         c) *Symbolic Cognition*
         d) *Verbal Comprehension*
      2) *Factors for Knowing Classes*
         a) *Figural Classification*
         b) *Semantic Classification*
      3) *Factors for Knowing Relations*
         a) *Eduction of Figural Relations*
         b) *Eduction of Symbolic Relations*
         c) *Eduction of Semantic Relations*
      4) *Factors for Knowing Patterns or Systems*
         a) *Spatial Orientation*
         b) *Eduction of Symbolic Patterns*
         c) *General Reasoning*
      5) *Factors for Knowing Implications*
         a) *Perceptual Foresight*
         b) *Conceptual Foresight*
      6) *Convergent-thinking Factors*
         a) *Factors for Producing Names*
            1. *Object Naming*
            2. *Concept Naming*
         b) *Factors for Producing Correlates*
            1. *Eduction of Symbolic Correlates*
            2. *Eduction of Semantic Correlates*
         c) *Factor for the Production of System*
            1. *Ordering*

        d) *Factors for the Production of Transformation*
           1. *Visualization*
           2. *Symbolic Redefinition*
           3. *Semantic Redefinition*
        e) *Factors for Production of Unique Implications*
           1. *Symbol Substitution*
           2. *Numerical Facility*
    7) *Divergent-thinking Factors*
        a) *Factors Involving Production of Units*
           1. *Word Fluency*
           2. *Ideational Fluency*
        b) *Factors Involving Spontaneous Shifts of Classes*
           1. *Semantic Spontaneous Flexibility*
           2. *Figural Spontaneous Flexibility*
        c) *Factor of Fluency for Producing Correlates*
           1. *Associational Fluency*
        d) *Factor Involving Production of Systems*
           1. *Expressional Fluency*
        e) *Factors Involving Divergent Transformations*
           1. *Figural Adaptive Flexibility*
           2. *Symbolic Adaptive Flexibility*
           3. *Originality*
        f) *Factors Involving Varied Implications*
           1. *Elaboration*

   c. *Evaluative Factors*—These abilities have to do with testing information and conclusions as to their suitability, acceptability, goodness, or correctness.
    1) *Factors Involving Judgments of Identity*
        a) *Figural Identification*
        b) *Symbolic Identification*
    2) *Factors Involving Judgments of Relations*
        a) *Logical Evaluation*
        b) *Symbolic Manipulation*
    3) *Factors for Judging in Terms of Systematic Consistency*
        a) Experiential Evaluation
        b) *Judgment*—The ability to make wise choices of action in a somewhat ambiguous situation.
    4) *Factor Involving Judgment of Goal Satisfaction*
        a) *Sensitivity to Problems*—The ability to recognize that a problem does exist.

It is clear that organizational and small group variables do not affect these ability variables in the same sense as they may influence the other variables in this panel. In this case we feel justified in placing an ability or aptitude set of categories in the overall picture for two reasons. First, the organizational requirements of role performers both in the group and in the organization affect the ability mix that is found in a particular group or organization through the processes of selection, promotion, attrition, etc. Secondly, the organizational and group structure and processes influence the exercise of these abilities and aptitudes. And as well, these abilities and aptitudes affect organizationally relevant behavior. Clearly much more taxonomic research has been done in the abilities and aptitude areas than in the other areas we have been exploring, but little research has been done on how these abilities variables fit into the larger picture.

E. *Dimensions of Temperament*—Temperament traits have to do with the manner in which actions occur. We are concerned here with the characteristics of the dispositions of the individuals in the groups in the organizational settings. This area is less clearly organized than the abilities area but there is some clear evidence that supports a breakdown such as the one that follows (Guilford, 1959). Further, it is relevant to consider temperament in this general panel of variables since it is a non-behavioral characteristic of individuals in organizational and small group environments which is influenced by these environmental factors and is in turn influential on organizational relevant individual behavior.

1. *Factors of General Disposition*
    a. *Confidence vs. Inferiority Feelings*
    b. *Alertness vs. Inattentiveness*
    c. *Impulsiveness vs. Deliberateness*
    d. *Restraint vs. Rhathmyia*—This dimension can be defined as self-controlled, serious, conscientious disposition vs. a happy-go-lucky and carefree disposition.
    e. *Objectivity vs. Hypersensitivity*
2. *Factors of Emotional Disposition*
    a. *Cheerfulness vs. Depression*
    b. *Emotional Immaturity vs. Maturity*
    c. *Nervousness vs. Composure*
    d. *Stability vs. Cycloid Disposition*
    e. *Poise vs. Self-consciousness*
3. *Factors of Social Disposition*
    a. *Ascendance vs. Timidity*
    b. *Socialization vs. Self-sufficiency*—This dimension is definable in terms of dependency vs. independence.
    c. *Social Initiative vs. Passivity*
    d. *Friendliness vs. Hostility*
    e. *Tolerance vs. Criticalness*
4. *Masculinity vs. Femininity*
5. *Personal Tempo*—Rate of movement
6. *Perseveration*—Mental inertia or lag (rigidity) vs. quickness and originality.

7. *Oscillation*—This concept reflects a consistent tendency for an individual to be variable in his behavior vs. being stable or uniform.
8. *Suggestibility*
   a. *Primary Suggestibility*—This dimension involves mainly motoric reactions consequent to verbal suggestions.
   b. *Secondary Suggestibility*—This dimension seems to involve unwarranted or illusory sensory or perceptual outcomes consequent to verbal suggestion.
   c. *Prestige Suggestibility*—This dimension is related to how strongly the individual accepts the opinions of authorities or peers.

Panel Six: Organizational Relevant Individual Behavior Variables

A. *Member Job Outputs*—This category of variables is concerned with both the quantity and quality of behavior in job output units. Job outputs can range from the number and quality of "widgets" assembled by an assembler to the number and quality of plans made by a corporate board chairman or university president. Included in this category are leadership behaviors as well as other organizationally relevant performances.
1. *Relative Number of Job Cycle Units Per Unit Time* (Repetitive Jobs)—This dimension reflects the relative number of cycles of behavior completed per unit time in order for the production of a unit of organizationally relevant behavior in repetitive type jobs.
2. *Relative Quality of Job Performance in Repetitive Type Jobs*—Quality is determined in and by organizational criteria.
3. *Relative Amount of Job Performance of Unequal Units of Job Performance in Complex Jobs*—The relative number of job performances of varying units of behavior including planning, (decision making), organizing and influencing the behavior of others. This category is guided by relativistic view of the distribution of this kind of behavior. That is any given organizaton or group may have changing requirements over time. The consideration here is how well the distribution of this behavior reflects the needs of the system.
4. *The Relative Quality of Performance of Unequal Units of Job Performance of Complex Jobs*—The qualitative complement to dimension #3.

B. *Member Participation*—The relative frequency of attendance when attendance is expected by the organization.
1. *Attendance Rates* (One minus Absence Rates)
2. *One Minus Turnover Rates*
3. *One Minus Lateness Rates*

C. *Strain Symptoms*—This category of variables refers to the behavioral forces generated within a system in response to stress. Phenomenologically in the individual they are indicated by discomfort and malfunction.

1. *Rate of Inappropriate (to the system) Behavior*—Frequency of dysfunctional behavior relative to the system's requirements.
2. *Rate of Inappropriate (to the individual) Behavior*

Panel Seven: Organizational Environment

Recently Sells (1963) has attempted to develop a classification listing of aspects of the "total stimulus situation" for the individual. We are here attempting to develop such a classification system for the organization. That is, we are intending to develop a category scheme for the variables that impinge on the organization from its environment.

A. *Natural Aspects of the Environment*
1. *Weather* in which the organization exists
2. *Gravity*
3. *Terrain* (rivers, lakes, deserts, altitude)
4. *Natural Resources*

B. *Availability of resources needed by the organization*
1. *Personnel Resources*
2. *Material Resources*
3. *Financial Resources*
4. *Market Resources*
5. *Technological Resources*

C. *Structure and Relations with Social Environment*
1. *Technological Structure*
2. *Amount of Contact with Non-Organizational Personnel*
3. *Dependence on Social Environment*
   a. *Degree to which the Social Environment Provides Consumers of Organizational Products or Services*
   b. *Degree to which the Environment Provides Integration of Organization to the Larger Social System*
4. *The Other Characteristics of the Social Environment that Influence Relationships and Behavior in the Systems, i.e. Urban-Rural Location, etc.*

Relationships Between Panels of Variables

In theory we expect that the first six panels of variables are mutually exclusive sets of variables that can be separated and considered as distinct classes. Variables in panels one and two are at the levels of organizational variables. Variables in panels three and four are at the level of the group and variables in panels five and six are at the level of the individuals embedded in the groups in the organizations. All six of these panels of variables are embedded in and affected by those variables found in panel seven, the organizational environment. The figure below represents the general approach of the present classification schema.

Figure 39.1 reflects several classes of hypotheses and something of the structure of the classificatory system. Variables within a panel are seen as being ideally mutually exclusive of each other (though at present they are probably not mutually exclusive since relatively little is known as to how they are related to each other).

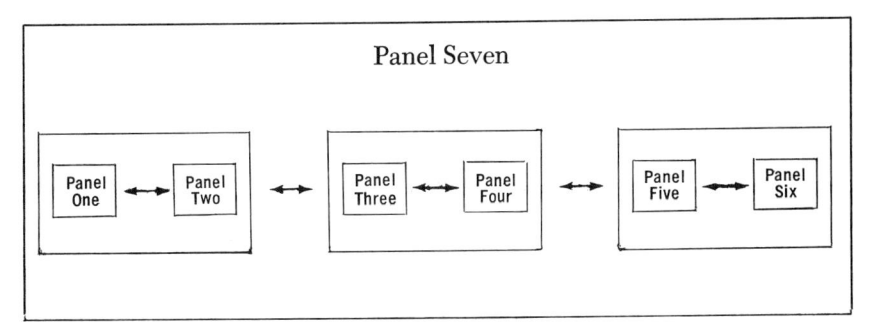

FIGURE 39.1. *Theoretical schema*

Panels one and two are panels where the set of variables within each of the panels are now probably not mutually exclusive. Both from our definitions especially in panel two and the definitions of Pugh *et al.*, 1963, one can see a good deal of definitional overlap between such concepts as control, communication and coordination. On the other hand, the fifth panel is probably the most adequately described area since much empirical and theoretical work has been done especially in the areas of abilities and temperament.

Each of the seven panels deals with characteristics which are classificatorially distinguishable from each other. All seven panels are highly relevant to the study of individuals in groups which are embedded in organizations which are embedded in their socioeconomic environment.

The first six panels are considered paired in Figure 39.1 because it is expected that the variables in the paired panels (1 and 2, 3 and 4, 5 and 6) are more likely to be directly and consistently related to each other since they are at the same level of analysis. There are, however, expectations that variables in panels closest to each other are more closely related to each other. Further, it is expected that variables in panel one are related to variables in panel six through their effects on variables in panels two, three, four and five and as well are conditioned by attributes of panel seven. That is, it is not likely that panel one variables directly affect panel six variables but work their effects through their resultant effects on panel two variables, which in turn affect panel three variables which affect panel four variables, etc. Further, it is implied that relationships between any two variables of differing panels should be cast in the present larger framework. That is to say that the present formulation does not expect to find any relationship of exactly the same size between a variable in one panel and a variable in another panel.

Specifically we expect larger relationships to occur between variables in panels closer together in the schema. For example, organization size, a panel one variable, should be more clearly related to variables of organization function or process such as communication control or coordination than with panel five variables such as attitude toward the organization, attitude toward the work group and achievement motivation. Further, we would expect that any connection between size and these panel five variables would be mediated by variables found in panels two, three and four and as well be conditioned by variables in panel seven. There will be tendencies for variables to be positively or negatively related but the amount of that relationship and sometimes the sign of that relationship will be dependent on the conditions, relations and interactions of other variables in those particular panels concerned, as well as variables from other panels.

Clearly then since there are so many variables described above and fitted into this scheme of classification we have but taken a large first step in developing a theoretical framework from which to work out the many as yet unanswered questions that remain.

Some of the important unanswered questions that are to be taken up in future reports include:
1. How adequately can we measure each of the variables specified above?
2. How adequate is this present schema? What does present evidence say as to its validity and appropriateness?
3. Have we exhausted the roster of variables necessary?
4. Specifically how do the variables *within a panel relate to each other*? What are the differences when different types of organizations are considered? What are the differences when different levels of the organizations are considered?
5. How do the variables *within a given panel relate to variables in other panels*? What are the differences when different types of organizations are considered? What are the differences when different levels of the organizations are considered?

Further specific questions occur; for example, how do the specific variables at the level of the organization (panels one and two) relate to the specific variables at the level of small groups (panels three and four)? How do variables from panel seven condition relationships between variables in the other six panels?

We have come to the end of this report with many questions as yet unanswered but it might well be that the significance of this report and the classification schema it presents lies in its ability to organize material thought to be too diverse to be considered together and as well to generate important questions that may now be researched and put into a perspective that aids our understanding.

REFERENCES

Bales, R. F., *Interaction process analysis: a method for the study of small groups.* Cambridge: Addison-Wesley, 1950.

Guilford, J. P., *Personality.* New York: McGraw-Hill Book Co., Inc., 1959.

Indik, B. P., *Organization size and member participation.* Unpublished doctoral dissertation. Ann Arbor: University of Michigan, 1961.

Indik, B. P., Some effects of organization size on member attitudes and behavior. *Human Relations,* 1963, 16, 4, 369–384.

Inkeles, A. and Levinson, D. J., The personal system and sociocultural system in large-scale organizations. *Sociometry,* 1963, 26, 2, 217–219.

Krech, D., Crutchfield, R. S. and Ballacey, E. L., *Individual in society.* New York: McGraw-Hill Book Co., 1962.

Mendeleev, D. I. as reported in Sienko, M. J. and Plane, R. A., *Chemistry.* New York: McGraw-Hill Book Co., 1957.

Pugh, D. S., Hickson, D. J., Hinings, C. R., Macdonald, K. M., Turner, C., and Lupton, T., A conceptual scheme for organizational analysis. *Administrative Science Quarterly,* 1963, 8, 3, 289–315.

Sells, S. B., *Toward a taxonomy of organizations.* Technical Report No. 2, Texas Christian University, 1962.,

Sells, S. B., *Approaches to the taxonomy of social situations: task or situation.* Technical Report No. 4, Texas Christian University, 1963.

Wolfe, D. M. and Snoek, J. D., A study of tensions and adjustment under role conflict. *J. Social Issues,* 1962, 18, 3, 102–121.

40 An Analysis of Organization Characteristics

ERICH P. PRIEN and WILLIAM W. RONAN

A report of a factor analysis of 38 measures of organization characteristics obtained for 107 small metal-working firms. Nine factors were derived and interpreted with reference to the results of other empirical studies. The results differ from those of other studies and there appears to be limited consensus. Factors which appear in three or more studies are: organization size, formalization, centralization of authority, extent of technology, and standardization with reference to skills and product complexity. The failure of researchers to interpret results more thoroughly seriously limits attempts to compare study results.

The analysis of organization characteristics, particularly with respect to organization functioning and performance, has been of concern to theorists in economics, administration, sociology, and psychology and has stimulated considerable research and speculation. In the past, interest in organization productivity often has focused primarily on the financial and operating dimensions (hard criteria) and only by implication on the human elements (soft criteria) of the organization. In this respect organizations are viewed primarily as economic systems.

In recent years social scientists have proposed different models to describe organizational behavior and performance, which would provide a basis both for prediction and, ultimately, control of an organization's functioning and a better understanding of human performance within organizations. These models have focused primarily on organizations as social systems, emphasizing the human element variables as a subject matter for study in order to explain organization performance and provide the basis for organizational measurement. Different researchers have focused on such variables as communication networks, motivational characteristics of individual members of the organization, reward and punishment, structure, leadership style, organization goals, and various perceptual measurements. Much of this research was initiated by an expressed need for organization change and since change was the ultimate end product, it became a focus for the research. Relatively little work has been undertaken for the sole purpose of describing and understanding the relationships which exist within an organization or across organizations, in particular, the interrelations of the hard and soft criteria.

The published literature reflects a considerable interest in the actions and decisions of top managements and the impact of individuals at that level within organizations. While interest in the executive has led, as a matter of expedience, to remedial and development programs, the effect of what has been accomplished is often not readily apparent or easily measured. The search for causal relationships has not been entirely fruitless and several approaches to the study of organizations have been implemented. Of particular interest are the studies by Palmer and Schroeder (1958), Boyles, Eddy, and Frost (1963), Seashore (1961), Seashore and Yuchtman (1968), and Indik (1965). The results of each of the above studies appeared to be equally promising.

Palmer and Schroeder surveyed 188 small industrial organizations obtaining questionnaire data on organization incentive policies and programs, and measures of employee response in categories conceptually relevant to the questions of policy and programs. Boyles, Eddy, and Frost obtained data from various departments within a single company that reflected various aspects of performance and organization functioning characteristics. Seashore (1961) obtained primarily attitudinal data and some indices of organization performance for semi-independent divisions of a single company. The study by Seashore and Yuchtman (1967) focused on measures of criteria at different levels—at the organization level and individual level.

Indik's (1965) study analyzed data primarily of an attitudinal-perceptual nature from three quite different organizations in a specific search for factors common to all three. These data too, were primarily from questionnaires although some hard criteria were included. These various research efforts do use many different variables, but in the later sections of this paper some common factors apparently emerge from all.

While a variety of research procedures exist, as outlined by Seashore (1961) and also by Forehand and Gilmer (1964), most of the research has emphasized incumbent perceptions and attitudes as basic data for analysis. The primary objective in the aforementioned studies is to relate characteristics of the psychological or social structure of an organization to some of the economic characteristics of the organization.

While constantly seeking to further our understanding of organization, most of the empirical studies have not been explicity designed to test the efficiency of hypothetical models. The notable exception is reflected by the work of Seashore (1961) and Seashore and Yuchtman (1967). However, as pointed out by Woodward (1965), there appears to be some confusion in the literature because of the diversity of discipline source, the individualistic approach and possibly because of the penchant for building on previous research by embracing the comparatively new while to some extent ignoring the findings of other workers.

On the other hand, the conceptualizations by Woodward (1965), Pugh, et. al. (1963), Hall (1963) and Inkson, Payne and Pugh (1967), have all proposed rather ingeniously devised models to understand organizations based upon the "Bureaucratic Model." The Pugh, et. al. (1963) conceptualization appears to be the most comprehensive and shares some common elements with the proposal of Seashore (1965) regarding both technique (factor analysis) and focus on levels of analysis (organization structure, group composition and interaction, and individual personality and behavior).

Pugh, et al. (1968) questioned the efficacy of the "Bureaucratic Model" on the basis of results obtained from a study designed to test the earlier proposal. The dimensionality proposed was partially reflected in their results and led to a more parsimonious proposed structure for organization comparisons.

The objective of this study was to quantify and interrelate two categories of organization level variables. The first category, consisting of independent, "input variables," includes organization conditions and variables resulting from management decisions or the resultant of cumulative management decisions and actions. The second category, consisting of dependent "outcome" variables, includes organization performance dimensions in both economic and psychological terms. While individual variables are labeled as if unidimensional, the assumption, in almost every case, is that a documented measurable characteristic is a result of the accumulation of several management decisions and actions. The existence, for instance, of a pension plan is not the result of a single analysis or decision, but represents an accumulation of analyses and decisions by a number of individuals in similar contexts considering both the common factors and probably some unique factors.

Certainly, the general orientation of the owners of the organization, the financial conditions best known to the chief financial executive, and the approach followed in union negotiations, will all contribute to the final decision which in a scheme as proposed here, provides a single score. The basic assumption of the present study is simply that the empirical description of organizations in terms of the relationships between psychological-social and economic variables is necessary to the understanding of organization functioning and ultimately to tests of theoretical propositions concerned with performance behaviors in organizations.

RESEARCH METHOD

The data for this research were collected in a multi-disciplined investigation of the characteristics of small metal-working firms,

(Lawyer, 1963). While all organizations included in the study were classified as being successful because of continuity of existence, varying degrees of economic success do exist.[1] Types of organizations included in this study are those which fall within the category of small businesses in the metal-working industry as defined by the Small Business Administration. Although all firms were surviving, the range extended from marginal operations to highly successful organizations. Some firms employed as few as 25 workers, others as many as 200 employees. The firms were located primarily in northern Ohio and management agreed to participate in the study.

For the study, interviews were completed with the top executive within each of the functional areas of the company operation. Interviews were structured about the area of responsibility of the individual. The areas investigated were: marketing, production, personnel management, accounting and finance, and a general interveiw covering factors leading to the creation by management of the specific organization characteristics and finally, some characteristics of the chief executive officer.

For the purpose of this study, variables were classified according to the input-outcome scheme described previously. Variables were selected which appeared to reflect the interests of the research and not items such as environmental factors which did not reflect current or recent management decisions. In this way, 38 variables (see Table 40.1) were selected which appear to be somewhat comparable to the characteristics measured in the few previous studies of this nature, plus those which previous research on leadership, motivation, and organizational productivity have suggested as being relevant.

While some previous research has been performed in this area, only the Seashore and Yuchtman (1968) study has been both across organizations and based on more than one or two economic and psychological-social variables.

ANALYSIS AND RESULTS

A total of 38 scores were obtained for each of the 107 firms included in this study. A complete matrix of product-moment correlations was computed and factor analyzed using a principal components method.

[1] Organization success can be described in either economic or psychological-social terms or as a combination. The characteristics of success which appear consistently Bass (1952), Caplow (1953), and Georgopoulos and Tannenbaum (1957) are: survival or continuity of operation and a complex of economic and psychological-social adaptation of flexibility. Minimal corporate success would be represented by static survival while levels of success would require achieving returns in other ways. Several of the variables used in this study are conventional outcomes in both the economic and social sense.

TABLE 40.1. *Organizational variables-patterned interview questions and direction of scoring*

Variable	Item and Source of Data	Score
	Accounting and Financial	
1*	Break even point, % capacity	
	Interview with President	
2*	When was company founded (age)	
3*	Number of employees (total)	
4	(% female)	
5*	Annual sales	
6*	(Growth % present (-) 3 years ago/3 years ago (+20)	
7	Long-term Company objectives	
	Increase sales	
	Gradual growth	1
	Maintain current status	
	No plans	0
	Dunn & Bradstreet Report	
8	Current Chief Executive	
	Company founder or with partner	1
	Any other style of acquisition	0
9	Previous Position of Chief Executive	
	Supervision or above	1
	Non-supervisory	0
	Marketing Management	
10*	Is company currently selling original line or service	
	Yes	1
	No	0
11	Source of idea for current major product	
	Self	1
	Elsewhere	0
12*	% of quotes resulting in contracts	
13*	Cost of advertising as % of sales -0.0 to 9.9	
14*	Extent of change of product since founding	
	Same product as when founded	1
	Added new products with opportunity	2
	Active program of product planning and development	3
15*	Company experience with product development	
	Successful	1
	Unsuccessful or uncertain	0
16*	Company experience with product diversification	
	Successful	1
	Unsuccessful or uncertain	0

TABLE 40.1. (continued)

Variable	Item and Source of Data	Score
17*	Dollar amount of average company sale	
	3-99	1
	100-199	2
	200-499	3
	500-999	4
	1,000-1,999	5
	2,000-9,999	6
	10,000-125,000	7
18*	Number of present and potential customers	
	91 - 100-199	
	92 - 200-299	
	93 - 300-399	
	94 - 400-499	
	95 - 500-599	
	96 - 600-699	
	97 - 700-799	
	98 - 800-899	
	99 - 900 and above	

Production and Personnel Management

Variable	Item and Source of Data	Score
19	Company conduct time studies	
	Yes	1
	No	0
20*	% of factory employees who are skilled	
21	Average hourly rate of factory employees	
22*	% of factory employees receiving average	
23*	Average length of service of production workers	
	less than 1 year	1
	1 - 5 years	2
	6 - 10 years	3
	11 - 15 years	4
	Over 15 years	5
24	Stability of employee job assignments	
	Stable	1
	Diverse	0
25	Quality demands of market	
	Extremely high	1
	High	2
	Ordinary	3
26	Company has a quality control function	
	Yes	1
	No	0
27*	Cost of inspection of % of production cost record range 0.0 to 9.9 to nearest tenth	
28*	Scrap rate as compared to industry	
	Higher than average	1
	About average	2
	Lower than average	3

TABLE 40.1. (continued)

Variable	Item and Source of Data	Score
29	Company has a formal personnel program	
	Yes	1
	No	0
30	Company use job descriptions	
	Yes	1
	No	0
31	Company use job evaluation	
	Yes	1
	No	0
32	Company uses merit rating	
	Yes	1
33	Company has an incentive plan	
	No	0
34	Number of benefit plans	
35	Company allows stock purchase	
	Yes	1
	No	0
36	Company has a pension plan	
	Yes	1
	No	0
37*	Operate under collective bargaining contract	
	Yes	1
	No	0
38	Company has regular employee promotion lines	
	Yes	1
	No	0

* Output Variables

Communalities were estimated using the highest multiple correlation obtained for each variable with any other combination of variables. The factor analysis incorporated an interative procedure to reestimate communalities and refactor until a point of stability was reached. The rotated factor loadings appear in Table 40.2. A Varimax rotation procedure was used to clarify the obtained factor structure. It should be noted at this point that these results also have limited generalizability, a criticism applicable to all the empirical studies published to date concerned with the problem of dimensionality of organization structure. It is through an integrative comparison of the various reports though that a comprehensive and sufficient taxonomy will eventually emerge.

The analysis of the data for the study reported here yielded nine factors. In interpretation, only items with loadings of .30 or higher were considered.

The proposed factor definitions with the accompanying relevant items (*indicates an outcome variable) are as follows:

FACTOR I. STANDARDIZATION

The variables which load on this factor reflect standardization of individual roles, tasks, and internal influences concerning management personnel practices. While variable 23 (length of service) appears on this factor it would be pure speculation to postulate a causal relation with other variables. Also, variable 23 is the only outcome which loads on this factor.

Variable		Loading
32	Company has a merit rating plan	45
31	Company uses job evaluation	42
35	Number of benefit plans	39
30	Company uses job descriptions	36
38	Company has regular employee promotion lines	35
23*	Average length of service of production employees	31
25	Quality demands of market	30

FACTOR II. CHANGE, PRODUCTS AND TECHNOLOGY

The variables which load highest on this factor are outcomes in terms of change in products and possibly technology. While variable 7 (Objective growth) appears there is no other indication of motives for expansion and diversification. Notably absent is any relation to "hard criteria" of effectiveness other than variable 13 (cost of advertising) which is obviously consistent with the concept of change. It appears paradoxical that the only concommitant of this type of change is an increasing cost unless a delay of impact of change is postulated.

Variable		Loading
14*	Extent of change of product since founding	−58
15*	Company experience with product development	−53
16*	Company experience with product diversification	−45
13*	Cost of advertising	−37
7	Company objective toward growth	−33
10*	Company is selling original line or service	30

FACTOR III. SUCCESSION

The variables loading on this factor appear to represent a small business phenomena or phase, that of succession or transition. There are two possible underlying causes, the retirement of the founder or imminent

TABLE 40.2. Factor loadings after rotation

Variable		1	2	3	4	5	6	7	8	9	h^2
1	Break even point 00% of capacity	-09	23	30	-02	-02	28	-21	24	00	33
2	Company age	08	15	36	20	-52	-37	20	20	01	68
3	Number of employees	10	04	-03	06	11	-19	79	-01	-06	69
4	Percent female	-09	-14	05	-47	-06	-02	-02	25	00	32
5	Annual sales	12	-05	-02	00	04	00	87	-20	05	81
6	Growth index	22	-23	-08	-22	08	23	21	-37	-18	43
7	Longterm company objectives	14	-33	01	-28	09	-06	16	-12	-26	33
8	Company founded vs acquired	24	-04	-72	-05	04	01	03	-03	23	58
9	Prior position of chief executive	01	-05	12	07	14	-07	03	01	-23	10
10	Company is selling original line	-02	30	03	-03	30	26	04	-02	-34	37
11	Source of idea of current product	01	00	-27	-13	-29	-03	07	-32	-06	28
12	Percent of quotes to contract	-07	11	-11	08	-36	-05	-10	-07	-08	19
13	Cost of advertising	-25	-37	-11	02	-60	-8	-05	17	-19	64
14	Product change since founding	05	-58	-08	-08	-02	05	11	13	-19	41
15	Company experience-product development	05	-53	-04	00	04	02	02	12	-03	31
16	Company experience-diversification	-07	-45	09	-07	-01	-02	-06	-15	05	24
17	Average sale	-02	10	-10	32	-11	10	06	-66	-09	59
18	Present and potential customers	06	-08	09	-16	-07	02	37	29	-19	30

Variable		1	2	3	4	5	6	7	8	9	h^2
19	Company conducts time studies	04	-06	02	-10	04	-41	15	25	-17	30
20	Percent of factory employees who are skilled	-02	10	-02	63	07	-02	-13	-25	-02	49
21	Average hourly rate of factory employment	19	-07	02	65	-05	-07	04	-02	-08	48
22	Percent who receive average wage	08	-13	06	-11	03	43	18	07	-12	28
23	Length of service of production workers	31	-11	-13	-09	13	-16	-27	23	-04	30
24	Stability of job assignments	-08	01	22	56	-17	-04	04	22	-16	47
25	Quality demands of market	30	15	-09	05	10	-28	04	-08	-11	23
26	Company has a quality control function	07	-01	00	-05	-30	02	-02	-05	12	11
27	Cost of inspection	-07	-03	03	07	-18	-03	-04	14	-62	46
28	Scrap rate as compared to Industry	-04	-11	-01	03	04	-02	-06	-25	-48	31
29	Company has a formal personnel program	05	03	-39	05	-12	-03	-02	-01	-04	18
30	Company uses job descriptions	36	-08	-15	02	-05	10	17	32	-14	33
31	Company uses job evaluation	42	-02	02	08	-12	07	13	06	11	23
32	Company uses merit rating	45	-04	-08	02	14	-01	03	-02	-01	23
33	Company has an incentive plan	17	-08	-02	04	05	13	36	08	11	20
34	Number of benefit plans	07	-01	26	-05	-04	-41	25	-02	01	30
35	Company allows stock purchase	39	03	05	13	-09	02	23	-17	13	28
36	Company has a pension plan	08	14	16	-04	06	36	10	-09	23	26
37	Company has a union	11	07	-11	34	09	04	22	09	09	22
38	Company has regular promotion lines	35	03	25	05	-06	-19	31	12	02	34

failure. This interpretation while informative about small businesses does not materially increase our understanding of organization structure but only that succession is an essential outcome.

Variable		Loading
8	Chief executive is the founder	− 72
29	Company has a formal personnel program	− 39
2	Company age	36
1*	Break even point as % of capacity	30

FACTOR IV. SPECIALIZATION

The variables which make up this factor reflect degree of functional specialization. The presence of skill level, stability of job assignments and a collective bargaining contract all indicate a degree of division of labor and specification of work roles.

Variable		Loading
21	Average hourly rate of factory employees	65
20*	% of factory employees who are skilled	63
24	Stability of job assignments	56
4	% of employees who are female	− 47
37*	Operate under a collective bargaining contract	34
17*	Amount of average sale	32

FACTOR V. MARKET STRATEGY

The most apparent characteristic of this factor is that four of the five variables are outcomes, and four of the variables relate to the marketing function or company products. The concept suggested by variable content is the choice of marketing strategy based in part on the existence of a unique and marketable product.

Variable		Loading
13*	Cost of advertising	− 60
2*	Company age	− 52
12*	% of quotes resulting in contracts	− 36
10*	Company is selling original line or service	30
26	Company has a quality control function	− 30

FACTOR VI. STANDARDIZATION

The variables loading on this factor reflect an emphasis on standardization of procedures and specification of management responsibility to employees. The inverse relation of variables 22 and 34 to the factor dimension suggests a trade off in younger companies toward material recognition and reward. At either extreme of the dimension, there is indicated a tendency to reduce recognition to a formula. This dimension differs from Factor I in that here the emphasis is on the individual whereas in Factor I the emphasis appeared to be more related to the task and impersonal manpower management.

Variable		Loading
22*	% of factory employees who receive average wage	43
19	Company conducts time studies	− 41
34	Number of benefit plans	− 41
2*	Company age	− 37
36	Company has a pension plan	36

FACTOR VII. ORGANIZATION SIZE

The dimension described by high loading variables emphasize organization size and suggest some possibly size related personnel management activities. This factor appears in six empirical studies referred to in this report. While variables 33 and 38 appear on this factor, the loadings are marginal and do not appear to warrant additional interpretation.

Variable		Loading
5*	Annual sales	87
3*	Number of employees	79
18*	Number of present and potential customers	37
33	Company has an incentive plan	36
38	Company uses job evaluation	31

FACTOR VIII.

The dimension underlying the variables which have significant loadings appears to be a reflection of the marketing-technology interface. While there is some overlap with Factor II, this factor is fairly definitely linked to a hard criterion (variable 6) of organization effectiveness.

Variable		Loading
17*	Amount of average rate	− 66
6*	Growth index	− 37
11	Company developed idea for current major products	− 32
30	Company uses job descriptions	− 32

FACTOR IX. QUALITY PRODUCTION

The variables which load on this factor reflect an emphasis on production of a quality product. Each variable is categorized as an outcome and variables 27 and 28 are also hard criteria of organization effectiveness. It should be noted that the scoring on variable 28 is reversed with reference to variable 27; high inspection costs are related to a low comparative scrap rate.

While the emphasis suggested here may appear to be an end in itself, minor loadings on variables 7, 8, and 9 suggest that the objective of organization growth is related.

Variable   *Loading*

Variable		Loading
27*	Cost of inspection as % of production cost	−62
28*	Scrap rate as compared to industry 1. high 2. low	−48
10*	Company is currently selling original line or service	−34

The results of this study suggest that organization performance or functioning can be studied from historical and descriptive data, and that present functioning of organizations shows differences related to such data. In studies of human performance the effects of differing organizations on similar jobs should be studied. However, the effects may be even more pervasive on work group performance or in the formulation of policies and procedures, in general, the milieu in which performance occurs. Another potential use is that the same descriptive indices could serve as dependent variables; for example, to assess management performance and decisions, clarifying goals or studying the effects on performance of changes within the organization.

Present knowledge in this area is obviously quite limited. The 38 variables used here could very likely be doubled to increase real meaning and clarification and, in addition, replications are demanded. However, the exploratory studies completed to date do show some comparability.

One factor that emerged from all the previously cited studies concerns organization size. Somewhat different variables loaded on the factor, but it was common to all. That it needs further clarification is evident from the fact that the results of the study by Boyles, et. al. showed two size factors probably because the variables were more directly related to hard criteria and were more similar than those of other studies.

Because of the difference in variables and how they were measured, it is difficult to make direct and unambiguous comparisons between the factors found in the different factor analytic studies of organization characteristics.

However, if research is to progress in the area of organizations and related human performance, it will be necessary to develop a set of "core variables" with which to compare the structure and functioning of organizations. Otherwise, each study is specific.

Perhaps the most meaningful criterion of the empirical studies reported to date is not of the research itself but of interpretation of the results. Whether because of prudent caution or as a result of lacking a conceptual model, the interpretations have largely focused on an elemental description, that of simply naming variables and variable relations within a factor. The search for meaning would seem to warrant a somewhat more penetrating analysis and search for the *continuum underlying* the variables. The practice of naming factors using as components just variable names appears typical and unfortunately in this area as both shortsighted and unduly restricting. A most welcome exception to this practice is the report by Pugh, et al. (1968). The study was conducted to test the conceptual framework of organizational structural differences offered earlier by Pugh, et al. (1963).

The comparison of results obtained in this study with those published previously is severely hampered by a lack of common variables used in the studies, differences in organizations (insurance offices, metal-working firms, English and American firms), and the different interests and focus of the researchers. Under these circumstances, findings common to several studies would be of prime interest because of the support of generality. In reviewing past work and interpreting somewhat speculatively several dimensions appear repeatedly. Prominent is the characteristic of organization size either in terms of business volume, number of employees, or scope of operation. What is reflected is the dimension of smallness-bigness with varying concomitant outcomes. The second characteristic is the degree of formalization which reflects the degree to which organizations are committed to fixed, publicly acknowledged operating procedures and plans. In the Pugh, et. al. (1968) study this dimension was further fractionated into role definition, information passing, and recording of role performance. Three additional factors have appeared, but with somewhat less generality, concerning centralization of authority, extent of technology (labor intensive *vs* capital intensive), and a work force characteristic type of business complex which resembles standardization. In this latter instance such elements as skill level, product complexity and assignment and group stability are prominent.

Other factors appear uniquely or in only two studies. Some are obviously a function of specific variables or sample characteristics and while interesting in the specific study, they do not lend clarity to the basic questions regarding organization structure and characteristics.

REFERENCES

BASS, B. M. Ultimate criteria of organizational worth. *Personnel Psychology*, 1952, 5, 157–173.

Boyles, B. B., Eddy, W. B., & Frost, C. F. *Organization data and multivariate analysis.* Paper, MPA Convention, Chicago: 1963.

Caplow, T. The criteria of organizational success. *Social Forces.* 1953, 32, 1–9.

Dunteman, G. H. Organization conditions and behavior in 234 industrial manufacturing organizations. *Journal of Applied Psychology,* 1966, 50 (4), 300–305.

Forehand, C. A., & Gilmer, B. von H. Environmental variation in studies or organizational behavior. *Psychological Bulletin,* 1964, 62 (6), 361–382.

Georgopoulos, B. S., & Tannenbaum, A. S. A study of organizational effectiveness. *American Sociological Review,* 1957, 22, 534–540.

Hall, R. H. Intraorganizational structural variation: Application of the bureaucratic model. *Administrative Science Quarterly,* 1962, 7, 295–308.

Indik, B. *Three studies of organizational and individual dimensions of organizations.* Technical Report No. 15, Office of Naval Research, Contract No. NR-404(10), May, 1965.

Inkson, K., Payne, R., & Pugh, D. Extending the occupational environment: The measurement of organizations. *Occupational Psychology,* 1967, 41, 33–47.

Lawyer, D. (ed.) *Small business success.* School of Business, Graduate Division, Western Reserve University, Cleveland: 1963.

Palmer, G., & Schroeder, R. H. *Incentive conditions and behavior in 188 industrial manufacturing organizations.* Technical Report No. 3, Office of Naval Research, Contract No. NR 475 (08) June, 1961.

Pugh, D. S., Hickson, D. J., Hinings, C. R. & Turner, C. Dimensions of Organization Structure. *Administrative Science Quarterly,* 1968, 13, 1, 65–105.

Pugh, D. S., Hickson, D. J., Hinings, C. R., Macdonald, K. M., Turner, C., & Lupton, T. A conceptual scheme for organization analysis. *Administrative Science Quarterly.* 1963, 8, 289–315.

Seashore, S. E. *Assessing organization performance with behavioral measurement.* Foundation for Research on Human Behavior. Ann Arbor, Michigan: 1964.

Seashore, S. E., Indik, B., & Georgopoulos, B. Relationships among criteria of job performance. *Journal of Applied Psychology,* 1960, 44, 195–202.

Seashore, S. E., & Yuchtman, E. Factorial analysis of organizational performance. *Administrative Science Quarterly,* 1967, 12, 377–395.

Woodward, Joan. *Industrial organization: Theory and practice.* Oxford University Press, London: 1965.

VII MODEL STUDIES FOR PERFORMANCE ANALYSIS

The research literature in psychology makes it patently evident that performance of any sort has a complexity that has received rather peripheral investigation. The Dunnette (1963) conceptualization presented earlier indicated the complexity of the prediction situation and, by implication, the need for complex research designs required to estimate the parameters involved. In spite of this and other attempts to indicate the desirable research effort there have been relatively few attempts to investigate performance and its prediction with broadly conceived multi-variate designs. Such designs do exist and this section is an attempt to show some of the more imaginative studies that appear to be required for fullest understanding of performance and its prediction.

One of the more ambitious studies of the sort visualized is that by Seashore and Bowers (1963). The description of the total effort cannot be presented because of space limitations, but "Design of Experiment" indicates the scope of the work involved. Attention is warranted by Table 41.1, which gives the list of independent and dependent variables considered worthy of evaluation. The lists shown are by no means exhaustive of the potential possibilities, but do indicate the complexity of the desireable frame-of-reference in creating research designs.

The second article, by Parker (1963), is another attempt to evaluate performance in a broader perspective. Here the performance is of *work groups* measured by several criteria and with independent variables of supervisory behavior, situational characteristics and, uniquely, employee perceptions of work related to employee goals. Here again, a pattern of complex interrelationship is revealed and relatively independent dimensions of performance.

Patton (1960) attempts, to bring order into an area that has offered quite thorny problems for attempts to arrive at some relevant performance evaluation of executive and management positions. Here the orientation is of such persons being responsible for events or outcomes ("goals") attributable to the work groups they manage. For example, clerical costs are a measurable index of unit functioning, and to assess performance, a goal might be some percentage reduction of such costs over a future time span. No attempt is made to understand behavior, but it is easy to imagine the possibilities for study if such a program were to be instituted in an organization, in particular, in terms of collecting critical incidents of effective and ineffective behaviors. However, this is still imaginative.

The article by Pickle and Friedlander (1967) illustrates an ingenious attempt to account for and predict the various components of manager job performance as reflected by organizational indices. Measures were obtained from various parties at interest to the firm managed by the executive. While the sought end product—the prediction of performance—is in itself interesting the conceptualization of the components of manager performance is quite unique.

A study by Scott and Taylor (1967) although reporting data relevant to another section of this book presents almost incidental data which is again unique. The observation of performance behavior independent of the performance measured in conventional terms strongly suggests that researchers have long overlooked those data which should be most important to psychologists.

The studies presented here, along with those in the section on performance dimensions, indicate the need for much broader studies of a multi-variate nature, in particular, that performance cannot be meaningfully understood in any global sense but must be investigated as an extremely complex phenomenon using complex designs and analyses.

REFERENCES

PATTON, A. How to appraise executive performance: Planned performance. *Harvard Business Review*, 1960, 38, 63–70.

SCOTT, W. E. and TAYLOR, S. A. *Some observations of human performance in a repetitive task.* Paper, Midwestern Psychological Association, 1967.

41 Design of the Experiment

S. E. SEASHORE and D. G. BOWERS

This section outlines the purpose of the experiment in terms of its conceptual foundation and the variables used. In addition it describes the approach to changing the experimental variables, the choice of organizational units for experimental and control purposes, and the plan for assessment of the results. The original design was not followed in all respects. The main points of discrepancy between the plan and the conduct of the work will be noted.

THE INDEPENDENT VARIABLES

The first task of the research team was the formulation of purposes in basic conceptual terms, and the conversion of these concepts into a language and form suitable for communication within the organization.

The theoretical framework for the experiment will not be spelled out here in great detail, as this information is available elsewhere. Likert's "modified theory of management" was adopted as a guide, and a few of the main elements of this system of propositions were selected as a focus for the work. Likert's modified theory does not encompass the whole of management theory and practice, but is confined to the specific but important problem of achieving mutual compatibility and adaptation between the requirements of the organization and the requirements of the individual members. It views the organization as having purposes, resources, technological possibilities and limitations, and internal dynamic processes of its own. In turn, the individual member is viewed as having fundamental purposes, resources, and the like, which tend to be more or less universal among people. One of the tasks of management is to find ways to maximize the valid congruence between individual motivations and organizational requirements. This congruence allows the individual voluntarily to give his energies and abilities to accomplishing the organization's (and his own) goals. The theory assumes that in our society the ego-motives are for most people prepotent, and further assumes that for most organizations the inherent conflicts of interest between the organi-

From *Changing the Structure and Functions of an Organization* by S. E. Seashore and D. G. Bowers. Ann Arbor, Michigan: Survey Research Center, 1963 (Chapter 4).

zation and the individual member are small enough to permit noncoercive collaboration.

An early memorandum of the Survey Research Center research team (fall 1958) summarizes the main themes to be incorporated in the experimental design:

> The basic requirement of the theory seems to be the creation of an organizational structure in which the forces deriving from membership in a group to which one is attracted are allowed to operate so as to create maximum organizational effectiveness. This attractiveness is created by satisfying what Dr. Likert considers to be an extremely important set of human motive-sources, namely, the desires for status, recognition, approval, acceptance, etc. (the ego motives). When this attraction emerges, persons (in line with the general group dynamics findings relating to attraction and conformity) will tend to behave in ways which implement the goals of the group.
>
> Our objective in the Banner study is to create an organizational structure in which these forces might emerge. The elements of this structure, in terms of our research design, may be thought of as the independent variables. The main elements are the following:
>
> 1. An organization in which the basic unit is the group (as opposed to the man-to-man pattern);
> 2. A high amount of mutual influence within each group;
> 3. Supportive (i.e., ego-enhancing) behavior on the part of all members of the group, and especially on the part of the supervsior;
> 4. A high amount of responsibility vested in the group for decisions in its special area (decentralization of decision-making);
> 5. Linking of the groups through a pattern of overlapping memberships.
>
> Given the above structure, the theory postulates adequate satisfaction of the ego motives, and forces should be set up to encourage members to behave so as to fulfill group decisions regarding method and goal. The satisfaction of the ego motives may be thought of as an intervening variable.

The limitations of this theory and experimental design should be noted in passing. There is obviously much more to the determination of organizational effectiveness than is implied by the foregoing scheme. Likert's theory is conceived to apply within the general framework of the classical line-and-staff, hierarchial organizational form, and is thought to be an enlargement upon, rather than a contradiction to, the familiar conceptions of scientific management, and human relations management. The theory assumes the existence of explicit lines of formal authority, provisions for division of labor and specialization, generally accepted purposes for the organization, and a plan of operations with respect to work flow, standards of performance, operations control systems, and the like. The modified theory pertains to the creation of an improved system of interpersonal relations and interpersonal influence which is compatible with the essential requirements of the work system, although not necessarily compatible with all of the manifestations and extreme applications of scientific management which arise from an overly narrow attention to the logic of the work system alone. The modified theory, if well applied, should enlarge the scope and effectiveness of rational management techniques rather than oppose them.

The research design, then, as far as independent variables are concerned, provided for introducing purposeful change with respect to four variables:

1. Increase in emphasis on the work group as a functioning unit of organization;
2. Increase in amount of supportive behavior on the part of supervisors;
3. Increase in participation by employees in decision-making processes within their area of responsibility;
4. Increase in amount of interaction and influence among work group members.

A fifth change, mentioned in the early documents as "linking of groups through a pattern of overlapping membership," came to be viewed as a method for achieving the above changes and not as an independent variable in its own right, and is accordingly not a topic for measurement or analysis in this study.

Change efforts were to be concentrated upon these four experimental variables. The plan called for the measurement of these variables before, during, and after the experimental period in order to assess the degree of success of the experiment. Plans were laid for assessment primarily through the use of the employees as participant-observers responding to questionnaires. The measurement methods are described elsewhere in this report. The variables which the questionnaires were designed to assess are detailed in Table 41.1.

TABLE 41.1. *Main variables in the experimental design*

Independent Variables: (*Variables to be Deliberately Altered*)	Dependent Variables: (*Criteria of Effectiveness*)
1. Increase in emphasis on the work group as a functioning unit of the organization:	1. Increase in employee satisfaction re:
A. Supervisors' use of group approach	A. Foreman B. Company as a whole

B. Employes' perception of belonging to a team that works together

C. Work group
D. Working conditions
E. Pay
F. Job security
G. Promotion opportunity

2. Increase in amount of supportive behavior by supervisors and peers:

   A. Supervisory support (achievement)
   B. Supervisory support (affiliation)
   C. Peer support (achievement)
   D. Peer support (affiliation)

3. Increase in participation by employees in decision-making processes:

   A. Amount of employee influence on what goes on in department
   B. Extent to which supervisor accepts influence from employees

4. Increase in amount of interaction and influence among work group members:

   A. Peer influence among employees
   B. Peer productivity pressure
   C. Peer waste-reduction pressure

2. Increase in productivity rate:

   A. Machine efficiency as percent of standard

3. Decrease in waste rate:
   A. Waste cost as percent of processed material cost

4. Decrease in absence rates:

   A. Instances of absence
   B. Days absent
   C. Late arrivals
   D. Early departures

THE CRITERION VARIABLES

The researcher faced with choosing dependent, or criterion, variables for an organizational experiment has a particularly difficult dilemma. His theoretical interests press toward criteria of organizational structure or process that are near the predictors in his conceptual scheme. At the same time, his concerns for enlarging the conceptual scheme press toward criteria representing the output of organizations, and these are likely to be distant from his predictors. The first choice maximizes his chance of getting significant relationships and is more likely to test and illuminate his theory; it also in most cases simplifies the problems of criterion measurement. The second choice offers the important gain of providing some link between the researcher's own limited theory and the ultimate criteria by which the risk of having criteria that are substantially confounded by factors not included in the theory. In the Banner study, this issue came down to the question whether to use near criteria (such as degree of goal-acceptance, strength of norms about high productivity, etc) or distant criteria (such as productivity, waste, etc.).

Measurements of both types of criteria were made in the study, but only the distant or output criteria are included in the present monograph. The basic study proposition was that increasing the four independent variables would increase the degree to which employees accept the norms and goals of their respective work groups and would increase their motivation to behave in ways that fulfill these norms and goals. It was assumed that the content of these norms and goals would be congruent with the purposes of the organization, and the following categories of criteria were chosen:

1. Employee satisfactions with various aspects of their working conditions, job rewards, and personal relations on the job;
2. Productivity rates and efficiency;
3. Waste rates;
4. Absence rates.

A number of other possibilities were considered and rejected, largely on the basis of unreliability of measurement, contamination of measures, cost of getting data, and similar practical reasons. The positive reasons for including absence and satisfaction are that these are relatively easy to measure, they are concerns of management and employees of self-evident importance, and they are relatively uncontaminated by extraneous sources of influence that might confound comparisons. The productivity and waste variables were chosen because of their prominence in the formal purposes of the firm. The specific measures actually used are itemized in Table 41.1, and described elsewhere in this report.

RELATIONS AMONG VARIABLES

The two sets of variables described in the foregoing pages are not the whole of Likert's modified theory, but only selected elements chosen for research purposes. A more complete formulation would have to provide for additional categories of variables (e.g., modifier variables, intervening variables, and successive echelons of criterion variables) and would also have to provide for relationships of more complex kinds (e.g., interactions, feedback loops, causal chains, and the like). In the interests of simplicity, the model for the Banner study was made very rudimentary; it assumed a simple additive relationship among the four independent variables, and treated the criteria as four representative examples of output criteria, to be treated separately in analysis.

EXPERIMENTAL AND CONTROL UNITS

Initially, the plan of the research distinguished among three populations for study. There was to be an early pilot introduction of the experimental changes in one department of the Banner home plant; when the work had proceeded far enough in this one department to provide an example and to provide experience in effective change methods, then the change program was to be extended to other departments in the plant. Another plant of the firm, engaged in similar manufacturing operations, but located in a distant city, was to serve as the control. The units for study were to be work groups, and also sets of these groups making up departments. There would thus be a number of experimental groups and departments, all at one location, to be compared with matched control groups and departments at the second location. Assessment of success in introducing change in the experimental units would be made both by measuring change over time and by comparing experimental and control units, and the consequent changes in the criterion variables would be similarly assessed.

This plan was substantially modified shortly after the field work began. The distant plant intended as a control proved to be sufficiently different in organization and technology from the home plant to preclude the matching of groups and departments between plants. Changes planned and then in progress at the control site were judged to make it unsuitable for comparison. It was then decided to confine the experimental changes to a single department of the home plant and to use the remaining departments and work groups as controls. As will be described later, this plan also broke down to some extent because of unforeseen difficulties and opportunities in carrying out the change program. In the end, three departments of the home plant became experimental units, with two other departments serving as controls. The plan to analyze both departments and also their component work groups could not be carried out. While five (out of seven) departments maintained their identity over the experimental period, many of the groups within these departments lost their identity because of changes in organizational structure. A few groups were dissolved when their work vanished under the press of technological changes; others merged and lost their separate identities; some changed so much in size or supervisory structure over the period of the study that they could not reasonably be considered to be the same work groups.

The analysis of results to be presented later in this report thus concerns three departments in which experimental change efforts were substantial, and these are compared with two control departments in the same plant.

RESEARCH POLICIES AND ROLE DEFINITIONS

The Union-Management Advisory Committee, created to guide the experiment, and composed of equal numbers from union and management, began work during 1958. In December of that year it prepared, in collaboration with Survey Research Center representatives, a statement, of "Proposals to Govern the Banner Experiment." Several of its provisions are mentioned below:

1. The Committee defined its own role not as a decision-making body, but a body to facilitate the exchange of information. Among other things, it would receive and review progress reports, exchange information on what groups outside the experimental department(s) were thinking and doing with respect to the experiment, and would develop and consider proposals for future modifications in the experimental plan and activities.
2. Provision was made for a representative from the Survey Research Center (hereafter called the SRC agent) to spend about three days a week at the plant. Among his principal duties would be the following:
To encourage the introduction of changes compatible with the experimental plan;
To report and discuss the results of surveys and observations at Banner;
To counsel individuals and groups in their interpretation of these data and observations;
To counsel individuals on their conduct of group meetings and other group activities;
To observe and record events related to the experimental plan.
3. Responsibility for introducing changes was stated to lie exclusively with the line management of Banner. "... decisions about proposed changes are to be made through the normal channels involving at least the parties normally involved .... perhaps improved procedures for decision-making would later be evolved..."
4. An attempt was made to identify the kinds of changes contemplated under the experimental plan: "... proposals made are to be directed toward improving productivity and quality, toward the reduction of costs, toward the improvement of morale, and toward the solution of problems that may [become known] from the results of the SRC survey."
5. Changes involving negotiable matters (pay, free time, working conditions, etc.) could be introduced on a trial basis, but the decisions to do so would come from the appropriate parties, i.e., union and management.

6. "If a change in one unit alters the work procedures of another unit, it will be necessary for all parties concerned to have an opportunity to participate in the decision. It is hoped that a spirit of cooperation will permit the trial of some of these proposed changes."

Not included in this statement of proposals, but understood by all parties, was the intention of having several questionnaire or interview surveys conducted by SRC. The purposes of these surveys would be:

1. To obtain measurements of change progress on some of the experimental variables;
2. To provide data on interpersonal relations and attitudes for use by plant people in directing or facilitating change;
3. To obtain measurements for use by SRC in basic research toward refinement of organizational theory.

No specific time duration was contemplated for the experiment except that it would probably continue for at least a year. The research team viewed the experiment as a semi-natural one involving events and change trends initiated before they arrived on the scene, coupled with a period of somewhat more intensified and focused change accompanied with measurements, and followed by further continuous change. The participation of the research team was to continue indefinitely, until one or another of the three parties—union, management, SRC—thought further activity by SRC to be unnecessary or undesirable. As it turned out, the active participation in these events at the plant by SRC began with the management seminars in the early months of 1958, and was terminated in September of 1960, with an additional field measurement taken in December of 1961.

The financial arrangements were that The Banner Company was to pay the SRC costs, with an agreed-upon ceiling for changes in any one month. Certain basic research costs above this ceiling were to be borne from other resources of SRC. Banner financial support ceased in the fall of 1960, with the suspension of field work. The terminal observations, measurements, and data analysis were supported by a research contract with the Air Force Office of Scientific Research and Development, as part of their interest in basic studies in organizational management.

THE APPROACH TO EXPERIMENTAL CHANGE

The conception of change processes and methods adopted by the research team derived from the previous experience of SRC in similar attempts to introduce modifications in organizational structure and process. The intent was to use concurrently a variety of change procedures without attempting in this study to evaluate them separately or to compare their effectiveness. The change program aimed to achieve direct modifications of organizational policy and structure, and also direct development of supervisors' knowledge and skill. These in turn were expected to alter the four experimental independent variables in the desired way. The immediate foci of change were to be the following:

1. *Policy change and clarification.* It was expected that some of the intended changes would appear incompatible with existing policies and practices, and would require steps by management to modify or clarify policy. Example: increasing the involvement of employees and work groups in decision-making would require that the supervisors be clearly authorized by higher management to transfer some of their decision function to others.

2. *Change in organizational structure.* The intended changes would involve some modification of work group membership, formation of new groups, introduction of new communication methods and channels, clarification and change in formal roles and job definitions.

3. *Cognitive change.* Some people, particularly the supervisors in the experimental unit, would have to acquire information, insight, and understanding with respect to the principles of participation management and their implications for supervisory behavior.

4. *Skill development.* Apart from knowledge of participation management, some people, including the supervisors, would have to improve their skill in interpersonal relations, particularly their skill in dealing with groups of subordinates, and in problem-solving through group processes.

These changes were to be introduced by the management and supervisors of the Banner plant in any ways they found feasible. They would be aided by the SRC agent, whose role as a change agent was to be limited to instruction and counseling. The chief methods for facilitating change were to be: (1) an increase in the number and variety of problem-solving and coordinating meetings at various levels, (2) seminars, conferences, and similar instruction and discussion meetings, (3) information given to supervisors at all levels concerning the earlier survey results, and (4) personal counseling and coaching by the SRC agent, and by supervisors at all levels. A key factor in these change activities would be the application of the "linking-pin" concept in the formation of groups; that is, an effort would be made to create effective groups with membership conforming to the formal organizational structure, and with overlapping membership to aid coordination vertically through the organization.

42 Relationships among Measures of Supervisory Behavior, Group Behavior, and Situational Characteristics

TREADWAY C. PARKER

Recently, an increasing amount of research in industrial psychology has been devoted to exploration of the psychological determinants of work group behavior. Several publications (Haire, 1959; March & Simon, 1958; Stogdill, 1959; Whyte, 1955; Zaleznik, Christensen & Roethlisberger, 1958) have presented theoretical models which emphasize the importance of interactions between worker needs and environmental conditions in determining group behavior. Typically, these models maintain that certain conditions in the work environment, e.g., wages, recognition, supervisory practices, operate as incentives in determining worker behavior.

Several empirical studies have dealt with the relationship between supervisory behavior and group behavior, which is the primary concern of this paper. Systematic research programs have established, beyond a reasonable doubt, that supervisory practices can affect both group performance and group attitudes (Herzberg, Mausner, Peterson & Capwell, 1957; Kahn & Katz, 1953; Pfiffner, 1955). Studies by Fleishman (1953); Fleishman, Harris & Burtt (1955); Halpin (1957); and Rush (1957), concentrated upon describing two categories of leader behavior, consideration and initiating structure, which were found to be related to group behavior in a wide variety of industrial and military settings.

While the need to consider the relationships of situational variables to group behavior in the industrial setting has been recognized (Katzell, 1957; 1962; Vroom & Maier, 1961), not until recently have investigations

From *Personnel Psychology*, 1963, 16, 319–334. The research described herein was performed in connection with the author's doctoral dissertation at New York University. I wish to express appreciation to Dr. Charles Doerr of McKesson and Robbins, Inc., for permission to conduct the study within that organization and to Dr. Richard S. Barrett, thesis chairman, for his helpful advice during the course of the study.

included such variables (Katzell, Barrett & Parker, 1961; Rosen & McCallum, 1962; Vroom & Mann, 1960). These studies indicate that situational variables can play a useful part in exploring the possible determinants of group behavior.

THE PROBLEM

The purpose of the present study was to explore relationships among group performance, situational variables, and supervisor behavior. The emphasis was upon illuminating the role of supervisory practices and situational variables in work group behavior. Relationships among four sets of variables including (a) group performance, (b) group attitudes, (c) supervisory behavior, and (d) situational variables were studied. The model which guided the investigation has been outlined elsewhere (Katzell, et al., 1961). Suffice it to say here that supervisory practices and situational variables were considered as work system inputs while group performance and attitudes were outputs. The following questions concerning relationships between these work system input and output variables were explored:

1. Is supervisory behavior related to group performance and attitudes toward supervision?
2. Are situational variables related to group performance and attitudes?
3. Is group productivity related to worker perception that job performance is instrumental to the attainment of desired goals?

METHOD

Research Setting

This study was conducted in a wholesale pharmaceutical company which operated 80 geographically decentralized warehouses located throughout the United States. The warehouse work groups operated under standardized work methods which had been installed on a company-wide basis. A foreman supervised each group which consisted of seval order-pickers and packers who filled and packed orders from stock shelved in the warehouses. The groups averaged 24 workers in size and 48 (60%) of them were unionized. The measures obtained on each group are described below.

Group Performance

The three measures of performance outlined below were selected as indicators of the job performance of each work group. Quarterly figures for each group on these measures were averaged for the 1959 calendar year:

Productivity—number of items processed per man-hour of production.

Filling Errors—number of order filling errors per 1000 man-hours of production.

Pricing Errors—number of order pricing errors per 1000 man-hours of production.

Internal consistency reliability estimates of the measures were computed by Tryon's method (Tryon, 1957) using the quarterly figures for each work group. The estimates were: Productivity, .93; Filling Errors, .90; Pricing Errors, .86.

Group Attitudes

The results of an attitude survey conducted during 1959 among the 80 participating work groups were made available to the writer for analysis. A total of 1716 employees completed a multiple-choice attitude questionnaire covering various aspects of the work situation. Product-moment intercorrelations among 30 items were factor-analyzed following the principal components technique (Hotelling, 1933). Fifteen components were extracted and analytically rotated to an orthogonal solution using the normalized varimax method (Kaiser, 1958). Six interpretable orthogonal factors emerged from the questionnaire analysis. Table 42.1 shows the questionnaire items included in the three attitude dimensions considered relevant to this investigation.

Unit item weights were used in developing scores for the factors in Table 42.1 and mean scores were derived for each of the 80 participating work groups on each factor. Internal consistency reliability estimates of the factor scores were: Attitude toward Supervisor, .85; Supervisory Recognition, .67; Performance Instrumentality, .58. The data in Table 42.3 indicate that the factor scores are rather highly correlated. However, in this study the three separate attitude dimensions were retained for purposes of further exploration.

Supervisory Behavior

During 1959, the company conducted training conferences for the foremen of the warehouse work groups. Prior to the training, the foremen were asked to complete the Leader Opinion Questionnaire (Fleishman, 1957), which was used as a measure of supervisory behavior. This 40-item instrument measured each supervisor's degree of consideration and initiating structure in dealing with his subordinates. Consideration refers to supervisory behavior which is flexible, responsive, and considerate of the needs and opinions of subordinates. Initiating structure is behavior intended to define workers' roles, establish a pattern of group organization, and prescribe work methods. Consideration is oriented toward the foreman-worker interpersonal relationship, while initiating structure is concerned with organizing workers to reach a particular work goal. The data in Table 42.3 indicate that consideration and initiating structure were independent in this sample of foremen ($r = .10$). The reliability estimates for the dimensions were: Consideration, .70; Initiating Structure, .69.

Situational Variables

The five situational variables described below were selected as relevant to the group output measures under investigation.

TABLE 42.1. *Group attitude dimensions*
$N = 1716$

Attitudes Toward Supervisor	Loading
My supervisor is one of the best people to work with.	.74
I can depend completely on promises made by my supervisor.	.72
My supervisor has a sincere and friendly interest in the personal welfare and problems of workers.	.68
My chances of getting a square deal and fair hearing from my supervisor are very good.	.65
Workers get all the help they need when they go to their supervisor for information on work problems.	.63
Corrections and criticisms are always made in a friendly and helpful way.	.51

Supervisory Recognition	Loading
I am encouraged in every way to offer suggestions for new or better ways of doing a job.	.63
My supervisor is always willing to try out good suggestions for better ways to do a job.	.57
Workers who make worthwhile suggestions are sure to get recognition for them.	.50
Workers who do unusually good work always get recognition for it.	.36

Performance Instrumentality	Loading
Under normal conditions, I can be very sure of holding my job as long as I do good work.	.72
I feel very secure in my job.	.57
I believe my work in McKesson offers an excellent opportunity to establish a satisfactory future for myself in the company.	.26

Wage Rates—Average hourly straight time wage paid during 1959.

Union Status—Work group union representation (union = 2, non-union = 1).

Percentage Male—Average percentage of male employees per group during 1959.

Community Size—Population of community in which group was located (1960 Census).

Group Size—Average number of employees per group during 1959.

A limited analysis of the situational variables was undertaken to determine if they could be described more parsimoniously by factor scores. The five variables were intercorrelated and a centroid analysis yielded the two orthogonal factors shown in Table 42.2.

The data in Table 42.2 indicate that two clusters exist within the situational variables analyzed. The first cluster, which includes community and group size, appears to be a measure of warehouse size. That is,

TABLE 42.2. *Analysis of situational variables*
$N = 80$
(Decimal points omitted in correlations)

Variable	Mean	S.D.	Intercorrelations*					Rotated Centroid Loadings		h^2
			1	2	3	4	5	I	II	
1 Wage Rate	1.74	.28		02	00	−03	01	.10	.85	.73
2 Union Status	1.60	.49	71		−04	02	04	.25	.74	.61
3 Percentage Male	73.9	16.1	53	32		07	−03	.00	.60	.36
4 Community Size	5.0	2.0	25	32	12		−04	.79	.14	.64
5 Group Size	24.0	11.0	23	33	14	62		.77	.19	.63

* Zero order correlations are below diagonal and residuals are above.

larger communities seem to necessitate larger warehouses and work groups to fill their needs. There is some possibility that a broader cultural factor, i.e., urbanization, may underlie this cluster of variables.

The second cluster, which includes wage rate, union status, and percentage male, appears to measure a syndrome of characteristics indicative of employment security. That is, work groups which are highly paid, unionized, and predominantly male seem to be operating in more secure employment situations that the lower paid, non-union, predominantly female groups. There is evidence (Katzell & Cureton, 1962) that this factor is negatively related to employee turnover, which suggests that it reflects employment security.

Regression equations were developed from the factor loading shown in Table 42.2 to estimate scores on warehouse size and employment security. The reliability estimates for the two scores were: warehouse size, .66; employment security, .74. The correlation of —.16 shown in Table 42.3 between the two factors indicates that they are independent within the sample of work groups studied.

RESULTS

The product-moment correlations among group behavior, supervisory behavior, and situational variables are shown in Table 42.3. A number of relationships among the variables shown in Table 42.3 are statistically significant and these are discussed below.

Supervisory and Group Behavior

The first question under study was whether supervisory behavior was related to group productivity and attitudes toward the supervisor. While such relationships have been found in other studies using similar

TABLE 42.3. *Intercorrelations among variables*
$N = 80$
(Decimal points omitted in correlations)

Variable	Mean	S.D.	1	2	3	4	5	6	7	8	9
1 Consideration	54.7	6.9									
2 Initiating Structure	51.9	7.1	10								
3 Warehouse Size	50.1	13.9	−06	22*							
4 Employment Security	100.1	31.9	−06	−21	−16						
5 Productivity	26.8	3.5	13	07	−25*	11					
6 Order Filling Errors	26.9	20.4	−11	15	27*	−24*	−16				
7 Order Pricing Errors	32.1	16.7	−10	23*	−03	−06	−11	28*			
8 Attitudes toward Supervisor	14.6	1.8	51**	22*	−09	−21	12	−04	−08		
9 Supervisory Recognition	27.6	10.9	45**	05	−15	−16	25*	−17	−03	47**	
10 Performance Instrumentality	77.7	8.1	24*	18	−23*	−12	52**	−15	05	41**	51**

* Significant beyond .05 level.
** Significant beyond .01 level.

variables (Comrey, Pfiffner & Beem, 1952; Comrey, Pfiffner & Beem, 1953; Kahn, 1956; Katz, Maccoby & Morse, 1950; Katz, Maccoby, Gurin & Floor, 1951), the measures used in those studies were more global in nature than those used here. Further studies concerned specifically with relationships between supervisory consideration, initiating structure, and group performance (Fleishman, Harris & Burtt, 1955; Fleishman & Harris, 1962) indicate that consideration and initiating structure are related to worker performance and attitudes.

The data in Table 42.3 indicate that in the present study both consideration and initiating structure were related to different aspects of group behavior. Supervisory consideration was correlated with favorable attitudes toward supervision but appeared unrelated to group performance. Initiating structure was weakly related to favorable attitudes toward supervision, order pricing errors, warehouse size, and job security. In short, supervisory practices seem related to group attitudes but not to group performance in the company studied.

Situational Factors and Group Behavior

Previous research conducted in this setting (Katzell, et al., 1961) indicated the importance of considering situational measures in studying work group behavior. The correlations in Table 42.3 indicate that the situational variables were weakly related to work group and supervisory behavior. Warehouse size was positively related to initiating structure and order filling errors but was negatively related to productivity and worker perceptions that productive behavior was instrumental to job security. These results, which are similar to those of Worthy (1950), suggest that the larger groups were supervised by foremen who were higher in initiating structure. Furthermore, the larger groups made more order filling errors and was less productive than the smaller groups. Generally, the larger work groups operating in urban settings were less effective than the groups located in smaller communities.

Employment security was negatively related to supervisory structure, order filling errors, and attitudes toward supervision but was unrelated to supervisory consideration and productivity. These correlations suggest that the unionized, highly paid, predominantly male work groups were supervised by low structure foremen and had relatively unfavorable attitudes toward them.

Group Performance and Perceived Performance Instrumentality

One hypothesis regarding group performance considers it as instrumental to worker goal attainment. That is, if workers feel that productive behavior leads to desired goals, e.g., job security, they will be productive.

Conversely, if work is perceived as not leading to desired goals no work motivation will be generated. Thus, job performance can function as a path for reaching desired goals such as job security. This "path-goal" hypothesis was tested and supported in a study by Georgopoulos, Mahoney, and Jones (1957). The same hypothesis was investigated in the present study and was supported by the correlation between performance instrumentality and group productivity. That is, the workers who perceived that job security depended on "doing good work" were the ones who worked most efficiently in the company studied.

Psychological Dimensions of the Work Situation

The intercorrelations in Table 42.3 were factor-analyzed to determine their underlying dimensions. Three centroids were extracted, iterated to obtain stable communalities, and graphically rotated to the orthogonal solution shown in Table 42.4.

TABLE 42.4. *Work situation dimensions*
$N = 80$
(Decimal points omitted)

Variable	Unrotated Centroid			Rotated Centroid			h^2
	I	II	III	I	II	III	
Consideration	56	25	−32	09	69	−01	48
Initiating Structure	13	37	36	11	06	52	28
Warehouse Size	−21	38	13	−25	−05	38	21
Employment Security	−10	−43	−17	03	−17	−44	22
Productivity	49	−39	30	68	01	−10	48
Filling Errors	−29	45	33	−23	−18	56	40
Pricing Errors	−09	21	27	−01	−10	35	13
Attitudes toward Supervisor	69	37	−19	20	76	17	65
Supervisory Recognition	68	12	−09	37	58	03	48
Performance Instrumentality	75	−12	36	78	29	14	71

The first factor in Table 42.4 has its heaviest loadings on group productivity and performance instrumentality but is virtually independent of situational and supervisory behavior measures. There is some suggestion that larger groups are less effective and that supervisory recognition received by employees is related to productivity, but the loadings of these variables are negligible. Based on the data in Table 42.4, it appears that the first factor may measure performance motivation. That is, productivity and performance instrumentality are hypothesized to be two facets of job motivation. In addition to a goal, e.g., job security, two further components which seem necessary for productive behavior to occur are (a) the perception that productive behavior leads to job security, and (b) the performance of the behavior to verify its goal instrumentality. In this study, the first factor in Table 42.4 seems to measure these two aspects of performance motivation.

The second factor loads on supervisory consideration, attitudes toward supervisor, and the degree of recognition given by supervisors to their workers, but it is almost completely independent of situational and group performance variables. Its pattern of loadings suggests that it measures the leadership climate existing within the work groups studied. Within a considerate leadership climate, a foreman treats his workers as his equal when making decisions, is responsive to their needs and opinions, and gives recognition for superior performance. This climate tends to equalize the distribution of power between foreman and worker and thereby may result in workers having favorable attitudes toward their foreman. With an inconsiderate leadership climate prevailing, the foreman is more rigid in pursuing his own ideas, more resistant to suggestions, and he makes decisions without consulting his subordinates. The inconsiderate foreman assumes more power relative to his subordinates which may result in less favorable worker attitudes toward him. The loadings on the leadership climate factor indicate that it is not related to the situational differences in the company nor to group performance as measured here.

The third factor has positive loadings on both types of errors, supervisory initiating structure, and warehouse size, but it is negatively correlated with employment security. Thus, the work quality of the larger groups is poorer and they are supervised by foremen who tend to initiate structure. Furthermore, there is a tendency for these groups to operate in the less secure employment situations present within the company. The loadings on this factor invite the speculation that the larger, less secure groups necessitate more directive supervision which may result in poorer quality work. While the psychological meaning of this complex factor is difficult to discern, it appears to measure worker autonomy. The positive loadings on errors, warehouse size, and initiating structure suggest that workers in larger groups are less careful about their work and are given less opportunity to plan their work since methods and procedures are likely to be prescribed by their foremen. In addition, because their positions are less secure, they may be unable to take much initiative in work planning. These relationships suggest an atmosphere in which the worker is in a dependent position and has little identification with his work. In short, lack of autonomy seems to create a situation in which there is little personal identification with group output and work quality is poor.

DISCUSSION

The results of the study suggest certain further explorations concerning the determinants of work group behavior. The dimensional analysis has uncovered clusters of psychological variables associated with worker attitudes, performance level, and performance quality. The finding that these organizational behaviors are relatively independent suggests that high output level, high product quality, and favorable employee attitudes are not necessarily incompatible as has been suggested. The dimensions isolated, i.e., leadership climate, performance motivation, and worker autonomy, may be useful for understanding group behavior.

A series of studies in which these three dimensions were systematically explored could determine their relationships with group behavior in a variety of situations. It is possible that the dimensions found in this study do not exist within other organizations or that different types of organizations have characteristic clusters of variables associated with their outputs which differ from those described here.

Performance Motivation

The typical industrial situation is designed to channel human behavior by the use of incentives. While it is relatively well recognized that incentives do evoke behavior, an important aspect of predicting the behavior seems to be a knowledge of the choice of paths to reach the incentive rather than the mere presence of the incentive itself.

The results of this study indicate that the perceptual aspect of motivation may predict actual behavior. That is, if worker goals and perceptions concerning what types of behavior lead to the goals are known, prediction of behavior seems possible. An analysis of the factors associated with goal path perceptions and choices might yield a better understanding of what determines human behavior in the industrial setting.

An important problem is the discovery of the determinants of goal path perceptions and choices. A simple testable model maintains that goal paths will be chosen according to their perceived utility for reaching the goals. For example, if job performance were judged to be the best path to a particular goal, performance should be at a high level. If, on the other hand, job performance were judged not be the best path to the desired goal, there would be little reason to expect performance to vary with changes in the goal. Goal path utility is a variable which has been largely ignored in seeking to understand human behavior in industrial work systems. The factors associated with this construct require systematic exploration.

Leadership Climate

Much research has been accomplished regarding leader behavior, leadership climate, and the effects of various types of leadership practices upon individual and group behavior. Leadership climate, as defined in this study, is a construct which describes the interpersonal climate between foreman and worker. One of its more important aspects is the degree of consideration shown by the foreman for his subordinates. Consideration on the part of the foreman implies an ability to accept the ideas, suggestions, and opinions of his subordinates. A supervisor who considers the ideas of his workers in making decisions creates an interpersonal climate in which communication channels are open and flexible. In short, a considerate leadership climate is one in which subordinates are included rather than excluded from decision-making activities. On the other hand, the supervisor who creates an inconsiderate leadership climate is likely to be rather rigid in pursuing his own ideas and to make decisions without consulting his subordinates. One of the primary differences between considerate and inconsiderate leaders seems to be the degree of psychological distance between leader and subordinate. The considerate leader seeks to reduce this distance while the inconsiderate leader does not attempt to reduce it.

Worker attitudes toward supervisors appear to vary as a function of supervisory consideration in the study reported here. In groups where the interpersonal climate is considerate, the attitudes of subordinates are favorable toward the supervisor and particularly in the recognition he gives for good performance. Conversely, in groups where the supervisor is less considerate, his subordinates have less favorable attitudes toward him. While worker attitudes seem to be an integral part of the leadership climate in the company studied, group performance is not included in this cluster of variables. However, there is sufficient evidence (Herzberg, et al., 1957) that supervisory behavior and group performance are related to suggest that, in certain situations, job performance may be perceived as instrumental to the attainment of certain types of supervisory behavior.

In summary, leadership climate as measured in this study reflects supervisory consideration and group attitudes toward the supervisor. This cluster of variables was independent of group performance in the company studied although this may not be true in other types of organizations.

Worker Autonomy

Autonomy in the work situation implies that individuals have certain freedom in planning and executing their work. Modern industrial methods have generally tended to reduce individual autonomy because most large systems require uniform behavior to achieve efficient operation. While there is little doubt that system efficiency is gained by limiting worker autonomy and requiring consistent, predictable behavior patterns, an important source of motivation may be lost in the bargain. Work situations which limit worker autonomy appear to reduce the worker's degree of identification with the product. That is, the degree of control the worker has over his job may be related to the degree of responsibility he feels for the final product.

Supervisory behavior is among the factors which may affect worker autonomy. For example, if a supervisor creates a relationship with his workers in which they are dependent upon him for direction (low autonomy), the workers often may tend to disassociate themselves from the group output since this type of foreman often has planned the work procedures without consulting his subordinates. On the other hand, a foreman who allows his workers some freedom in work planning and job procedures (high autonomy) is likely to create a situation in which workers feel that they have responsibility for their product. In short, high autonomy seems to facilitate worker ego involvement with the product, while low autonomy probably reduces such involvement.

The results of the present study indicate the existence of an organizational dimension which has been loosely defined as autonomy. This dimension is correlated with work quality in the company studied. The general finding is that the larger, less secure groups supervised by directive foremen make more order filling and pricing errors. However, while supervisory structure apparently plays an important role in worker autonomy and work quality, warehouse size is also related to work quality. The results suggest that in the larger groups workers may have less identification with group output than in the smaller more closely knit groups.

SUMMARY

A study relating supervisory behavior, group behavior, and situational variables was conducted among 80 work groups in a decentralized warehousing company. The principal findings were as follows:

1. Supervisory behavior was related to worker attitudes toward supervision but was not related to group performance.
2. Situational variables, including warehouse size and employment security, were related to group attitudes toward supervision and group performance measures.
3. Worker perception that job performance is instrumental to job security was related to group productivity.
4. Correlations among the variables studied yielded three independent

dimensions of organizational behavior loosely defined as performance motivation, leadership climate, and worker autonomy.

REFERENCES

COMREY, A. L., PFIFFNER, J. M., & BEEM, H. "Factors Influencing Organizational Effectiveness: I. The U. S. Forest Survey." *Personnel Psychology*, V (1952), 307–328.

COMREY, A. L., PFIFFNER, J. M., & BEEM, H. "Factors Influencing Organizational Effectiveness: II. The Department of Employment Survey." *Personnel Psychology*, VI (1953), 65–79.

FLEISHMAN, E. A. "The Measurement of Leadership Attitudes in Industry." *Journal of Applied Psychology*, XXXVII (1953), 153–158.

FLEISHMAN, E. A., HARRIS, E. F., & BURTT, H. E. *Leadership and Supervision in Industry*. Columbus, Ohio: Ohio State University, 1955.

FLEISHMAN, E. A. "A Leader Behavior Description for Industry." In Stogdill, R. M. and Coons, A. E. (Editors), *Leader Behavior: Its Description and Measurement*. Columbus, Ohio: Ohio State University, 1957.

FLEISHMAN, E. A. & HARRIS, E. F. "Patterns of Leadership Behavior Related to Employee Grievances and Turnover." *Personnel Psychology*, XV (1962), 43–56.

GEORGOPOULOS, B. S., MAHONEY, B. M., & JONES, N. W., JR., "A Path-Goal Approach to Productivity." *Journal of Applied Psychology*, XLI (1957), 345–353.

HAIRE, M. (Editor) *Modern Organization Theory*. New York: John Wiley & Sons, 1959.

HALPIN, A. W. "The Leader Behavior and Effectiveness of Aircraft Commanders." In Stogdill, R. M. and Coons, A. E. (Editors), *Leader Behavior: Its Description and Measurement*. Columbus, Ohio: Ohio State University, 1957.

HERZBERG, F., MAUSNER, B., PETTERSON, R. O. & CAPWELL, D. *Job Attitudes: Review of Research and Opinion*. Pittsburgh: Psychological Service of Pittsburgh, 1957.

HOTELLING, H. "Analysis of a Complex of Statistical Variables into Principal Components." *Journal of Educational Psychology*, XXIV (1933), 417–441, 498–520.

KAHN, R. L. & KATZ, D. "Leadership in Relation to Productivity and Morale." In Cartwright, D. and Zander, A. (Editors), *Group Dynamics*. Evanston, Illinois: Row Peterson, 1953.

KAHN, R. L. "The Prediction of Productivity." *Journal of Social Issues*, XII (1956), 41–49.

KAISER, H. F. "The Varimax Criterion for Analytic Rotation in Factor Analysis." *Psychometrika*, XXIII (1958), 187–200.

KATZ, D., MACCOBY, N., & MORSE, N. *Productivity, Supervision and Morale in an Office Situation.* Ann Arbor, Michigan: University of Michigan, 1950.

KATZ, D. MACCOBY, N., GURIN, C., & FLOOR, L. *Productivity, Supervision and Morale Among Railroad Workers.* Ann Arbor, Michigan: University of Michigan, 1951.

KATZELL, R. A. "Industrial Psychology." *Annual Review of Psychology.* VIII (1957), 237–268.

KATZELL, R. A., BARRETT, R. S., & PARKER, T. C. "Job Satisfaction, Job Performance, and Situational Characteristics." *Journal of Applied Psychology*, XLV (1961), 65–72.

KATZELL, R. A. "Contrasting Systems of Work Organization." *American Psychologist*, XVII (1962), 102–108.

KATZELL, R. A. & CURETON, E. E. "A Further Analysis of the Relations Among Job Performance and Situational Variables." *Journal of Applied Psychology*, XLVI (1962), 230.

MARCH, J. G. & SIMON, H. A. *Organizations.* New York: John Wiley & Sons, 1958.

PFIFFNER, J. M. "The Effective Supervisor: An Organization Research Study." *Personnel*, XXXI (1955), 530-540.

ROSEN, H. & McCALLUM, E. F. "Correlates of Productivity." *Personnel Psychology*, XV (1962), 429–439.

RUSH, C. H., JR., "Leader Behavior and Group Characteristics." In Stogdill, R. M. and Coons, A. E. (Editors), *Leader Behavior: Its Description and Measurement.* Columbus, Ohio: Ohio State University, 1957.

STOGDILL, R. M. *Individual Behavior and Group Achievement.* New York: Oxford Press, 1959.

TRYON, R. C. "Reliability and Behavior Domain Validity: Reformulation and Historical Critique." *Psychological Bulletin*, LIV (1957), 229–249.

VROOM, V. H. & MANN, F. L. "Leader Authoritarianism and Employee Attitudes." *Personnel Psychology*, XIII (1960), 125–140.

VROOM, V. H. & MAIER, N. R. F. "Industrial Social Psychology." *Annual Review of Psychology*, XII (1962), 413–446.

WHYTE, W. F. *Money and Motivation.* New York: Harper and Brothers, 1955.

WORTHY, J. C. "Organization Structure and Employee Morale." *American Sociological Review*, XV (1950), 169–179.

ZALEZNIK, A., CHRISTENSEN, C. R., & ROETHLISBERGER, F. J. *The Motivation, Productivity and Satisfaction of Workers.* Boston, Massachusetts: Harvard University, 1958.

43 Seven Societal Criteria of Organizational Success

HAL PICKLE and FRANK FRIEDLANDER

Management success is an elusive concept. It frequently represents a set of intermediate evaluations which, in turn, it is hoped are approximations of more ultimate criteria of *organizational success*. But, organizational success is an equally elusive concept. To most members of society, organizational success is an abstraction of the more specific people, processes, and products with which these members come into contact. In evaluating success, each segment of society would seem to view only that facet of the organization with which it interacts. In this sense, the organization is like the proverbial elephant which is defined and evaluated in a variety of ways, depending upon the particular part of it with which we have contact. For example, very different criteria of organizational success might be suggested by the organizational *owner*, its *customers*, its *suppliers*, its *employees*, its *creditors*, its *community*, and its *governments*. These seven parties are, in this paper, referred to as "parties-at-interest." They represent members of the society with which the organization transacts, members who may present contrasting demands upon the organization, and members whose needs must, in part, be satisfied if the organization is to fulfill its functions successfully, and if it is to survive.

Thus, the criterion in this study is one of the organization operating in such a manner as to successfully fulfill societal needs rather than a criterion of job success or employee success as conventionally set forth in most texts (Thorndike, 1949; Stone & Kendall, 1956; Krug, 1961). The ultimate criterion is not only *the total value of the man to his organization*, as suggested in the personnel literature, but also *the total value of the organization to its society*.

In addition to a focus upon multidimensional societal criteria of organizational success, the relationship of these several criteria to the abilities and personality characteristics of the manager of each organization was also of interest. Thus, our investigation followed the multiple predictor-multiple criteria design suggested by Guion (1961) and Dun-

From *Personnel Psychology*, 1967, 20, 165–178.

nette (1963) of analyzing the relationships between each of the manager characteristics (as predictors) and each of the success criteria.

Figure 43.1 depicts a schematic model of the managerial-organizational-societal interactions. The criteria of organizational success are the degree to which the needs of each of the seven societal members (parties-at-interest) are met. Organizational success, in turn, is a function of the manner in which the manager conducts the organization. This conduct is hypothesized to be in part dependent upon the manager's ability and personality characteristics.

Most previous attempts to measure the contribution of ability and personality characteristics to organizational success have utilized criteria of limited and insufficent relevance. Those studies which have been concerned with intermediate criteria of effectiveness have focused on manager evaluations, typically through the use of ratings which depict only a small slice of the manager's performance, are affected by the biases of the perceiver, and bear questionable relation to management results or organizational success. A second group of studies has utilized two broad types of criteria; organizational performance such as profit, cost, rates of productivity, and individual output, or criteria associated with human resources such as motivation, mental health, job commitment, cohesiveness, and attitudes toward employer. As Katzell (1957) pointed out in his review of industrial psychology, investigations in this area typically employ measures of satisfaction and performance. Our previous discussion has indicated that criteria of employee satisfaction and performance have relevance only to a small segment of the society which supports and interacts with the total business organization.

From this vantage, several questions may be raised. Are the satisfac-

FIGURE 43.1. Schematic model of the managerial-organizational-societal interactions.

tions of the several parties-at-interest sufficiently related so that concurrent satisfaction is prevalent? What is the impact of the manager's ability and personality characteristics upon the satisfaction of the seven parties-at-interest? If these satisfactions are unrelated, what combinations of manager abilities and personality characteristics will maximize the satisfaction of each of the seven parties-at-interest? More specifically, the purposes of this study were (1) to explore the relationships among the success criteria as seen by each of the seven parties-at-interest, (2) to examine the relationships between these several success criteria and the ability and personality characteristics of the managers of the organizations, and (3) to compare the degree to which combinations of manager ability and personality differentially predict each of the success criteria.

SAMPLE

The degree to which manager ability and personality affect the success of the organization would be expected to be related to the size of the organization. In large organizations, a variety of additional factors would undoubtedly attenuate the importance of the characteristics of any one manager, even though he might be at the highest level. Adequate preliminary tests of the contribution of manager characteristics to organizational success should, therefore, be made in an organization small enough to allow direct manager impact upon the conduct of the business. With these considerations in mind, the sample for this study included 97 small businesses, each employing from four to about 40 employees, and each having only one level of management. Thus, each manager in the sample had the highest line authority within his respective organization.

A random stratified technique was utilized in selecting small business establishments. The distribution of types of small businesses in the United States was determined from various census data. This distribution was approximated in a random selection of small businesses within the state of Texas. Since responses from two of the initial 97 business organizations were suspect, two additional organizations were substituted for these. The final sample of 97 small businesses was composed of 54 retail establishments, 26 service establishments, 8 wholesale establishments, 6 manufacturers, and 3 mineral extraction firms.

CRITERIA

A variety of methods was used in developing criteria relevant to the needs and satisfactions of the seven parties-at-interest.

Owners

The owner of each of the 97 business organizations responded to a questionnaire survey conducted in a structured interview. Owner satisfaction was considered to exist in two broad categories: (1) financial satisfaction, including dollar amounts, return on investment, return on hours of work, profit relative to other organizations, previous financial record, and growth potential; and (2) nonmonetary satisfactions including enjoyment and pride in ownership.

Customers

Customers were surveyed by the use of a questionnaire administered in an interview. The sample size of each organization was proportional to its total number of customers within a framework of a minimum of 15 and a maximum of 25 customers per organization. Customers rated the respective business on a five-point scale on each of the following features:

1. Location
2. Quality of goods and services
3. Variety of offering
4. Quantity available
5. Appearance of establishment
6. Hours
7. Days open
8. Knowledge of product
9. Availability of fashion
10. Speed of service
11. Prestige
12. Merchandise display
13. Various customer services
14. Satisfaction of complaints
15. Parking
16. Advertising
17. Dependability
18. Various employee factors
19. Price
20. Sales techniques
21. Congestion—inside and outside
22. Air conditioning

Employees

The SRA Employee Inventory, a measure of employee satisfaction, was administered to all employees of each organization, with a minimum of four and a maximum of ten employees per organization surveyed. A total of 513 inventories was completed by employees, representing an average of 5.29 employees per organization. A mean satisfaction score was computed for each of the 97 organizations.

Suppliers

Supplier satisfaction was measured in three categories: the supplier's cost of filling orders for the business organization, the organization's record of meeting its financial obligation to the supplier, and its record of stability in the continuity of relationship with the supplier. A total of 403 survey questionnaires was mailed of which 208 were completed and returned, representing an approximate 52 percent return.

Creditors

Levels of creditor satisfaction with each organization were obtained from statistical data gathered during interviews with banks, retain merchant associations, and Dun & Bradstreet.

Communities

Community satisfaction was measured in three categories: support of organizations in the community, support of charities and schools, and participation in political activities. These data were obtained through a questionnaire survey administered to the managers of the 97 organizations in directed interviews.

Governments

Relations with federal, state, and local governments were measured through the administration of a questionnaire to managers in the 97 organizations. Items in this section concerned communication with state and federal officials, the support of lobbying groups, questioning by Internal Revenue Service officials of income tax returns, penalties paid on taxes, or reprimands or censures by tax officials. In general, these items reflected the degree to which the organization carried out its explicit and implicit responsibilities with governmental agencies.

MANAGER CHARACTERISTICS

Two ability and eight personality characteristics of each of the 97 organization managers were measured through standardized testing instruments. Critical thinking ability was measured through use of the Watson-Glaser Critical Thinking Appraisal. Verbal comprehension was measured through responses to Test 1 of the Employee Aptitude Survey. Administration of the Gordon Personal Profile yielded manager scores on ascendency, responsibility, emotional stability, and sociability. The Gordon Personal Inventory also yielded scores on cautiousness, original thinking, personal relations, and vigor of each of the 97 managers.

RESULTS

In accordance with the three issues raised earlier, this section is divided into three parts. In each part the primary question is raised, the methodology is outlined, and the results are presented.

1. Are the satisfactions of the several parties-at-interest sufficiently compatible so that concurrent fulfillment of their needs is prevalent? To answer this question, we explored the relationships among the satisfac-

tions of the seven parties-at-interest. Person product moment correlations were computed among the several satisfaction criteria and are presented in Table 43.1.

It is apparent that the satisfactions of the seven parties-at-interest are not independent, although the correlations among them are of a moderately low magnitude. The lack of any significant *negative* correlations is gratifying and indicates that the satisfaction of any one party does not immediately imply gross dissatisfaction for any other party-at-interest. But, the lack of higher correlations does imply that the business firm will find it somewhat difficult to satisfy concurrently all or even a major share of its societal demands.

The highest correlation was found between owner satisfaction and customer satisfaction ($r = .37$), a finding substantiating the supposition that satisfied customers contribute toward the financial (and nonfinancial) satisfaction of the business owner. Owner satisfaction was moderately correlated with community satisfaction ($r = .23$) and employee satisfaction ($r = .25$). The latter figure might be viewed as a global employee performance-satisfaction measure, if we assume a high relationship between employee performance and the financial success of the owner. At a minimum it indicates that the owner's financial success is dependent, in part, upon employee satisfaction, although the direction of causality may be reversed. The fulfillment of employee needs is also related to the satisfaction of two other parties—the community and the customers.

As might be expected, government and creditor satisfactions were moderately correlated ($r = .20$). The needs of both of these parties are seen more as financial obligations which are fulfilled if continually

TABLE 43.1. *Intercorrelations of satisfactions of seven parties-at-interest with 97 business firms*

	\multicolumn{6}{c}{Satisfaction of}
	Community	Government	Customer	Supplier	Creditor	Employee
Owner Satisfaction	.23*	−.12	.37**	.14	.00	.25*
Community Satisfaction		.16	.04	.16	.14	.22*
Government Satisfaction			−.09	.11	.20*	−.07
Customer Satisfaction				.17	.23*	.23*
Supplier Satisfaction					.08	.17
Creditor Satisfaction						.08
Employee Satisfaction						

* $p < .05$.
** $p < .01$.

reduced to a minimum. Satisfaction of supplier needs did not correlate significantly with those of any other party-at-interest.

2. What are the impacts of the manager's ability and personality characteristics upon the satisfaction of the seven parties-at-interest? Pearson correlations were computed between satisfaction with the business firm by the seven parties-at-interest, and the two ability and the eight personality characteristics of the business manager. These relationships are presented in Table 43.2.

Managers high in verbal comprehension and (to a lesser degree) high in critical thinking skills operate business firms which provide higher fulfillment of societal needs. Business firms whose managers have high verbal comprehension provide satisfaction for the owner, the customer, and the supplier. Firms whose managers have high critical thinking skills provide high satisfaction for customers and employees.

The degree and consistency of the relationships between the manager's personality characteristics and the societal fulfillment which his firm provides were far less than for the manager's ability. Managers high in ascendency (active, assertive, self-assured), and high in original thinking (like to work on difficult, new, thought-provoking problems) operate business firms which provide high satisfaction for the owner. The fulfill-

TABLE 43.2. *Correlations of manager characteristics with the satisfactions of seven parties-at-interest*
($N = 97$)

| | \multicolumn{7}{c}{Satisfaction of} |
	Owner	Community	Government	Customer	Supplier	Creditor	Employee
Manager Ability							
Verbal Comprehension	.31**	.20*	.00	.30**	.27**	.20*	.12
Critical Thinking	.13	.11	.14	.22*	.10	.10	.24*
Manager Personality							
Responsibility	.02	.02	.08	.15	.03	−.08	.00
Vigor	.18	−.05	.00	.21*	.10	.08	.00
Ascendency	.29**	.14	−.03	.03	.06	.16	.12
Emotional Stability	.06	.02	.22*	−.03	−.17	−.03	.01
Sociability	.18	.14	−.04	.16	−.17	.10	.26**
Original Thinking	.26**	.06	−.13	.10	−.01	.07	.09
Cautiousness	−.07	.04	−.04	−.01	.00	−.17	.10
Personal Relations	−.09	.12	−.08	−.10	−.06	−.17	−.04

* $p < .05$.
** $p < .01$.

ment of governmental obligations and needs was increased by managers high in emotional stability. Managers high in vigor (energetic, like to work and move rapidly, accomplish more) tend to fulfill customer needs. Finally, employee satisfaction is heightened by managers high in sociability (gregarious, sociable, like to be with and to work with people).

3. What combinations of management abilities and personality characteristics will maximize the satisfaction of each of the seven parties-at-interest? Multiple regression methods were used to predict each of the seven criteria separately, allowing all ten management characteristics to enter into the equation. Ability and personality predictors were added to the regression equation as long as they added an increment significant beyond the .05 level to the multiple correlation. The degree to which each management characteristic is weighted in order to maximize satisfaction by each of the seven parties-at-interest is noted in the following equations.[1] Following each equation is the multiple correlation coefficient which results from this weighting.

Owner Satisfaction = .30 Verbal comprehension + .26 Ascendency − .17 Personal Relations ($R = .43$)
Community Satisfaction = .20 Verbal Comprehension ($R = .20$)
Government Satisfaction = .23 Emotional Stability + .19 Critical Thinking − .19 Original Thinking ($R = .32$)
Customer Satisfaction = .29 Verbal Comprehension + .20 Vigor ($R = .36$)
Supplier Satisfaction = .29 Verbal Comprehension − .20 Sociability ($R = .34$)
Creditor Satisfaction = .24 Verbal Comprehension − .21 Personal Relations ($R = .29$)
Employee Satisfaction = .27 Sociability + .25 Critical Thinking ($R = .36$)

Owner satisfaction can be predicted to a greater extent ($R = .43$) than other societal satisfactions from a knowledge of manager characteristics. Community satisfaction, on the other hand, seems least dependent ($R = .20$) upon the manager characteristics measured in this study. Verbal comprehension, appearing in five of the seven equations as the highest weighted skill, appears to be the most important manager characteristic in satisfying societal needs. Critical thinking skills enter into both employee and government satisfaction, but in neither of these does verbal comprehension skills seem primary.

A variety of personality characteristics in combinations with manager abilities adds to the maximization of societal fulfillment. For example, a manager high *both* in verbal comprehension and in vigor contributes

[1] All data were standardized prior to entry into the regression equations.

toward customer satisfaction to a significantly greater extent than managers high in only one of these characteristics. Similarly, the combination of critical thinking and sociability characteristics within a manager produces greater employee satisfaction than does either of these characteristics separately.

In several cases, personality characteristics take on negative weights in combination with abilities. Thus, while managers high in verbal comprehension contribute toward high owner and creditor satisfaction, minimization of high personal relations characteristics (trust, tolerance, patience, and understanding) will add further to owner and creditor satisfaction. Similarly, low manager sociability augments supplier satisfaction and low original thinking characteristics foster greater government satisfaction.

DISCUSSION

In a recent article, Stagner (1966) emphasized that one aspect of the (business) system, of great obvious importance, is its success in fulfilling its role or in meeting the challenges of its environments. Stagner goes on to raise some critical questions concerning the measure of this success, its potential multidimensionality, its relevance to the successful functioning of the business system, etc. Similarly, Bass (1952) stressed that measures of organizational value include the worth of the organization to the individual members and the worth of both individual members and the organization to society.

We have attempted to explore a variety of standards by which organizational effectiveness might be gauged. These criteria have gone well beyond the measures of employee performance or satisfaction typically utilized in most previous research. The effectiveness of an organization was based upon the degree to which it satisfied the needs of seven diverse members of the society with which it operates. An effective manager, then, was viewed as one who can and does maximize the extent to which the organization fulfills these seven sets of needs or demands.

It is clear from the low intercorrelations among societal satisfactions that organizational success is not a unitary concept. As Guion (1961) points out from the research vantage, "The fallacy of the single criterion lies in its assumption that everything that is to be predicted is related to everything else to be predicted—that there is a general factor in all criteria accounting for virtually all of the important variance in behavior at work and its various consequences of value." A parallel fallacy from the vantage of organizational goals and strategies is that everything that is to be maximized is related to everything else that is to be maximized.

Business organizations apparently have had some difficulty in concurrently satisfying all or even a major share of the societal demands made upon them. This "inadequacy" may be due to a variety of reasons—including nonrecognition of diverse societal needs, purposeful trade-off decisions intended to accentuate achievement of one or two criteria at the possible sacrifice of others, and temporary cyclical conditions which demand emphasis upon only select societal needs.

Typically, previous research and literature have served only to reinforce the manager's limited awareness of the many facets of organizational effectiveness. Little emphasis has been placed on the organization as an open system which must deal continuously with the variety of internal and external demands made upon it (Bennis, 1962). From this broader vantage, the manager's task is to relate the total system to its environment. To accomplish this, the manager must first recognize the boundary conditions of his organizational system and the various forms of exchange between the enterprise and its environment.

Underlying the low correlations among the seven societal criteria are the organizational values placed upon the various types of effectiveness. Managerial decisions may be based upon purposeful maximization of a particular criterion at the potential sacrifice of other goals on a permanent basis. Thus, trade-offs in the direction and thrust of organizational criteria may occur which may or may not return to a condition of equilibrium. In this sense, the manager may be seen as a system balancer (Bass, 1965). Burns and Stalker (1961), for example, suggest that use of either the organismic or mechanistic organizational models in the extreme and over an extended period of time may limit the growth and productivity of the organization.

The low relationships among the seven criteria, as well as between these criteria and manager personality characteristics, may also be due to the dynamic nature of the functions of organizations. The emphasis an organization places upon any particular one of its several functions may vary or even cycle over a period of time (Hage, 1965; Prien, 1966). Similarly, an effective manager at one point in time may be quite ineffective at a later date as the organization copes with the changing environment in which it exists.

The moderately high number of relationships between societal satisfactions and manager abilities (verbal comprehension and critical thinking) is reassuring when the distance between the operating manager of an organization and the seven parties which he attempts to satisfy through his organizational operation is considered. High verbal and critical thinking skills *do* make a contribution to a variety of successes. On the other hand, the sparsity of significant relationships between societal satisfactions and manager personality characteristics was disappointing.

We are unsure whether this lack should be ascribed to the "distance" mentioned above, to the design of the study, or to the frequently-cited inadequacies of personality tests as a means of predicting success in the industrial field.

Small organizations were intentionally selected for this study to allow any real relationships between manager characteristics and societal satisfactions to be discovered. The larger the business, the more the total organization represents far more than only one top level manager; and the more attentuated we would expect the relationship to be between manager characteristics and societal satisfactions. Further research aimed at exploring the issues cited in this study, however, need not be restricted to small business organizations. The characteristics of only those managers who conduct that specific segment of the organization which is related to each of the societal satisfactions might be studied. For example, what is the relationship between the characteristics of the employee relations manager and employee satisfaction—between the sales manager and customer satisfaction—between the public relations manager and community satisfaction—between the purchasing manager and supplier satisfaction? Such a design would treat each manager as the linking pin between his internal organizational operation and the relevant segment of his societal environment.

REFERENCES

Bass, B. M. "Ultimate Criteria of Organizational Worth." *Personnel Psychology*, V (1952), 157–173.

Bass, B. M. *Organizational Psychology*. Boston: Allyn & Bacon, 1965.

Bennis, W. G. "Towards a 'Truly' Scientific Management: The Concept of Organization Health." *General Systems*, VII (1962), 269–282.

Burns, T. & Stalker, G. M. *The Management of Innovation*. London: Tavistock Publications, 1961.

Dunnette, M. D. "A Note on The Criterion." *Journal of Applied Psychology*, XLVII (1963), 251–254.

Guion, R. M. "Criterion Measurement and Personnel Judgments." *Personnel Psychology*, XIV (1961), 131–140.

Hage, J. "An Axiomatic Theory of Organizations." *Administrative Science Quarterly*, X (1965), 289–320.

Katzell, R. A. "Industrial Psychology." In P. R. Farnsworth and Q. McNemar (Editors), *Annual Review of Psychology*, Volume VIII. Palo Alto, California: Annual Reviews, Inc., 1967.

Krug, R. E. "Personnel Selection." In B. von H. Gilmer (Editor), *Industrial Psychology*. New York: McGraw-Hill, 1961.

PRIEN, E. P. "Dynamic Character of Criteria: Organization Change." *Journal of Applied Psychology*, L (1966), 501–504.

STAGNER, R. "New Design for Industrial Psychology." *Contemporary Psychology*, XI (1966), 145–150.

STONE, C. H. & KENDALL, W. E. *Effective Personnel Selection Procedures*. Englewood Cliffs, New Jersey: Prentice-Hall, 1956.

THORNDIKE, R. L. *Personnel Selection*. New York: John Wiley & Sons, 1949.

VIII SOME GENERAL CONSIDERATIONS

The "criterion problem" has received and continues to receive considerable lip service, but even after many years of work it continues to plague research efforts. One of the major objectives of this book is to delineate the problems and, hopefully, encourage more investigative work in this area. In order for such work to be most effective there are certain general considerations that are important in planning and conducting research efforts. Some of these have been presented in the Toops and Dunnette articles. Those presented here are intended to add to, or elaborate upon previously presented information.

The importance of selecting or constructing an appropriate criterion is rarely questioned in any sort of research. However, the actual experimental evaluation of the use of *different* criteria in the interpretation of research results is virtually non-existent. The studies by Weitz (1961, 1964) represent one of the few attempts to investigate this crucial area. The studies show that the emphasis given to careful determination of an appropriate criterion are well warranted. As may be seen in the study reprinted here, (Weitz, 1964), the use of different criteria or measurement at different times can alter quite radically the interpretation of research results. Related to this is the material on criteria dimensions previously presented; it behooves any researcher to establish that his criteria is appropriate as to both time and the nature of measurement.

The next article, by Nagle (1953), is a general discussion, as is Thorndike's, but it presents important considerations in actual criterion development. In addition a consideration quite seriously neglected in most of the work in industrial psychology is discussed. This is the use of measures of *individual* morale, general attitudes, job fulfillment, or adjustment as criteria. As psychologists this is, or should be, an important consideration to us, but much of such work utilizes group measures with the intention of relating these to some economic aspect of organizational utility rather than arousing our specific interest in the individual's job adjustment. For the interested reader in this important area, there are probably not more than fifteen studies investigating, on a solid research basis, the individual correlates of occupational satisfaction.

Wherry's (1957) article reviews previous efforts in the field and, of particular interest, makes two important points. The first is the tendency to use batteries of predictors and quite simple criteria in most studies and, second, that criteria are probably often measuring the wrong thing.

A more recent presentation, Guion (1961), emphasizes many of the points that have been mentioned in this book, for example, the over-all criterion, and also brings in some new points. The Ghiselli and Haire (1960) concept of the "dynamic nature" of criteria is discussed, the influence of general economic conditions is presumed and, in particular, how human judgment is inevitably involved in certain aspects of the development or use of criteria.

Astin's (1964) work speaks of criteria in terms of "operational statements of the desired outcome." The general orientation is the effectiveness of some performance in achieving a desired goal. Astin is also quite explicit in showing the undesirability of combining measures into a single criterion and, finally, the ultimate need to relate "constructs" to responses in activities.

A more recent body of work is represented in the article by Lawshe and Steinberg (1955). This is an attempt to establish performance parameters by determining the abilities of incumbents. The procedure involves finding "critical" job duties and testing persons in the job with some appropriate test, in the study, a clerical test on such a job. Presumably job incumbents will attain higher scores on such critical aspects on the job. However, such studies still leave open the question of the measurements of *performance* but do represent an attempt to break away from what seems to have become a cul-de-sac, the criteria problem.

Gutzkow and Forehand (1961) present a conception of research in a field that has proven most difficult, executives. The model shown has, as far as the present authors are aware, never been fully tested but embodies most of the points made throughout this presentation.

The final article by Guion (1965) is a current demonstration of the concept of synthetic validity. This entire approach has, of course, tangents which have been developed much as Primoff's (J) coefficient approach, to meet specific problems.

In conclusion, the authors have attempted to show with the selected readings some of the major problems and considerations in a grossly neglected field. Most psychologists maintain that they study behavior but, more often than not, someone's opinion of behavior is accepted as a true measure. It appears that further progress in industrial psychology is directly dependent upon the study of performance behavior.

REFERENCES

Astin, A. W. Criteria centered research. *Educational and Psychological Measurement*, 1964, *24*, 807–827.
Ghiselli, E. E. & Haire, M. The validation of selection tests in light of the dynamic nature of criteria. *Personnel Psychology*, 1960, *13*, 225–231.
Primoff, E. S. The J-coefficient approach to jobs and tests. *Personnel Administration*, 1957, *30*, 34–40.
Weitz, J. Criteria for criteria. *American Psychologist*, 1961, *16*, 228–321.

44 The Use of Criterional Measures

JOSEPH WEITZ

Using paired-associate learning tasks of different difficulty level, it is shown that independent variables such as task order are more or less effective depending upon when the criterional measures are taken and the level of the criterion used. Similarly, the time of measurement and level of difficulty of the criterion are related to whether or not we find an effect of what is called "drive" in learning situations. An attempt is made to show how this approach may be useful in interpreting the meaning of independent variables.

How have criteria been used? In most instances only to show that an independent variable is or is not effective. Various studies might, for example, report such findings as these: partial reinforcement during acquisition leads to slower extinction, contact with a minority group leads to attitude change, client-centered therapy enhances the chances of effecting a cure. Such statements as the foregoing imply some criterion of extinction or attitude change or cure. How these particular criteria are chosen remains largely a matter of precedent or convenience. Further, once chosen, they are frequently ignored as sources of information concerning the operation of the independent variable. Very few investigators attempt to vary the criterional measure used in order to help explain the function of the input. These manipulations might be in terms of the time at which the measurement is taken, the level of the criterion, or the type of criterion chosen. If, in the examples given above, different conclusions are reached as a consequence of changing the criterion in any of the dimensions mentioned, then it should be possible to obtain new insights concerning the operation of such variables as partial reinforcement, minority group contact, or client-centered therapy.

In a recent article (Weitz, 1961) it was shown that the choice of the performance criterion determined to a large extent the conclusions reached concerning the effectiveness of an independent variable. The particular problem under consideration was the study of mediational effects in paired-associate learning when the response or the stimulus

From *Psychological Reports*, 1964, 14, 803–817. This research was supported by Grant Nonr 285 (51) from the Office of Naval Research. The author wishes to express his appreciation to Joel Aronson and Peter Greene for their assistance.

members of a first list had varying degrees of association to response or stimulus members in a second list. For the different conditions used in a study by Cramer and Cofer (1960) the mediation effect was or was not discernable depending upon the criterion of learning employed. That is, using criteria of different levels, ranging from 50 percent correct on one trial to a criterion of 100 percent correct on two successive trials, quite different conclusions were reached concerning the effectiveness of association in mediating responses on second list learning. It was further found with these data that a relationship existed between task difficulty and criterion difficulty. It appeared that more difficult tasks required an easier criterion (lower level) to show the hypothesized mediation effect and easier tasks required a more difficult criterion (higher level) to show this effect.

One of the major interests of the study to be reported here is further investigation of the relationship between task difficulty and criterional level. The term criterion will be used throughout this paper to mean that aspect of performance selected for measurement or, to put this another way, it is a particular representation of the dependent variable.

A second concern of the present study is an attempt to determine what relationships, if any, exist between criteria and those variables which might be thought of as related to drive. The word drive may be an inappropriate term here; however, when it is used it will always be defined by the operation or task used to identify it.

The reason for investigating the relationship of "drive" and criterional measures is not unrelated to the study of task difficulty and criteria. One might conceive of "drive" as affecting performance on a task in much the same way as does the difficulty of the task. That is, high drive (within limits) might be equated with easier tasks (better performance) whereas low drive might be thought of as having an effect similar to that resulting from an increase in the task difficulty (poorer performance).

The investigation of both of these aspects, task difficulty and drive, should be thought of as part of the larger problem of searching for generalizations concerning criterional measures. These are preliminary steps in determining the use of such measures for the better understanding of the operation of input variables.

PART I: TASK DIFFICULTY AND CRITERIA

Method

Procedure. The task in this part of the research involved paired-associate learning. Ss were to identify, by circling, the correct second member of a pair of words from among three response words. Two eight-pair lists of words were used. One list had high mean meaningfulness (m) values (Noble, 1952); the other contained low mean m values. Learning the list having word pairs of high m value was considered the easier task and the list containing the words with the low m values was considered the more difficult task. The procedure and the words for this part of the study were similar to those used by Cieutat (1961).

At the top of each page of the task booklet were 8 paired-associates of either high or low meaningfulness, listed in 4 columns of two pairs each. Below this were two columns of randomly chosen stimulus words from the above 8 pairs. Each column contained 35 stimulus words. Each stimulus word was followed by its correct response term (as indicated at the top of the page) and two other response terms selected from the remaining pairs. The order of the correct term and the particular incorrect terms was determined by chance. The stimulus words were selected randomly from those at the top of the page with the restriction that no stimulus word appeared twice in succession, either on any one page or going from one page to the next. The order of the stimulus words was newly randomized for each of 15 pages, but the same eight pairs in the same order appeared at the top of each page. This procedure was carried out for both the high and low m words. The first page contained the instructions and examples as shown below.

Paired-associates instructions.—This is a recognition task. At the top of each of the pages of the booklet, as on this page, is a series of pairs of words. Below this is a list of words consisting of the first member of a pair at the top of the page. The second member of the pair is one of the three words following the first member. You are to encircle the correct second member of the pair as shown in the example below. The first three words on the list in the example are correctly worked out. Now you finish the list and if you have any questions they will be answered. Do not turn this page until told to do so.

EXAMPLE

| glass-ears | chair-rose | job-pipe | book-clock |
table-couch	hat-shoe	bell-match	jar-dish
hat	rose; (shoe);* pipe	glass	ears; rose; pipe
bell	ears; couch; (match)	chair	shoe; rose; match
book	(clock); pipe; dish	job	couch; shoe; pipe
table	ears; couch; rose	book	clock; dish; ears
jar	clock; pipe; dish	hat	rose; shoe; match

* Words in parenthesis were actually encircled.

For one-half of the sample the paired-associate task of the high m value words was presented first and low m values second. In the other half of the sample Ss received booklets with the 15 pages of low *m* words first and the high *m* words on the last 15 pages.

The task was administered to Ss as a group. Before the booklets were passed out they were told, "Today you are going to work at a recognition task in order to collect normative data for college students." The booklets were then passed out and Ss were told to read the instructions while they were read aloud by the test administrator. Ss then completed the examples and were asked if there were any questions. Questions were answered and the testing began.

Fifteen 1-min. trials were given with enough time between trials to say, "Stop, turn the page, go." (This took approximately 3 sec.)

At the end of 15 trials Ss were told to stop and not turn the page until told to do so. They were then instructed as follows, "The next task is the same as the one you have just completed but the words will be different. Ready, turn the page, go." This procedure gave a 15-sec. break between the two tasks.

The scoring consisted of the number of correct responses on each trial.

Subjects. Ss were New York University college students in an advanced general psychology course. There were 34 Ss in all, 17 who had the high *m* words first and 17 who had the low *m* words first. As both males and females were tested, the data were analyzed separately for sex. It was found that there was very little difference between the groups; consequently, males and females were combined for all analyses to be reported.

This study was replicated with another group of college students (*N* = 37) from four colleges in Nashville, Tennessee. Eighteen had the high *m* words first and 19 had the low *m* words first. All Ss in this part of the study were tested individually.[1]

Results

Figure 44.1 shows the learning curves for the NYU sample. Figure 44.2 shows the curves for the Nashville group. It can be seen that these two sets of curves show marked resemblance to each other.

Considering task order as the independent variable, it can be observed that the largest difference between the performance of those taking the easy task first vs second occurs *early* in the trial sequence. On the other hand, for the more difficult learning task, if there is any difference at all, the maximal difference in performance between the two groups occurs somewhat *later*.

[1] The author is indebted to Dr. S. W. Cook who supplied Ss.

PART II: TASK DIFFICULTY-CONTROL STUDY

If there were differential positive transfer effects or even negative transfer effects due primarily to the relative difficulty of the initial learning and the second learning, then it would be possible to control for this by having the first and second tasks of equal difficulty. That is, transferring from low m paired-associates to other low m pairs or from high m pairs to other high m pairs.

Method

Procedure. For the control situation the testing procedure was the same as that in Part I, however, the lists to be learned and the sequence were different. It will be recalled that in Part I Ss learned either

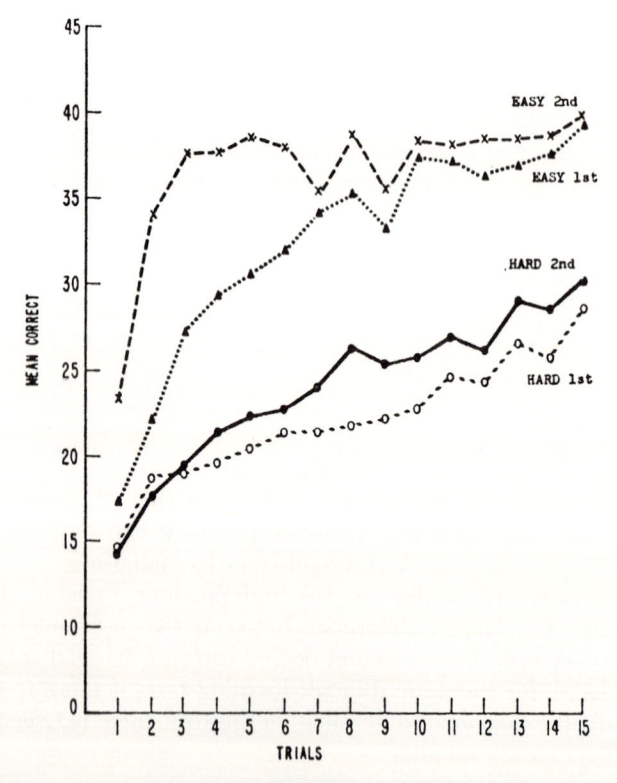

FIGURE 44.1. *Learning as a function of task difficulty and order, NYU Ss*

paired-associates of low *m* value first (*Hard*) and transferred to a list of high *m* value (*Easy*) or *vice versa*. That is the paradigms were: H to E or E to H. In the control study the paradigms used were Ha to Hb; Hb to Ha; Ea to Eb; Eb to Ea. The letters a and b are used to indicate different lists having equivalent *m* values.

Ha and Hb each had four of the pairs of words used in the H list in Part I. The other two sets of four pairs of words, making up the two lists

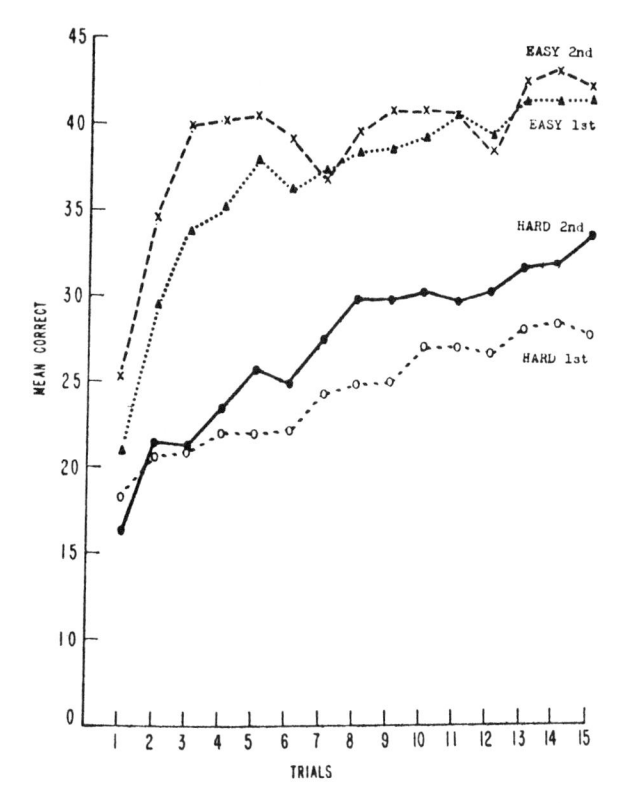

FIGURE 44.2. *Learning as a function of task difficulty and order, Nashville Ss*

of 8 pairs, were again taken from Noble's list. These additional pairs were the next 16 words in order of association value. The original pairs and the new pairs were combined to form the two lists Ha and Hb (low *m* values). The pairs were distributed in the two lists so that the *m* values were approximately equivalent for each pair and average *m* value for each list of eight pairs was approximately the same.

The same procedure was followed for the Ea and Eb (high *m*

values) lists. That is, Ea and Eb each had four pairs from the original E list and four new pairs. Again the two sets of four new pairs were the next 16 words in *m* value. The pairs for each list and the *m* value are shown in Table 44.1.

It should be noted that the relative ease or difficulty of association of any given *pair* of words is not known in the present study. As was stated before the assumption was made that the paired-associates with high *m* values would be easier to learn than those with the low *m* values. From the levels of the curves this appears to be true.

TABLE 44.1. *Paired-associates and* m *values*

Ha list and (*m* Values)	Hb list and (*m* Values)
GOJEY (.99) - NEGLAN (1.04)*	MEARDON (1.05) - BYSSUS (1.13)*
BALAP (1.22) - XYLEM (1.24)*	VOLVAP (1.22) - LATUK (1.26)*
QUIPSON (1.26) - TAROP (1.24)*	NARES (1.28) - GOKEM (1.27)*
ZUMAP (1.28) - SAGROLE (1.33)*	POLEF (1.30) - NOSTAW (1.34)*
RENNET (1.86) - ROMPIN (1.90)	BODKIN (1.31) - ULNA (1.50)
BRUGEN (1.79) - KAYSEN (1.82)	KUPOD (1.55) - DELPIN (1.60)
ATTAR (1.71) - MATRIX (1.73)	DAVIT (1.74) - WIDGEON (1.78)
WELKIN (1.53) - ICON (1.54)	MAELSTROM (1.84) - TUMBRIL (1.84)
Mean *m* H_a = 1.47	Mean *m* H_b = 1.44
Ea list and (*m* Values)	Eb list and (*m* Values)
KITCHEN (9.61) - ARMY (9.43)*	MONEY (8.98) - DINNER (8.33)*
OFFICE (7.95) - WAGON (8.12)*	JELLY (7.70) - HEAVEN (7.91)*
INSECT (7.39) - JEWEL (7.58)*	GARMENT (7.17) - VILLAGE (7.28)*
CAPTAIN (6.88) - ZEBRA (7.12)*	YOUNGSTER (6.75) - TYPHOON (6.83)*
YEOMAN (4.60) - QUOTA (4.68)	QUARRY (5.10) - EFFORT (5.13)
UNIT (5.32) - FATIGUE (5.33)	KEEPER (5.47) - KENNEL (5.52)
MALLET (5.61) - LEADER (5.94)	QUARTER (5.98) - REGION (5.98)
HUNGER (6.02) - ZERO (6.15)	INCOME (6.24) - UNCLE (6.57)
Mean *m* E_a = 6.73	Mean *m* E_b = 6.68

*These were the word pairs used in Part 1.

The paradigms Ea to Eb and Eb to Ea as well as Ha to Hb and Hb to Ha were used in order to combine the results of the learning on lists Ea and Eb when both were learned first (similarly Ha and Hb) and likewise combine the results on Ea and Eb (Ha and Hb) when both were learned second. If there were any difference in difficulty level between Ea and Eb lists or Ha and Hb lists, this procedure should operate as a satisfactory control.

Again 15 1-min. trials were given on each list followed by a second set of 15 trials of 1 min. each on the appropriate second list. The timing for all parts of the task was the same as that in Part I.

Subjects. Ss in this part of the study were 60 NYU students. Thirty were administered the two lists of low m paired-associates (either Ha to Hb or Hb to Ha) and 30 the two lists of high m value paired-associates (either Ea to Eb or Eb to Ea). In this part of the study Ss were tested in groups and again males and females were combined in the analyses.

Results

Figure 44.3 shows the results of this part of the study. From examination of these curves, again we see that the maximal difference in performance between easy task first vs easy task second occurs somewhat earlier in the trial sequence than does the maximal difference in performance between the hard task first vs hard task second.

The shapes of these curves resemble those in Figure 44.1. That is, for the easy task second, a very rapid rise reaching an asymptotic value early in the learning and for the easy task first a more gradual rise.

In the case of the performance on the harder task first, there is a more gradual slope and probably an asymptotic value is not reached in the 15 trials permitted.

It should be pointed out that the easy task in this part of the study has slightly lower average m value than the average m value of the initial 8 pairs used in Part I. On the other hand, the hard task here has a slightly higher average m value than the average m value for the initial eight pairs considered the hard task in Part I. Consequently, if ease and difficulty are related to m value, the *control* E task is slightly harder than the E task used in Part I and the *control* H task is slightly easier than the H task used in Part I. Assuming that the groups tested were approximately equivalent in learning ability, comparison of Figures 44.1 and 44.3 seems to corroborate the statement concerning difficulty level of the tasks.

Returning to Figure 44.1, let us assume that task difficulty (content) is the independent variable and now determine its effect under conditions of learning which are more or less facilitative. Considering task order as a variable related to ease or difficulty of learning, then it appears that learning a list first is a more difficult learning condition than learning it second. If we inspect the independent variable (task difficulty) under the easy condition (learning lists second), we find that the maximal difference in performance between the H and E lists is early, about Trial 3, whereas for the difficult condition (lists learned first) the maximal difference between H and E is somewhat later, about Trial 10.

While not so clearcut, a similar result is observed in Figure 44.3. That is for the "easy" condition (lists learned second) the maximal difference between H and E lists is earlier than it is for the "hard" condition (lists learned first). It may be that the difference here is not as marked as that in Part I due to the fact that the H and E tasks are closer to each other in difficulty level. If this is so, the places in the trial sequence where the maximal difference occurs should be closer together.

It seems from these preliminary studies, that in order to show an effect of an independent variable, where the task is relatively easy, or the conditions for learning are such that they facilitate learning, one can and perhaps must take the criterional measure early. On the other hand, if the task is more difficult or the conditions for learning are less facilitative, a later measurement of the criterion is more likely to show that the indipendent variable was effective.

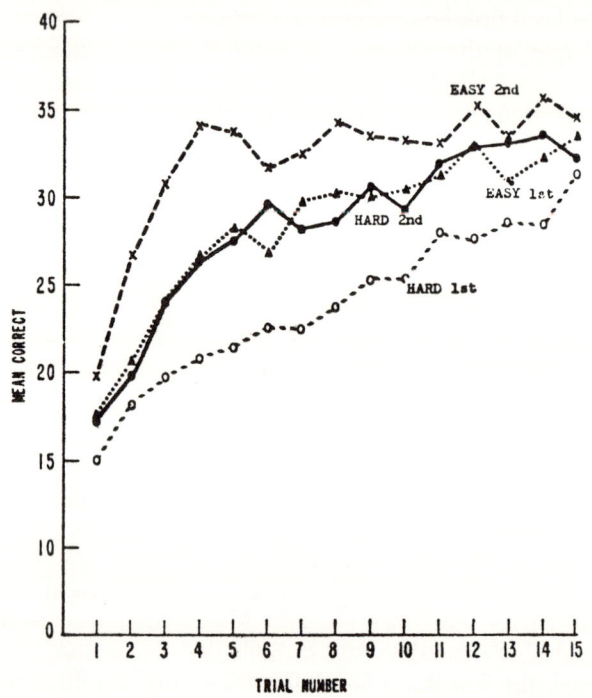

FIGURE 44.3. *Control condition for task difficulty*

Another way of looking at these data is to determine the number of trials required to meet various criteria. If we replot the data from Figure 44.1 to show the number of trials required to reach a particular mean number of correct responses[2] we obtain Figure 44.4.

Let us assume that we take as an arbitrary criterion of "good" performance or "learning," 24 correct responses. This choice is no more arbitrary than some of the criteria chosen for "success" or "learning." If we

[2] The plot was constructed by interpolating on trials for each mean number of correct responses shown.

USE OF CRITERIONAL MEASURES 571

examine Figure 44.4 we see that in using such a definition there is an average difference of approximately three and one-half trials to reach criterion between the hard task first vs hard task second groups. However, using this same criterion and comparing the number of trials required to reach criterion for easy task first vs easy task second, we find a difference of only about one and a half trials. We might conclude that with this (arbitrary) criterion there is a difference in performance related to task order for difficult tasks but not for simpler tasks. For the easier learning situation, it is not until we select a criterion of 30 or 32 correct responses

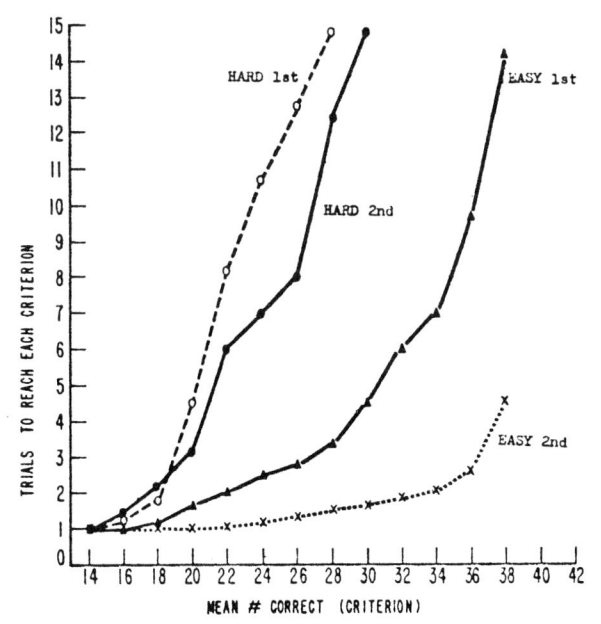

FIGURE 44.4. *Trials to criterion as a function of task difficulty and order*

that we find a difference in performance related to task order as large as that found for the more difficult task at the lower criterion level.

It seems then, that a more stringent criterion is needed to show an effect of an independent variable where the task involved is simple and a less stringent criterion to show a similar effect where the task is more difficult.

These data would further lead one to conjecture that the learning in this type of situation is composed of at least two parts: they might be called "task approach" and "task content." It seems that with an easy task, task approach is the more salient aspect early in the performance whereas with more difficult tasks the task content is the component more relevant in determining the course of the early learning. That is, with the simpler task, having had the experience of performing something like this before leads to very rapid learning on the second attempt. Presumably what is transferred is the method of attack or approach to the learning situation, whereas with a more difficult task this component (task approach) is not nearly as effective early in the performance, perhaps due to the level of difficulty of the task itself (task content). If task approach is operating as a positive transfer agent in the more difficult task, it is not apparent until later in the learning sequence.

In the learning situation in Part I of this study it is possible that there is greater positive transfer of task approach going from a difficult task to a simpler one than there is transferring from a simpler task to a more difficult one. In the latter case there may even be some interference. This, however, cannot fully explain the differential in performance due to task order since the control conditions show similar results. That is, transferring from an easy task to an easy task or from a hard task to a hard task gives results similar to those obtained in Part I of this study.

Analyses of these data and other studies from the point of view of when it is more efficient to take criterional measures might help us in determining something about transfer of training. For example, in the present study it appears that transfer of principles will be effective early or late in the transfer task depending upon the difficulty level of the tasks under consideration.

While we have no relevant data from this study, if we were to consider task content (elements of the material to be learned) as that which provides the basis of transfer, we might find differences in the effectiveness of this medium also dependent upon the task difficulty. An analysis of the appropriate time of measurement and level of criterion might give some insight into this matter. These comments are, of course, in the nature of hypotheses which will demand further investigation.

PART III: "DRIVE" AND CRITERIA

This part of the study was conducted on the same Ss used in Part I. Thirty-one of the 34 Ss in Part I completed not only the paired-associate task but also took what is called the Hand Skills Test. As was mentioned earlier, "drive" may not be an appropriate word to use in describing what the Hand Skills Test is measuring; but it will be used for the sake of convenience.

Procedure

The Hand Skills Test was described by Kipnis (1962). It was administered to Ss 2 days prior to the paired-associate learning task. The task consists of drawing sets of five tally marks as rapidly as possible. They were referred to as "fences." Ss were instructed to draw as many fences as they could in the time allowed. They were told that the task they were about to do was a simple hand-finger dexterity test. The work sheets, which consisted of pages containing numbered rectangular boxes, were then distributed.

Ss were instructed:

> In each of the boxes provided you are to draw a fence as shown in the example. It does not matter which way the four vertical lines are crossed. The test has four parts. The first part is 1 min. long and the remaining three parts are 4 min. each. The more fences you make the better your score. Any questions?

E answered any questions and then directed Ss to open their booklets and begin. After 1 min. E said:

> Stop! The next part will be 4 min. long. Remember the more you do the better your score. The minimum passing score on this part is 100 fences. Ready, turn the page, go!

E allowed 4 min. for this part and then repeated the above instructions with the exception that Ss were told that for the next 4-min. trial a passing score was 105 fences. For the last 4-min. trial S was told that a passing score was 110 fences.

The scoring for the Hand Skills Test consisted of the total number of "fences" made in the last 4-min. trial minus the number of fences completed in the first one-min. trial.

Kipnis (1962) found that the Hand Skills Test predicted achievement of low aptitude individuals. For this reason it was thought that perhaps this test was measuring something like drive. It appeared from his study that if one weren't bright he had better have stick-to-it-iveness or drive or something (perhaps willingness to please E) in order to do well. We shall refer to this test as measuring "drive" in the present study.

RESULTS

Ss were divided at the median score on the Hand Skills Test (one S at the median was included with the low group) and performance plotted on the paired-associate learning. Figure 44.5 shows the results.

There are 15 Ss in the high Hand Skills group and 16 in the low Hand Skills group. Compared to the low scorers, those with the higher (scores on the Hand Skills Test H.S.) perform at a higher level on both the easy and hard learning task. In this graph, order of task presentation is combined. When we control for both order and "drive" (H.S.) and plot the number of trials required to reach successive criteria[3] we obtain Figure 44.6.

We find a difference in performance between task order groups as large as 4 trials, using a criterion 36 correct for the high "drive" Ss. We can reach this same difference in trials to criterion for the low "drive" groups with a criterion of 30 correct. To put this another way, if we were investigating the effect of task order and chose as our criterion the number of trials needed to reach 30 correct for both the high and low

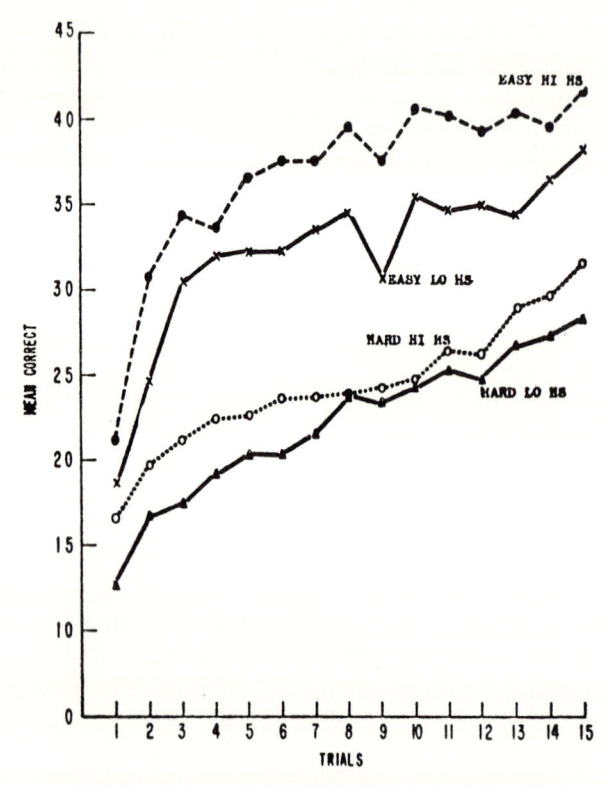

FIGURE 44.5. *Learning as a function of "drive"*

"drive" Ss, we would find a difference between task orders of approximately four trials to reach criterion for the low "drive" Ss but a difference of only about one trial for the high "drive" Ss. We might conclude from this arbitrary choice of a criterion that there was an effect of task order for the low "drive" group but not for the high "drive" group.

[3] Here medians are used since the Ns are 8 for high Hand Skills-E_2; 7, for high Hand Skills-E ; 7, for low Hand Skills-E_2; and 9, for low Hand Skills-E .

USE OF CRITERIONAL MEASURES 575

The same general picture, although not so clear cut, obtains for the more difficult paired-associate learning. That is, for those Ss manifesting high "drive" the criterion needed to show an effect of order is more stringent than that demanded under the condition of low "drive."

If we are interested in determining whether or not there are differences between performances of Ss with high and low "drive" under easy or more difficult learning conditions, we can analyze Figure 44.6 in another way. Let us consider easy task *first* as the more *difficult* learning condition. Now, comparing the performance on easy task first for those having high and low "drive," we can use a much lower criterion to obtain

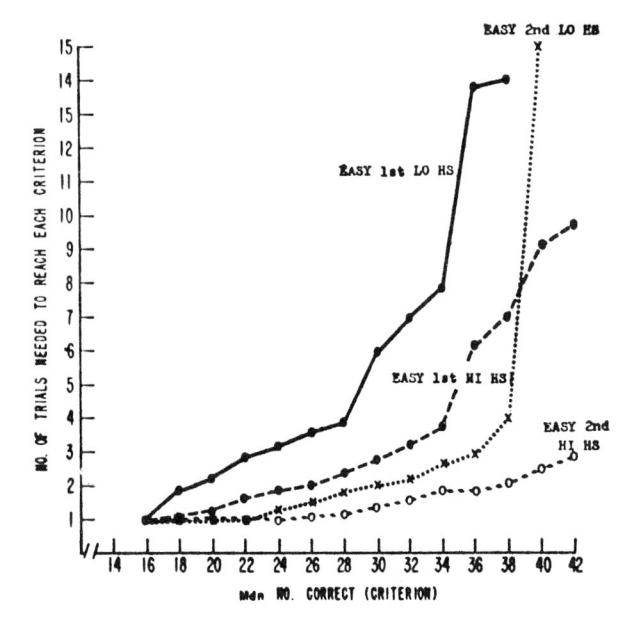

FIGURE 44.6. *Trials to criterion as a function of "drive"*

a substantial difference between Ss having these two "drive" levels than we can when we compare differences in high and low "drive" level for the *easier* task (easy task second).

DISCUSSION

It appears then, that if the task is relatively easy or Ss have relatively high drive as defined by the Hand Skills Test, a more stringent criterion is needed to show an effect of the independent variable. Further, criterional measures taken early in the learning sequence are more likely to show a difference between groups having different treatments when performing easy tasks. When the task is relatively difficult or the drive level is low, it appears that the converse is true.

From a reanalysis of other studies some support for this concept is found. One such study is by Woods and Holland (1961). They investigated the relationship between swimming speeds of rats in a water maze and learning rates under various motivational levels. Motivation here is determined by water temperature. That is, in some instances the water temperature was cool (20°C) and in other instances the water temperature of the maze was warmer (34°C). Using swimming speed as the independent variable and assuming that higher drive is present as a result of swimming in the colder water, we find that the difference between performances of fast and slow swimmers under conditions of high drive can be observed with a relatively high criterion (more successive correct choices). A lower criterion must be used to show differences between groups of different swimming speeds for the low drive condition.

Another study which seems relevant is one by Spence and Weyant (1960). Here the strength of the US was manipulated for Ss divided into high and low anxiety groups. If we replot the data, it appears that the conclusions drawn from the present study are reinforced. Under high drive (strong US), comparing the conditioned responses of high and low anxiety Ss, the major effect is early in the trial sequence whereas under the condition of low drive (weak US) the maximal difference between the response of high and low anxiety groups occurs later.

From other studies such as those by Clark (1962) and Walker (1960) we obtain similar findings. If one can consider drive as related to the US in the case of Walker and to stress in the case of Clark, upon reanalysis we find that for the high drive condition the effect of the independent variable is maximal with a more stringent criterion and under low drive conditions with a less stringent criterion.

When we consider the effect of an independent variable operating in easy and difficult task situations, we again find some corroborative evidence. Castaneda and Lipsitt (1959) report a study of children's performance on a simple or more difficult motor learning task. Stress vs no stress was introduced in both situations. If we now consider stress the independent variable, we find in the case of the simpler task the effect is more apparent using a difficult criterion and for the more difficult task the effect of the stress is more apparent with a criterion of a lower level.

In a human learning study by Lloyd (1960) we find that the effect of the independent variable (class words vs specific words) is greatest earlier for the experimental condition (easier task) than for the control (more difficult) condition.

In a study by Bahrick, Fitts, and Briggs (1957) which in part compared the performance of males and females on pursuit tasks of different levels of difficulty, it was found that on the easier task the maximal difference between the two groups is early in the performance sequence whereas on the more difficult task the maximal difference is later in the performance.

While these studies support the work reported here, it is still necessary to derive certain formulations for the identification of task difficulty. It now becomes desirable to determine whether or not these findings hold up over a wide range of task difficulty and what continuum should be used to identify independently difficulty level.

If these findings do continue to be supported, then we should be able to tell more about the effect of drive for example, in terms of *when* it is effective. From this it should be possible to say more about what "drive"[4] is doing. Is it, perhaps, having the same effect as reducing task difficulty? Would it affect task approach as a basis of transfer differentially on easy and difficult tasks? It might be hypothesized that with a difficult task and high drive, task approach might operate as it does in those situations where the task is less difficult and there is lower drive. Is it possible that the effect of drive is operating differentially on tasks of different difficulty levels so that on hard tasks it enables the individual to attack the problem without throwing up his hands in despair, whereas in easier tasks it permits the individual to maintain a relatively high level of performance without decrement due to boredom or other factors?

Obviously, many questions remain to be answered. However, the approach used here should enable one to obtain some answers.

REFERENCES

BAHRICK, H. P., FITTS, P. M., & BRIGGS, G. E. Learning curves—facts or artifacts? *Psychol. Bull.*, 1957, 54, 256-267.

CASTANEDA, A., & LIPSITT, L. P. Relations of stress and differential position habits to performance in motor learning. *J. exp. Psychol.*, 1959, 57, 25-30.

CIEUTAT, V. J. Group paired-associate learning: stimulus vs response meaningfulness. *Percept. mot. Skills*, 1961, 12, 327-330.

CLARK, R. E. The role of drive (time stress) in complex learning: an emphasis on prelearning phenomena. *J. exp. Psychol.*, 1962, 63, 57-61.

CRAMER, P., & COFER, C. N. The role of forward and reverse association in transfer of training. *Amer. Psychologist*, 1960, 15, 463. (Abstract)

KIPNIS, D. A noncognitive correlate of performance. *J. appl. Psychol.*, 1962, 46, 76-80.

[4] The effect, of course, may well be curvilinear. This discussion will assume linearity, at least within limits.

LLOYD, K. E. Retention of responses to stimulus classes and to specific stimuli. *J. exp. Psychol.*, 1960, 59, 54–59.

NOBLE, C. E. An analysis of meaning. *Psychol. Rev.*, 1952, 59, 421-430.

SPENCE, K. W., & WEYANT, R. G. Conditioning performance of high and low anxious Ss in the absence of a warning signal. *J. exp. Psychol.*, 1960, 60, 146-149.

WALKER, E. G. Eyelid conditioning as a function of intensity of conditioned and unconditioned stimuli. *J. exp. Psychol.*, 1960, 59, 303–309.

WEITZ, J. Criteria for criteria. *Amer. Psychologist*, 1961, 16, 228–231.

WOODS, P. J. & HOLLAND, C. H. Discrimination in a water maze. *Psychol. Rep.*, 1961, 9, 433–439.

45 Criterion Development

BRYANT F. NAGLE

SUMMARY

The three fundamental considerations in the development and construction of criteria have been surveyed. The problem of relevancy is explored, emphasizing the judgmental nature of this consideration. Relevancy has been analyzed by comparing the variance in the criterion with that in the ultimate criterion. In this respect relevancy may be considered the 'validity' of the criterion. Two sources of low relevance are indicated: omission of systematic variance in the criterion which is present in the ultimate criterion (criterion deficiency), and inclusion of systematic variance in the criterion which is not present in the ultimate criterion (criteron contamination). Reliability of the criterion is discussed with emphasis on its relation to validity, on the sources of unreliability, and on spurious reliability. The problem of combination of criterion measures is divided into scale unit equality and weighting of the sub-criteria. Little is contributed toward the problem of scale unit equality. The various methods which have been suggested for weighting sub-criterion measures are reviewed, and it is suggested that weighting be done by competent judges and that the sub-criterion weights be applied to the standard score conversions of the variables.

Last, a four step procedure for developing criteria is suggested. Some of the problems in this procedure are pointed out. The four steps are: define the activity, analyze the activity, define elements of success, and develop criteria to measure these elements. It is believed that only through a systematic procedure such as this in which the researcher is cognizant of the limitations and problems of what he is doing will the field of criterion research be advanced.

THREE CRITERION CONSIDERATIONS

Inherent in the phrase 'given a criterion' are many of the pitfalls of psychological research. This phrase, so common in the literature 10 years

From *Personnel Psychology*, 1953, 6, 271–288. The author is indebted to Dr. Erwin K. Taylor, Personnel Research Institute, Western Reserve University, for his constructive criticism of this article.

ago, overcame the problem of criterion development by ignoring it. The problem is no longer ignored. During World War II American psychologists were forced to exert a considerable portion of their efforts toward the construction and selection of criteria.

It is the purpose of this paper to survey the criterion literature published during the last 10 years and to suggest a systematic procedure for the development of criteria. The review of criterion literature has been organized about three theoretical considerations: relevancy, reliability, and combination of measures.

Before continuing it would be well to define what a criterion is. Horst says, "The measure of success or failure in an activity is what is technically known as a criterion" (17, p. 20). Similarly, Bechtoldt defines a criterion as, "... a means of describing the performance of individuals on a success continuum" (4, p. 357). As Brogden and Taylor see it, "The criterion should measure the contribution of the individual to the overall efficiency of the organization" (8, p. 139). Also representing the industrial bent is the definition given by Ghiselli and Brown, "By criterion is meant any attribute or accomplishment of the worker that can be used as an index of his serviceability or usefulness to the organization that employs him" (14, p. 62). We may say, then, that for a given activity, the criterion is an index by which we can measure the degree of success achieved by various individuals. Criteria are also used in industrial psychology to measure the success of an organization or of a program. This discussion is centered around the use of criteria to measure the success of individuals in the industrial situation.

How do criteria fit into the prediction process? Prediction might be thought of as consisting of two steps: validation and selection. In validation predictor variables are tested against a criterion. The criterion will give a metrical ordering of subjects in terms of success on the given activity. The predictor variables are matched against this metrical ordering to determine their relationship to success on the given activity. When one or more predictor variables shows a satisfactory relationship, such predictor variables are used to select those individuals likely to achieve success on the given activity. This last step is what is known as "selection."

It must be pointed out here that, while the goal of this process is prediction, the predictors themselves can never be anything but subsidiary to the criterion, for it is from the criterion that the predictors derive their significance. If the criterion changes, the predictors' validity is necessarily affected. If the predictors change, the criterion does not change for that reason. Likewise, it can be seen that if no criteria are used, one would never know whether or not the predictors were selecting those individuals likely to succeed. Research can be no better than the criteria used. One must, therefore, approach the prediction process in a logical fashion, developing criteria first, analyzing them, and then constructing or selecting variables to predict the criteria. When one or more variables show a satisfactory relationship to the criteria, such variables may then be used as selection instruments.

Three of the fundamental problems of criteria will be discussed here. These are: 1. The relevancy of the criterion, 2. The reliability of the criterion, and 3. The combination of criterion measures into a composite score. The exclusive emphasis on these three problems should not be interpreted as meaning that these are the only problems of criterion construction and selection. These three seem to the author to be the primary theoretical problems involved.

RELEVANCY

Relevancy, a term which seems to have been used first by Bechtoldt (4) and later by Ghiselli and Brown (14), Thorndike (28) and many others, refers to the extent to which an index of success (criterion) is related to the 'true' order of success in the given activity. In this respect relevancy is akin to validity, but to avoid confusion, use of the term relevancy seems desirable. Thorndike (28) has been helpful in clarifying this problem. He has spoken of the 'ultimate criterion', which may be thought of as the properly weighted embodiment of all the elements making for success in the activity. This is the 'true' order of success in the activity. Relevancy is the hypothetical correlation coefficient between the criterion used and the ultimate criterion.

In the preceding sentence an important point is introduced. Relevancy (validity of the criterion) is the *hypothetical* correlation coefficient between the criterion used and the ultimate criterion. It is hypothetical because one is forced to judge the relevance of the criterion used to the ultimate criterion. For example, in attempting to develop an index of success (criterion) for automobile driving, we may lay out a trial driving course and give a rating on the subject's proficiency in navigating the course. In laying out this course we must endeavor to duplicate the activity of driving in the non-experimental situation as closely as possible. Here we make judgments as to how closely our driving course approximates the everyday conditions of driving. Here also we must instruct the judge to look for certain things upon which to base his rating. We have made judgments that certain things constitute success in driving and tell him to look for those things. In all cases, when one accepts a measure as a criterion, he has judged that the measure has a certain degree of relevance to the ultimate criterion. Often times investigators fail to realize that they are making a judgment. Because they have a measure available which is somehow related to the given activity they are satisfied. What must be realized is that when a measure, or measures, is adopted as the criterion, one is implying that it is synonymous with success in the activity. By adopting certain measures the investigator has, consciously or unconsciously, judged them to be relevant to success in the activity.

Here would seem to be perhaps the greatest stumbling block to obtaining a 'true' criterion measure—one may only judge the validity of the criterion. Anyone familiar with the validity and reliability of judgments knows how serious is this shortcoming.

To have high relevancy, the systematic, non-error sources of variance in the criterion must be the same as those in the ultimate criterion. The systematic, non-error sources of variance will not be the same if the criterion does not include some variance present in the ultimate criterion, or if the criterion includes variance not present in the ultimate criterion. In other words, the criterion can suffer from omission of pertinent elements, or from inclusion of extraneous elements. These situations may be referred to as "criterion deficiency" and "criterion contamination" respectively (7).

If the criterion omits pertinent elements, predictive efficiency may not be as high as the correlation between the predictors and the criterion indicates. This will happen because the criterion, in its deficient form, is used to represent the ultimate criterion in the validation process. If we obtain a correlation of .90 between the predictors and the deficient criterion, and if the hypothetical correlation between the criterion and the ultimate criterion were .50, then the predictive efficiency will probably be less than .90.

If the criterion includes extraneous elements, predictive efficiency may not be as high as the correlation between the predictors and the criterion indicates. In cases where criterion contamination occurs, the predictors may correlate with the relevant variance in the criterion, or they may correlate with the extraneous elements in the criterion, or the predictors may correlate with both. To the extent to which the predictors correlate with the extraneous elements of the criterion, the validity coefficient will overestimate the predictive efficiency. In the extreme case where all the correlation is between extraneous elements and the predictors, subjects will be selected without regard to their chances of success in the activity. Therefore, extraneous elements in the criterion are a much greater handicap if they are predictor correlated. Inclusion of extraneous elements which do not correlate with the predictors only increases the error of measurement.

Bellows (5), Brogden and Taylor (7), and Thorndike (28) give numerous examples of criterion contamination. The research individual should be constantly on guard against these sources of criterion contamination. When one is aware that a certain extraneous element is likely to occur in a criterion, the influence of the extraneous element can usually be controlled experimentally or statistically. The real problem lies in anticipating the occurrence of such extraneous variables. This further emphasizes the need for careful consideration of the criterion measure or measures before such data are gathered.

RELIABILITY

As we have seen, there is almost never a quantitative statement of criterion relevancy because it is usually not possible to compare the criterion with a more representative measure of the given activity. But when it comes to reliability of criterion scores, there is a very definite possibility of obtaining a measure. Because one is able to measure the reliability of a criterion, there seems to be a tendency for writers to overemphasize its importance. This is not to imply that it is not important, but it must be remembered that high reliability, while desirable is not sufficient.

What is the relationship of criterion reliability to the validation process? First, the relevancy, as defined by a correlation coefficient (since relevancy is admittedly subjective, it does not seem realistic to analyze it as a correlation coefficient), cannot exceed the square root of the reliability coefficient of the criterion. This should emphasize the necessity of reasonably high reliability. Second, the obtained validity coefficient between the criterion and the predictor cannot exceed the square root of the product of the reliability coefficients of the predictor and the criterion (1). A reasonably high criterion reliability is necessary if any predictors are to show a significant relationship with the criterion.

The sources of criterion unreliability have received considerable attention in the literature (4, 14, 19, 28, 31). Among the most important influences upon criterion reliability are:

1. The size of the sample of performance.
2. The range of ability among the subjects.
3. Ambiguity of instructions.
4. Variation in conditions during measurement period.
5. The amount of aid provided by instruments.

The inherent instability of the given activity is a prime limitation on reliability. Careful consideration of the above sources of unreliability can lead to reliabilities which more closely approximate the reliability of the activity.

In addition to these sources of unreliability, there are several which are peculiar to the situation in which ratings are used as criteria:

1. The competency of the judges.
2. The simplicity of the behavior.
3. The degree to which the behavior is overt.

4. The opportunity to observe.
5. The degree to which the rating task is defined.

Spuriously high reliabilities are found frequently when criterion contamination occurs. Such reliabilities are termed spurious because the reliability contribution of the extraneous elements is meaningless, since the extraneous elements can add nothing in the way of relevancy. One cannot afford to ignore this spurious reliability, for if the reliability contributed by the extraneous elements were removed, surely some criterion reliabilities would become insignificant. Until such spurious reliability is eliminated, one does not know the reliability of the criterion. Whenever extremely high reliability is found in a criterion measure, one should be on guard for the presence of extraneous elements. It is also possible, though not so common, for extraneous elements to lower the reliability of a criterion.

COMBINATION OF CRITERION MEASURES

Since ultimate criteria are usually of a complex nature, it is usually necessary to use a multi-dimensional criterion to approximate the ultimate criterion. Seldom, however, can one criterion measure correspond to this multi-dimensional nature. The researcher is frequently faced, therefore, with the problem of using several criterion measures.

The use of several criterion measures raises the problem of whether scores should be left separate or combined into a single criterion score. The author is inclined to agree with Toops (29) that when several measures are to be used a unitary criterion score is indispensable. Use of a single criterion score may tend to minimize the number of predictors necessary and aid in the interpretation of predictor scores.

When several criterion measures are to be combined into a single criterion score there are two problems which arise:

1. Comparability of units along a scale.
2. Comparability of units from scale to scale.

Let us first consider equality of units along a scale. In an excellent treatment of the subject, Brogden and Taylor state, "From the criterion point of view, the scale-unit problem reduces to one of establishing units which represent equal increments in terms of the overall efficiency of the organization" (7, p. 180). When units along the scale are not equal one is assigning differing weights to the various portions of the criterion continuum. Thus, if the real difference between ratings of 5 and 6 is four times that of the difference between ratings of 2 and 3, then one is in effect weighting the difference between ratings 2 and 3 four times as heavily as that between 5 and 6. In the area of ratings this scale unit problem is an especially knotty one. There seems to be no acceptable method for judging the presence or absence of scale unit bias (7). In the matter of production data, the scale unit problem often disappears. Production data can be translated into dollars or work units which represent equal increments in terms of the overall efficiency of the organization. The thirteenth part scrapped represents just as great a loss to the organization as the first.

Comparability of units from scale to scale refers to weighting the various criterion measures so that the criterion composite will correspond to the ultimate criterion. When criterion measures are so combined, the individual criterion scales are usually referred to as sub-criteria and the combined scales as a criterion composite. Edgerton and Kolbe (10) suggest a number of ways of combining sub-criteria into a composite. These will be listed and discussed.

1. Weighting sub-criteria according to judgments of 'experts.' This method was first proposed by Toops (29). He had competent judges assign bids to the various traits in question. The experts are really called upon to analyze the nature of the ultimate criterion, then analyze the nature of the various sub-criteria, and weight the sub-criteria so that their composite will correspond as closely as is possible to what is believed to be the composition of the ultimate criterion. This amounts to weighting the sub-criteria on their judged relevancy.

2. Weighting in proportion to reliability (27). This reflects the undue emphasis that has often been placed upon reliability of criteria. The effect of this approach is to obtain the most reliable possible combination of the sub-criteria, without regard to relevancy.

3. Weighting in proportion to average correlation with other variables. This method tends to exaggerate the influence of any general factor there may be in the various sub-criteria. Again, relevancy is not considered.

4. Weighting so as to obtain maximum correlation with the predictors (18, 23). Both the sub-criteria and predictors are weighted to obtain the maximum possible correlation. This represents a perversion of the validation process. In the validation process the predictors are weighted to predict the criterion composite. The predictors should have no influence on the composition or weighting of the sub-criteria.

5. Extracting by factor analysis parts of criterion variates which may be due to the same factor. The purpose of this approach seems to be to include in the criterion composite just one measure of each factor. This is a desirable approach, but the problem remains of weighting the factors.

6. Weighting variates so that discrimination between all possible pairs of individuals will be as great as possible. This method is advocated by Edgerton and Kolbe (10). They state that, "Any method for combining several criterion variates into a single composite assumes that they are measures of the same thing" (10, p. 183). From this, the authors say one should expect, "... the differences among the variate values for any indi-

vidual, expressed in standard scores, to be small" (10, p. 183). The method gives the same results as Horst's method (16). The process assumes that the sub-criteria are measures of the same thing in a statistical sense (one factor). But the correct assumption is that the sub-criteria are measures of the same thing in a psychological sense (measures of success). This method may have some use when success is composed of one factor.

Other methods which have been discussed in the literature (14) are equal weighting of the sub-criteria, and multiple cutoffs. To this writer it seems that the only defensible method of combining sub-criteria is on the basis of relevancy. The more relevant the sub-criterion, the greater should be its weight. And since the relevancy must be judged, so the weights of the sub-criteria must be assigned by judgments. All weighting of sub-criteria on a relevancy basis is subjective.

When weights are assigned to the sub-criteria one must consider the influence of the standard deviations on the weights assigned. Should the weights given by judges to the sub-criterion variables be applied to the raw scores of the individual sub-criteria, or should they be applied to the standard score transformations? If the weights are applied to raw scores, the effective weights of the sub-criteria will differ from those assigned by the judges because of the influence of the varying standard deviations among the sub-criteria. But if the weights are to be applied to the standard scores of the sub-criteria, will the judges be able to think of the sub-criteria in terms of standard scores when they weight them? The problem reduces to one of what are the judges' conceptions of the sub-criteria as they stand before weighting. At present this seems an unanswerable problem. Many arguments can be advanced for both approaches, but this writer prefers to apply the sub-criterion weights to the standard scores of the sub-criteria.

The judge's job of weighting the sub-criteria will be simplified and made more meaningful if the sub-criteria are as independent as possible of each other. Factorially complex measures are difficult to analyze on a judgmental basis.

Brogden and Taylor (8) have proposed a new approach to the problem of combining sub-criterion measures which solves many of the difficulties discussed above. This new approach is applied in an industrial setting. It amounts to changing the scale units of all sub-criteria into dollar units. Their basic premise is that, "The general objective of industrial firms is to make money." (8, p. 139). Therefore, the contribution of an individual to the efficiency of the industrial organization is evaluated on a dollar basis. The individual worker's output, spoilage, accidents, damage to equipment, etc., can be expressed in dollar units. This approach solves the problem of scale unit differences. The fiftieth dollar saved is just as important as the sixth. This approach also solves the problem of weighting the sub-criteria. If an error costs six times as much to correct as the cost of producing one satisfactory piece, then each error is weighted six times as heavily as a satisfactory piece by virtue of the cost incurred. The scores obtained by an individual on each sub-criterion scale are directly additive to obtain a criterion composite. This dollar criterion solves the problems of combining sub-criterion measures, but it may be argued that the method does not include all relevant variables—those contributions to success which cannot be evaluated in terms of dollars and cents.

The preceding three sections have dealt with some of the considerations involved in evaluating criteria. There remains the problem of where and how does one obtain criteria. It is the purpose of this section to present an approach to this problem.

Many writers have urged that in the development of criteria one go beyond the state of asking for ratings of good and poor performers and try to determine the 'why' and 'how' aspects of success in the activity. Fiske (11) would first establish the goal of the organization and then specify the purpose of each position in the organization before asking why are some people successful. In the field of learning criteria, Brownell (9) says that in the more complex learning situations one should analyze the goal of the learning process and develop criteria to measure the attainment of the goal. The criteria are found by analysis of the purpose or goal of the learning process. Thorough-going analysis of the process should indicate the more specific goals. The problem then becomes one of developing measures of these specific goals. Other writers have also emphasized the need to seek the real reasons for success. What is suggested, then, by these authors is that one specify the purposes, goals, or objectives of the behavior first and then ask the question of why are some persons successful and others not.

Using this type of approach this writer has developed a four step procedure for criterion development:

1. *Definition of the problem.* In what type of activity are we seeking to determine success? The activity must be as closely defined as is possible if confusion is not to arise in subsequent steps.

2. *Activity Analysis.* The second step in this procedure is an analysis of the activity. This activity analysis may be sub-divided into four parts. First, a statement of the purposes of the activity should be made. What are the goals of the activity? Second, the types of behavior called for should be described. What does a man working at this activity have to do? Third, standards of performance in the activity should be stated. What levels of performance are required in the various behaviors of the

activity? Fourth, the relative importance of the various behaviors must be indicated. What is the relative importance of each behavior called for in the activity?

The similarity of the above activity analysis to job analysis is quite apparent. The use of a thorough job analysis done by a well-trained job analyst would be an appropriate way in which to complete this step. In this respect, Flanagan has written, "... the problems of job definition, job requirements, and criteria of success necessarily reduce to one and the same problem, at least with regard to their major outlines" (12, p. 40). The advancement of criterion research is limited to some extent, therefore, by the advancement of a more objective job analysis procedure.

3. *Definition of Success.* What must an individual do to be successful in the activity? What we are trying to develop here is a list of elements of an activity which will differentiate a successful individual from an unsuccessful one. The resultant group of elements when weighted may be thought to be equivalent to what has been spoken of as the ultimate criterion.

In this step we must ask the question of why are some persons successful and others not. By thoughtful analysis of the activity description in step 2 and by research, we should be able to identify the elements of the activity which are related to success. Ryans' work (26) suggests the possible use of the critical incident approach in this step.

When the success elements of the activity have been identified they should be weighted in accordance to their importance to success in the activity. It should be noted that the success elements are being weighted here, not sub-criteria. The sub-criteria are later combined in accordance with the weights established here. The effect of this is to place the weighting step in a more basic position.

There are several ways in which this weighting of success elements can be accomplished. Success elements could be weighted according to their dollar value. If a critical incident approach were used, the success elements might be weighted according to frequency of occurrence. Still another approach would be to have the experts who analyzed the activity weight the success elements. This author favors the latter approach. The use of a judging approach does not preclude the use of fiscal information as an aid to making such judgments.

4. *Development of sub-criteria to measure the elements of success.* The last step in this criterion development procedure is the development of sub-criteria to measure each of the elements of success. In some cases the sub-criterion measures developed will be identical to the elements of success. For example, an element of success on an industrial job may be infrequent absence. The number of times absent could be used as a sub-criterion measure for the success element, infrequent absence. To measure success elements for which there are no objective data, ratings will often have to be used. In such cases, the success element which the

rater is called upon to rate should be carefully defined for him. Sometimes success elements may not be amenable even to ratings.

It is in this step that the sub-criterion measures are subjected to analysis of the matter of relevancy and reliability to determine their acceptability. When we are unable to develop sub-criteria for some success elements, criterion deficiency occurs—the criterion omits some of the variance found in the ultimate criterion. On the other hand, sub-criterion measures designed to measure success elements may be contaminated with extraneous variance. In such a case criterion contamination occurs—a sub-criterion designed to measure a success element includes extraneous variance. Prolonged reflection upon the likely sources of contamination in a measure before the measure is developed is required. With ratings this problem is acute and difficult to diagnose. In the rating situation, therefore, the task of the rater should be carefully explained to him. Wherever the possibility of contamination exists the researcher must turn his thoughts toward experimental and statistical control of the sources of contamination. It is here, also, that we inquire into the reliability of the sub-criterion measure. Every effort must be made to obtain as reliable a measure as possible through consideration of the sources of unreliability previously listed.

When all the measurable sub-criteria are assembled they should be weighted according to the weights assigned to the success elements they are supposed to measure. The weights should be applied to the standard score transformations of the sub-criteria. For some success elements there may be no sub-criterion measures. Then we will have to temporarily leave out these elements, but still weight the other sub-criteria according to the original weights assigned to their respective success elements. When sub-criterion measures eventually are developed for the omitted success elements, these sub-criterion measures can be added to the composite criterion score according to the weights of their respective success elements.

Thus, this approach includes four steps:

1. Define the activity
2. Analyze the activity
    a. purposes of the activity
    b. types of behavior called for
    c. standards of performance in the activity
    d. relative importance of the various behaviors
3. Define success
    a. find the elements of success
    b. weight the elements of success
4. Develop sub-criteria to measure each element of success
    a. relevancy of each sub-criterion to its success element
    b. reliability of each sub-criterion
    c. combination of the sub-criteria

The importance of a thorough analysis of the activity and of a careful definition of success cannot be overemphasized. These steps must be done by psychologically trained persons well acquainted with the activity.

Does this approach seem too laborious? Couldn't a simple rating to determine "good" and "poor" performers do just as well? It must be admitted that considerable work is involved. Certainly an overall rating would be much easier and less time consuming. But it is felt that the procedure outlined here will lead to criteria of much higher relevancy than that achieved by overall ratings. There are two other major advantages of this four step approach as contrasted with an overall rating. First, this procedure holds out the hope for continued improvement of the criterion to increase relevancy. Second, the success elements provide a useful diagnostic instrument. These success elements can be invaluable in indicating training needs and serving as a counseling aid. On the other hand, practicality must be the deciding factor in many instances. Perhaps the activity in question is not important enough to warrant the expense of the more comprehensive criterion approach. Perhaps the simple, overall rating is good enough. The researcher who comes to this conclusion must realize that he is avoiding important problems, that he is settling for something easy but not quite so good, that the criterion for his criterion has become expediency.

It has been suggested that one might identify the elements of success by, ".... a factorial analysis of a set of criterion measures" (4, p. 364). While much can be said for this approach, it has two limitations. First, the factors obtained may not have psychological meaning and not exist as separate entities, and second, possible success elements for which we have no criterion measures will not be identified in the factorial analysis. In effect, step 3, definition of success, has been overlooked, and we are dealing only with the available criterion measures and forgetting about the success elements for which we have no criterion measures.

Bechtoldt has pointed out realistically that, "The development of an acceptable criterion is, in actual practice, accomplished by a series of successive approximations" (4, p. 379). When one obtains a criterion composite it is not time to sit back and relax, forgetting the criterion and its origin. The present inadequacies of job or activity analysis make it necessary to try repeatedly to analyze further the activity which was first done in step 2. The definition of success should also be subjected to periodic scrutiny to insure that all the elements of success have been obtained, that no false elements have been included, and that the proper weights have been assigned. The sub-criteria must be constantly watched to determine if extraneous elements are creeping into them. Also, sub-criteria will be subjected to more exacting tests as our knowledge of the nature of psychological measurement is expanded.

There have been a number of recent studies reported in the literature which deal primarily with analyses of criterion data. This seems to reflect an increased awareness of the crucial role of the criterion in research. Among the more important of these studies are two by Rothe (24, 25) analyzing the output rates of butter wrappers and chocolate dippers, one by Lawshe and McGinley (20) concerned with the independence and reliability of criterion measures for proofreaders, one by Gaier (13) about the criteria of success in medical school, and one by Hemphill and Sechrest (15) analyzing aircrew criteria and providing an example of how objective information may influence ratings.

While this paper is directed principally toward criterion development in the personnel selection field, most of what is said here can be used in criterion development in other areas (evaluation of training, marriage, organizations, equipment, personal adjustment, etc.). It is believed that the general methodology of criterion development, though not well systematized, is present now, but that the basis on which success is to be determined is still undecided and, in large measure, unexplored. A recent article by Bass (3) urges that the concept of success be extended beyond the confines of productivity to include the satisfaction derived from the activity by the individual and the contribution of the activity to society. While this is not a new idea, it reflects a growing awareness of and interest in the effects of an activity on the participants and society. As the basis of success is extended to include individual satisfaction and value to society, the psychologist will be faced with more complicated and more subjective methods of criterion measurement.

REFERENCES

1. ADKINS, DOROTHY. *Construction and analysis of achievement tests.* Washington: U. S. Government Printing Office, 1947.
2. ANASTASI, ANNE. The concept of validity in the interpretation of test scores. *Educ. psychol. Measmt.*, 1950, 10, 67–78.
3. BASS, B. M. Ultimate criteria of organizational worth. *Personnel Psychol.*, 1952, 5, 157-174.
4. BECHTOLDT, H. P. Problems of establishing criterion measures. In D. B. Stuit (Ed.), *Personnel research and test development in the Bureau of Naval Personnel.* Princeton, N. J.: Princeton Univer. Press, 1947. Pp. 357-380.
5. BELLOWS, R. M. Procedures for evaluating vocational criteria. *J. appl. Psychol.*, 1941, 25, 499-513.
6. BELLOWS, R. M. *Psychology of personnel in business and industry.* New York: Prentice-Hall, 1949.
7. BROGDEN, H. E., & TAYLOR, E. K. The theory and classification of criterion bias. *Educ. psychol. Measmt.*, 1950, 10, 159-186.

8. Brogden, H. E., & Taylor, E. K. The dollar criterion—applying the cost accounting concept to criterion construction. *Personnel Psychol.*, 1950, 3, 133–154.
9. Brownell, W. A. Criteria of learning in educational research. *J. educ. Psychol.*, 1948, 39, 170–182.
10. Edgerton, H. A., & Kolbe, L. E. The method of minimum variation for the combination of criteria. *Psychometrika*, 1936, 1, 183-187.
11. Fiske, E. W. Values, theory and the criterion problem. *Personnel Psychol.*, 1951, 4, 93-98.
12. Flanagan, J. C. Job requirements. In W. Dennis (Ed.), *Current trends in industrial psychology*. Pittsburgh: U. Pittsburgh Press, 1949. Pp. 32–54.
13. Gaier, E. L. The criterion problem in the prediction of medical school success. *J. appl. Psychol.*, 1952, 36, 316–322.
14. Ghiselli, E. E., & Brown, C. W. *Personnel and industrial psychology*. New York: McGraw-Hill, 1948.
15. Hemphill, J. K., & Sechrest, L. B. A comparison of three criteria of aircrew effectiveness in combat over Korea. *J. appl. Psychol.*, 1952, 36, 323–327.
16. Horst, P. Obtaining a composite measure from a number of different measures of the same attribute. *Psychometrika*, 1936, 1, 53-60.
17. Horst, P., et al. *The prediction of personal adjustment*. Soc. Sci. Res. Coun. Bul., 48, 1941. Pp. 20–36.
18. Hotelling, H. The most predictable criterion. *J. educ. Psychol.*, 1935, 26, 139–142.
19. Jenkins, J. G. Validity for what? *J. consult. Psychol.*, 1946, 10, 93–98.
20. Lawshe, C. H., & McGinley, A. D. Job performance criteria studies I. The job performance of proofreaders. *J. appl. Psychol.*, 1951, 35, 316–320.
21. Otis, J. L. The criterion. In W. H. Stead, and C. L. Shartle (Eds.), *Occupational counseling techniques*. New York: American Book Co., 1940. Pp. 73–94.
22. Patterson, C. H. On the problem of the criterion in prediction studies. *J. consult. Psychol.*, 1946, 10, 277-280.
23. Peel, E. A. Prediction of a complex criterion and battery reliability. *Brit. J. Psychol., Statist. Sect.*, 1948, 1, 84-94.
24. Rothe, H. F. Output rates among butter wrappers: I Work curves and their stability. *J. appl. Psychol.*, 1946, 30, 199-211.
25. Rothe, H. F. Output rates among chocolate dippers. *J. appl. Psychol.*, 1951, 35, 94–97.,
26. Ryans, D. G. A study of criterion data (a factor analysis of teacher behaviors in the elementary school). *Educ. psychol. Measmt.*, 1952, 12, 333–344.

27. THOMSON, G. H. Weighting for battery reliability and prediction. *Brit. J. Psychol.*, 1940, 30, 357-366.
28. THORNDIKE, R. L. *Personnel selection.* New York: John Wiley, 1949.
29. TOOPS, H. A. The selection of graduate assistants. *Personnel J.*, 1928, 6, 457-472.
30. TOOPS, H. A. The criterion. *Educ. psychol. Measmt.*, 1944, 4, 271-297.
31. VAN DUSEN, A. C. Importance of criteria in selection and training. *Educ. psychol. Measmt.*, 1947, 7, 498-504.

46 The Past and Future of Criterion Evaluation

ROBERT J. WHERRY

When we speak of the validity of a test, we have learned to ask, "Valid for what?" and "Against what criterion?" Whenever we lack answers to these questions we are apt to divert our attention to what might be called "potential validity." Thus we concern ourselves with reliability, objectivity, face validity, expert validity, or rational validity. Most psychometricians are apt to be less satisfied with this latter approach when dealing with tests.

In the field of criterion research, however, the standards tended to remain on this lower plane for many years. When Bellows (1) attempted to list criteria for a criterion, he included such criteria as:

1. reliability
2. accessibility and cost
3. acceptability to the sponsor

These criteria possess a crude practicality against which one could find few objections if other factors were held constant. They are scarcely standards of which a psychometrician could be proud in a technical sense. At this same time, the predominant classification of criteria was on an objective (work records, accidents) versus subjective (ratings, rankings) dimension. I would like to suggest that these criteria belong to the "dark ages" of criterion development. They constitute the substitutes for knowing what we are doing or even trying to do—our inability to sell something better because we do not know anything better. They seem to constitute an attempt to say, "We don't know what we are doing, but we are doing it very carefully, and hope you are pleased with our unintelligent diligence." I would predict that this approach will largely disappear because those who rely upon it will disappear.

Bellows also cited two other criteria for a criterion:

1. predictability
2. agreement with other criteria

The expansion of these two concepts represents a second historical period

From *Personnel Psychology*, 1957, *10*, 1–5.

in the development of criterion evaluation. They represent at best an attempt to prove that our criteria are really valuable for some purpose, but with considerable doubt as to the nature of that purpose. Each of these concepts has played a role in our thinking about criteria in the past two decades.

Predictability at first constituted but a kind of backward validation. Instead of using the criterion-predictor correlation to prove the validity of a test against a known criterion, we now reverse the procedure to prove the validity of our criterion by showing that it was predictable by a test judged to be valuable on rational grounds. One might conceive of this as a kind of eating one's cake and having it too. However, this concept has enabled us to realize the importance of the relation of the criterion to the predictor field. It leads to our classification of criteria along the dimension of simple to complex, to discussions concerning the difference between the selection of an appropriately factorially simple criterion for validating a single predictor instrument designed to accomplish a similar simple specific purpose, as contrasted with the selection of a complex or composite criterion when we wished to validate a battery of tests designed to measure many aspects of a job. It has also alerted us to the inadvisability of attempting to accomplish mutually antagonistic purposes at the same time.

The second principle, "agreement with other criteria," was similarly applied in a rather crude fashion at first. We attempted to show that ratings were good because they agreed with production ratings or vice versa. This paralleled the practice of validating one personality test against another, as objected to by our critic Whyte (3) in a recent issue of *Fortune*. Fortunately this rather stupid application has yielded to more sophisticated thinking—to a classification of criteria along the dimension of proximal to ultimate, and finally to some searching discussion of the problem of criterion equivalence. We have at this stage introduced a time dimension. We now seek agreement only in order to make intelligent substitution of criteria for each other in order to accomplish some agreed upon purpose equally well but more quickly or more cheaply or both—a procedure which relegates these practical criteria to a proper place of subordination to actual validity. This line of reasoning has in turn led to considerable discussion of the nature of ultimate criteria; e.g., the dollar criterion.

If we call the first period discussed the dark ages, we might speak of this period just ending as a renaissance. It is marked by the re-application of validity principles, earlier applied to testing, to the criteria themselves.

Bellows mentioned one further criterion. Acceptability to the personnel technician. I have chosen to treat this concept as designating an independent but eventually to be related stream of development. While the psychometricians were concerning themselves with the statistical problems discussed above, they were never able to escape the use of what are often derogatorily referred to as "clinical insights" or more elegantly as "rational theory." Everyone uses this approach when he selects a battery of predictors to try out or a criterion against which to conduct the tryout—both are picked on the basis of certain hunches or predictions as to their content. In the early forties we began to accept the idea that a man should be familiar with the job for which he desired to build a test battery—many psychologists wishing to do research in aviation learned to fly. This concept has led to an increasing emphasis upon job analysis and situational analysis. Unfortunately such systems have too often been truly clinical in the sense that all meanings were deeply hidden and reflected a non- or even anti-quantitative approach. Rational has meant merely armchair or untested or even anti-empirical. As of today there is real hope that these methods will become judgmental only in the sense that all measurement is essentially judgmental, that they will become empirically based and empirically checked in the best sense of mathematical theory building. Repeated factorial analyses of both predictor and criterion batteries have yielded or are yielding a sound set of elements upon which such systems can be based. The works of Dr. Primoff (2) of the U.S. Civil Service in analyzing both predictors and job performance in terms of elements and estimated weights and then testing his theoretically predicted relation via his J-coefficient against actual empirical validity coefficients seems to offer at least some hope that this stream of development can be incorporated into the other phases described earlier.

What then can we predict as to the next decade in criterion research and selection:

1. Continued study of the ultimate criterion with emphasis upon clarification of purpose, refinement of definition, and improvement in measurement methods.

2. Increased interest in the field of criterion equivalence; i.e., attempts to prove that more easily or cheaply obtainable criteria will actually accomplish the same results as would the ultimate criterion.

3. Improvement in methods of job and situational analysis techniques including a still better definition of the needed elements and of methods of estimating their presence and importance of both criteria and tests.

4. Studies to validate these rational approaches empirically so that they will represent true psychological scaling rather than mere clinical hunches.

5. Further attention as to how to select proper criteria to accomplish the specific task at hand; e.g., specifying in advance the population, predictor field, and the role of the new technique in the industrial setting, namely whether it is to replace or supplement the current techniques employed.

When and if we have accomplished the goals listed above—gotten our thinking clear and our goals identified and justified, I would predict a return to polishing jobs such as improvement of objectivity, reliability, and face validity, and even to such superpolishing activities such as correcting our correlation coefficients for sampling, attenuation, broad classes, and the like. Our sponsors or bosses may forgive us if we polish the brass on an instrument of proven value and efficiency, but I hope we are about to give up polishing instruments whose purpose and validity are in doubt. If we are measuring the wrong thing, it will not help us to measure it better.

REFERENCES

1. BELLOWS, ROGER M. Procedures for evaluating vocational criteria. *Journal of Applied Psychology*, 1941, 25, 499–513.
2. PRIMOFF, ERNEST S. *Test Selection by Job Analysis: The J-Coefficient, What it is, How it works.* Assembled Test Technical Series No. 20, U.S. Civil Service Commission Bureau of Programs and Standards, Standards Division, Washington 25, D. C., 1953, August.
3. WHYTE, WILLIAM H., JR. The Fallacies of "Personality" Testing. *Fortune*, 1954, September. P. 117 ff.

47 Criterion Measurement and Personnel Judgments

ROBERT M. GUION

In their review of the year's literature, Wallace and Weitz (1955) suggested that more talking was being done about "the criterion problem" than research. Despite all of the verbal attacks on this problem, they concluded, most workers still accept the most convenient criterion with the hope that it will turn out to be all right. The present note is in the tradition observed by the Wallace and Weitz survey; it is a discussion of an approach to the problem, not a report of concrete research!

A first point of view to be made explicit in this discussion is that the solution to the criterion problem does *not* lie in the typical efforts at statistical refinement. Much of this has been blind numerical manipulation. If we are honest, we will describe many of the very complex criterion refinements with words, "We don't know what we are doing, but we are doing it very carefully and hope you are pleased with our unintelligent diligence" (Wherry, 1957, p. 1).

THE PRESENT STATUS OF CRITERION MEASUREMENT

Most efforts at personnel prediction start (at least implicitly) from a judgment about the nature of some "ultimate criterion" (Thorndike, 1949; Fiske, 1951) of what may be called the general satisfactoriness of personnel performing some specified function within an organization. This ultimate criterion is a complex array of skills, interests, motives, attitudes, and other imponderables along with the whole gamut of specific behaviors appropriate to the job. Conceptually, the ultimate criterion can apparently be defined as "the total worth of a man to the company—in the final analysis." Such an abstraction is not measurable—at least not until the man's total career with an organization has finally been terminated!

Therefore, an acceptable substitute is usually deemed necessary. The search for such a substitute may begin by examining job descriptions and

From *Personnel Psychology*, 1961, *14*, 141–149.

by making some kind of subjective judgment or analysis of the needs of the organization. At best, the present status of techniques of job and need analysis leave much to be desired; typical techniques of job and need analysis are seldom the best when one is merely seeking some clues about possible criteria! Typically, in fact, the whole sequence of criterion selection goes something like this:

1. The psychologist has a hunch (or insight!) that a problem exists and that he can help solve it.
2. He reads a vague, ambiguous description of the job.
3. From these faint stimuli, he formulates a fuzzy concept of an ultimate criterion.
4. Being a practical psychologist, he may then formulate a combination of several variables which will give him—as nearly as he can guess—a single, composite measure of "satisfactoriness."
5. He judges the relevance of this measure: the extent to which it is neither deficient nor contaminated (Cf. Nagle, 1953).
6. He may judge the relative importance of each of the elements in his composite and assign some varying amount of weight to each.
7. He then finds that the data required for his carefully built composite are not available in the company files, nor is there any immediate prospect of having such records reliably kept.
8. Therefore, he will then select "the best available criterion." Typically, this will be a rating, and the criterion problem, if not solved, can at least be overlooked for the rest of the research.

In short, the sequence of events involved in the usual selection of a criterion involves a series of judgments on the part of the personnel research worker, culminating in the decision to use someone else's judgment as the criterion. This means, then, that the whole superstructure of personnel research—with its multiple correlations and confidence levels and other trappings of a quantitative, scientific methodology—is built upon the weakest of foundations: a residual judgment. (Parenthetically, it must be recognized that ratings may provide excellent criteria when properly applied and carefully worked out. But when ratings become the residual technique—the technique to use after everything else has been rejected because of *obvious* inadequacy—then one may be permitted a raised eyebrow when one reads in the journal, "The best available criterion was the instructor's rating." If a rating is indeed the best available criterion, then of course a personnel researcher must do the best he can under the situational limitations. But he should not delude himself that he has solved the criterion problem.)

Even in more desirable circumstances, where the finally selected criterion is not residual but does indeed conform to the judgments made in the first half-dozen steps of the sequence, the superstructure of research results may rest on a very shaky foundation. Ignore, if possible, the ever present possibility of poor judgment. There still remains the problem of changing circumstances. Changes in the general economy, in the company's competitive position, in the labor market, or (often overlooked) in the distribution of skills or traits within the organization itself are very likely to occur. Such changes may in turn influence one's "expert judgment" about the relative importance of the various elements that make up one's composite criterion measure. Consider, as one example, a company beset by customer complaints about quality of workmanship. If it initiates a personnel research program to help solve its problem, it will need a criterion—and the ultimate criterion must include not only the quality element but a quantity measure as well. In judging the relative importance of these two elements, at such a time, it is quite possible that a sound judgment might consider the quality measure to be perhaps two or three times as important as quantity. Selection research (and perhaps training or administrative changes) are then validated against this criterion, the variance of which is perhaps 70 per cent attributable to quality measures.

If the research is successful, and if the results are incorporated into the employment procedure (and other personnel practices), then in due time the organization should have a highly "quality-conscious" work force. Customer complaints should become markedly reduced and, as in other fairy tales, everyone should live happily ever after.

In most companies, however, there comes a time for a second chapter, and in this chapter the problem that has been solved is quickly replaced by a new one to solve. In the example company, for instance, the emphasis on quality may have resulted, in time, in a deliberate, careful work that moves slowly enough to endanger the company's competitiveness in pricing. While quality is still an important element, its relative importance may therefore shrink enough to reverse the earlier ratio. If this happens, then all of the validation work done with the original weighting needs to be done again with the revised criterion.

The argument of this note is simply that the judgment of relative importance of criterion elements is typically made too soon.

MULTI-DIMENSIONALITY OF CRITERIA

The variety of criterion selection outlined in the foregoing is based upon the idea of a single, over-all ultimate criterion which must somehow be duplicated in the criterion measure actually employed. This idea assumes a generality in criteria analogous to a general factor in intelligence.

Criteria, however, exist along many dimensions, not just one. A major landmark in our collective awareness of this point is the article by

Ghiselli (1956), "Dimensional Problems of Criteria." Although there has been much recognition of criterion dimensionality at any given time, Ghiselli has gone further in introducing the concept of "dynamic dimensions" of criteria. The concept here is that the dimensions along which performance occurs may change as a result of experience. This idea is supported by findings in one organization known to the writer. In the organization it was found that tests which can predict sales performance during the first year of employment are different tests from those which predict sales performance after five years. Clearly, first year sales and five year sales are not equivalent criteria. The reason is not as clear. What are the single, identifiable dimensions of sales performance that have changed in this period of time?

Such dimensions must be clearly defined and isolated if marked improvement in personnel selection techniques are to be made. This implies that personnel research must be multi-dimensional in its dependent, criterion measurement as well as in its independent, predictor measurement. The old insistence of the laboratory for a single dependent and a single independent variable may have worked well with rats and mazes, but it not appropriate to the study of the functioning of the human organism in his many-faceted world of making a living.

Successful multivariate research demands clear knowledge of each of the component parts. Each must be not merely definable, but reliably measurable as well. There is a profound difference between sound multivariable research, depending upon systematic handling of the variables included, and the verbal, conceptually over-cooked hash that is today's typical "composite criterion."

Too long and too frequently the doctrine is accepted that a single, over-all criterion is indispensable (Nagle, 1953; Toops, 1928). The second argument of this note is that this doctrine should be rejected; in many situations it is doubtful if the doctrine of a single criterion is even sensible, let alone indispensable.

A broad and useful definition of a criterion is behavior, or consequences of behavior, that one wishes to predict. The fallacy of the single criterion lies in its assumption that everything that is to be predicted is related to everything else to be predicted—that there is a general factor in all criteria accounting for virtually all of the important variance in behavior at work and its various consequences of value. Considering that there are two broad classes of criteria, satisfaction and performance (Katzell, 1957), this assumption is obviously silly in view of the often-noted failure to find significant correlations between these two classes of variables (Brayfield and Crockett, 1955). Even within the job performance domain, the assumption of a general factor is frequently not tenable. Within the domain of job satisfaction, evidence does suggest the existence of a general factor (Wherry, 1958). The same evidence, however, also points to a number of other reasonably invariant factors which also account for appreciable portions of the total satisfaction variance.

Where criterion elements or dimensions are shown to be related, then there may be some point in combining them into a general composite. Where they are clearly independent, however, then predictions should also be independent.

JOB AND NEED ANALYSIS

The indentification of criterion elements and the determination of their independence levels can be accomplished through some form of factor analysis. Factor analysis, however, requires data. The data from which clear identification of criterion elements must come are collected in job analysis and in the analysis of organizational needs.

The basic question of job analysis is, "What is the nature of the behavior called for by the job or the employment situation?" A corollary question in criterion selection is, "What is the degree of correspondence between the behavior called for and the behavior actually exhibited?" In analyzing needs, the basic question is, in a value-judgment sense, "What consequences should on-the-job behavior produce?" The corollary question for criteria is, "To what degree does each individual's behavior actually lead to these desired consequences?"

These questions indicate that criteria can be classified either as behavior data or as result-of-behavior data. Such a classification is related to, although not identical with, the job analysis classification suggested by McCormick (1959) with his job-oriented and worker-oriented job elements. It seems quite plausible that future research may find that job-oriented job analysis may be preferable for identifying the majority of the result-of-behavior criterion dimensions, and that these will be what Ghiselli (1956) termed the static dimensions, while the worker-oriented job analysis may be more effective in identifying the behavior dimensions, and that these may prove to be the "dynamic dimensions." This is, of course, mere speculation. What can be said now with conviction is that much work must be done to improve techniques of job analysis, and to develop and improve techniques of situational need analysis, before such dimensions can be clearly identified, isolated, and objectively and reliably measured.

THE ROLE OF JUDGMENT

The development of better techniques of job analysis with resulting increased emphasis upon actual worker behavior does not remove judgment from the process. The complete process of criterion development calls for two varieties of value judgment: (a) the judgment that a particular form of behavior or result of behavior is good or desirable[1] and (b) that one behavior or result is more or less or equally desirable compared with another.

A major problem in criterion development, therefore, is to find means by which these judgments can be improved. A whole program of personnel research will stand or fall upon the adequacy of the initial judgments which are made.

The first type of judgment can be made more effictively by persons who are well informed. The fund of information should include a clear formulation of the objectives of the organization (Fiske, 1951; Bass, 1952)—a matter for top level policy determination. It should also include definite facts about the relationships between specific behaviors on any given job and those organizational objectives—a matter of objective, descriptive research. Fiske (1951), as a matter of fact, suggests that clear policy plus competent research can eliminate the need for any more value judgments in criterion development.

This continues the fallacy of the single criterion by overlooking the second type of judgment, the designation of certain behaviors or results (criterion elements) as more or less valuable than others. It is this judgment which is most easily improved by the very simple and convenient expedient of postponing it as long as possible.

The sequence of events suggested here as typical of the present state of affairs places this judgment quite early in the personnel research process. This judgment is usually made prior to any research activity save that which may be associated with job analysis. The reliability of this judgment can be improved, however, by postponing it until validation data are in and until current needs of the organization, *at the time a prediction must be made,* are known.

This proposal can be made more explicit by suggesting a new sequence of events in criterion development and subsequent personnel research:

1. Analyze the job and/or the organizational needs by new, yet-to-be-developed techniques.
2. Develop measures of actual behavior relative to the behavior expected, as identified in job and need analysis. These measures are to supplement measures of the consequences of work—the so-called objective criteria commonly tried at present.

---

[1] Typically, this is a linear judgment; that is, it is judged that if more of something is good, then still more of that something must be better. The wisdom of this assumption needs to be questioned, but that, happily, is beyond the scope of this paper.

3. Identify the criterion dimensions underlying such measures by factor analysis or cluster analysis or pattern analysis.
4. Develop reliable measures, each with high construct validity, of the elements so identified.
5. For each independent variable (predictor), determine its predictive validity for *each one* of the foregoing criterion measures, taking them one at a time.

The first kind of judgment—that a given behavior or its result has some degree of value—is still implied in step 2. Any judgment of the relative importance of those considered to *be* important does not appear in this sequence of research events. This judgment would not be made, in fact, until administrative use is to be made of the research results. If we are concerned with selection research, for example, the judgment would be postponed until the time an employment decision must be made. The employment manager could, for each applicant, make a series of predictions about the kind of behavior to be expected or about the organizational consequences of hiring the applicant. It is likely that, for any given applicant, some predictions would be favorable and others less so. Other applicants might show different patterns, being predicted to be more successful where a first applicant seems risky. Only now, in this proposed sequence, is the judgment of the relative importance of the things to be predicted actually made. At this point, that judgment has the benefit of knowing the relative validites of the various predictions that are possible and the further benefit of knowing the immediate situational needs of the organization.

CONCLUSION

Improvement in personnel research of all kinds—including selection and placement but not these exclusively—will not be dramatic until the criterion problem is solved. This note has made no real, empirical progress in reaching that solution, but it has attempted to point out a serious obstacle and the path for avoiding it.

The basic argument of this paper is that (a) there are in many personnel situations dimensions of job performance and of performance consequences that are quite independent of each other, and that (b) the relative importance of these independent criteria ought not be judged prior to validation research—as is so commonly done in the development of "composite" criteria—but ought to instead be judged *after* the empirical data are in, at the time these data are to be used. The suggestion is that this will result in clearer criterion definition, more reliable criterion measurement, and greatly improved criterion prediction.

REFERENCES

Bass, B. M. "Ultimate Criteria of Organizational Worth." *Personnel Psychology*, V (1952), 157–174.
Brayfield, A. H. & Crockett, W. H. "Employee Attitudes and Employee Performance." *Psychological Bulletin*, LII (1955), 396–424.
Fiske, D. W. "Values, Theory, and the Criterion Problem." *Personnel Psychology*, IV (1951), 93–98.
Ghiselli, E. E. "Dimensional Problems of Criteria." *Journal of Applied Psychology*, XL (1956), 1–4.
Katzell, R. A. "Industrial Psychology." *Annual Review of Psychology*, VIII (1957), 237–268.
McCormick, E. J. "Application of Job Analysis to Indirect Validity." *Personnel Psychology*, XII (1959), 402–413.
Nagle, B. F. "Criterion Development." *Personnel Psychology*, VI (1953), 271–289.
Thorndike, R. L. *Personnel Selection*. New York: John Wiley & Sons, 1949.
Toops, H. A. "Selection of Graduate Assistants." *Personnel Journal*, VI (1928), 457–472.
Wallace, S. R. & Weitz, J. "Industrial Psychology." *Annual Review of Psychology*, VI (1955), 217–250.
Wherry, R. J. "The Past and Future of Criterion Evaluation." *Personnel Psychology*, X (1957), 1–5.
Wherry, R. J. "Factor Analysis of Morale Data: Reliability and Validity." *Personnel Psychology*, XI (1958), 78–89.

48 Studies in Synthetic Validity: An Exploratory Investigation of Clerical Jobs

C. H. LAWSHE and MARTIN D. STEINBERG

SUMMARY

This research has undertaken the task of attempting to establish test standards when accepted validation procedures are inapplicable. An elemental approach to job analysis has been used, test requirements for the elements have been established, and a procedure for their use is proposed.

BACKGROUND

The procedure for choosing tests for selection purposes in industry is fairly well agreed upon by industrial psychologists. Briefly, it consists of these steps: (a) discovering what the job requirements are, (b) picking tests that purport to measure these qualities, (c) trying out the tests on a sample of applicants or present employees, (d) identifying the "superior" job performers, and (e) examining test performance in relation to job performance to see whether or not the former predicts the latter. Numerous authors (4, 8) have pointed out the need for adherence to this procedure.

However, the extreme variability of job content, the small number of employees reporting to the same supervisor, and many related problems sometimes make the application of the more or less standard procedure completely unrealistic and virtually impossible. This is especially true in a great many office and clerical situations. Recognition of this fact prompted the senior author (5) in 1951 to propose the concept of *synthetic validity*. The term was used ". . . to denote the inferring of validity in a specific situation. The concept is similar to that involved when the time study engineer establishes standard times for new operations, purely

From *Personnel Psychology*, 1955, 8, 291–301.

on an *a priori* basis through the use of "synthetic times" for the various elements constituting the operation."

The Problem. Briefly stated, the problem is this: is it possible to discover the ability requirements of small work elements as measured by tests, and in turn to determine the test pattern that should be required of a person who is to perform some combination (possibly unique) of these elements? The research reported here dealt specifically with office or clerical activity.

PRELIMINARY WORK

Much preliminary work which laid the foundation for the present research needs to be reviewed.

The Job Description Check List. The *Job Description Check List of Clerical Operation*[1] was developed by Culbertson (1), refined by Dudek (3), and was used for job evaluation purposes by Miles (6). The *Check-List* consists of 139 operations or elements constituting clerical activity. The following four samples are illustrative:

1. Makes simple calculations such as addition or subtraction with or without using a machine.
16. Composes routine correspondence or memoranda, following standard operating procedures.
25. Compiles numerical or statistical data for tables, charts, rate schedules, or other uses with or without using a machine.
43. Approves or rejects applications, requests, claims, or other items, following operational policies or rules of action.

Culbertson's original work (1) together with subsequent use of the *Check-List* attests the fact that it adequately describes activities which make up the clerical field.

The Purdue Clerical Adaptability Test. The *Purdue Clerical Adaptability Test*[2] consists of the following seven sections: spelling, memory for oral instructions, arithmetic computation, checking, vocabulary, accuracy of copying (handwriting), and arithmetic reasoning. Research (7) has shown these seven sections to be reasonably independent and the scores to be stable.

[1] The detailed check-list has been filed with the American Documentation Institute. Order Document 3267 from American Documentation Institute, 1719 N Street, N.W., Washington 6, D. C. remitting $1.00 for microfilm (images 1 inch high on standard 35 mm. motion picture film) or $1.20 for photocopies (6 x 8 inches) readable without optical aid. Single copies of the printed form may be obtained gratis from the senior author.
[2] Marketed by the Occupational Research Center, Purdue University, Lafayette, Indiana.

Critical Test Requirements. Research conducted by Dawson (2) utilized 15 judges, familiar with clerical activity, to estimate the critical test requirements of each operation. That is, with respect to operation number one in the *Check-List*, judges were asked, "How critical is spelling (as measured by the first section of the *Purdue Clerical Adaptability Test*) to the performance of this operation?" Similarly, the same question was asked with respect to each of the seven tests for each of the 139 operations in the *Check–List*. As a result, certain test areas were designated as being "critical" for certain operations. Table 48.1 presents this information for the four sample operations listed earlier. Note that arithmetic computation and arithmetical reasoning were judged as being critical for the performance of operation number one. Some operations were judged to have no critical requirements in-so-far as these seven tests are concerned, while some operations were judged critical in all seven.

THE PRESENT STUDY

The present study utilized (a) the *Job Description Check-List of Clerical Operations*, (b) the *Purdue Clerical Adaptability Test*, and (c) Dawson's designations of critical requirements, for each operation. The sample studied consisted of 262 positions in 12 companies. Arrangements were made by mail and standardized instructions were supplied in connection with each of the following phases:

(a) Selecting office positions
(b) Having *Check-Lists* prepared
(c) Administering the test

Throughout, only five operations in each job were considered. These were the five operations designated as being most important or constituting the "core" by the supervisor. The use of these five is based partly on Miles' research (6) and partly on the rationale that it is the "highest level" or "most important" elements in a job that differentiate it from other jobs.

The current study rests upon one fundamental assumption; *i.e.*, in general, those incumbents who are currently employed in positions, by and large, possess those qualities which the positions demand of them.

TABLE 48.1. *Test sections judged critical for four sample operations*

Operation Number	Spell.	A.C.	Mem.	Check.	Vocab.	Copy.	A.R.
1		C					C
16	C				C		
25		C		C		C	C
43			C	C	C		

The rationale is that if an individual can not or does not "deliver" on the job, either the employee is replaced, or the job assignment is modified. Actually, we know that this is not universally true; there are no doubt many exceptions, but in general the assumption would seem to be valid.

Purpose. Specifically, then, this study sought to answer the question, "Are jobs which involve many operations with critical spelling demands presently "manned" by better spellers than are those jobs that involve few operations with critical spelling demands?" Similarly, the same question was asked with respect to each of the other six test areas.

RESULTS

In order to be able to present the data in expectancy chart form, the test authors' median (50th percentile) was employed. For example, those positions which had 4 or 5 operations judged critical in spelling, were found to have incumbents, 84% of whom scored above the median on the spelling test. Figure 48.1, then, is an expectancy chart; it indicates that the probability of finding a better than average speller or a 4 or 5 critical operation job is 84 in 100. Note that the probability of finding higher scorers in spelling diminishes as the number of operations with judged critical spelling requirements decreases.

Figures 48.2, 48.3, and 48.4 present similar facts for arithmetic computation, vocabulary, and arithmetic reasoning. In each instance it is evident that when a job includes several operations previously designated as having critical test requirements, the probability of finding a higher than average test scorer on that job is greater than in the case when the number of operations designated as critical is small. The differences represented in these four figures are statistically significant; *i.e.*, we are extremely confident that the results are stable and will occur again. Three sections of the test, memory for instruction, checking, and copying, did not yield similarly significant results. The first, memory, is an orally administered test, and variations in administration tend to make it unreliable when results from several administrators are pooled; in view of this fact it is not surprising that results in this study are negative. With respect to the other two, while no relationship was found in this study, it is possible that future research, using an ability or performance criterion, might demonstrate relationship.

SUMMARY DISCUSSION

Based upon this study, it would seem that we have made progress toward "synthetically" determining the test requirements for a particular job. The following procedures appear justified.

1. Apply the *Check-List* to the position.
2. Have the supervisor identify the five most important operations.
3. Determine how many of these five operations have critical requirements in (a) spelling, (b) arithmetic computation, (c) vocabulary, and (d) arithmetic reasoning.
4. Consult the expectancy charts presented below as Figs. 48.1–4. Determine the probabilities of finding a "better than average" scorer on each of the four tests.
5. Administer the *Purdue Clerical Adaptability Test* to applicants.
6. When the probability is high, look for a high scorer; when it is low, ignore this section of the test.

TECHNICAL SECTION

It seems desirable to the authors to point out some of the many possible sources of error variances, the first three of which stem from the fact that the data came from different plants:

1. *Variations in the application of the Check-List.* There is no assurance that the *Check-List* was uniformly applied, even though standardized instructions were provided. Any investigator who has undertaken multiple company research has observed marked variability in the rigor with which his plans are implemented.
2. *Variations in the test ability level of employees from company to company.* While systematic analyses of this matter were not undertaken, cursory observation of the data plus prior experience in multiple com-

NUMBER OF CRITICAL OPERATIONS	PROBABILITY OF EXCEEDING MEDIAN SPELLING SCORE
4 OR 5	84
2 OR 3	58
0 OR 1	45

FIGURE 48.1. *Expectancy chart showing the probability of finding a "better than average" scorer on the spelling section among employees currently employed on positions having various numbers of critical operations*

STUDIES IN SYNTHETIC VALIDITY 611

NUMBER OF CRITICAL OPERATIONS	PROBABILITY OF EXCEEDING MEDIAN ARITHMETIC COMPUTATION SCORE
1, 2, 3, 4, OR 5	41
0	23

FIGURE 48.2. *Expectancy chart showing the probability of finding a "better than average" scorer on the arithmetic computation section among employees currently employed on positions having various numbers of critical operations*

NUMBER OF CRITICAL OPERATIONS	PROBABILITY OF EXCEEDING MEDIAN VOCABULARY SCORE
4 OR 5	85
1, 2, OR 3	46
0	33

FIGURE 48.3. *Expectancy chart showing the probability of finding a "better than average" scorer on the vocabularly section among employees currently employed on positions having various numbers of critical operations*

NUMBER OF CRITICAL OPERATIONS	PROBABILITY OF EXCEEDING MEDIAN ARITHMETIC REASONING SCORE
2, 3, 4, OR 5	66
0 OR 1	46

FIGURE 48.4. *Expectancy chart showing the probability of finding a "better than average" scorer on the arithmetic reasoning section among employees currently employed on positions having various numbers of critical operations*

pany research support the contention that important company-to-company variations in test scores do exist.

3. *Variations in the extent to which the natural selection assumption is met.* That it is not a complete reality has been mentioned earlier. Systematic company-to-company variations are pointed out here.

4. *Error variance present in Dawson's designation of critical elements.* Dawson (2) demonstrated a certain unreliability in his results.

It seems to the authors that variance attributable to the above sources can operate only to mask any true relationships that might be operating. Consequently, those results presented here would seem to be conservative in that they are probably minimal statements of true relationships.

Statistical procedures. Chi squares are computed for all seven subtests of the *Purdue Clerical Adaptability Test.* Four were significant at the .05 level or better, and these are presented in Table 48.2. The breakdown under the heading "Number of Critical Operations" was suggested by Dawson (2), so results of this study are free from "fold-back" contamination from this source. The same lack of contamination holds for the separation of "low" from "high" scorers, since the dividing lines were based upon scores made by applicants for clerical jobs at Purdue University.

TABLE 48.2. *Original chi square data for four test sections*

Test Section	Number of Critical Operations	Low Scores	High Scorers	x^2	Significance Level
Spelling	4 and 5	5	26	16.661 with	.01
	3	21	24	4 d.f.	
	2	23	38		
	1	40	33		
	0	28	23		
Arithmetic Computation	4 and 5	6	5	11.167 with	.05
	3	11	13	4 d.f.	
	2	26	18		
	1	52	29		
	0	76	23		
Vocabulary	4 and 5	6	33	38.242 with	.01
	3	17	19	4 d.f.	
	2	27	26		
	1	44	30		
	0	39	19		
Arithmetic Reasoning	4 and 5	8	9	11.383 with	.05
	3	16	37	4 d.f.	
	2	16	30		
	1	31	29		
	0	45	36		

STUDIES IN SYNTHETIC VALIDITY 613

Attention is called here to the discrepancies existing between Figs. 48.1 through 48.4 and the corresponding sections of Table 48.2 in the breakdown of "number of critical operations." In short, the five categories in Table 48.2 have been compressed into three in Figs. 48.1 and 48.3 and into two in Figs. 48.2 and 48.4. For example, in Figure 48.1 the "2" category has been pooled with the "3" category and a probability of 58 reported for the new category. Referring to the "spelling" section of Table 48.2, if we compute the per cent of high scores for each category, these per cents in descending order are 84%, 53%, 62%, 45%, and 45%. While the reversal of the 53% for category "2" is not disturbing to the statistically sophisticated person, it does, none-the-less, present a problem to the industrial psychologist who feels the need to feedback his results to business men. For this reason, the authors have applied a somewhat dubious statistical procedure to prepare the material for presentation. Again considering the spelling section of Table 48.2, the percentage of the first category (4 and 5) was tested against the percentage of the second category (3). The difference was significant at the 10% level, so the first category was allowed to stand. (See the first bar in Figure 48.1.) Then, the percentage of the second category was tested against that of the third; since this difference was not significant at the 10% level a new category was created by pooling the old second and third and the appropriate probability of 58 was plotted in Figure 48.1. This same procedure was systematically followed throughout and Figures 48.1 to 48.4 are the result. As an added step, chi-squares were computed using the new categories. As expected and as shown in Table 48.3, all four were significant. The authors wish to go on record as being aware of the fact that neither of these procedures as applied is defensible *for purposes of testing hypotheses*. It is pointed out here, however, that the procedures have not been used for this purpose but rather to regularize the data for presentation to non-statistically trained people. In this respect the procedures seem justified.

TABLE 48.3. *Chi square data for four test sections using new categories*

Test Section	Number of Critical Operations	Low Scores	High Scorers	x^2	Significance Level
Spelling	4 and 5	5	26	15.80 with 2 d.f.	.01
	2 and 3	44	62		
	0 and 1	68	56		
Arithmetic Computation	1-5	95	65	8.24 with 1 d.f.	.01
	0	76	23		
Vocabulary	4 and 5	6	33	25.60 with 2 d.f.	.01
	1-3	88	75		
	0	39	19		
Arithmetic Reasoning	2-5	40	76	9.69 with 1 d.f.	.01
	0 and 1	76	65		

Interpretation. The copying section scores showed no relationship to the amount of copying ability judged to be required by the job. It is possible that copying is such a simple task that almost anyone can do it satisfactorily. Hence, even persons relatively low in copying ability might be retained on jobs which required this activity. Persons with high copying ability who were high on other abilities might be placed on jobs requiring the latter. The same explanation might be offered for the lack of relationship between the scores on the checking section and the amount of checking which is required by the job. The unreliability of the memory subtest scores has been mentioned above.

Further Work. Further work in this area has been initiated. A sample of jobs has been broken down according to the *patterns* of clerical skills required. The results have been promising, and we hope to report results in the near future.

REFERENCES

1. CULBERTSON, A. L. *The adequacy of an operational check list for the general description of clerical jobs.* Unpublished master's thesis, Purdue University, 1947.
2. DAWSON, ROBERT I. *A new approach to test validation for clerical jobs.* Unpublished PhD thesis, Purdue University, 1952.
3. DUDEK, E. E. *An operational approach to the valuation of office jobs.* Unpublished PhD thesis, Purdue University, 1948.
4. LAWSHE, C. H. *Principles of Personnel Testing.* New York: McGraw-Hill, 1948.
5. LAWSHE, C. H. Employee Selection. *Personnel Psychology*, 1952, 5, 31–34.
6. MILES, MINNIE CADDELL. Studies in Job Evaluation: 9. Validity of a check list for evaluating office jobs. *J. appl. psychol.*, 1952, 36, 97–102.
7. SINCLAIR, GORDON R. *The standardization of the Purdue Clerical Adaptability Test.* Unpublished master's thesis, Purdue University, 1950.
8. TIFFIN, JOSEPH. Industrial Psychology. (3rd edition) New York: Prentice-Hall, 1952.

49 A Research Strategy for Partial Knowledge Useful in the Selection of Executives

HAROLD GUETZKOW
and GARLIE A. FOREHAND

Two basic conclusions for guidance of research on executive selection seem available from today's evidence:
1. Criterion "problems" involved in appraising executive activity as it relates to individual or organizational performance will be a good many years yet in solving.
2. Executives differ tremendously in their styles, not only from each other, but in the fashion in which they exercise their leadership and decision making from situation to situation.

Difficulties in the valuation of performance and heterogeneity of performance style and situation are oft-cited complexities of executive selection. Perhaps these impediments to scientific selection procedures are not "problems" that can be solved by technological ingenuity. Rather, they are inseparable from the universe of variables that must be systematically explored in developing selection procedures; they must be incorporated into research on the problem.

Much successful personnel research has been based upon a relatively simple model. Two sets of variables figure operationally in the model: (1) individuals' performances on one or more predictor variables, and (2) a criterion, or set of values, assigned to personnel performance. An implicit intervening variable is the on-the-job behavior of the individuals being studied, as illustrated in Figure 49.1. The "result" most often sought is an index of the relationship between the predictor and the criterion, as shown by the solid arrow in Figure 49.1. Although this index can be obtained without observation of the intervening behaviors, a predictor can be valid with respect to given criterion only if (a) there is a relationship between the predictor and job-performance behavior, and (b) the predictable behaviors can be evaluated consistently and in comparable terms. The validity index, which describes operationally the rela-

From *Research Needs in Executive Selection*, R. Taguiri (ed.) Chapter 7. Boston, Mass. Harvard Graduate School of Business Administration, 1961.

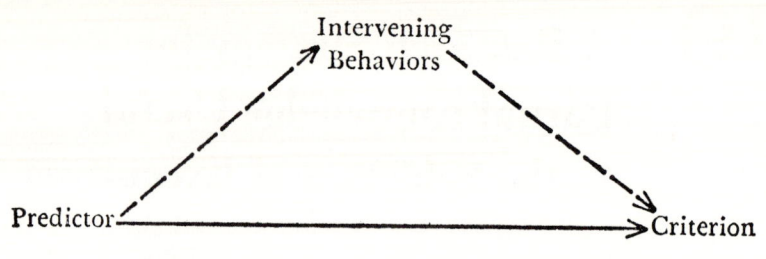

FIGURE 49.1. *A simple prediction model.*

tionship between predictor and criterion, actually summarizes the more complex relationships indicated by the broken arrows in Figure 49.1.

These conditions hold in a sufficient number of instances to make the prediction model a cornerstone of personnel technology. A machine situation, for example, may be designed so that a relatively small range of behaviors can result in satisfactory operation. The speed, efficiency, and accuracy of these behaviors may contribute directly to a valued index (e.g., productivity per time unit) of the operator's performance. It is relatively easy, moreover, to discover predictor variables which bear a close relation to these behaviors, for example, miniature job samples and measures of component aptitudes.

A richer schematization is necessary when we attempt to portray executive selection in terms of this model; the modification is presented in Figure 49.2. The following elucidation may be useful in deriving conclusions as to how executive selection differs from employee selection.

The assessment of "satisfactoriness" of executive performance is complicated because different sections of business or government agencies

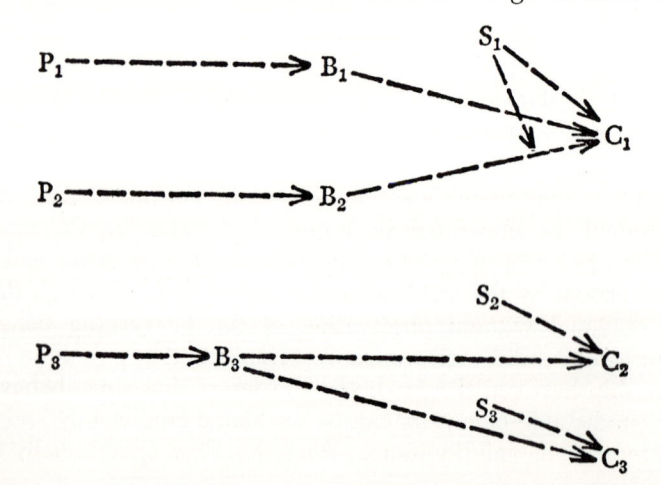

FIGURE 49.2. *The prediction model applied to executive performance.*

prize quite different—and sometimes contradictory—accomplishments (Cyert and March, 1959; Thompson, 1958). To compound this difficulty, little effort has been devoted as yet to the measurement of organizational outcomes, so that executive performance may be compared (Merrihue and Katzell, 1955). Hence, the simple model, with its single measurable "criterion," must be replaced by an array of criteria, as represented by C_1, C_2, ... in Figure 49.2, consequences which often can be appraised only quite subjectively.

The wide range of behaviors available to the executive in the conduct of his tasks is indicated in Figure 49.2 by the series B_1, B_2. ... Executives may use quite different styles in achieving the same outcome. Conversely, some executive performance, given a difference in organizational situation(s), may yield quite different consequences. As illustrated in the $P_1 - B_1 - C_1$ and $P_2 - B_2 - C_1$ sequences in Figure 49.2, it is possible for the executive to use one of a variety of styles (B_1 or B_2) in achieving a given consequence (C_1). The style preference of the executive then will determine whether P_1 or P_2 is a useful predictor of C_1—and prediction cannot be made without complementary knowledge of preference for style. On the other hand, a particular situation may interact with the behavior of the executive, so that under one set of circumstances quite a different consequence results from identical behavior, as is illustrated in the $P_3 - B_3 - C_2$ and $P_3 - B_3 - C_3$ sequences. The same behavior (B_3) interacts in one situation (S_2) to produce one type of performance prized by one part of the organization (C_2), but in another siutation (S_3) it may produce performance prized by a different part of the company or agency (C_3). The impact of situation, along with differences in style preference, make it impossible to use directly the simple prediction model in which one can proceed straight from predictor (P_k) to criterion outcomes (C_k).

This richer schematization suggests two conclusions about the course of research in executive selection. First, given the criterion problem, the research must not be expected to make integrations among the contradictory outcomes, nor be asked to develop an over-all, single index of the criterion. Instead, he should work with multiple criteria and develop more adequate measurements thereof so that the contradictory and overlapping nature of the consequences may be displayed to those in the organization who prize different outcomes. Second, the nature of executive performance necessitates a great deal more attention to behavior *per se* than has been traditional in personnel research; the path from predictor to criterion is too complex, depending upon style and situation, to permit efficient and consistent generalizations directly from one to the other. These conclusions call for a long-range program of research synthesizing the results of many studies. How can this be accomplished without conflict with the short-range technological needs which motivate such research in the first place?

Perhaps a clue to rapprochement between requirements of long-range synthetic research and short-range technological needs also may be found in the schematic model. If one can identify or postulate conditions which influence the choice of behavior style on the one hand and the valuation of behavior on the other, then a series of the arrows can be traced in Figure 49.2. A study which would accomplish such a result would be a valuable segment of a synthetic research program; it would also provide useful techniques for selection in situations in which the situational conditions apply. Further, it would seem quite feasible to work with a single or a limited set of criteria, especially those more amenable to measurement, objectively or through subjective ratings. Should not our present strategy for research, then, take advantage of practical opportunities in which segments of the complex of problems may be tackled, until we are prepared for grander, more wholistic studies?

As long as business, government, and other groups within our culture operate organizations—and it seems that operate them they will—it is necessary to select persons for executive positions. These selections are made usually on the basis of implicit theories about what characteristics of the individual and of the organizational situation, established for executive work, lead to what outcomes. When these theories are partially elaborated, as was done recently by Paul Lawrence (1958) for the management of a food chain store operation, they seem to consist of a set of variables about executive behavior which have organizational consequences. For example, Lawrence's top management group believed that more decentralized organizational decision making would allow district executives to make decisions more appropriate to the group of local stores that they supervised, which in turn would produce greater profits.

To be useful to practitioners, our research knowledge about executive selection need not be complete. Partial knowledge may be utilized within the framework of implicit assumptions already accepted by operating organizations. For example, suppose operating executives decide that more innovation is needed within a management position because an external situation is changing more rapidly than the present incumbent has been able to pace his adaptations. Then, knowledge about personal and situational characteristics which yield innovative behavior will be operationally useful *in the narrower context* of executive selection work, even if the more basic assumptions about innovation as a means for adaptation to changing environment are erroneous.

The discussion below presents systematic speculations about segments of a program of research on executive performance. This discussion focuses upon just a few of the behaviors which might be involved in executive performance in a given situation. It does not attempt to draw a complete picture of a proposed selection program. As will be suggested, however, the study of the hypotheses discussed can have immediate practical value as well as long-range theoretical significance.

SEGMENTS OF THE STUDY OF EXECUTIVE PERFORMANCE: COGNITION AND EXECUTIVE DECISION MAKING

With recent reawakening of interest in cognitive processes and problem-solving, it may be useful to consider the research potential in these areas for gaining partial knowledge about problems in the selection of executives. Psychologists have long emphasized the importance of the irrational characteristics of man, and this emphasis has become institutionalized within the last quarter-century in the so-called "human relations" approach. While research on intellectual processes has been among the more successful of psychological endeavors, it has been the economists and mathematicians who have institutionalized the rational emphasis in "operations research." Can the intellectual components of executive behavior be explored fruitfully for leads into more adequate executive selection?

Judgment. Is it possible to capture central elements in the valued capacity of experienced executives to "exercise judgment" when working in a decision making situation? Perhaps it will be helpful to conceive of "experience" as being composed of two processes, namely: (1) memory of particular specifics about a given administrative situation, and (2) skill in utilization of problem-solving abilities.

Knowledge of immediate situation. In another paper (Guetzkow, 1959), the senior author argues that in addition to an adequate general theory of the actual substance involved in decision making, the executive as practitioner must have relatively adequate estimates of the specifics or parameters of the given situation to make effective utilization of these more general theories, be they implicit or explicit. The organization's "old-timers" have an abundance of such specifics—they know the personalities of workers, customers or clients, and suppliers. They know the organization's climate and the detailed characteristics of the materials and monies used in fabricating a product or rendering a service. Memory of the specifics, which make *the* difference between Company A and Bureau X, would seem to be a most important ingredient in the exercise of judgment about what should be done—and when.

Abilities in problem solving. The proposal to consider "problem-solving abilities" as variables in executive selection requires research on the identification of relevant abilities and, in turn, the nature of the problem-solving process. Unfortunately, the experimental literature, as recently summarized by Duncan (1959), offers less than adequate help in illuminating the problem-solving process. Further, the "problem-solving situations" which confront executives may be different from those usually constructed for laboratory studies, in that the former are more often *indeterminate*: they have no built-in criteria of correctness. Research on administrative problem-solving may find some guidance in the conceptualizations of the problem-solving process proposed by theorists in the field; these conceptions themselves, however, must be subjected to empirical tests in a program of executive selection research.

Except for the assumption of sequentiality of the facets of problem-solving, it is still difficult to improve upon John Dewey's analysis of this activity (1910). Dewey postulated five "logically distinct steps" in problem-solving: "(i) a felt difficulty; (ii) its location and definition; (iii) suggestion of possible solution; (iv) development by reasoning of the bearings of the suggestion; (v) further observation and experiment leading to its acceptance or rejection." Administrative theorists, e.g., Simon (1945, 1957), Litchfield (1956), and Drucker (1954), have proposed similar schematizations as relevant to the "decision-making process" in administration.

Each theorist, of course, has his own idiosyncratic list of problem-solving phases. We are no exception. In our "Executive Judgment Study" we use the following list, couched in language consonant with the indeterminate nature of administrative problem-solving:

(a) Definition of a problem;
(b) Analysis of available data;
(c) Development of alternative solutions;
(d) Anticipation of consequences of the alternative solutions;
(e) Evaluation of the alternative solutions and their anticipated consequences.

These "facets" of the problem-solving process may be used as a guide for selection of variables in research on executive performance.

The clarifications gradually being made in the factor analysis of intellectual ability when related to this type of activity-analysis might further aid us in the choice of research variables. Perhaps the most intensive work in this field has been done by Guilford (1959). In Guilford's conception, intellectual factors are described in terms of the *operations* involved—memory, cognition, convergent thinking, divergent thinking, or evaluation. The factors may be further classified in terms of *products*, or the kind of thing remembered, known, or produced. Examples of products are units, classes, relations, systems, transformations, and implications. Cutting a third way, the factors may be classified by *contents*, or the type of material or content upon which the functions of memory and thinking operate. Some examples of contents are figural (perceptual), symbolic (without specified meaning), semantic (meanings or abstract ideas), and behavorial. An intersection of these three dimensions specifies a type of intellectual process; for example, evaluation (operation) of semantic (content) relations (product) is hypothetically identifiable as a statistically defined factor.

Without elaborating this scheme, we may display some parallels between it and the Dewey type of schematization of the problem-solving process. Let us concentrate upon semantic content, since dealing with meaning or abstract ideas is certainly an important, if not the most important, facet of an executive's intellectual functioning, and seek parallels in terms of operations and products. In this context, *defining a problem* might be seen as involving elements of both evaluation and cognition, corresponding to Dewey's concepts of "a felt difficulty" and "its isolation and definition." An evaluation factor of apparent relevance is called "sensitivity to problems"; it is measured by tasks of suggesting improvements in given social institutions (e.g., marriage) and in given items of apparatus (e.g., the telephone), and of seeing deficiencies in a plan. A cognition factor labeled "penetration" is defined by similar tasks, but seems to reflect the ability to "see beyond the immediate and obvious." The characteristics of sensitivity to problems and penetration, then, can be considered hypothetical components of executive judgment, and hence potential predictors of aspects of executive performance.

Analysis of available information in preparation for decision making implies, first of all, the systematic organization and collation of material—the type of operation that Guilford calls "convergent thinking." An exemplifying factor in this realm is one called "ordering," which is defined by success in arranging words, ideas, concepts, etc., into a sensible order. There is probably also an evaluation element in analyzing the available data—including evaluation of its relevance, sufficiency, and validity for the problem at hand. These "contents"—relevance, sufficiency, and validity—refer to relations between facts, premises, and objectives. A factor which falls in the "evaluation of semantic relations" realm is "logical evaluation," defined by syllogistic and logical reasoning tasks. It is quite possible that a similar factor involving heuristic or empirical relations rather than logical relations would be equally relevant to executive judgment. It is likely that such a factor could be operationally defined, although we have not come across one in our review of the factorial literature.

The talent for *developing alternative solutions*—the proverbial "imagination" of the executive—would appear to be one of eclectic productivity, of producing a wide range of ideas. Guilford denotes this type of intellectual operation "divergent thinking." Some examples of factors in this area are "ideational fluency," defined by uncritical productivity of ideas in varied situations, and "adaptive flexibility," defined by ability to change set to meet changing situational demands. In a similar fashion, the process of *anticipation of consequences* can be related to the cognition factor called "conceptual foresight," which is defined by tasks requiring the subject to "envision a situation in such a way that needs or consequences are anticipated"; *evaluation of alternative solutions* might be related to the evaluation factor of "judgment," defined as the "ability to weigh solutions and select the wisest and best ones."

This type of analysis could, of course, be elaborated considerably. These examples serve to illustrate, however, that testable hypotheses regarding predictors of executive performance can be inferred with some justification from schematizations of the problem-solving process and of intellectual functioning. Such "systematic speculation" perhaps can be of considerable value in areas where empirical findings offer few guides for developing hypotheses.

There are two aspects of intellectual work in executive decision making that at present can be but vaguely distinguished from the core of problem-solving, namely creativity and planning. Because of their close relation to the notions presented above, they will be discussed but briefly herewith.

Creativity and planning. Factor analytic studies reveal the existence of independent process within the "divergent thinking" domain, as it is labeled by Guilford and his colleagues. These consist of such components as "originality," "conceptual foresight," and "ideational fluency." How important is creativity to innovation? And then, in turn, how well do these abilities distinguish the executive operating within new industries or areas of service from the executive seeking continuity within a well-established bureau or enterprise?

Planning ability would seem to be an elaborate complex of intellectual processes, concerned with problem-solving as related to future events. In a factor analysis of Irving Lorge's Test of Planning Skill (in which the task is to "recommend a plan of action to solve the problems of low morale and low operating efficiency" of a hypothetical Air Base), the reliable variance (which unfortunately was estimated as low) seemed to be composed of a combination of four convergent and divergent thought processes: Elaboration, Originality, Judgment, and Ideational Fluency (Lorge, Fox, Herrold, and Davitz, 1959).

Choice: the terminal processes. By definition, the problem-solving process is said to be concluded by its outcome: choice of some answer, be it "no-decision" or one of the many alternative, more positive forms of problem solution, be it adequate or inadequate.

Risk taking. Recent work of the economists, stemming from their attempts to formulate the problem of choice in terms of expected utility, has highlighted the notions of risk preference in decision making. Recently at Michigan, Coombs and Pruitt seem to have demonstrated that there is preference for size-of-stake in risk taking, independent of preference for risk magnitude (1960). Is the terminal exercise of choice in decision making markedly influenced by these two facets of risk preference?

Uncerainty absorption. Perhaps there is validity in conceiving with Simon and his colleagues (1945) of the decision-making process within an organization as a structure of interlocked decisions, the more general of which serve as premises for the development of the more specific. Then, the ability of executives to set premises which may be used as fixed points for the decision making of his superiors and subordinates and laterally for his peers is an important ingredient in his intellectual work. Many times it may not be so important to have the "best" solution as to have a "satisfactory" one, which will allow the organization to continue functioning. Administrators must provide for absorption of uncertainty at various "stop-points" in the decision-making chain. The "indecisive" executive, who cannot bring himself to choice, often creates administrative chaos, because of the inability of his colleagues to absorb the unsettling uncertainty he allows to float within his organizational domain.

Value assertion. One form of premise in decision making is organizational goal. Goals may be considered as terminal points in means-means chains. It seems clear that any means in a means-means chain may be conceived by the decision makers as a goal or subgoal and thereby taken as basic assumption. One interesting proposition suggested about bureaucratic behavior (which applies equally well to industry and government) is the Weberian notion that means often become transformed into ends within large-scale organizations. Selznick (1957) and others (Thompson 1958) are concerned with the way in which end-values are inserted into organizational life. They feel that the essential core of administrative leadership is the formulation and adoption of the organization's goals.

Are the intellectual-intuitive processes involved in end-value assertion by executives within organizations different from those involved in means choice? Because goals usually are terminal in the means-means-ends chain, it may be that the open-ended component makes convergent intellectual processes inapplicable. But then from whence comes choice? Although we now have substantial descriptive materials on the "charters" of companies, perhaps research on the ways in which executives select with or without awareness among end-values would be helpful for selection purposes.

Evaluation of choice. The intuitive feeling of confidence in one's own choices is perhaps also worth exploring for leads in executive selection. It is difficult and expensive to appraise objectively the adequacy of many decisions. Yet it has been demonstrated within simpler, less complex materials that some individuals make considerably more valid estimates of the accuracy in their judgments in ambiguous situations than do others (Johnson, 1955). It also would seem that whether one is correct in the self-developed confidence one has in his own decisions is important in uncertainty absorption if those decisions serve as premises for the decisions of others.

The ability of an executive to "smell out" the "fishiness" of a given decision, his own or that of another, may be as important a determinant of effective decision making as his skill in handling the problem-solving process itself. Is confidence-in-decision the subjective feeling accompanying the narrow form of "judgment" described by Guilford as "the ability to weigh solutions and select the wisest and best one"? Is confidence-in-judgment the affect which accompanies an intuitive consideration of solutions against the background of experience, allowing the executive to tread sensitively among a variety of half-formulated, implicit choices?

RESEARCH PRACTICALITY

The limits imposed by the requirements of practical life on research enterprise depend upon the nature of the commitment of the organization to more adequate executive selection. Greenleaf[1] and his associates at American Telephone and Telegraph Company find it "practical"—albeit expensive—to follow up individuals for years after they have left the Bell System.

As hinted in the introduction, our most crippling limitation research comes from the lamentable state of our knowledge of criteria for individual and organizational performance. This state of affairs induced emphasis on the "segment" strategy proposed above. If we cannot predict through long chains of variables to fuzzy, poorly defined criteria, at least we can gain ground by studying segments of the total process which are judged important on *a priori* grounds by those who are responsible for selecting executives.

The findings that executives differ from each other in handling quite similar situations—and that each differs in style as he moves from one administrative situation to another—is more of a handicap to the social scientist who is interested in generalization than to the practitioner. In larger organizations it should be feasible to follow particular men as they make lateral shifts from one administrative situation to another. The current work of Mandell[2] in the Civil Service Commission with executives in the GS-15 classification will provide situational descriptions of posi-

[1] Personal communications (1961).
[2] Personal communications (1961).

tions within a large number of federal agencies. A possible extension of this work is the longitudinal study of these same positions as occupants change. Control work on those occupants who stay in the same positions over years perhaps could yield ways of describing the way in which administrative situations change, so that selection devices eventually might be firmly harnessed to changes in executive position demands. Bentz and his associates at Sears are using their regularly administered employee morale surveys to assess the impact of the style of their store executives as the latter move from store situation to situation.

A potentially useful research device for surmounting aspects of the criterion problem might develop in game-simulations of the operations of various management units within an organization, such as those being designed by Martin Shubik of General Electric (1958, 1959), and by Educational Testing Service in their "In-Basket Test" (Ward, 1959). The simulations hopefully represent essential functional characteristics of service and manufacturing units, whose consequences are of such complexity that they are amenable only to elaborate computational treatment. Might the decision-making styles of executives be explored within these simulated decisional worlds? The simulations might provide more satisfactory, if simplified, criteria than ever could be obtained in the intermeshed real world. In fact, if these simulated decision-making situations were useful for predicting executive performance, it would not be long before they would be used intermittently for executive training during the transition from one position in the company to another. It would be far wiser to have learning errors made in the simulations than in the dollar realities of company operations.

The development of procedures for executive selection often seems to become deadlocked in the confrontation of two seemingly irreconcilable propositions. The problems of designing such procedures are so complex that their solutions must rest upon a synthesis of years or decades of research on the "psychology of executive performance." Yet the immediate problems which motivate the costly research necessary for achieving such a synthesis will not wait years or decades for solutions. The strategy suggested is that research be designed so that emerging results can be useful for solving segments of the immediate practical problems, while at the same time contributing to an understanding of the over-all administrative process.

REFERENCES

1. COOMBS, C. H. & PRUITT, D. G. Components of risk in decision making; probability and variance preferences. *J. exp. Psychol.*, 1960, 60, 265–277.

2. CYERT, R. M. & MARCH, J. G. A behavioral theory of organizational objectives. In M. Haire (Ed.), *Modern organization theory: a symposium of the foundation for research on human behavior.* New York: Wiley, 1959, 76-90.
3. DEWEY, J. *How we think.* Boston: Heath. 1910.
4. DRUCKER, P. F. *The practice of management.* New York: Harper, 1954. (See esp. Ch. 28, 351–369).
5. DUNCAN, C. P. Recent research on human problem solving. *Psychol. Bull.*, 1959, 56, 397–429.
6. GUETZKOW, H. Conversion barriers in using the social sciences. *Administrative Sci. quart.*, 1959, 4. (See esp. 68–81).
7. GUILFORD, J. P. *Personality.* New York: McGraw-Hill, 1959. (See esp. 359–405).
8. JOHNSON, D. M. *The psychology of thought and judgment.* New York: Harper, 1955, 324–389. (See esp. 382–384).
9. LAWRENCE, P. R. *The changing of organizational behavior patterns: a case study of decentralization.* Cambridge: Harvard University Press, 1958.
10. LITCHFIELD, E. H. Notes on a general theory of administration. *Administrative Sci. quart.*, 1956, 1, 3–29. (See esp. 12–16).
11. LORGE, I., FOX, D., HERROLD, K., & DAVITZ, J. *Methods for the evaluation of the quality of rational decisions.* Paper read at the annual meeting of the American Psychological Association, Sept. 2, 1959.
12. MERRIHUE, W. V. & KATZELL, R. A. ERI—yardstick of employee relations. *Harvard Business Review*, 1955, 33 (6), 91–99.
13. SELZNICK, P. *Leadership in administration: a sociological interpretation.* Evantson, Ill.: Row, Peterson, 1957. (See esp. Chs. 3 & 4).
14. SHUBIK, M. *Simulation: its uses and potential.* Expository and Development Paper No. 2, Anticipation Project, Operations Research and Synthesis Consulting Service, General Electric Co., Ms. Part I, 1958 and Part II, 1959.
15. SIMON, H. A. *Administrative behavior: a study of decision-making processes in administrative organization.* New York: Macmillan, 1945.
16. SIMON, H. A. *Models of man: social and rational.* New York: Wiley, 1957. (See esp Section IV.)
17. TOMPSON, J. D. & McEWEN, W. J. Organizational goals and environment: goal-setting as an interaction process. *Amer. soc. Rev.*, 1958, 23, 23–31.
18. WARD, L. B. The business in-basket test. *Research Bulletin* RB-59-8, Educational Testing Service, 1959.

50 Synthetic Validity in a Small Company: A Demonstration

ROBERT M. GUION

IN BRIEF

Traditional methods of empirically validating tests for employee selection require large numbers of employees all doing essentially the same work. The small business organization is not able to meet this requirement; it is typically faced, therefore, with the options of not testing or of using clinical appraisals. An alternative has been proposed under the term "synthetic validity" in which empirical validation data can be used to infer the validity of a battery of tests even for situations in which the N is too small to permit conventional validation.

This report describes research in a small company in which nearly every employee has a job that is appreciably different from the jobs of other employees. Despite the diversity, however, there is some overlapping of job descriptions. Seven elements of work proficiency which appeared in many jobs in the company were identified. Ratings for each employee to whom an element applied were obtained, along with a rating on over-all effectiveness. A battery of tests was validated against this group of criterion ratings, taken one at a time.

The setting provided the opportunity for a demonstration of the concept of synthetic validity. Because of small N's, the results of the study cannot be taken as conclusive evidence of the superiority of synthetic validity over more traditional methods, but it can be taken as (1) a demonstration of the concept and (2) a model for the evaluation of the synthetic validity approach.

THE CONCEPT OF SYNTHETIC VALIDITY

Lawshe (1952) introduced the concept of synthetic validity in a symposium on industrial psychology in small business. Briefly, for small

From *Personnel Psychology*, 1965, *18*, 49–63. A part of this investigation was made possible by a grant of computer time from the University Computer Center at Berkeley.

business, the situation is this: (1) *N*'s are too small for traditional validation, and (2) clinical appraisals are, for many major jobs, much too expensive and frequently of uncertain predictive validity. The small company, wanting to capitalize upon developments in improved employee selection through testing, is just out of luck!

According to the synthetic validity idea, however, jobs can be analyzed into elements that are common to many dissimilar jobs. Tests can then be synthesized for any job—even a unique one—by using those tests found valid for the specific elements required by the job.

Schematically, this can be shown by Figure 50.1. In each column, the check marks indicate the two best of six predictors of performance in each of seven independent job elements. To hire an employee for a job consisting of elements I and IV, for example, tests A, B, and D would be used. If the next opening were for a job involving elements IV and V, then the test battery would consist of tests A, B and F.

Despite the attractive simplicity of this idea, little appears in the literature to describe its practical application. In one attempt to describe the concept, Lawshe and Steinberg (1955) showed, for example, that jobs judged to require high levels of spelling ability were jobs on which incumbents who had survived for a time scored higher on a spelling test than did the incumbents on other jobs; this is hardly, however, the problem in the employment office and is therefore not equivalent to the usual validity coefficient. In another study, Drewes (1961) constructed psychomotor tests from motion study principles and attempted to show that these tests, chosen in accordance with a motion analysis of a particular job, could do as well or better than other manipulative tests. Neither of these studies, however, could be considered a direct application of the synthetic validity concept to a small business.

PREDICTOR	\multicolumn{7}{c}{JOB ELEMENT}
	I	II	III	IV	V	VI	VII
A	X			X	X		
B		X		X			
C		X				X	
D	X						X
E			X			X	
F			X		X		X

FIGURE 50.1. *Schematic model for the concept of synthetic validity.*

THE SITUATION

The present study reports an application of the synthetic validity concept in a genuinely small organization; the total payroll, from president to stock boy, consisted of only 48 people when this study was begun. The firm, primarily an electrical wholesaler, maintains attractive "showrooms" where considerable retail trade is done. Commercial lighting, residential lighting, wiring, fixtures, large and small appliances, lamps, extension cords—in short, anything electrical is handled. Many jobs involve sales, but the job of a salesman selling wholesale to retailers or to contractors is not like that of one selling lamps or small appliances to a retail customer in a showroom. In no case are there more than three persons doing jobs that are really very much alike.

METHOD

The rate of hiring in such a small organization suggested that the desirable testing of applicants to determine predictive validity would require much too long to be useful as a demonstration of a technique. The study therefore used existing employees who had been with the organization for at least six months. A brief period of expansion followed the period of this study, making possible a total of thirteen new employees who could be used in a small cross-validation; with these, too, testing was done concurrently with the collection of criterion data.

Jobs were analyzed, criterion elements were identified, a test battery was chosen and administered in groups of about six to all employees, criterion ratings were obtained, and the tests validated. In the interests of simplicity, only the simplest methods of validation were used. Expectancy charts were developed and a system of predicting over-all job performance was devised using such expectancies. In cross-validation, the success record using this system was compared with the success record using conventional procedures.

Identification of Job Elements

For purposes of managerial reorganization for anticipated expansion, rather detailed job descriptions were available for all clerical jobs, all managerial jobs, and for most sales and warehouse jobs. Descriptions of nine of the job titles were studied carefully and lists of activities and types of responsibility were compiled. Examples from this preliminary list include "financial records keeping," "accept supervision," "plan," "gather information," "be familiar with product," and several others. The preliminary list was consolidated into ten categories of job responsibilities, each at three levels of responsibility. This list of job elements was discussed with the leading officers of the company. In several instances, the officers felt that certain of these elements were too nearly identical to permit reasonable discrimination. Others in the list (e.g., materials handling) were so routine that discriminations between individuals were not useful.

From this conference came a final list of elements of job proficiency identifiable as important aspects of the work done by at least some of the employees of this firm. There were seven such elements:

1. *Salesmanship:* The ability to sell, as shown by sales volume in relation to the potential sales within the individual's own selling area, the number of repeat customers, and the general size of orders.
2. *Creative Business Judgment:* The ability to identify or develop alternative courses of action and, subsequently, to make sound judgments either in action or in recommendations for action in such matters as buying, merchandising, or other business matters.
3. *Routine Judgment:* The ability to make correct decisions on matters governed by standard operating procedures such as credit clearance, display of merchandise, and other matters permitting latitude within the limits established by operating policies.
4. *Customer Relations:* The ability to work with the public in such a way as to insure a favorable attitude toward the company on the part of customers; i.e., the ability to handle people so that they will be satisfied or so that earlier dissatisfaction can be turned into satisfaction.
5. *Leadership:* The ability to exert a positive influence on the work of others; this element generally refers to a supervisory subordinate relationship.
6. *Detail Work:* The ability to catch small details, such as numbers or other symbols, quickly and accurately; this element is of greatest importance in the broadly clerical areas: filing, reading invoices, checking stock numbers, and so on.
7. *Work Organization:* The ability to plan effectively and to carry out the plans that are made; this ability is required only in those jobs where procedures must be chosen or developed by the person doing the work.

Finally, in recognition of the trial nature of this project, the list of criterion "elements" was expanded to include a general, over-all appraisal of the individual's worth to the organization based on his understanding of his own job, his desire to get ahead, and how far he has gone within the organization relative to the amount of time he has been in it.

The Criterion Ratings

An evening free from distractions and interruptions was scheduled with the two highest officers, the president and vice-president of the company. Unusual care was taken in obtaining the ratings because of the need to eliminate halo and because of the distractability of these raters in ordinary circumstances.

The raters worked at separate tables, near enough for conversation and separated enough for independence of judgment. Alternation ranking was used for the rating system so that all ratings on one job element were completed before going on to the next.

In rating on each element, the raters received a deck of cards; color coded for each rater. The deck included one card for every employee and, on the top, a general description of the job element on which the ratings were to be made. This description was to be studied and discussed before any ratings were made; the raters were instructed to reach agreement on the kinds of observable behavior they would consider in making their ratings *without mentioning or referring to specific cases*. When agreement was reached, they were to go through the deck, pulling out the cards naming persons whose jobs did not entail that job element; i.e., for whom the job element was irrelevant. There was occasionally some discussion about this matter. They next pulled out the cards of those whom they felt unable to rate. The remaining cards were, without further comment or discussion sorted by the alternation ranking method. The writer observed carefully this procedure, halting a rater who attempted to abbreviate the system and having him start over.

The procedure was perhaps overly elaborate, and it required many hours to complete. It was essential, however, that the halo effect be avoided: unless the performance on each of the rated job elements was reasonably independent, the concept of synthetic validity would have no applicability.

Rankings were converted to normalized scale values, the averages for the two raters were computed, and these averages were correlated, as shown in Table 50.1. Reliability estimates in the diagonal were determined by correlating the ratings of the two judges. The next to the last column shows the square of the mean correlations, determined by the use of z' transformations. This can be taken as an estimate of communality. The last column—the difference between this communality and reliability—represents an estimate of the unexplained systematic variance and offers an index of the degree of independence of these ratings—probably a conservative estimate. Salesmanship rating may be considered to be relatively independent, while ratings of creative business judgment were far more generalized.

Forty-eight employees, the total payroll at the time of the study, were tested in groups of six. The test battery consisted of three subtests of the Employee Aptitude Survey (Verbal Comprehension, Numerical Ability, and Accuracy), the Adaptability Test, the Management Aptitude

TABLE 50.1. *Intercorrelation among criterion elements*

	A	B	C	D	E	F	G	O	r_m^2	σ^2
A. Salesmanship	(.88)	.58	.83	.50	.18	.31	.27	.74	.28	.60
B. Creative Judgment		(.85)	.81	.82	.80	.64	.72	.85	.58	.27
C. Customer Relations			(.88)	.68	.63	.66	.51	.82	.52	.36
D. Routine Judgment				(.82)	.60	.77	.76	.78	.52	.30
E. Leadership					(.87)	.57	.67	.70	.38	.49
F. Work Detail						(.87)	.77	.56	.40	.47
G. Work Organization							(.95)	.52	.40	.55
O. Over-all Rating								(.89)	.53	.36

Inventory, the Guilford-Zimmerman Temperament Survey,[1] and the Graves Design Judgment Test—the latter introduced because some employees were to be selected for possible further training in interior decoration. In all, 19 test measures were obtained. Ratings were completed before the testing was begun.

The test-criterion validity matrix, with seven columns and 19 rows, required 133 validity statements. A very simple approach to validation was used. Each test score distribution was divided as nearly at the median as possible, identifying a high-scoring group and a low-scoring group. Those ranked in the top half on a given criterion rating were designated "superior" for that job element. Thus in each cell of the matrix, for a given test variable and a given criterion variable, the percentage of the high-scoring group who were superior could be compared to the percentage who were superior among the low-scoring group. Significance of the difference in each cell was determined by using a simple monograph (Lawshe & Baker, 1950). An abstract of the results is shown in Table 50.2. For clarity of presentation, only those values which were considered sig-

---

[1] The writer has elsewhere (Guion, in press) taken the stand that personality measures should not be used as instruments of personnel decision. In view of this position, the inclusion of the Management Aptitude Inventory, with four scales fitting within the tradition of personality and temperament measures, and the Guilford-Zimmerman Temperament Survey, with ten such scales—fourteen of nineteen "predictor" variables—may seem inconsistent. It should be noted, however, that the purpose of this study is the demonstration of an idea. Within this purpose, concurrent validity was most practical, and it seemed that personality measures had an excellent chance to correlate, at least concurrently, with the criterion ratings in this setting. There is no assumption that these concurrent validities reflect possible predictive validities in any sense.

The cooperating company did, of course, seek some payoff for practical personnel problems. The only use of tests recommended for practical decision problems, however, was as a source of questions about an applicant. If scores on a trait are low, then that fact may be taken as the basis for certain questions to be asked in examining the person's background behavior. The personnel decision is made, however, on the basis of facts in that background, not on the basis of test scores of unknown predictive validity.

nificant (the 5 per cent and the 1 per cent levels), or those which were considered to approach significance (the 10 percent level but falling short of the 5 per cent level), are shown.

Quite arbitrarily, it was decided to use the best two predictors, in combination, for each criterion element; the validity of such a combination was expressed in terms of multiple correlations, shown also in Table 50.2. These validities ranged from .82 for "Creative Business Judgment" to

TABLE 50.2. *Test-criterion validity matrix*

Test	Sales-man-snip	Creative Judg-ment	Customer Relations	Routine Judg-ment	Leader-ship	Detail Work	Work Organi-zation
EAS—Verbal					2.09†		
EAS—Numerical							
EAS—Visual							
Adaptability Test		1.62†					
Design Judgment Test		3.23**	1.82†		2.81†		
GZTS—G	1.73†			1.77†			
GZTS R						1.76†	
GZTS—A							
GZTS—S	2.21*						
GZTS—E			1.92†				
GZTS—O			2.84*	1.69†		3.01**	
GZTS—F			3.19**			2.35*	
GZTS—T							
GZTS—P					2.09†	3.01**	1.86†
GZTS—M	2.16*						
MAI—Int. Job Perf.					1.77†	2.27*	Note [a]
MAI—Leadership			2.27*				
MAI—Job Att.							
MAI—Relns Others							
R for best 2 tests	.53	.82	.80	(.31)	.65	.47	(—)

* Signif. at 5% level
** Signif. at 1% level
† Signif. at 10% level
[a] Note that 90% of those rated on this element had scores above the company median.

a nonsignificant .31 for "Routine Judgment." No such correlation was computed for "Work Organization" since only one test even approached the traditional significance levels. Moreover, the statistical tests applied on the other elements did not apply to this one. The "Intelligent Job Performance" scale of the Management Aptitude Inventory had a peculiar distribution for those rated on "Work Organization": 90 per cent of those rated on this element scored above the company's median on this test variable. Stated in a different way, of those who reached a level of responsibility where they must themselves do some planning and organizing, 90 per cent are above average with respect to whatever this test measures.

In short, the results suggested that two-variable expectancy charts could be established for five of the seven job elements and that another of the job elements could be considered in terms of position on a single test variable. The seventh, "Routine Judgment," was eliminated from further consideration because of the low validities of the tests.

For a visual presentation of the results, expectancy charts were developed—one of which is shown as Figure 50.2. For most tests the

Design Judgment	Adaptability	Chances in 100 of being rated superior on creative business judgment
47–72	16–29	80
37–46	16–29	75
47–72	7–15	50
37–46	7–15	25
13–36	any	0

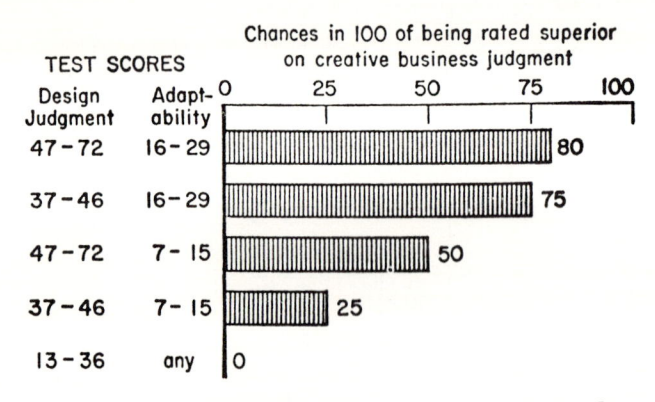

FIGURE 50.2. *Expectancy of success on the "creative business judgment" element considering the best two predictors together.*

expectancy charts were based on the same division used in validation, the division at the median. For the Design Judgment Test and the Leadership scale of the Management Aptitude Inventory, however, the distributions were rather flat; a division of the distribution into three roughly equal groups therefore seemed more realistic and was used.

THE APPLICATION OF THE SYNTHETIC VALIDITY DATA

The essence of the synthetic validity concept is not shown in a matrix of validity statements, but in the manner in which it may be used in making personnel decision. The balance of this paper will try to illustrate: (1) a practical and simple procedure for using the data already presented, and (2) a cross-validation design for the evaluation of a synthetic validity study.

During the data gathering stage and in the weeks that followed, the organization in which the study was done entered a period of expansion. By the end of a full year after the original testing was done, thirteen new persons had been hired and had worked long enough to be rated. The same two raters, again independently, were asked to rank each of these new people, on whichever elements were appropriate to their jobs, against their earlier rankings of the other employees. For each element, and for the over-all evaluation, each employee was, in effect, rated as either "superior" or as "not superior" in performance. For purposes of the cross-validation study, he was actually considered "superior" only if *both* judges so rated him—a requirement that divided the sample near the median. The same test battery was administered and an entirely mechanical, nonjudgmental procedure was followed to make "predictions" from test scores:

1. The person's job was analyzed. For one of the subjects, who will be used here as an example, the job responsibilities were for "Salesmanship," "Customer Relations," and "Attention to Details."
2. The person's test scores were noted for the two tests more important for each predictor, the appropriate expectancy charts were consulted, and expectancies, in terms of chances in 100 of being rated superior, were recorded.
3. Expectancies were then, for convenience, translated into simple integers, using the conversion table shown as Table 50.3.
4. The weights were added algebraically. Scores, expectancies, and weights for the illustrative subject are shown in Table 50.4. Since the sum of these integers is positive (the magnititude is given no significance in this study), it is "predicted" that this employee would in general be superior in the performance of this job.

This is, of course, but one of several systems that might have been devised. One might insist, for example, on minimum expectancies (perhaps about .35) for each job element. Or one might weight the elements differentially. Regression equations and other more sophisticated techniques could be adopted.

EVALUATION OF SYNTHETIC VALIDITY

How can we evaluate the concept of synthetic validity? It must be shown that this approach is at least as effective as traditional validation against a single criterion. First, we assume that any applicant superior on each, or at least most, of the assigned job elements, is also likely to be judged superior in over-all worth. A synthesized prediction of over-all worth based upon the sum of elementary, predictive weights should con-

TABLE 50.3. *Conversion integers for expectancies*

Expectancy	Conversion Integer
<25	−3
25–34	−2
35–44	−1
45–54	0
55–64	+1
65–74	+2
>74	+3

form to an actual overall rating quite well—better, in fact, than a direct prediction of over-all worth based upon traditional validation.

The original validation data included ratings on over-all effectiveness. A traditional approach to prediction would have involved the correlation of test variables with this single criterion measure. Such a correlation matrix was computed and an adaptation of the Wherry Doolittle technique was employed to identify an optimum test battery against the over-all criterion.

The method used was the Wherry-Doolittle-Holmes program for the IBM 7090.[2] This program, like the Wherry-Doolittle method, selects tests in the order of their contribution to a multiple R. It stops adding tests to the battery, however, when the additional variance does not add significantly to the R obtained at the preceding step.

Using this approach, the optimum battery for "predicting" over-all

TABLE 50.4 *Application of data for one employee*

Job Elements	Tests and Scores		Expectancies	Conversion Integers
Salesmanship	General Activity	23	53	0
	Sociability	23		
Customer Relations	Design Judgment	60	80	+3
	Objectivity	23		
Detail Work	Personal Relations	27	60	+1
	Intelligent Job Perf.	13		
			Total:	+4

[2] Professor J. A. Holmes of the University of California, Berkeley, developed this modification of the Wherry-Doolittle and, with the assistance of Mr. Price Stiffler, programmed it for the IBM 7090. The writer is indebted to these gentlemen for their assistance in this project. The program carries with it, although not reported in this study, a system of structure analysis aiding in a factorial interpretation of the selected battery.

effectiveness consisted of two tests: the Leadership scale of the Management Aptitude Inventory and the Personal Relations scale of the Guilford-Zimmerman Temperament Survey. The validities of these two measures, respectively, were .42 and .38; the shrunken multiple correlation was .53. Had a third variable been included, it would have been the score on the Design Judgment test, which had a validity of .23. The shrunken $\bar{R}$ with these three variables would have been .57, an increment not significant at the 1 per cent level.

On the basis of these results, an expectancy chart for over-all performance was developed, similar to those used for the individual job elements. It is shown in Figure 50.3.

Thus two sets of predictions could be made for each of the thirteen new employees. One was based on the sign of the sum of the integer weights, as shown in Table 50.4; the other was based on the expectancies of Figure 50.3. In both methods the group was dichotomized with one group designated as "predicted superior." The actual ratings also dichotomized the group into one subgroup of "superior" people in over-all effectiveness and another group. Table 50.5 shows a comparision of these two methods of prediction.

When prediction is based on elements, 76 per cent of the classifications prove correct. With the more traditional method only 46 per cent were correct. With only 13 cases, the difference is, of course, not statistically significant.

DISCUSSION

Several points seem worth considering. In the first place, it should be noted that the term "synthetic validity" is a logical misnomer—a fact

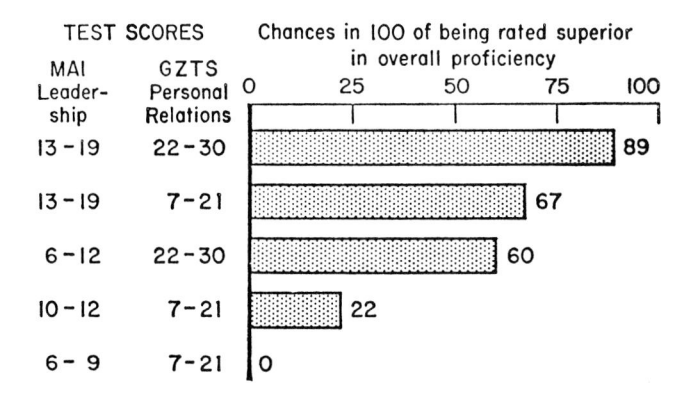

MAI Leadership	GZTS Personal Relations	Chances in 100 of being rated superior in overall proficiency
13-19	22-30	89
13-19	7-21	67
6-12	22-30	60
10-12	7-21	22
6-9	7-21	0

FIGURE 50.3. *Expectancy of over-all job success considering the best two predictors without prior division of job into component elements*

TABLE 50.5. *"Cross-validation" patterns*

Over-all Performance Predicted from Elements		Actual Over-all Rating	Over-all Performance Predicted from Over-all Data	
Superior	Other		Superior	Other
5	1	Superior	3	3
2	5	Other	4	3

which may in part account for the scarcity of research on this idea. Validity cannot be synthesized or created; it can only be observed and reported. It is not, however, *validity* which is synthetic; it is the *valid test battery* which is synthesized. "Synthetic validity" then should be considered a convenient shorthand statement for "synthesis of a valid test battery."

The relationship of this problem to that of over-all criteria should also be noted. Increasingly, the literature has shown evidence of disillusionment with the single criterion (Dunnette, 1963; Ghiselli, 1956; Guion, 1961). If more than one criterion element is to be used, however, then more than one predictor battery may be necessary. It follows, then, that the concept of synthetic validity is a potentially useful concept wherever multiple criteria are needed; as Balma (1959) has pointed out, the idea is as useful in large organizations as in small.

Some comments specific to the data presented are also needed. It was rather surprising to note the consistent validity of the Design Judgment test. This test was included in the study simply for convenience; it was needed for another purpose, the data were available, and it was more easily included in the analysis than excluded. The test was not developed, nor is it marketed, as a device for selecting astute business men, persons who can soothe customers, or those with supervisory potential. Its validity here can be explained on the basis of three possible hypotheses: (1) it might be a pure chance result; (2) there may be more artistry in the electrical business than suspected—an extremely plausible idea upon afterthought; or (3) the test measures a more fundamental judgment process than one specifically artistic. Its rather high validities, reaching as high as .82 in combination with another predictor, can in part be attributed to pure chance in a rather small sample; certainly such magnificent validities would not be expected to survive a legitimate cross-validation. It is, nevertheless, a measure which merits further investigation.

It is not pretended that conclusive evidence has been shown for superiority of synthetic validity over traditional situational validation. This report intended only to illustrate the way in which this idea can be put to use in a small company.

The idea is, however, exciting. It is reasonable to suggest that this concept can potentially provide very useful and valid generalization for employee testing to the effect that "a high level of X ability is associated with a high level of Y kind of job behavior." When there are enough such generalizations, and when they can be validly made, there will be less need for specific validation studies in each new situation, and employee testing can perhaps move farther along the continuum from a technology to a genuine science.

REFERENCES

BALMA, M. J. "The Development of Processes for Indirect or Synthetic Validity (A Symposium):1. The Concept of Synthetic Validity." *Personnel Psychology*, XII (1959), 395–396.

DREWES, D. W. "Development and Validation of Synthetic Dexterity Tests Based on Elemental Motion Analysis." *Journal of Applied Psychology*, XLV (1961), 179–185.

DUNNETTE, M. D. "A Note on *The* Criterion." *Journal of Applied Psychyology*, XLVII (1963), 251–254.

GHISELLI, E. E. "Dimensional Problems of Criteria." *Journal of Applied Psychology*, XL (1956), 1–4.

GUION, R. M. "Criterion Measurement and Personnel Judgments." *Personnel Psychology*, XIV (1961), 141–149.

GUION, R. M. *Personnel Testing.* New York: McGraw-Hill, in press.

LAWSHE, C. H. "What Can Industrial Psychology Do for Small Business (A Symposium): 2. Employee Selection." *Personnel Psychology*, V (1952), 31–34.

LAWHSE, C. H. & BAKER, P. C. "Three Aids in the Evaluation of the Significance of the Difference Between Percentages." *Educational and Psychological Measurement*, X (1950), 263–270.

LAWHSE, C. H. & STEINBERG, M. D. "Studies in Synthetic Validity: I. An Exploratory Investigation of Clerical Jobs." *Personnel Psychology*, VIII (1955), 291–301.

Name Index

Abelson, R. P., 94, 100
Adams, H. F., 157, 162, 168, 170, 171, 174, 177
Adjutant General's office, 84, 294, 295
Adkins, Dorothy, 207, 215, 216, 228, 591
Albee, G., 14, 15
Allport, F. H., 154, 156, 161, 167, 177, 189, 191
Allport, G. W., 156, 159, 162, 167, 177
Alpert, H., 5, 15
Amrine, H. T., 211–12, 229
Anastasi, Anne, 591
Anderson, T. W., 65, 67
Anderson, W. W., 327, 335
Andrews, L. P., 318, 336
Argelander, Annalies, 177
Argyris, C., 407, 414
Armstrong, T. O., 431n
Aronson, Joel, 562n
Asch, S. E., 127n, 134n, 183n, 186, 191
Astin, A. W., 560, 561
Ayres, L. P., 217, 229

Back, K., 184, 192
Bahrick, H. P., 577, 576–77
Baker, P. C., 632, 639
Balderston, C. C., 431n
Bales, R. F., 505
Ball, Richard S., 373, 415–18
Ballacey, E. L., 505
Balma, M. J., 73, 76, 188, 191, 286, 295, 638, 639
Banford, H. E., 358, 360
Barker, Roger G., 10, 15
Barkin, S. A., 433n, 437
Barnes, R. M., 211–12, 229, 261, 262, 266
Barrett, R. S., 187, 191, 404, 405, 533, 538, 545
Barron, F., 167n, 177
Barthol, R. P., 294, 296

Barton, A. H., 421, 423
Bass, Bernard M., 406, 414, 421, 424–37, 445, 467, 509n, 519, 554, 555, 556, 591, 603, 605
Baumgartel, H., 445, 467
Bavelas, A., 445, 467
Baxter, B., 3
Bechtoldt, H. P., 294, 295, 337, 345, 580, 581, 590, 591
Beem, H., 538, 544
Bell, G. B., 177
Bellows, Roger M., 3, 58, 67, 273, 337, 345, 582, 591, 594, 597
Ben-Avi, A. H., 347, 359
Bender, I. E., 155–56n, 158, 167, 175, 177, 179
Bennett, George K., 195, 230
Bennis, W. G., 555, 556
Benson, S., 150, 152
Bentz, V. J., 426, 437
Berdie, R. F., 74, 75, 76, 94, 96, 98, 99, 100
Bieri, J., 183n, 191
Bimed 17, 369
Bingham, W. V., 426–27, 437
Blair, J. L., 375n
Block, H., 127, 134
Bloom, B. S., 9, 16
Blum, M. L., 229, 437
Bonning, M. M., 179
Book, W. F., 130, 133
Bookwalter, K. W., 229
Bovard, E. W., Jr., 185, 192
Bowers, D. J., 521, 523–31
Boyle, D. J., 347, 359
Boyles, B. B., 507, 520
Bracken, H. von, 177
Brayfield, A. H., 1, 460, 467, 601, 605
Brecht, R. P., 431n
Briggs, G. E., 576–77
Brogden, H. E., 65, 67, 273, 285, 295, 580, 582, 584, 586, 591, 592
Brokaw, L. D., 245

NAME INDEX

Brown, C. M., 61, 64–65, 215, 229, 420, 430, 437, 580, 581
Brown, C. W., 67, 437, 592
Brown, W. F., 94, 101
Browne, C. G., 434, 437
Brownell, W. A., 592
Bruner, J. S., 187, 192
Bryan, W. L,. 130, 133
Buckner, D. N., 183, 193
Buehler, J. A., 184, 192
Bureau of the Budget, 467
Burgess, E. W., 374n
Burns, T., 555, 556
Buros, O. K., 336
Burtt, H. E., 295, 532, 538, 544
Butler, R. G., 358, 360
Buxton, C. E., 130, 133
Buzby, D. E., 178
Byrne, D., 184, 192

Campbell, J. T., 394, 403
Cantor, R. R., 178
Caplan, G., 14, 16
Caplow, T., 184, 192, 421, 423, 509n, 520
Capwell, D., 532, 542, 544
Carter, L. F., 67, 89, 91
Cartwright, D., 406, 414
Castaneda, A., 576, 577
Cattel, R. B., 47, 56, 60, 67, 130
Chalupsky, Albert B., 363, 368, 369
Channell, R., 199, 229
Chapin, F. S., 178
Chapman, J. C., 207, 229
Chapman, R. L., 445, 467
Chapple, E. D., 465, 467
Chowdhry, K., 173, 178
Christensen, C. R., 532, 545
Cieutat, V. J., 564, 577
Clark, R. E., 576, 577
Clarke, F. R., 292, 295
Cleaver, J. P., 437
Cleveland, E., 285
Clothier, R. C., 431, 437
Coburn, R., 110, 120
Coch, L., 406–407, 414, 445, 467
Cofer, C. N., 563, 577
Cogan, L. G., 154, 162, 178
Coleman, J. C., 154, 178
Colver, G., 110, 120
Committee on Ethical Standards for Psychology, 437
Comrey, A. L., 445, 467, 538, 544
Conklin, R. M., 178
Conrad, H. S., 141, 143, 147
Cook, S. W., 565n

Coombs, Clyde H., 63, 67, 90, 138–47, 622–23, 625
Cope, G. V., 383
Cottrill, Leonard S., Jr., 170, 374n
Coulls, J., 185, 194
Cox, J. W., 132, 133
Cramer, P., 563, 577
Creager, J. A., 309, 310
Crissey, Orlo L., 298n
Crockett, W. H., 460, 467, 601, 605
Cronbach, L. J., 75, 76, 187n, 192
Crutchfield, R. S., 505
Culbertson, A. L., 607, 614
Cureton, Edward E., 288, 295, 372, 404–5, 536, 545
Cureton, T. K., 229
Cyert, R. M., 617, 626

Dailey, J. T., 66, 68
Davis, R. C., 430–31, 432, 437
Davitz, J., 622, 626
Dawson, Robert I., 608, 612, 614
Dearborn, W. F., 130, 133
de Charms, R., 187, 192–93
Dent, J., 193
De Silva, H. R., 199, 229
Deutsch, M., 185, 192
Dewey, John, 620, 621, 626
Deyoe, G. P., 229
Dill, William R., 271, 337–45
Dorcus, Roy M., 236, 237, 245, 371, 377–82
Dorsey, J. M., 128, 134
Drewes, D. W., 628, 639
Drucker, P. F., 620, 626
Dudek, E. E., 363, 369, 607, 614
Dudek, F. J., 89, 91
Duncan, C. P., 619, 626
Dunnette, Marvin D., 2, 69–76, 77, 269, 521, 546–47, 556, 559, 638, 639
Dunteman, George H., 372, 406–14, 520
Dutton, H. P., 431n
Dymond, Rosalind F., 155, 156, 157, 158–59, 160, 163, 169, 173, 174–75, 178

Eagleson, B. M., 179
Ebel, R. L., 301, 303, 310
Eddy, W. B., 507, 520
Edgerton, H. A., 59, 67, 585, 592
Edwards, A. L., 266, 300, 301, 310
Einstein, Albert, 64
Elliott, R. M., 214, 229

NAME INDEX

Ellison, R. S., 318, 336
Endler, N. S., 74, 77
Ericksen, S. C., 347, 360
Ericson, E. E., 212, 330
Esso Standard Oil Company, 437
Estes, S. G., 154, 158, 165, 167, 178
Etzioni, A., 482, 482n
Eysenek, H. J., 315

Farnsworth, P. R., 128, 133, 468
Farguhar, W. G., 94, 101
Feldman, J. J., 327, 335
Ferguson, Leonard W., 178, 371, 383–90
Fernberger, S. W., 178
Feshbach, S., 185, 192
Festinger, L., 138, 147, 184, 192, 338, 345
Fields, S. J., 178
Fillmore, E. A., 128, 134
Finn, R. H., 369
Fiske, D. W., 87–88, 91, 94, 99, 100, 158, 163, 165–66, 179, 273, 285, 424, 437, 587, 592, 598, 603, 605
Fitts, D. M. 576–77
Flanagan, J. C., 269, 272, 286, 294, 295, 346, 360, 588, 592
Flieshman, Edwin A., 271, 294, 295, 346–59, 360, 361, 532, 534, 538, 544
Flexman, Ralph E., 346n, 347, 348, 361
Floor, L., 538, 545
Ford, G. L., 190, 194
Forehand, Charles A., 71, 77, 507, 520, 560, 615–25
Forman, R., 184, 192
Fox, D., 622, 626
Fraser, Russell, 311, 316
Fredericksen, Norman, 74, 77, 94, 100, 150, 195–228
Freeman, F. N., 203, 229
Freeman, H. E., 6, 16
Friedlander, Frank, 372, 373, 522, 546–56
French, E., 437
French, J. R. P., Jr., 407, 414, 445, 467
French, J. W., 246
Frenkel-Brunswik, Else, 171, 172, 178
Frost, C. F., 507, 520
Fruchter, B., 354, 361
Frutchey, F. P., 229

Gage, N. L., 156, 158, 173–74, 178
Gagné, Robert, 9–10, 16
Gaier, E. L., 75, 77, 296, 591, 592
Gates, G. S., 160, 178

Gaylord, R. H., 183, 192, 394
Gelser, G., 76
Georgopoulos, Basil S., 421, 422, 423, 442n, 460, 468, 509n, 520, 539, 544
Ghiselli, Edwin E., 2, 57–67, 69, 70–71, 72, 74, 75, 76, 77, 90, 91, 93–100, 101, 190, 191, 192, 288, 294, 295, 296, 298, 310, 318, 336, 426, 436, 437, 560, 561, 580, 581, 592, 601, 602, 605, 638, 639
Giese, W. J., 460, 467
Gilbert, A. C. F., 74, 77, 94, 100
Gilbreth, F. B., 122, 131–32, 133
Gilbreth, L. M., 133
Gilmer, B. von H., 507, 520, 556
Glassow, R., 229
Gleser, G., 75, 76
Glickman, Albert S., 182n, 184, 191, 192, 193
Goetz, B. E., 431n
Gollins, E. S., 183n, 192
Goodenough, Florence L., 178
Gottheil, E., 317, 335
Grant, D. L., 309, 310
Green, G. H., 178
Greenberg, B. G., 318, 336
Greene, H. A., 229
Greene, Peter, 562n
Greenly, R. J., 199, 230
Griffin, C. H., 73, 76, 295
Grooms, R. R., 74, 77
Grunes, W., 183n, 186, 192
Guetzkow, Harold, 71, 77, 560, 615–25, 626
Guilford, J. P., 179, 184, 192, 289, 295, 296, 324, 335, 346, 354, 356, 361, 500, 505, 620, 621, 622, 626
Guion, Robert M., 294, 296, 546, 554, 556, 560, 598–604, 627–39
Gulliksen, Harold O., 195
Gurin, C., 538, 545
Guttman, L. A., 138, 139, 146, 147, 476n

Haberstroh, C. J., 414, 445, 467, 468
Hage, J., 555, 556
Hagen, E., 345
Hagin, W. V., 347, 359
Hahn, Meton E., 15
Haire, Mason, 59, 183, 183n, 186, 187, 192, 288, 296, 532, 544, 560, 561
Hall, H. E., Jr., 177
Hall, R. H., 508, 520
Halpin, A. W., 544

NAME INDEX

Hanks, L. M., 164, 179
Harding, F. D., Jr., 309, 310
Harlow, H., 128, 133
Harman, H. H., 324, 335
Harper, N., 130, 133
Harris, E. F., 295, 532, 538, 544
Harvey, O. J., 189, 194
Hastorf, A. H., 155–56, 158, 177, 179
Haven, S., 45
Hag, E. N., 229
Hayden, R. G., 183n, 193
Hempel, W. E., 347, 354, 356, 357, 360, 361
Hemphill, J. K., 52, 56, 363, 369, 591 592
Heneman, H. G., Jr., 445, 468
Heron, A., 271, 293, 296, 311–15, 316
Herrold, K., 622, 626
Heryberg, F., 288, 296, 465, 467, 532, 542, 544
Heymans, G., 179
Hickson, D. J., 503, 505, 508, 519, 520
Hillix, W. A., 110, 120
Hilton, Thomas L., 271, 337–45
Hinings, C. R., 503, 505, 508, 519, 520
Holder, W. B., 266
Holland, C. H., 576, 578
Hollingsworth, H. L., 178
Holmes, J. A., 636n
Holzman, W. H., 94, 101
Hopkins, John J., 383–90
Horst, A. P., 59, 60, 67, 68, 278, 285, 371, 580, 586, 592
Hotelling, H., 534, 544, 592
Houston, R. C., 347, 348, 361
Hoyt, D. D., 94, 101
Hugh-Jones, E. M., 414, 467
Hull, Clark L., 60, 68, 69, 70, 77, 126, 229
Humphreys, L. G., 130, 133
Hunt, T., 179
Husband, R. W., 129, 133
Huse, Edgar F., 89, 135–37

Indik, Bernard P., 421, 422, 423, 442n, 460, 468, 485–505, 507, 520
Inkeles, A., 486, 488, 505
Inkson, K., 508, 520

Jacobsen, Tony L., 317–35, 336
Jaspen, N., 61, 68
Jaynes, William E., 391–403
Jenkins, John G., 46, 53, 56, 58, 68, 592
Jenkins, T. N., 296
Jenness, A., 179
Johnson, D. M., 624, 626

Johnson, O. C., 183, 192
Johnson, P. O., 289, 296
Jones, E. E., 187, 192–93
Jones, M. H., 236, 237, 245
Jones, N. W., Jr., 539, 544

Kahn, R. L., 538, 544
Kahneman, D., 72, 77, 98, 101
Kaiser, H. F., 324, 335, 409, 414, 447, 467, 534, 545
Kanner, L., 163, 179
Katz, B., 126, 134
Katz, D., 538, 544, 545
Katzell, Raymond A., 15, 288, 295, 372, 404–5, 422, 423, 460, 532, 533, 536, 538, 545, 547, 556, 601, 605, 617, 626
Katzell, R. B., 467
Kautz, R. L., 358, 360
Kellogg, W. N., 179
Kelly, E. L., 158, 163, 165–66, 179 183n, 347, 361
Kelly, G. A., 187, 193
Kendall, W. E., 546, 557
Kennedy, J. L., 445, 467
Kephart, N. C., 247n
Kerr, W. A., 155, 180, 445, 467
Kipnis, David, 149, 182–91, 193, 295, 296, 572–73, 577
Kipnis, Dorothy M., 182n, 184, 193
Kirchner, W. K., 70, 73, 76, 77
Kleiner, R., 185, 193–94
Klenimer, E. T., 88–89, 110–20
Klineberg, O., 127, 134
Knauft, E. B., 293, 296, 373, 419–20
Kogan, N., 183n, 193
Kolbe, L. E., 59, 67, 585, 592
Kornhauser, Arthur, 383
Krech, D., 505
Krug, R. E., 546, 556
Kuder, G. F., 195
Kurtz, Albert, 383

Lacey, J. I., 361
Lathrop, F. W., 229
Landis, C., 179
Langdon, J. N., 314, 316
Lawrence, Paul R., 618, 626
Lawshe, C. H., 188, 193, 213, 229, 560, 591, 592, 606–14, 627, 628, 632, 639
Lawyer, D., 509, 520
Leavitt, H. J., 445, 467
Lee, M. C., 75, 77, 99, 101
Leland, H., 9, 16
Lev, J., 447, 448

NAME INDEX

Levenstein, Sidney, 7–8, 16
Leventhal, H., 183n, 193
Levine, S., 6, 16
Levinson, D. J., 486, 488, 505
Lewin, K., 126, 185, 193
Lifson, Kalman A., 150–51, 247–66, 267
Likert, R., 422, 423, 445, 527
Lindahl, L. G., 212, 229
Lindgren, E., 285
Lindgren, H. C., 179
Lindquist, E. F., 195, 334, 336
Lippitt, R., 185, 193
Lipsitt, L. P., 576, 577
Litchfield, E. H., 620, 626
Lloyd, K. E., 576, 578
Lockhead, G. R., 88–89, 110–20
Lorge, Irving, 622, 626
Louttit, C. M., 415
Luft, J., 158, 165, 166, 179
Lupton, T. A., 503, 505, 508, 519, 520
Lykken, D. T., 75, 77
Lynch, H. R., 267

McBain, W. N., 62
McCallum, E. F., 533, 545
McClay, C. H., 229
McClelland, W., 156, 179
McClelland, David C., 12, 16
Maccoby, N., 538, 545
McCormick, E. J., 73, 76, 247n, 295, 298n, 369, 602, 605
McCormick, H. G., 229
MacCullough, A. V., 437
Macdonald, K. M., 503, 505, 508, 519, 520
McEwen, W. J., 626
McGinley, A. D., 591, 592
McGregor, D., 407, 414, 427, 437
Mack, R. W., 5, 16
McKenney, L. C., 431n
Mackie, R. R., 183, 193
MacKinnon, D. W., 153
McNear, Q., 134
McNemar, Q., 130, 143, 148
McPherson, M. W., 229
McQuitty, L. L., 75, 77, 286, 296
Mahoney, B. M., 539, 544
Maier, N. R. F., 445, 468, 532, 545
Maloney, 188
Mandell, 624–25
Mann, F., 74, 78, 545
Mann, R., 188, 193, 533
Manson, Grace, 383
March, J. G., 406, 410, 414, 445, 461, 467, 532, 545, 617, 626
Margolin, L., 261, 267

Margoluis, S., 292, 296
Martin, H. W., 179
Mausner, B., 465, 467, 532, 542, 544
Mead, G. H., 170, 179
Melton, A. W., 346, 361
Melville, S. D., 74, 77, 94, 100
Mendeleev, D. I., 505
Merrihue, W. V., 422, 423, 460, 467, 617, 626
Michael, C. M., 317, 335, 354, 361
Miles, C. C., 179
Miles, Minnie C., 607, 608, 614
Miller, Neal E., 12–13, 16, 55, 56, 358–59, 361
Moore, J. V., 187–88, 193
Moreno, Florence B., 156, 173, 179
Moreno, J. L., 156, 173, 179
Morse, N. C., 185, 193, 538, 545
Mortrud, L. C., 335, 336
Mosier, C. I., 295, 296
Moss, F. A., 179
Mundel, M. E., 247n, 261, 262–63, 267
Murphy, G., 131, 134
Murray, H. A., 157, 164, 180, 181, 185, 193
Musgrave, R. S., 177
Mussen, P., 180

Nagle, Bryant F., 559, 579–91, 599, 601, 605
Newcomb, T. M., 173, 178, 180
Newkirk, L. V., 212, 229, 230
Nichols, I. A., 347, 361
Noble, C. E., 564, 567, 578
Norman, R. D., 172, 173, 180
Norman, W. T., 94, 101
Norris, R. C., 63, 68
Notcutt, B., 154, 180
Nunnally, J., 70, 77
Nye, Charles T., 88, 102–9, 294, 296

O'Connor, N., 314, 316
Office of the Chief, Army Field Forces, U. S. Army, 437
Omwake, K. T., 179
Ornstein, George N., 271, 346–59, 360, 361, 362
OSS Assesment Staff, 180
Otis, Jay L., 2–3, 58, 60, 68, 79–86, 592
Owen, W. V., 247n, 298n

Palmer, George J., Jr., 320, 369, 406n, 407, 408, 412, 413, 414, 422, 445–67, 507
Parker, J. F., 347, 354, 356, 361
Parker, J. W., 190, 194
Parker, Treadway C., 404, 405, 521, 532–44, 545
Parsons, Talcott, 14, 16, 482, 482n
Patchen, M., 338, 345
Paterson, D. G., 127, 134, 214, 229, 337
Patten, E. F., 199, 230
Patterson, C. H., 345, 592
Patton, A., 521, 522
Payne, R., 508, 520
Peel, E. A., 592
Pepitone, A., 183n, 185, 193–94
Perloff, R., 394, 403
Perrin, F. A. C., 131, 134
Peterson, E., 431n
Peterson, O. C., 318, 327, 333, 336
Petterson, R. O., 532, 542, 544
Pfiffner, J. M., 538, 544, 545
Phillips, L., 12, 16
Pickle, Hal, 522, 546–56
Pigors, P., 431n
Plane, R. A., 505
Plowman, E. G., 431n
Polansky, N. A., 164, 180
Porter, L. W., 74, 77
Pressey, S. L., 415
Price, Phillip B., 317–35, 336
Prien, Erich P., 90, 91, 151, 152, 271, 363–69, 423, 506–19, 555, 557
Primoff, Ernest S., 73, 76, 77, 207, 295, 560, 561, 596, 597
Proffitt, M. M., 212, 230
Pruitt, D. G., 622–23, 625
Pugh, D. S., 503, 505, 508, 519, 520

Rabin, A. I., 180
Rahe, H., 110, 120
Ralph, R. B., 317, 336
Reeder, L. G., 6, 16
Reimer, E., 185, 193
Revans, R. W., 407, 410, 414, 460, 467
Ricciuti, H. N., 246
Rice, L. N., 87–88, 91, 94, 99
Rich, R. H., 437
Richards, James M., Jr., 317–35, 336
Robinson, Jacqueline, 179
Roethlisberger, F. J., 545
Rokeach, M., 180
Ronan, W. W., 90, 91, 270, 286–95, 423, 506–19
Rose, R. J., 75, 77
Rosen, H., 533, 545

Rosenberg, S., 183n, 192
Rothe, Harold F., 88, 102–9, 294, 296, 591, 592
Rubenstein, A. H., 407, 414, 445, 467, 468
Ruger, H., 129, 134
Rulon, P. J., 65, 68
Rush, Carl H., Jr., 68, 270, 273–85, 545
Russel, E., 183, 192
Ruter, H. W., 460, 467
Ryan, T. A., 437
Ryans, David G., 150, 195–228, 588, 592

Sarbin, T. R., 153
Satter, G. A., 63, 67
Saunders, D. R., 74, 78, 94, 98, 101
Sawatsky, J. C., 292, 296
Sayles, L. R., 465, 467
Schachter, S., 184, 192
Scheips, C. D., 369
Schell, H. A., 267
Schroeder, Ronald H., 422, 445–67, 507, 520
Schultz, D. G., 150, 152
Scodell, A., 180
Scott, M. G., 230
Scott, W. D., 431, 437
Scott, W. E., 522
Sears, R. R., 180
Seashore, C. E., 125, 128, 134
Seashore, E. E., 230, 468
Seashore, H. G., 74, 78, 89
Seashore, Robert H., 121–33, 134
Seashore, Stanley E., 421, 422, 423, 438–44, 460, 469–84, 507, 508, 509, 520, 521, 523–31
Sechrist, L. B., 591, 592
Sells, S. B., 9, 16, 486, 488, 489, 502, 505
Selznick, P., 623, 626
Severin, Daryl, 150, 183, 192, 194, 236–45
Shartle, Carroll, L., 61, 68, 285, 391–403, 407, 414
Sherif, M., 189, 194
Sherriffs, A. C., 156, 180
Singer, R. D., 185, 192
Siegel, Arthur I., 150, 152, 231–35, 294, 296
Sienko, M. J., 505
Silva, A. L. M., 154, 180
Simon, H. A., 406, 410, 414, 445, 461, 467, 532, 545, 620, 623, 626
Sinclair, Gordon R., 614
Skeels, H. M., 128, 134
Skodak, M., 129, 134

NAME INDEX

Smith, J. F., 347, 348, 361
Smith, K. M., 165, 181
Smith, Leo, 195
Smith, Patricia C., 55
Smith, W. R., 318, 336
Snoek, J. D., 505
Snyderman, Barbara, 465, 467
Sobol, R., 445, 467
Soskin, W. F., 166, 180
Spain, R. S., 318, 336
Spector, A. J., 185, 194
Spencer, K. W., 576, 578
Speroff, B. J., 180
Stagner, R., 94, 101, 554, 557
Stalker, G., 555, 556
Stalnaker, J. M., 317, 336
Stanton, H. M., 123, 124, 134
Stark, S., 337, 345
Stead, W. H., 285
Steinberg, Martin D., 560, 606–14, 628, 629
Steiner, I. D., 183n, 187, 194
Steinmetz, H. C., 180
Stephenson, W., 60, 68, 393, 403
Stiffler, Price, 636n
Stogdill, Ralph M., 372, 391–403, 532, 545
Stone, C. H., 445, 468, 546, 557
Stuit, D. B., 224, 230, 591
Sullivan, H. S., 170, 180
Super, Donald, 11
Sutter, E. L., 347, 348, 362
Sweet, Lennig, 161, 163, 180
Swenson, W. M., 285

Taft, Ronald, 149, 153–77, 180, 437
Tagiuri, R., 183n, 187, 192, 193, 615
Tannenbaum, A. S., 509n, 520
Taylor, Calvin W., 89, 317–35, 336
Taylor, Erwin K., 190, 194, 271, 273, 285, 295, 522, 579n, 580, 582, 584, 586, 591, 592
Taylor, S. A., 522
Terman, L., 179
Thibaut, J., 185, 194
Thomas, L. L., 363, 368, 369
Thompson, G. H., 593
Thompson, J. D., 617, 623, 626
Thorndike, Edward Lee, 58, 63, 65, 68
Thorndike, Robert L., 68, 230, 231, 235, 286, 296, 337, 345, 418, 425n, 546, 557, 559, 581, 582, 593, 598, 605
Thurstone, L. L., 133, 134, 138, 142, 144, 148, 285, 291, 297, 353, 362, 394, 447, 468
Tiedeman, D. V., 65, 68

Tiffin, Joseph, 109, 195, 199, 213, 229, 230, 247n, 298n, 614
Tinker, M. A., 128, 133
Tizard, J., 314, 316
Tobolski, F. P., 180
Toops, Herbert A., 2, 17–45, 58, 68, 75, 78, 214–15, 230, 273, 285, 337, 345, 584, 585, 559, 593, 601, 605
Townsand, J. C., 347, 348, 361, 362
Travers, R. M. W., 157, 158, 180
Travis, L. E., 128, 134
Tryon, R. C., 534, 545
Turnbull, J. G., 445, 468
Turner, C., 503, 505, 508, 519, 520
Turner, Weld W., 270, 298–309, 363, 369, 406, 468

Valentine, C. W., 180
Vance, Forest, 6
Van Dusen, A. C., 593
Van Zelst, R. H., 181
Vernon, P. E., 154, 156–57, 158, 162–63, 167, 168, 170, 171, 172, 173, 181
Viteles, M. S., 199n, 230
Votaw, D. F., 66, 68
Vroom, V. H., 73–74, 78, 445, 468, 532, 533, 545

Walker, E. G., 576, 578
Walker, Fred F., Jr., 25n
Walker, H. M., 447, 468
Wallace, S. Rains, 2, 46–56, 598, 605
Wallin, R., 126, 153, 181
Walton, W. E., 156, 181
Wantman, M. F., 317, 336
Ward, L. B., 625, 626
Warwick, Walter I., 6–7, 16
Watson, D. L., 181
Watson, Max, 17
Wedeck, J., 157, 163, 181
Wedell, C., 165, 181
Weingarten, Erica M., 181
Weitz, Joseph, 3, 55, 56, 559, 561, 562–77, 578, 598, 605
Wellman, B., 128, 134
Wesman, A. G., 317, 336
West, L. J., 110, 120
Weyant, R. G., 576, 578
Wherry, Robert J., 3, 37, 45, 270, 273, 285, 391–403, 560, 594–97, 598, 601, 605, 636n
White, J. B., 189, 194
White, R. T., 185, 193
White, Robert W., 11, 16

Whyte, William H., Jr., 532, 545, 595, 597
Wiersa, E., 179
Williamson, E. G., 375n
Wilson, C. L., 183, 193
Winer, B. J., 298n, 394, 403
Wolf, R., 157, 181
Wolfe, D. M., 505
Woodley, K., 151, 152
Woods, P. J., 576, 578
Woodward, Joan, 507, 520
Worthy, J. C., 545

Wrigley, C., 68, 296
Wyatt, S., 314, 316

Yoder, D., 431, 437, 445, 468
Young, K., 5, 16
Young, R. J., 292, 297
Yuchtman, Ephraim, 422, 469–84, 507, 509, 520

Zaleznik, A., 532, 545
Zander, A. F., 406, 414
Zigler, E., 12, 16
Zimmerman, W. S., 354, 361

Subject Index

Abilities
  critical thinking, 550, 552, 554
  intellectual, 311, 314–15, 498–500
  measurement of, 153–56
Absence
  index of, 281, 292, 293
  measure of, 135, 137
Absenteeism, 135–37, 292
Accessibility, and cost, 594
Accidents, lost time, 287, 292
Achievement
  measurement of, 197
  recognition of, 326
Activity analysis, 587–88, 589
Adjustment mechanisms, 125
Administrators
  behavior patterns of, 391, 402–3
  personnel, 396–97
  maintenance, 397–99
Advanced Management (periodical), 435–36
Affective field processes, 122, 125–27, 132
Alternative solutions, 621–22
American Institutes for Research, 14
Analysis, occupational, 60–63
Analytic judgments, 153, 162–63
Aptitude, 386
  index of, 383–84, 387–89, 390
  tests of, 73–74, 196–97
  variables, 495–96
Armed forces, and organizational worth, 429–30
Ascendency, of managers, 550, 552
Attitudes
  group, 533, 534
  individual, 485, 490
Authority structure, 490, 492
Autonomy, 543
Ayres Handwriting Scale, 217

Bank proof machine, 112
Barr scale, 417
Behavior, 1
  as criteria, 442–43, 601
  as global characteristic, 269
  individual, 496
    and suicide, 19

  variables, 485
  job, 83
  organizational, 406, 407, 413–14, 489, 501–2
  patterns of, 125–27, 391, 402–3
  supervisory, 533, 534–35, 537–38, 540, 543
  taxonomic schemata for, 486–87
Benefits
  health, 460
  insurance, 461
Bill collection requests, and productivity, 465
Blum Sewing Machine Test, 201, 202
Bonuses, 288, 339–40
Bureaucracy, 492, 494

Card punch machine, 112
Career progress, criterion for, 344–45
Case study, 376
Change
  adaptability to of groups, 491, 497
  cognitive, 531
Changing the Structure and Functions of an Organization (Seashore and Bowers), 523
Charity work, medical, 327
Check list, performance, 231–35
Choice evaluation, 623–24
Classification, 63–67
Clerical
  costs, 522
  functions, 363, 364–69
Clerical position description questionnaire, 363–69
Clinical
  insights, 595–96
  psychologists, 7
Cognitive thresholds, 125
Cold war, 64
Columbia City, 10
Communication
  as group function, 493, 494
  in industry, 43
  as organizational function, 490, 492
  structure of, 490, 492
Community, 546, 550, 551, 553
Community size, 536

Comparative empirical studies, 443
Competence, 11
Complex reactions test, 95
Composite criterion, 601
Conceptual foresight, as anticipation factor, 621-22
Concurrent validity, 48
Conflict control process, 491-92, 494
Consequences, anticipation of, by executives, 621-22
Construct validity, 55
Consultants, professional, 396
Consulting, 330-31
Contents, as factor classification, 620
Contingency factors, prediction of, 371, 374, 375, 376
Contingent prediction (see Prediction)
Control, as organizational variable, 490-91, 493
Control precision, in pilot performance, 354
Coordinate jobs, 64, 66-67
Coordination
 as function, 491, 493
 multilimb, 355-56
Coordinators, 400-1
Core variables, 422, 518-19
Correlation coefficient, 70, 72, 94
Costs
 clerical, 522
 maintenance, 479
 production, 479, 481
Counties, 42
Creativity, by executives, 622
Creditors, 546, 549-50, 551-52, 554
Criteria, 2, 28, 29, 46, 50, 51, 52-53, 559-60, 580, 601
 agreement of, 594-95
 behavior, 442-43, 602
 for career progress, 344-45
 classification of, 439-40
 composite, 601
 contamination of, 582
 for a criterion, 594-95
 deficiency, 582
 development, 602-4
 different, 559
 dimensionality, 58
 dynamic dimensions of, 601, 602
 establishment of, 83-84, 86
 global, 53, 273, 276-81
 hard, 440, 441-43, 506-7, 513, 517, 518
 hierarchy of, 440-42
 irrelevant, 52-53
 job analysis and, 81
 job-oriented, 50
 of job performance, 286-95, 298, 300-1, 302-3, 601-2
 long versus short run, 439-40
 management, 52
 material, 425-26
 measurement of, 204-5
 measures, 318-19, 570, 584-91
 modified prediction model and, 72
 multi-dimensional, 584, 600, 602
 multiple, 2
 of occupational adjustment, 312-13
 output, 441, 470
 parallel, 94
 partial, 53, 54
 pass-fail, 346
 penultimate, 441, 443, 470
 performance, 2, 346-47, 371, 615
 predictability as, 594-95
 prediction of, 59
 prediction model and, 70
 problem, 559
 production as, 383
 profile for sales success, 273
 profit as, 444n
 rating of, 630-34
 reliability of, 87, 89, 94
 research, 81-82, 596-97
 sales as, 273-85
 scores, 319-24
 selection of, 596-97, 599, 600
 social, 425-26
 soft, 506-7
 success as, 83, 416, 425
 time reference, 439
 ultimate, 428, 581, 584, 585, 596, 598, 600
 values, 440
 variables, 80, 83, 85-86, 486, 526-27
 variance, 100
 in worker selection, 58-60
Critical job duties, 560
Culture pattern, nonurban, 405
Customers, 546, 549, 551
Cutoffs, multiple, 586

Data-gathering, 44
Decision making, 399-400, 621
Diagnostic thoroughness, in medicine, 326
Dictionary of Occupational Titles (U. S. E. S.), 104
Differential prediction, 65
Dimensionality, individual, 60
Direction manual, for performance tests, 227-28
Disciplinary action, 287-88, 293, 294

SUBJECT INDEX

Discriminant function, 65–66
Dispersion scores, 141–43, 146, 147
Distance, psychological, 490, 493
Division of labor, 516
Doctor (see Physician)
Dramatic Production Test, 157
Drive, 563, 572, 573–74, 575, 577
D-scores, 90

Ecology, psychological, 10
Education
 of physicians, 332, 333–34
 and psychology, 13
Effectance, 11
Effectiveness (see Human effectiveness)
Ego psychology, 11
Emotional stability, of managers, 550, 552–53
Empathy test, 155, 156
Employees, as success criteria, 546, 549
Employee selection, validity of tests for, 627
Ends criteria, versus means, 439
Environments, 482n, 483
 organizational, 485, 488, 490, 502
 research on, 32–33
 variables, 39
Equal appearing intervals, method of, 216–17
Error
 in measurement, 93–94, 96, 99, 195
 in performance rating, 186
 in prediction, 93–94, 96, 99
 in pricing, 534
 rates, 114–15, 119
 and speed, 118
Esso Standard Oil Company, 435
Executive
 experience, 619
 selection, 615, 616–17, 618
 judgment study, 620
Experience,
 executive, 619
 as job criterion, 313
External judgments, 154

Failure, business, and selective regression equation, 35
Factor analysis, 270, 271
 as criteria determinate, 602
 iterative method of, 394
 of job performance, 286–95, 301–2, 304–8
 and performance dimensions, 298
 of sales success criteria, 278–89, 285

studies, 474–76
Factors
 biological, 127–29
 in clerical function tests, 364–68
 contingency, 374, 375–76
 in performance tests, 354–59
 products as, 620
 in validation studies, 73–74
 variable defined, 395
Female-employee syndrome, 404
Field experiments, 406–7
Filling errors, 534
Fold-back, 612
Frequency, as measure of absence, 137
Functions, human, classification of, 9–10

Global criteria, 53, 273
Global models, 2
Goal path utility, 541
Goals, 522, 541
 organizational, 469, 481–82, 483–84, 623
 penultimate, 471
 in sales, 481
Government, 546, 550, 551–52
Great Society, 8, 14
Grievances, 287, 293, 294, 410
Group, 487–88
 attitudes, 533, 534
 function, 493–95
 performance, 533–34, 537–39
 size, 536
 socialization process, 493
Guetzkow and Forehand model, 2

Halo effect, 346–47, 631
Handbook of Employee Selection (Dorcus and Jones), 236, 237
Handbook of Medical Sociology (Freeman, Levine and Reeder), 6–7
Hand Skills Test, 572–77
Hard criteria, 441–43, 506–7, 513, 517, 518
Hard versus soft criteria, 440
Health, 14
Health benefits, 460
Hierarchical levels, number of, 490
Honors, as pay, 39
Human effectiveness, 8–9, 11, 13, 14, 484
Human Functions, classifying, 9–10
Human motivation, 43–44
Human performance, 12
Human relations, 619

I-E tests, 125–26
Imagination, of executive, 621–22
Immediate situation, knowledge of, 619
Incentives, 541
Incentive system, 104, 108
Independent jobs, 64
Independent variable, 570
Index
  absence, 287, 292, 293
  aptitude, 383–84, 386–89, 390
  injury, 287
  pilot aptitude, 358
  validity, 615–16
Individual, 487–88
  behavior, 485, 490
  dimensionality, 60
  performances, 615
Industrial organization, 430–31
Industrial Organization and Management (Davis), 430–31
Industrial psychologist, 38, 47, 79–80, 83–84, 432
Industrial psychology, 1, 2, 55
  function of, 36
  goal of, 426
  progress in, 560
  validity for, 47
Information, analysis of in decision making, 621
Injury index, 287
Input variables, 508
Instability, emotional, and job adjustment, 314–15
Institute for Social Research, 444
Insurance benefits, 461
Intellect, 122, 127–29, 131, 132
Intellectual ability, 311, 314–15, 489–500
Intelligence
  occupation prediction and, 415, 417–18
  structural measurements and, 127–29
  tests, 129
Interaction
  empirically determined, 25
  social, 456
  trait, 23–25
Intraorganizational approach, to research, 406, 407
Intraorganizational investigations, 445
Irrelevant criteria, 52–53

J coefficient, 73
Jobs
  coordinate, 64, 66–67
  independent, 64
  successive 64, 66
Job adjustment, 313, 314–15
Job analysis, 81, 83, 84, 85, 220, 221, 377, 378–79, 599, 602
Job aversion, 460–61, 465, 466
Job behavior, 83
Job classification, differential prediction and, 65
Job concept, of industrial psychologist, 83–84
Job concept interview, 84–86
Job Description Check List of Clerical Operation (Culbertson), 607, 608, 610
Job duties, critical, 560
Job elements, 629–30
Job level, and mental ability test, 419
Job-oriented criteria, 50
Job output, 501
Job performance, 183, 185–86, 190–91, 236, 522
  as criteria, 601–2
  criteria for, 286–95, 298, 300–1, 302–3
  dynamic aspects of, 59
  and mental ability test, 420
  test, 236–45, 294
Job satisfaction, as criteria, 601–2
Job security, 536, 540
Job specification, role perception and, 62
Judges, good, 159–77
Judgments, 153, 154, 157, 162–63, 622
  creative business, 630
  and criterion development, 602–4
  executive, 619, 624
  expert, 600
  external, 154
  law of comparative, 138
  nonanalytic, 153, 157
  routine, 630
  work pace, 257–61, 264

Kinesthetic discrimination, in pilot performance, 357, 358
Knox Cube Test, 196
Kuder Preference Inventory, 158

Labor allocations, 412
Labor legislation, 429
Labor relations, 430–31
Lateness
  family responsibility and, 410
  productivity and, 465
Law of comparative judgments, 138
Leadership, as job element, 630

SUBJECT INDEX

Leadership climate, 540, 542
Learning, 121
Leisure planning, 333
Life insurance agencies, 471–73
Linking-pin concept, 531
LOMA-1, 419–20
Long versus short run criteria, 439–40
Lost time accidents, 287, 292

Maintenance administrators, 397–99
Maintenance costs, 479
Management, 533
 criteria, 52
 emphasis, 479
 modified theory of, 523, 524–25, 527
 quality, 384–85, 388–89
 success, 546
 success criteria and, 434–37, 438–39
 tasks of, 523
Managers, 555
 characteristics of, 548, 550, 552–54, 555–56
 job performance of, 522
 sales performance of, 469, 480
Maneuvers, in tests of pilot performance, 348–53
Manpower growth, rate of, 478–79
Market penetration, 478, 481
Market strategy, 516
Mass-empathy tests, 155
Material criteria, 425–26
Mathematics grade, 286–87, 292
Means criteria, versus ends, 439
Means-means chain, 623
Measurement
 objective, 299–300, 301
 of performance, 150–52, 231, 318, 326–34
 structural, 127–29
 theory, 138, 139
Mechanisms, adjustment, 125
Medicine, human effectiveness and, 14
Medical audit technique, 335
Medical College Admission Test, 317
Medical students, education and selection of, 317–18
Member job outputs, 501
Member participation, 501
Mental ability test, 419, 420
Mental health, psychologists in, 6–7
Mental retardation, 9
Mental Survey Quotient, 415
Merit rating, 313
Metal-working industry, 508–9
Miniature tests, 199–200

Minimal regression equation, 30
Minnesota Food Score Cards, 215
Minority-group compositions, 411
Moderator, 94, 96, 97–98, 99, 100
Modified theory of management, 523, 524–25, 527
Moss Social Intelligence Test, 156
Moss Social Situations Test, 157
Motivation, 11
 human, 43–44
 variables, 495
Motive acquisition program, 12
Motor Skills, 122, 131, 129–30
M. S. Q. (*see* Mental Survey Quotient)
Multi-dimensional criteria, 584, 600–2
Multi-dimensional measures, 271
Multilimb coordination, 355–56
Multiple cutoffs, 586
Multiple predictor–multiple criteria designs, 546–47
Multiple regression equation, 24
Multivariate research designs, 521, 522

National Education Association (NEA), 36
National Institute of Mental Health, 6
National Register of Scientific and Technical Personnel (questionnaire), 6
Natural environments, of organizations, 502
Need analysis, technique of, 599, 602
New cities (*see* Planned communities)
New members, productivity of, 478
Nonanalytic judgments, 153, 157
Nonbehavioral psychological variables, 495–501
Nonresponse bias, 447, 448, 461
Nonurban culture pattern, 405

Objective measures, of performance, 299–300, 301
Occupational analysis, 60–63
Occupational effectiveness, 72
Operating plan, for performance test, 222–25
Operations, as factor classification, 620
Operations research, 619
Optimization, 483
Ordering, as factor of information, 621
Organizations, 421, 487–89
 behavior of, 406, 407, 413–14 486–87
 effectiveness of, 423, 481–83, 554
 environments of, 485, 490, 502
 performance of, 372, 442–43, 470–71

Organizations (*cont.*)
  process of, 485, 489, 490–92
  size of, 410, 517, 518, 519
  as social-economic system, 422
  structure of, 485, 489, 490, 499, 531
  success and, 425, 428, 432–34, 554
Orientation
  physomatic, 327
  response, 356
Outcome variables, 508
Output criteria, 441, 470
Output rates, 102, 104–6, 108–9. *See also* Production
Owners, 546, 548–49, 551, 552–53, 554
Paired-associates learning task, 564–65, 572

Paired comparisons method, 216–17
Parsons (Hanson) State Hospital and Training Center, 9
Partial criteria, 53, 54
Parties-at-interest, 546, 547–48, 550–51, 552, 553
Pass-fail criterion, 346
Path-goal hypothesis, 539
Patients, special attention for, 327
Pay-skill level, 411
Pearsonian coefficient, 95, 106
Peer judgments, 154
Penultimate criteria, 441, 443, 470
Penultimate goals, 471
Perceptual role relations, 496
Performance, 12, 195, 219, 384–89
  administratative, 392, 401
  criteria, 2, 371
  determination, 372
  differences in, 372
  evaluation, 371–72
  group, 533–34, 537–39
  individual, 615
  level, 371
  measurement, 150–52, 208–20, 231, 299–300, 301, 318, 326–34
  motivation, 541
  observation, 149
  operating plan for test of, 222–25
  optimum, 483
  organizational, 372, 421, 422, 442–43, 470–71, 518
  perceived, 538–39
  personnel, 412–14
  pilot, 346–59
  physician, 271
  prediction, 87, 91, 371, 373
  ratings, 151, 152, 300, 306, 309
  reliability, 87, 88, 89, 91
  self-caused, 478

  tests, 150, 196
  See also Job performance
Performance check list, 231–35
Personality
  description of, 155–56
  disorder, 288, 292, 293
  system, 488
  trait, 142–43
Personnel
  administrators, 396–97
  performance, 412–14
  prediction, 598, 604
  problems of, 26–32
  research, 3
  selection, 203, 402–3
  technician, 595–96
Personnel Selection (Thorndike), 231*n*
Persons, as tests, 38–39
Pharmaceutical company, 533
Phi coefficient, 96
Physicians
  education of, 332, 333–34
  specialist, 318
Physique and Intellect (Paterson), 127
Physiological thresholds, 125
Physomatic orientation, of physician, 327
Picturization, 18
Pilot aptitude index, 358
Planned communities, 10
Planning
  by executive, 622
  leisure, 333
Policy change, 531
Porteus Maze Test, 196
Possessions test, 31
Predictability, 594–95
Predictability variable, 94
Prediction, 87, 91
  of contingency factors, 374, 375, 376
  of criteria, 59
  of occupations, 415, 417–18
  of performance, 373
  of personnel, 598, 604
Prediction model, 69, 70–73, 75–76
Prediction of Personal Adjustment (Horst), 374*n*
Predictive tests, 48, 49
Predictive validity, 51, 53
Predictors, 70, 71–72, 75, 76, 80, 580–81
  of criterion factors, 281, 283–84
  non-test, for sales success, 276
  reliability, 94, 98
Predictor-criteria relation, 2, 3
Prestige, 490
Prestige structures, of group, 493

SUBJECT INDEX

Pricing errors, 534
Private Practice in Social Work (Levenstein), 7–8
Problem definition, 587
Problem solving, 619, 620, 622
Production, 59–60
 costs of, 479, 481
 as criteria, 383
 high, 428
 foremen, 298, 299
 quality, 518
 rates of, 112, 113–14, 119–20
 records, 83
 See also Output rates
Productivity, 110, 312, 534
 job aversion and, 465
 training and, 119–20
Products
 change in, 513
 for factor classification, 620
Profile, 1, 18, 273
Profit, as criterion, 444n
Progress, 50
Promotions, 288, 292, 293
Psychological Corporation, 14
Psychological Services, Pittsburgh, 14
Psychological Services Center at Syracuse University, 15
Psychological tests, to study personality variables, 311, 312, 314–15
Psychological traits, 139–42, 144, 146, 147
Psychologists
 clinical, 7
 as good judges, 164–67
 industrial, 47, 432
 in mental health, 6–7
 personnel, 432, 433–34
Psychology, 5, 7, 8, 486
 education and, 13
 ego, 11
 industrial, 1, 2, 36, 55, 426, 560
 social institutions and, 6
 social orientation of, 5
Psychometric theory, 90, 93, 94, 96, 100
P-technique, 60
Public relations, 395–96
Publishing, by physicians, 331
Purdue Clerical Adaptability Test, 607, 608, 610, 612

Q-technique, 60
Quantitative scores, 18n
Questionnaire, morale, 140–41, 142, 143–44

Rankings, 186
Rate control, in pilot performance, 356–57
Rating, 149, 184
 of criterion, 630–34
 merit, 313
 of performance, 186, 306, 309
  global, 151, 152
  foremen, 300
 research, 182, 183, 189
 scales, 83
 of work pace, 247–66
Rating form, for performance tests, 222
Rating Form for Fastening, 216, 218
Rational theory, 595–96
Ready made tests, 236, 237, 239, 244–45
Recognition tests, 198
Reference keys, 394
Referrent variables, 23–24, 27
Relations
 customer, 630
 human, 619
 labor, 430–31
 semantic, 621
Relevancy, 581–83
Reliability
 of criteria, 583–84, 585
 as criterion, 594
Reliability coefficient, 99
Research
 criteria, 81–82
 designs of, 521–22
 human effectiveness and, 13
 intraorganizational approach to, 406, 407
 in medicine, 331
 operations, 619
 personnel, 3
 practicality of, 624–25
 rating, 182, 183, 189
 selection, 600
Residency, physicians, length of, 327–30
Resources, availability of, 502
Response orientation, in pilot performance, 356
Responsibilities, of physicians, 330
Responsibility, family, and lateness, 410
Results criteria, 470
Retirement, 30–32
Risk taking, 622
Role perception, job specification and, 62
Role relations, perceptual, 496

Salary
  as criterion of progress, 337–45
  formulae for occupations, 35
  growth, 338, 341, 342, 343–44
Sales aptitude, 383–84. *See also* Selling
Sales criteria, 273–85
Sales organization, goals in, 481
Sales personnel, authority-conflict
    and, 412
Sales routes, evaluation of, 379–82
Salesmen, selection and evaluation of,
    377, 378, 379, 380–81, 382
Salesmanship, as job element, 630
Sampling
  performance tests and, 206, 208, 217
  survey, 407, 408–9, 445–46
Satisfaction, with job, as criteria, 601–2
Satisfaction, of executive performance,
    616–17
Scale unit problem, 584–85
Schedule-procedure makers, 397
School rating, 286, 292
Scientific research, inductive methods
    of, 131
Scores, quantitative, 18n
Scoring, relative, 34
Scoring key, 18, 26
Security, of employment, 536, 540
Seguin Form Board, 196
Selection
  of executives, 615, 616–17, 618,
    619–20
  research, 69, 73, 76, 600
Selective regression equation, 18, 19,
    23, 26, 29, 35–37
Selectivity, employee, 412
Selling, 38, 53–54, 60, 82–83, 378–82,
    482
Semantic relations, 621
Sensory field, 122, 123–25, 131, 132
Shop rating, 286, 293
Simulated condition tests, 199–200
Situational variables, 531, 535–37, 538
Size
  of community, 536
  of group, 492, 536
  of organization, 416, 517, 518, 519
  output rates and, 108
  as variable, 490
Skills
  development of, 531
  motor, 122, 131, 129–30
Small group process, 489
Small-group process variables, 485
Small-group structure variables, 485,
    489, 492–93, 499
Sociability, of managers, 550, 553, 554

Social criteria, 425–26
Social effectiveness continuum, 12
Social environment, structure and
    relations, 502
Social institutions, 5, 6, 7–8, 13–14
Socialization
  organizational, 491
  process, of group, 493
Social objectives, 430–31
Social pathology, 8
Social security, 430–31
Social work, 7–8
Society, contribution to, by physicians,
    331
Sociocultural system, 488
Sociology, 486
Sociology of the profession, 7
Soft criteria, 506–7
Soft variables, 441, 442
Spatial orientation, in pilot perform-
    ance, 354–55
Specialization, 330, 516
Sponsor, 594
Standardization, 513, 516–17
Static dimensionality, 58
Status, 490, 493
Status scores, 141, 146, 147
Stencils, 33–34
Stimulus situation, total, 502
Stock, ownership of, 411, 413
Strain symptoms, 501, 502
Strong Vocational Interest Blank, 49
Students (*see* Medical students)
Sub-criteria, 585–87, 588–89, 590
Subgroups, 74–76
Success
  criterion, 416
  definition, 588, 589–90
  management, 546
  measurement of, 375–76
  minimal corporate, 509n
  organizational, 425, 428, 432–34,
    546–47
  of pilots, 346
  of physicians, 331, 333
Succession, 513–16
Successive jobs, 64, 66
Suicide, 19, 20
Supervision, 491, 494
Supervisors, 183, 185, 188, 190, 427–28
  technical, 397
  worker attitude toward, 542
Supervisory behavior, 533, 534–35,
    537–38, 540, 543
Supervisory ratings, 288, 289, 292,
    293, 294
Suppliers, 546, 549, 552
Support, employee, 412

SUBJECT INDEX

Supportiveness, 480
Survey Research Center, 524, 529, 530
Survival, 388, 443
Synthetic times, 606–7
Synthetic validity, 606–7, 609, 627–28, 629, 634–39
Systems, 422, 487

Tailor-made tests, 236, 237, 239, 244–45
Tasks
  approach, 571–72
  content, 571–72
  description, 9–10
  difficulty, 566–72
  interdependence, 490, 492
  specialization, 490, 492
  specification, 490, 492
Teaching aids, 204
Technology, 513
Temperament, dimensions, of, 500–1
Tenure, personnel, 411, 413
Tests
  of aptitude, 73–74, 196–97
  of complex reactions, 95
  of information, 195
  of intelligence, 129
  of job performance, 294
  of judgment, 154–56, 157–59
  non-personality, 236, 237, 239, 244–45
  parallel, 93, 94
  of performance, 150, 196, 227–28
  predictive, 48, 49, 98, 99–100, 191
  for selection, 606, 627
  of simulated conditions, 199–200
  trial, for sales personnel, 274–75
  validity of, 50–51, 54, 69–76, 419–20, 627
Test battery, valid, synthesized, 638
Test of Planning Skill (Irving Lorge), 622
Test requirement, critical, 608, 609
Test stencil, 31
Thefts, 461
Thematic Apperception Test (T. A. T.), 156
Therbligs, 132
Thinking
  convergent, 621
  original, 550, 552
Thresholds, 125
Thrift, employee, 460
Time, 209, 213, 221–22
  normal, 247
  studies, 247–66
Time reference criteria, 439
Time-series performance data, 479–80

Trade Tests, 28
Training transfer of, 124, 132
Traits, 125
  interaction, 23–25
  quantitative, 35
  rating of, 154
Trait dispersion score, 145–46, 147
Trait status score, 139, 143–45, 146
Transactions, between employees and companies, 461
Transfer of workers, 63–64
Types, 75

Ulstriths, 18, 19, 20, 21, 22n, 23, 27, 37, 40, 43, 75
Ultimate criteria, 428, 441, 444, 469–71, 581, 584, 585, 596, 598, 600
Uncertainty absorption, 623
Uni-dimensional scales, 141, 145
Uniques, 471
Union
  job aversion and, 465
  status, 536
Universals, 471
Utility, 48, 49, 51, 53, 54

Vacations, 39–40
Validation research, 72
Validity
  coefficient, 28, 88
  concurrent, 48
  construct, 55
  index, 615–16
  for industrial psychology, 47
  potential of, 594
  of performance tests, 206–8
  predictive, 51, 53
  significant, 51
  synthetic, 601–7, 609, 627–28, 629, 634–39
Value assertion, 623
Valued index of performance, 616
Variable relationships, 502–5
Variables
  aptitude, 495–96
  core, 422, 518–19
  and criteria, 486
  criterion, 80, 83, 85–86, 526–27
  environmental, 39
  factors defined by, 395
  genotypic, 486, 487
  independent, 570
  individual behavior, 485
  input, 508
  in job performance measures, 286–94

Variables (cont.)
 measurable, 486
 motivational, 495
 nonbehavioral, psychological, 495–501
 organization structure, 485
 outcome, 508
 predictabliity, 94, 96, 97–98, 99, 100
 referrent, 23–24, 27
 relevant, 495–501
 situational, 531, 535–37, 538
 soft, 441, 442
Variance, in ultimate criteria, 444
Verbal comprehension, of managers, 550, 552, 553–54
Vigilance test, 199
Vigor, of managers, 550, 553–54
Volume, 478, 481, 482

Wages
 disputes over, 30
 rates of, 536
Welfare, retirement, 456, 461
Wherry-Doolittle test selection method, 281, 283, 636
Wherry-Gaylord procedure, of factor analysis, 394

Wherry-Winer method, of factor analysis, 394
Wisconsin Miniature Test for Engine-Lathe Operations, 109
Work
 conditions of, 411–12
 detail, 630
 methods, 124–27, 129, 130, 131–32, 133
 organization of, 630
 pace, 247, 250, 251–52, 257–61
 situation, 539–40
Workers
 autonomy of, 542–43
 placement of, 63–67
 selection of, 57, 58–60, 60–63, 133
Work force
 quality conscious, 600
 reduction of, 411
 size of, 456–60
Work groups, 521, 538, 541
Work sample tests, 200–2

Yes-No questions, 21, 31
Youthfulness, 478–79